The Routledge
Handbook of Stylistics

The Routledge Handbook of Stylistics provides a comprehensive introduction and reference point to key areas in the field of stylistics. The four sections of the volume encompass a wide range of approaches from classical rhetoric to cognitive neuroscience, covering core issues that include:

* historical perspectives centring on rhetoric, formalism and functionalism
* the elements of stylistic analysis, including the linguistic levels of foregrounding, relevance theory, conversation analysis, narrative, metaphor, speech acts, speech and thought presentation and point of view
* current areas of 'hot topic' research such as cognitive poetics, corpus stylistics and feminist/critical stylistics
* emerging and future trends including the stylistics of multimodality, creative writing, hypertext fiction and neuroscience

Each of the thirty-two chapters is written by a specialist in the field and provides an introduction to the subject, an overview of the history of the topic, an analysis of the main current and critical issues, a section with recommendations for practice, and a discussion of the possible future trajectory of the subject.

The Routledge Handbook of Stylistics is essential reading for researchers, postgraduates and undergraduate students working in this area.

Michael Burke is Professor of Rhetoric at Utrecht University and author of *Literary Reading Cognition and Emotion: An Exploration of the Oceanic Mind* (Routledge 2011).

Routledge Handbooks in English Language Studies

Routledge Handbooks in English Language Studies provide comprehensive surveys of the key topics in English language studies. Each Handbook focuses on one area in detail, explaining why the issue is important and then critically discussing the leading views in the field. All the chapters have been specially commissioned and are written by prominent scholars. Coherent, accessible and carefully compiled, *Routledge Handbooks in English Language Studies* are the perfect resources for both advanced undergraduate and postgraduate students.

The Routledge Handbook of Stylistics
Edited by Michael Burke

The Routledge
Handbook of Stylistics

Edited by
Michael Burke

LONDON AND NEW YORK

First published 2014
by Routledge
2 Park Square, Milton Park, Abingdon, Oxon OX14 4RN

and by Routledge
711 Third Avenue, New York, NY 10017

Routledge is an imprint of the Taylor & Francis Group, an informa business

© 2014 Selection and editorial matter, Michael Burke; individual chapters, the contributors.

British Library Cataloguing in Publication Data
A catalogue record for this book is available from the British Library.

Library of Congress Cataloging in Publication Data
A catalog record for this book has been requested.

ISBN: 978-0-415-52790-3 (hbk)
ISBN: 978-1-315-79533-1 (ebk)

Typeset in Times New Roman
by Saxon Graphics Ltd, Derby

MIX
Paper from
responsible sources
FSC   FSC® C013056
www.fsc.org

Printed and bound in Great Britain by
TJ International Ltd, Padstow, Cornwall

Contents

List of tables and figures   ix
List of contributors   xi
Acknowledgements   xvii

Introduction   1
Stylistics: From classical rhetoric to cognitive neuroscience
Michael Burke

PART I
Historical perspectives in stylistics   9

1 Rhetoric and poetics: The classical heritage of stylistics   11
   Michael Burke

2 Formalist stylistics   31
   Michael Burke and Kristy Evers

3 Functionalist stylistics   45
   Patricia Canning

4 Reader response criticism and stylistics   68
   Jennifer Riddle Harding

PART II
Core issues in stylistics   85

5 The linguistic levels of foregrounding in stylistics   87
   Christiana Gregoriou

6 (New) historical stylistics   101
   Beatrix Busse

7 Stylistics, speech acts and im/politeness theory   **118**
   Derek Bousfield

8 Stylistics, conversation analysis and the cooperative principle   136
   Marina Lambrou

9 Stylistics and relevance theory   155
   Billy Clark

10 Stylistics, point of view and modality   175
   Clara Neary

11 Stylistics and narratology   191
   Dan Shen

12 Metaphor and stylistics   206
   Szilvia Csábi

13 Speech and thought presentation in stylistics   222
   Joe Bray

PART III
Contemporary topics in stylistics   **237**

14 Pedagogical stylistics   239
   Geoff Hall

15 Stylistics, drama and performance   253
   Andrea Macrae

16 Schema theory in stylistics   268
   Catherine Emmott, Marc Alexander, and Agnes Marszalek

17 Stylistics and text world theory   284
   Ernestine Lahey

18 Stylistics and blending   297
   Barbara Dancygier

19 Cognitive poetics   313
   Margaret H. Freeman

20 Quantitative methodological approaches to stylistics   329
   Olivia Fialho and Sonia Zyngier

21 Feminist stylistics   346
    Rocío Montoro

22 Literary pragmatics and stylistics   362
    Chantelle Warner

23 Corpus stylistics   378
    Michaela Mahlberg

24 Stylistics and translation   393
    Jean Boase-Beier

25 Critical stylistics   408
    Lesley Jeffries

PART IV
Emerging and future trends in stylistics   **421**

26 Creative writing and stylistics   423
    Jeremy Scott

27 Stylistics and real readers   440
    David Peplow and Ronald Carter

28 Stylistics and film   455
    Michael Toolan

29 Multimodality and stylistics   471
    Nina Nørgaard

30 Stylistics and comics   485
    Charles Forceville, Elisabeth El Refaie, and Gert Meesters

31 Stylistics and hypertext fiction   500
    Paola Trimarco

32 Stylistics, emotion and neuroscience   516
    Patrick Colm Hogan

Index   531

Tables and figures

Tables

1.1	The five canons of rhetoric	21
1.2	A six-part composition plan from the *Rhetorica ad Herennium*	23
2.1	Propp's functions of dramatis personae	38
2.2	Propp's distribution of functions among dramatis personae	40
3.1	Reference chain from 'The Attack'	49
3.2	Material processes	51
3.3	Mental processes	53
3.4	Summary of British action (Material processes)	55
3.5	Summary of Zulu action (Material Processes)	58
3.6	Summary of modal categories and narrative distribution	62
8.1	Non-cooperation in *Hamlet*	149
8.2	Transcription key	154
9.1	Some inferences involved in understanding an utterance of *'I was tired'*	160
13.1	Leech and Short's original categories of speech and thought presentation	223
13.2	Leech and Short's revised model of speech and thought presentation categories	224
30.1	Stylised examples of pictorial runes used in *Tintin and the Picaros* (adapted from: Forceville 2011, p. 877); the popped-up vein was identified in manga by Shinohara and Matsunaka (2009)	493

Figures

2.1	Bühler's tripartite model of communication	33
2.2	Jakobson's six basic functions of any communicative act	33
2.3	Jakobson's six associative functions of language	34
3.1	Relational processes	53
3.2	Summary of process types and constituents	55
7.1	Culpeper's control system for audience reading of dramatic character (2001, p. 35)	131
18.1	Generic space	304
18.2	Blend 1	306
18.3	Final blend	308
20.1	Percentage of quantitative and qualitative articles compared (*L&L* 2007–2011)	332

23.1   Concordance sample for *shoulder* retrieved with *WebCorp Live*   381
23.2   All forty occurrences of *shoulder* in *Nicholas Nickleby* (e-text from Project
       Gutenberg, www.gutenberg.org)   382
26.1   Representing speech and thought   434
31.1   A screen image of a lexia from *afternoon, a story* by M. Joyce   501
31.2   The first interactive screen of 'These Waves of Girls'   502
31.3   An image from 'These Waves of Girls'   512

Contributors

Marc Alexander is a Lecturer in English Language at the University of Glasgow. His work primarily focuses on cognitive and corpus stylistics, digital humanities, and the semantic development of English. He is the Director of Glasgow's STELLA Digital Humanities lab, and an Associate Director of the Historical Thesaurus of English.

Jean Boase-Beier is a Professor of Literature and Translation at the University of East Anglia. Her research focuses mainly on literary translation and stylistics. She is also a translator from German, and the editor of Arc Publications' *Visible Poets*, a series of bilingual poetry books.

Derek Bousfield is the Head of Languages, Information and Communications at Manchester Metropolitan University, UK. He has published on linguistic impoliteness, banter, and aggression in interaction and drama. He is a co-editor of the *Journal of Politeness Research: Language, Behaviour, Culture*.

Joe Bray is a Reader in Language and Literature at the University of Sheffield. He is the author of *The Epistolary Novel: Representations of Consciousness* (2003) and *The Female Reader in the English Novel* (2009), and editor of, among others, *Mark Z. Danielewski* (2011) and *The Routledge Companion to Experimental Literature* (2012).

Michael Burke is a Professor of Rhetoric at University College Roosevelt (Utrecht University). His books include *Literary Reading Cognition and Emotion* (2011) and *Pedagogical Stylistics* (Burke *et al.* 2012). He is a Routledge monographs series editor in linguistics (stylistics and rhetoric) and a former Chair of the International Poetics and Linguistics Association (PALA).

Beatrix Busse holds a Chair of English Linguistics at the English Department of the Ruprecht-Karls-Universität Heidelberg, Germany. She is a Visiting Fellow of the British Academy. Her scholarly interests include the history of English, (historical) pragmatics, stylistics, and corpus linguistics. Among her recent projects are speech, writing and thought presentation in the history of English, language and urban place, and language and medicine in Medieval and early modern texts.

Patricia Canning has taught undergraduate and postgraduate modules in linguistics as well as early modern literature at Queen's University, Belfast. Her published work reflects her interdisciplinary approach, synthesising functional stylistics, literary theory and phenomenology. She is the founder of the website read.live.learn, which promotes reading for wellbeing across Northern Ireland (www.readlivelearn.com).

Ronald Carter is a Research Professor of Modern English Language at the University of Nottingham. He has written, co-written, edited and co-edited more than fifty books and has published over one hundred academic papers in the fields of literary linguistics, language and education, applied linguistics and the teaching of English.

Billy Clark is a Senior Lecturer in English Language at Middlesex University. His most recent research has focused on pragmatic stylistics, the semantics and pragmatics of prosody, and the inferential processes involved in writing. His book on relevance theory was published by Cambridge University Press in 2013.

Szilvia Csábi received her doctorate in cognitive linguistics at Eötvös Loránd University, Budapest, Hungary. Her interests include textual analyses, especially from a cognitive linguistic perspective. She has co-authored three edited volumes and published several articles in these fields. She currently works at the Publisher of the Hungarian Academy of Sciences and Wolters Kluwer as managing editor of dictionaries.

Barbara Dancygier is a Professor in the English Department at the University of British Columbia in Vancouver. Her main research interests lie in the areas of cognitive linguistics and cognitive approaches to literary texts (theories of conceptual metaphor, mental spaces, and conceptual integration). Her recent book *The Language of Stories* (2012) proposes a blending analysis of narrative structure.

Catherine Emmott is a Reader in English Language at the University of Glasgow. Her publications include *Narrative Comprehension: A Discourse Perspective* (1997) and *Mind, Brain and Narrative* (2012, with Anthony J. Sanford). She is an Assistant Editor of the journal *Language and Literature*.

Kristy Evers is a graduate student at the University of Oxford where she is pursuing a graduate degree in English Language Studies. She is a former undergraduate student of Utrecht University (University College Roosevelt in Middelburg), where she majored in linguists, literature and rhetoric and where she was also editor-in-chief of the student literary magazine *RAW*. She is also the recipient of the 2013 UCR College Student Leadership Award.

Elisabeth El Refaie is a Senior Lecturer at the Centre for Language and Communication Research, Cardiff University. The focus of her research is on visual/multimodal forms of metaphor and narrative. She is the author of *Autobiographical Comics: Life Writing in Pictures*

Olivia Fialho is an Assistant Professor of Rhetoric at University College Roosevelt (Utrecht University). She wrote an interdisciplinary doctoral dissertation on self-modifying reading experiences (2012). She has published in the areas of the empirical study of literature, pedagogical stylistics and literary awareness, and recently on evidence-based learning (Fialho *et al.* 2011, 2012). She coordinates the PALA SIG on Pedagogical Stylistics.

Charles Forceville is an associate professor in the Media Studies Department at Universiteit van Amsterdam. His teaching and research focus on pictorial and multimodal metaphor and discourse. He aims to make humanities research and cognition studies mutually productive (see http://muldisc.wordpress.com).

Margaret H. Freeman is Emeritus Professor of English at Los Angeles Valley College and a co-director of Myrifield Institute for Cognition and the Arts (www.myrifield.org). Her many publications in cognitive poetics mark the expansion of her research from studies in cognitive linguistics to include phenomenology, cognitive science, and aesthetics.

Christiana Gregoriou is a stylistics lecturer at Leeds University's School of English. Her most recent publications include articles, books and edited collections on criminal stylistics. Her most recent critical stylistics monograph is on *Language, Ideology and Identity in Serial Killer Narratives* (2011).

Geoff Hall is a Professor of Sociolinguistics and the Head of the School of English at the University of Nottingham Ningbo China (UNNC), and editor of the journal *Language and Literature*. He has used stylistic approaches in teaching English in many differing countries and contexts. A revised second edition of his book *Literature in Language Education* (2005) is in preparation.

Patrick Colm Hogan is a Professor in the Department of English at the University of Connecticut, where he is also on the faculties of the programmes in Cognitive Science, India Studies, and Comparative Literature and Cultural Studies. He is the author of sixteen books including *What Literature Teaches Us About Emotion* (2011), *How Authors' Minds Make Stories* (2013), and *Ulysses and the Poetics of Cognition* (2013). He was also the editor of *The Cambridge Encyclopedia of the Language Sciences* (2011).

Lesley Jeffries is a Professor of English Language and the Chair of the Stylistics Research Centre at the University of Huddersfield. She is the author of a number of books and articles on textual opposition, critical stylistics and the stylistics of contemporary poetry. She is a co-editor of *Babel*: *the Language Magazine*.

Ernestine Lahey (BA St. Francis Xavier University, Canada; MA, PhD University of Nottingham, UK) is an Assistant Professor in Linguistics and Stylistics at University College Roosevelt, Utrecht University, the Netherlands. Her research interests lie mainly in the fields of (cognitive) stylistics and Canadian literature/culture.

Marina Lambrou is a Principal Lecturer in English Language and Communication at Kingston University, UK. Her research interests include stylistics with a focus on personal narratives, including trauma narratives, narratology and ethnography. Marina is a co-author of *Language and Media* (2009) and a joint-editor of *Contemporary Stylistics* (2007). She is the Guest Editor of the *Language and Literature* Special Issue: 'Narrative' (2014).

Michaela Mahlberg is a Professor of English Language and Linguistics at the University of Nottingham, UK. She is the editor of the *International Journal of Corpus Linguistics* and a co-editor of the book series *Corpus and Discourse* (Bloomsbury). Her most recent publications include the book *Corpus Stylistics and Dickens's Fiction* (2013).

Agnes Marszalek is a PhD research student in English Language at the University of Glasgow, funded by a scholarship from the Carnegie Trust for the Universities of Scotland. Her interests include humour, cognitive stylistics and psychological approaches to text analysis. Her current research focuses primarily on the reader's/viewer's experiences of narrative humour.

Andrea Macrae is a Senior Lecturer in Stylistics at Oxford Brookes University. She teaches stylistics, narratology and cognitive poetics. Her primary areas of research and publication include literary deixis, stylistics of performance, and metafiction.

Gert Meesters is an Associate Professor of Dutch Language and Culture at the University of Lille 3 – Charles de Gaulle. He co-founded Acme, the interdisciplinary group for comics research at the University of Liège, and publishes about comics and linguistic subjects.

Rocío Montoro is a Senior Lecturer in English Language at the University of Granada, Spain. She is the author of *Chick Lit: The Stylistics of Cappuccino Fiction* and *Key Terms in Stylistics* (with Beatrix Busse and Nina Nørgaard). She is currently working (with Dan McIntyre) on a new project on the *Language of Popular Fiction*.

Clara Neary is a Lecturer in English Language and Linguistics at the University of Chester. Specialising in literary and cognitive stylistics, she is particularly interested in the study of narrative empathy and the expansion of stylistic enquiry into genres such as autobiography.

Nina Nørgaard is an Associate Professor of Applied Linguistics in the Department of Language and Communication, University of Southern Denmark. She has published various articles on stylistics and multimodality, a monograph entitled *Systemic Functional Linguistics and Literary Analysis* (2003) and a reference book entitled *Key Terms in Stylistics* (2010). She is currently working on a second monograph entitled *Multimodal Stylistics*.

David Peplow is a Lecturer in English Language at Sheffield Hallam University. His research focuses on book clubs as sites of non-academic reading. He is currently considering how group identity affects literary interpretation in book clubs and how social reading may benefit vulnerable people.

Jennifer Riddle Harding is an Associate Professor of English at Washington and Jefferson College, Pennsylvania, USA. She has published in the *Poetics and Linguistics Association Journal, Style*, the *Hemingway Review*, and the *Journal of Narrative Theory*, as well as contributing to *Conceptual Blending and the Study of Narrative*.

Jeremy Scott writes, teaches and researches on the border between literature and language studies at the University of Kent. As well as his own fiction, he has published on narrative technique, literary representations of dialect, the relationship between narratives and identity, and portrayals of Englishness in fiction.

Dan Shen is the Changjiang Professor of English Language and Literature at Peking University, China. She is on the editorial or advisory boards of the British *Language and Literature*, the American *Style* and *Narrative*, and the European *JLS: Journal of Literary Semantics*. Apart from publishing five books in China, she has published *Style and Rhetoric of Short Narrative Fiction* with Routledge.

Michael Toolan has been Professor of English Language at the University of Birmingham since 1996, where he is currently the Head of the School of English, Drama and American and Canadian Studies. His research interests include literary stylistics and narrative.

Paola Trimarco is a Senior Lecturer at University Campus Suffolk, where she teaches Language Analysis, Critical Language Studies and Digital Textuality. Her publications include *The Discourse of Reading Groups: sociocultural and cognitive approaches* with J. Swann, D. Peplow and S. Whiteley (forthcoming), *Digital Textuality* (forthcoming), chapters in *Pedagogical Stylistics: current trends in language, literature and ELT* edited by M. Burke, S. Csábi, L. Week and J. Zerkowitz (2012) and in *Teaching the Short Story* edited by A. Cox (2011), as well as authoring three books for Penguin Readers.

Chantelle Warner is an Assistant Professor of German and Second Language Acquisition at the University of Arizona. Her research focuses on linguistic practices, and especially literary language and use as social sites of struggle over meanings, subjectivities, and aesthetics. She has published in the fields of German studies, stylistics, literary pragmatics, applied linguistics, and language pedagogy.

Sonia Zyngier has authored numerous papers on literary awareness, stylistics, and empirical research in literary education. She wrote an article on pedagogical stylistics for the *Elsevier Encyclopedia of Language and Linguistics* (2005) and is a co-editor of the *Linguistic Approaches to Literature Series* (John Benjamins). She has also co-authored *Scientific Methods for the Humanities* (2012).

Acknowledgements

Producing a handbook of this size and scope is no simple matter. Such a task must invariably draw substantially on the time, commitment and fortitude of many individuals. The timely production of this handbook therefore involved much hard work and cooperation across several institutions, groups of people and individuals. I am deeply indebted first to all of the contributors to this handbook who submitted on time, took heed of my suggestions for improvements and always remained agreeable. I would especially like to thank my former research assistant, Kristy Evers, for her attentive support in helping me to prepare the chapters for publication and for conducting a number of essential administrative tasks. At Routledge, I am grateful to commissioning editor Nadia Seemungal who initially approached me to edit this *Handbook of Stylistics* and allowed me free rein to come up with my own section heads, the chapter content in those sections and the authors to produce those chapters. I would also like to thank Sophie Jaques, senior editorial assistant, with whom I worked closely during the first half of this project, and editorial assistant Rachel Daw, who took over this project from Sophie and saw it through to its completion. I am also indebted to their colleagues in production and copyediting, in particular Louise Maskill, Geraldine Martin and Rob Brown, for doing such a wonderful job making this book. The publisher is indebted to Grove/Atlantic, Inc., for permission to reproduce an excerpt from *Rosencrantz and Guildenstern are Dead*, copyright ©1967 by Tom Stoppard. Further, the publisher is also grateful to the Trustees of Amherst College for permission to reprint the poetry of Emily Dickenson from *The Manuscript Books of Emily Dickenson: A Facsimile Edition*, R. W. Franklin, ed., Cambridge, Mass.: The Belknap Press of Harvard University Press, copyright © 1981 by the President and Fellows of Harvard College (copyright © 1951, 1955, 1978, 1979, 1980, by the President and Fellows of Harvard College; copyright © 1914, 1924, 1929, 1932, 1942, by Martha Dickinson Bianchi). The Wilfred Owen poem 'The parable of the old man and the young' appears in the form found in *Wilfred Owen: The war poems* (Chatto and Windus, 1994, p. 61). We are grateful to the book's publisher and its editor Jon Stallworthy for permission to reproduce it here. While every effort has been made to contact copyright holders, we would be pleased to hear of any that have been inadvertently omitted. I am also indebted to University College Roosevelt in Middelburg and the Humanities Faculty of Utrecht University, for encouraging and facilitating the production of both high quality research and valuable learning materials. My final thanks go to my wife Helle and my two children Louisa and Oscar for their patience, and for putting up with my long days of absenteeism (especially at weekends) while I was ensconced in my upstairs study at home editing and commenting on the thirty-two chapters that make up this handbook. This book is dedicated to my stylistics students –

past, present and future – for their inspiration, their motivation and their constructive criticism. For without them, there would be no book and no conceivable reason to have ever considered writing one.

Michael Burke
Middelburg, The Netherlands
September 2013

Introduction

Stylistics: From classical rhetoric to cognitive neuroscience

Michael Burke

This handbook is a reference work covering key topics in stylistics. It can also function as a textbook. Each of the thirty-two chapters provides an accessible, introductory overview to an area of the field. The book is intended for a broad audience: anyone, in fact, with an interest in language, literature or culture. However, the work is directed at beginners in the field, whether they are undergraduate students, graduate students or researchers and academics who work in other disciplines.

Stylistics

Stylistics, or 'literary linguistics' as it is sometimes called, is the study and analysis of texts; it is in particular, although not exclusively, the study and analysis of literary texts. The origins of stylistics go back to the poetics, and especially to the rhetoric, of the ancient classical world. In ancient rhetoric it is principally the third of the five canons which is of importance to stylistics. The ancient Greeks called this third canon '*lexis*', and the Romans referred to it as '*elocutio*'. We know it today as style (see Wales 2011, p. 372 for more on this).

First of all, textual 'material'/'data' was generated and/or discovered. Arguments were then formed from this material based on one of the three Aristotelian proofs: logos, ethos and pathos. This constituted the first canon of rhetoric. That material was then ordered for optimal effect in a given situation. This is the second canon. Thereafter, the textual material was stylised (the third canon). Finally, it was memorised (if it was a speech) and then delivered. These constitute the fourth and fifth canons respectively. The stylisation of the text in the third canon of rhetoric essentially took two forms. The first kind of stylisation was based on the clarity, preciseness and appropriateness of the language to be used. The second kind was based on style figures. These were either schemes (which deviate at the syntactic level of language) or tropes (which deviate at the semantic level). In addition to this, and linked to the category of appropriateness, there were three kinds of style which were thought to be appropriate in almost all speaking situations; these were the high style, the middle style and the low style. The high, florid style was often reserved for literature and poetry. It was also very persuasive, drawing as it did on pathos (one of Aristotle's three proofs) to influence thinking patterns. The low, plain style was mostly used for more mundane acts of discourse communication – for example, instruction in the classroom. The middle style was invariably a blend of both, to be used in intermediate situations.

There can be no doubt that the fundamental core of stylistics lies in the rhetoric of the classical world. The modern type of stylistics that we know today did not emerge until the beginning of the twentieth century. It was the Russian formalists, and especially Roman Jakobson, Viktor Shklovsky and Vladimir Propp, who were instrumental at the source of this development. What these scholars had in common was a desire to make literary scholarship more scientific and to find out what makes poetic texts poetic. To achieve this they put forward their structuralist ideas. Jakobson focused on the poetic function of language, Propp on the parts that make up stories and the repetitive/universal elements that occur within those stories, and Shklovsky on how literature and art defamiliarise or 'make strange'. It is clear that much of this work is a recycling of ideas from the ancient world of rhetoric and poetics. For example, Shklovsky's 'defamiliarisation' theory, which is the aesthetic idea that words that are ordered and presented in a fresh way can make a reader see a particular word, and the world to which it refers, in a fresh light, is simply a rhetorical style figure.

Russian formalism petered out in the early 1930s, but it continued in Prague under the heading of structuralism. Slowly but surely the Prague School turned away from formalism towards functionalism. It is this inclusion of context in textual meaning making that paved the way for much of the stylistics that occurs today. The text, the context and the reader are all now at the heart of stylistic scholarship. Stylistics nowadays is a field of study that confidently has one foot in language studies and the other in literary studies.

Contemporary stylistics goes far beyond the rhetoric, poetics, formalism, structuralism and functionalism of the past to embrace corpus, critical, cognitive, pedagogical, pragmatic, gender, multimodal and, most recently, neuroscientific approaches. This diversity might have the initial appearance of fragmenting the field. However, nothing could be further from the truth, because at many levels, interdisciplinarity study is what stylistics is designed to do. As stylistician Paul Simpson writes, 'stylistics is a method of textual interpretation in which primacy of place is assigned to language' (2004, p. 2). Stylistics thus still carries the methodological genes that it has inherited from its forebear, rhetoric. Its very purpose is its application to textual data, and its strength lies in its potential for such application. (For more on the 'many branches of stylistics', see Nørgaard, Busse and Montoro 2011, pp. 7–48).

Stylistic methodologies, both qualitative and quantitative, have become increasingly polished and honed over the years. Stylistician Ron Carter has said that stylistics should strive to be 'open, evidenced and retrievable' (2010, p. 68). This statement supports the falsifiability expectations that science expects, and in this sense it is relevant for stylistics. However, it is also true that stylistics in its more 'hands on', humanities-based, analytic sense is every bit as valuable. Another stylistician, Mick Short, writes that a good, stylistic foregrounding analysis should bring solid linguistic description to bear on autonomous critical statements from the world of literary studies of interpretation and evaluation (1996, p. 3). What a robust stylistic analysis can do here is point to the physical evidence in the text that can either support or falsify the disembodied verbal enunciation of the aforementioned literary critic/scholar.

Let us look at this point in more detail. A stylistician can arguably be viewed as a kind of empirical or forensic discourse critic: a person who with his/her detailed knowledge of the workings of morphology, phonology, lexis, syntax, semantics, and various discourse and pragmatic models, goes in search of language-based evidence in order to support or indeed challenge the subjective interpretations and evaluations of various critics and cultural commentators. Imagine a kind of Sherlock Holmes character, who is an expert grammarian and rhetorician and has a love of literature and other creative texts. Now imagine further that this linguistic sleuth reads a review of a novel on an internet blog, written by a cultural expert who is praising the story he has just read by using what you and I might call inflated language. That cultural expert might have written something along the lines of the following: 'the story succeeds in asphyxiating the waning reader in a hopeless series of disappearing alleys of claustrophobia'. Nice diction, our linguistic detective might think, but extremely vague, and perhaps even somewhat pretentious. Our sleuth then sets out to discover whether there is any linguistic evidence to support this claim, and/or to find counter-evidence in order to deny or falsify it. First, our stylistician-linguist reads the story, and in doing so she might, for example, indeed recognise the essence of what the cultural expert or critic meant with his vague words. This recognition would then confirm the interpretation and the subsequent evaluation of the critic. But what about the description? Where is the linguistic evidence to back up this claim? What role does the actual language use play in this story, and might it in some way be responsible from this essentially 'claustrophobic' interpretation that has been put forward by the cultural commentator?

Armed with her stylistic toolkit, our '*Sherlocke Stylistica*' sets out to see whether there might be, for example, an over-representation of such linguistic phenomena as closed vowels, mono-syllabic words, abstract nouns or minimalist syntax in the text, because if there is, the combination of such 'restrictive' or 'plain' linguistic features might be adding to, or even helping to create, the overall effect of perceived 'claustrophobia' in the reader. The stylistic detective can then present the linguistic data acquired by her systematic investigation to other stylisticians, and can offer a plausible and relatively objective interpretation for her fellow linguists to evaluate or corroborate by repeating her analysis. In this way, stylistics encourages literary criticism to be about more than just opinions. This is essentially what stylistics is all about. It is a kind of linguistic-forensic, literary discourse criticism.

The scope of this volume

This book is called *The Routledge Handbook of Stylistics*. Just as the name suggests, a handbook (or 'manual') is essentially a 'how-to-do' book. It is not a collection of academic article-like chapters based on current research. Once you have read this volume you should be able to confidently conduct your own stylistic analyses. This handbook is therefore both a reference work and a textbook for students and teachers alike. Teachers can use it as a textbook for a full course/module of study on stylistics, going through it sequentially, perhaps taking one or even two chapters per session. Alternatively, they can allow students to use it as a reference work, dipping in and out of it and reading specific chapters in support of an alternative textbook that they may be working from. Most chapters, and certainly those in Parts 2, 3 and 4 of the book, have a distinct structure to them. First, you are given a detailed historical overview of the theory under discussion. This 'historical perspectives' section is then followed by a clear outline of the method involved, together with examples to aid your understanding of the concept under discussion. Thereafter you are given a number of 'recommendations for practice'. This is an important section. The author who has written the chapter has come up with a number of fruitful small-scale research topics for you to have a go at. You should try at least one of these from every chapter. Preferably you will try more than one, because these will not only allow you to conduct a rewarding stylistic analysis, they will also give you the inspiration and confidence you may need to go in search of your own material for analysis.

Writing a stylistics paper can be a fraught and sometimes daunting endeavour. Thankfully, there are some additional guidelines available to take you through the process step by step (see, for example, Burke 2010). After the 'recommendation for practice' section in each chapter there is a section on 'future directions'. This will point you to where the stylistic research of the near future will be taking place in the area you are reading about. This is the research that *you* might very well be doing if you choose to stay in the field and write a PhD thesis or do research on a post-doctoral project. In a way, these sections are a kind of 'heads up' for newer and younger scholars in the field to show them the kind of cutting-edge research they should be producing. The chapters end with some essential suggestions for further reading. There is also a list of topics closely related to the one you have just been reading about that are covered elsewhere in this handbook, so if you find you are really interested in a particular topic, you will know what else to read in the handbook in order to enhance your knowledge of that topic.

This book covers thirty-two key stylistic topics that will take you from the very beginnings of stylistics, namely the classical world of ancient rhetoric, to its prospective future, the cognitive domain of neuroscience. All chapters have been written by handpicked stylistics experts from all over the world: from China, the USA, Canada, Brazil, the UK and mainland Europe, including Germany, France, Spain, Denmark, Hungary and the Netherlands. Many of these writers are in their prime and will still be teaching stylistics for the next twenty to thirty years. This publication is truly an international book, with international examples that are geared towards an international student audience. All the expert authors in this book actively teach stylistics in their universities, and it is this everyday pedagogical knowledge of how to guide students through the process of conducting a stylistic analysis that they bring to bear in their individual chapters, thereby helping you to take ownership of your own learning. As a result the chapters come to life, almost allowing students to hear the individual voices of each teacher as they are guided and stimulated to learn for themselves – after all, learning is not listening, or even reading, but rather 'doing', and this is why the 'recommendations for practice' sections in the chapters are so important for your own learning. It is also the reason why this section has not been tagged onto the end of each chapter as an afterthought, as is the case all too often in other handbooks and textbooks. Instead it is firmly embedded within the chapters, appearing as it does before the 'future directions' section.

The book is set out in four parts. We will now look in a little more detail at each part.

Part I   Historical perspectives in stylistics

Part I of this handbook, which consists of just four chapters, does not entirely follow the internal structure that most of the other chapters have, as described above. There is a lot of historical background to impart to you in these chapters, and as a result the focus lies here. What this opening section does do, however, is set the scene for you; it gives you all the background knowledge you will need to tackle the remaining twenty-eight chapters. These four chapters, and especially the first two, will continually point forward to the theories and methods that will come up in the rest of the book. This is to help you to draw comparisons, make links and understand just how the seemingly different parts of stylistic scholarship fit together. In the opening chapter in this first section Michael Burke takes us back to where it all began: the classical world of rhetoric and poetics. Aristotle is our main starting point, and you will be amazed at the things he was saying about style and narrative. That sense of wonder will be grounded in the realisation that things have not changed an awful lot in more than two thousand years. Reviewing the rhetorical work of figures like Cicero and Quintilian may very well give you pointers to future research in emerging domains. In Chapter 2, Michael Burke and Kristy Evers bring us into the early twentieth century to look at what we might call the beginnings of modern stylistics, namely formalism and later structuralism. You will be introduced to some of the key theories of the Russian formalists – people like Jakobson, Shklovsky and Propp – and you will see just how heavily these scholars drew on the ideas of the rhetorical and poetic ancient past to inform the development of theories on what makes language poetic. In Chapter 3 Patricia Canning takes us from formalism into the domain of functionalism. She applies the Hallidayan systemic functional grammar approach to stylistic analysis. In Chapter 4 Jennifer Riddle Harding examines the reader response theories that emerged as a result of earlier ideas on formalism, structuralism and functionalism. With these four building blocks – (1) ancient rhetoric and poetics, (2) formalism and structuralism, (3) functionalism, and (4) reader response theories – the scene is set to take on the second part of this handbook.

Part II   Core issues in stylistics

The second section of the volume, entitled 'Core issues in stylistics', runs from Chapter 5 to Chapter 13. As the title suggests, it is here that you will be introduced to the main aspects of stylistics. If Part I was the basement of a house built of stylistic knowledge, then Part II is the ground floor (or the first floor, if you are from North America). In Chapter 5 Christiana Gregoriou leads you through what is seen by many as 'the core of core issues' in stylistics – namely, foregrounding. In this chapter she puts into practice the theories that started to ferment in Chapters 1 to 4. In Chapter 6 Beatrix Busse sets out the basics of 'new historical stylistics', reminding us that stylistic study can be just as fruitful when analysing texts diachronically as the more standard synchronic mode of investigation. There then follow three chapters which are closely related: Chapter 7 on speech acts and (im)politeness theory, written by Derek Bousfield, Chapter 8 on conversation analysis and the cooperative principle by Marina Lambrou, and Chapter 9 on relevance theory by Billy Clark. Here the philosophical, discoursal and pragmatic elements of stylistic analysis are examined in depth. It is also here that you will see just how grounded in classical rhetoric many aspects of modern pragmatics are. In Chapter 10 Clara Neary shows us the subtleties of point of view and modality, and this narrative flavour is expanded in Chapter 11 with Dan Shen's clear exposition of narratological issues in stylistics. This section then ends with two chapters which deal with popular core principals in stylistics: these are stylistic studies into metaphor and metonymy, in Chapter 12 by Szilvia Csábi, and speech and thought presentation in Chapter 13 by Joe Bray. These chapters make an appropriate link to Part III of the handbook.

Part III   Contemporary topics in stylistics

Part III of the book contains Chapters 14 to 25. This section deals with the modern stylistics that is primarily taking place in the undergraduate university classrooms of today. The topics fall under the umbrella terms of the cognitive, the critical and the pedagogical. For this reason, the section is entitled 'Contemporary topics in stylistics'. If we proceed with our metaphor of 'stylistics as a house', we are now on the first floor (or the second floor, for North American readers). 'Pedagogical stylistics' is the title of Chapter 14, where the author Geoff Hall sets out a number of methods and approaches that show just why it is that pedagogical stylistics is at the very heart of stylistic scholarship. In Chapter 15 Andrea Macrae takes us through one of the most popular areas of stylistics at this moment in time: the stylistics of drama and performance.

Next come four chapters which all have a distinct cognitive flavour to them. Influences from cognitive psychology and cognitive linguistics have made cognitive approaches to stylistics extremely popular at the moment. In Chapter 16 Cathy Emmott, Marc Alexander and Agnes Marszalek look at the possibilities that schema, frame and script theory offer stylistics. We then have two very closely related chapters that theorise, from a stylistic perspective, how text processing and mental representations operate. These are Chapter 17 on text world theory, written by Ernestine Lahey, and Chapter 18 on blending, written by Barbara Dancygier. The fourth chapter in this short cognitive series, Chapter 19, acts as a kind of macro-level chapter, drawing together the topics discussed in the previous three chapters and much more. It is entitled 'Cognitive poetics' and is written by Margaret Freeman.

We then move to an empirical methods chapter (Chapter 20) written by Olivia Fialho and Sonia Zyngier, with a focus on the increasing significance of both qualitative and quantitative methods which have come to us from the social sciences. Part III ends with five chapters, all different in their approaches, but all at the cutting edge of practical stylistic scholarship today. The first of these is Chapter 21 on feminist approaches to stylistics, written by Rocio Montoro, and the second is Chapter 22 written by Chantelle Warner and dealing with literary pragmatics. The third of this five-chapter cluster is Chapter 23 on corpus approaches to stylistics, written by Michaela Mahlberg. Chapter 24 is on stylistics and translation and is written by Jean Boase-Beier. Finally, Chapter 25, written by Lesley Jeffries, is on the very popular topic of critical stylistics. Much research work is currently being done in all these five areas by students and scholars alike.

Part IV   Emerging and future trends in stylistics

If Part IV was the first floor of our 'house of stylistics', then Part IV is the newly renovated loft or attic apartment. In this final part of the handbook, entitled 'Emerging and future trends in stylistics', we encounter seven exciting developments in stylistic scholarship – modern trends that may very well make up the core of the field in ten years' time. In Chapter 26 Jeremy Scott introduces us to a 'productive' kind of stylistics in the form of creative writing. In Chapter 27 David Peplow and Ron Carter bring to our attention the importance of having real readers and reading groups in your experiments in order for you to be able to draw valid conclusions in stylistic and reader response studies. Chapter 28, written by Michael Toolan, takes us to the burgeoning world of stylistics and film, while Nina Nørgaard builds on this in Chapter 29 to show us the expanding visual domain of multimodality. Chapter 30, written by Charles Forceville, Elisabeth El Refaie and Gert Meesters, takes us into the relatively unexplored world of stylistics and comics, while Chapter 31 by Paola Trimarco introduces us to stylistics in the online world of hypertext fiction. The final chapter in the handbook is perhaps the most futuristic of all, but at the same time it is the most enticing. Written by Patrick Colm Hogan, this chapter on 'Stylistics, emotion and neuroscience' will point you firmly towards where stylistics is headed, and shed light on where it might very well be twenty years from now.

Concluding remarks

This handbook is set up to help you understand the basic principles and methods of the field, and to guide you through the process of doing stylistic analysis. The way the chapters are arranged means that ideally they should be read sequentially from 1 to 32 in a semester-long course on stylistics. However, they are written in such a way that you can, should you so wish, dip in and out of sections and chapters, making your own narrative and crafting stylistic pathways that fit your own interests. In this sense the book can act as a support to another textbook, filling in any gaps that remain open and making meaningful additions to the knowledge it imparts. There is also an innate interdisciplinary character to many of the chapters. For example, the final chapter on neuroscience includes parts that could quite easily have been placed in the very first chapter of the book, on classical rhetoric and poetics. The life of stylistics is a linear journey, from a source, through a path, to a goal, but at one and the same time it is also a loop, where the end can be the beginning, and the beginning the end.

Stylistics is a subject to be enjoyed. You should not lose sight of this fact when you are reading the chapters in this volume and writing your own analyses based on the many 'recommendations for practice' sections. Stylistics is going places, and now is the time for you to get on board. It is a welcome guest in many intellectual homes in many locations across disciplines such as communication studies, rhetoric, pragmatics, discourse analysis, applied linguistics, literary studies, film, television and theatre studies, museum studies and so on. Stylistics also has its own home, though, and that is the 'International Poetics and Linguistics Association' (PALA) which has seen more than thirty international conferences on stylistics come and go over the years (in locations from Malta to Middelburg, Budapest to Birmingham, and Huddersfield to Heidelberg). Its membership is now around seven hundred, and more than half of those scholars are under thirty. As the twenty-first century blossoms into its second decade, stylistics is moving out of young adulthood and into its prime. Notwithstanding the immense richness of its past and present – which you will read about in depth in the pages of this handbook – it is a certainty that the best years of stylistics still lie ahead.

References

Burke, M., 2010. Rhetorical pedagogy: Teaching students how to write a stylistics paper. *Language and Literature*, 19 (1), 77–98.

Carter, R., 2010. Methodologies for stylistic analysis: Practices and pedagogies. *In:* D. McIntyre and B. Busse, eds. *Language and style*. London: Palgrave, 55–68.

Nørgaard, N., Busse, B., and Montoro, R., 2010. *Key terms in stylistics*. London: Continuum.

Short, M., 1996. *Exploring the language of poems, plays and prose*, London: Longman.

Simpson, P., 2004. *Stylistics: A resource book for students*. London: Routledge.

Wales, K., 2011. *A dictionary of stylistics*. 3rd ed. London: Longman.

Part I
Historical perspectives in stylistics

Rhetoric and poetics

The classical heritage of stylistics

Michael Burke

Introduction

Without classical rhetoric and poetics there would be no stylistics as we know it today. This opening chapter introduces you to the fields of rhetoric and poetics, the classical forebears of contemporary stylistics. In doing so, it encourages you to go beyond this chapter and seek them out, to become better acquainted with them and to make them your allies, because a solid understanding of such past discourse and communication structures and models will both augment and enrich your current level of stylistic knowledge.

Almost every overview of stylistics in the past thirty years or so begins in the twentieth century, with Roman Jakobson and Russian formalism. This is understandable and in many ways it is appropriate and correct. However, choosing to start approximately one hundred years ago risks missing out on something that is of central importance to stylistics today, and to its continuing development into the multimodal and neuroscientific world of the twenty-first century. What this chapter seeks to accomplish is to offer you an indispensable contextual background to the field of stylistics, which many of the stylistics students of recent years have unfortunately been deprived of.

Jakobson's critical poetic work did not come into being spontaneously; it did not emerge out a void of nothingness. If you read his works you will see that he had a profound knowledge of both poetics and rhetoric, upon which he drew heavily. For example, in his famous 'Closing statement: Linguistics and poetics' essay he conducts a detailed stylistic analysis of Mark Anthony's famous monologue from Shakespeare's *Julius Caesar* (Jakobson 1960, pp. 375–376). In this analysis he observes levels of foregrounding that include paronomasia, polyptoton, apostrophe, exordium, *modus obliquus* and *modus rectus*, which are all key terms from the field of classical rhetoric.

In this chapter we will survey the main principles of both poetics and rhetoric. There will be a focus on history, theory and methodology. We will see how these ancient disciplines continue to affect and influence modern-day stylistics. The chapter will close with some pointers towards future directions in the field.

Historical overview

The great classical period of rhetoric and poetics began roughly in the fifth century BC with the beginnings of democracy in Athens. It continued right up to the fall of the Roman empire in the West, although the Roman tradition of rhetoric schools and their progymnasmata programme of learning (about which you will learn more later) continued in the Eastern Roman world right up until the fall of the Byzantine empire in the fifteenth century AD. After the fall of Constantinople, rhetoric continued to grow in status in the West and became part of the European trivium, which was the 'academic core', as it were, of schooling and learning, consisting of the three related disciplines of grammar, logic and rhetoric. This system lasted more or less in the same form through the Renaissance and Early Modern periods, only really disappearing in Europe in the early nineteenth century. However, rhetoric continued to be taught as a learning tool in the United States, and even today every US college worth its salt offers freshman courses in rhetoric, argumentation and composition.

It is perhaps fair to say that rhetoric, with its inherent link to style, is more important to modern day stylistics than poetics. It is for this reason that a relatively short overview of poetics will now be given, followed by a longer survey of classical rhetoric.

Classical poetics

The three main concepts that we will encounter in this section are: (i) mimesis (which is the opposite of diegesis); (ii) catharsis (which incorporates the emotions of pity and fear); and (iii) plot structure (including the key notions of *hamartia*, *peripeteia* and *anagnorisis*). These terms no doubt seem very strange to you in their ancient Greek form. However, they do all have straightforward English equivalents, which we will learn about in the course of this section and which you can use instead.

When the word 'poetics' is mentioned, there is really only one name that can follow: Aristotle. This fourth century BC *homo universalis* will be our starting point. From him, we will go on to consider the work of two Roman literary theorists, Horace and Longinus. Of course, there were many prolific Greek lyric poets and playwrights before Aristotle, including, Homer, Hesiod, Pindar, Sappho, Aeschylus, Sophocles, Euripides and Aristophanes. However, it is Aristotle who is thought to have written the first book-length work of critical literary theory in the ancient Hellenic world (of course, there may have been earlier ones, of which Aristotle makes no mention, which are now lost to us). The main theoretical points that Aristotle focuses on are, as listed above, mimesis (broadly translated as 'imitation', 'copying' or 'representing'), catharsis (a kind of 'cleansing' or 'clearing away') and plot structure. We will look at all three of these, starting with mimesis.

Perhaps paradoxically, it was not Aristotle who first wrote on mimesis but his mentor and teacher Plato. If you recall, Plato was the man who, if he had had his way, would have banned all poets from his ideal state for being generally useless and also a threat to people's perception of reality. As such, poets were surplus to requirements in his hypothetical utopian republic. Therefore, if we wish to know more about Aristotle's mimesis, we will first have to briefly consider Plato's views on this topic. Not surprisingly, Plato writes about poetry not in the context of praising its worth, but to critique it and demonstrate its dangers to society. He reflects on mimesis in different places in his magnum opus, *The Republic*. For example, in Book 3 (pp. 392–395) he deliberates on the kind of literature that the future citizens of his ideal state should study. He then distinguishes between two types of narration. The first is when an author speaks in the voice of his characters. This he defines as mimesis: the author is 'imitating' their voices. The second is when the author speaks in his own voice. This is 'narration', which Plato calls 'diegesis'. You can see here the clear beginnings not just of narratology and narrative theory, but also the essential groundwork for speech and thought presentation, a key area in stylistics (see Chapters 11 and 13 in this volume for more on these topics).

Plato returns to the notion of mimesis in Book 10 of *The Republic* (2000, pp. 597–600) in a discussion of his famous 'theory of forms', where he relates mimesis to the negative idea of mere 'copying'. This is somewhat different to the gloss mimesis is given in Book 3, where identification with character and character voice is central. In Book 10 poetic mimesis is presented as a superficial and essentially worthless practice, distracting people from seeing the true forms. As such it is a danger to the state, something that should be rooted out and banished.

Let us now turn to Aristotle and his views on mimesis. What makes Aristotle's discussion different is that, unlike Plato, for him poetics is the object of study itself and not a side argument in a larger philosophical theory. In the *Poetics*, believed to be the first work of literary criticism in the Western tradition, Aristotle tackles the thorny issues of the nature of poetry and how its parts can be classified, categorised and understood. In this sense, Aristotle's approach is very much a formalist one. However, the *Poetics* is not a prescriptive handbook. In fact, its concerns are aesthetic and psychological, because it seeks to understand how poetic discourse works on an audience, something with which current studies into 'stylistics and real readers' are also concerned (see Chapter 27 in this volume for more on this). Like rhetoric, Aristotle sees poetry as an art, in the sense of a skill/craft (*technê*), and this becomes clear in the course of his work. This differs to Plato, who mainly saw poets as slaves to the Muses – individuals who sat around waiting to be touched by the creative hand of inspiration. Where Aristotle thought that poets create things by means of their intellect and applied reason, Plato believed that they copy things with the help of their irrational mood swings and general ignorance.

Another significant difference is that where Plato saw poetry and drama as morally perilous and therefore a threat to society; Aristotle saw them as useful and practical and therefore helpful to society. Plato thought that emotions were best kept deep inside a person, but Aristotle wanted them expressed and out in the open, believing that this would be of benefit for both the individual concerned and for the community in general. Although Plato does give us a clear definition of mimesis in the *Republic*, Aristotle does not do so in his *Poetics*, so we can only assume that he is also referring to the imitative or representative power of both verbal and visual art forms.

Aristotle was also interested in why it is that human beings instinctively appear to delight and take great pleasure in artistic imitations. In this sense Aristotle takes mimesis to a new level, turning it into a kind of natural, basic instinct that exists alongside other social, cultural and individual phenomena. We do not only like to observe pleasurable things in art; we also like to observe things that are confrontational, such as acts of murder and human degradation, which we would not wish to encounter in real life.

The main bulk of the surviving chapters of the *Poetics* focus on the poetics of drama and on tragedy in particular. There was apparently a second book in the *Poetics* on the subject of comedy, but this is lost. There is also very little written in the *Poetics* about the third genre, 'epic'. This leaves the *Poetics* as essentially a discourse on tragedy. Aristotle defines tragedy as

> … a representation of action that is serious, complete and of some magnitude; in language that is pleasurably embellished, the different forms of embellishments occurring in

separate parts; presented in the form of action, not narration, by means of pity and fear bringing about the catharsis of such emotions.

[1449b]

'Catharsis' is a major concept in Aristotle's *Poetics*, even though nowhere in the book is it a given a solid definition. As a result, and in many ways similar to mimesis, views differ on its translation and on its semantic scope. The most general description involves the notion of a 'clearing away' or 'cleansing' of both body and mind. This is how catharsis is said to work.

Imagine that instead of hanging out in the pub with your friends you decide to go to the theatre. There you watch a tragedy. It could be something from ancient times, such as *Oedipus Rex* by Sophocles, something more recent like Shakespeare's *Hamlet*, or something relatively modern like Kesey's *One flew over the cuckoo's nest* or Miller's *Death of a salesman*. On stage you see the protagonist/hero suffering, not as a result of deliberate, immoral deeds but because of fate. As a result you start to empathise with him/her and to pity his/her situation. That pity then transforms into fear for yourself and your loved ones as you subconsciously trigger a kind of 'I hope that kind of thing never happens to us' scenario in your head. At any stage in this process you can be moved to tears both by what you have witnessed and by the fear and anxiety you have experienced. This experiencing of intense emotion at what might be called a benign artistic distance, rather than in real life, is what 'cleanses' your mind, body and perhaps even your soul, allowing you to function better in your everyday life for the benefit of yourself, your loved ones and your fellow citizens.

Let us now look at the third of Aristotle's poetic theories, plot structure, which is in many ways connected to both mimesis and catharsis. Three key elements in Aristotelian plot structure are *hamartia*, *peripeteia* and *anagnorisis*. *Hamartia* is essentially a 'mistake' or 'error', often translated in poetic terms as an innate 'tragic flaw' in a specific character, often the protagonist. *Peripeteia*, or 'peripety' as it is referred to in English, pertains to a 'reversal of circumstance' – a change of fortune. It comes as a surprise to the character, but it is a necessary development in the plot. *Anagnorisis* refers to an act of 'recognition'. This is a place in the plot where the character realises what he/she has done (often as a result of his/her *hamartia* or earlier mistake or tragic flaw). For example, the character Oedipus Rex, in the play of the same name, does not know that he has inadvertently killed his own father (whom he thought was a stranger) and married his mother (whom he thought was the Queen of Thebes, the head of a city state from which he believed he did not hail). The reason for his misperception is that as a small baby he was taken from Thebes to Corinth, some distance way, where he was raised as the child of the king and queen of that city state. When in later life he travelled to Thebes as a young man, he did not know that his real mother and father lived there and that he would be destined to commit two prophesised heinous acts: patricide and incest.

The events in his past, the transgressions against the gods that had been committed by his ancestors, imbued him with *hamartia* (he is a tragic hero destined to suffer). The reversal or 'peripety' in the story occurs when a messenger comes to court in Thebes to tell Oedipus, who is essentially a good man, that his mother in Corinth is dead. Oedipus is relieved because this news means that he will not fulfil the prophecy that he will end up sleeping with his mother and killing his father. However, his lingering fears about the prophecy, together with a malicious plague of infertility that has suddenly descended on the city since he married the queen, slowly start to disclose the facts of the matter to him as the messenger gives him more information than he expected. The truth is revealed. The next stage *anagnorisis*, i.e. 'recognition', follows quickly after *peripeteia* as Oedipus realises who he truly is and what he has done. This is a stage where he passes from ignorance to knowledge.

Upon hearing the news his wife, who is also his mother, kills herself, and on finding her body Oedipus gouges out his own eyes and is doomed to wander the earth until the end of his days, becoming a wretched, worthless creature. For an audience watching the events unfold, the individuals in that gathering will almost certainly feel pity for the hapless Oedipus. This in turn may lead to tears. They might also project aspects of the events witnessed on the stage onto themselves and their loved ones according to different 'what if' scenarios. Upon leaving the theatre, the audience members might feel purged or cleansed of certain subconscious feelings they might have had. This is the catharsis of which Aristotle writes.

Aristotle was prescriptive with regard to which elements the ideal plot should entail. For example:

i.   the plot should consist of a single issue (not a double one) and the representation of action should be serious and complete (with a beginning, middle and end), and it should be represented in embellished language where necessary
ii. plots can be simple or complex. In simple plots/actions the change of fortune comes about without the elements of reversal or recognition; however, complex plots/actions need reversal and recognition
iii. the hero's change of fortune (*peripeteia*) has to be from happiness to misery (and not the other way around). There were few happy endings in the ancient Greek world, unlike the Hollywood of today
iv. the cause is not depravity or wickedness but a character error/flaw (*hamartia*)
v.   the hero must be a relatively good man
vi. the action of the play unfolds over one day, no longer, which means that a lot of the story has to have already taken place when the play starts. This is reported in speech about past events and flashbacks
vii. the deed that is committed must be among family members or good friends/loved ones, not among strangers
viii. there is a predictable and necessary 'surprise' – recognition/discovery (*anagnorisis*).

In this structured approach we see a kind of organic unity that in some ways might (mimetically) imitate nature; the parts naturally make up the whole, which makes it beautiful.

Aristotle's *Poetics* had a huge influence on later Renaissance writers. However, they made the error of thinking that like his *Art of rhetoric*, his *Poetics* too was a precise composition plan for how to construct the ideal tragedy. It was not. Long before the Renaissance, Aristotle's *Poetics* had a huge influence on the Roman poets and playwrights. In Roman poetics and literary criticism there are two names that spring to mind: Horace and Longinus. Of course, there are many great Roman poets, such as Petronius, Ovid, Virgil, Juvenal and many more, some of whom also wrote theoretical treatises, but Horace's *The art of poetry* and Longinus's *On the sublime* are much cited works, and were already important didactic tools in antiquity. They will therefore constitute the mainstay of this next section.

Horace, a first century BC Roman, believed that the poet had to sweat in order to create great works of literary art. The archetypal long-haired bohemian artist who sits around most of the day waiting for inspiration to strike would be a depiction that Horace would neither recognise nor agree with. Natural ability was admittedly an asset, but without hard endeavour there could be no successful writer. Good writers were studious craftsmen, not carefree nonconformists. In order to become good writers, students had to read the Greek poetic masters like Homer, making these stories their own. They then had to learn to imitate the style and syntax of writers like Homer in their own words and draft compositions, in much the same fashion as the young men in the rhetoric schools had to do. Indeed, modern-day stylistics and/or rhetoric-based creative writing modules and courses at universities also do just this. (For more on creative writing and stylistics, see Chapter 26 in this volume). Horace focused not so much on plot, as Aristotle did, but rather on character. Main characters had to be morally good individuals, and this knowledge and insight into what makes an ethically upright character came to the poet not just as a result of his hard work, but also as a consequence of his wide reading and subsequent knowledge of the world. This idea that being well read can make you a better citizen is something that is still topical today (see, for example, Nussbaum 1998).

Arguably, Horace's main theoretical input was the notion of 'decorum', the idea that in poetry everything should be fit and proper and appropriate. In many ways Horace is a kind of proto-'relevance theorist' for poetics (for more on relevance theory in stylistics see Chapter 9 in this volume). For Horace, decorum ranged from the nature or genre of the subject matter right down to the more micro-level matters of words and meter. Characters should also be true to life. His ideas on decorum also extended to the mind. Although he valued the eye above the ear (i.e. looking at/watching something rather than listening to it), when it came to being capable of actively stimulating the mind, heinous acts like the killing of innocents, acts of rape and so on should always take place offstage and never be performed in full view of the audience, because this was not fitting. Of course, what all this shows is just how committed Horace was to the notion of mimesis: that art should imitate nature, and that incompatibility in these matters should be avoided at all costs.

Like Aristotle, Horace was also interested in literary emotions. One idea which he undoubtedly took from the rhetoricians was that if you wish to move your audience, then you must feel and express that same emotion yourself. Horace was certainly influenced by rhetoric. This can be seen in many areas including his nature–nurture discussions. Horace said that although one needed a rich vein of natural talent in order to embark on the road to becoming a successful poet, if such native genius remained uncultivated, then it was worthless. This essentially rhetorical principle of talent honed by craft is something that we can also find in the ideas of Longinus.

Probably written in the third century AD, *On the sublime* has been traditionally attributed to Longinus. However, scholars nowadays are no longer sure who wrote the text, or even when it was written. Nonetheless the text itself, although fragmentary (several sections and subsections having been lost over the years), is an important window on Roman literary criticism and theory. *On the Sublime* is certainly inspired by the method of learning that was prevalent in the Roman rhetorical schools. Style, the third canon of rhetoric, prescribed three levels: plain style, middle style and grand style. Students were advised to use each of these styles in particular contexts. It is the grand style that interests us here in this discussion on the sublime.

Poetic sublimity can be defined as a kind of passionate style/language-based force that has the power to delight, engage and transport readers and hearers to states of bliss. Longinus claims that there are five sources of sublimity. These are set out in Chapter 8 of his work and are then investigated further in the subsequent chapters. The first two of these five sources rely on nature; one could say they depend on the innate genius of the poet. The other three are all nurture-like; they are all down to hard work, skill and craft. The first of the five sources is 'the ability to form grand conceptions'. This is classed as a natural gift. The second, which is also classed as innate, concerns 'the stimulus of powerful and inspired emotions'. The third source, which is the first of the nurture/craft inputs, is 'the proper formation of the figures of thought and figures of language'. The fourth source is 'noble diction', which refers to the choice of words, language and imagery. Fifthly, and lastly, comes 'dignified and elevated word arrangement'.

From a stylistic perspective we can see how the latter three, which are by far the most rhetorical in nature, have their counterparts in modern stylistics. Figures of thought and language have the effect of deviating from normal language usage (schemes will deviate at the syntactic level of language and tropes will deviate at a semantic level). This is firmly in the territory of foregrounding, a core concept in stylistics (for more on this see Chapter 2 on 'formalism' and Chapter 5 on 'foregrounding' in this volume). 'Noble diction' and 'prominent word arrangement' at the sentence level also involve foregrounding, as well as creative text production.

We have started to see here how many of these poetic ideas rely on rhetoric and the method of instruction that was being conducted in the rhetorical schools of the ancient Greek and Roman worlds. Let us now look more closely at classical rhetoric itself.

Classical rhetoric: History, theory, method

The following overview will consist of two parts, the first about history and the second concerning methods and theory. The first part is there to offer a little bit of historical context. It is the second part that is of the most importance to you, the practicing stylistician of today.

A short history of classical rhetoric

There is no appropriate way to compress a historical overview of rhetoric into a short section like this. For this reason, this brief account will be largely based on important individuals in the development of the field. The subject deserves a more extended account, which you will find elsewhere (see, for example, Burke forthcoming).

Classical scholars tend to agree that the formal codification of rhetoric, as a heuristic system, was first written down in the second quarter of the fifth century BC (around 475 BC) by a man named Corax. He came from the city of Syracuse on the island of Sicily, which in those days was part of the ancient Greek world. Corax taught the people of Syracuse how to structure their speeches logically and deliver them persuasively in front of a jury in the law courts in order that they might successfully reclaim their possessions which had been stolen by a recently deposed dictator name Thrasybulus. Corax charged a fee for his services. He soon became a wealthy man (as did his star pupil Tisias).

Most forms of rhetoric can only exist within a democratic political system. As we have seen, the tyrant of Syracuse was deposed, and as a result the people could argue publically about what was right and wrong in their view, and why. Athens was one of the few democratic city-states in ancient Greece (the others were monarchies, dictatorships or oligarchies), and good thinkers and speakers were needed to further the ends of the political and judicial city-state. It was not long before teachers of rhetoric such as Protagoras from the north of Greece and Gorgias of Lentini (in Sicily) were arriving there to make a living. (Gorgias was said to have been taught by Tisias, who in his turn had been taught by Corax). These were the first Sophists: itinerant teachers who for payment would teach the young and wealthy men of Athens how to speak and argue eloquently in the public arena.

Even though Athens was a democracy for most of the fifth and fourth centuries BC, there were still many rich aristocratic families within Athenian society who had been in charge during previous, less democratic periods. Therefore, the situation was quite simple: in a democracy, those who can speak well and put forward clear, solid arguments in front of either juries or political assemblies will win the day in both courtrooms and parliament, which were, and still are, the two core seats of power in democratic systems. Young male aristocratic Athenians had money but no power, while the new teachers of rhetoric, who were sprouting like mushrooms in the city, had the skills to teach rhetoric but were relatively poor. In a society where eloquence meant power, it is easy to understand why things developed the way they did.

In many of Plato's works you can find his mouthpiece Socrates attacking the Sophists, including Protagoras and Gorgias. Plato found them morally corrupt and therefore essentially worthless. His main argument was that Sophists can teach people to win public debates and discussions with weaker arguments by the use of unfair tactics such as 'style' and 'emotion'. Plato believed that people should reason logically, ethically and truthfully, without the use of stylistic and/or affective embellishments. In short, Plato believed that the people who had been trained by the Sophists dazzled their interlocutors with lexical and syntactic trickery, rather than reasoning logically with them. Plato also believed in the philosophical notion of 'truth' and despised the oratory of the professional and political world. In a way this is somewhat ironic, since if you have ever read any of Plato's works you will have noticed that they are written in a skilful rhetorical fashion, and quite often Socrates is not always the ethical debater we might expect him to be. In addition to this, Plato was an aristocrat who is reported to have disliked democracy, especially since he saw the democratic system as being partially responsible for the trial and execution of Socrates, his friend and teacher.

In the fourth century BC, schools of rhetoric started to emerge in Athens. Perhaps the most famous of these was the one run by the somewhat conservative but essentially ethical Isocrates, which in its day rivalled Plato's philosophical Academy that was also located in Athens. Isocrates trained affluent young men to serve the state wisely, and what he showed in his teaching was that real rhetoric involved not just logic and reason, but emotion and style as well. In effect, he concluded that reason and emotion on the one hand and content and style on the other were more or less inseparable, so it was pointless to continue to complain about the emotive and stylistic aspects of rhetoric. Several of Isocrates' speeches still exist, including ones on educational policy like 'Against the Sophists', and they make for fascinating reading. He almost certainly wrote an 'art of rhetoric'-type handbook too, but it is lost to us. Many great and famous orators flourished in this period, not least the lawyer Lysias, who was also attacked by Plato in his works, and the statesman Demosthenes, who was said to have been the greatest public speaker of all time, despite a debilitating speech impediment that he suffered throughout most of his childhood. Demosthenes was born in 384 BC and died in 322 BC. These are also the dates of birth and death of a person who, for us in the twenty-first century, is, and always will be, intrinsically linked with classical rhetoric: Aristotle.

Aristotle, a Macedonian by birth, arrived back in Athens after the Macedonians under Phillip II (and later his son Alexander the Great, whom Aristotle tutored as a boy) had conquered the Greeks and put an end to democracy and seemingly to much of rhetoric too. He founded a school called the Lyceum (close to the place where Isocrates had founded his school of rhetoric), where, in addition to subjects like biology, physics and geometry, the students also studied poetics and rhetoric. Aristotle had learned from what he saw around him. As a young man he had spent twenty years studying and teaching at Plato's philosophical school, the Academy in Athens, before he was asked to leave. There, under the tutelage of Plato, he learned to distrust rhetoric and rejected it for its purported phoniness. However, on his return as an older and wiser man, he saw on the streets of Athens and in the other schools, such as Isocrates' school of rhetoric, that 'rhetoric-in-practice' was not a logical search for some philosophical notion of truth, but rather an innately human communicative process which, in addition to employing logic, also centrally involves character and emotion, as Isocrates had already noted. Aristotle went on to produce his *Art of rhetoric,* which he may have used in his teaching at the Lyceum. It is the oldest complete treatise on rhetoric that we have today.

Aristotle had a huge influence on the Roman scholars, not least Marcus Tullius Cicero, who began his own investigations into rhetoric during the first century BC. As a leading lawyer of his day during his early life (as a member of the equestrian order), and as a member of the senate in later life, rhetoric was the tool of his trade and he needed to be able to use rhetorical techniques effortlessly. Cicero believed that rhetoric had a tripartite function: to teach (*docere*), to persuade (*movere*) and to delight (*delectare*). Thankfully for us, Cicero was also a prolific writer and in addition to all the letters he wrote and all his defence and prosecution speeches, we also have a number of his treatises on rhetoric – for example, *de Inventione* (*On invention*) and *de Oratore* (*On the orator*).

Several other Romans wrote on the subject of rhetoric over the next four hundred years, including the historian Tacitus and the late Roman St. Augustine of Hippo, who in his *Christiana doctrina* (*The Christian doctrines*) added a final chapter which sought to teach the new priests of the emerging Christian faith how to persuade the pagan masses. However, arguably the most important Roman rhetorician was a man who came from the Iberian peninsula and lived during the first century AD. He moved to Rome and set up a school of rhetoric, where in time he became the first ever professor of rhetoric. His name was Marcus Fabius Quintilianus, but we know him today as Quintilian. When Quintilian finally retired from teaching generations of young Roman boys, mostly of whom later became lawyers, he decided to write down his teaching methods. The result was a handbook in twelve volumes called the *Institutio oratoria* (translated as *The institutes of oratory* or sometimes more loosely as *The orator's education*).

Quintilian's main focus on rhetoric was ethical education. This was needed, given that most of his students were aspiring lawyers. He wrote of 'the good man speaking' and did his upmost to keep this ethical dimension alive in rhetorical practice. In the later Roman period of the second, third and fourth centuries AD, many rhetorical schools sprang up throughout the empire. A system that many teachers used was known as the *progymnasmata*. This entailed a series of rhetorical assignments that grew in length and degree of difficulty. Usually, *progymnasmata* employed a fourteen-level model. The students would start with something simple, like constructing and performing their own fable based on a traditional one. The assignments would then get gradually longer and more complex. The fourteenth and final assignment would often be something like writing and performing a defence speech, and thereafter a prosecution speech, in a court of law. Such a stylistic-rhetorical programme of learning can still be employed today in contemporary stylistic and rhetoric-based creative writing courses to great pedagogical effect.

After the fall of the Roman empire in the fifth century AD at the hands of marauding Germanic tribes (especially the Visigoths), the art of rhetoric continued to flourish in Byzantium, the surviving Eastern part of the Roman world. When it too fell at the hands of the Ottoman Turks in the fifteenth century AD, around a thousand years after the Western Roman empire had collapsed, knowledge of rhetoric began to flow back to the West where it had been largely abandoned, fuelling the early Renaissance. Around this time a complete copy of Quintilian's *Institutio oratoria*, which had been lost for centuries, was found in a monastery in Switzerland. The work quickly became embedded at the core of the European Renaissance educational curriculum, and in the two hundred years that followed, the book is reported to have gone through a hundred reprints.

One of the most influential rhetoricians in this period was Erasmus of Rotterdam. While studying and teaching in England at Cambridge University, he introduced his work *De Copia* (meaning 'abundance'), which was to serve as a handbook in the grammar schools of England for many years. This work encouraged students to expand their Latin vocabulary (for the purposes of lexical variation), apply style figures (schemes and tropes) and basically make their written and spoken style more eloquent and engaging. Another continental scholar who had an influence on the teaching of rhetoric in England was Juan Luis Vives, who was appointed professor of rhetoric at Oxford by Cardinal Wolsey. However, the turbulent religious history of that time meant that his stay was a short one.

As we have learned, the university educational system in England and most of continental Europe in the Early Modern period was broadly based on the trivium. The trivium was an elementary programme that all students had to undertake. It was a bit like an undergraduate BA programme (or just the first/freshman year of that programme) where students only study three subjects. As mentioned earlier, the trivium consisted of grammar, logic and rhetoric, to be learned in that order, and was designed to give students the basic tools to be successful both in their higher-level quadrivium studies and in everyday life itself, after their formal education had ended. (The quadrivium consisted of the four fields of arithmetic, geometry, music and astronomy.)

Rhetoric flourished in the grammar schools of Europe right up to the early nineteenth century. Around this period, however, the teaching and study of rhetoric seemed to dry up after more than two thousand successful years of practice. Rhetoric did continue, and flourish, in the United States; indeed, modules like rhetoric, composition and critical thinking still form an essential component in the first-year programmes at many top-ranked US colleges and universities, especially in those undergraduate institutions with a strong tradition in the liberal arts and sciences. Rhetoric was also still taught in Eastern Europe and it was no doubt taught at Moscow University, where a young Roman Jakobson encountered the basic principles which would go on to form and develop his thinking on formalism and, stylistics.

In a sense, rhetoric did continue in Western Europe in the nineteenth and early twentieth centuries, in both muted and mutated forms. One such area was literary criticism and early linguistics. Prominent figures were Charles Bally, who published a two-volume treatise on stylistics in 1909 entitled *Traité de stylistique française*, and Leo Spitzer who wrote *Stilstudien* (1928). It is with these individuals and their works that we see the beginning of modern stylistics.

The theory and method of rhetoric

There are a number of basic principles that underlie classical rhetoric. The most important of these is the system of the five canons. Another basic rhetorical principle concerns the three traditional kinds of persuasive discourse, also known as 'genres'. We will now look at these more closely.

The five canons of rhetoric

Etymologically, the English noun 'rhetoric' is derived from the Greek word *rhēma* (meaning 'a word'), which in turn is linked to *rhētor* ('a teacher of oratory'). Both are ultimately derived from the Greek verb *eirō* (which means 'I say'). Originally, therefore, the notion of rhetoric was firmly rooted in language. However, rhetoric is also about structure and strategy. Structure can be viewed at both a macro and micro level. The former pertains to the arrangement of the whole process of rhetoric, while the latter refers to the discourse itself, irrespective of whether this is spoken or written text. The macro level is expressed by means of the five canons of rhetoric. These are the five logical steps in the process of producing a persuasive discourse. These steps are: (i) the discovery or 'invention' stage; (ii) the arrangement stage; (iii) the stylisation stage; (iv) the memorisation stage; and (v) the delivery stage. Below is a table which also shows the Latin and Greek terms that are used by several scholars. You do not need to learn these, but it is handy if you can at least recognise them since some traditional scholars insist on retaining them.

Table 1.1 The five canons of rhetoric

	English term	Meaning	Latin name	Greek name
1	discovery	coming up with materials for agruments	*Inventio*	*heúrisis*
2	arrangement	ordering your discourse	*Dispositio*	*taxis*
3	stylisation	saying/writing things well and in a persuasive manner	*Elocutio*	*léxis/phrases*
4	memorisation	strategic remembering	*Memoria*	*mnémē*
5	delivery	presenting your ideas	*Pronunciatio/ Actio*	*hupókrisis*

If you are a native speaker of English, or indeed of any European Romance language, the Latin terms should all be recognisable to you. The Greek terms should not be completely strange to you either. We might perhaps all be expected to know what a 'heuristic' is, and we understand that 'taxis' means 'place' or 'order', just as our word 'taxonomy' refers to the science of classification. Of course, 'lexis' is 'word', which is closely linked to style, and this is something to which we will pay extensive attention in this chapter.

Let us now look at the first canon, discovery/invention. For courses and modules in 'composition' and 'academic writing', this canon is arguably the most important of the five. Every argumentative piece of written or spoken discourse needs a standpoint or proposition. This can be your thesis statement. Once you have decided on what this is going to be, next you need to go about gathering, discovering or generating arguments, also known as 'proofs', in support of your proposition. Aristotle was the first to point out in his *Art of rhetoric* that there are two categories of arguments, or 'means of persuasion' as he called them, which are available to writers and speakers. We can refer to these broadly as 'internal' and 'external' resources. The internal resources are also sometimes referred to as 'artistic' or 'technical' proofs, while the external ones are 'non-artistic' or 'non-technical' proofs. 'Art', as in the title *Art of rhetoric*, means 'skill'. Therefore, artistic proofs are arguments or proofs that need skill and effort in order to be brought into being. Non-artistic proofs are arguments or proofs that need no skill or real effort to be created; rather, they simply need to be recognised – taken off the shelf, as it were – and employed by a writer or speaker.

Let us look first at the external proofs, since this category is by far the simplest. The non-technical means of persuasion (known in Greek as the *atechnoi pisteis*) are not, strictly speaking, really part of the art of rhetoric at all. As described above, you just need to know what they are, where they are and how to employ them. Speaking on the subject of the rhetoric of law, Aristotle said that there were five non-technical proofs to legal oratory. These were laws, contracts, oaths, witnesses and torture (illogically, in the classical Greek world the only credible evidence that could be given by slaves was that elicited under torture). For you, a twenty-first century student, these external proofs still exist, although they are somewhat different to the ones Aristotle listed. For example, you might think of reference books in libraries, academic search engines on the internet, articles in refereed academic journals, data, statistics, testimony and so on. These are all modern-day external sources or non-artistic proofs.

The internal mode of persuasion, the 'technical' or 'artistic means', is known in Greek as the *entechnoi pisteis*. This is central to the art of rhetoric and includes three modes: (a) rational appeal (logos); (b) emotional appeal (pathos); and (c) ethical appeal (ethos). We will now look at these more closely.

Logos centres on whether arguments are what we call deductive or inductive, fallacious or non-fallacious, syllogistic or enthymemic. These are all relatively complex concepts and beginner students would not be expected to know what they are (see Burke, forthcoming, for more on this). What we can say right now is that, broadly speaking, logos is about producing arguments in support of your thesis statement that are solid, honest and valid, rather than ones that are weak, false and invalid. The main means of argumentation in logos are realised by use of rhetorical examples and enthymematic reasoning. With regard to the first of these, it does not matter if you do not have a lot of rhetorical examples. Rhetoric is not like statistics or inductive reasoning in general, where numbers matter. Instead, it is the vividness and the relevance of the examples that you choose to employ in your speech or writing that matters. This visual intensity and community significance can be achieved by deploying analogical examples from history and/or fiction that your intended audience will easily recognise. In a way, there is a distinct crossover here between logos and pathos.

Enthymemic reasoning involves a premise being ellipted or supressed from a syllogism. Often this is the main premise (a syllogism is made up of a major premise, a minor premise and a conclusion, and their arrangement must produce a logically valid pattern of reasoning). The ellipted (main) premise in the enthymeme (which is the syllogistic logical equivalent in rhetoric) acts to persuade people because they infer what is not there and fill it in themselves. It is the act of providing the answer that not only makes people feel good about themselves, at a subconscious level, but which also persuades them: it is a kind of self-persuasion. The inferential part of enthymemic reasoning keys into contemporary ideas in pragmatics. This is especially the case with regard to inference. (For more on the diverse pragmatic aspects of stylistics see Chapters 7, 8, 9 and 22 in this volume.)

Pathos, the second of the proofs, can be said to deal with the psychology of persuasion, focusing on how emotions are triggered by language and performance and then channelled within the minds of the people in an audience. Modern theories of communication and persuasion from the field of social psychology will tell you that pathos persuades more often than any of the other proofs. Irrespective of our intelligence, at times we all process information 'mindlessly', peripherally, unthinkingly. Indeed, we are probably neurally wired by evolution to employ such cognitive shortcuts in our everyday lives.

Ethos is concerned with character. It has two aspects. The first concerns the esteem in which the speaker or writer is held. We might see this as his/her 'situated' ethos. The second is about what a speaker/writer actually does linguistically in his/her texts to ingratiate him/herself with the audience. This second aspect has been referred to as 'invented' ethos. Situated ethos and invented ethos are not separate; rather, they operate on a cline. For example, the more effective your invented ethos is, the stronger your situated ethos might become in the long run, and vice versa.

The second canon of rhetoric is concerned with ordering or arranging the text or text elements. There is no real consensus as to how many parts a text should have. Aristotle, for instance, thought that there were only two parts to a speech: he said you should first state the case, and then prove it. This is a bit on the minimalist side. You may recall Corax, who for a fee helped the citizens of Syracuse to get their belongings back by writing speeches for them. It is said that he used a four-part system that included: (1) an introduction, (2) some background information, (3) the arguments, and (4) a conclusion. This simple model would fit many basic student essays even today. A famous model of discourse presentation that went on to be very influential during the Renaissance period is the one set out in the first century BC handbook *Rhetorica ad Herennium*. This manual, the author of which is unknown (although it was once attributed erroneously to Cicero), stipulates that there are six distinct parts to a speech or piece of written discourse. They are shown in the table below, together with the original Latin terms.

Table 1.2 A six-part composition plan from the *Rhetorica ad Herennium*

1. introduction (*exordium*)	Where you foster good will, make your audience receptive and attentive and state your standpoint
2. background (*narratio*)	Where you set the scene (past facts)
3. brief list of arguments (*divisio/partitio*)	Where you state your arguments briefly
4. arguments in favour (*confirmatio*)	Where you put forward your arguments in detail
5. counter arguments (*confutatio*)	Where you deal with the views of your opponents
6. conclusion (*peroratio*)	Where you end appropriately (summarising and employing style figures)

One of the reasons that rhetoric fell out of favour in Western Europe in the nineteenth century was that it was said to have become too prescriptive, too dogmatic, too narrow. These accusations were not without substance. However, this was never the ideal for what rhetoric should be. The notion of rhetoric as a narrow, prescriptive methodology would have been completely alien to great rhetoricians of antiquity such as Demosthenes and the wily Cicero. Claims that rhetoric was always prescriptive can be rebuffed with a single word: *kairos*. It is in this discussion of the second canon of rhetoric, arrangement, that we can observe how *kairos* works.

In our modern world, we have only one conception of time, namely, the idea that it moves forward in a linear and fixed fashion. The ancient Greeks, however, had two. In addition to the linear sense of time, which the Greeks called *kronos* (and from which we get our word 'chronology'), the Greeks also had *kairotic* time from the word *kairos*. *Kairos* is about locative time, time in and at a specific moment. It is also essentially about context. It is the pragmatic utterance *avant la lettre*, as can be observed in a number of chapters in this volume (see, for example, Chapter 22 on literary pragmatics). Every textual utterance will differ depending on the contextual elements involved in that utterance. Everything depends on the speaker, the message, the audience, the audience's relationship with the speaker and with the issue, as well as the speaker's relation towards the issue and with his/her audience. If that was not enough, the mode of the message is also important. Perhaps most important of all are the time and place of the utterance.

The Romans called *kairos* '*occasio*', from where we get our word 'occasion', and this points to another important aspect of *kairos*. A good speaker needs to be situationally attuned to the possibilities of *kairos*. A moment might arise suddenly and unexpectedly when he can deliver a speech that he has been working on. A speaker has to have all sensory channels open at all times, looking for such opportunities. There is no telling how long a *kairotic* window might stay open; it may be mere seconds, or it might last for years. It will all depend on the context and the nature of the subject matter. A speaker will also have to be situationally sensitive to the audience. If he feels that the audience is in a certain mood, he will have to deviate from the planned order and content of his speech and insert new parts and/or restructure sections until he/she notices that the audience is starting to move psychologically back towards him. If he sticks to a set linear structure, he will probably lose the debate and the day. Alterations in a discourse can result in the six-part structure that was mentioned above being reduced in number and/or given different or unusual places in the arrangement.

Once textual material has been generated (the first canon of rhetoric) and then preliminarily arranged in a discourse (the second canon), it can be stylised. The third canon of rhetoric therefore deals with style. It is this canon which we can say has had the greatest influence on the structuring and development of modern day stylistics. Below, we will look at: (i) the notion of style itself, (ii) grammar and clarity, (iii) the levels of style, (vi) style figures, and finally, (v) imitation.

Style has always been, and still is, an elusive concept. Etymologically speaking, the word derives from the Latin '*stilus*', an ancient writing implement. For the Romans, style, or *elocutio* as they called it, was a system for producing and thereafter performing persuasive acts of discourse. The elusiveness of style lies in the age-old dispute as to whether style is extrinsic or intrinsic in nature; whether it is the icing on the cake – in effect, an optional extra – or whether it is an inherent part of the cake itself. Although no definite, all-encompassing answer can be given to this question, most contemporary views on the form/content debate support the idea of inseparability. Style, it would therefore seem, is not a discretionary extra in linguistic exchanges; rather, it is part of the essence of communication itself. As Marshall McLuhan, the twentieth century philosopher of communication, once put it, 'the medium is the message'.

In the *Art of rhetoric* Aristotle writes extensively on style. He deals with such phenomena as 'clarity', 'amplitude', 'propriety', 'rhythm', 'syntax' and 'metaphor'. These are concepts still relevant to modern stylistic scholarship. Aristotle's *Art of Rhetoric* can be said to have paved the way for the publication of *On Style,* written by Demetrius of Phaleron, former student of Aristotle and Theophrastus at the Athenian Lyceum. This work is the first that we know of to focus exclusively on style genres and style figures. In a way, we might view it as the first systematic stylistics textbook on foregrounding.

The main grammatical aspects of style depend on correctness, clarity and appropriateness. Correctness, also known as 'purity', is very much grammar-based and prescriptive. Clarity, also known as 'perspicuity', requires that a writer or speaker should use words in their ordinary/everyday sense, avoiding the use of obsolete, technical or colloquial terms. Appropriateness is about what is correct in a certain situation. These ideas are repeated and expanded on in both modern day pragmatics and in stylistics (for further evidence of this, see in this volume Chapter 7 on speech acts, Chapter 8 on conversational analysis and the cooperative principle and Chapter 9 on relevance theory).

The style of a text should fit the audience, occasion, subject matter and so on, as we saw in our earlier discussion on *kairos*. This idea goes back to the notion that certain subject matters require a certain style. Ancient orators and writers would adopt an appropriate high, middle or low style, depending on the discourse context and the make-up of their audience. The low style, also known as 'plain' or 'Attic' style, was the most ordinary speech. It was said to be often used for instruction and teaching. It had very little ornament, and the narrative was straightforward. It was often a simple exposition of the facts. It employed so-called 'loose' sentences, which is also known as 'paratactic' style. This is a chat-like style, which is fast and casual with little or no punctuation and many run-on sentences. We see it in use today in text messaging and in the interactive discourse of social media such as *Twitter* and *Facebook*.

The high style is sometimes known as 'florid' or 'Asiatic' style ('Asiatic' in the sense of the Greek cities of Asia Minor, where it was cultivated). It was used for lofty issues and required the employment of a lot of style figures. It often employed what is known as a 'periodic' style. Unlike its opposite, paratactic style, discourse in the periodic style was well structured, well punctuated and generally formal in nature. It was said to be the most effective style to move, delight and produce emotion in listeners and readers. The middle style, as might be expected, was a mix of both low and high styles.

We saw above how style figures are important for a high or florid style. They are significant for stylistic analysis too. Style figures can usually be divided into the categories of 'schemes' (from the Greek for 'to form/shape') on the one hand and 'tropes' (from the Greek for 'to turn') on the other. Schemes are broadly concerned with deviations in syntactic structure, involving a transfer of order, while tropes often constitute deviation in semantics, entailing a transfer of meaning. Schemes can be categorised in different ways, such as schemes of 'balance', 'inverted word order', 'omission', 'repetition' and so on. Similarly, tropes can be grouped by metaphor-type figures (e.g. similes, oxymora, hyperboles, etc.), and puns or word-plays. Other more general groupings can also be made, such as those pertaining to 'brevity', 'description', 'emotional appeals' and so on. In addition, style figures can be grouped as to whether they are figures of thought or language, as we saw in Longinus's earlier classification. All style figures fall under the stylistic heading of 'foregrounding', namely, parallelism, repetition and deviations (see Chapter 2 in this volume on 'formalist stylistics' and Chapter 5 on 'foregrounding' for more on this).

Classical rhetoricians believed that rhetoric was learned in three stages, to be studied in this order: (i) by means of the study of principles; (ii) through imitation of the work of others; and (iii) through practice in writing. This strategy, involving (i) knowledge, followed by (ii) analysis, followed by (iii) production, not only follows a recognised contemporary pedagogical norm (see for example Bloom's '*Taxonomy of educational objectives*' (1956)); it also forms a sound basis for the successful creative writing classroom of today, with its foundation of testable, principle-based creativity. We can also see here some clear overlap with the principles of poetics described earlier in this chapter, not least the three nurture-based inputs that are part of the five principles of the sublime set out by Longinus: (i) the proper formation of the figures of thought and figures of language, (ii) noble diction, and (iii) dignified and elevated word arrangement.

The fourth and fifth canons set out the performative aspects of rhetoric and concern mainly oral rather than written production. These are the memorising and delivery of a speech. Delivery places a focus on intonation, prosody, voice, rhythm and gesture, all factors that the Roman orators made an art of in themselves. Indeed, when he was asked what the most important aspects of rhetoric were, the ancient Athenian Demosthenes, the greatest speaker of all time, answered, 'delivery, delivery, delivery'. In order that great delivery be achieved one must practice, and then when you are finished you must practice again. The canon of delivery in its written form impinges on the multimodal dimension of stylistics (for more on this, see in this volume Chapter 29 on multimodality and Chapter 31 on hypertext fiction). The visual persuasive tools of fonts, layout, typography, graphology and so on are all essentially aspects of the fifth canon of rhetoric, the delivery and performance of the discourse.

The three genres of rhetoric

In addition to the five canons, the three traditional kinds of persuasive discourse are also central to a good understanding of classical rhetoric. In ancient times three distinct 'genres' or kinds of oratory developed. The first was forensic oratory, the rhetoric of the law courts, which is also referred to as judicial oratory. The second is deliberative oratory. This is the rhetoric of the political arena, also known simply as political rhetoric. The third, which we have not really encountered thus far, is known as epideictic oratory. This is the rhetoric of praise or blame, also called display, demonstrative, ceremonial or panegyric oratory. These three categories of oratory are also known as the 'special' topics.

Speakers often belong to one particular group, depending on their profession. Having said that, there is often a lot of crossover. For example, people like Corax, Tisias, Lysias, and Cicero from the ancient world all practiced some form of law, as did famous fictional characters such as Perry Mason, Atticus Finch, Horace Rumpole and Mr. Tulkinghorn. These individuals all belong to the category of forensic orators. Political speakers like Demosthenes and, more recently, Winston Churchill and John F. Kennedy are deliberative orators too, as is Barack Obama.

Both forensic and deliberative genres have their own separate focus, expressed in so-called 'means' and 'topics'. Deliberative oratory is said to be about what is 'good/worthy' or 'useful/ advantageous' for society. The opposites are also topics. Ideally, a speaker should 'exhort' or 'dehort' an audience either to do − or not to do − something. For example, a deliberative orator might plead that 'we need to build a new road' or 'we should not pull down those houses in the centre of town in order to create a park'. The subject matter can also be much more serious, such as 'we have to go to war against a state that uses chemical weapons on its own citizens'. This kind of political oratory is about what should happen in relation to upcoming events: it is concerned with future time. Forensic oratory, the rhetoric of the courtroom, is about the past: who did what to whom, when, how and why, and who witnessed it. Its topics are justice and injustice, what is right and what is wrong.

The third and final genre is epideictic oratory. This is the oratory of praise and blame, of honour and dishonour. In a praise speech, often called an encomium, one focuses on the virtues of an individual. A speaker often points out how noble he/she is and how he/she has achieved things better than others have done, endured things for longer and under more demanding circumstances, and so on. These days you will hear epideictic oratory at venues such as at graduation ceremonies and weddings. Another type of praise speech is the eulogy. In this case the person being praised has died. Eulogies are most often heard at funerals. In a way, detailed obituaries in newspapers are also a form of epideictic rhetoric. In the past, the discourse of blame used to be heard as often as the discourse of praise. Individuals were lambasted for their lack of virtue, their ignoble behaviour, their gluttony, greed, immorality and callousness. These speeches are often called invectives. These days they are not often heard, because of the fear of being sued for either libel, if the invective is written, or slander, if it is spoken. Political satire is a good way to circumvent such repressive laws.

This brings us to the end of our overview of classical poetics and rhetoric. In all honesty we have only started to scratch the surface of these two subjects. Nonetheless, it should be relatively clear how both ancient poetics and ancient rhetoric have influenced the stylistics we know today, and why they justifiably constitute the classical heritage of stylistics.

Recommendations for practice

Poetics

1. In order to understand Aristotle's notion of plot a little better, try applying his structural requirements to a popular film of recent years. You can choose your own – and indeed you should do – but just to get you going, try one of these first: *Gladiator*, *Rocky*, *Terminator*, *Angel Heart*, *American Beauty*, the *Harry Potter* series, *Atonement*, *The Unforgiven*, *Hamlet*, *King Lear*, *Apocalypse Now*, the *Star Wars* series, or *The Godfather*. You may recall that some of the structural components of Aristotle's plot were: (a) a plot should consist of a single issue (not a double one) and the representation of action should be serious, complete (with a beginning, middle and end) and be represented in embellished language where necessary; (b) the hero's change of fortune has to be from happiness to misery and not the other way around; (c) the cause is not depravity or wickedness but a character error/flaw; (d) the hero must be a relatively good man; (e) the play/film takes one whole day, no longer (so a lot of the story has taken place once the play starts); (f) the deed that is committed must be among family members or loved ones and not among strangers; (g) there is a predictable and necessary 'surprise' – recognition/discovery. Now ask yourself whether the film or play that you have chosen broadly fits Aristotle's framework. Which categories listed above are missing? Do you think the acts of peripety and recognition are powerful enough to instigate pity and fear (leading to catharsis) in the average film goer from your country/culture? Try to give examples as to why or why not.

Rhetoric

1. Have a look at a stylistic analysis that you have carried out in the past. See where you have made observations pertaining to foregrounding: either parallelism, repetition or deviation. Now do some investigative work into the vast array of style figures that are available in classical rhetoric. (See for example the 'Forest of Rhetoric' website hosted at Brigham Young University in Utah, USA http://rhetoric.byu.edu/). Return to your original observation/analysis in your essay/paper and try to give it more detail by referring to the style figure(s) concerned. Does this extra level bring to light new descriptive observations that the general umbrella classifications of parallelism, repetition or deviation did not? Does this alter your original interpretation in this part of your analysis? If so, how?

2. Choose a short story from the twentieth or twenty-first century and go on a style figure hunt. Try to find five different schemes and five different tropes. Explain what the style figure is – i.e. give a short description – and then say whether you think it is aesthetically pleasing/persuasive or not – i.e. did it grab your attention, move you, make you think of things beyond the text and/or guide you to draw new links with other aspects of the story? Also, try to say whether the short story you have chosen is primarily written in the plain, middle or high style. Does the style remain constant through the story or does it change? Are these changes in important places (like the end of the story)? If so, what effect might this have on you as a reader, and what effect do you think it might have on other engaged readers?

Summary and future directions

Rhetoric has exerted a considerable influence on the stylistics that we know today, in terms of foregrounding, relevance theory, narratology, metaphor, literary pragmatics, multimodality and many more areas. For example, foregrounding, a key concept in stylistic analysis, is firmly rooted in the style figures of classical rhetoric. Indeed, a cogent case can be made that by limiting ourselves to only three terms in our foregrounding analysis, namely parallelism, repetition and deviation, we are left with a potentially impoverished linguistic analysis that only allows the analyst to make somewhat shallow and superficial analytic observations. Were he/she to have the whole range of schemes and tropes at his/her disposal, the stylistician would be able to observe whether or not certain repetitions or parallelisms were based on schemes of balance, inversion, omission and so on, or whether certain tropes were pun-like, metaphor-like, word plays, etc. In short, it would allow sub-levels of analysis to take place that could bring to light patterns of linguistic evidence that might support an earlier evaluation or interpretation which might otherwise have eluded the analyst had he/she restricted his/her analysis to the surface level of foregrounding analysis and the three main terms. A wider and deeper range of tools should yield a more detailed and perhaps even more accurate stylistic analysis.

In the past thirty years or so there has been little mention of rhetoric in the stylistics classroom, or in the research conducted by stylisticians. This has been an unfortunate omission, as students during this period have been deprived of much useful knowledge. There are great modern stylisticians writing today who have based much of their stylistic scholarship on a thorough grounding in rhetoric. These include, most prominently, Geoffrey Leech (1969; 2008) and Walter Nash (1989). Other stylisticians who have employed rhetoric in their stylistic analyses include Leech and Short (1981), Wales (1993) and Verdonk (1999). All five of these scholars have now retired from teaching. A new generation of rhetorical stylisicians is needed. Perhaps you, the very students reading this chapter, might make up that new cohort.

Some might ask – but what is the point of looking back? Scholarship and research should be about 'onward and upward'. It might very well be a good thing that tools, methods and perspectives have narrowed over the years in some respects. This might have been necessary in order to change a paradigm or advance a set of ideas within the field. However, sometimes, and especially when one has reached a methodological or theoretical impasse, it is beneficial to step back and look at the original blueprint, as it were, of human communication, a design which has at its core the fundamentals of Aristotelian rhetoric and poetics. The stylisticians of the 1970s and 1980s listed above knew of these tools and could fall back on them when necessary. Scholars working in the field since the mid-1980s, however, often cannot, since poetics and rhetoric have largely not been explicitly taught but have instead disappeared under the burgeoning fields of narrative, in the case of poetics, and pragmatics, in the case of rhetoric.

It is time to reintegrate the key tools of rhetoric and poetics into the modern stylistician's toolkit, for he/she will need them to both pick out finer detail and map out larger and more innovative frameworks as stylistics steps boldly into the fields of creative writing, multimodality, hypertext fiction and cognitive neuroscience. It is for this reason that this chapter on rhetoric and poetics has been situated as the first chapter in this handbook, in order to lead you into the modern world of stylistics that will unfold in the upcoming chapters. When you are reading those chapters, ask yourself 'does this sound a little like classical rhetoric or classical poetics?' If it does, explore that link further, because it may well give you new and unexpected tools with which you can conduct your stylistic analysis more thoroughly than might otherwise have been the case.

Related topics

cognitive poetics, creative writing, emotion and neuroscience, formalism, foregrounding, literary pragmatics, metaphor and metonymy, narratology, pedagogical stylistics, real readers

Further reading

Burke, M., forthcoming. *Rhetoric: The basics*. London: Routledge.

An accessible introduction to the field of rhetoric, complete with exercises and examples which will help you understand the significance of rhetoric in such diverse contemporary fields as stylistics, pragmatics, literary theory, communication studies, social psychology and cognitive neuroscience.

Burke, M., 2012. Systemic stylistics: An integrative rhetorical method of teaching and learning in the stylistics classroom. *In:* M. Burke, S. Csábi, L. Week and J. Zerkowitz, eds. *Pedagogical stylistics: Current trends in language, literature and ELT.* London: Continuum, 77–95.

This chapter sets out a pedagogical model which shows how rhetoric feeds into stylistics, which in turn feeds into the practice of the modern creative writing classroom. It shows the inseparability of these three fields and is embedded within the pedagogical framework of Bloom's taxonomy of learning.

Leech, G., 1969. *A linguistic guide to English poetry.* London: Longman.

A pioneering study in its day, which maintained the important role of rhetoric in stylistic analysis. The result is a series of stylistic analyses that are deep, rewarding and poignant. It offers rhetorical tools to help young stylisticians to at least double their existing analytic toolkit (see also Leech's later 2008 work which preserves important links to rhetoric.)

Nash, W., 1989. *Rhetoric: The wit of persuasion.* Oxford: Blackwell.

A companion to rhetoric applied to literary studies and especially to stylistic analysis. A skilful reminder of the power and importance of the *ars rhetorica* for the budding stylistician.

Online resources

The Perseus Digital Library http://www.perseus.tufts.edu/hopper/

English versions of all of the classical texts mentioned in this chapter can be found online at *The Perseus Digital Library*, a web resource which covers the history, literature and culture of the Greco-Roman world. It is hosted at Tufts University (editor-in-chief G. R. Crane). The current version is Perseus 4.0, also known as 'The Perseus Hopper' (last accessed September 22, 2013).

The Forest of Rhetoric (*silva rhetoricae*) http://rhetoric.byu.edu/

This useful online rhetorical resource is hosted by Brigham Young University and edited and updated by Dr. Gideon Burton. It is essentially a beginner's guide to the many terms that abound in the world of classical rhetoric (last accessed September 22, 2013).

References

Aristotle, 2000. Poetics. *In:* P. Murray and T. S. Dorsch, trans. and eds. *Classical literary criticism.* London: Penguin, 57–97.

Aristotle, 2006. *Art of rhetoric.* J.H. Freese, trans. Loeb Classical Library, Cambridge, Mass: Harvard University Press.

Bally, C., 1909. *Traité de stylistique Française*. Heidelberg: Carl Winters.

Bloom, B. S., 1956. *Taxonomy of educational objectives*. Boston: Allyn and Bacon.

Burke, M. forthcoming. *Rhetoric: The basics*. London: Routledge.

Burke, M., 2012. Systemic stylistics: An integrative rhetorical method of teaching and learning in the stylistics classroom. *In:* M. Burke, S. Csábi, L. Week and J. Zerkowitz, eds. *Pedagogical Stylistics: Current trends in language, literature and ELT*. London: Continuum, 77–95.

Burke, M., 2008. Advertising Aristotle: A preliminary investigation into the contemporary relevance of Aristotle's *Art of Rhetoric*. *Foundations of Science*, 13 (3), 295–305.

Burke, M., 2010. Rhetoric and persuasion. *In:* P. C. Hogan, ed. *The Cambridge encyclopaedia of the language sciences*. Cambridge: Cambridge University Press, 715–717.

Cicero, 1968. *De inventione; De optimo genere oratorium, Topica*. H. M. Hubbell, trans. Loeb Classical Library, Cambridge, Mass: Harvard University Press.

Cicero, 2001. *On the orator: Books I and II*. E. W. Sutton and H. Rackham, trans. Loeb Classical Library, Cambridge, Mass: Harvard University Press.

[Cicero], 1954. *Rhetorica ad herennium*. H. Caplan, trans. Loeb Classical Library, Cambridge, Mass: Harvard University Press.

Demetrius, 1996. *On style*. D. C. Innes and W. Rhys Roberts, trans. Loeb Classical Library, Cambridge, Mass: Harvard University Press.

Erasmus, D., 1963. *On copia of words and ideas (De duplici copia verborum ac rerum)*. D. B. King and H. D. Rix, trans. and eds. Milwaukee, WI: Marquette University Press.

Horace, 2000. The art of poetry. *In:* P. Murray and T. S. Dorsch, trans. and eds. *Classical literary criticism*. London: Penguin, 98–112.

Isocrates, 2000. Against the sophists. *In: Isocrates: volume II*. G. Nordlin, trans. and ed. Loeb Classical Library, Cambridge, Mass: Harvard University Press, 159–177.

Jakobson, R., 1960. Closing statement: Linguistics and poetics. *In: Style in language*. T. A. Sebeok, ed. Cambridge, Mass: The M.I.T. Press, 350–377.

Leech, G., 1969. *A linguistic guide to English poetry*. London: Longman.

Leech, G., 2008. *Language in literature: Style and foregrounding*. London: Longman.

Leech, G. and Short, M., 1981, *Style in fiction*. Longman: London.

Longinus, 2000. On the sublime. *In:* P. Murray and T. S. Dorsch, trans. and eds. *Classical literary criticism*. London: Penguin, 113–166.

Murray, P. and Dorsch, T. S., eds. 2000. *Classical literary criticism*. London: Penguin.

Nash, W., 1989. *Rhetoric: The wit of persuasion*. Oxford: Blackwell.

Nussbaum, M., 1998. *Cultivating humanity: A classical defence of reform in liberal education*. Cambridge, Mass.: Harvard University Press.

Plato, 2000. *Republic* (Books 2, 3 and 10). *In:* P. Murray and T. S. Dorsch, trans. and eds. *Classical literary criticism*. London: Penguin, 15–56.

Quintilian, 2001. *The orator's education*, 5 vols. D. A. Russell, trans. and ed. Loeb Classical Library, Cambridge, Mass: Harvard University Press.

Spitzer, L., 1928. *Stilstudien*. 2 vols. Munich: Max Hueber.

St. Augustine, 1958. *On Christian doctrine (De doctrina Christiana)*. D. W. Robertson Jnr., trans. Library of Liberal Arts, Indianapolis, IN: Bobbs-Merrill.

Verdonk, P., 1999. The liberation of the icon: A brief survey from classical rhetoric to cognitive stylistics. *Journal of Literary Studies*, 15 (3/4), 291–304.

Wales, K., 1993. Teach yourself rhetoric: An analysis of Phillip Larkin's 'Church Going'. *In:* P. Verdonk, ed. *Twentieth century poetry: From text to context*. London: Routledge, 134–58.

2

Formalist stylistics

Michael Burke and Kristy Evers

Introduction

This chapter will focus on formalist stylistics. It will begin by setting out the historical context of formalism. It will then introduce the main protagonists and discuss their most important theories. Our main focus will be on three Russian theoreticians: Roman Jakobson and his theory of 'the poetic function of language'; Viktor Shklovsky and his concept of 'estrangement/defamiliarisation'; and Vladimir Propp and his structural/morphological ideas on plot components in folktales. Thereafter we will consider the structuralist work of the Prague School and in particular the notion of foregrounding. Lastly, we will look at a linguistic branch of formalism as proposed by Noam Chomsky. We will conclude by reflecting on some of the shortcomings of formalism and the criticisms that it has received in recent years.

Historical background

The origins of stylistics, as we saw in the previous chapter, are to be found in the poetics and especially in the rhetoric of the classical world. In the words of stylistician Paul Simpson: '… there is indeed a case for saying that some stylistic work is very much a latter day embodiment of traditional rhetoric' (2004, p. 50). Having said this, and as Simpson himself points out, there is a particular field of academic enquiry that began at the beginning of the twentieth century and which has had a lasting and profound impact on contemporary stylistics (p. 50). This is commonly known as Russian formalism.

There were two schools that can lay claim to the founding of the Russian formalism movement: the Moscow Linguistics Circle, founded in 1915, and the Petrograd Society for the Study of Poetic Language (*Opayaz*), based in current day St. Petersburg, which was founded a year later. Influential members of these schools included the aforementioned Jakobson, Shklovsky and Propp. These are the three theorists that we will focus on. However, this does not mean that there weren't other influential voices involved in this movement; Tomashevsky, Tynyanov, Eikhenbaum and Brik all made significant contributions to formalism which should not be underestimated (for an engaging synopsis of the diverse theories that came out of Russian formalism see Cook 1994, pp. 130–140). The movement would continue to flourish long after the Bolshevik revolution until around 1930, when it was finally suppressed by the dogmatism of Stalinist communism.

The formalists were interested in the poetic form of literary language and were inspired by the early ideas of the Swiss linguist Ferdinand de Saussure, and also by a number of aesthetic ideas that were emerging from the world of visual art. The most important of these was symbolism, which came about as a reaction to the preceding movement of naturalism/realism. In this sense, we can see that the formalists opposed Plato's and Aristotle's ideas on mimesis (i.e. art imitating nature), which was described in the previous chapter when 'poetics' was discussed. In a nutshell, and in line with the symbolists of the time, the formalists felt that art should not mirror the natural world; instead the notion of 'truth' should be represented indirectly through the imagination and through dreams. It is perhaps a cruel irony that after the dissolution of Russian formalism around 1930 the doctrine of social realism would engulf the communist world and dominate Soviet society until the demise of the USSR in 1989.

The formalists were particularly interested in formal linguistic differences between poetic and non-poetic language. This area is often known as the 'literariness' debate, and includes discussions on what would come to be known in the Prague School as 'foregrounding'. In addition to such motivated choices at the lexical level, they were also fascinated by the structure of narrative. Here we can see how the Russian formalists were concerned with both rhetoric and poetics: the former at the word level (which can be equated with the third canon of rhetoric, dealing with style) and the latter at the narrative level (mirroring the second canon of rhetoric, concerned with structural arrangement and motivated disposition).

One thing that bound these formalists together was their desire to see literature studied in a much more scientific way. The word 'scientific' here does not mean that they generated hypotheses from qualitative data which were then tested empirically/quantitatively for falsification, as the term implies today in contemporary empirical approaches to stylistics (see Chapter 20 in this volume for more on quantitative methods); rather, it meant that they wished to align literary studies more with linguistics. In this way, they could focus on formal observations that could be made in a sentence at the diverse levels of phonology, morphology, lexis, semantics and syntax, and in doing so they could anchor all evaluative and interpretative claims in solid textual description. It was thought that if the study of literature could be made more scientific, then it would command more respect in the intellectual world and benefit in diverse ways from its new, elevated scientific status.

It is interesting to note from an English language perspective that in spite of formalism being a seminal early twentieth century literary and linguistic movement, it was almost exclusively unknown in the West, and in particular in English literary studies, until the major ideas were translated into French in the 1960s by the Bulgarian literary theorist Tzevetan Todorov.

Roman Jakobson and the poetic function of language

If any one person may be referred to as 'the father of modern stylistics', then it is Roman Jakobson. Jakobson studied at Moscow University and later became one of the key figures in the Moscow Linguistic Circle, which he co-founded. He left Russia in 1920 when the political situation worsened and moved to Prague where he went on to co-found the Prague Linguistic Circle, also known as the Prague School. The Prague School, although formalist in its beginnings, would end up focusing on pragmatics, something that is much more in line with functionalism (see Chapter 3 of this volume for more on this topic). At the outbreak of World War II Jakobson found himself fleeing politics and war once again, this time to end up in the United States. It was only then that scholars in the West started to find out about his work, when it was translated into a number of languages. Throughout his life Jakobson and his colleagues conducted research and developed theories on language communication. Jakobson was particularly interested in the poetic function of language.

Jakobson is best known for the model of communication that he presented as a lecture in 1958 and which was published in a collection of essays from that conference in 1960, entitled *Closing Statement: Linguistics and Poetics* (in Sebeok 1960). This model was an extension/ revision of Bühler's earlier tripartite model of communication from 1934. This model consisted of three parts.

Figure 2.1 Bühler's tripartite model of communication

What is interesting to note from the previous chapter is that this twentieth century model of communication is a somewhat pale imitation of what the orators of the classical world knew as *kairos*, which had its emphasis not merely on the speaker, message and audience but also on the time and place of the discourse act, as well as the attitude that the audience held towards both the speaker and the issue/message.

Jakobson changed Bühler's model in two different ways. First, he added three extra parts. These are the context, the contact and the code. The first refers to the context that is alluded to, the second refers to the contact between the addresser and the addressee, and the third refers to the code or language used in the utterance. We could be critical at this point and say that although at first sight this appears to be a ground-breaking intuition, what Jakobson was doing was simply applying the full scope of rhetorical *kairos*, which he almost certainly knew about, to account more fully for the pragmatic situation surrounding the discourse act/ utterance. This is what Jakobson's model looked like.

Figure 2.2 Jakobson's six basic functions of any communicative act

After Jakobson had made these additions to the model he gave each part an associated 'function'. The addresser has the emotive function, which refers to language directed towards the addresser himself. The addressee has a conative function, which refers to language directed towards the addressee. The context has a referential function, which is concerned with the background and circumstances. The message has a poetic function, which focuses on the message itself. The contact has a phatic function, which is concerned with the contact between the speakers. Finally, the code has a metalingual function, which attends to particular language use. In the figure below these six functions can be observed.

Figure 2.3 Jakobson's six associative functions of language

A text will usually have one dominant function, but more functions can be at work at the same time. Jakobson argued that literary texts and other verbal arts often focus on the message of the text: the poetic function. However, the poetic function is not only limited to literary texts, and not all literary texts are restricted to only having a dominant poetic function. He also noted that factual texts such as history books are not like poetic texts, because they are focused on the context: the referential function. Jakobson himself was most interested in the poetic function of literary texts, because he wanted to study just what it is that makes a text literary – in short, what constitutes 'literariness'.

Jakobson defined the poetic function of language with the following, somewhat dense formula: 'the poetic function projects the principle of equivalence from the axis of selection into the axis of combination' (p. 358 in Sebeok 1960). This will sound like gobbledygook to the average person, so it needs some unpicking. What Jakobson essentially means here is that poetic language is all about the selection and combination of words in sentences. First, let us look at the paradigmatic notion of selection. Imagine a line or two from a poem with a couple of key words missing. Here, for example, are the opening two lines to Phillip Larkin's poem 'Pigeons' (lines 1–2).

> On …… slates the pigeons shift together,
> Backing against the …… rain from the west

We have omitted two adjectives here as in a 'cloze test' style exercise. There are a number of lexical items that could easily be inserted (in a paradigmatic fashion) into these slots. This is what Jakobson means by the phrase 'axis of selection'. Some of these words might fit semantically, but they will be wholly inappropriate because they are either too mundane, too literal or too clichéd. For example, you might choose 'grey' slates or 'sloping' slates. These are probably not good poetic choices because they are too predictable. The same would be true if you to choose 'torrential' rain for the second line – or, worse still, 'wet' rain. The missing words in Larkin's poem are in fact 'shallow' slates and 'thin' rain. We might have been guessing all day and still not come up with the two poetic forms 'shallow slates' and 'thin rain', and yet they both make perfect sense to us. 'Shallow' in some senses can be a kind of un-steep sloping, and 'thin' can conjure up imagery of drizzle or even its opposite, piercing rain. In short, they both work. When it comes to poetic form, therefore, it seems plausible to suggest that the words used in such key paradigmatic, selection slots are at one and the same time both wholly unpredictable and yet, once they are read, instantly recognisable and aesthetically appropriate.

Another skilful strategy of the poet is that both 'shallow' and 'thin' are semantically related. If this link is appraised by the reader, either consciously or subconsciously, it might send him/her off searching for possible extra meanings. There are further links from the words in the slots to other words in immediate context of the surrounding lines. The word 'shallow' alliterates with the word 'shift' later in the line. There is also a glimpse of a half-rhyme with the word 'thin' and the succeeding word 'rain'. The fact that both these words are monosyllabic and end with the letter 'n' strengthens the effect. We could go looking for more links at a deeper, phonetic level or even a semantic level, where we might start to find associations between phenomena in this short text fragment that mainly exist high above the ground, such as rain, pigeons, roof slates and so on. Indeed, the subject matter of these lines, to do with battening down the hatches against the onslaught of the elements, ties into a key metaphor that runs through most of Larkin's poetry, namely that LIFE IS SLOW DYING (see Burke 2005). We can conclude from all this that the way Larkin uses language here is an apt example of how Jakobson's poetic function works.

You may recall that Jakobson's somewhat impenetrable formula read as follows: 'the poetic function projects the principle of equivalence from the axis of selection into the axis of combination'. We can now unpick this with our Larkin example in mind and point clearly to the three parts of the equation. First of all, we have the patterns of language that a writer/ poet chooses and employs which help to establish general connections across a text. This is the principle of equivalence. Second, we have the words chosen by the writer/poet from a (paradigmatic) string of possible lexical items. This is the axis of selection. Third and finally, there are the words that are (syntagmatically) combined across the poetic line. This is the axis of combination.

What makes a text literary? This was a question that occupied much of Jakobson's time. The answer, according to him, lay principally in the text itself, in formalism and textualism. The rigidity and the somewhat myopic focus of formalism would meet with resistance in time, as we will see later in this chapter. Before that, though, let us move on to look more closely at the second figure from the Russian formalist movement that we have chosen to highlight: Viktor Shklovsky.

Viktor Shklovsky and defamiliarisation

Viktor Shklovsky lived in St. Petersburg and studied at the St. Petersburg State University. There he founded the Petrograd Society for the Study of Poetic Language in 1916. In addition to being a literary scholar and theoretician, he was also involved in the fields of film and children's literature. In 1925 Shklovsky published one of his most important works, his *Theory of Prose*. However, a number of circumstances, not least the political isolation of the Soviet Union at the time, kept the book from having a significant impact on the Western literary world. Some have suggested that it could have been the book of the century if it wasn't for two factors. The first was its fairly late translation into English; it was not until 1990 that the book was translated and entered the English speaking world. The second was the outmoded phase that formalism went through from the 1930s onwards.

One of Shklovsky's most important ideas from the *Theory of Prose* was his principle of 'defamiliarisation'. Shklovsky argued that as things become more familiar, we stop paying attention to them. In some cases we stop noticing them entirely. This is what happens to everyday language; it gets automatised. Shklovsky thought that it was the function of literary texts, and all other arts, to make people perceive the world from new and different perspectives. In short, he believed that poetic language has the power to de-automatise; to shake us out of our everyday visual and cognitive lethargy. He thought that the employment of style figures (both schemes and tropes) that foreground at the levels of meaning and syntax would help achieve this effect. These he saw as linguistic devices. As we saw in the previous chapter, this idea is not a million miles away from what Longinus had prescribed some two thousand years earlier in the last three of his nature-based categories with regard to producing sublime discourse.

In addition to defamiliarising, Shklovsky also thought that poetic discourse had the effect of estranging or alienating its readers. If something in literature seems familiar, then one should look at it with a renewed sense of vision. For example, we all know what a daffodil is, but a careful reading of Wordsworth's poem about said flower persuades us to look at it differently: to apprehend novel aspects that will lead to a fresh conceptualisation of the flower. Following Shklovsky, we could say that poetic language should ideally succeed in revealing the innate 'daffodilness' of a daffodil. A paradoxical element that arose from Shklovsky's theory is that the over-use of the unfamiliar in poetry can, in time, make it become familiar and conventional. We all know about dead metaphors, for instance. Therefore, a continuous cycle of renewal is necessary. Exactly how this should be achieved is not made entirely clear.

In 1925 Shklovsky also introduced the key terms of *fabula* and *sjužet* into the field of narrative studies. *Fabula* refers to the chronological order of events in a story, while *sjužet* refers to the order of the events as they were narrated; for example, this might involve things like flashbacks or gaps in the narration. These two terms fall into the two 'levels' of narrative: the deep level and the surface level. The deep level is the abstract level that contains the *fabula*, while the surface level is the actual level that contains the *sjužet*. Readers will read the *sjužet* and slowly work out the *fabula* by looking at the logic of all the events and actions.

You may recall from the previous chapter that Aristotle wrote in his *Poetics* that a story had to have a beginning, a middle and an end, and that they should be represented in that order. In such simple narratives the *fabula* and *sjužet* can be, and usually are, the same. However, in most cases of literature or film they are not equivalent. Let us show you an example. One of the most celebrated films of the twentieth century was *Citizen Kane*. The film opens with the death of the protagonist, and the story is then told in flashbacks which are intermingled with a journalist's ongoing investigation into who Kane really was and what made him tick. In this example, we can say that the *fabula* of the film is the way the events occurred in chronological order (at a deeper level of narrative), while the *sjužet* is the way the story is told in a flashback style (a more surface level of narrative).

Both terms, *fabula* and *sjužet*, are referred to here with the original Russian names. This is because there are no satisfactory English equivalents. The term 'plot' is sometimes used to represent *sjužet*. However, when we look closely at the meanings of both words, plot does not seem to be a good substitute. Whereas in *sjužet* the exact order of the events narrated are recounted, in plot usually only the highlights are mentioned. A plot can even be described in only one sentence or a few propositions, while *sjužet* cannot.

There have also been critiques in more recent times of the *fabula* and *sjužet* pattern, especially from post-structuralists (e.g. Culler 1981, Derrida 1979). These criticisms concerned the order and hierarchy of the two terms. Such critiques from deconstructionists are to be expected, since two of the things that they have regularly railed against are: (a) the hierarchies that exist between words, and (b) the fact that many concepts have oppositions.

Derrida tried to eradicate these positions by making up new words which he claimed would account for both sides of a concept while privileging neither. We think it is fair to say that this attempt has had a very mixed reception across the academic world.

Fabula can also be viewed in the sense of underlying (universal) structural character roles, such as heroes, villains, princesses and so on. This leads us to the third of the featured Russian formalists in this chapter, Vladimir Propp, and his 'morphology of the folktale'.

Vladimir Propp and the morphology of the folktale

Vladimir Propp was born in St. Petersburg, where he attended university. He studied Russian and German philology. He later became a secondary school teacher in these subjects, and in 1932 he started to teach at the State University of St. Petersburg. He was an important member of the Russian formalist group, extending the scope of formalism into narrative studies.

Propp is best known in the field of formalism for his 1928 work *Morphology of the Folktale*. In this work he aims to create a structural framework for Russian fairy tales by applying a formalist methodology. What attracted him to investigate these tales is their apparent similarity in plot. The question of universality quickly arose. Propp essentially wanted to come up with a description of the fairy tale in itself. Despite the fact that his main focus was on Russian fairy tales, his framework of analysis can be applied to other stories as well, as other scholars have shown since. This will be discussed at the end of this section.

Propp limited his data collection to one hundred tales. He argued that this was the right amount of material for two reasons. First, there is no use in researching more tales that represent the same components every time. Repetition is prominent in the tales. Second, the research would otherwise simply become too unwieldy. The material Propp used for his research were fairy tales from Afanás'ev's collection of four hundred tales (Afanás'ev was the Russian equivalent of the German brothers Grimm). Propp decided to take the fairytales with numbers 50 to 151, or, using the enumeration system of the fifth and sixth editions, numbers 93 to 270. This gave him a relatively random sample. After gathering this data, he set out to compare the tales by creating a so-called 'morphology'. Propp ended up with four main theses which he explicates in his work. These are reproduced below, accompanied by a short description and outline of each.

> Thesis #1. 'Functions of characters serve as stable, constant elements in a tale, independent of how and by whom they are fulfilled. They constitute the fundamental components of a tale' (Propp 1968, p. 21).

Every tale is divided into different components by looking at the smallest narrative units, the so-called motifs. Propp describes these by looking at the functions of the dramatis personae, because he observes that even though these dramatis personae and their attributes change, the actions and functions do not. The ways in which the functions are realised may be different, but the function itself remains the same. Therefore, it is important to look at *what* is done by the characters, rather than *who* does it or *how* it is done. The *what*, the function, is the constant factor, while the *who*, the dramatis personae, and the *how* are variable factors.

> Thesis #2. 'The number of functions known to the fairy tale is limited' (Propp 1968, p. 21).

As we can see in the second thesis, Propp believes that the number of functions is restricted. After the setting of an initial situation, thirty-one functions are recognised by Propp. He explains every function by giving (i) a short summary, (ii) an abbreviated definition often in one word, and (iii) a so-called 'designation', which is a conventional sign that he allocated to the function. The table we have constructed below constitutes a synopsis of the information set out in Chapter 3 of Propp's work on 'the functions of dramatis personae' (1968, pp. 25–65).

Table 2.1 Propp's functions of dramatis personae

THE FUNCTIONS OF DRAMATIS PERSONAE

	Short Summary	*Abbreviated Definition*	*Designation*
	Members of family are enumerated or future hero is introduced	Initial situation	α (alpha)
1	One of the members of a family absents himself from home	Absentation	ß (beta)
2	An interdiction is addressed to the hero	Interdiction	γ (gamma)
3	The interdiction is violated	Violation	δ (delta)
4	The villain makes an attempt at reconnaissance	Reconnaissance	ε (epsilon)
5	The villain receives information about his victim	Delivery	ζ (zeta)
6	The villain attempts to deceive his victim in order to take possession of him or of his belongings	Trickery	η (eta)
7	The victim submits to deception and thereby unwittingly helps his enemy	Complicity	θ (theta)
8	The villain causes harm or injury to a member of a family	Villainy	A
	8a. One member of a family either lacks something or desires to have something	Lack	A
9	Misfortune or lack is made known; the hero is approached with a request or command; he is allowed to go or he is dispatched	Mediation, the connective incident	B
10	The seeker agrees to or decides upon counteraction	Beginning counteraction	C
11	The hero leaves home	Departure	↑
12	The hero is tested, interrogated, attacked etc., which prepares the way for his receiving either a magical agent or helper	The first function of the donor	D
13	The hero reacts to the actions of the future donor	The hero's reaction	E
14	The hero acquires the use of a magical agent	Provision or receipt of a magical agent	F
15	The hero is transferred, delivered or led to the whereabouts of an object of search	Spatial transference between two kingdoms, guidance	G

THE FUNCTIONS OF DRAMATIS PERSONAE

	Short Summary	*Abbreviated Definition*	*Designation*
16	The hero and the villain join in direct combat	Struggle	H
17	The hero is branded	Branding	J
18	The villain is defeated	Victory	I
19	The initial misfortune or lack is liquidated	Liquidation	K
20	The hero returns	Return	↓
21	The hero is pursued	Pursuit	Pr
22	Rescue of the hero from pursuit	Rescue	Rs
23	The hero, unrecognised, arrives home or in another country	Unrecognised arrival	O
24	A false hero presents unfounded claims	Unfounded claims	L
25	A difficult task is proposed to the hero	Difficult task	M
26	The task is resolved	Solution	N
27	The hero is recognised	Recognition	Q
28	The false hero or villain is exposed	Exposure	Ex
29	The hero is given a new appearance	Transfiguration	T
30	The villain is punished	Punishment	U
31	The hero is married and ascends the throne	Wedding	W

The first seven functions can be seen as the preparatory part of the tale. Function 8, which has two options, is important, since it is said to give momentum to the tale. In the first option, which Propp labels 8, the complication action is started with the act of villainy. Propp lists nineteen villainous alternatives (1968, pp. 30–31). In the second option, which Propp labels 8a, an important character in the story either lacks or desires something. All stages follow from here.

Thesis #3.   'The sequence of functions is always identical' (Propp 1968, p. 22).

Taking Propp's third thesis into account, it is important to note that not all tales have to contain all functions. However, if a tale is missing some functions, the order of the other functions does not change. Therefore, the sequence will always be the same. There are very few exceptions, which can all be accounted for and precisely formulated.

Thesis #4   'All fairy tales are of one type in regard to their structure' (Propp 1968, p. 23).

In Propp's final thesis he states that the tales he has investigated are actually all the same fairy tale. Different variations of the tale can be seen, but they are all in essence the same tale. This is because the same functions and the same order are always presented.

Propp recognised seven different dramatis personae (or character types), who each have their own 'sphere of action' (1968, pp. 79–80). These are listed in the table below.

Table 2.2 Propp's distribution of functions among dramatis personae

THE DISTRIBUTION OF FUNCTIONS AMONG DRAMATIS PERSONAE		
	The sphere of action of …	*The Constituents*
1	The villain	– Villainy (A) – A fight or other forms of struggle with the hero (H) – Pursuit (Pr)
2	The donor (provider)	– The preparations for the transmission of a magical agent (D) – Provision of the hero with a magical agent (F)
3	The helper	– The spatial transference of the hero (G) – Liquidation of misfortune or lack (K) – Rescue from pursuit (Rs) – The solution of difficult tasks (N) – Transfiguration of the hero (T)
4	The princess (a sought-for person) and her father *"The princess and her father cannot be exactly delineated from each other according to functions. Most often it is the father who assigns difficult tasks due to hostile feelings towards the suitor. He also frequently punishes (or orders punished) the false hero"* (Propp 1968, pp. 79–80)	– The assignment of difficult tasks (M) – Branding (J) – Exposure (Ex) – Recognition (Q) – Punishment of a second villain (U) – Marriage (W)
5	The dispatcher	– Dispatch (connective incident, B)
6	The hero or victim-/seeker-hero *The first function (C) is characteristic of the seeker-hero, the victim-hero performs only the remaining functions*	– Departure on a search (C↑) – Reaction to the demands of the donor (E) – Wedding (W)
7	The false hero	– As above includes (C↑) followed by E and then special function L

However, there are three different options for how these spheres of action of the dramatis personae can be divided among the actual characters in the tale (Propp 1968, pp. 80–1). The first option entails that the character exactly conforms to the sphere of action. The second is that one character acts in multiple spheres of action. One character can be involved in two or more spheres at the same time, or can change from one sphere to another over the course of time. A character can also involuntarily play a role in another sphere. Here one might imagine an antagonist who guides the hero by accident, making this antagonist an involuntary helper. It is important to keep in mind that the intentions and feelings of the characters do not matter. Only their actions are important. The third option contains the distribution of one sphere among multiple characters. Often the sphere of action of the princess is divided between herself and her father. Other, more frequent characters in this category involve helpers. These might be living things, referred to as magical helpers, or objects and qualities, referred to as magical agents. Both act the same way, but they are are referred to slightly differently for purposes of convenience.

Long after formalism had ceased to be influential in literary criticism, several scholars outside the realm of literature started to use Propp's framework, and not just those working in the humanities. Among these was Claude Lévi-Strauss, known as the father of modern anthropology. Lévi-Strauss used Propp's model for his study on, and interpretation of, classical myths. Lévi-Strauss later reviewed Propp's model and came up with some improvements. One of his points of critique was that Propp's sequence rule is too strict. Sometimes an order of actions may be appointed to different sequences, for it is not always straightforward to see which function belongs to which action. For example, a struggle and a difficult task could well be assigned to one and the same action. Why then does the rule of sequence importance insist on a clear-cut outcome? Furthermore, Lévi-Strauss also argued that several functions can be seen as unnecessary, because they are repetitive. For example, think about function B ('the hero is approached with a request') and function M ('a difficult task is proposed to the hero'). He also found this redundancy in the dramatis personae of villain and false hero. You can see in function 28, represented by the conventional sign 'Ex', that Propp has already made them functionally equivalent. Lastly, it is interesting to note that several of the functions consist of relational pairs, such as departure (↑) and return (↓), and a difficult task (M) and the solution (N). Propp did mention these pairs, but he never took this analysis a step further to create a particular set of rules.

This concludes our brief overview of the three main players in Russian formalism. We will now look at how formalism continued and changed under the auspices of the Prague structuralists.

The Prague structualist school and foregrounding

While working with the Prague School in the 1920s and 1930s Jakobson became interested in the notion of foregrounding, a concept which had been developed by a Czech colleague, Jan Mukařovský, who was a key figure in the Prague School. The word Mukařovský used for foregrounding was *actualisation.* It was Garvin who came up with the term 'foregrounding' in his 1964 translation of the works of the Prague School scholars. Put simply, foregrounding highlights the poetic function of language, in particular its ability to deviate from the linguistic norm and to create textual patterns based on either parallelism, repetition or deviation from a norm. This idea was not only built on Shklovsky's earlier work on 'making strange' (defamiliarisation); it was in effect a modern description, at a meta-level, of the basic workings of schemes and tropes from classical rhetoric.

The Prague School may have started as a formalist movement, where the emphasis in meaning making was mainly on the logical and semantic message/text, but the school and its members quickly became functionalists. Like formalism, functionalism is concerned with the text, but it is also interested in the role that context plays in the process of meaning making. In short, with the advent of functionalism in the Prague School there was a gradual move from text to context, from form to function, from semantics to pragmatics and from logic to rhetoric.

We have seen how foregrounding is about parallelism, repetition and deviation. Stylistician Mick Short has argued in his book *Exploring the language of poems, plays and prose* (1996) that deviations can be made on seven levels: discoursal, semantic, lexical, grammatical, morphological, phonological and graphological (pp. 36–58). Short also shows how a distinction can be made between internal and external deviations. Internal deviations are foregrounded by the norms and expectations of the text itself, while external deviations rely on the norms and expectations of language (or the main literary genre) in general. For example, an external discoursal deviation is when a text begins *in medias res* or when a poem is presented in a non-poetic, unexpected form, such as, for example, a newspaper article or shopping list (pp. 59–63).

Formalism: Recent approaches and criticisms

Since the time of the Russian formalists there have been a number of formal/structural approaches within both literary and linguistic studies. One such formal view of language was that proposed by the celebrated academic and intellectual Noam Chomsky (1957, 1965, 1966). His generative grammar (also referred to as 'universal' or 'transformational' grammar) is based on rules that Chomsky thought underpinned the generation of grammatical sentences. Some early stylistic analyses were conducted using generative grammar (e.g. Ohmann 1964), but not very many. By this time stylisticians had discovered the importance of context and pragmatics, and as a result the idea of only looking at the form of a literary text seemed like a step backwards. Chomsky also wrote on generative phonology and metrics (Chomsky and Halle 1968) and this study is still influential today in the work of some stylisticians (see, for example, Fabb 1997, 2002).

A formal view of literature was proposed by Jonathan Culler within the framework of what he termed 'structuralist poetics'. Structuralism was closely related to formalism and the work of the Prague School, reaching a peak of popularity in the 1960s. It was also influenced by the much earlier work of Ferdinand de Saussure (see de Saussure 2002) and especially his ideas on the sign: the two intertwined notions of the signifier (form) and the signified (concept). Culler's 1975 work entitled *Structuralist poetics* made an important leap forward. Although grounded in many of the precepts of Chomskian generative grammar, it also started to take the reader into account (albeit a theoretical idea of a reader rather than real readers – for more on 'real readers' in stylistic analysis see Chapter 27 in this volume). Culler introduced the term 'literary competence', which he defined according to the idea that the reader's knowledge of the literary conventions is important for the interpretation of the literary text. Despite taking the reader on board, the approach was widely thought to be still too formalistic, because it didn't consider other important aspects of the context such as culture and history. Soon thereafter Culler moved on from structuralism to embrace the post-structuralist ideas of Derridean deconstruction, as referred to earlier.

Recommendations for practice

1. Try working out the timeline of both *fabula* and *sjužet* in the films *Memento* and *Pulp Fiction*. Try to create visual graph-like representations.
2. Take Jakobson's idea of paradigmatic slots (the axis of selection) and set up your own experiments with real subjects. Ask them to guess what the missing word is. You can either choose to tell them that it is a line from a poem or from some other discourse (or both). Consider using a control group. Devise a hypothesis and test it. What are the outcomes of your experiments? Did you manage to falsify your hypothesis?
3. Take Jakobson's six components of basic communicative functions and compare them with the element of *kairos* mentioned in the previous chapter. Is there overlap in

categories? Try to put into words what extra (if anything) Jakobson's model offers us that *kairos* does not (and vice versa).

4. In order to help you understand Propp's model better, apply it to any simple story you know. This can be a fairy tale or a myth, but it can also be a children's story or cartoon. Some suggestions are *The Gruffalo*, *Room on the Broom*, *Stickman*, *Harold and the Purple Crayon* or something similar. You could also apply it to an episode of a children's series such as *Shaun the Sheep* or *Tinga Tinga Tales*. Fill in any missing roles or events you come across with plausible characters and actions in order to make the story fit Propp's framework.

5. Follow Lévi-Strauss and review Propp's categories. Review (a) his four theses, (b) his thirty-one functions of dramatis personae, and (c) his seven 'distribution of functions' among the dramatis personae. See if you can locate even more overlap than Lévi-Strauss did. Compare and contrast what you have discovered with other students in your class (work in small groups). Can you agree who among you is correct, and, if so, why? In addition to collapsing and/or eliminating categories, you may feel that an important category has been overlooked by Propp. Argue your case to your fellow students and your lecturer. Make sure you have a good number of examples from both literature and film as supporting evidence.

Future directions

So what of the future for formalism? There have been many criticisms of formalism, which may be summed up by saying that it only looks at the autonomous nature of the text, and in doing so it makes decidedly spurious claims to scientific objectivity. As a result, the pragmatic and contextual elements which are crucial to meaning making are ignored, as are the real readers who read/process a text. It is difficult to talk of future directions within the framework of formalism with the exception of the earlier mentioned formal stylistic work being done on metrics. This being said, we may very well be on the eve of a formalist revival. The reason for this is that deconstruction/post-structuralism has almost certainly run its course. The essentially nihilistic idea that anything can mean anything has become jaded. Often in philosophical cycles, when one extreme has been exhausted someone comes along and once again 'discovers' the extreme at the other end of the spectrum. Maybe, for better or worse, the new days of textualism and the rebirth of the author are just around the corner. We shall see.

Related topics

Functionalist stylistics, linguistic levels of foregrounding, metaphor and metonymy, narratology

Further reading

Culler, J., 1975. *Structuralist poetics: Structuralism, linguistics and the study of literature*. London: Routledge and Kegan Paul.

The first full length study of structuralism in literary criticism. The main argument made in the book is essentially for more linguistics in literary analysis, meaning more conventions, codes and models. The notion of 'literary competence' also makes its first appearance here.

Jakobson, R., 1960. Closing statement: Linguistics and poetics. *In:* T. A. Sebeok, ed. *Style in language.* Cambridge, Mass.: M.I.T Press, 350–377.

Jakobson's *Closing Statement* was first presented at a conference held in Indiana, USA in 1958. Two years later, it was published in Sebeok's collection of conference essays *Style in Language.* It contains his acclaimed revisions of Bühler's model of communication as well as a wonderful rhetorical-stylistic analysis of Mark Anthony's exordium from Shakespeare's *Julius Caesar.*

Propp, V., 1968. *Morphology of the folktale.* L. Scott, trans. Austin: University of Texas Press.

In *Morphology of the folktale* Propp describes his most important ideas and models concerning the structure of Russian folktales. This condensed work is accessible and easy to read.

Shklovsky, V., 1925. *Theory of prose.* B. Sher, trans. Elmwood Park: Dalkey Archive Press.

Theory of prose is probably Shklovsky's most significant work. It contains ideas, such as his theory of defamiliarisation, that are important to both formalism and structuralism. It also sets out his thoughts on the internal laws that he believed governed literature.

References

Bühler, K., 1934. *Sprachtheorie: Die darstellungsfunktion der sprache.* Jena: Fischer.

Burke, M., 2005. How cognition can augment stylistic analysis. *The European Journal of English Studies,* 9 (2), 185–96.

Chomsky, N., 1957. *Syntactic structures.* The Hague: Mouton Publishers.

Chomsky, N., 1965. *Aspects of the theory of syntax.* Cambridge. Mass.: MIT Press.

Chomsky, N., 1966. *Topics in the theory of generative grammar.* The Hague: Mouton Publishers.

Chomsky, N. and Halle, M., 1968. *The sound pattern of English.* New York: Harper and Row.

Cook, G., 1994. *Discourse and literature.* Oxford: Oxford University Press.

Culler, J., 1975. *Structuralist poetics: Structuralism, linguistics and the study of literature,* London: Routledge and Kegan Paul.

Culler, J., 1981. *The pursuit of signs: Semiotics, literature, deconstruction.* Ithaca, NY: Cornell University Press.

Derrida, J., 1979. Living on: border lines. *In:* G. Hartman, ed. *Deconstruction and criticism.* London: Routledge and Kegan Paul, 75–176.

Fabb, N., 1997. *Linguistics and literature.* Oxford: Blackwell.

Fabb, N., 2002. *Language and literary structure: The linguistic analysis of form in verse and narrative.* Cambridge: Cambridge University Press.

Garvin, P. L., 1964. *A Prague school reader on esthetics, literary structure, and style.* Washington D.C.: Georgetown University Press.

Jakobson, R., 1960. Closing statement: linguistics and poetics. *In:* T. A. Sebeok, ed. *Style in language.* Cambridge, Mass.: M.I.T Press, 350–377.

Larkin, P., 1988. Pigeons. *In:* A. Thwaite, ed. *Collected Poems.* London: Faber and Faber, 109.

Lévi-Strauss, C., 1973. *Structural anthropology 2.* M. Layton, trans. New York: Basic Books.

Ohmann, R., 1964. Generative grammars and the concept of literary style. *Word,* 20, 424–439.

Propp, V., 1968. *Morphology of the folktale.* L. Scott, trans. Austin: University of Texas Press.

Saussure, F. de., 2002. *Writings in general linguistics.* M. Pires, trans., S. Bouquet and R. Engler, eds. Oxford: Oxford University Press.

Sebeok, T.A. ed. 1960. *Style in language.* Cambridge, Mass.: M.I.T Press.

Shklovsky, V., 1925. *Theory of prose.* B. Sher, trans. Elmwood Park: Dalkey Archive Press.

Short, M., 1996. *Exploring the language of poems, plays and prose.* Harlow: Addison, Wesley. Longman, Ltd.

Simpson, P., 2004. *Stylistics: A resource book for students.* London: Routledge.

Todorov, T., ed. 1965. *Théorie de la littérature.* Paris: Seuil.

3

Functionalist stylistics

Patricia Canning

Introduction

In Shakespeare's *Macbeth* the only certainty regarding the death of the reigning monarch, King Duncan, is that he was killed. This much is explicit in the play text ('our royal master's murdered!' II.iii.83). Arguably, we pretty much 'know' that the eponymous hero did it, even though this information is merely implied ('I have done the deed' II.ii.14). However, as I have demonstrated elsewhere (Canning 2010) it is not clear from the text of the play that Macbeth actually did anything to anyone. While not wishing to make an affective judgement on interpretation, how do we account for intuiting any knowledge from a text when events are not explicitly delineated in black and white, as it were? In Macbeth, as in every literary text, actions, events, states of being and the like are key aspects of the 'story' encoded therein. For example, consider your personal response to David in the following (very) short story:

'While waiting for the bus, David idly kicked an old tin can.'

We might think David was a bit bored, but relatively harmless. We may even expect to find the words 'kicked', 'old', 'tin' and 'can' in the same sentence. However, we might think differently about David if we read that,

'While waiting for the bus, David viciously kicked an old tin can.'

The modifying adverb 'viciously' suggests a more insidious action which may negatively influence our opinion of David. But what if we replaced the object in the first example, 'an old tin can', with 'his little brother'? The more generous amongst us may deduce that David is impulsive or bored, while others may intuit or import some contextual clues (such as the nature of sibling relationships) and deduce that he has an axe to grind with his 'victim'. If we remove the circumstantial adjunct ('while waiting for the bus'), to leave 'David kicked his little brother', we may simply conclude (without any circumstantial indicators to 'explain' David's behaviour) that David is downright horrible. The 'story' of David building in our minds is shaped by the linguistic formulations that tell it. However, it also relies on factors external to language – our perception of violence as socially unacceptable, for example, or our understanding of functional (or dysfunctional) familial relationships, and so on. In other words, language does not function in a vacuum– it does not 'do' or mean everything in and of itself. Functionalist stylistics is concerned with the relationship between the forms of language as a system and the context or situation of its production, as well as the social, cultural and political (what we may collectively call ideological) factors that impact upon its construction and reception. In other words, functional stylistics deals with the connections between what Leech (2008, p. 104) calls 'language and what is not language'. In what follows, I aim to develop these connections by exploring what it is that language can 'do'. I begin with an outline of the historical background to functional stylistics as a discipline, before moving on to consider its functionality in real, practical terms.

Historical perspectives

Traditionally, functionalist stylistics has often been regarded as distinct from formalist linguistics (Saussure 1916, Chomsky 1957, 1986) insofar as the latter is concerned with (among other things) the *semantic* function of the formal properties of the language system, that is, its *propositional meaning* (see Burke and Evers, Chapter 2 in this volume). On the other hand, functionalist approaches (Halliday 1994, Halliday and Hasan 1976) are fundamentally concerned with the ways in which the formal properties of language are used *pragmatically*. Saussure developed the concept of language as a semiotic system which involved the simultaneous selection from a vertical axis of 'choice' (what he termed 'paradigmatic relations') and a horizontal axis of combination ('syntagmatic relations'). Functionalists developed the structural model of language to account for the variety of *uses* of language, and in so doing they explored the motivations behind the selections and combinations that gave rise to their meaning *potential*. The distinction – or rather, the continuum that connects the two schools of thought – could be loosely understood as being along an axis of language and language use. For functionalists, the context of a language event is as important as the formal features of which it is comprised. Building on Malinowski's (1923) work on the importance of situational context, and Firth's 'Personality in language and society' (1950), Halliday (1971, 1985, 1994, 2004) has often been credited with developing the key concepts of functionalist stylistics. In his work *An Introduction to Functional Grammar* (1994), Halliday developed the idea that language has three primary roles or functions which intersect to make meaning. The example 'David kicked an old tin can' has three interrelated functions in Halliday's terms (1994, p. 34): it contains a 'message' (the information about David and his action), it is an 'exchange' ('a transaction between a speaker and a listener or writer and reader'), and it is a means of 'representation' ('a construal of some process in ongoing human experience'). Thus, Halliday observes, language has a tripartite function, which can be broken down into three interconnecting 'metafunctions' as follows:

a. *Ideational* – to express ideas and experience (clause as *representation*)
b. *Interpersonal* – to mediate in the establishment of social relationships (clause as *exchange*)
c. *Textual* – to provide the formal properties of language (clause as *message*)

While all three metafunctions can be explored independently, it is important to note that each simultaneously informs the production and interpretation of meaning to differing degrees, so that, as Eggins (2004, p. 21) puts it, a text's pivotal nature is the 'meeting point of contextual and linguistic expression'. The fact that these three metafunctions overlap means that any study of a text's meaning potential can make good use of all of them, offering a more robust analysis than would otherwise be the case with one or another.

Thus, I aim to explore the scope of functionalist linguistics through an application of some of the contiguous stylistic models through which the metafunctions are traditionally espoused. I am particularly interested in the ways in which they intersect to encode and express ideas, particularly ideas about race. Using H. Rider Haggard's *King Solomon's Mines* as a point of departure, I will explore the ways in which transitivity, a feature of the ideational metafunction, offers a way of reading behind Haggard's text to uncover a colonial worldview. Firstly, however, drawing from Halliday and Hasan (1976), I will examine how cohesion, a feature of the textual metafunction, helps readers to 'make sense' – from a particular point of view – of the characters the text describes. My argument will be that cohesion helps structure our perceptions of the social relationships that obtain between characters. Moreover, the interpersonal metafunction offers a framework (modality) through which these relationships are reinforced and modulated. In short, I aim to show how the metafunctions of language intersect to take account of a text and the context of its production – what Malinowski (1923) calls the 'context of situation' – in a specific social and cultural milieu.

Textual metafunction

Each of the metafunctions of language can be elucidated through particular grammatical features or models. Part of the *textual* metafunction of language, *cohesion* (Halliday and Hasan 1976) refers to the way in which sentences are related or linked together in order to make sense. This 'internal organisation' (Eggins 2004, p. 29) is realised *grammatically* through a series of cohesive devices such as conjunction, ellipsis, substitution and reference, and relies on the reader's ability to make the necessary linkages between the two (or more) elements that are semantically tied together. Cohesion is also realised *lexically* through the repetition of certain words or collocation (Firth 1957, Hoey 2005, Toolan 2009), which is to say words that would reasonably be expected to co-occur (like 'old', 'tin', and 'can' in the example above). Texts exhibiting a high number of cohesive ties will be processed much easier and faster than texts with less cohesion (compare Hemmingway with Joyce, for example) because less effort is required to make sense of the text. An important feature of cohesion, and of functionalist stylistics generally, is that while the 'internal organisation' of a text serves as the basis for establishing cohesion, its cohesiveness derives not only from the formal properties within the text itself but also from situational knowledge, or as Halliday and Hasan (1976, p. 20) put it, 'the relations BETWEEN the language and the relevant feature of the speaker's and hearer's (or writer's and reader's) material, social and ideological environment'. Thus, cohesion in a text can often signal non-textual or situational influences. The following section explores these principles in Haggard's novel and looks at the ways in which cohesive ties can function 'environmentally' to steer the readers' interpretation in a particular direction.

H. Rider Haggard wrote *King Solomon's Mines* in 1885 during a time of great imperial growth and colonial expansion in Africa. Haggard travelled to South Africa from England to take up a position of employment in 1875 and remained there until shortly after the first Boer war of 1880–81. While he was there he witnessed the British army's defeat by the Zulus in 1879. Haggard's novel charts the adventures of its British narrator Allan Quartermain and his compatriots Sir Henry Curtis and Captain John Good as they travel through the African continent. All three set off in search of Curtis's brother, who has disappeared while treasure hunting *en route* to King Solomon's mines. They are assisted by a native, Umbopa (also known as Ignosi) who, we are told, 'was different from the ordinary run of Zulus' (48), being 'very light-coloured for a Zulu' (46), a description that, as the narrative continues, suggests a contiguous relationship between Ignosi's 'assumption of dignity' (47) and his uncharacteristically Western (almost noble) traits. The extract under analysis is from the chapter titled 'The Attack' (reproduced in the appendix) and demonstrates the cultural significance of the textual metafunction. Stylistically, it makes for interesting reading, not least in terms of the ways in which the two factions – the British and the Zulus – are presented or referenced. Reference is a type of cohesion described by Halliday and Hasan (1976, p. 305) as 'a semantic relation linking an instance of language to its environment', and a simple reference chain, that is, a collated list of all of the terms of reference to a specific person or social group in a text, often makes characterisation and the nature of social relationships more transparent. In the Haggard text, it offers insights into how characters are to be perceived: as Halliday and Hasan (1976, p. 305) acknowledge, the social context within which meaning takes place is made up of 'realities [which] may reside in the persons and the objects that figure in the immediate vicinity'. Without wishing to overcomplicate the analysis by differentiating between the types of reference (endophoric or in-text reference, and exophoric or external reference), the chain below isolates the various nomenclatural items used by Haggard (the italicised references are ambiguous and may refer to both factions). His choices exhibit some striking polarities:

The British:

us – Good – he – us – I – We – you – Quartermain – you – you – we – you – me – I – I – I – I – me – I – I – I – I – I – Quartermain – Good – you – me – I – one – one – one – myself – I – I – I – I – we – I – the regiments – the white man – we – Sir Henry – Good – the latter – him – I – we – we – we – us – we – Ignosi – we – we – our first line of defence – our second – our third – our people – *the mass of struggling warriors* – *men* – our first line of defence – the second – our people – our third line – the assailants – men – *the dense mass of struggling warriors* – Sir Henry – a kindling eye – he – Good – himself – myself – I – I –his tall form – he – a messenger – myself – we – our men – the right defence – us – Ignosi – me – the reserve regiment – the Greys – itself – Ignosi – the captains – I – myself – I – Ignosi – I – I me – we – the flying groups of our men – us – I – I – I – me – I – I – I – I – I – I – myself – my prostrate form – I

The Zulus:

the three columns – the main or centre column – the other two – the serried phalanxes – the plain – that tall fellow – him – my friend – an orderly – him – him – the neck – him – the chest – he – my man – his orderly – the officer – his force – him – the general – poor man – his arms – his face – the force – the general – he – the dense mass – eight or ten men – they – an ominous roar – similar roar – the other two divisions – the mass of men – they – they – several men – that mighty rush of armed humanity – they – they – the advance – the attacking force – their breath – they – they – the battle – *the mass of struggling warriors* – *men* – the attacking force – that third impenetrable hedge of spears – *the dense mass of struggling warriors* – the soldiers – the attacking force – it – its reserves – the left attack – swarms of the enemy – the advancing foe – a huge ruffian – eyes – his head – the horrid apparition – him – himself – he – the matter

The first obvious difference here is the abundance of personal pronouns in representations of the British (eighty-four in total). Notwithstanding the fact that the narrative viewpoint is Quartermain's (which largely accounts for the heavy bias in pronominal distribution overall), there is a comparative lack of pronominal referencing (he, him, they) when it comes the Zulus (seventeen instances) who are more often than not presented as a homogenous entity ('that mighty rush of armed humanity', 'the left attack', 'the advancing foe'). Secondly, the Zulus are referred to inanimately on thirty occasions ('the three columns', 'the serried phalanxes', and so on) compared to only thirteen instances of inanimate reference to the British. The table below exhibits the distribution of reference items in full.

Table 3.1 Reference chain from *The Attack*

	British	Zulus
personal pronouns	I (33); we (12); me (6); myself (5); you (5); us (5); he (3); him (1); himself (1)	they (7); him (6); he (3); himself **TOTAL (17)**
proper nouns	Good (4); Ignosi (4); Quartermain (2); Sir Henry (2); the Greys (1) **TOTAL (84)**	
nominal animate reference	our people (2) – the white man – the regiments – the mass of struggling warriors – men – a messenger – our men – the captains – the flying groups of our men **TOTAL (10)**	the general (3) – several men (2) – that tall fellow – my friend – an orderly – my man – his orderly – the officer – poor man – eight or ten men – the mass of men – men **TOTAL (15)**
nominal inanimate reference	our first line of defence (2) – the latter – our second – our third – the second – our third line – the assailants – his tall form – the right defence – the reserve regiment – itself – my prostrate form **TOTAL (13)**	the attacking force (3); the three columns – the main or centre column – the other two – the serried phalanxes – the plain – his force – the force – the dense mass – an ominous roar – a similar roar – the other two divisions – that mighty rush of armed humanity – the advance – the tollas or throwing knives – the mass of struggling warriors – that third impenetrable hedge of spears – the dense mass of struggling warriors – the soldiers – it – its reserves – the left attack – swarms of the enemy – the advancing foe – a huge ruffian – the horrid apparition – the matter **TOTAL (31)**
meronymic reference	a kindling eye **TOTAL (1)**	the neck – the chest – his arms – his face – their breath – eyes – his head **TOTAL (7)**

Furthermore, meronymic reference – that is, where characters are referred to in terms of body parts – is unequally weighted towards the Zulus (seven instances to three). Taken together with the high occurrence of inanimate reference to the Zulus, the issue of cohesive referencing raises questions about how both factions are ideologically constructed and perceived. It is my view that Haggard's selections embody colonial or imperial ideas about racial otherness by presenting a depersonalised struggle between a human British faction and the subhuman Zulus. In other words, to return to Halliday and Hasan's contention above, language is linked here to environment. The next section explores this phenomenon.

'Colonialism', say Tiffin and Lawson (1994, p. 3), like its counterpart, racism, 'is an operation of *discourse*, and as an operation of discourse it interpellates colonial subjects by incorporating them in a system of *representation*' (my italics; see also Althusser 1984, Bhabha 1994 and Said 1979). Haggard's novel perpetuates a colonial worldview by establishing a dichotomy of cultural difference between the British and the African characters, with the latter being described as 'heathenish' (65). The two factions are polar opposites in the novel, 'the proud white man' often pitched against the 'poor Hottentot' (101), a dichotomy that is nevertheless threatened with dissolution through the ambivalent character Ignosi. A discourse of 'otherness' finds expression in colonial stereotypes, whereby the Zulus, or 'natives', as the narrator often refers to them, are constructed as savages ('native' is an eighteenth-century cognate of the term 'savage'), while the British leaders are constructed as the civilised and civilising force. It could be argued that the author tacitly engages in what Said (1979) calls 'Orientalism', the discursive construction of racial otherness through the perpetuation of European (or Occidental) ideas about the text's non-European characters. Said (1979, p. 2) proposes that Orientalism is 'based upon an ontological and epistemological distinction between the Orient and (most of the time) the Occident'. Said bases his critique of Orientalism on the assumption that the Orient is 'not an inert fact of nature [but] an *idea* that has a history and a tradition of thought, imagery and vocabulary that have given it reality and presence in and for the West' (1979, pp. 4–5, my italics). Haggard's novel could be understood to embody Orientalist ideas by making a distinction between the Orient and the West in terms of relationships of 'power, of domination, of varying degrees of a complex hegemony' (Said 1979, p. 5). These ideas underpin the actions in the Haggard text and develop the ideologically skewed story presented through the reference chain and summary (Table 3.1) that accords with a colonial worldview of the indigenous native as stereotypically uncivilised and 'other'. An exploration of these underpinning ideas can help us make sense of the cohesive ties and their unequal distribution in the text. The following section, then, deals with the ideational metafunction elucidated through the model of transitivity.

Ideational metafunction

I suggested earlier that stories are made up of actions, events, goings-on and the like. In order for a story to make sense, these salient aspects need to cohere both grammatically *and pragmatically*. For instance, if we were to take the clause 'David kicked an old tin can' and reverse the participants to read 'an old tin can kicked David', our story would be of a very different type altogether. In effect, there is nothing grammatically wrong with this clausal structure. Pragmatically, we may feel that it doesn't 'make sense' because we know that historically tin cans don't act on humans. However, we are propelled by this incongruous construction into a different kind of *experience*. Perhaps there is a science fiction novel in which an old tin can may well kick a human participant. The point is that however incongruous the 'reality' or story, the *representation* of action and event, as well as the participants responsible for and affected by that action and event, are captured neatly here by the clause. We don't have to have experienced in reality something that we encounter in language – this is why literature provides a wonderful conduit for experience, so that, as writers like Pessoa (2001, p. 145) acknowledge, 'reading about the risks incurred by a man who hunts tigers, I feel all the risk worth feeling, save the actual physical risk'. Our incongruous example works because as Halliday (1994, p. 106) puts is, 'language enables human beings to build a mental picture of reality, to make sense of what goes on around them and inside them.' Here, Halliday is referring to the *ideational* metafunction, the area of language that accounts for encoding and representing ideas and experience. In this way, transitivity can be considered in Halliday's terms as 'clause as representation'.

Transitivity is a more complex stylistic model in the context of this metafunction than would be suggested by its traditional grammatical role in determining whether or not a verb takes a direct object. We can use the transitivity system to account for patterns of *experience* in a text because reality is made up of experiential processes – doing, sensing, being, happening and becoming – and so the transitivity system, according to Halliday (1994, p. 106), 'construes the world of experience into a manageable set of PROCESS TYPES.' The process is realised through the verb or verb phrase (although it can be implied through a nominalised verb) while other constituents satisfy the Participant roles (agent and affected) and the Circumstances of the clause (the 'where', 'when', 'how'). Following Berry (1975), Halliday's breakdown of process types makes the distinction between inner and outer experience so that processes of 'sensing', for example, are contrasted with processes of 'doing'. However, whereas Berry retains the primary distinction between Mental and Material processes (or 'inner' and 'outer' experience), Halliday and others (Halliday and Mattheissen 2004, Simpson 1993, 2004, Eggins 2004) make further subdivisions, some of which I will outline below with examples.

Material Processes are processes of doing and usually involve the entity (or thing) that does the doing, as well as the entity (or thing) affected by the doing. These roles are termed 'Actor' and 'Goal' respectively, and there are different kinds of material process which account for the scope of 'materialness'. If we return to our original example of 'David kicked an old tin can', David is the Actor and 'an old tin can' is the Goal element. However, there are a few other ways of expressing this same process – so that, for example, we take the focus off David by foregrounding the Goal as in 'an old tin can was kicked *by David*'. As functionalist stylistics is as much about *choice* as anything else, we can see from the table below the different material process types and their various permutations.

Table 3.2 Material processes

Material Process Type	Clausal Configuration			Agency
(a) Action-intention	David	kicked	an old tin can	Agency explicit
	Actor	Process	Goal	
(b) Action-intention (passive voice)	An old tin can	was kicked	by David	Agency backgrounded
	Goal	Process	Actor	
(c) Action-intention (passive voice)	An old tin can	was kicked		Agency deleted
	Goal	Process		
(d) Action-Supervention	An old tin can	rolled		Agency excised
	Actor	Process		

In each of the examples, the only constant element is the Process, the 'doing'. The Actor role is more or less present as we read down the table; in a) it is clear what David is doing and to whom, while in b) his active role is 'backgrounded' through a passive formation and the Goal, or affected entity, is given focal prominence. In c) the Actor is deleted from the clause, although the passive formation allows us to ask 'by whom'. In d) the Process is represented as involuntary, in that it implies no external agent, whereas the use of 'kicked' requires one (see Simpson 1993, pp. 92–95 for an ergative interpretation of such processes). The final column in the table relates to the degree (presence or absence) of agency that results from the formulation to which it corresponds. The more explicit the Participants, the more explicit the responsibility for the 'doing'. It is not difficult to see how grammatical configurations like those above can influence our interpretation of the same event and could have political or cultural leverage in a range of discursive practices (see Fowler 1981, Fowler, Hodge, Kress and Trew 1979, Kress and Hodge 1979).

Each of the permutations can take a Circumstantial component, a deletable element which offers specific information about the 'where', 'when', and 'how' of the experience. The positioning of the Circumstance may have a bearing on how we perceive the information in the clause, as the bold type in this example from Haggard's novel demonstrates:

> '**Slowly, and without the slightest appearance of haste or excitement**, the three columns crept on'.

This Circumstance/Actor/Process construction has the deictic effect of placing the reader in the moment while also 'backgrounding' 'crept', the action encoded in the Material process. This example throws up an interesting feature of Material (and other) processes that is worthy of note here, which is their ability to reflect the scope of the action through a 'Range' constituent. Put simply, the Range elaborates on the process by extending it. At times, the Range feels a bit like a Goal and a bit like a Circumstance. In the above example from Haggard, 'crept' is the process, but 'on' specifies the extent of the 'creeping' and thus satisfies the Range. Further Range elements can be found in the following examples in bold type:

a) 'Ella made **a mess**'
b) 'I made **the best of a bad job**'
c) 'We kept **up a steady fire**'

The Range is typically, but not exclusively, a cognate of the verb in the process, as is the case in a) with 'a mess' and 'made'. Other examples are 'sing' and 'a song' or 'done' and 'the deed'. Examples b) and c) are from Haggard's text and constitute Goal-less Material processes. In both, the Range elements substitute for the affected entity. Without making any further critical comment at this stage, readers may be shocked to know that the fairly innocuous noun phrase in b), 'the best of a bad job', euphemistically encodes the Material process of killing.

Mental processes are processes of 'sensing' – thinking, feeling, perceiving – and the transitivity configurations necessitate different kinds of participants. In a Mental process, there are two potential participants, the Senser (the entity that does the sensing), and the Phenomenon (the 'thing' sensed). Generally, the Senser is an animate entity, but inanimate objects can be endowed with consciousness by assuming the role of Senser, as in 'the book was watching me from its home on the shelf'. In reality this cannot happen, but anyone who has ever lagged behind in their studies would probably understand the pragmatic significance of such a statement. Mental processes are divided into three 'principal sub-types' (Halliday 1994, pp. 118), namely Perception (seeing, hearing etc.), Affection, sometimes known as Reaction (liking, fearing etc.), and Cognition (thinking, knowing, understanding etc.). Examples are outlined in table 3.3.

A significant feature of Mental processes is their ability to encode presupposed 'facts' through projection. For instance, a simple clause like 'I saw my man standing' (from the Haggard text) presupposes the 'fact' of a man standing. The projected element, itself a Material process, is mediated through a Mental process and construed as given. In the same way, the projected clause (in bold), 'She believed **her brother ran a competitive race at the Olympics**' is taken as fact – it is true that 'she' *believed* this to be fact, but whether it was fact *in reality* is open to interpretation (the 'fact' of his race being 'competitive' as well as the 'fact' of him running at the Olympics). The point is that the projected clause *may* be construed as accepted fact.

Table 3.3 Mental processes

Mental Process Type			Clausal Configuration
(a) Mental-Perception	I	saw	my man standing
	Senser	*Process*	*Phenomenon*
(b) Mental-Affection	Fiona	loves	Matchbox Twenty
(Also known as Mental-Reaction)	*Senser*	*Process*	*Phenomenon*
(c) Mental-Cognition	She	believed	her brother ran a competitive race at the Olympics
	Senser	*Process*	*Phenomenon*

Perhaps one of the most complex process types, Relational processes denote states of being. In Halliday's terms (1994, pp. 119), there are 'two parts to the 'being': something is being said to 'be' something else', and a relationship exists between the two things. The nature of the relationship can be captured by three primary categories of process as follows:

a. *Intensive* – marks a relationship of equivalence (*x is y*)
b. *Possessive* – marks a relationship of ownership (*x has y*)
c. *Circumstantial* – marks a relationship of 'time, place, manner, cause, accompaniment, role, matter or angle' (130) *(x is on y, x is at y,* and so on)

Each Relational process has two modes, an attributive mode (denoting an attribute) and an identifying mode. In the attributive mode 'some entity is being said to have an attribute' (128), as in 'my daughter is clever'. The quality 'clever' does not define her; in other words, it is not the identifying trait putting her in a class of one, but is an attribute which puts her in a class of clever people. The Identifying mode, on the other hand, singles her out as being identified by that quality as 'clever' does in 'my daughter is the clever one'. Figure 3.1, below, offers examples that account for both modes.

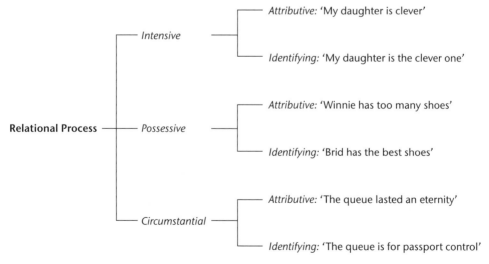

Figure 3.1 Relational processes

The clause constituents for Relational Processes are Carrier (the entity to whom the attribute is ascribed) and Attribute. In the Identifying mode, the participants, Identified and Identifier, are self-explanatory.

Behavioural processes sit between Material and Mental processes and account for 'physiological and psychological behaviour' (Halliday 1994, pp. 139) such as coughing, dreaming, looking (in contrast to 'seeing' which is Mental) and such like. Key constituents of Behavioural processes are self-explanatory in that there is a 'Behaver', a process and a Circumstance if applicable. Like Material and Mental processes, Behavioural processes can take a Range element. Examples of Behavioural processes are as follows:

a)   He **sighed** heavily
b)   I **took** a deep breath
c)   Maura **dreamt** of Barcelona

In b) the process is extended through the Range element 'a deep breath' which qualifies the process 'took'. As in other processes with a Range, the behaviour appears 'participant-like'. This is also the case with some Circumstantial components, particularly those of Manner, like 'Barcelona' in example c) above (see Halliday 1994, pp. 139).

Verbal processes account for 'saying', not just of the human communication kind, but of 'any kind of symbolic exchange of meaning' (Halliday 1994, pp. 140). Clausal constituents include the 'Sayer', the entity who verbalises, and the 'Verbiage', that which is said or communicated. Verbal processes take an additional participant role that accounts for the person who receives the Verbiage and is predictably known as the 'Receiver'. Examples of Verbal processes are:

a)   Conor **shouted** at the referee
b)   Daniel **called** out to Katie
c)   Declan's notice **told** everyone to 'Keep Out'

In a) there is no Verbiage component – 'at the referee' is a Circumstantial element. Verbal processes can also take a Range constituent as in b), signalled by 'out'. 'Katie' is the 'Receiver', or the person to whom the Verbiage (ellipted here) is directed. Example c) is an instance of an inanimate 'Sayer', the 'notice', while the Verbiage component is satisfied by the order 'Keep out'. Interestingly, like Mental processes Verbal processes can be multi-layered in that they can project other non-Verbal processes. The highlighted Relational-Intensive process in 'Gerard told us that **his children were the cleverest in the class**' is an example of a projected process. Whether the projected Relational process is true in fact or not is completely anterior to the 'truth' of him making the statement.

Existential processes function to state that something exists, as in 'There was a murder'. This construction offers no participant clues – 'there' acts not as a Circumstance (as is often the case with 'there' in other processes) but as a 'dummy subject' (Simpson 2004, pp. 25), while 'a murder' functions as the 'Existent'. Existential processes can circumvent cause and effect relationships by eliding the participant roles and using nominalised verbs that encode other process types, such as the Material process of 'murdering' in the example above. Encoded actions are in bold in the following examples:

a)   **There was a shout** across the hall
b)   Stephanie heard **there was a car crash**
c)   The end **is** near

In a) the 'shout' merely exists, although it is reasonable to assume that some animate entity created it, while in b) the (projected) Existential process 'there was a car crash' implies rather than asserts agency. Finally, in c) the process is simply stated as a 'fact'.

In summary, then, the spectrum of processes and participants is outlined in Figure 3.2 below.

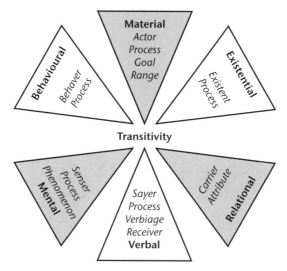

Figure 3.2 Summary of process types and constituents

I now want to bring these process types to life through the Haggard extract. I stated earlier that the cohesive reference chain suggested a favourable bias toward the British faction. As many of these reference items feature as participants in transitivity configurations, it makes sense to assess the context of their occurrences by exploring who or what did what to whom or what. A simple transitivity analysis of the physical role the British played in the attack yields the following Material processes, shown in Table 3.4 below.

Table 3.4 Summary of British action (material processes)

			The British		
Clause	Actor	Process	Goal	Circumstance	Range
i	I (would)	clear	the plain	in twenty minutes	
ii	(Suppose) you	try	Ø		a shot
iii	you	go	Ø	to that tall fellow there	
iv	you	miss	him		
v	you	(don't) drop	the ball	within ten yards	
vi	I	covered	him		
vii	I	took	him	halfway down the neck	
viii	Ø	find	him	in the chest	

			The British		
Clause	Actor	Process	Goal	Circumstance	Range
ix	I	pressed	Ø		
x	I	did	Ø		a rash thing
xi	I	let drive	Ø	with the second barrel	
xii	I	had made	Ø		no mistake
xiii	Sir Henry and Good	took	Ø		up their rifles and began to fire
xiv	the latter (Good)	browning	the dense mass	before him with a Winchester repeater	
xv	we	put	some eight or ten men	*hors de combat*	
xvi	we	kept	Ø		up a steady fire
xvii	(we)	accounted	Ø	for several men	
xviii	(we)	produced	Ø	upon that mighty rush of armed humanity	no more effect
xix	Ø	was pressed	our first line of defence		back
xx	Ø	were driven	our people	back and up	
xxi	our third line	came	Ø	Ø	into action
xxii	he	rushed	Ø	Ø	off
xxiii	(he)	flung	himself	into the hottest of the fray	
xxiv	I	stopped	Ø	where I was	
xxv	the reserve regiment	extended	itself		
xxvi	I	found	myself	involved in a furious onslaught upon the advancing foe	
xxvii	I (found myself)	involved	Ø	in a furious onslaught	
xxviii	I	made	Ø		the best of a bad job
xxix	(I)	toddled	Ø	along	to be killed
xxx	we	were plunging	Ø	the flying groups of our men	through
xxxi	I	rose	Ø	to the occasion	
xxxii	I	flung	myself	down	
xxxiii	(I)	settled	the matter	from behind with my revolver	

For the purposes of clarification, the processes in bold type represent non-real actions – that is, they are imagined or anticipated, but not realised. Absent participant elements are represented by ø where necessary. The extract from which these process types are taken depicts a violent battle between the British and the Zulus, the culmination of which is a 'dreadfully heavy' loss. The British claim to 'have lost quite two thousand killed and wounded', while 'they [the Zulus] must have lost three' (209). Given such losses, it would not be surprising to find a high incidence of Material processes in the text, particularly from the British soldiers as they inflict the heaviest losses. As would be expected, there are thirty-two Material processes enacted by the British. Nearly half of these (fifteen) affect a participant, which accords with the high Zulu death toll. However, of these fifteen, only eight posit the Zulus as Goal. With the exception of one clause that is hypothetical (iv) the remaining seven of these fifteen processes are either self-reflexive (the British fulfil both Actor and Goal in clauses xxiii, xxv, xxvi, xxxi) or they feature as Goal in clauses with no Actor (xix, xx). Interestingly, the eight clauses in which the Zulus occupy the Goal element (i, iv, vi, vii, viii, xiv, xv, xxxii) can be split further to account for five that present the Zulus as animate, although one of these ('him', clause iv) is hypothetical. The remaining three (of eight) present the Zulus as inanimate (i, xiv, xxxii). This breakdown of clausal constituents means that there are only four instances out of thirty-two Material processes where the Zulus are explicitly presented as the affected Goal and in which the British occupy the role as Actor (vi, vii, viii, xv). Let us have a closer look at these clauses below.

vi. 'I **covered** him'
vii. 'I **took** him halfway down the neck'
viii. '[I calculated to] **find** him in the chest'
xv. 'We **put** some eight or ten men *hors de combat*'

The Material processes (in bold) are interesting because they are metaphoric and thus euphemistic; all of them are lexically under-specific and semantically vague, and none definitively suggest murder ('covered', 'took', 'find', 'put'). However, that is precisely what they are employed to represent. To give a flavour of their context in the narrative, examples vi, vii and viii feature in the paragraph below:

> This piqued me, so, loading the express with solid ball, I waited till my friend walked some ten yards out from his force, in order to get a better view of our position, accompanied only by an orderly, and then, lying down and resting the express upon a rock, **I covered him**. The rifle, like all expresses, was only sighted to three hundred and fifty yards, so to allow for the drop in trajectory **I took him** half-way down the neck, which ought, I calculated, **to find him** in the chest (203–4).

The action 'I covered him' is so far post-positioned as to render it almost peripheral to the seven syntactically prominent clauses that precede it. Similarly, 'I took him' is semantically ambiguous and mitigates the force of the murderous action against the Zulu victim. While it is grammatically explicit that the British protagonist is responsible for the killing of this Zulu man (he fulfils the role of Actor in a Material process in which the Zulu man is Goal), the action is obscured through the choice of verb 'find'. Arguably, 'find' is not typically used to convey such wilful action as murder because it implies a degree of involuntary control. One can actively 'look', but cannot purposefully 'find'. Its inclusion here, then, is significant. Moreover, an interesting pattern of under-specificity is developed through the following sixteen Material processes (all of which encode murder by the British): 'clear the plain', 'covered', 'took', 'find', 'pressed', 'let drive', 'made no mistake', 'browning', 'put [men] *hors de combat*', 'kept up a steady fire', 'accounted for', 'produced no more effect', 'found myself involved', 'made the best of a bad job', 'rose to the occasion', and 'settled the matter'.

If we shift our focus to the actions of the Zulus (mediated through the British narrator), we find similar instances of euphemistically encoded action. However, on closer examination, a systematic pattern of selection emerges as is captured by Table 3.5 below.

Table 3.5 Summary of Zulu action (Material processes)

			The Zulus		
Clause	Actor	Process	Goal	Circumstance	Range
i	the three columns	crept	Ø		on
ii	the main or centre column	halted	Ø		
iii	the other two	circumvent	our position		
iv	my friend	walked	Ø	some ten yards	
v	he	stood	Ø	quite still	
vi	(he)	gave	me		every opportunity
vii	my man	standing	Ø	unharmed	
viii	his orderly	was stretched	Ø	upon the ground, apparently dead	
ix	the officer I had aimed at	began to run	Ø	towards his force	
x	he	ran	Ø		
xi	the poor man	threw	his arms		up
xii	(the poor man)	fell	Ø	forward on to his face	
xiii	the force	began to fall back	Ø	in confusion	
xiv	the other two divisions	were engaging	us		
xv	the mass of men	opened	Ø	out	a little
xvi	(the mass of men)	came	Ø	on towards the hill	
xvii	they	advanced	Ø		
xviii	they	came	Ø	on	
xix	they	came	Ø	on	
xx	they	were driving	the outposts		in
xxi	the attacking force	had to come up	the hill		

			The Zulus		
Clause	Actor	Process	Goal	Circumstance	Range
xxii	(the attacking force)	came	Ø	slowly	
xxiii	they	came	Ø	on	
xxiv	the tollas or throwing knives	began to flash	Ø	backwards and forwards	
xxv	the mass of struggling warriors	swayed	Ø	to and fro	
xxvi	men	falling	Ø	thick as leaves in an autumn wind	
xxvii					
xxviii	the dense mass of struggling warriors	swung	Ø	backwards and forwards	
xxix	Ø	was pressed	the attacking force	back down	
xxx	it (the attacking force)	retreated	Ø	upon its reserves	
xxxi	Ø	had been repulsed	the left attack		
xxxii	swarms of the enemy	succeeded	Ø	at this point	
xxxiii	a huge ruffian	making	me	with a bloody spear	straight at
xxxiv	the horrid apparition	came	Ø		
xxxv	he	took	Ø	right over my prostrate form	a header

Astonishingly, of thirty-four Material processes, only nine carry a Goal element and thus affect any other entity. Of these nine Goal-directed processes, the Goal is animate in only four of them. They are as follows (in bold):

vi.   He gave **me** every opportunity
xiv.   The other two divisions were engaging **us**
xxvii.   The assailants lost **many men**
xxxiii.   A huge ruffian making straight at **me** with a bloody spear

In the first example the Zulu is Actor and the British narrator is Goal. However, the nature of the process, 'gave', is a metaphoric construction that evades explicit qualification – the Zulu warrior is depicted as giving himself sacrificially to the British soldier who kills him (on the second 'opportunity' after missing the first), thus playing an active role in effecting his own murder. The implication of such 'willingness' on the part of the Zulu may function to naturalise his murder. As the narrative point of view is Quartermain's, it is perhaps no surprise that he construes himself as merely hitting a target that has presented itself. In the second example, the process, 'engaging', like the 'making' in the fourth example, is a rather weak verb and plays down the role of the natives in effecting any real 'damage' to their British counterparts. In the third example the Zulus occupy both Actor ('the assailants') and Goal ('many men') roles, which make them appear responsible for their own demise. In the Zulu attack on the British, it becomes difficult to tell who is responsible for the retreat of the English faction:

'To and fro swayed the mass of struggling warriors, men falling thick as leaves in an autumn wind; but before long the superior weight of the attacking force began to tell, and **our first line of defence was slowly pressed back**, till it merged into the second. Here the struggle was very fierce, but again **our people were driven back and up**, till at length, within twenty minutes of the commencement of the fight, our third line came into action' (206).

Compare this to the British attack on the natives:

'Sir Henry and Good now **took up** their rifles, and **began to fire**, the latter industriously **'browning'** the dense mass before him with a Winchester repeater, and I also had another shot or two, with the result that so far as we could judge we **put** some eight or ten men *hors de combat* before they got out of range' (205).

In the first extract, the natives are completely elided or at best obscured in the passive configurations (in bold type) and collective noun phrases such as 'mass of struggling warriors', 'men falling', 'the superior weight of the attacking force' and 'the struggle'. Their primary actions throughout the battle scene are intransitive and involve moving around – 'crept', 'halted', 'circumvent', 'walked', 'stood', 'stretched', 'fell', 'swayed', 'retreated', and so on – but they really don't *do* anything. On the other hand, what the British 'do' is positively glossed through adverbs like 'industriously' and metaphorical substitutions such as 'came into action', that imply diligence, progression and productivity, rather than murderousness. In contrast, the Zulus are presented as inept or perhaps untrained and their actions encode little or no causation – from an Orientalist perspective their inefficacy could well offer some justification for colonialism, which relies on the (Western) assumption that the native is uncivilised, uneducated and ultimately, radically 'other'. Glimpses of this dichotomy can be discerned in the detail of the descriptions, such as the battle armoury that divides the natives who use primitive 'tollas' or 'throwing knives' and 'spears', while the British have more advanced (and lethal) weapons ('Winchester repeater', 'express' and 'solid ball'). Armed primitively, heavily depersonalised ('the horrid apparition') and ultimately homogenised ('the force', 'they', 'the mass', 'the assailants', 'swarms of the enemy'), the natives appear to offer no real threat to the mighty British. The British, for their part, are a powerful force, although their murderous actions are heavily mitigated to accord with this lack of indigenous threat and, one could argue, to maintain the civilised Occidental stereotype. Even detailed depictions of one-to-one combat are similarly biased:

'Getting dead on, as I thought, a fine sight, **I pressed**, and when the puff of smoke had cleared away, I, to my disgust, saw my man standing unharmed, whilst his orderly, who was at least three paces to the left, was stretched upon the ground, apparently dead' (204).

'I pressed' tells us nothing and causation has been ellipted – we merely infer that whatever Quartermain 'pressed' resulted in the death of his 'friend', the Zulu orderly. The latter's death is described through a Relational Circumstantial process, 'was stretched upon the ground'. Of course, we can assume that the bullet killed him (as opposed to the narrator who discharged the gun), but the point is that agency is not explicit – the key action of the bullet hitting and killing the orderly has been ellipted, a pattern that discursively constructs the British as effective without being brutal ('I pressed'). Throughout the extract the narrator is careful not to be construed as savage himself and goes some way towards naturalising the British onslaught, even presenting the execution of a Zulu general as a game to be won: 'Two to one you miss him, and an even sovereign to be paid … that you don't drop the ball within ten yards'. The 'naturalness' of the British-led actions may offer ideological justification for colonialism. The same naturalising discourse governs the linguistic choices that construe the Oriental stereotype, metonymically captured through a perpetuation of the naturalness of the 'savage' tag as inherently bound up with physiology. The following quotation taken from the final stand of the British (with their supporting native army) subtly demonstrates this:

> 'At this moment, however … I felt my bosom burn with martial ardour … numbers of sanguinary verses from the Old Testament, sprang up in my brain … my blood … **went beating through my veins, and there came upon me a savage desire to kill and spare not**. I glanced round at the serried ranks of warriors behind us, and … **began to wonder if my face looked like theirs**.' (224)

The killing instinct, when it does surface in the British narrator, seems to happen outside of his control and is impelled by his Christian faith. This is interesting as colonialism is often predicated on the desire to bring the indigenous population into Western Christianity. Significantly, Quartermain draws a parallel between his irregular 'savage desire' and the native army that surrounds him, alluding to what Bhabha (1994, p. 86) calls 'mimicry', or the fear of 'going native' ('I began to wonder if my face looked like theirs'). The ambivalence between the coloniser and the colonised (consider Ignosi) may compel the narrator to consistently reaffirm the differences between the British and their African counterparts through the language choices examined above. This is certainly the case with intransitive processes conveying the Zulu natives as inept, and the heavily mitigated euphemistic processes that depict the natives' demise under the direction of the British. I want to develop this contention briefly in the following section through an exploration of the interpersonal metafunction.

Interpersonal metafunction

Modality, a key exponent of the interpersonal metafunction, refers to a 'speaker's attitude towards, or opinion about, the truth of a proposition expressed by a sentence [and] extends to their attitude towards the situation or event described by a sentence' (Simpson 1993, p. 47). The concept of 'attitude' is central to modality (see Fowler 1996, p. 168), and so a consideration of the 'truth' value of the propositions of Haggard's omniscient narrator may well shed some light on the attitudinal biases raised in the analyses of cohesion and transitivity above. As such, modality is inherently bound up with point of view (Fowler 1996), as Neary's chapter in this volume aptly demonstrates. It makes sense, therefore, to consider modality in terms of its contribution to the emerging point of view in our analysis thus far. Modality (see Uspensky 1973, Fowler 1996) can be categorised in four primary ways to account for the level of obligation or duty in a statement ('deontic' modality), its truth-value ('epistemic' modality), level of desire ('boulomaic' modality) and the degree of perception ('perception' modality). The table on the following page outlines the prominence of modal markers in the Haggard extract according to the four principal types.

Table 3.6 Summary of modal categories and narrative distribution

Deontic Modality *(expressions of duty)*	Boulomaic Modality *(expressions of desire)*	Epistemic Modality *(expressions of belief)*	Perception Modality *(expressions of perception)*
'that the threefold assault should be delivered simultaneously'	'Oh, for a gatling'	'their object being, no doubt'	'See how near you can go to that tall fellow who appears to be in command'
'Suppose you try a shot'		'but whether it was the excitement of the wind, or the fact of the man being a long shot, I don't know'	'Getting dead on, as I thought, a fine sight'
'which ought, I calculated, to find him in the chest'		'his orderly ... was stretched upon the ground, apparently dead'	'the officer ... began to run towards his force, in evident alarm'
'seeing that if I stood where I was I must be done for'		'This time I had made no mistake'	'Swarms of the enemy ... had evidently succeeded at this point'
		'I also had another shot or two, with the result that so far as we could judge we put some eight or ten men *hors de combat*'	'I found myself involved in a furious onslaught'
		'Ignosi ... accounted for several men, but of course produced no more effect'	'I toddled along to be killed as though I liked it'
		'The issue was doubtful'	'All I can remember is the dreadful rolling noise of the meeting of shields'
		'From that moment on the issue was no longer in doubt'	'a huge ruffian, whose eyes seemed literally to be starting out of his head'
		'I'm sure I do not know what happened'	'The time seemed all too short to me'

The most common type is epistemic modality (perception modality is a sub-category of epistemic modality), which reflects degrees of truth or certainty. In practically all of the instances in which the linguistic expression of murder is more explicit (notwithstanding the mitigated Material processes through which they are conveyed), the clauses are heavily modalised: 'so far as we could judge', 'I had made no mistake', 'apparently dead', 'as I thought', 'all I can remember', and 'I found myself'. However, if we have another look at the extract above which depicts the actual fighting (the extract which begins 'To and fro swayed the mass of struggling warriors'), there is, surprisingly, almost no modality. In a move away from the stylistic patterning of the rest of the extract, this section and the three paragraphs that follow it are devoid of what Uspensky calls '*verba sentiendi*' (words of 'feeling'), and so incorporate no judgement or subjective reflection. It is, in fact, almost Hemminway-esque in its bald, generic style. It is perhaps no surprise that such savage hand-to-hand combat is represented as mere fact, without judgement, without excuse and without evidence of the subjective consciousness through which the rest of the extract is, in the ironic sense of the term, framed.

Conclusion

I suggested earlier that ideas about racialised otherness could be discerned through the representation of action in the text. The transitivity analysis of the British characters' actions makes these underpinning ideas more transparent; the British are systematically presented as acting materially in the battle, and thus as effectual, but crucially they are also presented as civilised and non-barbaric. Their 'actions' are murderous, yet the Material processes that convey them are semantically vague and heavily mitigated ('I settled the matter'), unthreatening ('I made the best of a bad job') and non-barbaric ('I pressed'). In representing such a fierce and violent battle, it seems strange to encounter what amounts to a 'killing me softly' narrative.

I have argued here that Haggard's novel is motivated by environmental and ideological factors in perpetuating an Orientalist world-view. Through a functionalist stylistic toolkit that makes use of the ideational, interpersonal and textual metafunctions of language, I have shown how patterns in a literary text can shed some light on the context of situation that impels and informs a text's production and interpretation. Through an exploration of Haggard's novel, I have demonstrated the reciprocity and scope of the metafunctions outlined and developed by key thinkers in stylistics. I have shown how ideas about stereotypes can find their way into a literary work, and how the clause as message and the clause as experience intersect to bring Haggard's literary masterpiece to life. Through an exploration of transitivity and cohesion, I hope to have provided a multi-dimensional reading of both the literary and pragmatic stories that Haggard's novel articulates and encodes, as well as accounting for the cultural milieu in which it was produced. By reading the text as bound up within the context, it could be successfully argued that rather than being an adventure story that began from the Western pursuit of African riches, Haggard's novel encodes a second story – an environmental one that expounds colonial views and presents the British attack on African natives as a political and moral victory.

If stylistics encourages what O'Toole calls a 'hermeneutic spiral', that is, a 'dialectic between precise description of the details of linguistic form and less precise intuitions' (Birch and O'Toole 1988, p. 12), then functionalist stylistics offers a way of reading around the spiral, of interacting with it. It offers insights into possible motivations for the text's existence. In short, functional stylistics offers a way of reading between and beyond a text's formal properties. As well as providing a 'powerful method for understanding the ways in which all sorts of 'realities' are constructed through language', stylistics – and particularly functionalist stylistics – provides a way of answering the implicit question, 'what is the point of this text?' The external forces that impel a text can be crucial determiners of the hermeneutic spiral that results from the dialectic relationship between linguistic form and intuitive feeling to which O'Toole refers. For instance, holding a particular worldview – whether on the nature of aggression towards younger siblings, the relationship between social class and culture, or on the importance of nationalism – can and does influence how we read and use language. To refer to the opening sentence of this chapter, whatever 'it' was that Macbeth 'did' tells us nothing other than there was an event, a 'doing' of something. Our cultural knowledge (of the character, of Shakespeare's play, of the history of monarchy, and even of the linguistic construction 'he did it' to which negative connotations – of blame, for instance – are often attached) allows us to infer that while on the (decontextualised) surface 'it' says nothing at all, the 'it' in *Macbeth* says everything.

Recommendations for practice and future directions

The capacity for functionalist stylistics to see through the text to the underlying ideas that shape its construction allows us to engage with language in ways that go beyond the words on the page. In this way, it provides a robust and cogent way of bringing multi-layered stories together so that the meaning potential therein can be most fully realised. Such robustness can also find practical application in other areas of research such as forensic linguistics, offering insights into authorship (of literary and non-literary texts) by examining linguistic patterning through an amalgam of the various metafunctions. Furthermore, where possible it can supplement psychological profiling, offering profitable analyses in the field of criminology.

Functionalist stylistics is also practically useful for expounding literary theory, as this short introduction has demonstrated. Bringing both hermeneutic approaches together enriches analyses of text and context and ascribes equal importance to sociological, literary and linguistic perspectives.

Related topics

Critical stylistics, feminist stylistics, formalist stylistics, linguistic levels of foregrounding, metaphor and metonymy, multimodality, narratology, point of view and modality, stylistics, emotion and neuroscience.

Further reading

Said, E., 1979. *Orientalism*. London: Vintage.

Said's work expounds the essentially ideological practice of reading Orientalist stereotypes from an Occidental viewpoint.

Simpson, P., 1993. *Language, ideology and point of view*. London and New York: Routledge.

Simpson offers extremely accessible and engaging analyses of language use, and gives examples of its dynamic meaning potential.

Halliday, M. A. K., 1994. *An introduction to functional grammar*. 2nd ed. London: Arnold.

This is an indispensable introduction to functionalist stylistics and includes a fully comprehensive account of the transitivity model.

Fowler, R., Hodge, R., Kress, G. and Trew, T., eds. 1979. *Language and control*. London: Routledge and Kegan Paul.

This is a very useful study of a range of discursive practices and uses transitivity, amongst other functionalist stylistic models, to uncover political and ideological biases in journalistic discourse.

References

Althusser, L., 1984. *Essays on ideology*. London: Verso.
Berry, M., 1975. *An introduction to systemic linguistics: Structures and systems*. London: Batsford.
Birch, D. and O'Toole, M., 1988. The power of functional stylistics. *In:* D. Birch and M. O'Toole, eds. *Functions of style*. London: Pinter, 1–11.
Bhabha, H. K., 1994. *The location of culture*. London: Routledge.
Canning, P., 2010. *Styling the Renaissance: Language and ideology in early modern England*. London: Continuum.
Chomsky, N., 1957. *Syntactic structures*. The Hague: Paris: Mouton.
Chomsky, N., 1986. *Knowledge of language: Its nature, origins, and use*. New York: Praeger.

Eggins, S., 2004. *An introduction to systemic functional linguistics.* 2nd ed. London: Continuum.

Firth, J. R., 1950. Personality and language in society. Reprinted 1957 in J. R. Firth, *Papers in linguistics 1934–1951.* London: Oxford University Press.

Firth, J. R., 1957. *Papers in linguistics 1934–1951.* London: Oxford University Press.

Fowler, R., 1981. *Literature as social discourse.* London: Batsford.

Fowler, R., 1996. *Linguistic criticism.* 2nd ed. Oxford: Oxford University Press.

Fowler, R., Hodge, R., Kress, G. and Trew T. eds. 1979. *Language and control.* London: Routledge and Kegan Paul.

Greenblatt, S., Cohen, W., Howard, J. E. and Maus, K. E. eds. 1997. *The Norton Shakespeare.* New York and London: W.W. Norton & Company.

Haggard, H. R., 1998. *King Solomon's mines.* Oxford: Oxford University Press.

Halliday, M. A. K., 1994. *An introduction to functional grammar.* 2nd ed. London: Arnold.

Halliday, M. A. K., 1996. Linguistic function and literary style: An inquiry into the language of William Golding's *The Inheritors.* In: J. J. Weber, ed. *The stylistics reader: From Roman Jakobson to the present.* London: Arnold, 56–86.

Halliday, M. A. K. and Hasan, R., 1976. *Cohesion in English.* London: Longman.

Halliday, M. A. K. and Matthiessen, C. M. I. M., 2004. *An introduction to functional grammar.* 3rd ed. London: Arnold.

Hoey, M., 2005. *Lexical priming: A new theory of words and language.* London: Routledge.

Kress, G. and Hodge, R., 1979. *Language as ideology.* London: Routledge and Kegan Paul.

Leech, G., 2008. *Language in literature: Style and foregrounding.* Harlow: Pearson Longman.

Malinowski, B., 1923. The problem of meaning in primitive languages. In: C. K. Ogden and I. A. Richards, eds. *The Meaning of meanings.* London: Routledge and Kegan Paul.

Pessoa, F., 2001. *The book of disquiet.* London: Penguin.

Said, E., 1979. *Orientalism.* New York: Vintage.

Saussure, F. de, 1916. *Cours de linguistique generale. In:* C. Bally and A. Sechehaye, eds. W. Baskin, trans. 1977. *Course in general linguistics.* Lausanne and Paris: Payot. Glasgow: Fontana/Collins (*passim*).

Simpson, P., 1993. *Language, ideology and point of view.* London: Routledge.

Simpson, P., 2004. *Stylistics: A resource book for students.* London: Routledge.

Tiffin, C. and Lawson, A., eds. 1994. *De-scribing empire: Post-colonialism and textuality.* London: Routledge.

Toolan, M., 2009. *Narrative progression in the short story: A corpus stylistic approach.* Amsterdam and New York: John Benjamins.

Uspensky, B., 1973. *A poetics of composition.* Berkeley: University of California Press.

Appendix

Chapter XIII: The Attack (Battle)

(203) Slowly, and without the slightest appearance of haste or excitement, the three columns crept on. When within about five hundred yards of us, the main or centre column halted at the root of a tongue of open plain which ran up into the hill, to enable the other two to circumvent our position, which was shaped more or less in the form of a horse-shoe, the two points being towards the town of Loo, their object being, no doubt, that the threefold assault should be delivered simultaneously.

'Oh, for a gatling!' groaned Good, as he contemplated the serried phalanxes beneath us. 'I would clear the plain* in twenty minutes.'

'We have not got one, so it is no use yearning for it; but suppose you try a shot, Quartermain. See how near you can go to that tall fellow who appears to be in command. Two to one you miss him, and an even sovereign, to be honestly paid if ever we get out of this, that you don't drop the ball within ten yards.'

This piqued me, so, loading the express with solid ball, I waited till my friend walked some ten yards out from his force, in order to get a better view of our position, accompanied only by an orderly, and then, lying down and resting the express upon a rock, I covered him. The rifle, like all expresses, was only sighted to three hundred and fifty yards, so to allow for the drop in trajectory I took him half-way down the neck, which ought, I calculated, to find him in the chest. He stood quite still and gave me every opportunity, but whether it was the excitement or the wind, or the fact of the man being a long shot, I don't know, but this was what happened. Getting dead on, as I thought, a fine sight, I pressed, and when the puff of smoke had cleared away, I, to my disgust, saw my man standing unharmed, whilst his orderly, who was at least three paces to the left, was stretched upon the ground, apparently dead. Turning swiftly, the officer* I had aimed at began to run towards his force, in evident alarm.

'Bravo, Quartermain!' sang out Good; 'you've frightened him.'

This made me very angry, for if possible to avoid it, I hate to miss in public. When one can only do one thing well, one likes to keep up one's reputation in that thing. Moved quite out of myself at my failure, I did a rash thing. Rapidly covering the general* as he ran, I let drive with the second barrel. The poor man threw up his arms, and fell forward on to his face. This time I had made no mistake; and – I say it as a proof of how little we think of others when our own pride or reputation are in question – I was brute enough to feel delighted at the sight.

(205) The regiments who had seen the feat cheered wildly at this exhibition of the white man's magic, which they took as an omen of success, while the force to which the general had belonged – which, indeed, as we afterwards ascertained, he had commanded – began to fall back in confusion. Sir Henry and Good now took up their rifles, and began to fire, the latter industriously 'browning' the dense mass before him with a Winchester repeater, and I also had another shot or two, with the result that so far as we could judge we put some eight or ten men *hors de combat* before they got out of range.

Just as we stopped firing there came an ominous roar from our far right, then a similar roar from our left. The two other divisions were engaging us.

At the sound, the mass of men before us opened out a little, and came on towards the hill up the spit of bare grass land at a slow trot, singing a deep-throated song as they advanced. We kept up a steady fire from our rifles as they came, Ignosi joining in occasionally, and accounted for several men, but of course produced no more effect upon that mighty rush of armed humanity than he who throws pebbles does on the advancing wave.

On they came, with a shout and the clashing of spears; now they were driving in the outposts we had placed among the rocks at the foot of the hill. After that the advance was a little slower, for though as yet we had offered no serious opposition, the attacking force had to come up hill, and came slowly to save their (206) breath. Our first line of defence was about half-way up the side, our second fifty yards further back, while our third occupied the edge of the plain.

On they came, shouting their war-cry, 'Twala! Twala! Chielé! Chielé! (Twala! Twala! Smite! Smite!). 'Ignosi! Ignosi! Chielé! Chielé!' answered our people. They were quite close now and the tollas or throwing knives began to flash backwards and forwards, and now with an awful yell the battle closed in.

To and fro swayed the mass of struggling warriors, men* falling thick as leaves in an autumn wind; but before long the superior weight of the attacking force began to tell, and our first line of defence was slowly pressed back, till it merged into the second. Here the struggle was very fierce, but again our people were driven back and up, till at length, within twenty minutes of the commencement of the fight, our third line came into action.

But by this time the assailants were much exhausted, and had besides lost many men killed and wounded, and to break through that third impenetrable hedge of spears proved beyond their powers. For a while the dense mass of struggling warriors swung backwards and forwards in the fierce ebb and flow of battle, and the issue was doubtful. Sir Henry watched the desperate struggle with a kindling eye, and then without a word he rushed off, followed by Good, and flung himself into the hottest of the fray. As for myself, I stopped where I was.

(207) The soldiers caught sight of his tall form as he plunged into the battle, and there rose a cry of –

'Nanzia Incubu!' (Here is the elephant!) 'Chielé! Chielé!'

From that moment the issue was no longer in doubt. Inch by inch, fighting with desperate gallantry, the attacking force was pressed back down the hillside, till at last it retreated upon its reserves in something like confusion. At that moment, too, a messenger arrived to say that the left attack had been repulsed; and I was just beginning to congratulate myself that the affair was over for the present, when, to our horror, we perceived our men who had been engaged in the right defence being driven towards us across the plain, followed by swarms of the enemy, who had evidently succeeded at this point.

Ignosi, who was standing by me, took in the situation at a glance, and issued a rapid order. Instantly the reserve regiment round us (the Greys) extended itself. Again Ignosi gave a word of command, which was taken up and repeated by the captains, and in another second, to my intense disgust, I found myself involved in a furious onslaught upon the advancing foe. Getting as much as I could behind Ignosi's huge frame, I made the best of a bad job, and toddled along to be killed, as though I liked it. In a minute or two – the time seemed all too short to me – we were plunging through the flying groups of our men, who at once began to (208) re-form behind us, and then I am sure I do not know what happened. All I can remember is a dreadful rolling noise of the meeting of shields, and the sudden apparition of a huge ruffian, whose eyes seemed literally to be starting out of his head, making straight at me with a bloody spear. But – I say it with pride – I rose to the occasion. It was an occasion before which most people would have collapsed once and for all. Seeing that if I stood where I was I must be done for, I, as the horrid apparition came, flung myself down in front of him so cleverly, that, being unable to stop himself, he took a header right over my prostrate form. Before he could rise again, I had risen and settled the matter from behind with my revolver.

4

Reader response criticism and stylistics

Jennifer Riddle Harding

Introduction

A famous philosophical question goes something like this: when a tree falls in the woods, if there's nobody there to hear it, does it make a sound? To understand the emphasis of reader response theory, one might analogously ask: does a text have any meaning if there's no reader there to interpret it? This was the basic issue that originally motivated reader response theory in the 1970s, when theorists reacted to an earlier dominant paradigm that regarded texts as self-contained icons, and readers' interpretations as irrelevant in critical analyses. In order to understand what inspired the turn to reader response criticism, let's first consider the paradigm that was dominant prior to the 1970s.

These earlier literary critics, referred to as formalists or practitioners of New Criticism, maintained that critical focus should be on texts. In his formalist classic *The Well Wrought Urn*, for example, Cleanth Brooks warned that critics should be wary of 'yielding to the temptation to take certain remarks which we make about the poem – statements about what it says or about what truth it gives or about what formulations it illustrates – for the essential core of the poem itself' (1947, p. 1221). In this view, the work of literature (formalists tended to call all works 'poems') was exalted while its interpretation was not. The emphasis was on the 'essential core' of the work, not on the readers' generative process of reading, understanding, and appreciating it.

Formalist critics warned particularly about the misleading interpretations that could result from investing too much authority in readers' emotional responses. William Wimsatt Jr. and Monroe Beardsley labelled this emphasis on emotion the 'Affective Fallacy', which they described in their book *The Verbal Icon*. Wimsatt and Beardsley argued that it would be fallacious to consider the emotional impact of a text on a reader; a reader's affective response should be considered, in this view, inconsequential to the critical study of the text. As the authors contended, 'The Affective Fallacy is a confusion between the poem and its results (what it *is* and what it *does*)'. A focus on 'psychological effects', they believed, could only produce 'impressionism and relativism' (1954, p. 1246).

A formalist wariness of the 'Intentional Fallacy', also outlined by Wimsatt and Beardsley, conveyed a similar suspicion of investing too much authority in authors' stated or perceived intentions. In this view, just as readers' emotional or psychological reactions to a text could be messy and irrelevant to critical interpretation, so too could a focus on an author's stated or inferred intentions lead to a misleading and unclear interpretation of the text. The pressure to largely ignore both author and reader in favour of the text itself produced readings of canonical texts that treated them as self-contained units consisting of internal structures that had only limited connection to 'external' factors such as an author's biography or a reader's reaction to the text – or, for that matter, to history, culture, ethnicity, or identity. The emphasis was on textual form over most other factors, hence the label 'formalism'.

Though there were earlier voices who insisted on the importance of the reader, the influence of reader response as a critical movement became pronounced in the 1970s as more writers reacted to the dominant formalist paradigm by placing a new emphasis on the role of the reader. Instead of ignoring the reader, or considering her responses messy and subjective, reader response theorists put readers squarely in the centre of discussions of textual meaning by focusing on readers' acts of interpretation. Where classic formalist approaches analysed the text as a static and self-contained object, the practitioners of reader response introduced a theory that focused on readers *doing* something with, to, and through literary texts. Rather than seeing this act of interpretive *action* as a 'confusion' between text and results, as Wimsatt and Beardsley maintained, reader response practitioners viewed examining how readers make meaning from a text as the essential avenue that led to discovering the meaning – or meanings – of a literary text. In his summary of reader response approaches, Steven Mailloux observes, '[the critics] construct a theory consisting (in more or less detail) of an account of interpretation, a model for critical exchange, and a model of reading' (1982, p. 23).

With a common focus on readers, and strong emphasis on readers' acts of interpretation, the group of theories collectively known as 'reader response' approaches are otherwise quite numerous and heterogeneous. Therefore it is difficult to describe core premises, a common methodology, or a shared perspective among reader response critics. In fact, it is difficult to construct a fixed list of reader response critics, as critics who are sometimes listed in reader response lists are at other times labelled not as reader response critics but as narrative theorists, semiotic critics or structuralists. An inclusive list of influential critics who have been associated with the reader response approach includes, in alphabetical order, Roland Barthes, David Bleich, Stephen Booth, Jonathan Culler, Umberto Eco, Judith Fetterley, Stanley Fish, David Hirsch, Norman Holland, Wolfgang Iser, Hans Robert Jauss, Gerald Prince, Peter Rabinowitz, Michael Riffaterre, Louise Rosenblatt and Jane Tompkins.

Ultimately, it is more accurate to think of reader response as a critical orientation rather than a coherent category of techniques and beliefs. This orientation predicts that if asked whether a text can 'mean' even if there's no reader there to interpret it, a reader response critic – unlike a formalist critic – would say no. The text contains meaning only insofar as a reader engages with the text to interpret its meaning.

Historical perspectives

In the next few paragraphs, I will briefly discuss five theorists whose work represents a range of approaches within the field, providing a glimpse into the variety of techniques that have been labelled 'reader response'. The theorists will be considered in the order that their major books were published. These brief descriptions are based on influential texts written mostly in the 1970s and very early 1980s; the intent is to succinctly capture a range of theories as they were proposed during the most active period of reader response criticism, and to simulate a synchronic 'conversation' among theorists by describing the theories they proposed in their most influential books written in that era.

Each of these individuals continued to write and theorise after the heyday of 'reader response' approaches described below – and in many cases theorists eventually refined or even refuted the earlier theories that characterised them. In the second half of this chapter I will consider the evolution of reader response approaches after the 1980s.

Norman Holland: The Dynamics of Literary Response, 1968

Norman Holland embraced Freud's theory of psychoanalysis, and adapted some of the major concepts of psychoanalysis to explain the reading experience. Psychoanalytic theory was originally developed by Sigmund Freud to treat mental disorders, but it had a lasting impact on the way that theorists in many fields throughout the twentieth century, and even today, think about the mind, psychological development and personality. Freud proposed that each person develops through a series of childhood stages when the locus of pleasure can be associated with one part of the body, such as the mouth or the penis (the psychosexual stages of development). Freud also proposed that the mind can be understood as conscious regulation of unconscious impulses that exist in a part of the mind that is inaccessible, that memories can be repressed into this 'unconscious', that many actions can be explained as defences against threatening feelings or memories, and that dreams and fantasies provide windows, albeit largely symbolic ones, into unconscious impulses or fears. Today, references to the Oedipus complex, to unconscious sexual feelings, to the symbolic nature of dreams, or to 'defence mechanisms' allude to Freud's original theories.

In applying Freud's theory to the reading experience, Holland proposed that literature represents a 'transformation' of material into psychological experiences for the reader. In Holland's analyses, a work may represent a fantasy, or enact defence mechanisms, or allow the reader to gain pleasure through a merging of self with the text's world. He believed that the psychoanalytic meanings of a text could be described as the most basic meaning, for as he put it, 'the psychoanalytic meaning underlies all the others' (1968, p. 27). His theory allowed for a very individualised reading experience that is reflective of psychological experiences common to humans, but ultimately based in the psychological history and needs of individual readers. Reading a text, in Holland's view, provides a way to negotiate desires and fears and ultimately to reaffirm the self.

In a reading of 'Dover Beach', for example, Holland explained that the poem offers a series of disturbing images and concepts that are nonetheless obscured by 'defences' that leave the reader with a feeling of peace. He demonstrated how particular lines direct a reader's attention away from sexual activities and refer only obliquely to negative experiences. The poem, he observed, is structured by a dualism that both excites and soothes. He read the poem as a defensive fantasy in which the final scene 'deflects our attention from a pair of lovers in a sexual situation and sublimates it into a distant, literary, and moral experience, a darkling plain from Thucydides' (1968, p.121).

Jonathan Culler: Structuralist Poetics, 1975

Drawing on linguistics and European structuralist theory, Culler proposed a technique for examining literature by treating it as a 'language'; in other words, he believed that the key to analysing a reader's understanding of a literary text lay in uncovering the 'rules and norms' (1975, p. 31) that constitute the system the readers have assimilated. As Culler described it, the goal of this approach was 'to render as explicit as possible the conventions responsible for the production of attested effects ... to determine the nature of the system underlying the event' (1975, p. 31).

With his plan to describe the system that belonged to readers, not authors, Culler defined his readers as having literary competence. To achieve literary competence, Culler wrote, a reader 'requires an acquaintance with a range of literature and in many cases some form of guidance' (1975, p. 121). Developing competence means assimilating the rules and norms of the system, which readers then use to understand additional texts. The job of the critic in this paradigm is then to uncover this system, which often means examining a category of texts sharing features rather than analysing individual texts.

In one chapter called 'Poetics of the Lyric', Culler demonstrated this technique through an examination of the lyric poem. He considered how knowledge of the lyric, and of poetry more generally, structures a reader's expectations. Culler examined how the conventions of the lyric would guide readers to expect poetic distance, unity, and significance and thus to arrive at interpretations of poetic elements like figurative language and rhythm shaped by those expectations.

Judith Fetterley: The Resisting Reader, 1978

Judith Fetterley added a new dimension to the reader/text relationship: the idea that the language of the text, and the reader interpreting it, should not necessarily work together in harmony. Fetterley's feminist approach instead encouraged readers to uncover and then resist the gender norms and stereotypes encouraged by so many classic texts written by men, focusing especially on American texts written by Hawthorne, Fitzgerald and others. She exposed the implicit sexism and patriarchal values embedded in these texts that, once exposed, could be analysed and critiqued. Her critique also extended to previous discussions of the reader, many of which used the generic pronoun 'he' to describe readers and assumed that readers represented a standard – in other words, male – understanding of the world. Fetterley wrote, 'American literature is male. To read the canon of what is currently considered classic American literature is perforce to identify as male' (1978, p. xii). Fetterley argued that because they have been taught through previous reading experience to read as if they were male, women find themselves 'in effect no one' (1978, p. xxii) unless they learn to resist the text.

In a reading of 'Rip Van Winkle', for example, Fetterley focused on the characterisation of Rip's wife, Dame Van Winkle. She described the sexist treatment of Dame Van Winkle who is characterised as the nagging shrew who opposes her husband's irresponsible behaviour. Meanwhile Rip Van Winkle, though wildly irresponsible and boyish, is characterised sympathetically. The wife is symbolically aligned with the unwelcome British government in Rip's colonial America; by the end of the story, Rip and his town have overthrown them both. By making readers more aware of the learned tendency to cheer Rip and disparage Dame Van Winkle, Fetterley encouraged readers not simply to accept this stereotyped 'nag' as a norm for women, but to resist the text's judgments of these characters and to unpack the implied association between marital domination and governmental domination.

Wolfgang Iser: The Act of Reading, 1978

Iser's model of reading profiled the participation of the reader in the creation of meaning; he saw the text as 'virtual', existing between two different poles – the artistic pole (associated with the author) and the aesthetic pole (associated with the reader).

Central to Iser's theory was his observation that texts have gaps (which he called 'Leerstellen' in the original German version). These gaps, he wrote, are filled by the reader who participates in or interacts with the text. The gaps disappear once the reader has made the connections – both to other parts of the text, and to pre-existing knowledge structures – necessary to arrive at meaning and fill the gaps. Once the gaps are filled, the text is transformed into an aesthetic object that results from the reader's imaginative interaction with the text. He wrote, 'communication in literature, then, is a process set in motion and regulated, not by a given code, but by a mutually restrictive and magnifying interaction between the implicit and explicit, between revelation and concealment' (1978, p. 168).

In a reading of Fielding's *Tom Jones*, Iser applied this model by showing that characters represent certain modes of thought that the reader can recognise and evaluate – the readers, in other words, help to complete the characters by judging them, so that a definite meaning is possible. Iser also showed how the reader can recognise possibilities in the text that are negated. In this and other readings, Iser's emphasis was on the dynamic participation of the reader.

Stanley Fish: Is There a Text in this Class? 1980

Though Stanley Fish appears last in this chronological list, he was one of the most influential of the reader response critics, particularly in the United States. In fact, in the United States the reader response school of criticism was sometimes called the 'School of Fish'. He wrote many influential works of reader response criticism prior to *Is There a Text in This Class?* However, after 1976 Fish enhanced his previous discussions of the reader by proposing an even more extreme position: that the text did not exist without the reader. I will therefore focus primarily on Fish's book *Is There a Text in This Class?* which he wrote after he moved his theory in this direction.

Fish adamantly believed that a text was a process of doing, an activity, not a thing. In *Is There a Text in This Class?* Fish proposed that the same readers can have the same response to the same text because they belong to the same interpretive community. Fish defined an interpretive community as 'those who share interpretive strategies not for reading (in the conventional sense) but for writing texts, for constituting their properties and assigning their intentions. In other words, these strategies exist prior to the act of reading and therefore determine the shape of what is read rather than, as is usually assumed, the other way around' (1980, p. 171). In other words, Fish claimed that readers *write* texts because the act of reading produces the meaning anew each time, and the reader's predispositions determine the textual meaning, not vice-versa. Mary Louise Pratt characterised his approach as 'the collapsing of subject and object' (1980, p. 221).

Fish's radical position about the text itself represented the most extreme departure from the formalists: he proposed that without the reader, the text does not exist at all. He proposed a version of reader response theory in which the text actually comes into existence because of the reader's attention and processing. Unlike other critics who envisioned readers responding to cues and structures in texts, or at times resisting them, Fish actually saw the reader as the person creating – in his description, *writing* – the text anew with each reading. In his analyses of textual examples, Fish read very closely, dwelling on line-by-line interpretations in describing how readers respond to a text and adjust their interpretation with each new word and line.

Points of disagreement

The five books described above were published by different theorists writing at different times and in different countries, although describing them together simulates a conversation or argument between them. In many ways these theorists, and others whose books and articles have been characterised as 'reader response', were engaged in different enterprises. Nonetheless, there were points of disagreement that can help us to understand how they compared with each other. As with any argument that encompasses many voices and positions, it is helpful to ask – what are the stases, or points of disagreement? Certain arguments arose over where to draw the lines between theories and critical schools. For example, Jane Tompkins argued that reader response criticism was 'a close relative' of deconstructive criticism (1980, p. 224), while others have argued that theorists produced readings more akin to formalism than most reader response critics would want to admit. These arguments about the boundaries of the field are not as important as two primary points of disagreement that help differentiate the theorists at work in reader response – reader identity, and the reading process.

Who are the readers?

Reader response critics have made claims about the experiences readers have while they read different kinds of texts. However, these claims beg the question – who are these readers that are being described, and how much can critics really say about them? It is very difficult to make claims that describe the common experience of even a small group of people. It may not even be accurate to say that all 'readers' are literate, since people can have stories read to them or view imagistic representations of stories. In order to say something concrete about readers, critics had to make certain assumptions or generalisations about them.

Certain critics, in describing readers, focused on the skills that readers bring to a text, and which are shared widely (how widely may be an arguable point) by educated members of a culture. Thus, Culler described a 'competent reader' who could interpret a text based on knowledge about structures and language, Iser described a 'participating reader' who engaged actively with the text while constructing its meaning, and Fish described an 'informed reader' who had a certain level of base knowledge about literary traditions and ideas.

Readers were also profiled in some cases for their individual qualities, while in other cases for their membership in groups. Holland, for example, described an 'idiosyncratic reader' who brought certain unique psychological variables to a text, while Fish posited the existence of 'interpretive communities' consisting of readers who shared experiences and reading strategies. Judith Fetterley specifically criticised her counterparts for not accounting for the unique circumstances of female readers, and described the strategies a woman could employ to become a 'resisting reader'.

What is the reading process?

Reader response critics were keenly interested in describing what readers were *doing* when they read a text. Of course, this process is difficult to describe even by the person doing the reading. Imagine trying to describe the reading process as you experience it – reading letters, words, and sentences, while simultaneously imagining characters and worlds, while simultaneously bringing to bear ideas or information that is relevant to the text, while simultaneously monitoring (perhaps unconsciously) the temperature, light, and sounds of the room. After all of this, perhaps interrupted and renewed many times, the reading process eventually leads to understanding or appreciation or pleasure or confusion. In short, the process is very difficult to describe first-hand, and the reader response critics attempted to describe the process on behalf of other readers.

Needless to say, there were disagreements. Some disagreements amounted to sniping about technique. It was not uncommon, for example, for one theorist to claim that another theorist wrote excellent analyses of texts but that the analyses did not follow directly from his ideas: Fish made this criticism of Michael Riffaterre (1980, p. 65), and Mary Louise Pratt made it of Fish (1983, p. 222).

A related issue that lies at the very heart of reader response theory is how any reader can 'do' reading. Even though critics in the 1970s generally agreed that the act of interpretation should be the paramount concern of critics, this did not settle the issue of how such interpretation actually occurred – in fact, agreement on the importance of interpretation opened the door for very different descriptions of the reader experience.

For Holland, personal psychology was an important guide to the reading experience, while for other critics such as Fish and Culler, the important factors were prior experiences with texts and reading contexts. Iser focused on the reader's active participation while reading the text, while Fetterley went even further to describe the reader's need to resist textual cues.

Whether describing readers or the reading process, reader-response critics often made generalisations about readers and reading experiences, and opened themselves to criticism that they were really just describing their own experiences with the texts. Nonetheless, if reader response critics had not been willing to make confident and at times bold claims about readers and reading, they would have had very little to say about the interpretation of literary texts. As it turned out, their various bold and divergent claims were important and influential.

Current contributions and research

While it may not be common to meet someone who identifies as a reader-response critic in the twenty-first century, that is perhaps because the movement has been very influential, rather than because it is forgotten. Attention to readers has been folded into so many disparate and interesting approaches that now the emphasis on readers' interpretation is no longer a defining feature of a unified theoretical school, but a common praxis among many schools of criticism. I will describe these schools of criticism first, and then consider the role that reader response theory has played in shaping pedagogy.

Cognitive approaches

Generally speaking, the variety of techniques known collectively as 'cognitive approaches' – whose literary practitioners align themselves with fields called cognitive linguistics, cognitive narratology, cognitive poetics, cognitive rhetoric, or cognitive stylistics – are those techniques used to describe how the human mind is represented in, and acts upon, a variety of texts.

Cognitive approaches draw on advances in the cognitive sciences, a cluster of mind sciences (especially neuroscience and cognitive psychology) that have burgeoned in range and influence since the 1980s. Thanks in large part to technologies such as functional magnetic resonance imaging (fMRI), eye tracking devices, and software that captures precise response times, these fields have offered new insights into the workings of the brain and the relationship between thinking and behaviour. Advances in genetics and medicine have also provided additional insights into conditions that affect cognition, such as autism, and cognitive deficits resulting from brain damage, such as anterograde amnesia. New theories and models have arisen as a result of these insights. For researchers interested in considering how texts model the human mind, and in how humans make sense of texts, these insights and theories have provided a variety of new approaches to examining texts.

Because textual characters represent human beings, insights into the workings of human minds have been used to examine the thoughts, interactions, language, and behaviour of 'people' in texts. In *Why We Read Fiction* (2006), for example, Lisa Zunshine has applied the psychological concept of 'Theory of Mind' to characters including Clarissa Dalloway in *Mrs. Dalloway*, showing that Mrs. Dalloway's interpretation of other characters' behaviour is a direct consequence of her understanding of minds – her ability to 'mind read'. Zunshine also argues that reading itself is practice of readers' 'mind-reading' abilities.

Other theorists are most interested in understanding how readers make meaning from texts – not only how they put the words together to understand the sentences, but also how the cues in the text allow them to imagine the worlds inhabited by characters. I count myself among the critics most interested in this central question – how do readers make meaning from words and other visual cues like typography?

One cognitive model used by many critics to explain the meaning-making process is the conceptual blending model described by Gilles Fauconnier and Mark Turner in their book *The Way We Think* (2003). The idea of conceptual blending, or the integration of separate domains at a detailed cognitive level, has been used to describe readers' understanding of metaphor, paratext, images, perspective, and many other textual phenomena. Schneider and Hartner's recent collection *Blending and the Study of Narrative* (2012) demonstrates the variety of texts and topics examined using the conceptual blending model.

Although they are informed by cognitive science that was simply unavailable in the 1970s, cognitive approaches inherited the reader response interest in readers and their acts of interpretation.

Gender/ethnic/queer studies approaches

Gender, ethnic, and queer studies approaches examine the power structures inherent in texts and the normative functions of texts. Feminist critiques often consider the representations of gender and the power differences encoded and at times reinforced both explicitly and implicitly by texts. In addition to an examination of power structures, queer studies approaches examine how texts function to normalise (or destabilise) sexual identity and certain types of sexual relationships, such as heterosexual marriage, and ethnic studies approaches examine how texts portray racial identity and attitudes toward racial difference, such as white supremacy. In general, theorists from these approaches are interested in how texts contribute to constructions of race, gender, or sexual orientation, and in the reader's relationship to these textual constructions.

With Judith Fetterley's *The Resisting Reader* laying the preliminary groundwork, subsequent studies examining reader response have at times focused on the fraught relationship between a reader and the text. From this perspective, readers are not simply passive recipients of meaning or even active constructors of meaning, but also people with gender, race, and sexual identities (i.e. normal human beings) who must negotiate a relationship with texts that only sometimes represent or reinforce their individual identities. At times readers 'read against' the dominant racial, sexual, or ethnic messages of a text in order to negotiate a meaning that is true to the text, but which also foregrounds the reader's ability to make meaning from the text and thereby actively question, resist, or reject these textual messages. This approach has been extended to a range of identity groups besides women – for example, to men in the collection *Engendering Men: The Question of Male Feminist Criticism* (1990), edited by Joseph A. Boone and Michael Cadden.

Some studies have combined literature with a range of other cultural texts that can be 'read', and/or have incorporated autobiographical writing into the account of reading. For example, writing from the perspective of his identity as a gay man, Wayne Koestenbaum has incorporated autobiographical writing into his critical studies of a range of cultural texts, for example in his book *Humiliation* (2011), positing the relation between his gay identity and his reading and viewing of cultural texts and situations.

Reception studies/new historical approaches

Evidence of readers' responses to texts can provide a glimpse into the reading process as reported and described by various readers. One approach known as reception studies considers the way that a particular text has been *received* by readers – how it was reviewed when first published, whether it won awards or other accolades, how many editions were printed, whether it sold widely in its time or since then, whether it has been studied or neglected over time, and so on. All of these issues are part of the reception history of the text, and reveal the experiences of real readers with the text as well as their attitudes toward its quality.

In order to find historical documents related to reader reception, researchers have at times conducted archival research, and the availability of technologies like the worldwide web and digitised databases have made these historical resources accessible and searchable, fuelling renewed interest in examining historical readers who have read, and sometimes reviewed or responded to, literary texts.

Some theorists have used evidence about various kinds of reception to consider how texts affected actual readers, and the culture at large, at the time of their publication and in subsequent eras. For example, in the book *Mightier than the Sword: Uncle Tom's Cabin and the Battle for America* (2012), author David S. Reynolds describes the effect that the abolitionist book had on readers and on American culture before the American Civil War.

Interesting historical groups of readers have also been examined, such as the literary clubs described by Elizabeth McHenry in her book, *Forgotten Readers: Recovering the Lost History of African American Literary Societies* (2002). As McHenry describes, these clubs consisted of African American members who met regularly in the nineteenth century to read and discuss books.

Narrative/rhetorical approaches

Narrative theorists, and rhetorical theorists, have a longstanding interest in the audience of readers that encounter a text, and in both theoretical subfields a variety of theoretical constructs have been developed to describe the reading audience and/or its individual members. Narrative and rhetorical theorists have also observed that authors may imagine readers, and texts may allude to or suggest readers, who can then act as models or representatives for the actual reading audience encountering the text.

In his essay 'Introduction to the Study of the Narratee' (originally published in French) in the collection of reader response essays edited by Jane Tompkins (1980), Gerald Prince detailed a theory of narrative that created a role for the narratee, or the textually inscribed listener or reader to whom the story is narrated by the narrator. In a refined model developed by Peter Rabinowitz (1977), four audiences were identified: the actual (flesh-and-blood) reader, the ideal audience, the narrative audience (constructed by the text), and the narratee. In his own more recent clarification of this model, James Phelan writes that 'the concept of the flesh-and-blood reader allows the rhetorical [narrative] approach to recognise that differences among individual readers can lead to their different responses and interpretations, while the concept of the authorial audience allows the rhetorical [narrative] approach to consider the ways in which readers can share the experience of reading narrative' (2007, p. 5). Increasing attention has been paid to the effects narrative can have on actual readers, for example generating emotions such as empathy, as described by Suzanne Keen in *Empathy and the Novel* (2010).

Traditional rhetorical theory not only has a much longer history than reader response theory (extending back to Aristotle), but has typically examined a wider range of texts than literary approaches. Literary texts are examined under the umbrella of rhetorical theory, along with political, educational, instructional, and other kinds of texts that can be imagistic or auditory in nature. Because rhetorical theorists are primarily concerned with explaining the persuasive power of texts of all kinds, they are keenly interested in considering the actual effects that texts have on audiences, such as convincing them to vote for a particular candidate, conserve water, or value education. Rhetorical theorists, including Linda Flower and her colleagues in the book *Reading to Write: Exploring a Cognitive and Social Process* (1990) have also developed models for readers and writers who want to understand and perhaps achieve social and cultural effects from texts.

Empirical approaches/studies of real readers

To study the experiences of real readers, researchers may rely on readers' self-reports, and/or on measurements of their experiences collected using eye tracking tools, response time software, or other measurement devices. Quantitative studies can be conducted on readers in laboratory settings, while qualitative studies rely on interviews and/or surveys and questionnaires.

An example of an early qualitative study of romance readers was conducted by Janice A. Radway and published in her book *Reading the Romance* (1984). Radway interviewed dozens of women who avidly read popular romance novels, compiling hours of interview testimony as well as answers to questionnaires. In an extended analysis based on these interviews, Radway described the sociological and personal importance of the romance genre, as well as processes of romance selection and reading described by her participants.

Laboratory studies of real readers who process texts have also contributed to the understanding of real reader response. In some cases, empirical studies of readers are conducted by scientists trained in psychology or linguistics who are interested in learning more about literary reading comprehension and other text processing strategies. These studies are designed around hypotheses and conducted on voluntary participants. The results are evaluated using quantitative statistical analyses. Inductive studies of this type can provide findings that may have implications for literary criticism, though the scientists themselves do not intend to provide 'readings' of literary texts.

Some literary critics also conduct empirical studies on readers, collecting data and analysing it with statistics, with the goal of providing literary readings. An example is presented in the book *Graphing Jane Austen* by Joseph Carroll, Jonathan Gottschall, John A. Johnson and Daniel J. Kruger (2012). Using an online questionnaire, the authors gathered responses from 519 respondents to questions about 435 characters in 134 novels. The authors then analysed the responses for patterns, and used the data to make claims about 'agonistic structure', or the organisation of characters into protagonists, antagonists, and minor characters in various novels. They then used this data to argue that agonistic structure is more important than character gender in determining reader response to characters, and that the agonistic structure of novels fulfils an adaptive (in Darwinian terms) social function.

Pedagogy

Reader response certainly has an important place in the classroom setting. A focus on the reading experience can be tremendously helpful and rewarding for students, as students in literature classes realise they are participant readers whose experiences with texts can be validated and mediated by the classroom experience. Readers become more conscious of their unique reading strategies and reactions, particularly when they are asked to complete responses, participate in free writing, or respond to questions. The initial response to a text can be an important first step for students in considering how the text informs, interests, controls, decentres, reinforces, misleads, challenges, hides from, upsets, and/or convinces them in their role as readers.

Additional classroom activities and discussion may expand the range of these analyses as readers have the opportunity to compare their own responses to the reactions of others, and to assiduously study textual details together, sharing insights and observations and receiving guidance from an expert reader. In short, the classroom is perhaps the most wide-ranging active space for readers to engage in 'reader response', and to hone their skills in close reading while gaining skills and information that can shape and facilitate the quest for meaning in future literary interpretation.

Beyond reaction and discussion in a classroom setting, additional research can lead students to make even more complex observations about topics like cognitive activities, historical readers, or individuated responses that represent the domains of newer approaches to reader response – in other words, further research expands the consideration of reader response in relation to other contexts. Researching and writing on a text often involves re-reading it in part or in its entirety, which enriches the initial reading through further observation of detail.

If there is one downside to an emphasis on reader response in the classroom, though, it is the potential for responsive criticism to engender a mistaken belief that any and every reading is a valid interpretation based on opinion. While all readings, including misreadings, are 'real readings', the goal of many teachers is to encourage and model close readings that depend on tight connections between textual details and interpretation. The original reader response critics did not believe that any and every reading was equally valid, but they did authorise a range of approaches to the same text, and some validated a vast array of readings by noting that different readers could approach the same text differently, perhaps because they belonged to different interpretive communities or had different individual psychologies. As Donald E. Hall worries, 'readers with little knowledge of the texts of reader-response critics sometimes use the category to justify their own hasty, impressionistic work' (2001, p. 47).

To keep this tendency in check, teachers may redouble their attention to textual evidence, insisting that consistent support from the text is necessary to validate readings. The point of reader response criticism has never been to validate impressionistic or speculative readings that depart wildly from the text itself, but to consider how readers who bring personal, cultural, cognitive, social, scholarly, and historical knowledge to a text may go about interpreting a text that is made up of words, structures, and ideas.

Recommendations for practice

Whether in the classroom or in textual analysis and theory, reader response analysts may generate fruitful discussions by considering a range of questions. Today, as Ross C. Murfin notes, critics who work in the tradition of reader response often identify themselves as 'reader-oriented' critics (1998, p. 528). These critics may identify primarily with another approach, but nonetheless incorporate issues of reader comprehension and interpretation into their analyses.

In my own work, I have investigated individual texts from a perspective that is a combination of the cognitive, narratological, and historical approaches. I am most interested in determining how readers bring their meaning-making capacities, pre-existing concepts, historical knowledge, emotional inclinations, and genre experiences to a text. Reading, as I see it, is a creative process in which a reader detects textual cues by engaging actively with the text. Mine is a participatory model reminiscent of Wolfgang Iser's approach, but with a strong investment in recent cognitive theories and models.

One facet of my research involves counterfactuals, or 'what might have been' scenarios, which play a role in many kinds of discourse (Harding 2007, 2011); these scenarios, I believe, require reader participation because they depend on the reader's ability to imagine two contrasting situations. The situations are not developed completely by the text, but instead are evoked by specific linguistic constructions that cue readers to imagine contrasting scenarios – one actual, one 'counterfactual'. By noting the importance of both fleeting and elaborate counterfactuals in certain texts, I make claims about the relationship between counterfactuals and characters' emotions like relief and regret, the author's thematic emphasis on possibilities and irrevocable choices, and the readers' understanding of and attitude towards narrative possibilities.

This provides a brief example of a cognitive approach with a strong orientation toward reader-response. In the following section, I discuss how a reader-oriented critic might start with broad questions, and adopt various critical lenses, to generate ideas about reader interpretation of the novel *Atonement* by Ian McEwan. Starting with these broad questions, I discuss a range of issues related to the text and its interpretation that, once brought into the foreground, could generate useful material for reader response analyses.

Individual differences and prior experiences

1. To what extent does a reader's personal history affect the reading of this text? A critic might take a range of approaches in considering this question, from psychoanalytic to feminist to cognitive. The plot of the novel *Atonement* includes an interrupted sex scene between two main characters, a rape that is blamed on the wrong man, and a rape victim who marries her rapist; a theorist might consider how male and female readers react differently to these parts of the text. Depending on gender or certain attitudes about sex and rape, readers might align with different characters or make certain ethical judgments of the text and its author. Alternatively, a theorist might consider how a reader's own sexual experiences affect his or her reading of these events and related details in the story.

2. One might also consider how prior knowledge of Ian McEwan's other novels – such as *On Chesil Beach* (2007), which also includes an interrupted sex scene – might lead readers familiar with McEwan's works to read *Atonement* with certain expectations or conditioned attitudes. Similarly, some readers could have seen the film version before reading the book, which would undoubtedly impact on their reading responses to McEwan's text.

Misunderstandings, resistance, or double meanings

3. Are there elements of this text that are available or unavailable for certain readers? You might start by considering whether the text seems to invite certain kinds of readers but not others into its meanings. Are there, for example, words, phrases, or concepts that might simply be unavailable to some readers based on their personal history? Does the text distance anyone? Would someone who is a woman, or gay, or from a minority group, or disabled, need to 'read against' the text in order to understand and critique its meanings? The book does, for example, tend to portray Briony and Cecilia's mother as a stereotypical 'cold absent mother' whose lack of oversight creates the situation for many of the traumas the characters experience. Do we need to 'read against' this stereotyped portrayal of the mother to resist blaming her for the events in the text? Similarly, the text normalises heterosexual love and sex – what impact does that normalisation potentially have on gay readers?

4. Certain knowledge domains could be particularly important for readers. Much of the action takes place in England and France during World War II; a theorist might consider how detailed knowledge of the war, or lack thereof, might affect the reading experience. Similarly, elements of the plot are enhanced by a knowledge of British law in the 1940s, which many readers are likely to lack. Does this matter? Does the author take steps to reach out to less-informed readers?

Linguistic and structural meanings

5. What individual words, phrases, and other schemes are available sources of meaning in this text? I always suggest to my students that they look to the title as a starting point for investigating important words and phrases in a text. In this case, atonement is obviously an important word and idea. Why is that? It would be interesting to find where the word atonement actually appears in the text, and to check if related words like 'compensation' or 'apology' or 'penance' appear in the story as well, and at what points.

6. The main character Briony, speaking as a writer, also informs us that the phrase 'at the double' became a marker of historical accuracy. She learned from a veteran that 'at the double', rather than 'on the double', would have been used by British soldiers in World War II. Are there other phrases that signal the historical veracity in this text? If so, what are they?

7. For reasons that will become apparent in the next section, the themes of truth, falsehood, and creative license are central to this text. It would be interesting to conduct a close reading to discover whether any words and phrases help mark the status of different sections of the text in relation to these categories. For example, are sections that later turn out to be 'false' narrated with more frequent indicators of perceptual ambiguity or instability?

In general, detecting highly significant linguistic elements requires either close reading, or the use of a digitised text that can be searched.

Cognitive and affective considerations

8. How might this text and its voices affect a reader cognitively and emotionally?

In the second part of *Atonement*, lovers Cecilia and Robbie are separated by a mistaken rape accusation, a resulting jail term for Robbie, and then later by World War II. They eventually reunite. At the end of *Atonement*, it is revealed that this reunion was actually constructed and written by another character in the book, the narrator Briony, who as a character in Part I was responsible for the false rape accusation and the jail term that separated them. As a narrator in Part III, she presents the preceding section as a fictional version that she wrote in contrast with 'actual' facts, stating that Robbie and Cecilia both died as a result of the war before being reunited. The book thus creates a complex interplay of 'fact' and fiction (which is situated completely within a novel that readers know is fictional). The readers must interpret the same events – the events detailed in Part II – first as actual and then later as a version that the narrator has written for us because she wishes that it had been true.

Such complex juggling and re-coding of narrative events requires a lot of the reader, and I could imagine analyses that would help explain the reader's navigation of this material. This book is tricky on a cognitive level, but also tricky on an emotional level. Do readers blame Briony, and get irritated at her, for 'tricking' us into thinking that Part II is real? On another level, do we blame McEwan and get irritated with him for writing a book that is essentially a trick? Or does the book resonate emotionally regardless of its cognitive trickery? After all, the love affair is beautifully described, Briony's shame and regret provides a counterbalance to her destructive tendencies, and her life ends with dementia, which will erase her memory and abilities altogether. If you find yourself ready to respond to these issues, then you might be ready to do this type of cognitive or narratological reading.

Studies of real readers

9. How do actual readers of this text respond to it?

Empirical studies could be designed to test readers' responses to different parts of the text, or to investigate the reading process itself. It might be interesting, for example, to ask readers to respond to the same questions at different points in the text, gauging their attitudes toward certain characters as their understanding of these characters change.

10. How has *Atonement* been received?

Ample reviews of *Atonement* exist, and there is another set of reviews of the movie adaptation. I could imagine an interesting project that examined reception of *Atonement*. The novel seems noteworthy for its acceptance by both general and critical audiences.

Future directions

There are a number of ways that reader response theory may develop. If the current trend is any indication, the phrase 'reader response' itself may become more and more outdated, but the critical orientation toward readers will continue strongly in many branches of criticism. I'll now describe a few developments that may be indicators of the next generation of reader-response approaches.

In cognitive studies, recent activity in the areas of consciousness and embodiment portend interesting developments for cognitive criticism. Previous work on consciousness in literature includes David Lodge's *Consciousness and the Novel* (2004), but there seems to be potential for many more interesting studies of this sort, especially since new findings are being discovered every day by cognitive scientists. Michael Burke's recent book (2011) is one example of how cognitive and emotive developments in embodiment have generated new ways of understanding the literary reading process. Along with this continued attention to the mind, there has been a renewed interest in emotion – we seem to have come full circle since Wimsatt and Beardsley warned of the 'Affective Fallacy'. Patrick Colm Hogan's book *Affective Narratology* (2011) is a recent example of this focus on the emotional experiences of readers.

I also foresee more studies of reading practices, particularly empirical studies. A recent topic of interest in narrative theory has been a consideration not just of reading, but of re-reading. How does the meaning of a text change with subsequent readings, and depending on whether those readings are spaced or close together? Studies of this sort have implications for pedagogy; in classrooms, readers who have intimate knowledge of a text (professors) must often relate to first-time readers, in some cases attempting to relive the experience of reading the text for the first time so that they can discuss, quiz, and test first-time readers. How can teachers and professors fairly and effectively teach those who are reading a text for the first time?

Digital and online technologies will no doubt continue to have an influence on how readers are studied, opening up many interesting possibilities for future research. As technology also produces more formats in which texts may appear (text on a digital device, audio, a combination of text and audio), we may see empirical studies on how the reading experience is affected by technological formats. As more empirical studies and more historical texts are digitised, more information is available to investigate historical readers and their cultural contexts.

In short, the techniques and ideas for studying readers and the reading process seem to be growing rapidly rather than shrinking. Access to digitised historical materials, improved techniques for quantitative research, refined models of reading and the mind, and an interest in a wider range of texts and reading groups have all contributed to the growing field of reader response. It is not the study of readers and reading, but only the label 'reader response' that has become out-dated.

Related topics

Cognitive poetics, formalist stylistics, functionalist stylistics, pedagogical stylistics, feminist stylistics, rhetoric and poetics, stylistics and blending, stylistics and real readers

Suggestions for further reading

Burke, M., 2011. *Literary reading, cognition and emotion: An exploration of the oceanic mind.* London: Routledge.

In this volume Burke seeks to chart what happens in the embodied minds of engaged readers (both real and hypothesised) when they read literature.

Hogan, P. C., 2011. *Affective narratology: The emotional structure of stories.* Lincoln: University of Nebraska Press.

Hogan argues for the importance of emotional structure in stories, and the importance of stories in emotional development, by examining a range of genres across cultures.

Keen, S., 2007. *Empathy and the novel.* New York: Oxford University Press.

In this work, Keen analyses how reading fiction encourages empathetic response, and she argues for the importance of a wide range of genres in promoting empathy in readers.

McHenry, E., 2002. *Forgotten readers*. Durham: Duke University Press.

In this historical look at African American reading clubs of the late nineteenth century, McHenry demonstrates the relationship between reading and citizenship.

Zunshine, L., 2006. *Why we read fiction*. Columbus: Ohio University Press.

In this application of 'theory of mind', a psychological model that accounts for the understanding of other peoples' feelings and intentions, Zunshine examines the importance of 'mind reading' to the understanding of fiction.

References

Boone, J. A. and Cadden, M., eds. 1991. *Engendering men*. London: Routledge.

Brooks, C., 2010. The heresy of paraphrase. *In:* V. B. Leitch, W. E. Cain, L. Finke, B. Johnson, and J. McGowan, eds. *The Norton anthology of theory and criticism*, 2nd ed. New York: W.W. Norton, 1217–1229 (original book *The Well Wrought Urn* published 1947).

Burke, M., 2011. *Literary reading, cognition and emotion: An exploration of the oceanic mind*. London: Routledge.

Carroll, J., Gottschall,J., Johnson, J. A. and Kruger, D. J., 2012. *Graphing Jane Austen*. New York: Palgrave MacMillan.

Culler, J., 1975. *Structuralist poetics: Structuralism, linguistics and the study of literature*. Ithaca: Cornell University Press.

Fauconnier, G. and Turner, M., 2003. *The way we think*. New York: Basic Books.

Fetterley, J., 1978. *The resisting reader*. Bloomington: Indiana University Press.

Fish, S., 1980. *Is there a text in this class?* Cambridge: Harvard University Press.

Flower, L., Stein, V., Ackerman, J., Kantz, J. M., McCormick, K. and Peck, W. C., 1990. *Reading to write*. New York: Oxford University Press.

Freund, E., 1987. *The return of the reader*. New York: Methuen.

Harding, J. R., 2007. Evaluative stance and counterfactuals in language and literature. *Language and Literature*, 16 (3), 263–280.

Harding, J. R., 2011. He had never written a word of that: Regret and counterfactuals in Hemingway's 'The Snows of Kilimanjaro'. *The Hemingway Review*, 30 (2), 21–35.

Hall, D. E., 2001. *Literary and cultural theory*. New York: Houghton Mifflin Company.

Hogan, P. C., 2011. *Affective narratology*. Lincoln: University of Nebraska Press.

Holland, N., 1968. *The dynamics of literary response*. New York: Oxford University Press.

Iser, W., 1978. *The act of reading: A theory of aesthetic response*. Baltimore: The Johns Hopkins University Press.

Koestenbaum, W., 2011. *Humiliation*. London: Picador.

Keen, S., 2007. *Empathy and the novel*. New York: Oxford University Press.

Lodge, D., 2002. *Consciousness and the novel*. Cambridge, M.A.: Harvard University Press.

Mailloux, S., 1982. *Interpretive conventions*. Cornell: Cornell University Press.

McEwan, I., 2003. *Atonement*. New York: Anchor.

McEwan, I., 2007. *On Chesil Beach*. New York: Doubleday.

McHenry, E., 2002. *Forgotten readers*. Durham: Duke University Press.

Murfin, R.C., 1998. What is reader-response criticism? *In:* J.P. Riquelme, ed. *Tess of the D'urbervilles*. Boston: Bedford St. Martin's, 521–537.

Phelan, J., 2007. *Experiencing fiction*. Columbus: The Ohio State University Press.

Pratt, M. L., 1983. Interpretive strategies/strategic interpretations: On Anglo-American reader response criticism. *Boundary*, 2 (1/2), 201–231.

Prince, G., 1980. Introduction to the study of the narratee. *In:* J. Tompkins, ed. *Reader-Response Criticism*. Baltimore: Johns Hopkins University Press, 7–25.

Radway, J.A., 1984. *Reading the romance*. Chapel Hill: The University of North Carolina Press.

Rabinowitz, P., 1977. Truth in fiction: A reexamination of audiences. *Critical Inquiry*, 4, 121–141.

Reynolds, D. S., 2012. *Mightier than the sword*. New York: W. W. Norton & Company.

Schneider, R. and Hartner, M. eds. 2012. *Blending and the study of narrative*. Berlin: de Gruyter.

Tompkins, J. ed. 1980. *Reader-response criticism*. Baltimore: The Johns Hopkins University Press.

Wimsatt, W. K. and Beardsley, M. C., 2010. The Intentional Fallacy. *In:* V. B. Leitch, W. E. Cain, L. Finke, B. Johnson, and J. McGowan, eds. *The Norton anthology of theory and criticism*, 2nd ed. New York: W.W. Norton, 1232–1246 (original book *The Verbal Icon* published 1954).

Wimsatt W. K. and Beardsley, M. C., 2010. The Affective fallacy. *In:* V. B. Leitch, W. E. Cain, L. Finke, B. Johnson and J. McGowan, eds. *The Norton anthology of theory and criticism*, 2nd ed. New York: W.W. Norton, 1246–1261 (original book *The Verbal Icon* published 1954).

Zunshine, L., 2006. *Why we read fiction*. Columbus: The Ohio University Press.

Part II

Core issues in stylistics

The linguistic levels of foregrounding in stylistics

Christiana Gregoriou

Introduction: The theory of foregrounding

In technical but also in non-technical contexts, 'foregrounding' refers to the property of perceptual prominence that certain things have against the backdrop of other, less noticeable things. In the visual and perhaps more obvious sense of the term, we can see foregrounding manifesting itself as a psychological effect generated by particular aspects of say images, thereby drawing the viewer's attention to themselves or parts of themselves. For instance, one would expect bright colourful objects to be more noticeable in an environment compared to those objects in dull colouring. To give another example, it is for foregrounding-related effects that poster advertising designers manipulate the size and position of words and objects within the poster space to direct the observer's focus on particular aspects of the product advertised, and all while distracting potential buyers away from possibly discouraging aspects of this same product. Important product-related images, such as smiling faces of supposed product users and images of the product itself, often feature prominently as large and centrally placed elements on the poster page. On the other hand, discourse that relates to limited product-related surveys, or even wording such as 'patent pending', often has to be included in advertisements for legal reasons, but it is backgrounded, hidden in tiny print at the bottom of designs, away from the viewer's main attention. To give a last example, as Kress and van Leeuwen (1998) pointed out in their analysis of newspaper front pages, within a Western framework of reading, the top half of such pages is likely to yield information that is 'ideal' and therefore foregrounded, in contrast to the bottom half that yields information that is 'real' and therefore backgrounded. At the same time, however, the page's right half (from a reader's viewpoint) gives information that is also foregrounded, this time in the sense of being 'new', whereas the page's left-hand side provides 'given', backgrounded information. In short, we are led to 'read' 'the foreground [as] more important than the rest' (Short 1996, p. 12). This is probably linked to fact that from the reader's perspective, the top right-hand corner of such front pages is where our hand, and therefore our eyes, need to go when flicking the newspaper open. It appears that it is not just the choice of front page stories that matters; the story length and, just as importantly, its placement on the page, matter just as much.

We now turn to the linguistic and also more specifically literary sense of the term. '[F]oregrounding refers to a form of textual patterning which is motivated specifically for literary-aesthetic purposes' (Simpson 2004, p. 50). Here, Simpson interprets the effect along the lines of literary art, and only when it is motivated for artistic purposes can we think of it as 'foregrounding'. Shklovsky's (1925; 1965) perceptual 'defamiliarisation' concept (*ostranenie*) is linked to foregrounding in suggesting that the purpose of all art is to force our attention to the very artfulness of things (see also Chapter 2 in this volume). By undoing the familiarity of things (hence enabling 'de-familiarisation'), observers are led to examine what otherwise would fall in a sort of automatic, habitual kind of attention.

Linking this to the act of literary reading, defamiliarisation is a notion that Cook (1994) describes as literature's 'schema-refreshing' property. A notion that forms part of schema theory is the idea that knowledge is organised in a person's head and gets activated when triggered. Schema-refreshment therefore refers to the process whereby conventional ways of viewing the world (meaning our 'schemata') become disturbed and are accordingly refreshed. The schema disturbance itself depends on the reader whose schemata these are, rather than on an intrinsic quality that necessarily belongs to the text itself. In short, we do not all react to texts the same way, because we do not all share the same exact schemata. The reason for this is that schemata are structured around experiences that are bound by our individual language, culture, age, gender and so on. In other words, texts often comply with other patterned ones, and only when they violate schemata for us as readers and hence 'stick out' (see Leech 1969, p. 57) from the crowd are they likely to be viewed as artistic enough in themselves. This property can be interpreted on the level of genre, but also at the level of the world, and of language itself. Literary texts can generate foregrounding and hence an artistic tone by violating what Stockwell describes as text, world or language schematic expectations (2002, p. 80). Text schematic violations are what I would describe as 'generic' violations, meaning that they are violations related to the formulas that various text types adhere to. World violations, being to do with how the world works and the expected order of things, are understood in direct relation to the experience of the reader. I would correlate this violation type with what I refer to as 'social' violations, though I would not want this latter type to exclude non-human acts. Language schematic violations I correlate with 'linguistic' violations of various sorts, and it is such deviations that form the focus of most of this remaining chapter (see Gregoriou 2007 for my tripartite generic/social/linguistic distinction, particularly in relation to deviance and the reading of crime fiction).

One last set of terms is worthy of note here, which again bears much relevance to the concept of literary foregrounding, namely 'figure' and 'ground'. These ideas stem from the gestalt psychology of the early twentieth century. This is a distinction that explains our human capability to perceive shapes in our environment as not flat, and therefore as differentiable from one another (Stockwell 2002, p. 15). 'Figures', Stockwell asserts, are self-contained objects featuring in their own right, their well-defined edges separating them from the 'ground'. Figures also move in relation to the ground, they are more detailed, they are in sharper focus and so on. To return to the stylistic relevance of this distinction, literary text readers conceptualise fictional characters as figures against the backdrop of grounded settings; they are seen as characters moving across space and therefore they emerge as foregrounded figures against their (back)ground. It is the difficulty in keeping hold of figures against the ground, and not knowing what the foregrounded focus is and where it needs to move, that often makes the process of reading poems in particular pleasurably challenging. Perhaps contradictorily, it is the same process that makes reading poetry potentially less appealing than the process of reading, say, a novel.

Linguistic foregrounding can take a number of different forms. 'Capable of working at any level of language, foregrounding typically involves a stylistic distortion of some sort, either through an aspect of the text which deviated from a linguistic norm or, alternatively, where an aspect of the text is brought to the fore through repetition or parallelism' (Simpson 2004, p. 5). In other words, foregrounding can take the form of what have come to be known as 'deviation' and 'parallelism' in stylistic (and rhetorical) circles. Parallelism refers, rather straightforwardly, to linguistic repetition of some sort, whereas deviation refers to an encounter with something different from what is expected, or indeed different from regulations of some kind. Admittedly, 'deviation', a term I use synonymously with 'deviance', is a slippery notion which is hard to define. Definitions referring to deviation as a departure from a 'norm' often encounter criticisms asking whether 'norm' is itself a straightforward term. One could think that 'deviance' is easier to define in the context of sociology, the term here being linked to the breaking of social rules. As Downes and Rock (1995, p. 4) put it, however, 'ambiguity' is a crucial facet of rule-breaking; judgements over what true deviance is, and whether a particular episode *is* truly deviant, are dependent on context, biography and purpose. In other words, these authors argue that one's social behaviour is likely to be thought of as deviant, as opposed to normal, on the basis of surrounding factors and background contexts, and there is no clear position from which 'deviance' can be objectively classified as such. For example, one's behaviour may be deemed criminal in one context and not in another, while one man's 'hero' is another's 'villain' (see also my social deviance analyses in Gregoriou 2007). As such, criminality as an instance of social deviance can be quite hard to define in itself, with behavioural factors being unable to explain the labelling of 'criminality' independent of context. As Downes and Rock themselves put it, in this view, 'deviance is messier than science' (1995, p. 4), not to mention a political phenomenon; deviance is an exercise in power, and even more so an exercise in the application of rules in direct relation to this power (Downes and Rock 1995, p. 7). In the same way that it is difficult to define the term 'deviance' in this social context, literary linguistic deviance is also hard to discuss irrespective of context. Where literature is concerned, 'context' encompasses such things as genre, period and also reader perspectives and schemata.

Both deviation and parallelism can, language-schematically speaking, take place on a number of linguistic levels, and I will illustrate each level, drawing from non-literary examples to start with. Besides, foregrounding is not an effect that is related to (visual and verbal) art alone. My first non-literary source is a small corpus of chat-up lines borrowed from car advertising campaign commercials screened during the TV breaks of a UK ITV dating show. Inspired by Mahlknecht (2012), I also draw examples from a second corpus consisting of recent movie taglines, using a list compiled by Nudd (2011). Chat-up lines and movie taglines function as slogans for people and films respectively, since (self- and product/ service-) advertising is a genre utilising rhetorical devices to the full. Hence, chat-up lines and taglines rhetorically aim to persuade people to do things – to go ahead and (conversationally) engage with (most usually) the man, or to watch the film in question. After I have engaged with these two genres in the form of illustrating the various deviation and parallelism levels, I will turn to analysing a literary example, namely Keyes' (1994 [1966]) *Flowers for Algernon*. This will be done in linguistic foregrounding terms (for further illustration and foregrounding examples taken from advertising slogans, band names, jokes, prose, poetry, and rhymes, see Gregoriou 2009, Chapters 2 and 3; for a further overview of linguistic foregrounding across genres, see Burke 2014).

Deviation

When a text deviates from norms set outside it in relation to its context, the deviation can be deemed to be 'external'. For example, the tagline from the film *Naked Gun 33 1/3: The Final Insult* (1994), which reads 'From the brother of the director of Ghost', is externally deviant in that it is unexpected and unique. Taglines are supposed to advertise the film by telling you something about its content. The *Naked Gun 33 1/3* tagline is singularly uninformative in this respect. The tagline is externally deviant in other ways too. In keeping with the witty tone of the film that it is advertising, the 'filmic crew', as it were, is mocking itself by referring to the director as being closely related to an assumedly more famous one, humorously suggesting that the actual director is not as good as the one who made the film *Ghost*. It also suggests that this presumed relationship is the only good thing that the film has to say about itself. Intertextually and metatextually speaking, the tagline mocks its own film in relation to other films, where a director's success is mentioned as a way of drawing the audience in (though as noted, doing this is unsuitable for the tagline genre anyway). Arguably, the tagline is also grammatically deviant since it is a minor, i.e. non-standard, sentence, although it is still understandable – as are most of the taglines given in this chapter. Admittedly, grammatically non-standard taglines are in line with the genre.

Another example of such external deviation is found in the tagline of the film *House of Wax* (2005), which reads 'On May 6th ... see Paris die!' In contrast to other films who cast celebrities as a commercial tactic, *House of Wax* humorously advertises itself not so much on the basis of its star, celebrity socialite Paris Hilton, but on the basis of the fact that it features her supposedly 'dying', a jibe at the perceived negative image this celebrity has. As it is the character Hilton plays who dies, and not the celebrity herself, the filmic tagline is also semantically deviant since it is non-literal. Semantic deviance is a type of deviance I will return to later. For external deviance to work, then, a certain familiarity with the tagline genre and its context is needed. One can only become aware of a norm being broken if one is familiar with the norm in question to start with. Deviation of historical period (Leech 1969, p. 51), meaning the use of words inappropriate for the relevant historical context, is, by definition, deviation that can also be described as external.

In contrast to external deviance violating primary norms, internal deviance violates secondary norms, meaning those that the text itself has set, and this type of deviance is therefore based on some sort of repetition/parallelism. *A Fish Called Wanda* (1988) is a film taglined 'A tale of murder, lust, greed, revenge, and seafood'. Although grammatically this is a paralleled tagline in the sense of its listing five nouns in a row, it is also internally deviant on the lexical/semantic level. The word 'seafood' is incongruous in this context; it does not fit the crime narrative schema created by the other listed words – 'murder', 'lust', 'greed' and 'revenge' – and therefore pleasurably breaks the pattern the tagline itself has set. The *Arachnophobia* (1990) filmic tagline, 'Eight legs, two fangs, and an attitude', is also internally deviant. Another minor sentence, it lists three noun phrases in a grammatically paralleled manner, with the last of the three deviating from the semantic and lexical norm set by the first two. The pre-modifying determiners (two numerals and an indefinite article) precede two spider body parts ('legs', 'fangs') and a final non-body part ('attitude'), with the reader's attention being drawn to the action of the film while also hinting at its comedic nature. *Army of Darkness* (1992) also features an internally deviant tagline. 'Trapped in time. Surrounded by evil. Low on gas' is syntactically and semantically paralleled in listing three adjective phrases, the last of which is semantically as well as grammatically internally deviant. The first two expressions are metaphorical in concretising 'time' and 'evil', but the last is metaphorical only in terms of the orientational conventional metaphor of 'low gas' suggesting either a literal or a figurative lack of fuel/energy. Grammatically speaking, the first two minor sentences feature adjectival verbal participles ('trapped', 'surrounded') prior to the postmodifying prepositional phrases ('in time', 'by evil'), with the last instead featuring such a phrase ('on gas') but following a simple adjective ('low') instead, hence the syntactic deviance.

Text types depend on particular kinds of discourse structures. For instance, whereas autobiographies are written on behalf of a real-life first person narrator whose actual story is shared with the readers, dramatic plays often take the form of fictional conversation among imagined characters, inviting the reader-viewers to take on the position of over-hearers of this imaginary conversation. Texts that deviate from the sort of discourse situation that is expected of them can be said to deviate 'discoursally'. To use the earlier terminology, such texts therefore often deviate text-schematically, generically and, by definition, externally. Furthermore, for them to deviate from the discourse structure that other texts within the same genre abide by, they also break rules that are set elsewhere, outside of themselves. The tagline from the film *Armageddon* (1998), namely 'Earth. It was fun while it lasted', is arguably externally discoursally deviant, as is the tagline for *Independence Day* (1996) which reads 'Earth. Take a good look. It could be your last.' Here, moviegoers are unexpectedly placed in a discourse situation where they 'overhear' the storyworld's 'earth' being directly addressed, and this is done as if a disaster is actually truly about to strike. Note that moviegoers normally expect taglines to take the form of imperatives such as 'Be afraid. Be very afraid' (*The Fly,* 1986) or descriptive declarative statements of the sort 'The true story of a real fake' (*Catch Me If You Can,* 2002). In the last two examples, viewers are being engaged in a discourse situation whereby they are addressed rather directly. The above *Armageddon* and *Independence Day* taglines address the movie's fictional earth-living beings instead. *Saw 2*'s (2005) 'Oh yes, there will be blood' tagline is also externally deviant on a discoursal level, itself functioning as a response to an imagined reader needing reassurance that the film would be bloody enough for them.

The tagline from the movie *Postcards from the Edge* (1990) – 'Having a wonderful time, wish I were here' – is externally and discoursally deviant in drawing on a postcard-sending genre rather than the tagline genre, suggesting a rather different discourse scenario compared to the one expected of the filmic genre. Also a minor sentence, this tagline is arguably lexically deviant in that we get 'I' and not the expected 'you', the narrative voice supposedly suggesting that it is strangely no longer situated within its own 'origo' (meaning 'origins'); it is not 'here', wherever 'here' is. Similarly, the *Sicko* (2007) tagline – 'This might hurt a little' – is externally and discoursally deviant in echoing a doctor–patient discoursal situation. This movie is Michael Moore documentary about the American healthcare system, and the tagline is in keeping with the filmic theme in suggesting the sort of pain-warning that one might hear in a doctor's surgery. However, the expression here also attracts a metaphorical meaning in its suggestion of the reaction of discomfort ('hurt') that the film itself will generate. 'This' deictically refers not to any painful doctor's action that is to come, but to Moore himself who is warning us that his documentary is worrying to watch. In this sense, the tagline also generates semantic deviance as a result of the polysemous word 'hurt'.

Any strangeness of the written form would be classified as a form of graphological deviation (Leech 1969, p. 47). Aspects to consider here include the arrangement of words on the printed page, the use of punctuation, spacing, capitalisation and so on. The *Buffalo Soldiers* (2001) filmic tagline – 'War is hell ... but peace is f*#!%!! boring' – is externally graphologically deviant in its inclusion, but also in the unconventional spelling, of a taboo word, something which was probably enforced legally. The word in question, being ill-fitting for the context, is what generates lexical deviation, while we also get grammatical parallelism in the repetition of the subject-verb-complement grammatical structure in each of the two clauses coordinated by 'but'.

There is a large number of grammatical rules in English, and so the number of foregrounding possibilities via grammatical deviation is also very large (Short 1996, p. 47). Such deviation can take place at the syntactic level of grammar – for instance, where words are found in an unusual order. As mentioned, because taglines are mostly in non-standard grammatical form, they generate grammatical deviation by generic default. However, grammatical deviation can also take place at the morphological level, for instance where word morphemes are found in unusual isolation or in unusual combination. In the chat-up line 'Are you from Tennessee, cause you're the only ten I see', the 'Tennessee' word is split into invented morphemes, suggesting that the female addressed originates from a state named after a compound word, which is itself made up of words metaphorically alluding to the woman being graded as the one and only visible 'ten'. The line also draws on semantic deviation in suggesting a metonymic 'one to ten' scale along which people can be assigned in terms of their looks. By repetition in terms of the wording and by default the sounds (/ˈtɛnəsɪ/), the line also draws on phonological deviation and parallelism.

The *Christmas Vacation* (1989) tagline 'Yule crack up' is morphologically, lexically and phonologically unusual in using the word 'Yule', meaning 'Christmas', as in 'Christmas break down'. It is also semantically deviant in using 'Yule' in a context where the word can be read as an invented and phonetically spelt blend out of 'you' and 'will' (/jʊl/), as in 'You'll have fun'. In a third sense, the tagline's semantic deviance can depend on its literalising of the 'crack up' phrasal verb (meaning, among other things, 'to have a good time') with its inclusion of the word 'crack', which alludes to Christmas crackers cracking. The polysemous meaning of 'crack' in this context generates all sorts of puns. The tagline can ultimately be read in three ways: in reference to some sort of Christmas-related problem that the characters will face, the viewers having fun watching the film, or the characters literally 'cracking up' their crackers at Christmas. In this sense the tagline is manipulating different sorts of discourse situations, and can be discoursally read as deviant.

Short (1996, p. 43) defines semantic deviation as drawing on meaning relations that are paradoxical or logically inconsistent, metaphors fitting this characterisation. Quality maxim flouts (see Grice 1975) are quite common in the chat-up line corpus. In 'Is there an airport nearby or was it just my heart taking off?', the metaphor is drawn of a heart supposedly physically taking off in emotional excitement, in the same way in which an airplane would. Similarly, in 'You're so hot. When I look at you, I get a tan', the female is likened to the sun; her 'hotness' is interpreted on the level of attractiveness instead of warmth/sunlight, with the multiple meanings of 'hot' helping to create the pun. Finally, in 'I didn't know angels could fly so low', 'I must be in heaven, cause I'm looking at an angel', and 'I must be lost cause I thought paradise was further south', the female is supposedly treated as an angel, or at least is figuratively likened to one. *The Big Lebowski*'s (1998) tagline 'Her life was in their hands. Now her toe is in the mail' draws on grammatical parallelism in the repetition of the same sort of sentence structure: subject (premodifying possessive pronoun 'her' followed by a noun), verb (form of simple verb 'to be') and adverbial (prepositional phrase starting with 'in'). The tagline also employs deviation on the semantic level. Whereas the first of the two paralleled minor sentences is metaphorical ('life' cannot literally be held in someone's hands), the second is literal in the filmic fictional context. The *Dazed and Confused* (1993) 'See it with a bud' tagline is semantically deviant also, since it is interpretable in a number of ways. There is deliberate semantic ambiguity as to whether the polysemous word 'bud' refers to drugs ('bud' is slang for 'marijuana'), 'buddies' (as in 'friends') or even the beer Budweiser. Similarly, the tagline from *Dumb and Dumber* (1994) depends on semantic deviation: 'For Harry and Lloyd, every day is a no-brainer'. It literalises the metaphorical expression of something being a 'no-brainer', meaning 'easy'. The title-reference to the two main characters as 'dumb' activates a schema inclusive of 'brains', and therefore drives a somewhat literal interpretation of the expression, suggesting that the two characters literally lack brains. The tagline draws on the underlying metaphor of lacking intelligence corresponding to a lack of 'brains'. In other words, the 'no-brainer' expression comes to be schematically and linguistically refreshed. The *Erin Brockovich* (2000) tagline – 'She brought a small town to its feet and a huge corporation to its knees' – is grammatically paralleled and semantically deviant, personifying both the small town and the corporation it is juxtaposed with. Finally, *Grosse Pointe Blank* (1997) also features such a semantically foregrounded tagline. In the line 'Even a hit man deserves a second shot', the noun phrase 'second shot' acquires a meaning other than its metaphorical one, which alludes to 'chance'. The meaning triggered by the 'hit-man' stimulated schema is literalised to mean 'fire a shot from a gun'. In this context, the word 'deserves' acquires a more sardonic meaning.

The most obvious example of lexical deviation is where one neologises, meaning that one invents a word that did not previously exist (Short 1996, p. 45). Other types of this sort of deviation include the conversion of a word from one grammatical class to another, and the use of a word in a context where it does not normally belong. The lexically deviant taglines in my corpus mostly utilise the latter type. The *Chicken Run* (2000) film's 'Escape or die frying' tagline is lexically deviant in using 'frying' where one would expect 'trying', using a word inappropriate for its context. The tagline is interpretable as literalising the 'die trying' expression into 'die frying', and it can therefore be said to be semantically deviant also. Furthermore, it also draws on the popular dietary phenomenon of 'fried chicken'. Finally, it can be described as phonologically deviant in that it utilises an imagined rhyme with the word we expected; 'dying' rhymes with 'frying' (/ˈaɪːŋ/). The *Gladiatress* (2004) tagline – 'Does my gluteus maximus look big in this?' – is externally and discoursally deviant since it is inappropriate for its context, and it therefore violates both schematically and generically. It is arguably also grammatically deviant in taking the form of an interrogative; as previously noted, declarative statements and imperatives are more common for the tagline genre. Of course, this filmic slogan is particularly lexically deviant in its use of words and language fitting for an entirely different context. 'Gluteus maximus' is Latin for the expected English word 'bum'; the former term is normally used solely in technical/medical contexts to refer to the large muscles that make up the buttocks. Instead, here it is used in the context of a female (appropriate given the film title) supposedly checking to ensure her gladiator outfit does not make her bum look big. Similarly, in the *Gremlins 2: The New Batch* (1990) tagline 'Here they grow again', we get the word 'go' for 'grow'. The line draws on phonological parallelism in that the word we would expect is a near homophone to the one we get (/gəʊ/ and /grəʊ/), but also on lexical and semantic deviation in that the word 'grow' is found in a context where it is unexpected, and it literalises the expression in question. Beside, gremlins do indeed 'grow' in the film.

Irregularities in the way in which words are pronounced fall under phonological deviation. Alliteration, assonance and rhyme are not only classes of phonological deviation; as Short (1996, p. 54) points out, they are also examples of phonological parallelism as well. Our attention is attracted to the level of the words' unusual sound, but this is most often done via sound repetition. The tagline from *The Truman Show* (1998) 'On the air. Unaware' is phonologically foregrounded in that the first and second minor sentences (which are also grammatically deviant) are phonetically similar (/ən ðɪ ˈɛə ʌnəˈwɛə/), and indeed rhyme (/ɛə/). The *Volcano* (1997) tagline 'The coast is toast' also internally rhymes (/ˈkəʊst/ and /ˈtəʊst/) and is hence phonologically foregrounded, not to mention the fact that it is semantically deviant in drawing on the metaphorical image of toast burning, presumably in a parallel with the film's volcano. The *Alien3* (1992) tagline 'The bitch is back' is alliterative (repeating /b/), as is *Schindler's List*'s (1993) 'The list is life' (repeating /l/). The latter also assigns a metonymic meaning to the word 'life' and draws on semantic deviation in doing so. The tagline from *Hot Shots! Part Deux* (1993), namely, 'Just deux it!', also draws on phonological foregrounding (repeated /də/) in that the word we would expect ('do') is a near homophone to the one we get (the French word for 'two', i.e. 'deux'). This tagline also draws on lexical and semantic deviation because 'deux' is found in an unexpected English language context. Furthermore, it also literalises the expression in question in that the film is a sequel to a previous movie. Finally, the *Redneck Zombies* (1987) tagline 'They're tobacco chewin', gut chompin', cannibal kinfolk from hell!' is phonologically deviant in phonetically misspelling words. It also rhymes, and phonetically repeats a number of stop consonants (the /k/, /t/), among others (such as /tʃ/). The tagline is also phonologically deviant in its onomatopoeic effect, with the phonemes echoing the chewing sounds the words refer to and thereby vividly re-enacting the film's cannibalism.

One thing worth highlighting through this deviance analysis is that norm violation rarely occurs on one linguistic level alone, but mostly takes place on a number of different levels simultaneously, not to mention that it also interacts with various forms of parallelism. It is to more examples of such parallelism that I now turn.

Parallelism

Parallelism is to do with 'the introduction of extra regularities, not irregularities, into the language' (Leech 1969, p. 62). The repetition on the level of grammar is called grammatical parallelism, and on the level of sound it is known as phonological parallelism. The *Alien vs. Predator* (2004) 'Whoever wins, we lose' tagline is phonologically as well as grammatically paralleled. It carries assonance (repetition of /ɪ/) and alliteration (repetition of /w/), but it also takes the form of two paralleled clauses structured in the form of a pronoun ('whoever', 'we') followed by an intransitive verb ('wins', 'lose'). The tagline of *Cool Runnings* (1993) – 'One dream. Four Jamaicans. Twenty below zero' – is semantically as well as syntactically paralleled. All numerals ('one', 'four', 'twenty below zero') are followed by a head noun ('dream', 'Jamaicans'), with the ellipted 'temperature' being filled in schematically by readers at the tagline's end.

Meaning repetition can be described as semantic parallelism, while the repetition of actual words is known as lexical parallelism. The *Wayne's World* (1992) tagline – 'You'll laugh. You'll cry. You'll hurl' – is lexically paralleled as well as grammatically paralleled, and it also features an internal deviation, breaking its pattern at the end. Movie goers encounter a schema disruption here. 'Hurling' is an atypical and undesirable effect in response to watching a film, hence the tagline being externally deviant in mockingly suggesting it is an attractive one. *The Royal Tenenbaums* (2001) features the grammatically paralleled tagline 'Family isn't a word. It's a sentence'. It not only repeats the subject-verb-complement syntactic structure, but it is also a semantically foregrounded tagline in drawing on 'word' and 'sentence' from the semantic field of 'language', with 'sentence' being polysemic and interpretable as 'a legal term of punishment'. In addition to violating language schemata, the tagline also violates world schemata; 'family' is not a 'sentence' in either the grammatical or the legal sense.

According to Short's parallelism rule (1996, p. 14), in addition to the prominence of parallel structures, they also invite the reader to search for meaning relations in terms of the parts that are varied. Even more importantly, parallelism has 'the power not just to foreground parts of a text for us, but also to make us look for parallel or contrastive meaning links between those parallel parts' (Short 1996, p. 15). *The Terminator* (1984) tagline, 'The thing that won't die, in the nightmare that won't end', is grammatically and lexically paralleled in that we get both structure and words repeated. It is the repetition of structure ('the A that won't B, in the C that won't D') that invites readers to find meaning relations between the A and C pairing ('thing' and 'nightmare') and also the B and D pairing ('die' and 'end').This results in a near-synonymous reading of 'thing' as something frightening and 'end' as something inevitably negative. The words 'thing' and 'end' do not in themselves necessarily carry negative associations; it is the parallelism that forces them to carry meanings aligned with the words 'nightmare' and 'end' respectively, thereby making the tagline suitable for the action thriller genre. The tagline from the film *Dude, Where's My Car?* (2000) – 'After a night they can't remember comes a day they'll never forget' – is also grammatically parallel, with the two structures following 'after' and 'comes' being syntactically identical: 'After an A they B, comes a C they D'. The parallelism here enables readers to spot a contrastive pairing relationship between A and C ('night' and 'day'), and between B and D ('can't remember' and 'will never forget').

Foregrounding in *Flowers for Algernon*

It was back in 2004 during a 'creativity symposium' at Nottingham University that Ron Carter light-heartedly used the term 'steam stylistics' to refer 'in the most positive sense, to that body of stylistic work which continues to achieve thorough, convincing, and mind expanding results year on year without the aid of new advances in computer technology, or reference to cutting-edge research in cognitive science' (Gavins 2005, p. 405). The term was used in contrast to the more recent corpus or computational stylistic tradition, which relies on computer technology when engaging in linguistic analysis of texts. It is the traditional, 'steam stylistic' tradition that I follow when analysing a literary example in the current sub-section, as a way of illustrating the relevance of linguistic levels of foregrounding while engaging with the study of literary art.

Originally published in the form of a short story, Keyes' (1994 [1966]) book-long *Flowers for Algernon* exhibits the mind style of an intellectually disabled character, thirty-two-year-old Charlie Gordon, as he undergoes a scientific experiment to increase his IQ, which is considered low at sixty-eight. Charlie's story is paralleled with that of an experimental mouse, Algernon, who also gets an increased IQ under the same experimental conditions as Charlie. However, the mouse goes on to lose his new-found intelligence and ultimately get ill and die, leaving Charlie to place flowers on the mouse's grave. I use Fowler's (1977) term 'mind style' to refer to the style employed by real-life author Keyes. The term seems fitting since the exceptionality of the book's language reflects the exceptionality of the portrayed mind behind the language (for more on 'mind style' see, for instance, Leech and Short, 1981 and Gregoriou 2007, 2009). Furthermore, Keyes' book takes the form of a series of chronologically written reports put together by the implied author and character-narrator Charlie while he undergoes the relevant scientific treatment. The book is in the first person narrative mode, and reads much like an interior monologue. The language is particularly foregrounded toward the novel's start. The story initially takes the form of non-standard English, violating language schemata, and is therefore externally deviant linguistically speaking, suggesting a character with particular kinds of deficiencies. I employ the foregrounding framework as previously outlined in order to explain how linguistic techniques effectively show Charlie to be unintelligent at first, then growing in intelligence, only to parallel Algernon's experience and return to a state of unintelligence toward the novel's end. Unlike the taglines and chat-up lines from the previous section, foregrounding here has a more clearly artistic function, not to mention a possible metaliterary and critical function; in portraying the mind of the mentally disabled, the language defamiliarises and raises awareness about the nature and limitations of mental disability sufferers. Nevertheless, and despite being taught a lot in American schools, the novel is often critiqued in the critical disability writing literature for being reductive, not unlike other such fictional texts about the mentally disabled (see, for instance, Cline 2012). Besides, *Flowers for Algernon* portrays the disabled as somewhat static, the book being based on the assumption that Charlie's IQ would not improve without scientific experimentation. Furthermore, the novel uses the mentally disabled Charlie as a mere vehicle through which to tell other, non-disabled stories, such as the story of animal and human experimentation and its ethical consequences. This is not atypical for disabled literature, of course, and the same issues may be raised for numerous such books and films (for important work in cultural disability studies, see any book by David Mitchell and Sharon Snyder; for another literary paper on the representation of disability in *Flowers for Algernon* see Sklar 2012). However, despite the controversy that the book raises, it is nevertheless interesting in terms not only of its language but also for its depiction of literature and character. It is a novel analysable on the basis of my tripartite linguistic, social and generic deviance model (Gregoriou 2007). It exhibits unusual language, portrays a socially unconventional character, and is also generically deviant in being unlike other novels published in its time; it takes on the report-form and relies on a discoursal situation generically unexpected for the context of fiction. The book is therefore externally as well as discoursally deviant. From a linguistic perspective, the book exhibits foregrounding techniques on a number of levels, which perhaps justifies and explains why it won not only the Hugo but also the Nebula Award when it was first published.

At first glance, one could easily mistake the book's early narrative for that of a dyslexic writer, though it is not just the spelling that proves problematic for Charlie:

progris riport 1 march 3

Dr Strauss says I should rite down what I think and remembir and evrey thing that happins to me from now on. I dont no why but he says its importint so they will see if they can use me. I hope they use me becaus Miss Kinnian says maybe they can make me smart. I want to be smart. My name is Charile Gordon I werk in Donners bakery where Mr Donner gives me 11 dollers a week and bred or cake if I want. I am 32 yeres old and next munth is my brithday. I tolld dr Strauss and perfesser Nemur I cant rite good but he says it dont matter he says I shud rite just like I talk and like I rite compushishens in Miss Kinnians class at the beekmin collidge center for retarted adults where I go to lern 3 times a week on my time off. Dr. Strauss says to rite a lot evrything I think and evrything that happins to me but I cant think anymor because I have nothing to rite so I will close for today ... yrs truly Chalie Gordon. [...]

He has a wite coat like a docter but I dont think he was no docter because he dint tell me to opin my mouth and say ah. All he had was those wite cards. His name is Burt. I fergot his last name because I dont remembir so good. [...]

He shaked his head so that wasn't rite eather. [...]

He said Miss Kinnian tolld hum I was her bestist pupil [...]

I said how can I tell storys about pepul I dont know. She said make beleeve but I tolld her thats lies.[...]

Then I drawed some picturs for her but I dont drawer so good. [...]

Well do you know he put Algernon in a box like a big tabel with alot ot twists and terns like all kinds of walls and a START and a FINISH like the paper had. Only their was a skreen over the big tabel. And Burt took out his clock and lifted up a slidding door and said lets go Algernon and the mouse sniffd 2 or 3 times and startid to run.

Keyes (1994 [1966], pp. 1–5)

The above excerpts are linguistically deviant in a number of ways. Charlie is incoherent and insecure (there is a lot of epistemic and deontic modality), his grammar is simplistic and child- or speech-like ('Well do you know'), featuring overlong, compound sentences coordinated with 'and' and 'but', and non-standard features such as double negatives ('I dont think he was no docter'). Typical first or second language learning error-type features appear, including the regularisation of not only irregular verbs ('shaked' for 'shook' and 'drawed' for 'drew') but also irregular adjectives ('bestist' for 'best', after regular 'biggest' for 'big'). Charlie does not, at this stage, appear to be capable of generating grammatically complex constructions, and also does not consistently punctuate sentences, a deviation that can be described as graphological. Also, there are missing apostrophes, inserted commas, full-stops and commas throughout, many sentences trailing off each other, often with no capital letters where one would expect them ('he says it dont matter he says I shud rite'). The non-standard syntax and punctuation are also accompanied by some morphological deviation, namely compound words being split into their morphemes (such as 'evrey thing' for 'everything'), and certain free morphemes being unexpectedly combined into new words themselves (such as 'alot' for 'a lot').

The text is particularly lexically and phonologically deviant in its use of phonetic misspellings (such as 'rite' for 'write' and 'happins' for 'happens'), new words being created as a result of the spelling, pronunciation and simplification. Nevertheless, Charlie's spelling, being relatively phonetic and mostly consistent, is interesting in itself. One could argue that it is the antiquated and illogical system of English spelling that fails him, as it does many new writers of this language, rather than the other way round. Notice, for instance, how much more phonetic Charlie's spelling of the word 'compositions' is; 'compushishens' is used for /kəmpəˈʃɪʃəns/, the 'sh' spelling consistently transcribing the /ʃ/ phoneme which he appears to be using when pronouncing the last two syllables. Another lexical deviation of Charlie's lies in his use of certain words where near synonyms would be expected instead. In reference to the process of writing and remembering for instance, Charlie uses 'good' as opposed to 'well' ('I cant rite good' as opposed to 'I can't write well' and 'I dont remembir so good' as opposed to 'I don't remember so well'), again a choice that is importantly consistent.

97

Semantic deviation is noticeable too. For instance, Charlie seems to be unaware of the word 'doctor' having both an academic and medical sense, and appreciates only the latter meaning on the basis of his limited schemata; he does not understand how someone can call themselves a 'doctor' but not ask him to open his mouth, as doctors he has previously encountered have asked him to do. Also, in being asked to write fiction for others to observe his imagination at work, Charlie appears to struggle to differentiate between 'make-believe' and 'lies'; to him, the two are synonymous.

Charlie appears not only to be underlexicalised, but he also lacks certain schemata, and is unable to process multiplicity of meaning on a semantic level. Elsewhere, for instance, he struggles with the word 'majors': 'I dint know they had majers in collidge. I thot it was only in the army' (p.15). Readers are put in the position of reading correctly all the signs that Charlie fails to process. For example, readers can work out that the mouse is required to find his way out of a maze in the excerpt above. Charlie is developing a schema for this, but he is lacking the relevant vocabulary with which to capture the concept. Elsewhere Charlie admits to not understanding certain words: 'Burt says its about art and polatics and riligon. I dont know what those things are about' (p.14). He also seems to have problems with pragmatic processing: 'She says she woud never let them do things to her branes for all the tea in china. I tolld her it wasnt for tea in china. It was to make me smart' (p.12). Literal-minded Charlie struggles to process the relevant idiom here, hence the misunderstanding. He is also oblivious to mockery from his bakery colleagues and supposed friends: 'Some times somebody will say hey lookit Frank, or Joe or even Gimpy. He really pulled a Charlie Gordon that time. I dont know why they say it but they always laff and I laff too' (p.17). In frame theory terms (Emmott 1997), Charlie misreads the frames that we read correctly; we can 'repair' his frames, but he cannot do so as yet.

As the experiment gets under way, Charlie's intelligence grows and his sentence structure becomes more complex. He starts to correct his own spelling, words getting crossed over and re-spelt in the text itself, and at the same time punctuation is being introduced, he acquires more schemata and a larger lexicon, and ultimately becomes able to reflect on and question things around him, including authority: 'I dont think its right to make you pass a test to eat' (p. 23). His memory also improves and he experiences a wider range of emotions, and comes to process concepts that he previously could not. He is now enabled to handle pragmatic concepts and therefore comes to some important realisations, as can be seen in his assertion that 'I never knew before that Joe and Frank and the others liked to have me around just to make fun of me' (p. 30). As is evident in this last example, the spelling and punctuation also eventually become standardised with Charlie getting to grips with their complexities on a conscious level, while the writing becomes more assertive and confident. The text is no longer externally deviant here; in fact it can be described as internally deviant. By becoming standardised, the writing breaks its own internal norms. A different kind of discoursal deviance is also introduced, where Charlie dissociates himself from his old self, referring to the mentally disabled Charlie in the third person. This occurs not only in the context of his now accessible childhood memories ('I see Charlie, standing in the center of the kitchen', p. 51) but later even as a presence in his own space and time ('That's when I saw Charlie watching me', p. 174). Ultimately, Charlie grows in intelligence to such an extent that he gets depressed when confronted with the difficult reality of his past, present and future. Furthermore, he realises that, like Algernon's, his own intelligence is temporary, and therefore he isolates himself in a sense of despair.

In the final pages of the book, Charlie's writing disintegrates, returning to the externally deviant norm in play at the start of the story. Charlie vaguely remembers the intelligent version of himself, referring to him in the third person at this stage, discoursally deviating again: 'And when I close my eyes I think about the man who tored the book and he looks like me only he looks different and he talks different but I dont think its like me because its like I see him from the window' (p. 216). Charlie eventually becomes infantilised again, forgetting the words, schemata and memories he once had. Ironically, however, he is also naively blissful again, feeling optimistic about his future: 'Im going to have lots of friends where I go' (p. 216). The book ends on a tragic but simultaneously positive note.

Overall, the foregrounding analysis of *Flowers for Algernon* sheds light on the authorial technique by which our attention is drawn to the limitations of language and also the limitations of people. Furthermore, foregrounding also shows its worth as a vehicle by which the author reminds us that high intellect comes at a price, and that the disabled mind is one to learn from, not one to pity.

Future directions

Classic linguistic foregrounding analysis is a method that reveals how wonderfully complex language use can be. Furthermore, in helping to explain reader reactions to literary as well as non-literary texts, it can be put to use in various contexts and for various functions. It can be employed in educational arenas such as creative writing classes and language/literature teaching in general (see the 'Recommendations for practice' sections in Chapters 1, 2, 14 and 26 in this volume). Such analysis can also be utilised in the study or mastery of any powerful creative language use, including such discourses as advertising, journalism and political oratory, among others.

Related topics

Formalist stylistics, metaphor and metonymy, rhetoric and poetics, schema, script, and frame theory

Further reading

Burke, M., 2014. Literary linguistics. *In:* N. Braber, L. Cummings, D. Hardman and L. Morrish, eds. *Introducing language and linguistics*. Cambridge: Cambridge University Press.

This chapter has a main focus on foregrounding both at and below the sentence level. It uses examples from literature, advertising and popular culture to explain notions of parallelism, repetition and deviation from the phonetic level up to the syntactic level.

Gregoriou, C., 2009. *English literary stylistics*. Basingstoke: Palgrave.

This book-guide introduces students to the stylistics of prose, fiction and drama, and also illustrates framework application to non-literary texts. It includes a chapter as well as several exercises on foregrounding.

Gregoriou, C., 2007. *Deviance in contemporary crime fiction*. Basingstoke: Palgrave.

This monograph introduces the different kinds of deviance employed by contemporary crime fiction, and offers a relevant framework that is applicable to the analysis of all contemporary genre fiction.

Leech, G. N. and Short, M., 1981. *Style in fiction*. London: Longman.

A leading stylistic textbook reprinted in 2007, this book offers linguistic analytical techniques for the analysis of prose fiction.

Short, M., 1996. *Exploring the language of poems, plays and prose.* London: Longman.

This very accessible textbook by a leading authority in the area of stylistics examines reader interaction with three literary genres in turn, and includes useful checksheets for students to use, including one for foregrounding analysis.

References

Burke, M., 2014. Literary linguistics. *In:* N. Braber, L. Cummings, D. Hardman and L. Morrish, eds. *Introducing language and linguistics.* Cambridge: Cambridge University Press.

Cline, B. W., 2012. You're not the same kind of human being: The evolution of pity to horror in Daniel Keyes's *Flowers for Algernon. Disabilities Studies Quarterly,* 32 (4). Online. Available at http://dsq-sds.org/issue/view/98 (Accessed 4 April 2013).

Cook, G., 1994. *Discourse and literature.* Oxford: Oxford University Press.

Downes, D. and Rock, P., 1995. *Understanding deviance: A guide to the sociology of crime and rule-breaking.* 2nd ed. Oxford: Clarendon Press.

Emmott, C., 1997. *Narrative comprehension: A discourse perspective.* Oxford: Oxford University Press.

Fowler, R., 1977. *Linguistics and the novel.* London: Methuen.

Gavins, J., 2005. The year's work in stylistics 2004: Old dogs, new tricks. *Language and Literature.* 14 (4), 397–408.

Gregoriou, C., 2007. *Deviance in contemporary crime fiction.* Basingstoke: Palgrave.

Gregoriou, C., 2009. *English literary stylistics.* Basingstoke: Palgrave.

Grice, H. P., 1975. Logic and conversation. *In:* P. Cole and J. Morgan, eds. *Syntax and semantics III: Speech acts.* New York: Academic Press, 41–58.

Keyes, D., 1994. [1966] *Flowers for Algernon.* London: Orion.

Kress, G. and van Leeuwen, T., 1998. Front pages: Analysis of newspaper layout. *In:* A. Bell and P. Garrett, eds. *Approaches to media discourse.* London: Blackwell, 186–219.

Leech, G. N., 1969. *A linguistic guide to English poetry.* London: Longman.

Leech, G. N. and Short, M., 1981. *Style in fiction,* London: Longman.

Mahlknecht, J., 2012. 'The shortest story ever told: The art and rhetoric of the movie tagline.' paper presented at *International Society for the Study of Narrative Conference*, Las Vegas, Nevada, USA, March.

Nudd, T., 2011. 66 Great Movie Taglines from the past 30 years. *In: Adweek,* April, online. Available from: http://www.adweek.com/adfreak/66-great-movie-taglines-past-30-years-130595 (Accessed 3 July 2012).

Shklovsky, V., 1925, *O Teorii Prozy*, Moscow: Federatsiya.

Shklovsky, V. 1965. Art as technique. Trans., L. Lemon and M. J. Reis, eds. *In: Russian formalist criticism.* Lincoln: University of Nebraska Press.

Sklar, H., 2012. The many voices of Charlie Gordon: On the representation of intellectual disability in Daniel Keyes's *Flowers For Algernon'.* Paper presented at *International Society for the Study of Narrative Conference* in Las Vegas, Nevada, USA, March.

Short, M., 1996. *Exploring the language of poems, plays and prose,* London: Longman.

Simpson, P., 2004. *Stylistics: A resource book for students.* London: Routledge.

Stockwell, P., 2002. *Cognitive poetics: An introduction.* London: Routledge.

6

(New) historical stylistics

Beatrix Busse

Introduction: Why analyse historical discourse from a stylistic perspective?

One answer to the question of this section's title could be: simply because there are too few historical stylistic studies which focus on how meaning is made in historical language data – a fact also stated by Hall in 2012. Diachronic stylistic studies, he claims, should include a variety of valued, canonical and non-canonical texts from different centuries, languages and countries of origin other than English and England (Hall 2012, p. 7). In addition, Hall (2012, p. 7) stresses the pedagogical potential of stylistics in general, which also carries a historical component, since students generally have a genuine interest in past stages of a language and historical discourse practices. However, they often lack the tools to investigate them. It is the responsibility of historical stylisticians to take on this pedagogical task.

There is also a general line of argumentation in favour of a proposed need to increase diachronic stylistic investigations. For example, such studies would put into perspective the sometimes overrated and ahistorical promotion of the allegedly unprecedented novel linguistic character of the new media, such as emailing, text-messaging or internet chat in forums. It can be stated as a fact that there are always preceding discursive/generic diachronic lines of communicative practices, even in new media discourse. The past is in the present, and past discourses influence and are intertextually connected with those of today. Carter (2012) hints at this underlying 'diachronic presence' when he describes new media practices as a way in which 'speakers' 'appropriate a so-called 'between' language which is not simply standard English (nor simply written or spoken English)' (Carter 2012, p. 111). Hence, it may be the role of (historical) stylistics to analyse and explain how in these highly dynamic and diverse media, 'speakers' 'give creative expression to their feelings of friendship, intimacy [or] resistance' (Carter 2012, p. 111). Also, and perhaps even more importantly, it is the task of a historical stylistic endeavour to explain why new media discourses play such a crucial role in today's society as well as to trace their origins, intertextual links and potential for social styling against the background of established conventions.

Outlining my framework of *new historical stylistics*, I have recently provided additional reasons for why stylistics should 'go historical' and follow innovative pathways. I argue (B. Busse 2010a) that historical stylistics needs to embrace the most recent developments in stylistics in general – especially the branches of corpus stylistics, cognitive stylistics and multimodal stylistics – and the to-date unparallelled facilitated access to the plurality of historical language data which is a result of both new technologies and enormous digitisation efforts. There are today new ways of engaging with historical texts and literature, and due to outstanding findings and new developments in (historical) corpus linguistics, stylistic investigations of historical data have at their disposal novel ways of searching, browsing, comparing and linking language data. At the same time new questions can be asked, and finding answers to these questions will also affect investigations of contemporary discourse, despite the challenges involved in a historical corpus stylistic approach. The carte blanche of historical text analysis given to us as stylisticians will do away with what I would like to call the somewhat intuitively-based, impressionistic, unsystematic 'firstness discourse', in which it is often claimed, for example, that a particular stylistic trend or a particular narrative strategy is typical of or first appeared in a certain century or literary period. Relying on the main tenets of stylistics – systematic, detailed, retrievable and rigorous analysis – and on the core stylistic question of how a text comes to mean, a 'new historical stylistician' is now in a position to chart the development of specific stylistic features over time in much more detail. Simultaneously, it is possible to accept the concept of evolving grammars and styles, and to recognise that language usage, styles and styling have always had fuzzy boundaries. They have not always been simply generic, but also rather situational, localised and dynamic.

This last point relates to one of the main goals of this chapter. Building on my 'new historical stylistics' (B. Busse 2010a) framework, I am now going to situate it within the 'mobilities' paradigm and conceptualise historical discourses and styles as functions of 'place-making'. As such, I also address some of the issues Carter (2012) identifies to be among the future challenges of stylistics. 'New historical stylistics' has thus become 'mobile new historical stylistics' and is therefore part of the mobility turn (Sheller & Urry 2006), where places are conceptualised as progressive, open and hybrid (Hall 2009), and where bodies, objects, flows and social processes are continuously combined in new ways (Massey 1991, 1999). Hence, cultural dynamics are regarded as mobilities in which discourses index social value, in particular situations and communities of practice past and present, and in which the analyst – in the sense of a twenty-first-century Sherlock Holmes – serves as a profiler and mediator of discourse patterns on all levels of language and interaction as well as in context. They aim to illustrate that, in theory, method, data collection and interpretation it is no longer possible to draw on fixed and stable social or linguistic categories when historical discursive (and multimodal) styles and profiles are investigated. The focus on mobile discourse profiles shows further interdisciplinary connectivity, because these are crucial to understanding meaning-making and how human beings put stylistic resources to work creatively; as part of their ideologies, as representation and as expressions of materiality.

Critical issues and topics: Mobile new historical stylistics and place-making

Diachronic/historical stylistics has so far focused on the meticulous qualitative stylistic investigation of historical literary texts, and on charting changing or stable styles and their linguistic characteristics, practices and representations in literary language or particular genres: 'linguistic features in texts may pattern to function as generic codes over time, exhibiting more or less variation to be distinguished as genres and subgenres' (Fitzmaurice 2010, p. 680). Diachronic/historical stylistics has combined a number of approaches from stylistics. It has both tested these on historical data and asked how meaning potential is created in historical texts (Adamson 1995, 1999).

In addition, diachronic/historical stylistics has been very much a qualitative enterprise for a long time, relying mainly on the analyst's intuition, meticulous reading and philological work. This endeavour has included establishing styles in a particular author's work, in a particular period or genre, with a focus on particular aspects of rhetoric or classic linguistic features such as syntax or phonology. For example, Adamson (1999) relates the history of style in the Early Modern English period to the development of a standard language as well as the complex political, historical and philosophical contexts of stylistic change. She outlines key concepts, such as *de copia*, *of amplifying* or *perspicuity*, in Renaissance ideas. She also illustrates the stylistic instruments which construe and reflect them in Early Modern English literature. Thus, she draws our attention to the importance of studying historical origins and sources which address style and rhetoric, for example in the ancient rhetorical treatises of Quintilian and Cicero (see Chapter 1 in this volume on classical rhetoric and poetics for further details).

Stylistics in general has most certainly reacted to recent trends in linguistics and developed into a discipline which embraces, for example, corpus stylistics, pragmatic stylistics and multimodal stylistics. Modern historical linguistics (Mair 2006) has also investigated historical language data from a socio-pragmatic and cognitive perspective, drawing on fruitful developments in historical corpus linguistics. Furthermore, modern linguists probably recognised much earlier than linguists investigating contemporary language that literary texts need to be seen as an indispensable source of data for analysis, and this is not only because they have been forced to include literature as a classic component of historical corpora (due to the non-existence of spoken records for historical periods). As such, modern historical linguists follow (historical) stylisticians by stressing the Sinclairian view that 'no systematic apparatus can claim to describe a language if it does not embrace the literature also; and not as a freakish development, but as a natural specialisation of categories which are required in other parts of the descriptive system' (Sinclair 2004, p. 51). Literary discourse is an important accessible source of data 'that may be evaluated as evidence for the communicative practices among members of historical speech communities' (Fitzmaurice 2010, p. 680).

In historical corpus linguistics, style is often seen as a quantitative unit describing the occurrence of linguistic phenomena – for example, in different genres or text types, with the aim of describing changing and stable genre conventions. The focus is not so much on stylistic effects on the reader and on particularly relevant micro-contexts. Taavitsainen (2001, 2009), for example, uses Biber's (1988) multidimensional corpus linguistics study on the styles of contemporary written and spoken English for historical genre analysis (see also Conrad and Biber 2001). Biber and Finegan (1989, 1992), in return, show that the style of written registers, such as prose fiction, become more 'literate' in the eighteenth century and then again more 'oral' in the nineteenth and twentieth Centuries, respectively. Biber's (2004) multi-dimensional analysis of literary genres from 1600 to 1900 reveals patterning in the grammatical marking of stance. Fitzmaurice (2000) examines the historical pragmatic functions of modal auxiliaries as a means of expressing subjectivity in seventeenth-century prose.

In her account of historical pragmatic approaches to 'literary discourse', Fitzmaurice (2010) stresses the diversity of genres that encompass literary discourse as well as the internal variation of literary texts. She explains how what could loosely be called 'historical literary discourse analysis' is either based on a traditional historical pragmatic framework, or else draws on a community of scholars whose work is grounded in philosophical pragmatic literature (by Habermas or Searle) or sociological work (by Bourdieu or Bakhtin). Despite the fact that these perspectives on literary discourse exist fairly independently, a few points of intersection, even with a (new) historical stylistic approach, can be observed, such as a focus on the interaction between author and reader and a contemporary audience, and a focus on communicative functions of earlier literary texts. Accordingly, historical literary pragmatic investigations include a theoretical focus on politeness, conversation analysis and especially speech-act theory (Jucker & Taavitsainen 2010, Hillis Miller 2001). What is more, historical drama represents contexts par excellence for the analysis of pragmatic conventions and routines as well as their deviations from them (Fitzmaurice 2010, p. 692; Fitzmaurice 2002). Also, Chaucer and Shakespeare have received major attention in both quantitative and qualitative historical pragmatic investigations of literary texts (Pakkala-Weckström 2010, Busse & Busse 2010). A historical stylistic dimension is also sometimes provided by exploring pragmatic functions of lexico-grammatical categories such as deixis or discourse markers (Fitzmaurice 2010, p. 683). Frequently investigated features furthermore include and pronominal forms of address in literary texts (U. Busse 2002, B. Busse 2006, Calvo 2003, Magnusson 2007). While Fludernik (2000) examines discourse markers in Malory's *Morte D'Arthur* and shows how they organise narratives, Taavitsainen (1998) illustrates how these are used to mark particular structural aspects of the narrative. Jane Austen's use of interjections as means of characterisation.

Fludernik (1993, 1996) in particular has explicitly shown the importance of systematically investigating the diachronic aspects of narrative patterns. Her work is crucial for exposing how orally oriented narrative structures have been gradually replaced by a more complex interplay of discourse presentation modes indicating experientiality and subjectivity (see also B. Busse 2010b). She also focuses on how focalization, person and tense and narrative scene shift patterns. Adamson's qualitative analysis (1995) offers insight on why what she calls a free style of discourse presentation appears earlier than in nineteenth-century narrative fiction. Elsewhere, Tandon (2003) investigates Gricean principles in the examination of Jane Austen's fiction and Roger Sell (2000, p. 117) also points out that literary discourse can serve as authentic communication for historical literary pragmatics because it is interactive, marked by a difference from ordinary communication and situated within the cultural, social, literary and religious contexts of the time.

Situating a new historical stylistic approach within the mobility paradigm is admittedly a challenge, because the mobility paradigm builds on recent assumptions or mobility modes (Büscher and Urry 2009, p. 100) which have been generated by modernity, new technologies and the fact that people seem to be on the move more than ever before. On top of this, the mobility paradigm does not explicitly incorporate the functions and effects of discourse. However, a 'new historical stylistics' (B. Busse 2010a) framework, which uses the potential of stylistics and bridges the complex interrelationships between stylistic and modern historical linguistic approaches, theories and tools to raise – among other things – methodological awareness, does have some points of intersection with the mobility paradigm, which can be productively exploited. For example, these allow us to stress how – on a broader qualitative and quantitative scale – literature, discourse and stories in historical data in general come to bear meaning, or to show how past ways of styling influence the present. Also, the procedural, multi-modal and multi-contextual dynamic character of discursive meaning-making in new historical stylistics, which can be changed and reshaped in a variety of (cultural) contexts, situations, places or times (Britain 2004, 2010; Coupland 2007, p. xi), is a common denominator.

Büscher and Urry (2009) describe the mobility paradigm as follows:

> It [the mobility paradigm] enables the 'social world' to be theorized as a wide array of economic, social and political practices, infrastructures and ideologies that all involve, entail and curtail various kinds of movement of people, or ideas, or information, or objects.
> *(Büscher and Urry 2009, p. 99)*

A mobilities turn is part of the critique of such a humanism that posits a disembodied cogito and especially human subjects able to think and act in some ways independent of their material worlds.

(Büscher and Urry 2009, p. 99)

Following these quotations, mobility and movement can be seen as characteristic components of the past. As such, they find their expressions not solely in sociolinguistic categories of variation and change, language contact and the like, because language usage and (social) styling in historical discourses can no longer be seen as dependent on, for example, fixed 1:1 correlates between language usage and social variables. Generally speaking, these are too static to determine linguistic practices of a historical community and to chart 'the social detail that vivifies language usage' (Moore 2012, p. 67) in general. Therefore, a mobile new historical stylistics framework also embraces the historical social styling outlined by Coupland (2007) as interactivity in ('spoken') historical discourse. Style is not just the measurable linguistic profile which deviates from or is parallel to certain norms, but it is also a communicative and social practice (Carter 2012, Coupland 2007, Moore 2012). Therefore genres and the historical developments of them, for example, are no longer a fixed, absolute set of conventions; instead they are dynamic and related to changing social institutions and purposes. It is crucial to take the 'communities of practice' (rather than the speech community) into account in which language usage/the use of particular styles/the use of genres take place. Coupland (2007) and Moore (2012) point out that only in a specific community of practice can linguistic features become socially meaningful (Moore 2012, p. 71). This entails understanding the social concerns of a historical community and how they are embodied in historical social styles (Moore 2012, p. 71), as well as which linguistic features occur in interaction with others (Moore 2012, p. 68). While it is always possible that speakers – past and present – exhibit particular stylistic effects or characteristics outside their socio-economic classification, the social meaning of a linguistic feature (and a genre) is typically underspecified until it enters into a speaker's or a group's social practice (Moore 2012, p. 68). The social meaning of a linguistic feature is embedded in the specific context of its use; which means that we situate meaning relative to the other social or linguistic feature. The following example from Shakespeare's *Hamlet* may give us an idea of what mobile social styling entails from a historical perspective.

King	But now, my cousin Hamlet, and my son,
Ham	[Aside] A little more than kin and less than kind
King	How is it that the clouds still hang on you?
Ham.	Not so, my lord, I am too much in the sun.

(Hamlet 1.2.64–7)

Hamlet only resorts to the conventional title 'my lord' to address the King. Even if we did not know the social relations between Hamlet and Claudius, their choice of address formulae would – at least superficially – allow us to infer that Claudius's position is higher up the social ladder than that of Hamlet because he addresses Hamlet by his personal name and with the help of kinship terms. However, Hamlet's choice of form of address carries more contextually grounded functions as well. It carries a more nuanced and pointed social styling as he resorts to the – in Early Modern English – rather neutral, semantically frozen and most frequently occurring vocative form, the generalised 'my lord'.

For a diversity of reasons, agents of discourses also adhere to certain conventions of social styling and use generic patterning. For example, Lowth (1762) in his *Short Introduction to English Grammar* is one among many so-called prescriptive grammarians of the eighteenth century who condemn the use of the split infinitive. However, this practice of 'verbal hygiene' (Cameron 2012) also had a social function to instruct 'social upstarts' in correct language usage.

Hence, the presence of historical discourse formations in contemporary discourse on the one hand, and the fact that 'we accept that the linguistic forces which operate today and are observable around us are not unlike those which have operated in the past' (Romaine 1982, p. 122), on the other, enable us to transfer our modern conceptions of discourse to the past. These observations also allow us to see discourses as collective and individual cultural understandings of the stories and values associated with them (Canning 2012, p. 1). The five independent mobilities outlined by Büscher and Urry (2009, p. 101) – corporeal travel, physical movement, imaginative travel, virtual travel and communicative travel – are also of historical and contextual importance because they reflect and construe the materiality of discourses. They are therefore functions of particular instances of social styling and ideologies. These can be seen as social practices which are constructed, perpetuated, and opposed in discourses past and present. As such, they become material, and expressions of both power and of routines, in addition to being sign-making and communicative practices (Warnke 2013).

Historical sources are materially visible as soon as they are said: They are constitutive of discursive acts of so-called mobile historical 'place-making'. When human beings invest in a portion of space, and then become attached to it in some way, space becomes 'place' (Cresswell 2004, p. 24). Place is thus something which people have made subjectively and personally meaningful, and place-making includes reiterative social practices, inclusiveness, performability and dynamic quality. Friedmann (2010, p. 154) adds to this list the idea of the place being cherished or valued. In the words of Lefebvre (1974, pp. 48–49), the production of a meaningful space comprises the three dimensions of the 'perceived-conceived-lived triad (in spatial terms: spatial practice, representations of space, representational space)' (Lefebvre 1991, p. 40). To account for the specific qualitative and multi-modal discourses of an urban place, Warnke (2013, pp. 192–194) modifies these dimensions to come up with three modes of urbanity which interact and are interdependent, namely: a) dimension, b) action, and c) representation. Whereas 'dimension' spatial dimensions in developed and open space, 'action' is interpersonal and takes into account 'lived experience, interaction and use of space by its inhabitants' (McIlvenny *et al.* 2009, p. 1879). 'Representation' embraces the ways in which meanings are construed by means of cognitively represented and socially construed sign-making (Warnke 2013).

In a next step, historical discourse can be described by the interaction of these three dimensions, since they are construed in their materiality while simultaneously creating it. Historical discourses therefore happen not only in a place (that is, in a situation, a genre, a novel by a particular author), but they also create places in interaction by making meaning and construe value. For example, due to the geographical location of the borough of Brooklyn, NY, divided from Manhattan by the river, discourses of place-making about and in some, mainly gentrified, Brooklyn neighbourhoods construct the so-called Doppelgänger motif characterised by a feeling of 'Brooklyn vs. Manhattan'. In B. Busse (forthcoming), I trace the linguistic and multimodal means of reflecting on people's sense of belonging as stylistic place-making activities in Brooklyn, New York. One aim is to find out how and to what extent features on all (and not just dialectical) levels of language and repetitive patterns index, that is, 'enregister' (Johnstone 2009) social value and construe 'Brooklyn-as-a-brand-name' today and in the past. This includes not only face-to-face interactions, but also the realm of '"imagined presence" – realised through objects, people, information and images travelling, carrying connections across, and into multiple other spaces from time to time' (Büscher and Urry 2009, p. 100).

In her study of 'Pittsburghese', Johnstone (2009) invokes the concept of enregisterment to explain the historical development of local dialect use and awareness in Pittsburgh. She shows that that there is a promoted or enregistered dialect called 'Pittsburghese' which has also become commodified. Among other factors, the currently existing variety as well as the ubiquity of items for sale displaying local speech peculiarities are examples of the process Johnstone describes. Basing her claims on a wealth of historical and contemporary linguistic data, Johnstone (2009) illustrates that in terms of Silverstein's (2003) 'orders of indexicality', a fixed one-to-one correlation between linguistic variation and demographic facts – Silverstein's first order of indexicality, which is also used as an ideological scheme by dialectologists – may not be sufficient to explain when, why and how particular ways of speaking come to be discursively construed with a dialect in general, and Pittburghese in particular, in popular imagination and discourse.

Therefore, new researchable entities and the investigation of how they come to mean include the styling of style, places, and areas. Interdisciplinarity, which has always been fostered by stylistics, is a prerequisite as mobile new historical stylistics finds mobile profiles – that is, it moves on a continuum of quantitative and qualitative pattern identification. It finds underlying grammars, profiles, orders and rules by drawing on a variety of contexts, but at the same time it is also interested in qualitatively describing the tools, strategies and methods that are used in local historical discourse to achieve and coordinate particular effects, styles and places. To be moved by the research, to follow people and to focus on the mobile historical discourse profiles therefore incorporates the interplay between patterns and creativity, norms and deviations, global and local, multiple and yet local and practical ordering of social and material realities and representations (Büscher and Urry 2009, p. 103).

Computer-assisted text analysis helps to establish patterns of foregrounding in historical literary texts along dimensions which might otherwise go unnoticed (Kohnen 2006, p. 73). The investigation of large amounts of data also provides us with a framework and a norm against which the results of a mobile new historical stylistic investigation can be qualitatively measured to establish the discursive practices of a particular genre, the linguistic profiles of an author, the stylistic realisation of a particular linguistic function in a text, or keywords and how these work thematically. Although quantitative historical semantic analyses – useful for the historical analyses of speech acts, for example – are still in the process of being developed, there are a number of highly useful tools such as the *Oxford English Dictionary* (1992) and the *Historical Thesaurus of the Oxford English Dictionary* (2010) which can also be fruitfully exploited for a mobile new historical stylistic investigation (see B. Busse 2012b). In addition, new quantitive and/or qualitive historical stylistic investigations of functional or discursive phenomena, such as speech, writing and thought presentation (B. Busse 2010a, 2010b, McIntyre and Walker 2011, Semino and Short 2004), clusters as local textual functions (Mahlberg 2007, Mahlberg 2012), style and ideology in Reformation England (Canning 2012), stance (B. Busse 2012a) in historical literary texts and an investigation of historical newspaper discourse from a stylistic perspective (Studer 2008).

Thus, this methodology relates to the quantitative side of the theory of foregrounding; that is, it comprises establishing forms in historical data which then need to be enhanced with meaning. As such, literary creativity in historical data in general relates to established inter-

and intra-textual norms (Leech 2007), and it can be measured through the interrelationship between both quantitative and qualitative research endeavours. The quantitative identification of patterns can be seen as a platform which, among other things, leads to a systematic, detailed micro-linguistic (qualitative) investigation of the aforementioned social styling. In order to measure and describe the levels of foregrounding (including deviation and parallelism) in a historical dimension, it is impossible to argue on a one-to-one basis that what occurs in a big historical reference corpus constitutes the ordinary or the norm. However, a more delicate and contextually based analysis is also necessary which deals with context and envisages the notion of the already mentioned 'emergent grammar' or emergent styles (Taavitsainen and Fitzmaurice 2007). Styles in historical texts are not always stable in terms of form-to-function or function-to-form, but instead they may be constantly modulated within a historical framework. What constitutes a writer's motivated choice may, over the course of time, become a norm and therefore highly frequent. Hence, it is valid to be more micro-linguistically/ stylistically oriented. In addition, Leech's (1985) distinction between deviation on a primary, secondary, and tertiary level needs to be seen as interdependent in exploring the effects of linguistic processes in historical contexts. Language norms, discourse specific norms and text-internal norms all play a role in evaluating stylistic change and stability within a historical dimension. We also need to bear in mind that a bottom-up corpus linguistic approach is very much determined by and focuses on lexis. Hence, complex discourse frameworks cannot immediately be identified with the help of generally available programmes for text analysis.

Nevertheless, Cameron (2011) draws our attention to the fact that an exaggerated focus on empiricism in humanities scholarship (Carter 2012) in general and in the analysis of literature in particular, which was proposed by Gottschall in 2008, may neglect the sensitivity that is needed in literary analysis. Frequency of usage plays a role in a particular community of practice in relation to the significance of the 'variants' themselves and what they mean, especially because some social variables are cognitively stored. Also, in historical pragmatics, a number of recent discussions have revolved around the interrelationship between low- and high-frequency items, or even the debate about the need for quantitative figures to chart historical-pragmatic change and variation on a longer diachronic scale (B. Busse 2012a). Consequently, a frequently visible genre-bias and a focus on mass media (Warnke 2013) resulting from the way corpora are structured, for example, may not always lead to the desired outcome. Number-crunching alone or statistics taken out of context do not say much about how a historical text comes to mean stylistically. Concomitantly, stylistic place-making in historical discourse can be highly individual, dynamic, local and pragmatic or creative, which is one of the reasons why mobile new historical stylisticians should also be interested in low frequency items, in the qualitative meanings which sit in places and which can only be detected by means of reading and philological work. Curzan and Palmer (2006, p. 21) also point to the limits of corpora and search engines and regard an informed historical investigation as completed only according to the following maxim: 'Research begins where counting ends' (Curzan and Palmer 2006, p. 21). The nuanced usages of forms of address in Shakespeare (B. Busse 2006) mentioned above is one example.

New criticism, with its focus on the aesthetic value of texts in their socio-historical, cultural, and political contexts, in conjunction with these historically situated philological approaches (and their re-considerations through theories from anthropology, history, or political history) is of equal value to new historical stylistic analysis (Taavitsainen and Fitzmaurice 2007, p. 22f.). Depending on which theory is construed to be relevant, that theory shapes and constraints the qualitative reading of the text as a communicative and contextual event. New historicism, and Stephen Greenblatt's (1988, p. 1) famous phrase 'to speak with the dead', actually sees this interplay between a text and its context as indispensable for the interpretation process. That is, in order to understand Shakespearean English in its full complexity, it is important to know about the Elizabethan world picture, the Early Modern preoccupations with language, and so on. It is through this reciprocal relationship and the 'new philology' (Taavitsainen and Fitzmaurice 2007, p. 22) that even more recent linguistic/ stylistic approaches and methods can be further enhanced.

Very importantly, the mobility paradigm comes up with new methodologies. One is a so-called 'physical traveling with their research objects' (Büscher and Urry 2009, p. 103) and a claim for a 'multi-sighted ethnography' (Marcus 1995). The other puts emphasis on being 'moved by and moved with their subjects' (Büscher and Urry 2009, p. 103). Of course, we are not witnesses of older stages of a language and it is impossible for us to observe, for example, the actions of historical figures when acting as mediators of the past. However, it is possible to convey some of the material contexts of past speakers by addressing a plurality of interdisciplinary methods to face the challenges involved. These may include experts from a plethora of disciplines whose concerns intersect those of new historical stylistics, including the digital humanities as well as historians.

Within this framework, the validation of data, analysis and interpretation is indispensable (Taavitsainen and Fitzmaurice 2007). A mobile new historical stylistic analysis of texts from older stages of the English language also presupposes a comprehensive knowledge of the period, of the context, of reading habits and dissemination processes of texts and of the language in which the text was produced. The question of what constitutes representative data is not trivial, because it also includes knowledge of genre conventions, existent editions, copy texts and spelling variation (Taavitsainen and Fitzmaurice 2007, p. 21f.).

There is a variety of contextual information guiding our reading: generic knowledge, encyclopaedic background knowledge and knowledge of schemas and scripts, as well as about belief systems. It is impossible to question contemporary historical speakers. However, it is possible to include historical material – that is, contemporary sources (Nevalainen and Raumolin-Brunberg 2004, p. 8f.) – in the interpretation process, despite the time and effort it may take, and so 'follow the people' (Marcus 1995). Although historical descriptions of, or comments on, a particular grammatical or linguistic phenomenon are often normative rather than descriptive, they nevertheless show us what was considered to be of importance and can give us vital c(l)ues to the purposes of usage. Contemporary sources, such as dictionaries, grammars, and rhetorical handbooks serve to enhance modern (linguistic) theories and methods. They may serve not as an interpretative agenda, but rather act as interpretative help.

A new historical stylistic analysis

The following excerpts and data represent place-making in and about some neighbourhoods of Brooklyn, New York. Current linguistic practices of place-making are assessed and exemplified, and it will be shown how these strategies are diachronically motivated (see B. Busse forthcoming).

If place is something that is made meaningful by human beings, 'enregisterment' (Johnstone 2009, B. Busse and Warnke 2014), being the way in which local language usage is indexically linked with social meaning, can be seen as a place-making activity too. There are different reciprocal indexical relationships between complex multimodal discourses and their interpretation as well as their evaluation with an ideological scheme, personal and social identity and locality and place. For example, linguistic features may become 'enregistered'. 'Metapragmatic practices' (Silverstein 1993) also show which particular linguistic features encode local identity and place. In addition, specific values of a place and how they are created and enregistered through language as well as other semiotic modes may also describe this relationship.

In the following conversational exchange from the TV series *Sex in the City*, which is set in Manhattan, New York, the borough of Brooklyn is conceptualised as a place one does not want to live in.

Narrator (Carrie):	Meanwhile, across town, a couple who had won the baby race, had lost their bedroom, to their baby.
Miranda:	Wait, we saw that one! Charming, midtown, two bedroom. Why don't they say what it really is: crack-house on an airshaft. Scout, off! Off!
Steve:	Hey, listen to this one: in our price range, three bedroom.
Miranda:	I'm putting my shoes on.
Steve:	Outdoor space…
Miranda:	I'm getting my bag.
Steve:	…finished basement…
Miranda:	It's a house?!
Steve:	…in Brooklyn!
Miranda:	Ok, shoes are off. What did I tell you about that side of the paper?
Steve:	What, it's a good place!
Miranda:	Steve, we're not moving to Brooklyn. I'm a Manhattan girl, I don't like anything not Manhattan.
Steve:	Hey, I'm Queens and I'm pretty cute. Let's just look at it.
Miranda:	Sleeping in the dining room isn't so bad. We're near the kitchen. [Cat miaws. Dog barks.]

Excerpt from Sex and the City – *'Out of the Frying Pan' (2004)*

We find Miranda and Steve checking newspaper ads for a new flat because they 'house' in a far too small Manhattan apartment with their child and dog. While Steve considers the borough of Brooklyn to be an option for a more spacious home to live in, Miranda adamantly rejects the idea of 'moving to Brooklyn.' The initially anticipated activity, climactically built up in the present continuous constructions announcing her getting dressed is therefore immediately destroyed through her blunt statement: 'shoes are off,' indicating immobility. One does not go flat-hunting, let alone live, in Brooklyn. Miranda further (stereotypically) creates the antagonism between Brooklyn and Manhattan through an identifying relational process: 'I'm a Manhattan girl,' and a multiply-negated mental process in which she stubbornly, if not childishly, claims that 'I don't like anything not Manhattan' and indicates that she would rather prefer sleeping in the dining room than moving to Brooklyn. Apart from the humour that is created through the constructed schema opposition between Brooklyn and Manhattan, this also illustrates that Brooklyn has to be imagined side by side with Manhattan.

In contrast to the construction of Brooklyn as a 'no go' stand practices of enregisterment in gentrified neighbourhoods of Brooklyn, such as Williamsburg, Park Slope or Brooklyn Heights, which create a positive Brooklyn identity and in which Brooklyn, or certain parts of Brooklyn, are construed as valuable places. The practices of enregisterment can be seen on road signs which have marked Brooklyn motorway exits on the Brooklyn or Williamsburg Bridge since the beginning of the new century. They attribute local identity to Brooklyn as a place through their celebration of fixed, authentic and historical expressions. Borough

President Markowitz comments on the function of these road signs in 2003: '"Once you enter Brooklyn, there's no good reason why you should ever leave." […] These signs are just another great example of the Brooklyn attitude, and they capture the spirit, energy and enthusiasm alive and well all across Brooklyn. It also gives people one last chance to turn their cars around and stay in the promised land.' (See the link http://www.barrypopik.com/ index.php/new_york_city/entry/how_sweet_it_is_brooklyn_street_signs/ for more.

One popular sign reads 'How sweet it is!', referring to the catchphrase of Brooklyn entertainer and *Honeymooners* television star Jackie Gleason. His quote on a highly public road sign reinforces the sense of local identity, illustrates the success of Brooklynites in the media scene and simultaneously stresses Brooklyn's historical past and tradition.

Another sign (which you can find at http://www.flickr.com/photos/jag9889/5483202296/) reads 'Leaving Brooklyn, Fuhgeddaboudit!' This is an urban hip colloquial dialectal expression which means something to the effect of 'the issue is not worth the time, you better stay!' It is even written down in the phonological pronunciation. This re-enregisterment of the famous Brooklyn accent is also practised by the first-person narrator Nathan in Paul Auster's (2006) *The Brooklyn Follies*: 'that unmistakable accent so ridiculed in other parts of the country, which I find the most welcoming, most human of all American voices' (Auster 2006, p. 12).

The strategy of contrasting Brooklyn with Manhattan also has historical precedents in which Brooklyn is indexed as a contrast to the then City of New York. The night before the city of Brooklyn and the other boroughs of New York as well as the City of New York became united on 1 January 1898, the editor and owner of the famous Brooklyn newspaper the *Brooklyn Daily Eagle*, St. Clair McKelway, was asked to give a speech for the mayors and citizens of the City of Brooklyn. This speech is reported in direct speech in the *Brooklyn Daily Eagle* from 2 January 1898. McKelway's stance is expressed in two neologisms – 'Brooklynisation' and 'New Yorking' – as in, 'The Brooklynisation of New York, not the New-Yorking of Brooklyn is what we should expect' (*Brooklyn Daily Eagle* 02/01/1898, p. 4). Despite the fact that McKelway attributes a stronger role to Brooklyn in the unification process, it becomes obvious that the comparison between Brooklyn and Manhattan/New York, as well as their opposition, are mutually dependent as a Doppelgänger motif. The 'special purpose' (Leech 1983, p. 101) of the use of the negative in 'not the New Yorking' is to let Brooklyn shine and stand out. It is only through these contrasts that both the cancellation of the propositions are seen via recourse to Manhattan/New York, in concert with the positive propositions relating to Brooklyn. The narrator Nathan in Auster's (2006) *The Brooklyn Follies* also explains one character's decision to move to Brooklyn by drawing on the contrast: 'He chose Brooklyn because it was New York and yet not New York' (Auster 2006, p. 50).

Like any urban space (B. Busse and Warnke 2014), Brooklyn is a highly condensed and heterogeneous territory in which different place-making activities and discursive strategies can be assessed within a historical framework. The example analysed here can illustrate why parts of Brooklyn – especially those dimensionally facing Manhattan – have been given so much press and how parts of Brooklyn have been enregistered as *cool* places or 'place[s] of creative consumption' (Zukin 2010, p. 35), always standing in opposition to Manhattan.

Recommendations for practice

1. Contextualise the following four excerpts from Shakespeare's plays. Then analyse and interpret the use of pronominal and nominal forms of address and discuss to what extent address strategies are place-making. Pay special attention to the performative effects of the usage of pronouns and vocative forms.

Beatrice:	I wonder that you will still be talking, Signior Benedick, nobody marks you.
Benedick:	What, my dear lady Disdain, are you yet living?

(Much Ado About Nothing 1.1.116ff.)

Claudio:	Benedick, didst thou note the daughter of Signior Leonato?

(Ado 1.1.162)

Benedick: [...]	Do you question me, as an honest man should do, for my simple true judgement? Or would you have me speak after my custom, as being a profess'd tyrant of their sex?
Claudio:	No I pray thee, speak in sober judgement.

(Much Ado About Nothing 1.1.161ff.)

Hamlet	Now, mother, what's the matter?
Gertrude	Hamlet, thou hast thy father much offended.
Hamlet	Mother, you have my father much offended.

(Hamlet 3.4.8f.)

Goneril [to Edmund]:	Decline your head: this kiss, if it durst speak, / Would stretch thy spirits up into the air.

(King Lear 4.2.22–23)

2. Contextualise the following excerpts. Analyse the modes of speech, writing and thought presentation and their effects. Use the model presented in Leech and Short (2007), Semino and Short (2004) and B. Busse (2010b).

I expected Miss Matty to jump at this invitation; but, no! Miss Pole and I had the greatest difficulty in persuading her to go. She thought it was improper; and was even half annoyed when we utterly ignored the idea of any impropriety in her going with two other ladies to see her old lover.

(Gaskell 2007 [1853], p. 38)

3. The following two excerpts are taken from Zadie Smith's 2012 novel *NW*. Analyse the narrator's comments on the use of language in North-West London and focus on the historical dimensions of place-making patterns.

She knows the way people speak around here, that *fucking*, around here, is only a rhythm in a sentence.

(Smith 2012, p. 12)

Michael exercising his little store of hard-won colloquialisms, treasure of any migrant: *at the end of the day, know what I mean, and if that wasn't enough, and I says to him, and I was like, that's a good one, I'll have to remember that one.*

(Smith 2012, p. 17)

Future directions

Linguistic style is choice (B. Busse 2010a) and mobile historical discourse profiles move along methodological continuums of quantitative and qualitative as well as synchronic and diachronic investigations. Motion, mobility and fluidity are added to the central components of change – in both place and time. Along a cline of literariness (Carter 2012), 'texts' to be investigated may range from literature to historical semiotic landscapes (Landry and Bourhis 1997, p. 25; Backhaus 2007, Jaworski and Thurlow 2010). Furthermore, standard, fixed and static concepts of style, place, speaker or the linguistic variable (Labov 2006, Moore 2012) need to be challenged by stressing the fluid continuum on which these concepts can be situated.

With regard to new research objects for mobile new historical stylistics, attention to mobile or transitional places where people and discourse were, have been or are arriving (Saunders 2010) is required. This also includes the styling of urbanity within a diachronic framework. In addition, research on cultural heritage, tourism and the historical stylistic formations of these components of historical mobility touches upon an equally new framework of cultural stylistics (B. Busse forthcoming), especially because 'thinking in placing' is something which people have made subjectively and personally meaningful in order to create a sense of belonging (Cresswell 2004, p. 24). Hence, Augé's (2008) anthropological place is endowed with movement as if 'unfolding through time' (Hall 2009, p. 573). Representation and declaration in the Searlean sense (Searle 2010) are in smooth transition. Mobility can be materialised in particular places (Hubbard 2006) as well as in discursive conventions, both past and present. Goffman's (1969) claim that the (qualitative) researcher has to go 'where the action is' no longer implies any single setting or location. A threefold cline of a disciplinary movement beyond – interlinguistic, interhuman and interdisciplinary – is guaranteed.

Related topics

Corpus stylistics, literary pragmatics, multimodality, pedagogical stylistics, rhetoric and poetics, speech and thought presentation.

Further reading

Adamson, S., 1999. The literary language. *In:* R. Lass, ed. *The Cambridge history of the English language. Volume 3: 1476–1776*, Cambridge: Cambridge University Press, 539–653.

This article is representative of an earlier philological focus on historical stylistic investigation. It links the history of literary style during the Early Modern English period to the history of the standardisation of English.

Busse, B., 2010a. Recent trends in new historical stylistics. *In:* B. Busse and D. McIntyre, eds. *Language and style: In honour of Mick Short*. Basingstoke: Palgrave Macmillan, 32–54.

This article consolidates new stylistic and linguistic approaches to the analysis of historical language data and suggests a methodological triangulation for diachronic stylistic investigations. It is accompanied by a hands-on analysis of discourse presentation in nineteenth-century narrative fiction.

Busse, B., 2012a, Historical text analysis: Underlying parameters and methodological procedures. *In:* A. Ender, A. Leeman and B. Wälchli, eds. *Methods in contemporary linguistics,* Berlin: De Gruyter Mouton, 285–308.

This article focuses on the mythological challenges that a historical linguist/historical stylistician has to face when historical language data is investigated from a stylistic perspective. It is accompanied by a complex quantitative and qualitative investigation of stance adverbials in the corpus of Shakespeare's plays.

References

Adamson, S., 1995. From empathetic deixis to empathetic narrative: Stylisation and (de-)subjectivisation as processes of language change. *Transactions of the philological society*, 92 (1), 55–88; reprinted with minor changes in S. Wright and D. Stein, eds. 1995. *Subjectivity and subjectivisation*. Cambridge: Cambridge University Press.

Adamson, S., 1999. The literary language. *In:* R. Lass, ed. *The Cambridge history of the English language. Volume 3: 1476–1776*. Cambridge: Cambridge University Press, 539–653.

Adamson, S., 2001. The rise and fall of empathetic narrative. *In:* W. van Peer and S. Chatman, eds. *New perspectives on narrative perspective*. New York: State University of New York Press, 83–99.

Augé, M., 2008. *Non-places: An introduction to supermodernity*. 2nd edn. J. Howe, trans. London: Verso.

Auster, Paul. 2006. *The Brooklyn Follies*. New York: Henry Holt.

Backhaus, P., 2007. *Linguistic landscapes: A comparative study of urban multilingualism in Tokyo*. Toronto: Multilingual Matters.

Biber, D., 1988. *Variation across speech and writing*. Cambridge: Cambridge University Press.

Biber, D., 2004. Historical patterns for the grammatical marking of stance: A cross-register comparison. *Journal of Historical Pragmatics*, 5 (1), 107–136.

Biber, D. and Finegan, E., 1989. Drift and the evolution of English style: A history of three genres. *Language*, 65, 487–515.

Biber, D. and Finegan, E., 1992. The evolution of five written and speech-based English genres from the 17th to the 20th centuries. *In:* M. Rissanen, O. Ihalainen, T. Nevalainen and I. Taavitsainen, eds. *History of Englishes: New methods and interpretations in historical linguistics*. Berlin/New York: Mouton de Gruyter, 688–704.

Blakemore Evans, G., 1997. *The riverside Shakespeare*. 2nd ed. Boston: Houghton Mifflin.

Britain, D., 2004. Geolinguistics: Diffusion of language. *In:* U. Ammon, N. Dittmar, K.J. Mattheier and P. Trudgill, eds. *Sociolinguistics: International handbook of the science of language and society, vol. 1*. Berlin: De Gruyter Mouton, 34–48.

Britain, D., 2010. Language and space: The variationist approach. *In:* P. Auer and J. E. Schmidt, eds. *Language and space: An international handbook of linguistic variation. Volume 1: theories and methods*. Berlin: De Gruyter Mouton, 142–163.

Brooklyn Public Library, 2003. *Brooklyn Daily Eagle Online* 1841–1902. Online. Available at http://eagle.brooklynpubliclibrary.org/Default/Skins/BEagle/Client.asp?Skin=BEagle (Accessed 15 April 2013).

Büscher, M. and Urry, J., 2009. Mobile methods and the empirical. *European Journal of Social Theory*, 12 (1), 99–116.

Busse, B., 2006. *Vocative constructions in the language of Shakespeare*. Amsterdam: John Benjamins.

Busse, B., 2010a. Recent trends in new historical stylistics. *In:* B. Busse and D. McIntyre, eds. *Language and style: In honour of Mick Short*. Basingstoke: Palgrave Macmillan, 32–54.

Busse, B., 2010b. *Speech, writing and thought presentation in a corpus of 19th-century narrative fiction*. Unpublished 'Habilitationsschrift', University Bern.

Busse, B., 2012a. Historical text analysis: Underlying parameters and methodological procedures. *In:* A. Ender, A. Leeman and B. Wälchli, eds. *Methods in contemporary linguistics,* Berlin: De Gruyter Mouton, 285–308.

Busse, B., 2012b. A celebration of words and ideas: The stylistic potential of the historical thesaurus of the Oxford English Dictionary. *Language and Literature*, 21 (1), 84–92.

Busse, B., (forthcoming). Enregisterment in Brooklyn, New York. *Journal of Sociolinguistics*.

Busse, B. and Warnke, I. H., 2014. *Grundlagen der urban Linguistics: Konzeption, methodologie, forschungsfelder*. *In:* B. Busse and I. A. Warnke, eds. *Handbuch sprache in urbanen Raum* (Language and urban space). Vol. 20. Berlin: De Gruyter Mouton.

Busse, U., 2002. *Linguistic variation in the Shakespeare corpus: Morpho-syntactic variability of second person pronouns*. Amsterdam/Philadelphia: John Benjamins.

Busse, U. and Busse, B., 2010. Shakespeare. *In:* A. H. Jucker and I. Taavitsainen, eds. *Historical pragmatics*. Vol. 8, Berlin: de Gruyter Mouton, 247–284

Calvo, C., 2003. Pronouns of address in *As You Like It. Language and Literature,* 1 (1), 5–27.

Cameron, D., 2011. Evolution, science, and the study of literature: A critical response. *Language and Literature,* 20 (1), 59–72.

Cameron, D., 2012. *Verbal hygiene*, 2nd edn. London: Routledge.

Canning, P., 2012. *Style in the renaissance: Language and ideology in early modern England.* London: Continuum.

Carter, R., 2012. Coda: Some rubber bullet points. *Language and Literature*, 21 (1), 106–114.

Conrad, S. and Biber, D., eds, 2001. *Variation in English: Multi-dimensional studies.* London: Longman.

Coupland, N., 2007 *Style: Language variation and identity.* Cambridge: Cambridge University Press.

Cresswell, T., 2004. *Place: A short introduction.* Oxford: Blackwell.

Cresswell, T., 2006. *On the move: Mobility in the modern Western world.* London: Routledge.

Curzan, A. and Palmer, C. C., 2006. The importance of historical corpora, reliability and reading. *In:* R. Facchinetti and M. Rissanen, eds. *Corpus-based studies of diachronic English.* Berlin: Peter Lang, 17–34.

De Certeau, M., 1984. *The practice of everyday life.* S. Rendall, trans. Berkeley: University of California Press.

De Certeau, M., 2000. Walking in the city. *In:* G. Ward, ed. *The de Certeau reader.* Oxford: Blackwell, 101–119.

Evans, M., (in press). Pronouns of majesty: A study of royal we and other self-reference pronouns during the reign of Queen Elizabeth I. *Journal of Historical Pragmatics.*

Fitzmaurice, S., 2000. Like talking on paper? The pragmatics of courtship and the eighteenth-century familiar letter. *Language Sciences,* 22 (3), 359–383.

Fitzmaurice, S., 2010. Literary discourse. *In:* A. H. Jucker and I. Taavitsainen, eds. *Historical pragmatics.* Vol. 8, Berlin: de Gruyter Mouton, 679–704.

Fludernik, M., 1993. *The fictions of language and the languages of fiction.* London and New York: Routledge.

Fludernik, M., 1996. *Towards a 'natural' narratology.* London: Routledge.

Fludernik, M., 2000. Narrative Discourse Markers in Malory's *Morte d'Arthur. Journal of Historical Pragmatics.* 1 (2), 231–262.

Fludernik, M., 2003. The diachronization of narratology. *Narrative*, 11 (3), 331–348.

Fludernik, M., 2007. Letters as narrative: Narrative patterns and episode structure in early letters, 1400 to 1650. *In:* S. Fitzmaurice and I. Taavitsainen, eds. *Methods in historical pragmatics.* Berlin: Mouton de Gruyter, 241–266.

Friedmann, J., 2010. Place and place-making in cities: A global perspective. *Planning Theory & Practice,* 11 (2), 149–165.

Gaskell, E., 2007. [1853]. *Cranford.* Jenny Uglow, ed. Watson, London: Bloomsbury.

Goffman, E., 1969. *Where the action is.* London: The Penguin Press.

Gottschall, J., 2008. *Literature, science and the new humanities.* New York: Palgrave Macmillan.

Greenblatt, S. J., 1988. *Shakespearean negotiations: The circulation of social energy in Renaissance England.* Berkeley: University of California Press.

Hall, G., 2012. A celebration of style: An introduction to the special issue by the current editor of Language and Literature. *Language and Literature*, 21 (1), 5–8.

Hall, T., 2009. Footwork: Moving and knowing in local space(s). *Qualitative Research*, 9 (5), 571–585.

Hillis Miller, J., 2001. *Speech acts in literature.* Stanford: Stanford University Press.

Hubbard, P., 2006. *City.* London: Routledge.

Jaworski, A. and Thurlow, C., eds. 2010. *Semiotic landscapes: Language, image, space.* London: Continuum.

Johnstone, B., 2009. Pittsburghese shirts: Commodification and the enregisterment of an urban dialect. *American Speech*, 84 (2), 157–175.

Kohnen, T., 2006. Historical corpus linguistics: Perspectives on English diachronic corpora. *Anglistik*, 17 (2), 73–91.

Labov, W., 2006. *The social stratification of English in New York City.* 2nd edn. Cambridge: Cambridge University Press.

Landry, R. and Bourhis, R. Y., 1997. Linguistic landscape and ethnolinguistic vitality: An empirical study. *Journal of Language and Social Psychology*, 16 (1), 23–49.

Leech, G., 1983. *Principles of pragmatics.* London: Longman.

Leech, G., 1985. *A linguistic guide to English poetry.* 2nd edn. Harlow: Longman.

Leech, G., 2007. *Language in literature: Style and foregrounding.* London: Longman.

Leech, G. and Short, M., 2007. *Style in fiction: A linguistic introduction to English fictional prose.* 2nd edn. Harlow: Pearson.

Lefebvre, H., 1974. *La production de l'espace*. Paris: Anthropos.

Lefebvre, H., 1991. *The production of space*. D. Nicholson-Smith, trans. Oxford: Blackwell.

Lowth, R., 1762. *A short introduction to English grammar*. London: J. Hughs.

Magnusson, L., 1999. *Shakespeare and social dialogue: Dramatic language and Elizabethan letters*. Cambridge: Cambridge University Press.

Magnusson, L., 2007. A pragmatics for interpreting Shakespeare's sonnets 1 to 20: Dialogue scripts and Erasmian intertext. *In:* S. Fitzmaurice and I. Taavitsainen, eds. *Methods in historical pragmatics*. Berlin/New York: Mouton de Gruyter, 167–184.

Mahlberg, M., 2007. Corpus stylistics: Bridging the gap between linguistics and literary studies. *In:* M. Hoey, M. Mahlberg, M. Stubbs and W. Teubert, eds. *Text, discourse and corpora: Theory and analysis*. London: Continuum, 219–246.

Mahlberg, M., 2012. *Corpus stylistics and Dickens's fiction*. London: Routledge.

Mair, C., 2006. *Twentieth-century English*. Cambridge: Cambridge University Press.

Marcus, G. E., 1995. Ethnography in/of the world system: The emergence of multi-sited ethnography. *Annual Review of Anthropology*, 24, 95–117.

Massey, D., 1991. A global sense of place. *Marxism Today*. (June), 24–29.

Massey, D., 1999. Cities in the world. *In:* D. Massey, J. Allen and S. Pile, eds. *City worlds*. London: Routledge, 93–151.

McIlvenny, P., Broth, M. and Haddington, P., 2009. Communicating place, space and mobility. *Journal of Pragmatics,* 41, 1879–1886.

McIntyre, D. and Walker, B., 2011. Discourse presentation in Early Modern English writing: A preliminary corpus-based investigation. *International Journal of Corpus Linguistics,* 16 (1), 101–130.

Moore, E., 2012. The social life of style. *Language and Literature*, 21 (1), 66–83.

Nevalainen, T. and Raumolin-Brunberg, H., 2004. *Historical sociolinguistics: Language change in Tudor and Stuart England*. London: Longman.

Pakkala-Weckström, M., 2010. Chaucer. *In:* A. H. Jucker and I. Taavitsainen, eds. *Historical pragmatics*. Vol. 8, Berlin: de Gruyter Mouton, 219–246.

Romaine, S., 1982. *Socio-historical linguistics: Its status and methodology*. Cambridge: Cambridge University Press.

Saunders, D., 2010. *Arrival city*. London: Random House.

Searle, J., 2010. *Making the social world: The structure of human civilisation*. Oxford: Oxford University Press.

Sell, R., 2000. *Literature as communication*. Amsterdam/Philadelphia: John Benjamins.

Semino, E. and Short, M., 2004. *Corpus stylistics: Speech, writing and thought presentation in a corpus of English writing*. London: Routledge.

Sheller, M. & Urry, J., 2006. The new mobilities paradigm. *Environment and Planning*, 38 (2), 207–226.

Silverstein, M., 1993. Metapragmatic discourse and metapragmatic function. *In:* J. A. Lucy, ed. *Reflexive language: Reported speech and metapragmatics*. Cambridge: Cambridge University Press, 33–58.

Silverstein, M., 2003. Indexical order and the dialectics of sociolinguistic life. *Language and Communication*, 23, 193–229.

Sinclair, J., 2004. *Trust the text: Language, corpus and discourse*. London: Routledge.

Smith, Z., 2012. *NW*. London: Penguin.

Studer, P., 2008. *Historical corpus stylistics: Media, technology and change*. London: Continuum.

Taavitsainen, I., 1998. Emphatic language and romantic prose: Changing functions of interjections in a sociocultural perspective. *European Journal of English Studies*, 2 (2), 195–214.

Taavitsainen, I., 2001. Changing conventions of writing: The dynamics of genres, text types, and text traditions. *European Journal of English Studies,* 5 (2), 139–150.

Taavitsainen, I., 2009. The pragmatics of knowledge and meaning: Corpus linguistic approaches to changing thought-styles in Early Modern medical discourse. *In:* A. H. Jucker, D. Schreier and M. Hundt, eds. *Corpora: pragmatics and discourse*. Amsterdam: Rodopi, 37–62.

Taavitsainen, I. and Fitzmaurice, S. M., 2007. Historical pragmatics: What it is and how to do it'. *In:* S. M. Fitzmaurice and I. Taavitsainen, eds. *Methods in historical pragmatics*. Berlin: De Gruyter Mouton, 11–36.

Tandon, B., 2003. *Jane Austen and the morality of conversation*. London: Anthem Press.

Warnke, I. H., 2013. *Urbaner diskurs und maskierter protest: Intersektionale feldperspektiven auf gentrifizierungsdynamiken in Berlin Kreuzberg. In:* C. S. Roth and C. Spiegel, eds. *Angewandte diskurslinguistik: Felder, probleme, perspektiven*. Berlin: Akademie-Verlag, 189–222.

Zukin, S., 2010. *Naked city: The death and life of authentic urban places*, Oxford: Oxford University Press.

7

Stylistics, speech acts and im/politeness theory

Derek Bousfield

Introduction

The study of stylistics can be an enigmatic, alluring and eclectic one. Stylistics, as originally envisaged and practiced, explored the linguistic construction of the style of writing of literary authors, ostensibly as an approach to ascertain whether it was possible to assign authorship definitively to unattributed or questionably attributed literary works. Given that literature itself, no matter who authors it, exists primarily to – literally or metaphorically – comment critically and creatively on what it means to be human in the social and physical world in which contemporary readers find themselves (to comment on 'the human condition', in effect), it was no great leap either in application or of academic interest for stylistics, and those who practice it, to begin exploring how and why readers engage with, appreciate, understand and respond to literary texts, their themes, characters, plot developments and narrative resolutions. After all, it stands to reason and resists counter-argument that how you understand, appreciate and evaluate a literary text relies in no small part on the way, or the *style*, in which that text is written or otherwise communicated, and how the characters are presented linguistically to you as reader, hearer, or audience member.

With regards to fictional characters, the style (or way) in which characters are described, and, indeed, the style (or way) by which characters themselves interact all reveal how we, within the cultural context in which we receive the information, are being invited to see, to understand, to appreciate, empathise, sympathise or antipathise with those characters, and what they literally, metaphorically or metonymically represent (see Chapter 12 in this volume). Therefore, a stylistic approach to understanding characters should – indeed, *must* – explore the language that those characters themselves are presented as using.

However, language itself is no straightforward or concise tool of communication. What we say in real life interaction is often very different to what we mean (see Chapter 8 in this volume, and discussion below), and one reason why we diverge from otherwise direct and to-the-point communication is as a result of the need to maintain the 'face' (Goffman, 1955, Brown and Levinson 1987) of our interactants (see further discussion below). Brown and Levinson's (1987) now classic approach to politeness is both predicated upon and fundamentally explained by our 'need' to maintain the face – that is, the public or interactional social standing, and the personal feeling of self-worth – of our interactants, so that they too will be predisposed to maintain ours. This tends, in some cultures, to lead towards indirectness, falsehoods and incomplete ways of saying things: all quite inconcise, not very straightforward ways of communicating which are caused, or at least *directed* by, this need to maintain others' face (see below, though also see Bousfield 2008, 2010, Culpeper 2011 for discussions on face-threat and face-attack). When people use, or, more noticeably, don't use politeness (especially when we expect it), we rightly or wrongly infer character traits about them, or wider situational reasons for their behaviour. Furthermore, if individuals go so far as to use impoliteness, we – again rightly or wrongly – infer character traits about them, or infer wider situational reasons for their behaviour. This is as true in fictional dialogue as it is in real-world interaction. Indeed, language is clearly not only a tool of communication, but a technique for forging and protecting or threatening and damaging interpersonal relationships, for establishing or challenging power relations, and for constructing notions of belief, self, and identity. Nowhere is this more readily apparent and visible than in literature in all its forms and all its glory, for, as mentioned above, literature comments on what it means to be human. As such, literature must reflect, even if metaphorically, how we *do being human* – including how we use and misuse language.

To this end it is worth noting that the study of pragmatics, among other subjects, is intimately interested in how users of language use their linguistic skills and communicative repertoires to, as Austin put it (1962), 'do things with words' – that is, how language is used by its users beyond the function of being merely a means of communication. This is where pragmatic theories of speech acts, face, politeness and impoliteness meet and merge with stylistic theories of characterisation (Culpeper 2001) and narrative development (Labov and Waletzky 1967). In the rest of this chapter I will outline the background and application of speech acts, concentrating the discussion on one specific form of speech act – that of threatening – and explaining how the use of such speech acts adds to audience understanding of the face-threatening, face-attacking ('impolite') behaviour of characters, and how such behaviour adds not only to our understanding of the characters themselves, but to the ways in which the dramatic narrative itself is propelled forward. What is argued in this chapter is theoretically applicable to all types of speech act beyond those of threats. As such, I will therefore explore how language operates as a 'characterisation' device – that is, as a system by which we are invited to infer particular traits and characteristics about any given dramatic character according to *what* they say and *how* they say it.

Having characters do things with words: Speech acts, face-work and im/politeness

The fact that what the characters say (and how they say it) has a bearing on how we view them is hardly contentious. While there are some largely silent and dialogue-free pieces of drama (the 1970s TV show *Secret Army,* and the love story told semiotically with images and music only during the first seven minutes of Disney/Pixar's fantastic *Up* spring most readily to mind), such experiments have been fleeting and short-lived. The vast majority of drama, especially character drama, relies heavily on what the characters say (and how they say it) to one another. With this principle in mind, it is important for us to recognise that it has long been understood that what characters say (and how they say it) is susceptible to, and analysable by, *some* of the same models and methods which are applicable to naturally occurring, real-life or day-to-day interactive language use. One of the most fundamental is the theory of 'Speech Acts' (Austin 1962, Searle 1975).

Austin (1962) in his seminal work 'How to do things with words' first recognised (academically, that is) that when we speak we don't just make statements about the world, or convey information from one person's cognitive centres to another person's. We can also *DO* things with such words and interactions. Consider the following:

(i)   I like red wine
(ii) I drive a silver Audi
(iii) I now pronounce you man and wife
(iv) "Get your trousers on, you're nicked!"   *(Regan in* The Sweeney, 'The Ringer', *1975)*

Austin recognises that the types of utterance in (i) and (ii) above are of a different quality and have a different interactional use than those in (iii) and (iv). The utterances in (i) and (ii) are what he terms 'constatives' – they make reference to a (semi-)permanent or persistently 'constant state of affairs' in the world that can be proven to be either 'true' or 'false' based on observational or other solid evidence. For example, if you hear me utter (i) above, and then see me turn up my nose, become an unhealthy shade of green and proceed to vomit after taking a sip of red wine, you could reasonably conclude that (i) is false. Likewise, if you see me regularly drive to and from work in a silver Audi, you could reasonably conclude that (ii) is true. These utterances refer to (albeit potentially short-lived) 'constant' states of affairs in the world. By contrast, the utterances in (iii) and (iv) are 'performatives' and are not 'true' or 'false' in the same way as constatives. To exemplify, if these phrases (iii, and iv) are uttered in an appropriate context, by an authorised person (i.e. if there is an appropriate authority figure uttering either (iii) or (iv) above), with appropriate persons present to whom the utterance is addressed, then all we can say is that they *happen*, and if they happen successfully (see below) then they change the world in however small a way (in that in (iii) two people are now joined together in matrimony in faith and law where they were not before, and in (iv) one person is now under police arrest where he or she was not before). We cannot say that they are 'true' or 'false' as we can with (i) and (ii). When such as (iii) and (iv) are uttered, however, Austin recognised that there must be a series of (contextual) conditions that must be in effect in order for them to *happen successfully* or 'felicitously', as he put it. After all, it is not legally, religiously, or socially binding if I wander around the streets randomly yelling 'I now pronounce you man and wife' to every pair of strangers I happen to come across. There are numerous reasons why such attempts at matrimony, either holy or civil, would fail – not least because (a) I am not a religious or civil authority, with the training or power to join two such people in matrimony, (b) the two people to whom I am addressing the remark may not want, or be able, to get married, and (c) the utterance is actually part of a wider, longer, religious and/or legal process, and hence just blurting it out at any chosen point does not *de facto* or *de jure* constitute marriage. Indeed, in understanding that for a speech act to be a genuine, allowable, acceptable, or 'felicitous' speech act that does have an effect and thus changes the world, in however small a way, Austin proposes the following:

Austin's felicity conditions for speech acts

> A: i)   There must be a conventional procedure having a conventional effect.
>   ii) The circumstances and persons must be appropriate.
> B: The procedure must be executed (i) correctly, (ii) completely.

C: Often
    i)   The persons must have the requisite thoughts, feelings and intentions *and*
    ii) If consequent conduct is specified, then the relevant parties must do it.

(Austin 1962, pp. 14–15)

As such, utterances like those in (iii) above would only be considered 'legal', 'valid', or 'felicitous' speech acts if the words were uttered at the appropriate time, in the appropriate place and by, and to, the appropriate persons. Whether such speech acts are successful or not, or are perceived to be successful or not by either the other characters in the drama or by the audience/viewer, is significant. This significance (a) is dependent on who, how, why, when and where the utterance is said, and (b) adds to our understanding of characterisation (the processes by which we are stylistically invited to understand any particular character and what they represent). All this is explored in detail below.

First, though, it is important to note that the dichotomy between constatives and performatives is overly simplistic in terms of understanding the actions (or not) that utterances can perform. There are different *types* of speech act. Again, the type of act used – be it a promise, offer or threat (for example) – can tell us huge amounts, stylistically, about how we are being invited to 'interpret' a particular character. Hence, it is worth us looking at these now.

Types of speech act

Searle's (1969, 1975) research into Speech Act theory has identified different 'types' of speech act (although, as I will show, the 'typing' of speech acts is perhaps best seen as identifying points of reference for utterances, rather than indicating that each utterance is 'either' – 'or'). These types can be categorised as follows:

Representatives

These are speech acts via which the speaker or producer expresses or communicates their beliefs. The speaker *represents* their understanding of the world or reality in some way. E.g. 'My wife and I went to see our friends for a meal last night. They were in good spirits.'

Assertives

Those types of speech acts that commit a speaker to the truth of the central proposition. Examples would include repeating an idiomatic lesson, e.g. reciting a statement of faith, belief or prayer, or asserting a lay or legal belief about how the world, society or culture works. E.g. 'It is illegal to drink and drive.'

Directives

These are speech acts which cause, or are uttered in an attempt to cause, the hearer (or rather, the main recipient) to take a particular course of action. Prototypical speech acts of this type include requests, advice, commands and, crucially for us, conditional threats (as in, if you do/ don't do Act *a*, I will perform Act *b* which is detrimental to you). E.g. 'Girls, tidy your rooms or I'll ring Santa to tell him to put you on the naughty list.'

Commissives

Speech acts which commit the speaker to some future action, examples of which include promises, oaths and, again, crucially, threats.

Expressives

Speech acts by which the speaker or producer communicates (or attempts to communicate) or otherwise *expresses* the speaker's emotions and/or attitudes towards the main proposition. Such utterances might be thanks, excuses, explanations and congratulations.

Declaratives

Those speech acts which change (others' understandings of, or actual, socio-cultural) reality in line with the proposition being expressed. Example declarative speech acts include *declarations* (naturally), christenings, baptisms or other naming ceremonies, pronouncements, admissions (e.g. of guilt, status, or belief) and suchlike.

When they are uttered, they change the world in however small a way. This is what is meant by words and phrases 'doing' something. In (iii), if my fiancée and I were to stand in front of a suitable religious figure, in a religious building, with our family and friends present, and the religious figure was to utter the declarative 'I now pronounce you man and wife' then the world has changed in a small but significant way. That is, my fiancée and I are no longer engaged to be married; we are now, as a result of that declarative phrase being said in the appropriate context, married because all the conditions above have been met, and hence the speech act is 'felicitous'. (This did indeed happen in 1999.) Hence, the world changed. Someone from the audience jumping up and shouting 'That's false!' (which did *not* happen to us in 1999), while likely to cause something of a stir, is nevertheless not a statement on the world (or even a very good challenge to it) as it would be in (i) and (ii), above. It would be disruptive, but it would not change the fact that we were married *as the fact that the words have been said in the appropriate context to the appropriate people by the appropriate person is the crucial element in us being married.* Saying 'That's false!' is not, in this case, a statement on the truthfulness of our matrimonial state; rather, it would be a (very weak) challenge to the religious authority that had just joined my fiancée and myself together.

Likewise, when Regan, a police officer in ITV's landmark 1970s TV series *The Sweeney*, tells a suspect who Regan has just gone to arrest *in* the suspect's bedroom to 'Get your trousers on, you're nicked!', he has, by virtue of uttering the words as a police officer, placed his suspect under arrest on suspicion of having committed a crime (at least in *The Sweeney*'s dramatic fictional text world). The text world has changed (by what can be seen as both a *directive* (*put your trousers on*) and a *declarative* (*you're nicked* = *I'm placing you under arrest*)); the suspect is no longer a free man, but is now under legal arrest, purely as a result of the utterance being made. Furthermore, and perhaps more pertinently for us here, we would be able to infer what type of policeman Regan is by *what* he says and *how* he says it – arresting his suspect using such informal language is unorthodox (even legally questionable by early twenty-first century standards) but definitely straightforward and with little finesse. This is likely to lead us to assume that Regan himself is also unorthodox, straightforward and with little finesse – which would be a correct set of inferences in his case (see below for more on *what we say* and *how we say it* in terms of understanding character).

Despite this analysis of Regan's very straightforward speech act, there are issues with speech act theory in that what is said directly is not always what is actually meant. That is, there are ways of performing speech acts *indirectly*. Again, when speech acts are performed directly or indirectly, this can give rise to a different but important set of understandings about a character that we're being invited to make (see discussion below).

Indirectness and implicitness

As will be becoming readily apparent, one issue with speech acts is that they are not easily (or even preferably) pigeonholed into one or the other type of speech act category. One primary reason for this is that, as Austin (1962) was to come to recognise, there is *no direct correlation* between the *form* of an utterance and its *force* (what is meant). For example, the utterance *Could you open a window?* could function as it appears – as a request (a commissive), or as an admonition (I could be criticising you for not having opened the window earlier – which would be functioning in the same way as a declarative, e.g. '*Open the window!*'), or some other type of action such as a sarcastic comment about you having the windows open when the snow or rain is pouring in (which would function as an (implied) expressive) and so on. Similarly, the phrase *I'm quite good at decorating*, which appears to be a simple statement (a constative, not unlike *I like red wine* or *I drive a silver Audi*) could actually have the intent and function of an offer of help (hence acting as a *commissive*) – in effect, it could be viewed as an indirect offer of help.

Recognising this mismatch between *form* and *force*, Austin attempts to account for both the direct and indirect nature by which Speech Acts could function. He theorises a tri-partite explanation of every speech act, by way of explaining how the form of one utterance could have the function of another. The tri-partite, or three-part elements of speech acts are:

> *Locution* – or what is actually *said*;

> *Illocution* – or what was *meant* by what was said; and

> *Perlocution* (or perlocutionary effect) – which is the effect on the hearer(s) of what was said *and* what was meant (and recognised as being meant by the hearer).

With direct speech acts, the locution largely matches the illocution. For example, the (at least) two speech acts in Regan's now classic and oft quoted line *Put your trousers on. You're nicked!* are considered direct because the first locution *put your trousers on* propositionally matches the illocution (= 'I want you to put your trousers on', or, more formally, 'I want you to get dressed'), while the second locution *you're nicked* propositionally matches the illocution (= 'you're nicked', or, more formally, 'I'm placing you under arrest on suspicion of having committed a crime').

However, with regards to *indirect* and even *implied* speech acts, the match between the locutions and the illocutions in the following extract take more cognitive work to fully unlock and understand. These examples are taken from the film *The Book of Eli* (Hughes Brothers, 2010) – a movie about one man's quest to deliver a religious text to a safe haven on Alcatraz in San Francisco Bay as he travels across a post-apocalyptic landscape. In this scene Eli is ambushed by a marauding gang of survivors who want to rob and, it is implied, kill and eat him. However, Eli is not prepared to let them rob him, much less harm him. He has just walked through a road underpass and out of the darkness into the light, where he has been confronted by the gang.

1. Gang leader: Whatcha got there in that pack?
2. Eli: What pack?
3. Gang Leader: (*snorts*) You gotta gun. (*turns to other gang members*) Shit, it ain't loaded.

One gang member sniggers

4. Gang leader: Ahh they never are. (*looks at Eli*) Ain't that right, old man?

Gang leader hefts his metal pole. Eli tenses at this, then relaxes and appears to glance behind him down the road over his shoulder and through the dark tunnel underpass behind him. He turns back to face the gang leader.

5. Gang leader: Open the pack and tip it out on the road nice and slow.

Eli takes a slow step back.

6. Eli: Can't do that.

Three second pause while the gang leader looks at the ground then at Eli.

7. Gang leader: Take off the fucking pack and put it on the ground OR DIE!

Eli does not move and stays silent.

8. Gang leader: (*steps forward and pushes Eli*) Are you listening to me?
9. Eli: I am now.
10. Gang leader: Good.
11. Eli: Are you listening to me?
12. Gang leader: Yeah.
13. Eli: Good. Put that hand on me again and you won't get it back.
14. Gang leader: (*laughs and turns to his gang*) Can you believe THIS FUCKING GUY? Alright, you wanna do it the hard way –

Gang leader moves to put his hand on Eli. Eli moves lightning fast. With a flash of steel the gang leader's hand is sliced off above the wrist by Eli wielding a large but previously concealed blade. The gang leader and the other gang members all look shocked.

15. Gang leader: (*staggering back holding stump*) How'd you do that? HE JUST CUT MY HAND OFF! (*collapses onto ground, voice breaking in pain*) WHAT ARE YOU STANDING AROUND FOR? KISS HIM!
16. Gang member: (*muffled, through gas mask*) What'd he say?
17. Eli: (*backing slowly into the shadowed darkness of the tunnel underpass*) He's in shock. I think he meant 'kill him'.

Gang members come at Eli with an assortment of weapons but are dispatched quickly by the protagonist. Eli walks back to the gang leader who is still on the ground but slowly working his way towards his severed hand.

18. Eli: (*moving severed hand away with his foot*) I told you you weren't going to get that back.
19. Gang leader: Yeah, you did. Who are you?

While the gang leader's utterance in turn 7 is a *more* obvious form of a directive speech act of conditional threat – with the locution (*put the pack on the ground or die*), more or less matching the illocution ('by which utterance I mean if you don't do as I say and put the pack on the ground, I and my gang members, who are obviously armed, will kill you for it'), Eli's own threat speech act (in turn 13) is much more *indirect*, even *implied* – as the locution (*Put your hand on me again and you won't get it back*) does not appear to have a clear and sincere threatening illocution beyond 'I don't like you poking me with your hand', in conjunction with the potentially bizarre 'if you poke me with your hand once again I will keep your hand'. There are a number of reasons why Eli's own threat appears less 'felicitous' than the gang leader's. First, hands are generally not considered to be objects that can be confiscated if misused. Second, Eli does not appear to be visibly armed to the gang members, who are obviously armed themselves, and who outnumber Eli by a factor of six to one. In effect, the gang leader and the gang members appear *not* to believe Eli –to their cost. In both cases the threats both the gang leader and Eli make to one another are not *the* most obvious, direct versions that could have been made. Indeed, the most obvious versions would be both formally and interactionally odd: Gang leader: 'I hereby threaten you that if you do not put the pack down on the ground, myself and my gang will kill you', and Eli: 'If you place your hand on me again I will hack it off with my blade'. In both cases, because the form of the words doesn't fully match the force, extra cognitive work is required by both characters and audience members to fully unlock the illocutionary force of *what was meant* by their implied threats.

The mismatch that typifies 'indirectness' between what was said (locution) and what was meant (illocution) is explained by reference to Grice's (1975) co-operative principle. Grice's (1975) Cooperative Principle (hereafter shortened to CP) assumes a tacit understanding between interlocutors to co-operate in an interactive event in a meaningful way.

> *[...] a rough general principle which participants will be expected* (ceteris paribus) *to observe, namely: Make your conversational contribution such as is required at the stage at which it occurs, by the accepted purpose or direction of the talk exchange in which you are engaged.*
>
> *(Grice 1975, p. 45).*

This 'rough general principle' means that Grice is suggesting that in conversational interaction, people work on the assumption that a certain set of interactional 'rules', expectations or 'maxims' is in operation, unless they receive indications to the contrary. All utterances, the gang leader's and Eli's included, occur in a (text-world) context, and for our purposes, interpreting character often involves interpreting a character's utterances *in relation* to the (understanding) of the context in which they occur. Pragmatic inferencing – understanding what was *meant* beyond what was *said*, in context – is at the heart of Grice's (1975) Cooperative Principle, which seeks to explain why it is that we often do not say exactly what we mean, but our interlocutors are by and large able to understand the meaning just the same. Grice postulated that the four conversational or interactional 'maxims' which all interlocutors assume are in operation whenever interaction takes place are:

Maxim of quality

- Try to make your contribution one that is true
- Do not say what you believe to be false
- Do not say that for which you lack adequate evidence

Maxim of quantity

- Make your contribution as informative as is required (for the current purpose of the exchange)
- Do not make your contribution more informative than is required

Maxim of relation

- Be relevant

Maxim of manner

- Be perspicuous
- Avoid obscurity of expression
- Avoid ambiguity
- Be brief (avoid unnecessary prolixity)
- Be orderly

It is worth noting that while the first three maxims refer to what is said, the maxim of Manner relates not to *what* is said, but to *how* what is said is actually said. Further, we should recognise that no speaker ever produces *all* their utterances in direct accordance with these maxims. Indeed, Grice understood that many speakers consistently break or transgress one (or more) of these maxims when they speak, and they do so *purposefully* in order to communicate illocutionary meaning beyond what they actually say by their locution.

There are two main ways in which speakers generate illocutionary meaning beyond their actual locutionary utterances. These are *flouting* a maxim, and *violating* a maxim. Flouting a maxim is the intentional and blatant non-observance of a maxim at the level of what is said. This is overt – that is, it is designed to be noticed by the speaker's interlocutor(s) and is therefore designed to generate a *conversational implicature* for particular effect (Grice 1975, p. 49, *my emphasis*). On the other hand, violating a maxim is the unostentatious or covert non-observance of a maxim. In violating a maxim, the speaker '...will be liable to mislead' (Grice 1975, p. 49).

To put it another way, *flouting* occurs when a speaker (a) breaks a maxim and (b) intends the hearer to understand that it is being broken. In this way extra (illocutionary) meaning in generated beyond what was actually said (in locutionary terms). *Violating* occurs when a speaker (a) breaks a maxim (or maxims); *and* (b) intends the hearer not to understand or perceive that the speaker is breaking it. Often the speaker's intention is to *mislead* the hearer. For example, *telling a lie* violates the Maxim of Quality; *giving vague or ambiguous answers* can violate the Maxims of Manner and Quantity.

In the cases of the threats from *The Book of Eli* scene above, Grice's (1975) maxims of quantity and manner are both flouted. Neither participant gives enough technical information on what they are proposing – they are not fully informative (which is a *quantity* maxim issue) or, in Eli's case, fully clear (which is a *manner* maxim issue) in their threats. As such, there is a level of ambiguity in what they have said in relation to what they mean. However, whilst Gricean implicature can tell us *how* implied speech acts (in this case, threats) work, they cannot tell us *why* the threats were not successful.

However, Searle's (1979) expansion of Austin's (1962) work does help us understand why Eli's threat in particular is not taken seriously – which, as a result, leads to the confrontation in which Eli is forced to sever the gang leader's hand and kill all the gang members. This explanation in turn helps us as audience members to read or 'interpret' both Eli's character and that of the gang leader (and other gang members). Searle identifies a series of further *felicity conditions* beyond those that Austin identified (see discussion above). These felicity conditions lie behind speech acts, and the fulfilment of all of them is necessary for a speech act to be considered a valid, effective, legal or 'felicitous' speech act. These fuller felicity conditions are:

> *Propositional Act* – what the speaker proposes to do – either directly or indirectly – by uttering the locutionary aspect of their speech act

> *Preparatory condition* – what actions, events, beliefs, understandings or similar need to be in place for the speech act to have an effect – and be in a situation where they can make the proposition occur, if necessary

> *Sincerity condition* – the speaker needs to mean the proposition

> *Essential condition* – the speaker commits to ensuring the proposition comes to pass

Essentially, then, the speech act of *threatening* – either directly or indirectly, explicitly or implicitly – would have the following felicity conditions:

> *Propositional act*: Speaker (S) proposes to do a particular action (A) to hearer (H)

> *Preparatory condition*: S believes A is *not* in H's best interests and that S *can do* A

> *Sincerity condition*: S intends to do A

> *Essential condition*: S undertakes an obligation to do A to H

In the case of Eli's threat to the gang leader – *Put that hand on me again, you won't get it back* – the conditions can be broken down like so:

> *Propositional act*: Eli proposes to 'keep' the gang leader's hand if the gang leader touches Eli again. The 'keeping' of the hand is not *explicit*; rather, it is an *implied* severing of it based on a *flout* of Grice's (1975) maxims of *quantity* and *manner.*

> *Preparatory condition*: Eli believes severing the gang leader's hand is not in the gang leader's best interests, and that Eli *can* sever the gang leader's hand if necessary.

> *Sincerity condition*: Eli *intends* to sever the gang leader's hand if he is touched by the gang leader again.

> *Essential condition*: Eli *undertakes* an obligation to sever the gang leader's hand if he is touched again.

Essentially, the gang leader and his gang – in being obviously armed and outnumbering Eli – evidently find it difficult to accept the *preparatory*, *sincerity* and, therefore, *essential* felicity conditions behind Eli's implied locutionary threat. Indeed, a mismatch between what one character understands or believes and what another may understand or believe is often a main driving force behind the propulsion of narrative plot and drama – it creates a *complicating action* (see Labov and Waletzky 1967) – because our narrative structure expectations are that such a mismatch in belief or understanding between two or more characters requires, demands, or even predicts resolution. Hence, stylistic analysis of pragmatic phenomena like *speech acts* can assist us in the analysis of both character and narrative plot development.

However, all of this leaves open the question of why we, as human interactants or dramatic characters, don't simply say what we mean, explicitly, directly and in full, in every case. Why didn't Eli just say 'touch me again and I'll cut your hand off'? (And why did the gang leader feel the need to push Eli again?) While there is a level of 'efficiency' to more brief utterances, the real answer to why we are not more explicit, direct and fulsome in our utterances lies in the linked concepts of 'face' and 'im/politeness'.

Face, politeness and impoliteness

Originating in academic circles with Goffman, face can be defined as 'the positive social value a person effectively claims for himself by the line others assume he is taking during a particular contact' (Goffman 1967, p. 5). In other words, 'face' relates to our feelings of *self-worth*. Scollon and Scollon (2001) argue that there can be no communication, no interaction, without face being an issue. That is, whenever one person speaks to or otherwise communicates with another, the face – this positive social value that each person claims for themselves, their feeling of 'self-worth' and 'respect' – is at risk of threat or damage to face for one, both, or all of the interactants. In order to account for how we orient our utterances to obviating the risk to our sense of face, Brown and Levinson ([1978] 1987) postulated a concept of linguistic politeness which was based on an elaborated version of face. Following and extending a train of thought first suggested in Durkheim (1915), Brown and Levinson (1987) suggested that each member of a culture, group or society had two interlocking aspects to face: 'positive face' and 'negative face' (1987: 61–62). They explain them as follows:

> *Positive face*
> Positive face is the want of every member that his [or her] wants be desirable to at least some others.
>
> *(Brown and Levinson 1987, p.62)*

> *Negative face*
> Negative face is the want of every 'competent adult member' that his [or her] actions be unimpeded by others.
>
> *(Brown and Levinson 1987, p.61)*

In essence, positive face is the desire to be *approved of* by others – to be liked, or at least not to be disliked or hated, whereas negative face is the desire to be *free from undue imposition* – to be liberated in thought, deed, ownership of goods, and action, and (or at least) not unnecessarily restrained.

Brown and Levinson (1987) suggested that there is a general *reciprocal* consensus regarding face needs among members of a society, culture or group. This reciprocity of face awareness and management indicates that in the main, any given member of a group, culture or society will attempt to maintain (or enhance) the face needs – both positive (approval) and negative (freedom) – of the other members of the group, culture or society because in doing so, that other member is then more likely to reciprocate with maintenance of the original member's face needs. Hence, face maintenance is reciprocal.

While Brown and Levinson provide a wealth of examples suggesting their underlying premise has considerable and demonstrable merit, other researchers such as Culpeper, Bousfield and Wichmann (2003), Bousfield and Locher (2008) and Bousfield (2008, 2010) have categorically shown that the opposite can, and does, occur. What is meant by this is that there are situations, peoples, circumstances or groups that do not have at their core the reciprocal face needs suggested above.

Indeed, despite Leech's contention that '[...] conflictive illocutions tend, thankfully, to be rather marginal to human linguistic behaviour in normal circumstances' (Leech 1983, p. 105). Culpeper *et al.* (2003, p. 1546) demonstrate that conflictive illocutions are anything but 'marginal' and have been observed in a wide variety of everyday discourses. Locher and Bousfield (2008) consider impoliteness to be 'ubiquitous'. As such, many and various researchers since Brown and Levinson (1987) and Leech (1983) have been at pains to point out that 'any adequate account of the dynamics of interpersonal communication, including models of politeness, should *also* consider hostile as well as cooperative communication' (see Bousfield 2008, p. 71). Nowhere is this more pertinent than in models of interpersonal communication that can be, and are, adopted by stylistics for the reading and understanding of character and plot. As we can see from the above extract from *The Book of Eli*, the main protagonists – Eli, and the gang leader – are far from engaging in linguistic instantiations of face reciprocity. In matter of fact, they are not only *not* being polite, they are being linguistically rude, aggressive, or following the current terminological flow, 'impolite', in that each seeks – via the speech acts of threats – to attack or threaten the face of the other. In each case the threats, being conditional threats (Turn 7. Gang leader: 'Take off the fucking pack and put it on the ground OR DIE!'; Turn 13. Eli: 'Put that hand on me again, you won't get it back'), attack both the positive face of the other (the desire to be approved of), and the negative face of the other (the desire to be unimpeded). In Turn 7 the gang leader uses taboo language both as a face-attacking linguistic strategy (see Culpeper 1996) and as an emphatic and positive-face threatening booster (see Holmes 1984) to the main thrust of the negative-face threatening propositions ('take off the pack' and 'put it on the ground'). These utterances are positive face threatening because the use of taboo language aimed at the target does not show or maintain approval of the target; rather, it attacks and diminishes such approval, and these utterances are also negative face-threatening since Eli is given no choice, no freedom of action, by the gang leader in being told to *take off the [...] pack* (a command with the same effect as a directive) and *put it on the ground* (another command with the same effect as a directive) *or die* (as discussed, an implied threat leading to the linguistic impoliteness output strategy of the gang leader attempting to 'threaten/frighten'; see Culpeper 1996). In effect, face-threat and face-attack are used as linguistic strategies to gain and maintain power and control of the situation (see Bousfield and Locher 2008), and this analysis tells us a huge amount regarding the way in which we are invited to read or interpret the gang leader's character. Further, such face-attacking strategies constitute what has been termed *impoliteness*. Bousfield (2010, p. 112) defines impoliteness like so:

> I take impoliteness as constituting the issuing of intentionally gratuitous and conflictive face-threatening acts (FTAs) that are purposefully performed:
>
> 1) Unmitigated, in contexts where mitigation (where mitigation equates with politeness) is required and/or

2) With deliberate aggression, that is, with the face threat exacerbated, 'boosted', or maximised in some way to heighten the face damage inflicted.

Furthermore, for impoliteness to be considered successful impoliteness, the intention of the speaker (or 'author') to 'offend' (threaten/damage face) must be understood by those in a receiver role.

Under the above definition, it should be obvious that the gang leader's utterance in Turn 7 (at least) is a prime candidate for recognition as 'impoliteness' (a technical term which encompasses outright linguistic aggression). Culpeper *et al.* (2003) and, by extension, Bousfield (2007b) postulate a series of predictable response tokens to such impoliteness. One is to meet and counter impolite aggression with impoliteness in return. This is what Eli (eventually) does in Turn 13. He utters his own conditional speech act of threat which attacks the gang leader's own positive and negative face. Eli's threat, 'Put that hand on me again, you won't get it back', attacks positive face as it indicates disapproval of the last time the gang leader put his hand on him with the use of 'again', and it attacks negative face as it implies loss of the hand – an attack on the 'freedom' of the gang leader to keep his own belongings, including his own body parts. We should also note as an aside that Eli is already conceptually and linguistically objectifying the gang leader's hand by describing it as '*that* hand' not 'your hand'. 'Your hand' implies non-detachability via a process of schematic recognition of body parts (generally, they stay attached). However, by using distal deixis 'that hand' indicates physical and emotional distance on Eli's part toward the hand of the gang leader; an emotional and physical expression that, seconds later, we find in actuality to be the case. Even analysis of language at the phrasal level can give stylistic insight into the mindset of individual characters within a scene.

It has been alluded to throughout, but of course the question remains as to how all this speech act usage and conversational implicature leads to notions and expressions of im/politeness to provide us with a process for audiences to 'read' or interpret individual characters in drama.

Language as a stylistic characterisation device

Culpeper (2001) leads the contemporary field of research with respect to the analysis of fictional (or dramatised) characters based on their dialogue. Working from within both linguistic and psychological paradigms, Culpeper produces an easily applicable framework for analysis by taking a wholly cognitive stylistic approach. In summary, he argues that readers or audiences/viewers of dramatic fiction embark on a process of inferencing about or understanding characters based on both pre-existing (also known as 'top-down') expectations that they have about the character/character type in question, and data-driven, (or in this case dialogue-driven, 'bottom-up') evidence that adds to, confirms, or fine-tunes our understanding of that specific character, or challenges it (in a believable way, to add to the progression of the narrative's plot development as well as characterisation). From this process (which I explicate below) he argues that we develop and apply a 'control system' for the reading of dramatic characters in texts or performance. His control system for comprehending character (see Figure 7.1) relies on PRIOR KNOWLEDGE (the application of top-down, schematically held understandings of the types of individual with which we're presented) and TEXTBASE and SURFACE STRUCTURE – essentially what the character says, and how s/he says it, respectively. His model is represented in Figure 7.1.

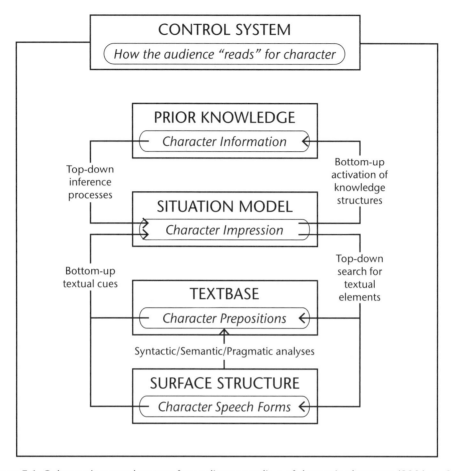

Figure 7.1 Culpeper's control system for audience reading of dramatic character (2001, p. 35).

In more detail, then, Culpeper's CONTROL SYSTEM (see Figure 7.1, above) suggests that we rely on both PRIOR KNOWLEDGE (pre-existing information about a character or character-type that we hold already) *and* the TEXTBASE (what the character says at any given point) and SURFACE STRUCTURES (how the character says what they say) to stylistically 'read', 'interpret' and understand character types and motivations.

Prior-knowledge – Top-down processing

This element of the model relies on our socially or culturally held view of certain 'prototypical' types of person, animal, or other entity in the world at large. With a healthy degree of relativity dependent upon the individual reader or viewer, such entities have shared characteristics by which they are 'understood' in society and the world in which we all live (even if the 'type' of character is a mythical, non-real entity, so long as the concept is alive and shared by members of society). Reference to these types is, in effect, an efficient way for a dramatic storyteller getting his or her (or their) message across as to what type of person you're dealing with.

For example, if a 1970s policeman, a medieval lord, a nineteenth century factory worker, the father of an abducted character, a lone traveller, a fairy princess, a post-apocalyptic gang member or even a dragon enters an appropriate dramatic-narrative scene, certain pre-existing assumptions are triggered based on our schematic, shared-background assumptions as to what such characters generally are (already understood to be) like, and what 'role' they (are generally assumed to) play in their text-world. As we get to know the individual character (via textbase and surface structure information; see below), we 'fill out' or add to our schemata for both the type of character they represent and the specific individual with which we are presented.

Textbase and surface structure – Bottom up processing:

This element relies on what a character says (the textbase) and how they say it (surface structure). For example, our character, the 1970s policeman *Regan* saying 'Put your trousers on, you're nicked!', while this is *propositionally* similar to the hypothetical and potentially more schematically expected utterance 'I'm arresting you on suspicion of X crime', is nevertheless delivered in a rather more informal or no nonsense style. Regan's textbase – what he says and, in speech act terms, what he *does* (arresting a suspected criminal) – by and large matches the audience's general understanding of what we expect of policemen generally. However, *how* he does it, in terms of how he utters the speech act of arrest – 'You're nicked!' – deviates from our expectations, and therefore Regan deviates from our schematic assumptions of policemen. We are able to 'fill out' or add to our specific 'Regan' schema which we carry forward to the next interaction he has, in that we now expect him to be a brash, forthright, unrepentant, unreconstructed, rough, tough, no-nonsense police officer.

Recommendations for practice

1. Consider how we can use the above pragmatic phenomena, and our understanding of them, to 'read' the characters of 'Mills' and 'Kidnapper' in the following transcription of a very famous scene from the 2008 film *Taken*. Further, try to explain why Mills' threat was not deemed successful by the kidnapper. However, what does this threat, and its unsuccessful reception, mean for how we are being invited to read (a) Mills' character and (b) the necessary plot development for the remainder of the film? (In more detail: Explain why there is a mismatch between our (as audience/viewers) top-down processing of Mills, and that of the Kidnapper as he reads Mills from Mills' threat. Further, ascertain the significance of this mismatch in contributing to the failure of Mills' threat, and the consequent construction of a narrative complicating action requiring resolution as the film unfolds.)

    Context: *Bryan Mills has just been speaking on the phone, from his home in the US, to his daughter who has gone on holiday with a female friend to Paris. As he was speaking to her, human traffickers broke into the apartment where they were staying and abducted Mills' daughter's friend and moments later, Mills' daughter. After Mills hears his daughter being abducted he hears her phone being picked up and detects breathing, but no voice. He begins speaking to whoever is now on the other end of the line, holding his daughter's phone:*

Mills

I don't know who you are. I don't know what you want. If you're looking for ransom I can tell you I don't have money, but what I do have are a very particular set of skills. Skills I've acquired over a very long career. Skills that make me a nightmare for people like you. If you let my daughter go now, that'll be the end of it. I will not look for you, I will not pursue you. But if you *don't*, I will look for you, I *will* find you ... and I will *kill* you.

5 second pause, then:

Kidnapper *(voice over phone)*

Good luck

(sound of phone being smashed before line goes dead)

2. In terms of further recommendations for practice, consider the centrality and critical importance of the use of pragmatic phenomena in character-to-character dialogue: consider how implicatures, face-oriented comments whether polite or impolite, and different speech acts (promises, offers, declaratives, for example) are all used. Find excerpts from dramatic texts of your choice in which one character uses one or more of the above. Explain how the character uses the pragmatic phenomena and then explain why the character uses them – what effect does their usage have on other characters and on us, as readers/viewers/audience members? What does a pragmatic analysis tell us in each case? Would we have been able to understand this without a pragmatic analysis? Do the pragmatic phenomena contribute to an understanding which creates a complicating action?

Future directions

Im/politeness research within pragmatics is taking a multimodal turn, not unlike the direction we see in stylistics (see McIntyre 2008) – consideration of character actions and the wider semiotics of specific scenes will all aid the reader/viewer/audience in understanding how we are being invited to understand the use of pragmatic phenomena.

Related topics

Conversation analysis and the cooperative principle, formalist stylistics, metaphor and metonymy, relevance theory, rhetoric and poetics.

Further reading

Archer, D. and Bousfield, D., 2010. See better, Lear? See Lear *better*! A corpus-based pragma-stylistic investigation of Shakespeare's *King Lear*. In: B. Busse and D. McIntyre, eds. *Language and style: In honour of Mick Short*. Basingstoke: Palgrave Macmillan, 183–203.

Here Archer and Bousfield attempt to show how a pragmastylistic reading of characters in terms of the dialogue they speak can be enhanced and corroborated by corpus stylistic analyses.

Bousfield, D., 2007a. Never a truer word said in jest: A pragmastylistic analysis of impoliteness as banter in Shakespeare's *Henry IV, Part I*. *In:* M. Lambrou and P. Stockwell, eds. *Contemporary Stylistics*. London: Continuum, 209–220.

In this chapter, I demonstrate how the application of pragmatic phenomena, specifically impoliteness, can give greater insight into the development of central characters before other evidence. In this case, we see Prince Hal developing autonomy and independence from Falstaff long before it is recognised as the case in *Henry IV, Part II*.

McIntyre, D., 2005. Logic, reality and mind style in Alan Bennett's *The Lady in the Van. Journal of Literary Semantics*, 34 (1), 21–40.

McIntyre provides an insightful argument by demonstrating that a stylistic analysis of characters' inferencing processes (as evidenced by their dialogue) allows the reader/audience/viewer to themselves infer the mental health and cognitive state of said characters. In this case, McIntyre demonstrates mental illness on the part of the titular character from Bennett's play, and is able to surmise that her part in a fatal road traffic accident years earlier is to blame for her mental instability.

McIntyre, D., 2008. Integrating multimodal analysis and the stylistics of drama: A multimodal perspective on Ian McKellen's *Richard III. Language and Literature*, 17, 309–334.

In this paper, McIntyre demonstrates how stylistics can profit from consideration of characters' movements, positioning on stage or screen, and direction of gaze/gesture. McIntyre shows how McKellan's portrayal of Richard III disambiguates the meaning of long-contested utterances in Gloucester's initial monologue and further explores how a multimodal analysis allows us to see how McKellan breaks the 'fourth wall' to directly address, and involve, the audience in Gloucester's devious plots to murder his way to the throne.

Short, M., 2007. How to make a drama out of a speech act: The speech act of apology in the film *A Fish Called Wanda*. *In:* D. L. Hoover and S. Lattig eds. *Stylistics: Prospect & retrospect*. Amsterdam: Rodopi, 169–189.

Short provides a timely reminder of the value of considering speech act theory in particular, and pragmatics in general, to produce effective and convincing stylistic analyses.

References

Archer, D. and Bousfield, D., 2010. See better, Lear? See Lear *better*! A corpus-based pragma-stylistic investigation of Shakespeare's *King Lear*. *In:* B. Busse and D. McIntyre, eds. *Language and style: In honour of Mick Short*. Basingstoke: Palgrave Macmillan, 183–203.

Austin, J. L., 1962. *How to do things with words*. Oxford: Oxford University Press.

Bousfield, D., 2007a. Never a truer word said in jest: A pragmastylistic analysis of impoliteness as banter in Shakespeare's *Henry IV, Part I*. *In:* M. Lambrou and P. Stockwell, eds. *Contemporary Stylistics*. London: Continuum, 209–220.

Bousfield, D., 2007b. Beginnings, middles and ends: A biopsy of the dynamics of impolite exchanges. *Journal of Pragmatics*, 39 (12), 2185–2216.

Bousfield, D., 2008. *Impoliteness in interaction*. Amsterdam/New York: John Benjamins.

Bousfield, D., 2010. Researching impoliteness and rudeness: Issues and definitions. *In:* Locher, M. and Graham, S. L., eds. *Interpersonal Pragmatics*. Berlin: Mouton de Gruyter, 101–134.

Bousfield, D. and Locher, M., eds. 2008. *Impoliteness in language*. Berlin: Mouton de Gruyter.

Brown, P. and Levinson, S. C., 1987. *Politeness: Some universals in language usage*. Cambridge: Cambridge University Press.

Culpeper, J., 1996. Towards an anatomy of impoliteness. *Journal of Pragmatics*, 25 (3), 335–361.

Culpeper, J., 2001. *Language and characterisation: People in plays and other texts*. London: Longman.

Culpeper, J., 2011. *Impoliteness: Using language to cause offence*. Cambridge: Cambridge University Press.

Culpeper, J., Bousfield, D and Wichmann, A., 2003. Impoliteness revisited: With special reference to dynamic and prosodic aspects. *Journal of Pragmatics*, 35 (10/11), 1545–1579.

Durkheim, E., 1915. *The elementary forms of the religious life: A study in religious sociology*. Trans J. Ward Swain. New York: Macmillan.

Goffman, E., 1955. On face-work: An analysis of ritual elements of social interaction. *Psychiatry: Journal for the Study of Interpersonal Processes,* 18 (3), 213–231.

Goffman, E., 1967. *Interaction ritual.* Chicago: Aldine Publishing.

Grice, P. H., 1975. Logic and conversation. *In:* P. Cole and J. Morgan, eds. *Speech acts (Syntax and Semantics 3)* New York: Academic Press, 41–58.

Holmes, J., 1984. Modifying illocutionary force. *Journal of Pragmatics*, 8 (1), 345–365.

Labov, W. and Waletzky, L., 1967. Narrative analysis: Oral versions of personal experience. *In:* J. Helm, ed. *Essays on the verbal and visual arts.* Seattle: University of Washington Press, 12–44.

Leech, G. N., 1983. *Principles of pragmatics.* London: Longman.

Locher, M. and Bousfield, D., 2008. Impoliteness and power in language. *In:* D. Bousfield and M. Locher eds. *Impoliteness in language.* Berlin: Mouton de Gruyter, 1–17.

McIntyre, D., 2005. Logic, reality and mind style in Alan Bennett's *The Lady in the Van. Journal of Literary Semantics*, 34 (1), 21–40.

McIntyre, D., 2006. *Point of view in plays: A cognitive stylistic approach to viewpoint in drama and other text-types.* Amsterdam: John Benjamins

McIntyre, D., 2008. Integrating multimodal analysis and the stylistics of drama: A multimodal perspective on Ian McKellen's *Richard III. Language and Literature*, 17, 309–334.

Scollon, R. and Scollon S. W., 2001. *Intercultural communication: A discourse approach.* London: Blackwell.

Searle, J . R., 1969. *Speech acts. An essay in the philosophy of language.* Cambridge: Cambridge University Press.

Searle, J. R., 1975. A taxonomy of illocutionary acts. *In:* K. Günderson, ed. *Language, mind, and knowledge.* Minneapolis: University of Minneapolis Press, 344–369.

Searle, J. R., 1979. *Expression and meaning: Studies in the theory of speech acts.* Cambridge: Cambridge University Press.

Short, M., 2007. How to make a drama out of a speech act: The speech act of apology in the film *A Fish Called Wanda. In:* D. L. Hoover and S. Lattig eds. *Stylistics: Prospect & retrospect.* Amsterdam: Rodopi, 169–189.

8

Stylistics, conversation analysis and the cooperative principle

Marina Lambrou

Introduction

Conversation analysis (CA) and the cooperative principle (CP) are two approaches associated with understanding structure and order in naturally occurring speech, and in particular, how speakers communicate cooperatively. While historically they are placed within differing sub-fields of linguistics, with CA in sociolinguistics and the CP in pragmatics, the emergence of *pragmatic stylistics* as a branch of stylistics combines approaches 'to answer questions about how (literary) language is used in context and how it contributes to the characterization of the protagonists in a literary piece of art or how power structures are created and so on.' (Nørgaard, Busse and Montoro 2010, p. 39). Studying spoken interaction in literary texts is likely to consider both the CA model and the CP together even though they are interested in different aspects of verbal communication. CA and the CP can be successfully applied as analytic tools to literary dialogue in drama and novels to gain insights into characterisation and characters' relationships with each other, and help us understand not only how coherence in spoken communication is maintained but also how meaning is intended by one speaker and inferred by another. This chapter describes CA and the CP, and illustrates how they can be applied for the analysis of spoken interaction in literary texts beyond the mechanics of turn-taking. The chapter also outlines historical perspectives as well as current contributions to the application of CA and the CP to the stylistic analysis of texts representing speech.

Conversation analysis

Conversation is a social activity that is prevalent in all human interaction. It can be simply defined as a form of linguistic communication that humans participate in to develop and maintain relationships. A conversation can be defined as 'any stretch of continuous speech between two or more people within audible range of each other who have the mutual intention to communicate' (Crystal and Davy 1975, p. 86). A further definition sees conversation as 'instances of speech exchange organization with variable turn order, turn size and turn content peculiar to a given occasion and the participants involved' (West and Zimmerman 1982, p. 515).

One approach to studying everyday talk developed out of a branch of American sociology called *ethnomethodology*, and in particular the work of Harold Garfinkel (1967). Garfinkel was concerned with making sense of common everyday behaviour and how 'social action is accomplished through the participant's use of tacit, practical and reasoning skills and competencies' (Woofitt 2005, p. 73). The study of talk was concerned with the analysis and interpretation of everyday, spoken interaction and the 'communicative competencies that informed ordinary, everyday conversation' (2005, p. 73). This was developed by Sacks and colleagues in their seminal paper *A simplest systematics for the organization of turn-taking for conversation* (Sacks, Schegloff, and Jefferson 1974). The study investigated how people organise their speech to allow them to get through a conversation without constantly interrupting or overlapping with other speakers so that all the speakers and listeners cooperate to take over from each other smoothly and rapidly. Not only did they attempt to identify the existence of fundamental 'rules' to spoken interaction, but also how talk can accomplish goals if used strategically. Sacks, Schegloff and Jefferson (1974) analysed naturally occurring conversation as a distinct form of spoken interaction and developed a model of conversation called Conversation Analysis. They found that conversation is 'realised through sets of practices which speakers can deploy in order to undertake particular actions in particular contexts and which will be recognised as achieving the appropriate action by other participants' (Liddicoat 2007, p. 5). Sacks *et al.* (1974) also found similar patterns, and concluded that conversation is a turn-taking activity based on a number of facts:

1. Speaker-change recurs, or at least occurs
2. Overwhelmingly, one party talks at a time
3. Occurrences of more than one speaker at a time are common, but brief
4. Transitions (from one turn to a next) with no gap and no overlap are common. Together with transitions characterised by slight gap or slight overlap, they make up the vast majority of transitions
5. Turn order is not fixed but varies
6. Turn size is not fixed but varies
7. Length of conversation is not specified in advance
8. What parties say is not specified in advance
9. Relative distribution of turns is not specified in advance
10. Number of parties can vary
11. Talk can be continuous or discontinuous
12. Turn-allocation techniques are obviously used. A current speaker may select a next speaker (as when he addresses a question to another party), or parties may self-select in starting to talk (pp. 700–701)

These patterns in turn-taking show that conversation is not randomly organised: participants need to work at making sense of what is going on to produce an orderly structure. Moreover, for successful conversational goals, participants should also make the content of their talk relevant and appropriate for their listeners and be sensitive to 'recipient design', whereby 'the talk by a party in a conversation is constructed or designed in ways which display an orientation and sensitivity to the particular other(s) who are the co-participants' (Sacks *et al.* 1974, p. 727). However, it should be noted that different cultures may have variations in the turn-taking organisation proposed by Sacks *et al.*, an extension which was developed in relation to conversational data from British and American English. (See Graddol, Cheshire and Swann 1994, p. 173.)

An example of naturally occurring conversation is presented in below – a conversation between two friends, Alexis and Emilios, as they reminisce about their younger days. (See Appendix for transcription key.)

1	E	We're always do crazy things like that of course Dover as well
	A	Oh oh yeah drove to Dover
	E	=we went down to Dover just for the night=
	A	=and we
5		stood on cliffs
	E	Yeah and the silly Turkish boy
	A	[laugh]
	E	[ ] oh my God he's like hanging off the edge of the cliffs you know
	A	=quite
10		literally hmm=
	E	='Are you alright?' 'Yeah yeah'. 'Can you get back please'
		Hmm. He goes 'Will you look at me doing this?'
	A	So many places aren't there?
	E	Hmm there's more there's Southend...
15	A	=Southend=
	E	There's definitely more...

Natural conversation between friends. (Author's data, Lambrou 2005)

This excerpt shows some of the normal non-fluency features associated with conversation, such as errors, pauses and unclear speech as well as overlapping/ simultaneous speech and rapid turn-taking showing a high involvement style. Coherence in the talk is maintained through the collaborative formation of the conversation, reflecting the speakers close relationship through shared experiences (see Lambrou 2003, 2005). Note also the backchannelling or feedback the speakers give to each other to indicate they are listening and engaged. (See Crystal and Davy 1969, 1975 for a discussion of normal non-fluency features.) In work on oral narratives of personal experience, Lambrou (2003) applied the CA framework to the dynamic conversation that occurred in peer group interviews. Specifically, the conversational talk that took place before, during and after the actual narration between informants was examined to understand how collaborative storytelling strategies take place, despite the constraints of a formal interview setting.

Conversational structure in a dialogue

In the fictional dialogue of literary works, one way of maintaining realism in the talk between characters is to present talk with the structure and features of real, naturally occurring interaction. This would mean presenting dialogue with a turn-taking organisation as proposed by Sacks *et al.* (1974) with occasional non-fluency errors such as interruptions, hesitations, pauses, errors and slips of the tongue to reflect real talk. To illustrate this point, it is useful to compare the natural conversation above with a literary representation of a conversation, below. This excerpt from Thomas Hardy's *Far from the Madding Crowd* is a conversation between a jealous Bathsheba and her husband Troy as they discuss the lock of a woman's hair that Troy keeps in his watch:

1	'…It is the hair of a young woman I was going to marry before I knew you'
	You ought to tell me her name, then.'
	'I cannot do that.'
5	'Is she married yet?'
	'No.'
	'Is she alive?'
	'Yes.'
10	'Is she pretty?'
	'Yes.'

From Far from the Madding Crowd *(Hardy 1874)*

This excerpt from Hardy presents a series of adjacency pairs (see section on the Cooperative Principle, below, and Schegloff 2007 for a description of adjacency pairs) in a question-answer format with none of the hesitations, interruptions or overlaps that one that might expect in such a difficult conversation. Instead, Troy's one word answers show his attempt to maintain control by revealing as little information as possible.

Another short excerpt from a literary conversation, this time from Jane Austen's *Pride and Prejudice* between Elizabeth Bennet and her father, includes some features of natural talk.

1	'Oh, papa, what news—what news? Have you heard from my uncle?'
	'Yes I have had a letter from him by express.'
	'Well, and what news does it bring—good or bad?'
	'What is there of good to be expected?' said he, taking the letter from
5	his pocket. 'But perhaps you would like to read it.'
	Elizabeth impatiently caught it from his hand. Jane now came up.
	'Read it aloud,' said their father, 'for I hardly know myself what it is about.'

Chapter 49. Pride and Prejudice *(Austen 1813)*

In this extract, there is use of repetition ('what news—what news' l. 1) and the use of ellipsis signalled by the use of a dash, which creates an abruptness in the grammatical structure of the sentence (l.3). However, there are none of the usual interruptions or overlaps found in emotional and dynamic interactions, which illustrates that conversational features are rarely reproduced in fictional representations of conversation. Toolan acknowledges the difference between natural and fictional conversation, which is 'tidied up', but there are also 'literary conventions at work governing the fictional representations of talk, so that the rendered text is quite other than a faithful transcription of a natural conversation' (1989, p. 195). The lack of normal non-fluency features is perhaps more evident in a dramatic dialogue, which Short (1996) points out is 'written to be spoken' (p. 174), and where they do occur 'they are perceived by readers and audience as having a *meaningful* function precisely because we know that the dramatist must have included them *on purpose*' (p. 177). Short illustrates this argument with an analysis of a short extract from *A Man for all Seasons*, in an exchange between Lord Norfolk and Chapuys:

1	NORFOLK	One moment, Roper, I'll do this! Thomas– (sees CHAPUYS) Oh. (He stares at CHAPUYS, hostile)
5	CHAPUYS	I was on the point of leaving, your Grace. Just a personal call. I have been trying ... er, to borrow a book – a book but without success – you're sure you've no copy, my lord?

Robert Bolt A Man for All Seasons, *Act II (1960)*

In this meeting, the awkwardness between the characters is conveyed in several ways: Norfolk stops dead mid-sentence and utters 'Oh' in surprise at seeing Chapuys unexpectedly (1.2). Chapuys tries to extricate himself from Norfolk's presence by pretending he is there to borrow a book, but his discomfort is shown by a pause and the use of the filler 'er', his repetitive use of 'a book' and a sharp clause change indicated by two dashes (ll.4–5). While these are characteristics of natural, unrehearsed speech, they are used dramatically by the author to show the uneasiness in the relationship between Norfolk and Chapuys. (Also, see Chapter 7 in this volume on stylistics, speech acts and im/politeness theory).

Explorations of conversational talk in literary work have been discussed in a number of scholarly works, each with a specific focus. Thomas (1997), for example, investigates how Waugh (1930) in *Vile Bodies* exploits the comedy arising from misunderstandings in telephone communication brought about by the medium's lack of visual aids and the characters' consequent reliance on verbal cues only. As Thomas points out, analysis of this conversation has tended to focus on what the characters *do not* say to each other, and how inhibited they are in their expression, which perhaps reflect their mental states. In other work on Waugh's *Black Mischief,* Thomas's analysis of multiparty talk notes that a character's intentions can be conveyed in the turn-taking organisation of multiparty talk where:

> temporary alliances may be forged and minor victories achieved ... despite the apparent triviality and surface politeness of the talk, the characters are capable of dealing fairly brutally with one another by attending to others or deliberately excluding them.
>
> *(2002, p. 681)*

Conversational exchange that conveys more that just the content of talk is outlined further in the following sections on the CP, which attempt to understand the interplay between characters, talk and their relationship with each other not just through the mechanics of interaction but also through inferences that are based on what people *say*.

Powerful *and* powerless speakers *in dramatic dialogue*

Some of the earliest work on CP in stylistics tended to focus on characters and their relationships with and intentions towards other characters. By analysing the sequence of turns and revealing through interpretation how they are meaningful, Short (1996) offers a useful set of questions to identify the most *powerful* and *powerless* speakers through a quantitative analysis of the interaction. Short's list of questions considers the natural characteristics of conversation, such as turn-taking length, topic control and interruptions, to help understand and gain insights into what is really taking place between speakers. In the list of questions, reproduced below, he indicates his intuitions with an 'X' in the relevant columns and asks whether our intuitions coincide with his:

	Powerful speakers	Powerless speakers
Who has most turns?	X	
Who has the least?		X
Who has the longest turns?	X	
Who has the shortest?		X
Who initiates conversational exchanges?	X	
Who responds?		X
Who controls the conversational topic?	X	
Who follows the topics of others?		X
Who interrupts?	X	
Who is interrupted?		X
Who uses terms of address not marked for respect (e.g. first name only)?	X	
Who uses terms of address marked for respect (e.g. title + last name)?		X
Who allocates turns to others?	X	

Identifying *powerful* and *powerless* speakers in dramatic dialogue (from Short, 1996, p. 206)

Short applies these questions to a conversation from Shakespeare's *Richard III* between the Duke of Buckingham and King Richard in the presence of Lord Stanley, and reveals the subtle distribution of power and status between these characters (see Short 1996, pp. 206–210 for the analysis).

Textual cues in characterisation

An understanding of characters and their relationships with one another is also the focus of Culpeper's (2001) work on language and characterisation in drama (see also Chapter 7 in this volume). Culpeper's interest lies with the '*process* of characterisation, rather than with the character – the output of that process' (p. 1). He explains that this can be gained by considering several factors: how a reader's prior knowledge contributes to characterisation; how a reader infers characteristics from the text; and what textual cues exist in characterisation. His model of characterisation suggests that both top-down and bottom-up processing take place when readers engage with a text, and it is the interaction between these two cognitive processes that helps to form an impression of a character. Put simply, the pre-existing schemas of top-down processing can be drawn from real-life experiences and from fiction, while bottom-up processing relies on analysing textual cues for linguistic behaviour, including lexical items such as *keywords* or what Enkvist (1973) calls *style-markers* that are *spoken* by the character. (See McIntyre (2010, p. 167) for an illustration of this type of cognitive processing using the example of Priestly's (1947) play *An Inspector Calls*.)

Culpeper's investigation of the textual cues for presenting another dimension of characterisation takes a multi-disciplinary approach that includes CA and pragmatics. In his analysis of the conversation in *Richard III* between King Richard and the Duke of Buckingham (discussed above), Culpeper analyses the distribution of talk between characters by applying the CA model not only to understand how participants interact with each other but also to understand 'implicit' information about a character that is derived by inference through both verbal and non verbal cues. So, while Short's analysis provides insights mostly into the distribution of power between characters, Culpeper's also reveals additional information about the participants, such as King Richard's deliberate avoidance of the issues altogether, and conversely, Buckingham's 'robust' character in his tenacity to pursue his claim. (For a full discussion of this analysis, see Culpeper, 2001, pp. 175–180. See also Chapter 7 in this volume for a description of politeness and the notion of 'positive face' and 'negative face' for further insights into the relationships between characters through conversational dialogue).

While CA offers one level of understating of the characters when applied to literary dialogue in drama, the interplay between characters and their relationship can also be conveyed beyond the organisation of talk. The following section explores the concept of a CP for how participants communicate in a meaningful and cooperative way, and provides a further analytic tool for the exploration of conversational talk.

The cooperative principle

The study of cooperation in conversation was the focus for H.P. Grice (1975) in *Logic and conversation*, which developed out of language use and pragmatics for how individuals communicate cooperatively. This study was presented in his classic series of William James lectures at Harvard in 1967, which was eventually published together with his other influential work as *Studies in the way of words* in 1989. According to Grice, exchanges should be 'cooperative efforts' and have 'a common purpose or set of purposes, or at least a mutually accepted direction'. He proposed a general Cooperative Principle to account for how cooperation can take effect. He defined the CP as follows: 'Make your conversational contribution such as it is required, at the stage at which it occurs, by the accepted purpose or direction of the talk exchange in which you are engaged' (p. 45). Grice proposed four sets of rules or 'maxims' for the Principle that must be adhered to, listed below:

Quantity: 1. Make your contribution as informative as is required for the current purpose of the exchange)
2. Do not make your contribution more informative than is required

Quality: 1. Do not say what you believe to be false
2. Do not say that for which you lack adequate evidence

Relation: 1. Be relevant

Manner: 1. Avoid obscurity of expression
2. Avoid ambiguity
3. Be brief (avoid unnecessary prolixity)
4. Be orderly.

Grice's Maxims of Conversation *(1975, p. 57)*

Although Grice presents the maxims as imperatives, Cooper points out that 'they do not rule conversation in any sense. We rarely fail to observe the maxims casually, for no reason, but we do fail to observe them intentionally for a variety of reasons' (1998, p. 57). One of the reasons is when we say something indirectly so that participants may fail to fulfil a maxim, and this can be achieved in several ways by:

a. *violating* a maxim, whereby the hearer is not aware that what is said is breaking the maxim, for example, by a speaker lying or changing the topic, so that they may be misled as a result; or
b. *flouting* a maxim, whereby the hearer is aware the maxim is being broken, and also, there is additional meaning that the hearer has to interpret.

Grice called this additional meaning that has to be interpreted *conversational implicature*. Often the meaning is intuitive but the hearer needs to go through a process of recognising whether the utterance is appropriate and then interpret what is actually being said. The fact that conversational implicature takes place shows that individuals often fail to conform to the maxims of conversation, and that the intended meaning is not always inferred because pragmatic meaning does not always equate with the conventionally agreed meaning of semantic denotation. (Grice distinguished between *conversational implicature*, which 'must be capable of being worked out', and *conventional implicature*, which can be grasped intuitively (1975, p. 51) and is not derived from pragmatic principles like the maxims. See Levinson 1983.)

Conversational implicature can often be found in the unexpected reply in an adjacency pair. Adjacency pairs are common discourse features in conversational structure and can be described as a pair of utterances where the second contribution is functionally dependent on the first, such as those found in a greeting or a question–answer sequence. For example:

Cooperative example

A: How's work?
B: Okay, thanks.

However, naturally occurring speech often contains sequences that seem uncooperative if we only consider what the speaker says, as in the second contribution below:

Uncooperative reply

Bi: I can't wait for my holiday

or

Bii: Get lost!

Here, B's replies flagrantly flout the maxim of *relation* (Bi) and *relation* and *manner* (Bii). The hearer would be able to make an intuitive interpretation of what is being meant by working through a two-stage process of first recognising whether the utterance is appropriate or relevant, and secondly, interpreting what is actually being said. Levinson (1983) points out that despite this *apparent* failure of cooperation, we try to interpret the reply as 'nevertheless co-operative at some deeper (non superficial) level' (p. 102) by trying to make a connection between the utterances. An inference or conversational implicature is made to interpret what is meant. In the example above, B's indirect replies imply he is unhappy at work.

Unexpected replies are often used as a stylistic device to create humour because they flout and violate conversational maxims, as can be seen in Richard Curtis's screenplay for the film *Four Weddings and a Funeral* (1994). This brief exchange between Charles, the main protagonist and a wedding guest takes place at one of the weddings:

1	Charles	How do you do? My name's Charles
	Wedding guest	Don't be ridiculous. Charles died years ago.
	Charles	Must be a different Charles, I think.
	Wedding guest	Are you telling me I don't know my own brother?
5	Charles	No.

From Four Weddings and a Funeral *(1994)*

Charles's initial greeting is met with the startling 'Don't be ridiculous...' (1.2), which flouts the maxims of *relation* and *manner* for the abrupt way in which it is delivered. This unexpected response gives Charles no choice but to violate the maxim of *quality* by saying 'No' (1.5) to the wedding guest's question, 'Are you telling me I don't know my own brother?' as a way of avoiding any further confrontation and confusion. Grice noted that there are additional maxims such as 'Be polite' that are normally observed in conversational interaction (1975, p. 47). This double meaning of cooperation – as in Grice's technical meaning and the more general meaning of the word– is, according to Davies (2007), problematic and causes issues with interpretation. Davies argues that:

> The use of these two terms in the same area of linguistics has muddied the waters, and it is perhaps unsurprising that some confusion has occurred [...] CP is assumed to take on a meaning rather closer to that of the general meaning of 'cooperation' – thus leading to what I have termed 'cooperation drift'.
>
> *(p. 2328)*

The earlier sections in this chapter outlined how the dialogue of drama and novels draws on the rules of conversation analysis to produce realistic scenarios for characters as well as highlight the interpersonal relationships between them. However, interesting stylistic effects can be achieved by exploiting the rules and norms of interaction, such as flouting and violating conversational maxims so that talk is not always coherent or meaningful, bringing to the text a level of realism that is found in natural conversation. An extreme example would be a total subversion of the conversational maxims, where the conversation is purposeless, in terms of not being goal-orientated, as well as being nonsensical and incoherent. This style of writing belongs to a particular genre of drama, *The Theatre of the Absurd*, and is associated with writers such as Harold Pinter and Tom Stoppard. A well-known example is Stoppard's *Rosencrantz and Guildenstern are Dead* (1967), where the darkly humorous but illogical dialogue between the main protagonists, Rosencrantz and Guildenstern, intentionally bewilders the audience who are trying to make sense of the plot:

1	Ros	What's the matter with you today?
	Guil	When?
	Ros	What?
	Guil	Are you deaf?
5	Ros	Am I dead?
	Guil	Yes or no?
	Ros	Is there a choice?
	Guil	Is there a God?

From Tom Stoppard's Rosencrantz and Guildenstern are Dead *(1967, p. 33)*

The prolonged flouting of the conversational maxims foregrounds the continuous wordplay between the characters, who appear to be completely *in sync* with each other despite their uncooperative answers. Despite this 'layering' through banter, Rosencrantz and Guildenstern are able to maintain a dialogue even if it does appear to be incoherent and we assume the playwright is observing pragmatic principles at a 'higher' level.

Conversational maxims and characterisation

Exploiting conversational maxims can also provide insights into characterisation, as discussed earlier in the chapter, as the interplay between characters in how they communicate and respond with each other highlights their relationship with each other. In the classic showdown between Elizabeth Bennet and Lady Catherine de Bourgh in Austen's *Pride and Prejudice* there are numerous examples of flouted conversational maxims in the final clash of words. In both examples below, Elizabeth deliberately refuses to answer Lady Catherine's questions about her intentions in relation to marrying Mr Darcy. It is important to bear in mind that Lady Catherine is a member of the upper classes and is of a higher social ranking than Elizabeth. The social norms of the time would expect her questions to be answered politely.

Lady Catherine de Bourgh	'Has he, has my nephew, made you an offer of marriage?'
Elizabeth Bennet	'Your ladyship has declared it to be impossible.'

And:

Lady Catherine de Bourgh	'You are then resolved to have him?'
Elizabeth Bennet	'I have said no such thing. I am only resolved to act in that manner, which will, in my own opinion, constitute my happiness, without reference to *you*, or to any person so wholly unconnected with me.'

Pride and Prejudice *by Jane Austen (1813) Chapter 56*

Both of Elizabeth's replies can be described as dispreferred answers to Lady Catherine's forthright questions: in the first example the usually respectful Elizabeth flouts the maxim of *relation* by not being relevant and answering 'yes' or 'no', whereas in the second example Elizabeth flouts the maxims of *quantity, relation* and *manner* because she says more than is required, is not being relevant and is not being particularly brief in her reply. Elizabeth's refusal to cooperate with Lady Catherine confirms Elizabeth's outspokenness, intelligence and verbal skills, while also revealing her true feelings for Mr Darcy. The assumption that speakers tacitly agree to cooperate by conforming to the conversational maxims to achieve the same goals is not what is important to Elizabeth in this exchange.

An unusual way of communicating can also provide profound insights into a character, particularly if the character has a condition that affects how they interact and socialise with others. This is apparent in the narrative style of the fifteen-year-old protagonist Christopher Boone in Mark Haddon's *The Curious Incident of the Dog in the Night-Time* published in 2003. Christopher has an autistic spectrum disorder (ASD), identified as Asperger's syndrome though this is never explicitly stated in the book. As the story progresses, it becomes evident through the style of narration and conversational interaction that Christopher is different. Semino (2014) in her chapter *Language, mind and autism in Mark Haddon's The Curious Incident of the Dog in the Night-Time* discusses many of these salient linguistic features in an attempt to understand how the character's mind is constructed. In her discussion she concludes that Christopher 'seems to have difficulties with the maxims of Quantity and Relation' because 'he has difficulties providing information at the level of detail that would normally be expected from a fifteen-year-old' and provides detailed descriptions of his observations 'that will not turn out to be relevant to any subsequent developments in the plot' (p. 9). Semino argues that:

> the ways in which Christopher provides irrelevant and inadequate information, both as a character and as a narrator, are nonetheless informative for the reader, as they lead to inferences about why he behaves like this (and not just in the above extract, but consistently, or consistently enough, throughout the novel). Readers are likely to conclude that Christopher's communicative behaviour is involuntary rather than deliberate, i.e. not a narratorial or conversational strategy but the result of a genuine inability to assess what information is relevant and how much detail is required. In Gricean terms, Christopher's behaviour does not, I would argue, constitute a violation or flout of the relevant maxims (since both are intentional strategies), but rather an 'infringement'.
>
> *(p. 20)*

An 'infringement' can be described as being committed by a 'speaker who, with no intention of generating an implicature and with no intention of deceiving, fails to observe a maxim is said to 'infringe' the maxim' (J. Thomas 1995, p. 74). Clearly, Christopher's cognitive impairment is carefully constructed through his style of communication and readers are able to understand that the central character is different, even interpreting that he has autism spectrum disorder. (Interestingly, tests using relevance theory are now being applied for the diagnosis of ASD because Relevance Theory can predict levels of communicative competence among subjects with autism. See Happé 1993 for a fuller discussion, and Chapter 9 of this volume on Stylistics and relevance theory.)

Another fictional character who has generated much discussion for his peculiar style of interaction is Sherlock Holmes, created by Sir Arthur Conan Doyle. Noted for his obsessive interest in solving cases and his extraordinary powers of deduction, relational thinking and observation, there is evidence to suggest that he may also be on the autism spectrum (though this would not have been conceptualised as such in Doyle's time). This is particularly evident in how Doyle constructs the character through a particular style of conversation and interaction, as seen in Holmes's first meeting with Dr Watson in *A Study In Scarlet*, first published in 1887. Prior to their meeting a mutual friend, Stamford, attempts to prepare Watson for Holmes's idiosyncratic manner, saying that Holmes is 'a little queer in his ideas

[…] His studies are very desultory and eccentric, but he has amassed lot of out-of-the way knowledge which would astonish his professors' and 'he can be communicative enough when the fancy seizes him'. These clues to characterisation forewarn both the readers and Watson, and they are evident in the dialogue that follows between Watson and Holmes:

---

1   "Dr. Watson, Mr. Sherlock Holmes," said Stamford, introducing us.

"How are you?" he said cordially, gripping my hand with a strength for
which I should hardly have given him credit. "You have been in Afghanistan,
5   I perceive."

"How on earth did you know that?" I asked in astonishment.

"Never mind," said he, chuckling to himself. "The question now is about
10   haemoglobin. No doubt you see the significance of this discovery of mine?"

"It is interesting, chemically, no doubt," I answered, "but practically—"

"Why, man, it is the most practical medico-legal discovery for years. Don't
15   you see that it gives us an infallible test for blood stains. Come over here
now!" He seized me by the coat-sleeve in his eagerness, and drew me over to
the table at which he had been working. "Let us have some fresh blood," he
said, digging a long bodkin into his finger, and drawing off the resulting drop
of blood in a chemical pipette. "Now, I add this small quantity of blood to a
20   litre of water. You perceive that the resulting mixture has the appearance of
pure water. The proportion of blood cannot be more than one in a million. I
have no doubt, however, that we shall be able to obtain the characteristic
reaction." As he spoke, he threw into the vessel a few white crystals, and
then added some drops of a transparent fluid. In an instant the contents
assumed a dull mahogany colour, and a brownish dust was precipitated to the
bottom of the glass jar. "Ha! ha!" he cried, clapping his hands, and looking as
delighted as a child with a new toy. "What do you think of that?"

"It seems to be a very delicate test," I remarked.

(From http://www.gutenberg.org/files/244/244-h/244-h.htm*)*

Sherlock's verbose style and use of medical and scientific terms foreground this character immediately to readers, and to Watson, as someone who is highly intelligent but also eccentric. Moreover, his extended turns at 15 flout Grice's maxims of *quantity* and *manner* and provide further evidence of Holmes's unusual but engaging character.

Conversational implicature, state of mind and *Dramatic Irony*

We have seen that characterisation can be achieved by interpreting textual cues in the conversation, and that what one says and what one means are not always in agreement, giving rise to implicatures. In drama, Culpeper (2001) explains that sometimes implicatures can be worked out by both characters on the stage and the audience, or they may only be worked out by the audience, leaving the other characters on the stage oblivious as to what is going on. This is referred to as *dramatic irony*:

> At one level we have the playwright conveying some sort of message to the audience: within that message we have an embedded level of discourse where character A conveys a message to character B. Character A can flout maxims and generate implicatures for character B, implicatures which the audience can usually also work out. However, character A can also generate implicatures which only the audience can work out, and dramatic irony results.
>
> *(p.181)*

This is illustrated in *Hamlet* in several ways: the character Hamlet colludes with the audience by informing them of his plans and actions through soliloquies and through the dramatic device of the aside, where he speaks directly to the audience. In Act II, Scene 2, Hamlet's nonsensical replies to Polonius are understood by the audience, who know that Hamlet is deliberately feigning madness:

1	Lord Polonius	[Aside] How say you by that? Still harping on my daughter: yet he knew me not at first; he said I was a fishmonger: he is far gone, far gone: and truly in my youth I suffered much extremity for love; very near this. I'll speak to him again. What do you read, my lord?
5		
	Hamlet	Words, words, words.
10	Lord Polonius	What is the matter, my lord?
	Hamlet	Between who?
	Lord Polonius	I mean, the matter that you read, my lord?
15		
	Hamlet	Slanders, sir: for the satirical rogue says here that old men have grey beards, that their faces are wrinkled, their eyes purging thick amber and plum-tree gum and that they have a plentiful lack of wit, together with most weak hams: all which, sir, though I most powerfully and potently believe, yet I hold it not honesty to have it thus set down, for yourself, sir, should be old as I am, if like a crab you could go backward.
20		

From Act II, Scene 2 of Hamlet

Hamlet's unwillingness to cooperate is very clear. Each time Polonius asks Hamlet a question (ll.6, 10; 14), Hamlet deliberately violates the maxims of conversation with the effect that Polonius misinterprets Hamlet's responses. This can be seen in Table 8.1.

Table 8.1 Non-cooperation in *Hamlet*

Polonius (question)	Hamlet (answer)	Maxim violated
What do you read, my lord?	Words, words, words	*Relation, Quantity*
What is the matter, my lord?	Between who?	*Relation*
I mean, the matter that you read, my lord?	Slanders, sir: for the satirical rogue says here that old men have grey beards, that their faces are wrinkled, their eyes purging thick amber and plum-tree gum and that they have ... if like a crab you could go backward.	*Manner, Relation, Quantity*

Polonius is unaware that Hamlet is deliberately misunderstanding his questions in a show of pretence, which further convinces him that Hamlet is mad. Unfortunately, this unusual behaviour eventually leads to tragedy for both Polonius and Hamlet.

A deliberate and dramatic flouting of maxims can also be found in Act 4 Scene 1 of *Othello*, in the dialogue between Iago and Othello. In this scene, Iago skilfully manipulates Othello into believing that Othello's wife Desdemona has been unfaithful. Iago's flouting of maxims throughout by giving uncooperative and dispreferred answers shows how implicatures are triggered in the hearer, which forces the hearer to process the gap in what is said to try to interpret what is meant. Having sown the seed of doubt in Othello's mind, Iago slowly succeeds in getting his revenge (although Othello's own insecurities also contribute to his downfall). Iago succeeds by not stating *explicitly* what he is thinking, which leads to tragic consequences and the demise of all three characters.

Act 4, Scene 1
Enter Othello and Iago

1	Iago	Will you think so?
	Othello	Think so, Iago?
	Iago	What,
		To kiss in private?
5	Othello	An unauthoriz'd kiss.
	Iago	Or to be naked with her friend abed
		An hour, or more, not meaning any harm?
	Othello	Naked in bed, Iago, and not mean harm?
		It is hypocrisy against the devil:
10		They that mean virtuously, and yet do so,
		The devil their virtue tempts, and they tempt heaven.
	Iago	So they do nothing, 'tis a venial slip;
		But if I give my wife a handkerchief–
	Othello	What then?
15	Iago	Why, then, 'tis hers, my lord; and, being hers,
		She may, I think, bestow't on any man.
	Othello	She is protectress of her honour too,
		May she give that?
	Iago	Her honour is an essence that's not seen,

20		They have it very oft that have it not:
		But for the handkerchief,–
	Othello	By heaven, I would most gladly have forgot it:
		Thou said'st, (O, it comes o'er my memory,
		As doth the raven o'er the infected house,
25		Boding to all) he had my handkerchief.
	Iago	Ay, what of that?
	Othello	That's not so good now.
	Iago	What if I had said I had seen him do you wrong?
		Or heard him say—as knaves be such abroad,
30		Who having, by their own importunate suit,
		Or voluntary dotage of some mistress,
		Convinced or supplied them, cannot choose
		But they must blab–
	Othello	Hath he said anything?
35	Iago	He hath, my lord; but be you well assur'd,
		No more than he'll unswear.
	Othello	What hath he said?
	Iago	Faith, that he did … I know not what he did.
	Oth.	But what?
40	Iago.	Lie.
	Othello	With her?
	Iago	With her, on her, what you will.
	Othello.	Lie with her, lie on her?–We say lie on her, when
		they belie her, – lie with her, zounds, that's fulsome!
45		Handkerchief-confessions-handkerchief! To confess,
		and be hanged for his labour. First, to be hanged, and
		then to confess; I tremble at it. Nature would
		not invest herself in such shadowing passion without
		some instruction. It is not words that shake me thus.
50		Pish! Noses, ears and lips. Is't possible?–Confess?
		–Handkerchief? – 0 devil! [*He falls down*].

There has clearly been a shift in the power relationship between these characters, because despite Iago's lower status and shorter turns, his clever manipulation of Othello through insinuation and the flouting of conversational maxims shows him to be more powerful than Othello at this juncture in the play. (This dialogue can be mapped onto Short's checklist for powerful and powerless speakers, presented earlier in the chapter. for an interesting discussion.)

Recommendations for practice

Perhaps the best way to gain insights into the applications and interpretations of conversation analysis and Grice's maxims in literary dialogue is for students to undertake their own analysis. Several of the examples provided in this chapter, which have not been analysed in detail but presented to exemplify characterisation, provide useful excerpts for exploration. These include the dialogue in the previous section from *Othello*, Act 4 Scene 1, between

Othello and Iago, and the dialogue from Doyle's *A Study in Scarlet*, between Sherlock Holmes, Dr Watson and Stamford.

For each excerpt:

1. Analyse the interaction using Short's checklist of questions (i.e. who has the most turns; who has the fewest; who has the longest turns, etc.) to identify *powerful* and *powerless* speakers. See the section '*powerful and powerless speakers in dramatic dialogue*'. What is really going on between the characters? Is the distribution of power subtle or clearly evident?

2. Analyse the interaction using Grice's Conversational Maxims presented in the section '*conversational maxims and characterisation*'. Identify any examples of dispreferred responses to questions, and examples of any flouting or infringement of maxims. What further insights into characterisation does this analysis provide? What is revealed about the relationship between these characters from the way they communicate with each other?

3. Both Shakespeare's and Conan Doyle's works have been adapted for the screen and television. Analyse the film and television version of the above scenes to compare interactions. (It may be necessary to produce a transcript if the screenplay is not available.) Analyse these dialogues using Short's checklist of questions, then apply Grice's maxims – as in questions 1 and 2. How do the two dialogues compare to the original written versions? Does characterisation and the relationship between the protagonists remain the same? If there are differences, where can these be found?

Future directions

Since Grice first proposed the Cooperative Principle and the notion of conversational maxims, there have been further developments on the theory of talk which have produced several post-Gricean models of implicature. These models, which Nørgaard, Busse and Montoro (2010) describe as 'arguably, reductionist in outlook' (p. 69), reduce the number of Grice's maxims to a smaller number. One post-Gricean development is Sperber and Wilson's *Relevance Theory* (1995). Sperber and Wilson felt that the Gricean maxims were vague and overlapping, and proposed a radically different approach that replaces Grice's *Relation* or *Relevance* maxim with something more efficient. Further developments of Grice's maxims, known as neo-Gricean approaches, also set out to revise Grice's maxims to reduce overlaps and redundancy. The most well-known approaches were those proposed by Horn (1984, 2007), Horn and Ward (2004) and Levinson (1987, 1995, 2000). Building on the work of Grice, Horn proposed two principles: Q Principle for Quantity and R Principle for Relation:

Q Principle

> Make your contribution sufficient
> Say as much as you can (given R)

R Principle

> Make your contribution necessary
> Say no more than you must (given Q)

The Q Principle subsumes Grice's maxims of *Quantity* and the first two maxims of *Manner* (1. Avoid obscurity of expression and 2. Avoid ambiguity), and the R Principle subsumes the maxims of *Relation* and one of the maxims of *Manner* (3. Be brief). For Horn, the maxim of *Quality* cannot be reduced and is outside this analysis. (See Clark 2013 for a fuller discussion of Horn and also Levinson's models, which are not discussed here.) Chapman's (2012) stylistic analysis of the implicatures in Sayers's *Gaudy Nights* applies Horn's theory of communication to understand 'implicit aspects of the communication between characters in a text, or between narrator and reader (pp. 21–22).

There is no doubt that the CP is a key aspect of Grice's framework in his *Theory of Conversation* and that current approaches have developed from it, some retaining much of the spirit of Grice's approach (e.g. Horn and Levinson's neo-Gricean approaches), while others diverge quite significantly (e.g. the post-Gricean *relevance theory*). This chapter has dealt with Grice's original ideas, and further information on relevance theory can be found in the following chapter in this volume (Chapter 9) and in Clark (2013).

Related topics

Narratology, relevance theory, stylistics, drama and performance, speech acts and (im) politeness theory

Further reading

Levinson, S. C., 1983. *Pragmatics*. Cambridge: Cambridge University Press.

Levinson presents a detailed discussion of conversational implicature with a critique of its applications in Chapter 3 of *Pragmatics*.

Mandala, S., 2007. *Twentieth century drama dialogue as ordinary talk: Speaking between the lines*. London: Ashgate.

See Mandala for her linguistic study of dialogue in four modern plays (by Pinter, Rattigan, Wesker and Ayckbourn) that engage with and exploit naturalistic models of speech.

Piazza, R., 1999. Dramatic discourse approached from a conversational analysis perspective: Catherine Hayes's *Skirmishes* and other contemporary plays. *Journal of Pragmatics*, 31 (8), 1001–1023.

Piazza presents a pragmatic perspective of the use of conversational repair strategies in dramatic discourse.

Toolan, M., 1989. Analysing conversation in fiction: An example from Joyce's *Portrait*. In: R. Carter and P. Simpson, eds. *Language, discourse and literature*. London: Routledge, 195–211.

Toolan's analysis of a conversation from Joyce's *Portrait of the Artist as a Young Man* provides a stylistic analysis of conversational structure, focusing on the distribution of 'moves' and the different strategies employed by different characters.

Spitz, A., 2010. The music of argument: The portrayal of argument in Ian McEwan's *On Chesil Beach*. *Language and Literature*, 19 (2), 197–220.

Spitz explores the underlying conflict of real-life talk in McEwan's *On Chesil Beach* to understand how authenticity can be achieved in fictional dialogue.

Thomas, B., 2012. *Fictional dialogue: Speech and conversation in the modern and postmodern novel*. Nebraska: University of Nebraska.

Thomas brings together a range of theories to explore fictional dialogue from literature, popular fiction, and nonlinear narratives to understand the development of the characters and their intentions through their speech.

References

Austen, J., 2010. [1813] *Pride and prejudice*. Oxford: Oxford University Press.

Bolt, R., 1960. *A man for all seasons*. Harlow, Essex: Heinemann.

Chapman, S., 2012. Towards a neo-Gricean stylistics: Implicature in Dorothy L. Sayers's *Gaudy Night*. *Journal of Literary Semantics*, 41 (2), 139–153.

Clark, B., 2013. *Relevance theory*. Cambridge: Cambridge University Press.

Cooper, M.M., 1998. Implicature, convention and *The Taming of the Shrew*. In: J. Culpeper, M. Short and P. Verdonk, eds. *Exploring the Language of Drama: From Text to Context*. London: Routledge, 54–66.

Crystal, D. and Davy, D., 1969. *Investigating English style*. Bloomington: Indiana University Press.

Crystal, D. and Davy, D., 1975. *Advanced conversational English*. Essex: Longman Group Ltd.

Culpeper, J., 2001. *Language and characterisation: People in plays and other texts*. London: (Longman) Pearson Education.

Curtis, R., 1994. *Four weddings and a funeral*. Online. available at http://www.script-o-rama.com/movie_scripts/f/four-weddings-and-a-funeral-script.html (Accessed 8 April 2012).

Davies, B., 2007. Grice's cooperative principle: Meaning and rationality. *Journal of Pragmatics*, 39 (12), 2308–2331.

Doyle, A. C., 1897. *A study in scarlet*. London: Ward, Lock & Co. Online. Available at http://sherlock-holm.es/stories/html/stud.html#Chapter-1 (Accessed 3 April 2012).

Enkvist, N. E., 1973. *Linguistic stylistics*. Berlin: Mouton.

Garfinkel, H., 1967. *Studies in ethnomethodology*. Cambridge: Polity.

Graddol, D., Cheshire, J. and Swann, J., 1994. *Describing language*. 2nd edn. Maidenhead, Berks: Open University Press.

Grice, H. P., 1975. Logic and conversation. In: P. Cole and J. Morgan, eds. *Syntax and semantics, III: Speech acts*. New York: Academic Press, 41–58.

Grice, H. P., 1989. *Studies in the way of words*. Cambridge, MA: Harvard University Press.

Haddon, M., 2003. *The curious incident of the dog in the night-time*. London: Vintage.

Happé, F. G. E., 1993. Communicative competence and theory of mind in autism: A test of relevance theory. *Cognition,* 48 (2), 101–119.

Hardy, T., 1994. [1874] *Far from the madding crowd*. London: Penguin.

Horn, L., 1984. Toward a new taxonomy of pragmatic inference: Q-based and R-based implicature. In: D. Schiffrin, ed. *Meaning, form and use in context (GURT '84)*. Washington: Georgetown University Press, 11–42.

Horn, L., 2007. Neo-Gricean pragmatics: A Manichaean manifesto. In: N. Burton-Roberts, ed. *Pragmatics*. Basingstoke: Palgrave, 158–183.

Horn, L. and Ward, G., eds. 2004. *The handbook of pragmatics*. Oxford: Blackwell.

Lambrou, M., 2003. Collaborative oral narratives of general experience: When an interview becomes a conversation. *Language and Literature*, 12 (2), 153–174.

Lambrou, M., 2005. *Story patterns in oral narratives: A variationist critique of Labov and Waletzky's model of narrative schemas*. Unpublished PhD Thesis. Middlesex University.

Levinson, S .C., 1983. *Pragmatics*. Cambridge: Cambridge University Press.

Levinson, S. C., 1987. Minimization and conversational inference. In: J. Verschueren and M. Bertuccelli-Papi, eds. *The pragmatic perspective*. Selected papers from the 1985 International Pragmatics Conference. Amsterdam: John Benjamins, 61–129.

Levinson, S. C., 1995. Three levels of meaning. In: F.R. Palmer. ed. *Grammar and meaning. Essays in honour of Sir John Lyons*. Cambridge: Cambridge University Press, 90–115.

Levinson, S. C., 2000. *Presumptive meanings: The theory of generalized conversational implicature*. Cambridge, MA: MIT Press.

Liddicoat, A. J., 2007. *An introduction to conversation analysis*. London: Continuum.

Mandala, S., 2007. *Twentieth century drama dialogue as ordinary talk: Speaking between the lines*. London: Ashgate.

McIntyre, D., 2010. Dialogue and characterization in *Reservoir Dogs*. In: D. MacIntyre and B. Busse, eds. *Language and Style*. Basingstoke: Palgrave, 162–182.

Nørgaard, N, Busse, B and Montoro, R., 2010. *Key terms in stylistics*. London: Continuum.

Piazza, R., 1999. Dramatic discourse approached from a conversational analysis perspective: Catherine Hayes's *Skirmishes* and other contemporary plays. *Journal of Pragmatics*, 31 (8), 1001–1023.

Sacks, H., Schegloff, E. A. and Jefferson, G., 1974. A simplest systematics for the organization of turn-taking for conversation. *Language*, 50 (4), 696–735.

Schegloff, E., 2007. *Sequence organization in interaction*. Cambridge: Cambridge University Press.

Semino, E. A., 2014. Language, mind and autism in Mark Haddon's *The Curious Incident of the Dog in the Night-Time. In:* M. Fludernik and D. Jacob, eds. *Linguistics and literary studies*. Berlin: de Gruyter.

Short, M., 1996. *Exploring the language of poems, plays and prose*. Harlow, England: Longman.

Sperber, D. and Wilson, D., 1995. *Relevance*. Oxford: Blackwell.

Spitz, A., 2010. The music of argument: The portrayal of argument in Ian McEwan's *On Chesil Beach. Language and Literature*, 19 (2), 197–220.

Stoppard, T., 1967. *Rosencrantz and Guildenstern are dead*. London: Faber and Faber.

Thomas, B., 1997. Telephone conversation from *Vile Bodies. Language and Literature*, 6 (20), 105–19.

Thomas, B., 2002. Multiparty talk in the novel: The distribution of tea and talk in a scene from Evelyn Waugh's *Black Mischief. Poetics Today*, 23 (4), 657–684.

Thomas, B., 2012. *Fictional dialogue: Speech and conversation in the modern and postmodern novel*. Nebraska: University of Nebraska.

Thomas, J., 1995. *Meaning in Interaction,* London: Longman.

Toolan, M., 1989. Analysing conversation in fiction: An example from Joyce's *Portrait. In:* R. Carter and P. Simpson, eds. *Language, discourse and literature*. London: Routledge, 195–211.

Waugh, E., 1930. [1936] *Vile bodies*. London: Penguin.

West, C. and Zimmerman, D. H., 1982. Conversation analysis. *In:* K. Scherer and P. Ekman, eds. *Handbook of methods in nonverbal behaviour research*. Cambridge: Cambridge University Press, 506–541.

Wooffitt, R., 2005. *Conversation analysis and discourse analysis*. London: Sage.

Appendix

Table 8.2 Transcription Key

?	question or uncertainty
" "	indicates direct speech
"italics"	captures the marked change in voice quality when speaker mimics another using direct speech
(names and places)	names and locations not given but indicated in brackets
[ ]	non-transcribable speech
[laughs]	paralinguistic and non verbal information
=	overlapping talk
...	pauses of under 3 seconds

9

Stylistics and relevance theory

Billy Clark

Introduction

Relevance theory is arguably the most influential approach to pragmatics to have developed from the work of Grice (1989). It has been applied in a wide range of areas, including accounts of reasoning in general, developmental psychology, and the understanding of conditions such as autistic spectrum disorders. The majority of relevance-theoretic work has been concerned with developing accounts of linguistically encoded meanings (linguistic semantics) and how these interact with contextual assumptions in understanding utterances (pragmatics). Accounting for interpretations is a key focus of work in stylistics, so it is natural that relevance-theoretic ideas have been applied to stylistics, providing accounts of particular texts and of particular phenomena involved in the production and comprehension of texts. It has also contributed to more general theoretical debates, for example about the nature of 'literariness' and authorial intention, and it is beginning to contribute to accounts of formal literary interpretation and formal and informal evaluation. As has often been pointed out (e.g. by Pilkington *et al.* 1997 and Wilson 2011), the aim is not to provide particular interpretations or evaluations, but to explain the processes involved in arriving at these. Relevance theory can also contribute to accounts of textual production and editorial processes, and to pedagogical work of various kinds. This chapter says something about previous, ongoing and possible future work in each of these areas.

Overview: From Grice to relevance theory

Relevance theory arose directly from critical discussion of the ideas suggested by Grice (1989; for introductions to Grice's work, see Chapman 2011, pp. 68–88, Clark 2013, Chapter 2, Levinson 1983, p. 97–166, and Chapters 7 and 8 in this volume. For a discussion of Grice's intellectual life see Chapman 2005). In common with many approaches, relevance theory retains the broadly Gricean view that pragmatic principles, grounded in rationality, guide the interpretation of utterances (these also guide production but work in relevance theory, in common with other approaches, has focused mainly on interpretation).

Relevance theory departs from Grice in not assuming 'maxim-like' principles. Instead, it assumes two principles understood as law-like generalisations about human cognition and communication: the 'cognitive principle of relevance', and the 'communicative principle of relevance'. This places relevance theory within the group of approaches currently described as merely 'post-Gricean' rather than 'neo-Gricean', since it does not preserve the assumption that pragmatic principles are maxim-like (as do, e.g., Horn 1984, 2004, Levinson 1987, 2000).

Relevance theory also departs from Grice's approach in assuming that pragmatic principles are involved in deriving explicit content (what Grice called 'what is said') and in understanding nonverbal communication. It is easy to see that Gricean or other pragmatic principles could explain how Andy works out what Beth is explicitly communicating in (2) and how he works out what she intends by her nonverbal behaviour in (3):

(2) Andy: Has Colin brought that book back yet?
    Beth: He'll be round later.

(3) Andy: I think the last bus has gone. Will you get home OK?
    Beth: *[points to her bicycle helmet in the corner of the room]*

In (2), Andy has to work out that *he* refers to Colin and that the intended sense of *round* is one which means that Colin will be visiting later (rather than that he will be spherical). Relevance theory assumes that these are inferred in the light of accessible contextual assumptions and constrained by (relevance-theoretic) pragmatic principles. Equally, Andy's interpretation of Beth's nonverbal behaviour in (3) is guided by pragmatics and accessible contextual assumptions (key ones here being about Andy's expectation of an answer to the question he has just asked).

Relevance theory also assumes that there is more to working out what someone has explicitly communicated than just disambiguation and reference assignment, as assumed by Grice. Among other things, we might need to recover ellipsed material as in (4), work out in what ways the referent of *it* is 'the same' (and as what) in (5), and decide how long *some time* will be in (6):

(4) And Colin.

(5) It's just the same.

(6) This will take some time.

More generally, relevance theory assumes what has been called the 'underdeterminacy thesis' (see, for example, Carston 2002, p. 48–83), according to which what is linguistically encoded by an expression vastly underdetermines what it can explicitly and implicitly communicate.

Critical issues and topics

This section provides a very brief overview of key relevance-theoretic ideas. Relevance theory assumes that a 'Relevance-Guided Comprehension Heuristic' is triggered by the recognition of an ostensive stimulus, i.e. by an action clearly intended to communicate something. The heuristic is stated as follows:

(7)   Relevance-Guided Comprehension Heuristic
    a.   Follow a path of least effort in deriving cognitive effects: test interpretations (disambiguations, reference resolutions, implicatures, etc.) in order of accessibility.
    b.   Stop when your expectations of relevance are satisfied.

When we recognise an ostensive stimulus, we follow a path of least effort in looking for an interpretation ('deriving cognitive effects') and stop when our expectations of relevance are met. So what are our expectations of relevance? The claim is that an act of ostensive communication creates a presumption that the communicator thinks it will be worth our while to pay attention and to put in the effort required to process it. More precisely, the communicator must think that interpreting this stimulus will be more worthwhile than processing any other stimulus which we could pay attention to instead.

We can see how this works informally by considering again example (3) above, where Beth points in the direction of her bicycle helmet. Beth must think that it is worth Andy's while to process her stimulus. In this situation, Andy will expect Beth's pointing to have something to do with his question about her getting home. As soon as Andy spots the helmet and makes the necessary inferences about Beth planning to cycle home, he will have arrived at an interpretation which meets his expectations. To understand this more formally, we need to understand the technical definition of the term 'relevance' and the nature of the 'expectations of relevance' mentioned above.

Relevance is defined within relevance theory in terms of cognitive effects and processing effort. Other things being equal, the more cognitive effects a stimulus has, the more relevant it is – and conversely, the more effort required to achieve those effects, the less relevant it is. We can illustrate this by imagining Beth's three possible responses here:

(8)   Andy: Have you checked the weather forecast for tomorrow?
    Beth: a. Yeh, I did.
           b. Yeh, I did. It's going to be sunny all day.
           c. Yeh, I did. It's going to be sunny all day and it was sunny on this date in 1864.

(8a) has some relevance for Andy because he can derive effects from it (he now knows, for example, that Beth has checked the weather forecast and has some evidence about what the weather will be like tomorrow). (8b) is more relevant than (8a) because he can derive further effects (that it is predicted to be sunny and whatever follows from that). Other things being equal (importantly, assuming that nothing follows for Andy from information about the weather conditions on the same day in 1864), (8c) is less relevant than (8b) as Andy has to process the second conjunct, from which nothing significant follows.

Relevance theory does not claim that interpreters assume that utterances are as relevant as possible. Rather, the Communicative Principle of Relevance states that they assume that the act is 'optimally relevant', i.e. that it provides enough effects to justify the effort involved and does not require unjustified effort.

Following the relevance-guided comprehension heuristic, then, a hearer moves along a path of least effort, accessing contextual assumptions, testing hypotheses about intended senses and referents, possible implicatures and so on, looking for an interpretation which the communicator could have intended to give rise to enough effects to justify the effort involved in deriving them. As soon as he finds such an interpretation (or until he gives up, if he cannot find one), he stops.

We can illustrate this by considering Beth's utterance in example (2) above ('*He'll be round later*'). Andy can assume very quickly that the referent of *he* is Colin, given that he has just mentioned Colin. If he assumes that his being '*round*' means that he will be visiting Andy and Beth's home later, he can derive enough effects to justify the processing effort (assuming that Beth thinks Colin will be coming to return the book) and he can stop looking for an interpretation.

The reference to processing effort plays a key part in relevance-theoretic explanations, as can be seen by comparing pairs of utterances which differ only in the amount of processing effort they require. The most commonly-discussed examples involve repetition or the addition of linguistic material which does not affect the proposition likely to be inferred, such as the word *now* in many contexts:

> (9)   a.   I'm making the tea.
>   b.   I'm making the tea now.

In a context where the hearer is likely to infer that the speaker of (9a) is making the tea at or just after the time of utterance, *now* contributes no more than an explicit indication of something the hearer would have inferred anyway. Nevertheless, most people report a strong intuition that (9b) communicates something different or more than would be communicated by (9a). This might involve contrasting this time with other possibilities, or highlighting something which follows from the fact that this moment is when the tea is being made. For another example, we might imagine Beth in example (3) above adding the phrase *I'm saying* at the start of her utterance:

> (10) I'm saying he'll be round later.

Without this phrase, Andy will realise that Beth is saying that Colin will be round later. With this phrase, he will infer something extra, perhaps that she is stressing her commitment to this so that Andy will be more likely to believe it, perhaps that Andy is acting as if he doesn't follow, perhaps that she is unsure whether Colin will really show up. For relevance theory, the key notion is that extra effort must lead to extra effects.

The assumption is not that interpretation is a linear or 'one-step-at-a-time' process. Rather, all of the processes of accessing contextual assumptions, forming hypotheses about disambiguations, generating possible implicatures and so on are seen as carrying on in parallel and as adjusting each other. More generally, hypotheses about explicit and implicit content are accessed and tested alongside each other. In (3), for example, Andy will be considering hypotheses about what Beth meant to communicate explicitly by saying '*he'll be round later*' (that Colin will visit their home later) at the same time as testing hypotheses about what this implicates (that he might return the book).

Analysing texts

So how do we go about analysing texts using relevance theory? A natural assumption might be simply to approach texts and explain all of the inferential processes involved in understanding them. This section begins by pointing out why this approach is impractical and then considers a number of aspects of communication which have been approached from a relevance-theoretic point of view.

Accounting for individual texts

The impracticality of attempting to account for every inferential process involved in analysing particular texts follows from the large amount of time and space needed to explain even fairly straightforward everyday inferential processes (a similar point applies, of course, to any method of stylistic analysis). Consider, for example, what is involved in understanding a straightforward everyday utterance such as:

(11) I was tired.

An account of how this utterance is understood in a particular context will have to include at least an account of how the interpreter works out:

a.   the referent of *I*
b.   how tired the referent of *I* was
c.   when the referent of *I* was tired
d.   which contextual assumptions are required to arrive at an interpretation
e.   what set of implicatures follow from this
f.   what other implications follow from this

A relevance-theoretic account would involve a characterisation of the mutual adjustment processes involved in accessing and adjusting contextual assumptions, testing and developing hypotheses about word senses, reference assignments, and so on. Table 9.1 presents an abbreviated version of the beginning of an account in the underspecified context suggested by the exchange in (12) (missing out implications which Andy will derive on his own initiative and which Beth need not have intended):

(12) Andy: Did you not put the bins out last night?
     Beth: I was tired.

A fuller account would discuss how Andy follows each of these paths, adjusting hypotheses in the light of each other and recognising when enough effects have been derived to justify the effort involved in arriving at them (strictly speaking, these have to be effects which Beth could and would have chosen to communicate). The key here is for Andy to access the strongest implicature (that Beth is suggesting that her tiredness explains her not having put the bins out). Another key point to notice is how much I have written without yet providing a full account of how this utterance is understood.

   Now imagine that the words from Beth's utterance (12) appear as the opening sentence of a novel. The complexity of the inferential processes is much greater. The reader might not be able to work out the referent of *I* at this stage, but he or she will assume that this can be fleshed out later. Confidence in reference assignment will depend on the availability of other contextual assumptions, e.g. the reader might know that the book is a first-person narrative about a particular character. Other inferential processes might reflect assumptions or expectations created by what the reader knows about the author, the book (e.g. whether it is thought of as 'popular' writing, a 'literary' text, etc.) and so on. Of course, novels and many other texts have more than one reader. Another task for stylistics is to explore how different readers respond differently to particular texts. This vastly increases the task of accounting for inferences associated with texts.

Table 9.1 Some inferences involved in understanding an utterance of '*I was tired*'

Referent of I?	How tired?	Time?	Contextual assumptions?	Implicatures?
Beth is most accessible referent – test this hypothesis first	Adjust assumptions about how tired Beth usually is before bedtime	The most accessible time is just before Beth went to bed last night	Andy has asked Beth whether she forgot to put the bins out	It is because Beth was tired that Beth did not put the bins out
	Beth must have been more tired than usual		Andy went to bed before Beth last night and expected Beth to put the bins out	Beth would have put the bins out if she hadn't been so tired
	Beth must have been tired enough that she forgot or could not summon the energy to put the bins out		Andy has noticed that the bins did not go out last night	Beth hopes Andy will empathise with her tiredness and feel less negatively about her
			Andy's utterance suggests a kind of reprimand	Beth thinks it is unfair that Andy has implicated a negative attitude given her tiredness
			Andy is wondering why Beth didn't put the bins out	

Given the impracticality of aiming to spell out the details of every inference involved in responding to particular texts, relevance theorists have focused on specific aspects of the inferential processes involved in understanding texts. In some cases the aim is to give a partial account of how a particular text works. In others the aim is to account for a particular communicative phenomenon and consider how it works in a range of texts. The rest of this section looks briefly at a selection of these, beginning with the notion of 'salient inference', which relates directly to the just-discussed practical difficulties in accounting for inferential processes. Two important areas which have been explored by relevance theorists but which are not discussed further here are nonverbal communication (discussed by Wharton 2009) and multimodal communication (see, for example, Forceville 2010, Yus 1998, 2009).

Salient inferences

One approach to dealing with the complexities involved in explaining inferences suggests that:

> ... it is in principle always worth exploring all of the inferential processes involved in understanding a text, but it is not practical to do so. Where analysts notice something marked or unusual about an interpretation, this calls for an analysis of inferential

processes. But cases that seem simpler are in principle of interest too. It will be up to the analyst to decide in each case whether and where to develop an account of inferential processes.

(Clark 2009, p. 184)

One situation in which inferential processes are worth investigating is where audiences become more aware than usual of the inferential processes they are engaged in. This applies to jokes, creative uses of everyday language and literary texts.

Clark (2009) explores how such salient inferences are involved in reading William Golding's *The Inheritors*. The same approach could be applied to William Faulkner's *The Sound and the Fury* (for previous discussion by stylisticians, see, for example, Fowler 1986, p. 127–146, Leech and Short 1981, p. 162–166). In the first section of this novel, readers are aware of the difficult and complex inferences required to cope with the mind style of the character Benjy. Among other things, Benjy has an idiosyncratic way of describing events, does not clearly distinguish two separate characters called Quentin, and makes random leaps in time while telling his story. When beginning the second section, it seems much easier to follow the mind style of Benjy's brother Quentin. However, as the section unfolds, we discover that Quentin's narrative presents its own difficulties. It also makes leaps in time and fails to make a number of things clear, including linguistic details such as when one sentence ends and another begins. It is only in the third section that the novel finally begins to follow a more conventional structure and to be relatively clear about what is happening when. An account of the contrasting nature of the inferential processes at various stages of reading and rereading would help to explain key effects of the novel. Most importantly, some of the effects of the text follow from the reader's varying awareness of the kinds of inferences involved in reading the text.

Metarepresentation

Metarepresentation is an important notion in human cognition and communication, and one which is often seen as closely connected with the evolution of human language and communication (see, for example, Sperber 2000). It refers to the ability to embed representations within other representations (e.g. representing a thought as being entertained by someone else, as in *Dave thinks that Emma thinks that...*) Several aspects of individual communicative acts can be understood as involving metarepresentation. These include understanding utterances as attributed to others, as in (13), ironic utterances such as (14) and the complexities involved in understanding fictional 'layering' as in (15) and (16):

(13) Andy: What did Colin say?
      Beth: He's tired and doesn't want to go out tonight.

(14) Andy: The government has announced that it's revising the whole education
              system from top to bottom.
      Beth: Teachers will love that.

(15) I have just returned from a visit to my landlord – the solitary neighbour that I shall
     be troubled with.

(Emily Brontë, Wuthering Heights*)*

(16) Mr. Earnshaw once bought a couple of colts at the parish fair, and gave the lads each one. Heathcliff took the handsomest, but it soon fell lame, and when he discovered it, he said to Hindley –

'You must exchange horses with me: I don't like mine; and if you won't I shall tell your father of the three thrashings you've given me this week, and show him my arm, which is black to the shoulder.'

(Emily Brontë, Wuthering Heights*)*

In (13), Beth is communicating that Colin has said that he's tired and doesn't want to go out. In (14) Beth is dissociating herself from the thought that teachers will love the government announcement, which she finds ridiculous. In (15) Emily Brontë is presenting the narrator Mr. Lockwood's utterance. In (16) Brontë is presenting Mr. Lockwood telling us that the housekeeper Ellen Dean told him that Heathcliff said the words reported here.

MacMahon (2009a, 2009b) discusses metarepresentation with reference to Jane Austen's *Northanger Abbey*. As well as considering metarepresentation in general and with regard to the novel, MacMahon considers how metarepresentation relates to 'decoupling', as discussed by Cosmides and Tooby (2000). Decoupled representations are separated from those associated with 'architectural truth'. To take a simple example discussed by MacMahon (2009a, p. 527), suppose I think that:

(17) My daughter believes fairies exist.

I can entertain this proposition without believing the embedded and attributed proposition that:

(18) Fairies exist.

However, I can still draw conclusions from (18) and work out other things which my daughter might believe. This is, then, a 'decoupled' proposition since I can represent it and derive inferences from it without believing that it is true.

MacMahon argues that fictional works play a key role in cognition by allowing complex and extended decoupled representations and reasoning.

Implications and implicatures

Leech and Short (1981, pp. 231–254) discuss how a Gricean approach can be applied both to inferences about what characters implicate to each other and to what authors are implicating to audiences. To take just one example, we might consider Orsino's utterance at the beginning of *Twelfth Night* in two ways:

(19) If music be the food of love, play on.

First, we might say that Orsino is implicating a love of music. At another level, we might say that Shakespeare is implicating that Orsino is pretentious. Clark (1996) suggests that this might partly be accounted for by the relevance-theoretic distinction between implications and implicatures. An implication is a logical conclusion derived from one or more assumptions. An implicature is a communicated implication. Suppose, for example, that I am running late for a lecture which starts at 11am. As I approach my university campus, I ask a stranger what time it is and she replies:

(20) Ten past eleven.

In this situation, I can derive the implication that I am late for my lecture but the speaker cannot be intentionally communicating this since she cannot know about the timing of my lecture.

Suppose, by contrast, that (20) is uttered by a colleague who knows that my lecture begins at 11am. In this situation we are likely to say that the speaker is intentionally communicating that I am late, and so this is an implicature of her utterance. The conclusion that Orsino is pretentious is an implication of Orsino's utterance but an implicature of Shakespeare's script.

Figurative language

Unlike Grice's traditional approach, relevance-theoretic work on metaphor does not assume that literalness is any kind of 'norm' or that metaphorical utterances fall into a natural kind (see, for example, Carston 2002, pp. 349–358, Wilson and Sperber 2012, pp. 97–122). Metaphorical utterances share properties with loose talk or approximations, where we do not assume that the speaker commits herself to all of the implications of the proposition she expresses. (21) and (22) are examples which have this property but are not metaphorical:

(21) He is six feet tall.

(22) Aberdeen is sixty miles from here.

In (21), we do not assume that he is exactly six feet tall. In (22), we do not assume that Aberdeen is exactly sixty miles away. What is important is to work out relevant implications of these utterances (that the person referred to is approximately six feet tall, that it would take around an hour to drive to Aberdeen, etc.). Metaphorical utterances are accounted for in the same way:

(23) He's a wild animal.

(24) You're on fire tonight.

In (23), we do not assume that the referent of *he* is a non-human creature but we do assume that he is hard to control, and so on. In (24), we assume not that the referent of *you* is ablaze but that he is full of energy, hard to miss, performing well, and so on. Metaphorical utterances are understood in similar ways to other utterances and are not seen as different in kind from other kinds of utterance. The key thing in understanding (23) and (24) is being able to access the intentionally communicated implications.

Similarly, the relevance-theoretic account of irony does not assume any special mechanisms and does not assume that irony is a natural kind. The key ideas exploited in irony are that some utterances implicitly represent the thoughts or utterances of others (are 'attributed' to others) and that some attributed utterances implicitly convey an attitude to the thought or utterance represented, i.e. they are 'echoic'. As Wilson and Sperber put it:

> An utterance is echoic when it achieves most of its relevance not by expressing the speaker's own views, nor by reporting someone else's utterances or thoughts, but by expressing the speaker's attitude to views she tacitly attributes to someone else.
>
> *(Wilson and Sperber 2004, pp. 272–273)*

An utterance is ironic when it is both implicitly attributed and implicitly dissociative.

Here is an example of a non-ironic attributed thought:

(25) Andy: What did Colin say?
     Beth: You're wonderful.

Here, Beth might be representing her own thought or she might be attributing this thought to Colin. If the latter, then this is an attributive utterance.

Here is an example of a non-ironic echoic utterance:

(26) *(Before Beth asks Colin to help her organise a party)*
     Andy: You can always rely on Colin.
     (After Colin has been a great help in organising the party)
     Beth: You CAN always rely on Colin.

Here Beth is implicitly attributing the thought to Andy and implicitly agreeing with it.

For an utterance to be classed as ironic, it should be not only implicitly attributive and implicitly expressing an attitude to the attributed thought, but also implicitly dissociative:

(27) *(Before Beth asks Colin to help her organise a party)*
     Andy: You can always rely on Colin.
     (After Colin has been no help at all in organising the party)
     Beth: You CAN always rely on Colin.

Here, Beth is implicitly dissociating herself from a thought she is implicitly attributing to Andy, and so she is being ironic.

There have been several applications of relevance theory which focus on figurative language in texts. To take two examples, Pilkington (2000) (discussed below) considers in some detail what might be communicated by the metaphor of WRITING AS DIGGING in Seamus Heaney's poem 'Digging', and MacMahon (1996) explores irony and related phenomena in discussing Browning's verse monologue 'My Last Duchess' (for critical discussion of the relevance-theoretic account of irony, see Morini 2010).

Strong and weak communication

Relevance theory reflects the vagueness and open-endedness of verbal communication by recognising that utterances do not generally encode one strong 'explicature' (an explicitly communicated assumption) and a small number of strong implicatures. Rather, what is communicated can vary with regard to how wide a range of propositions is communicated and how strongly each is communicated. Communicated assumptions can be stronger or weaker in two ways. First, there might be more or less evidence for a particular assumption. Second, the communicator's intention to communicate them can be more or less manifest.

Songs and literary texts often give rise to relatively weak explicatures. A common way in which this arises is when the referent of a personal pronoun is not accessible to the reader or listener. This is common in the lyrics to pop songs, where the referent of pronouns such as *you* and *me* can be taken in a range of ways, e.g. as the singer addressing the listener, as a persona adopted by the singer addressing the listener or another implied listener, and so on (for discussion, see Durant 1984, pp. 202–209). We can also illustrate this by considering poetry, such as this extract from the poem *In Vain* by Emily Dickinson:

(28) I cannot live with you,
     It would be life,
     And life is over there
     Behind the shelf
     The sexton keeps the key to,
     Putting up
     Our life, his porcelain
     Like a cup
     Discarded of the housewife,
     Quaint or broken;
     A newer Sèvres pleases,
     Old ones crack.

(Dickinson 1990, p. 29)

As with song lyrics, we can think about what follows if the referent of *I* is Emily Dickinson herself, a poetic persona who we might imagine in a range of ways, and so on. Similarly, we can follow different inferential paths depending on who we assume is the referent of *you*. As with much poetry, some of the key effects of Dickinson's work arise because of indeterminacies such as these.

Implicatures also vary in strength. Relatively strong implicatures are ones which are members of a relatively small set of communicated assumptions, and ones which need to be recovered in order for the utterance to be seen as relevant. Consider, for example, Beth's utterance in (29):

(29) Andy: Do you want a piece of cake?
     Beth: I have a nut allergy.

If Andy knows that the cake contains nuts, he will recover this contextual assumption and use it along with the explicature of Beth's utterance to recover the implicature that Beth does not want a piece of cake. This implicature will follow even if Andy knows that the cake does not, in fact, contain nuts. Beth's utterance makes clear that she thinks it does and that she does not want a piece of cake because of this. Beth has provided strong evidence for this and it is hard to see how the utterance would be relevant if she did not intend to communicate this.

While Beth's rejection of the cake is strongly implicated, no implicature is absolutely guaranteed and we can imagine situations where this would not follow. Imagine, for example, that there is another item of food available and that this other item contains nuts. Beth's utterance might, then, communicate that she wants a piece of cake because she cannot eat the other food that is available. And there are other possibilities.

Other strong implicatures which Andy can derive from Beth's utterance include those in (30):

(30) a. Beth cannot eat anything which contains nuts.
    b. Beth cannot eat peanut butter.

Andy can be quite sure that these follow and that Beth intended to provide evidence for them. Others are not so strong, such as those in (31):

(31) a. Beth is disappointed that she can't eat the cake.
    b. Beth wishes the cake did not contain nuts.
    c. Beth will want something else to eat.
    d. Beth has to think carefully about food.
    e. Beth's life is more complicated than she would like it to be.

These also vary in strength. (31e), for example, is clearly less strongly evidenced than (31a).

Poetic effects

Some utterances achieve relevance by giving rise to a wide range of relatively weak implicatures rather than a narrower range of fairly strong ones. Sperber and Wilson (1986, pp. 217–224) suggest that poetic effects 'result from the accessing of a large array of very weak implicatures' (Sperber and Wilson 1986, p. 224). Pilkington (2000) developed this notion and applied it to a number of questions about literary interpretation as well as to analysing specific texts. His most well-known example is his discussion of Seamus Heaney's poem 'Digging' (Pilkington 2000, pp. 102–104) where he explores the range of weak implicatures derivable from the metaphor of digging applied to the pen being held in the poem. The poem ends with the lines:

(32) Between my finger and my thumb
    The squat pen rests.
    I'll dig with it.

Before this, the poem discusses the speaker's father and grandfather digging, giving rise to a complex range of implicatures about the nature of their digging, their place in a wider community, assumptions about digging as an activity with a long tradition, as hard work, as something requiring concentration, and so on. The weak implicatures generated by the ending include assumptions about writing resembling digging and '... a note of guilt or unease ... as well as a note of assertion and what might almost be termed defiance' (Pilkington 2000, p. 103). These follow partly from accessible assumptions about how writing is in fact not like digging. A key point Pilkington makes is that it is risky even to begin to list these potential implicatures since '... it mistakenly suggests that all these assumptions are strongly communicated and equally strongly communicated...' whereas many '... are weakly implicated or made marginally more manifest' (Pilkington 2000, p. 103).

Lexical pragmatics

A recent development in relevance theory concerns how words are understood in context. A standard assumption when thinking about word meanings is to differentiate 'concept words' such as *book*, *shadow* and *island*, which are thought to indicate specific concepts, from words which require inferences before we can recognise what they contribute to interpretations, such as pronouns and referring expressions. Many concept words are ambiguous, of course, and part of the task of understanding utterances containing them is to access the intended sense. This task has been seen as an inferential one that is guided by pragmatic principles. The traditional view is that this captures more or less all of the inferential processing required when understanding utterances of concept words.

By contrast, recent work in relevance theory developing ideas suggested by the psychologist Barsalou (1987, 1993) and later work by Glucksberg *et al.* (1997), has suggested that inferential processing is routinely involved in understanding uses of any word in a context, including concept words (see, for example, Carston 1997, 2002, Sperber and Wilson 1998, Wilson and Carston 2007). The examples in (33) to (35) provide a simple illustration of this.

(33) They used to think the earth was flat.

(34) You'll need a flat surface to roll the dough on.

(35) My front tyre is flat.

The word *flat* is used in different ways in these three examples, none of which correspond to the mathematical notion of flatness. In (33), the intended sense is not much different from 'not spherical' and the existence of mountains was not seen as inconsistent with the 'flat-earth' view. In (34), a different kind of surface is clearly intended and the intended sense will be 'relatively even' in a different way. In (35), *flat* means containing no (or relatively little) air. We might address this by arguing that the word *flat* is polysemous. However, even if we think of these uses as involving different senses, we still have to make inferences to see exactly what is meant. The polysemy view is also less attractive given that we would need to propose a great deal of polysemy to cover all of the possible senses.

Current thinking in relevance theory (see, for example, Carston 2002, pp. 320–367) suggests that understanding any concept word involves adjustment processes which both 'broaden' and 'narrow' original encoded senses. Each of the above examples could be used to illustrate broadening. In (33), the intended sense of *flat* extends to allow some parts of the earth to be higher than others. In (34), the surface will be suitable even if the surface is not completely smooth and some parts of it are not at exactly the same level as others. In (35), all that is required is that there is relatively little air in the tyre. Equally, we could say that there is narrowing in each case since *flat* is a different concept when applied to land, kitchen surfaces or tyres.

This new approach to word meanings has led to a new account of metaphorical utterances. This approach retains the idea that literalness is a matter of degree rather than a categorical 'either/or' notion, and that interpreting a metaphorical utterance involves selecting which of a range of possible conclusions are being intentionally communicated. A key part of the account now is a focus on how concept adjustment is involved in representing a word's meaning on the way to deriving implicatures. Consider again the use of *dig* in the last line of Seamus Heaney's poem 'Digging' (*I'll dig with it*). According to the earlier approach, the focus was on how to know which (weak) implicatures the poem is communicating (e.g. that the writer will explore things with his pen, that he will work like a craftsman, and so on) and not to derive those not intended (e.g. that he will turn over soil with it). On the new approach, the focus is on inferring an adjusted notion of the concept DIG from which the intended implicatures can be derived.

This view of lexical pragmatics might be applied in other ways. The notion of adjustment can continue throughout the reading process. The reader's notion of the concept {DIG} is changing as she or he reads the poem and this might continue to be adjusted afterwards as the reader continues to think about it. In a novel, a particular concept might be being adjusted over considerable time. We might see a key aim of many writers of fiction and non-fiction as being to adjust particular concepts in the minds of readers. We might also see how a character's understanding of a particular concept evolves, or consider the differences between concepts as entertained by different characters.

Local and global inferences

An important notion used by relevance theorists in accounting for textual interpretation is a contrast between 'local' and 'global' inferences. At its simplest, we might choose as an example of the former the very local inference about the co-reference relationship between *a young man* and *he* in the first sentence of Dostoevsky's 'Crime and Punishment':

> (36) On an exceptionally hot evening early in July a young man came out of the garret in which he lodged in S. Place and walked slowly, as though in hesitation, towards K. bridge.
>
> *(Fyodor Dostoevsky,* Crime and Punishment*)*

We could then contrast this with inferential conclusions that we reach on the basis of having read the entire book, perhaps about the nature and limits of human reason. The evidence for the local inference comes from just the first sentence itself. Evidence for the conclusions about human reason come from the book as a whole. Of course, things are more complicated than this extreme contrast suggests. Evidence for particular conclusions can be more or less local and more or less distributed in a text, and evidence also comes from contextual assumptions not provided by the text. We can develop accounts of how understanding of a text develops as new evidence confirms, disconfirms or adjusts existing hypotheses about characters, narrative development, and so on. (For discussion of this with reference to a short story by Raymond Carver, see Clark 1996; for discussion of ideas about local and global relevance in accounting for genre, see Unger 2006).

Beyond analyses

The main contributions of relevance theory to stylistics have been in accounting for particular communicative phenomena and in analysing particular texts. This section indicates some areas where relevance theory can be applied beyond the analysis of texts.

Literariness

Furlong (1996, 2001) has applied relevance theory in considering the nature of literariness. Considering what it is that makes an interpretation literary, she develops a distinction between 'spontaneous' and 'non-spontaneous' interpretations. Spontaneous interpretations are the kind made by most people in most everyday interactions. In these cases, addressees follow the relevance-theoretic comprehension procedure until their expectations of relevance are met and then move on to pay attention to other phenomena in their environment. We can illustrate this with the interaction in (37):

(37) Andy: I'm just off to the shop.
     Beth: Can you get butter while you're there?

Andy can quickly understand that Beth would like him to buy butter while he's at the shop and will quickly make inferences about how much butter to buy. Having inferred this, he is likely to move on towards the shop and not think much more about Beth's utterance, even though nothing stops him from going on to think further about what Beth might have thought or intended (e.g. what she might want the butter for).

If Andy decides to think consciously about all the possible implications and implicatures of Beth's utterance, considering all of the evidence he can find, perhaps going out of his way to look for more evidence, then he is engaged in 'non-spontaneous interpretation'. This more laborious approach, perhaps even involving explicit writing down of assumptions and a quest for more relevant contextual assumptions, is typical of formal literary interpretation. We can, of course, respond to literary texts with fairly spontaneous interpretations and we can develop non-spontaneous interpretations of non-literary texts. This means that we cannot make an absolute direct link between non-spontaneousness and literariness. However, non-spontaneousness can be seen as part of what makes an interpretation literary and we can use this notion to distinguish texts as more or less literary with regard to how likely they are to give rise to non-spontaneous interpretations. A fuller understanding of notions of literariness could be developed by considering the role of cultural assumptions about literariness, the nature of textual production and presentation, and so on.

Pilkington (2000) sees literariness as partly to do with 'poetic effects' (as discussed above) and partly to do with what philosophers call 'qualia' (roughly, conscious and subjective experience) or affective states which are created by literary texts. He admits that discussion of emotions and affect is necessarily speculative at this stage, but he insists that an account of this is required for an account of literariness. Referring to the 'wide array of minute effects' which Sperber and Wilson (1986, p. 224) describe in discussing poetic effects, he says:

> Although this 'wide array of minute cognitive effects' may characterise and distinguish poetic effects from other kinds of stylistic effects in terms of propositions, it is not clear that the affective dimension can be reduced to such cognitive effects.
>
> *(Pilkington 2000, pp. 190–191)*

Authorial intention

Relevance theory also has something to say about the notion of authorial intention. Wilson (2011) points out that work in relevance theory has assumed that the task of a pragmatic theory is to explain how readers, hearers and viewers attempt to work out what communicators intend to communicate. This goes against the assumptions of theorists such as Wimsatt and Beardsley (1946) who would surely have said that relevance theorists are guilty of the 'intentional fallacy'. Wilson suggests that at least some of the same principles involved in ordinary communication carry over to literary communication, suggesting that inferential approaches to pragmatics:

> ... have amply confirmed the importance of the communicator's intentions in all varieties of verbal communication, and at both explicit and implicit levels. Literary texts, like ordinary everyday utterances, are full of lexical and syntactic ambiguities, referential and lexical indeterminacies, unarticulated constituents, loose, hyperbolic or metaphorical

uses of language, ironies, witticisms and indications of attitude. Both literary texts and ordinary utterances must be treated as pieces of evidence about the communicator's intentions, and interpreted in a context which is not fixed in advance but constructed as part of the interpretation process.

(Wilson 2011, p. 72)

Wilson also points out that interpreting any utterance involves going beyond the communicator's intentions, i.e. that 'interpretation' goes beyond 'comprehension'. Wilson illustrates this with the following exchange between two people who have just met:

(38) Bob: Were you brought up in England?
     Sue: I was brought up in Cornwall.

As Wilson points out, Sue might have no idea what Bob will derive from this information beyond accessing the contextual assumption that Cornwall is in England and so concluding that she did grow up in England. If Bob accesses further assumptions about Cornwall and derives conclusions about Sue's experiences growing up, he is going beyond recognising Sue's original intentions ('comprehension') and establishing the fuller relevance of the utterance for himself (deriving a fuller 'interpretation').

Wilson suggests that the distinction between comprehension and interpretation is important in accounting for literary works, and links this to the notion that communication can be stronger and weaker. As we move from relatively stronger implicatures, where we can be confident that the speaker or author intended them, to weaker ones where we take more responsibility, we also move from initial comprehension towards a fuller interpretation.

Literary criticism and the evaluation of texts

Two areas not much explored so far are the inferences involved in literary criticism and in formal and informal evaluation. A forthcoming paper (Clark, in press) considers how relevance-theoretic assumptions might be applied in developing fuller accounts of these by considering Chekhov's story *The Lady with the Little Dog*, often described as a masterpiece and often striking readers as fairly trivial on first reading. Clark suggests that the nature of inferences made after reading makes it easy for readers to continue thinking about the story and deriving inferential conclusions, and that this partly accounts for how the story comes to be valued by readers and critics. A suggestion for future work is that a fuller account of how the story becomes more popular and more valued might combine relevance-theoretic notions with Sperber's (1996) proposal for an 'epidemiology of representations' studying how particular ideas spread through populations.

Writing and pedagogy

In common with other pragmatic theories, there has been relatively little work within relevance theory on how written and spoken texts are produced. There has also been relatively little relevance-theoretic work on pedagogical stylistics. Owtram (2010) addressed both of these areas in discussing the application of relevance theory to the teaching of writing. This work focuses mainly on helping students to think about how different linguistic choices lead to different kinds of effects for readers. More recently, Clark and Owtram (2012) discuss different ways in which they have applied ideas developed in this work with different groups of students. They also make suggestions about how a fuller account might be developed of the nature of inferential processes made by writers. They note that both relevance theory and Grice say something about the way in which communicators and addressees represent what each other are thinking, even though they are often thought of as focusing mainly on interpreters. The next step will be to develop a fuller account of these inferential processes, spelling out some of the inferences writers make about what readers will infer.

Recommendations for practice

As with other areas of stylistics, the best way to develop understanding of relevance theory is to apply it in analysing texts for yourself. You might begin by working through some of the inferential processes involved in particular texts, keeping an eye out for places where the inferential processes are particularly salient or where they seem to connect with effects of the text.

1. You might, for example, look at Emily Dickinson's poem *In Vain* and consider different inferential paths which follow from different assumptions about the referents of the pronouns. Follow this up by considering how the availability of a range of different paths contributes to an overall understanding of the poem. You might then look at other discussions of the poem and explore connections with your inference-based analysis. Does the account you have developed help to account for literary critical responses or complement other stylistic analyses? (Two examples of stylistic work on Dickinson which are not based on relevance theory are Freeman 1997 and Hamilton 2005.)

2. Another approach might be to look at particular ideas from relevance theory (e.g. relevance-theoretic accounts of metaphor or irony, the contrast between implications and implicatures, strong and weak communication) and explore how these are exploited in particular texts. Clark (2012) uses the notion that implicatures vary in strength in exploring the work of Raymond Carver, showing that the effects of editorial changes can be understood as adjustments to the strength of particular implicatures. One way to explore the effects of a text is to consider where the text provides evidence for stronger and weaker implicatures and the effects of the availability of a relatively wide range of relatively weak implicatures in particular cases.

3. There has not yet been much work on the stylistics of texts which exploit relevance-theoretic accounts of lexical pragmatics and the account of metaphor developed in the light of this. It would be interesting to see how much these ideas can help us to understand specific texts. Consider, for example, how the concept {LIFE} is developed and adjusted in Emily Dickinson's *In Vain* and explore the implicatures derived as a result of this. You might try this, or you could explore a specific notion as it develops in another text.

Future directions

There is scope for considerable further work in all of the areas discussed above. Analysing particular texts is, of course, a task that can go on forever, simply because humans can go on producing and developing new texts, new kinds of texts, new communicative techniques, and new ways of responding to them. At the same time, theoretical understanding of communicative phenomena will continue to evolve and lead to new analytical techniques. We can expect new work and new kinds of work with regard to all of the communicative phenomena, theoretical ideas and pedagogical practice mentioned above. Relevance theory has developed within the wider context of cognitive science and we can also expect future developments in cognitive science more generally to influence the theory.

Related topics

Cognitive poetics, conversation analysis and the cooperative principle, speech acts and im/politeness theory, literary pragmatics, pedagogical stylistics.

Further reading

Clark, B., 2013. *Relevance theory*. Cambridge: Cambridge University Press.

A comprehensive introduction.

Sperber, D. and Wilson, D., [1986] 1995. *Relevance: Communication and cognition*. Oxford: Wiley-Blackwell.

The classic source on relevance theory. It is not aimed at a general audience and is best approached after having read more accessible introductions.

Wilson, D. and Sperber, D., 2004. Relevance theory. *In:* L. R. Horn and G. Ward, eds. *Handbook of pragmatics*. Oxford: Wiley-Blackwell, 607–632.

An accessible overview.

Wilson, D. and Sperber, D., 2012. *Relevance and meaning*. Cambridge: Cambridge University Press.

A collection of essays, including recent discussions of metaphor and irony.

Yus, F., *Relevance theory online bibliographic service*. Online. Available at http://www.ua.es/personal/francisco.yus/rt.html

A regularly-updated comprehensive list of work on relevance theory.

References

Barsalou, L., 1987. The instability of graded structure: Implications for the nature of concepts. *In:* U. Neisser, ed. *Concepts and conceptual development: Ecological and intellectual factors in categorization.* Cambridge: Cambridge University Press, 101–140.

Barsalou, L., 1993. Flexibility, structure and linguistic vagary in concepts: Manifestations of a compositional system of perceptual symbols. *In:* A. Collins, S. Gathercole, A. Conway and P. Morris, eds. *Theories of memory.* Hove: Lawrence Erlbaum Associates, 29–101.

Carston, R., 1997. Enrichment and loosening: Complementary processes in deriving the proposition expressed? *Linguistische Berichte*, 8, 103–127.

Carston, R., 2002. *Thoughts and utterances*. Oxford: Wiley-Blackwell.

Chapman, S., 2005. *Paul Grice: Philosopher and linguist*. Basingstoke: Palgrave Macmillan.

Chapman, S., 2011. *Pragmatics*. Basingstoke: Palgrave MacMillan.

Clark, B., 1996. Stylistic analysis and relevance theory. *Language and Literature*, 5 (3), 163–178.

Clark, B., 2009. Salient inferences: Pragmatics and *The Inheritors*. *Language and Literature*, 18 (2), 173–212.

Clark, B., 2012. Beginning with *One More Thing*: Pragmatics and editorial intervention in the work of Raymond Carver. *Journal of Literary Semantics*, 41 (2), 155–174.

Clark, B., 2013. *Relevance theory*. Cambridge: Cambridge University Press.

Clark, B., in press. Before, during and after Chekhov: Inference, literary interpretation and literary value. *In:* S. Chapman and B. Clark, eds. *Pragmatics and literary stylistics*. Basingstoke: Palgrave Macmillan.

Clark, B. and Owtram, N., 2012. Imagined inference: Teaching writers to think like readers. *In:* M. Burke, S. Csábi, L. Week and J. Zerkowitz, eds. *Pedagogical stylistics: Current trends in language, literature and ELT.* London: Continuum, 126–141.

Cosmides, L, and Tooby, J., 2000. Consider the source: The evolution of adaptations for decoupling and metarepresentations. *In:* D. Sperber, ed. *Metarepresentations: A multidisciplinary perspective.* Oxford: Oxford University Press, 53–116.

Dickinson, E., 1990. *Selected poems.* Mineola NY: Dover Publications.

Durant, A., 1984. *Conditions of music.* Basingstoke: Palgrave Macmillan.

Forceville, C., 2010. Why and how study metaphor, metonymy and other tropes in multimodal discourse? *In:* R. Caballero Rodriguez and M. J. Pinar. Sanz, eds. *Ways and modes of human communication.* Ciudad Real, Albacete, Spain: Universidad de Castilla-La Mancha, Servicio de Publicaciones y AESLA, 57–76.

Fowler, R., 1986. *Linguistic criticism.* Oxford: Oxford University Press.

Freeman, M.H., 1997. Grounded spaces: Deictic *–self* anaphors in the poetry of Emily Dickinson. *Language and Literature*, 6 (1), 7–28.

Furlong, A., 1996. *Relevance theory and literary interpretation.* PhD thesis PhD. University College London.

Furlong, A., 2001. Is it a classic if no one reads it? *In: Proceedings of the 24th annual meeting of the Atlantic Provinces Linguistics Association (APLA).* Moncton NB: Université de Moncton, 54–60.

Glucksberg, S., Manfredi, D., and McGlone, M. S., 1997. Metaphor comprehension: How metaphors create new categories. *In:* Ward, T., Smith, S. and Vaid, J., eds. *Creative thought: An investigation of conceptual structures and processes.* Washington DC: American Psychological Association, 327–350.

Grice, H. P., 1989. *Studies in the way of words.* Cambridge MA: Harvard University Press.

Hamilton, C., 2005. A cognitive rhetoric of poetry and Emily Dickinson. *Language and Literature*, 14 (3), 279–294.

Horn, L. R., 1984. Towards a new taxonomy for pragmatic inference: Q- and R-based implicature. *In:* D. Schiffrin, ed. *Meaning, form, and use in context: Georgetown University Round Table on Languages and Linguistics*, Washington DC: Georgetown University Press, 11–42.

Horn, L.R., 2004. Implicature. *In:* L. R. Horn and G. Ward, eds. *The handbook of pragmatics.* Oxford: Wiley-Blackwell, 3–28.

Leech, G. and Short, M., 1981. *Style in fiction* (2nd edn. 2007), London: Longman.

Levinson, S. C., 1983. *Pragmatics.* Cambridge: Cambridge University Press.

Levinson, S. C., 1987. Minimization and conversational inference. *In:* J. Verschueren and M. Bertuccelli-Papi, eds. *The pragmatic perspective.* Amsterdam: John Benjamins, 61–129.

Levinson, S. C., 2000. *Presumptive meanings: The theory of generalised conversational implicature.* Cambridge, MA: MIT Press.

MacMahon, B., 1996. Indirectness, rhetoric and interpretive use: Communicative strategies in Browning's 'My Last Duchess'. *Language and Literature*, 5 (3), 209–223.

MacMahon, B., 2006. Relevance theory: Stylistic applications. *In:* E. K. Brown, ed. *Encyclopedia of language and linguistics.* 2nd edn. Oxford: Elsevier, 519–522.

MacMahon, B., 2009a. Metarepresentation and decoupling in *Northanger Abbey*: Part I. *English Studies*, 90 (5), 518–544.

MacMahon, B., 2009b. Metarepresentation and decoupling in *Northanger Abbey*: Part II. *English Studies*, 90 (6), 673–694.

Morini, M., 2010. The poetics of disengagement: Jane Austen and echoic irony. *Language and Literature*, 19 (4), 339–356.

Owtram, N., 2010. *The pragmatics of academic writing: A relevance approach to the analysis of research article introductions.* Oxford: Peter Lang.

Pilkington, A., 2000. *Poetic effects: A relevance theory perspective.* Amsterdam: John Benjamins.

Pilkington, A., MacMahon, B. and Clark, B., 1997. Looking for an argument: A response to Green. *Language and Literature*, 6 (2), 139–148.

Sperber, D., 1996. *Explaining culture.* Oxford: Wiley-Blackwell.

Sperber, D., 2000. Metarepresentations in an evolutionary perspective. *In:* D. Sperber, ed. *Metarepresentations: A multidisciplinary perspective.* Oxford: Oxford University Press, 117–137.

Sperber, D. and Wilson, D., [1986] 1995. *Relevance: Communication and cognition.* Oxford: Wiley-Blackwell.

Sperber, D. and Wilson, D., 1998. The mapping between the mental and the public lexicon. *In:* P. Carruthers and J. Boucher, eds. *Language and thought: Interdisciplinary themes.* Cambridge: Cambridge University Press, 184–200.

Unger, C., 2006. *Genre, relevance and global coherence: The pragmatics of discourse type*. Basingstoke: Palgrave Macmillan.

Wharton, T., 2009. *Pragmatics and non-verbal communication*. Cambridge: Cambridge University Press.

Wilson, D., 2011. Relevance and the interpretation of literary works. *UCL working papers in linguistics* 23, 69–80. Online. Available at http://www.ucl.ac.uk/psychlangsci/research/linguistics/publications/uclwpl23 (Accessed 21 April 2013).

Wilson, D. and Carston, R., 2007. A unitary approach to lexical pragmatics: Relevance, inference and ad hoc concepts. *In:* N. Burton-Roberts, ed. *Pragmatics*. Basingstoke: Palgrave Macmillan, 230–259.

Wilson, D. and Sperber, D., 2004. Relevance theory. *In:* L. R. Horn and G. Ward, eds. *Handbook of pragmatics*. Oxford: Wiley-Blackwell, 607–632.

Wilson, D. and Sperber, D., 2012. *Relevance and meaning*. Cambridge: Cambridge University Press.

Wimsatt, W. K. and Beardsley, M. C., [1946] 1954. The intentional fallacy. *In:* W. K. Wimsatt, ed. *The verbal icon: Studies in the meaning of poetry*. Lexington KY: University of Kentucky Press, 3–18.

Yus, F., 1998. Relevance theory and media discourse: A verbal-visual model of communication. *Poetics*, 25, 293–309.

Yus, F., 2009. Visual metaphor versus verbal metaphor: A unified account. *In:* C. Forceville and E. Uriós-Aparisi, eds. *Multimodal metaphor*. Berlin: Mouton de Gruyter, 145–172.

10

Stylistics, point of view and modality

Clara Neary

Introduction

This chapter comprises an introduction to one of the most intensively researched areas of stylistic enquiry, that of narratorial *point of view* and its interaction with the linguistic system of modality. Just as in everyday speech we typically use the phrase 'point of view' to refer to a particular person's *perspective* of an action or event, this figurative understanding of the phrase underlies the use of the term in stylistics, as it does in literary, linguistic, art and film theory. However, theories of point of view in narrative are many and varied, with the high levels of research conducted generating a correspondingly high number of differing and often competing definitions which have complicated its discussion somewhat (see Wales 2011, p. 326). As such, this chapter commences with an introduction to and a simultaneous consolidation of existing theories of point of view which allow us to arrive at a workable definition of the term that can act as a basis for consideration of the relationship between point of view and modality. The initial survey will be based upon the three 'bands' of research into point of view as helpfully identified by Simpson (1993). The last of Simpson's research 'bands' – which includes the seminal work of Uspensky (1973) and Fowler's four-part taxonomy of point of view (1996 [1986]) – provides a useful springboard for consideration of the relationship between point of view and *modality*. As Simpson (1993) and others demonstrate, the concept of modality can be utilised to systematically identify the linguistic means by which various differing points of view are manifested in narratives. As such, the interactions between point of view and modality will be discussed in detail, and will include an outline of the four modal systems found in English and the provision of illustrative examples which enable the formalisation of a grammar of point of view through placement within a modal frame. Finally, a consideration of future research into narrative point of view will illustrate the growing trend towards expanding its application.

Point of view

Point of view in literature refers to the 'angle of telling' of a narrative act – that is, the perspective from which events and/or thoughts are related. A pivotal concern in literary criticism since the rise of the novel throughout the eighteenth century, the increasing internalisation of narrative viewpoint characteristic of literary production since the early twentieth century has stimulated much research into this complex construct. Central to the concept of narrative viewpoint is the distinction between *who tells* and *who sees*. In the case of a first-person narrative, for example, events are both 'told' and 'seen' by the same entity, an 'I-narrator'; in third-person narration, the 'story-teller' and the 'viewer' are separate entities. Point of view is an effect produced by the process of narration, with perspective being embedded in the very act of narration even in its most basic form. Consider, for example, that you and a friend are sitting in a sparsely furnished room, facing one another across a table. The only additional object in the room is a coat-stand in the corner. Both of you are asked to describe the room to each other. *You* might commence with a description of the colour of the walls or the carpet; you may mention the coat-stand to your *right*. *Your friend*, sitting across from you, will possibly describe the same things, including the coat-stand to his/her *left*. Immediately, then, there is a difference in the *spatial* perspective being offered: you are both describing the same coat-stand, but its spatial location differs according to your visual perspective. This is a very simple example of how point of view effects are encoded in a narrative, and *spatial point of view* is just one of a number of different types of viewpoint. For instance, your description of the room might be limited to a categorisation of its physical features; your friend, however, noting the sparsity of the surroundings, might describe the room as depressing or gloomy. You are both reporting on the very same room, but your friend has now augmented the narration of their spatial point of view with a description of their *psychological point of view*.

Now, consider that an omniscient entity is peering through the ceiling of that room and describing the scene below to an external listener: he/she/it might relay the speech act in which you gave your physical description of the room, as well as the psychological viewpoint expressed by your friend. However, this omniscient narrator might also relate how you have secretly become bored with your friend's company and wish they would stop depressing you with their description of how 'gloomy' the room is! The purely 'objective' account of the events taking place in the room – the representation of the words used by you and your friend – has been augmented by a rendering of your own, necessarily 'subjective', thoughts. While your friend's psychological point of view has been narrated through either direct or indirect *speech* presentation, your psychological viewpoint has been narrated through either direct or indirect presentation of your *thoughts*. The mode of narration remains third person, but the narratorial viewpoint *reflects* your internal consciousness.

What should be evident from this scenario is, firstly, that point of view can operate on a number of different planes (for example, *spatial* and *psychological*) and secondly, that point of view can vary depending on the mode of narration (first-person versus third-person, for example). Given this, Herman *et al.*'s definition of point of view as 'the physical, psychological and ideological position in terms of which narrated situations and events are presented' is a useful one (2005, p. 442). It may also be obvious from the above scenario that a number of different types of narration are possible. For example, the third-person narrator had access to your internal consciousness, but not that of your friend. Hence the narrator's omniscience has been restricted to reflect *only* your point of view. If the narrator then proceeded to relate your friend's thoughts – perhaps they're wondering how they got stuck in such a grim room with someone they never liked anyway – this would demonstrate the narrator's full omniscience.

In order to flesh out this basic understanding of point of view, the next section will detail the various planes on which point of view operates in narrative; having done so, the following section will proceed to focus specifically on point of view on the *psychological* plane, the most fertile site for linguistic creativity and hence enquiry, and the one in which the grammatical system of *modality* plays a key role.

Types of point of view

Probably the most influential model of point of view in narrative is that originally proposed by narratologist Boris Uspensky (1973), and later redeveloped by Roger Fowler (1996, p. 160–184). Essentially, it offers a four-part taxonomy of the different types of point of view, namely *spatial*, *temporal*, *psychological* and *ideological*. *Spatial* point of view refers to the 'viewing' position adopted by a narrator: in the scenario described above, you described the spatial location of the coat-stand in the room as being on your *right*, while your friend described it as being on his/her *left*. This disparity is an indicator of different spatial viewpoints. Spatial point of view, then, can be defined as point of view in its most literal, non-metaphorical sense. As it represents the visual angle from which an action, event or object is perceived, Chatman (1978) refers to it as *perceptual* point of view. Spatial point of view has close and obvious parallels with films and the visual arts, in that it refers to the virtual 'camera angle' adopted by a text, be that a 'bird's-eye' view, a close up, etc. Next, *temporal* point of view is concerned with how time is perceived by the narrator; specifically, as Fowler states, it relates to 'the impression which a reader gains of events moving rapidly or slowly, in a continuous chain or isolated segments' (Fowler 1986, p. 127). As such, techniques of temporal viewpoint include *analepsis* (flashbacks), *prolepsis* (flashforwards) and narrative gaps. As the spatial location of an object or event is at least partially dependent on *when* it is perceived, Uspensky (1973) conflates both categories into that of spatio-temporal viewpoint. In any case, the primary linguistic indicators of spatial and temporal point of view tend to be markers of the linguistic system of deixis. The *ideological* plane of point of view, or what Chatman (1978) defines as *conceptual* point of view, is most aptly defined by Simpson who perceives it as 'the way in which a text mediates a set of particular ideological beliefs through either character, narrator or author' (2004, p. 78). These ideological beliefs can be expressed through the 'mouthpiece' of a character, narrator or author, though it must be noted that they may or may not be condoned by the author. However, as Simpson remarks, there is an inherent difficulty in attempting to categorise ideological point of view, given that *all* texts embody ideological perspectives on some level through their representations of particular types of story world and choice of the genre of representation. Given that ideology, by its very nature, is embedded in *all* language choice, Fowler's definition of ideological point of view as 'the set of values, or belief system, communicated by the language of the text' (1996, p. 165) is rendered somewhat redundant. As Simpson remarks, a fully operational model of ideological point of view has yet to be developed (2004, p. 78).

Returning again to the scenario in which you and your friend are sitting in a room: in giving a physical description of the room, you might describe the colour of the carpet as 'blue' while your friend might label it 'cerulean blue'. Both statements are equally true, but the disparity in visual and cognitive perspective suggested by the differing colour labels occurs because you and your friend are separate entities, with differing attitudes and differing beliefs, values and knowledge systems. In a narrative representation of the scenario, told by the 'presence' peering in through the ceiling of the room, each of you can be considered a *medium* through which a point of view is potentially reflected, with the resultant point of view operating on the *psychological* plane. The *psychological* plane of point of view refers to the ways in which a narrative can be refracted through an individual consciousness or perception, be that of a character or a narrator. As such, depictions of the spatial and temporal viewpoint can also be considered representations of a character/narrator's psychological point of view because that character/narrator's belief and knowledge systems will influence their understanding, and hence their representation, of their spatio-temporal viewpoint. It is worth noting at this stage that the differing types of viewpoint – spatial, temporal, ideological and *particularly* psychological – are often depicted in narrative through a stylistic technique known as *speech and thought presentation*. Essentially, speech and thought presentation encompasses the various ways in which events, actions and states in a narrative can be described through, variously, direct or indirect speech or thought representation or the narrative report of a speech or thought act. (For an in-depth consideration of this technique, see Chapter 13 in this volume. See Short (1996) for a checklist of further linguistic indicators of point of view in a narrative.)

Psychological point of view

Point of view on the *psychological plane* is probably the most fertile in terms of literary and associated linguistic creativity, being a crucial technique for characterisation. Unsurprisingly, then, it has been the subject of a great deal of linguistic research. Simpson (1993) identifies three distinct 'bands' of research on psychological point of view in narrative: the *structuralist*, *generative* and *interpersonal* approaches. *Structuralist* approaches attempt to identify and define the abstract principles which underlie literary production, while *generative* approaches are characterised by their detailed analysis of individual sets of sentences, from which a theory of narrative communication can be 'generated'. While remaining mindful of the dangers of condensing such broad and complex strands of research into a one-sentence summary, for the purposes of this chapter, the differences between the two can be delineated as follows: the *structuralist* approach effectively focuses on the *macrostructures* of literary communication, while the generative approach concentrates on its *microstructures* (see Simpson 1993, p. 35). The *interpersonal* approach can be considered something of a 'middle ground': firmly pragmatic in orientation, it is concerned with identifying the linguistic techniques that make up the 'character' of a text. Given that the chief concern of the interpersonal function of language is to isolate the linguistic features which add communicative 'texture' to a text – what Simpson refers to as 'the compositional techniques of message construction' (1993, p. 38) integral to, for example, the process of characterisation – the resulting band of research is the most appropriate for this study of point of view in narrative. However, research carried out through the structuralist and generative approaches is not without its merits and has provided an invaluable foundation upon which the interpersonal approach to point of view has been built. Singled out for attention here is the influential framework of viewpoint proposed by narratologist Gérard Genette (1980).

Firstly, Genette (1980) helpfully identifies the two different positions which a narrator can occupy relative to a story: a *homodiegetic* narrator is an *internal* participant in the story he/she is narrating, while a *heterodiegetic* narrator is *external* to the narrative action. Identification of this structural contrast has proven crucial to the development of subsequent typologies of point of view. Secondly, Genette's (1980, pp. 188–192) three-tier typology of psychological viewpoint, which he refers to as narrative 'mood', has greatly influenced research in this area. Eschewing the term 'point of view' on the basis of its purely visual connotations, Genette favours the alternative phrase *focus of narration*. His resultant typology of viewpoint identifies three different types of focalization: *zero focalization* (also known as *nonfocalized narrative*), *internal focalization* and *external focalization*. *Zero focalization* refers to what Genette terms 'classical narratives', in which the omniscient narrator appears to know, and say, more than any of the characters. *Internal focalization* occurs in narratives where narratorial omniscience is restricted; such restriction can be *fixed* (confined to the perspective of one character), *variable* (varying between the perspectives of two or more characters) or *multiple* (in which the narrator provides more than one perspective on the same event). *External focalization* describes narratives in which the narrator reveals less than is known by the characters and does not give access to a characters' internal consciousness. Influential as it has been, this typology of viewpoint is not without its limitations. As McIntyre notes (2006, pp. 32–37), firstly, the visual connotations of the term 'point of view' are not overcome by adoption of the semantically similar term 'focalization'. Furthermore, Genette's contention that the distinction between *who sees* and *who speaks* is entirely extraneous to consideration of point of view effects seems to be a 'logical impossibility' (McIntyre 2006, p. 36). Moreover, the theory of focalization fails to comment meaningfully upon how point of view effects are produced in a narrative (see Simpson 1993, p. 34, McIntyre 2006, p. 36). Finally, little attempt is made to describe the interrelationship between *homodiegetic/heterodiegetic* narration and external focalization (see Simpson 1993, p. 34).

The interpersonal approach to psychological point of view

Given its particular focus on identifying the linguistic construction of narrative point of view effects, the *interpersonal* approach to research in this area overcomes at least one of the major problems of Genette's structuralist typology. However, Genette's framework is illustrative of a general trend towards defining point of view effects in terms of the type of narration that is taking place, a trend that is evidenced in the majority of theories of viewpoint put forward by those adopting an interpersonal approach to research in this area. Once again, the most influential framework of types of narration is that originally devised by Uspensky (1973) and later revised by Fowler (1996 [1986]).

Uspensky (1973) was among the first to develop a theory of narrative viewpoint, and he began by distinguishing between two different types of narration: *internal* and *external*. *Internal* narration refers to narration that is restricted to the 'subjective viewpoint' of a particular character or characters in the narrative. *External* narration, on the other hand, is ostensibly 'objective' and can include commentary on the characters, actions and events depicted in the narrative. First-person narration is inherently subjective, but subjectivity is also possible in third-person narration, especially if the narrator prioritises the viewpoint of a particular character or set of characters. As McIntyre (2006, p. 23) notes, Uspensky's classification of narrators has two 'clear consequences' for viewpoint effects: firstly, that internal narration is inherently restricted, and secondly, that external narration prioritises the perspective of the narrator rather than that of any specific character or characters.

Fowler (1996 [1986]) endeavours to address the issues inherent in Uspensky's (1973) framework by putting forward a more nuanced classification of types of narration. As such, he sub-divides the latter's categories of internal and external narration. *Internal Type A* narration is 'narration from a point of view within a character's consciousness, manifesting his or her feelings about, and evaluations of, the events and characters of the story' (Fowler 1996, p. 170). Essentially, then, this mode of narration is highly subjective, located as it is entirely within a participating character's consciousness and expressing their thoughts and feelings on the other characters and events taking place in the narrative. Technically, examples of Internal Type A can be found in first- or third-person narratives. However, because the interior of a character's consciousness is most convincingly described through first-person narration, Internal Type A can be considered a predominantly first-person narrative mode. Its characteristic subjectivity is typically achieved through the use of *verba sentiendi* (words denoting thoughts, feelings and perceptions) and what Simpson describes as a 'foregrounded modality' (1993, p. 39), a concept that will be elaborated upon shortly.

Internal Type B narration, according to Fowler, presents 'the point of view of someone who is *not* a participating character but who has knowledge of the feelings of the characters – a narrator, or the so-called 'omniscient' author' (Fowler 1996, p. 170; emphasis added). As such, it is always presented in the third person. As the focus is on the interior consciousness of a character(s) and not on the author's perception of the character(s), Simpson rightly notes that authorial modality is not evident in examples of Internal Type B narration; however, as the author is supplying us with a character's thoughts and feelings, *verba sentiendi* are still present (1993, p. 40).

The external modes of narration developed by Fowler are linked, as Simpson notes, by 'the general avoidance, on the part of the narrator, of any description of characters' thoughts and feelings' (1993, p. 40–41). *External Type C* narration is predicated upon the narrator's avoidance of any overt account of or engagement with a character's thoughts or feelings, or, as Fowler himself stipulates, 'at least, avoidance of any claim to the fidelity of such an account' (1996, p. 177). As such, Type C may be considered the most impersonal and 'objective' form of third-person narration. Its 'refusal' to report upon a character's internal consciousness is marked by the absence of *verba sentiendi*; similarly, authorial modality cannot be present in a narrative which ostensibly denies the author a voice.

External Type D narration differs from its Type C counterpart in that Type D highlights 'the persona of the narrator … perhaps by first person pronouns, and certainly by explicit modality' (Fowler 1996, p. 178). Type D narration is characterised by the author 'pretending' not to have access to the character's thoughts or feelings, a ruse carried out through the use of non-factive verbs such as 'seemed' and 'appeared' and so-called 'words of estrangement', a phrase Uspensky coined to include adverbs of manner such as *evidently*, *apparently* and *perhaps*, as well as metaphors and comparisons. As Simpson remarks, External Type D narration is 'most intriguing and most problematic', and its effect is striking, with the impression being created 'of a narrator who controls the telling of the story and who has definite views on the characters and events of the story, though, curiously, at the same time has no privileged access to the thoughts and feelings of those characters' (1993, p. 42).

McIntyre (2006, pp. 28–29) is quick to point out the problems inherent in Fowler's typology. Firstly, the distinction between External Type C and D is too subtle, based as it is upon the assertion that in Type D the narrator foregrounds 'the limitations of authorial knowledge' (Fowler 1996, p. 170). However, these limitations are also inherent in Type C, given Fowler's insistence that Type C narration not only avoids engaging with a character's *verba sentiendi* but also evades 'any claim to the fidelity of such an account' (Fowler 1996, p. 177). In any case, as McIntyre proceeds to note, the categorisation of External Type C narration is effectively redundant given that it is rare to encounter a text that purposefully neglects to depict the internal state of a single character. One might also debate the usefulness of such a distinction to literary interpretation: would a reader's awareness that the narrator is only *pretending* not to have access to a character's thoughts or feelings throughout the duration of a text actually affect their interpretation of the text? The end result is, after all, the same: no access to the character's *verba sentiendi*. Furthermore, as McIntyre states, there is no allowance made for alternative modes of narration, such as second person narration. Moreover, Fowler's categorisation of narrators appears to be based on an assumption that the type of narration is unvarying throughout the course of a narrative, which is not the case (see McIntyre 2006, pp. 28–29).

Although Fowler's taxonomy of narratorial modes is elegant and certainly comprehensive, at times some of its classifications are somewhat 'counter-intuitive', as Simpson (1993) points out. For example, a text which conveys an objective, even 'alienated' viewpoint, may have to be classified as an *Internal Type A* narrative simply because that 'isolation' is both experienced and reported by a character who is a participant in the action, rather than by an external narrator (Simpson 1993, p. 54). As such, Simpson expands upon Fowler's framework, integrating into it the concept of modality. This 'modal grammar of point of view' (Simpson 1993, p. 55) endeavours to overcome the problems inherent in Fowler's model by offering a more nuanced and integrated framework and one which, most importantly, can account for the various differing viewpoints expressed in narrative by identifying the linguistic techniques which underpin them. The next section outlines the grammatical system of modality, and delineates the four types of modal system found in the English language. The section following this will introduce Simpson's (1993) modal grammar of point of view.

Modality

Thus far, we have considered the various types of narration, emphasising throughout their centrality to point of view effects in narrative. For example, we have noted how an Internal Type A narrative results in the expression of a highly 'subjective' viewpoint, focalized through the internal consciousness of a participating character, while External Types C and D avoid any representation of a character's thoughts or feelings, thereby projecting an ostensibly 'objective' viewpoint. We have also noted the linguistic techniques which evince each of these narrative modes, and which act as a potential means of identifying which mode is in operation. These techniques namely involve the employment of *verba sentiendi* and *modality*, the presence or absence of which greatly affects the mode of narration and hence the presentation of point of view. Referring to words that denote feelings, thoughts and perceptions, *verba sentiendi* are relatively easy to recognise and identify. However, thus far a rather informal definition of modality has been in operation; in order to fully understand and appreciate its centrality to viewpoint effects in narrative, it is necessary to elaborate upon this concept further. This is the intention of the current section.

As Fowler notes (1996, p. 167), there are numerous ways in which grammatical structures can convey modal commitment, including modal auxiliaries, modal or sentence adverbs, evaluative adjectives and adverbs, generic sentences and verbs of knowledge, evaluation and prediction. Simpson suggests that the identification and classification of the different *types* of modality found in English would constitute 'a useful supplement' (1993, p. 47) to Fowler's framework and prove extremely useful to the resultant development of a modal grammar of point of view. As modality refers to a speaker's (or, given the current context, a narrator's) attitude towards or opinion regarding 'the necessary or contingent truth of propositions' (Lyons 1977, p. 791) – which, as Simpson notes, also extends to the speaker's/narrator's 'attitude towards the situation or event described by a sentence' (1993, p. 47) – it can be considered part of the *interpersonal* function of language (see Halliday 1994, Halliday and Hasan 1989).

The four modal systems of English are as follows: the *deontic* system and its close relative the *boulomaic* system, and the *epistemic* system and its subsystem *perception*. The *deontic* system of modality contains those words that express a speaker's attitude towards the degree of duty or obligation attached to carrying out certain actions. This system is hence integral to communicative strategies of social interaction, most notably to strategies of persuasion and politeness. The deontic system of modality is expressed through the use of modal auxiliaries (e.g. *must, should, may*) or through adjectival and participial combinations such as 'BE …

THAT' and 'BE … TO' constructions (e.g. *He is allowed to come; It is essential that he come*), all of which have the potential to convey what Simpson terms a 'continuum of commitment from permission through obligation to requirement' (1993: 48).

The *boulomaic* system of modality is closely related to the deontic system, involving as it does the expression of 'desire'. It is conveyed through the use of modal lexical verbs – such as *hope, wish* and *regret* – which express a speaker's wishes and desires. Adjective and participle combinations with 'BE ... THAT' and 'BE ... TO' can also be employed (e.g. *It is hoped that he will come*; *It is good that he is coming*), as can modal adverbs which are related to modal lexical verbs (e.g. *Hopefully, he will come*).

Epistemic modality is regarded by Simpson as 'possibly the most important regarding the analysis of point of view', as it is concerned with 'the speaker's confidence or lack of confidence in the truth of a proposition expressed' (1993, p. 48). It can be conveyed in a number of ways: through use of modal auxiliaries (e.g. *He could be wrong*); modal lexical verbs (e.g. *He supposes he is right*); adjectives in the 'BE ... THAT' and 'BE ... TO' constructions (e.g. *It is certain that he is wrong*); and through epistemic modal adverbs (e.g. *maybe, possibly, perhaps, probably, certainly* etc.). Categorical assertions, it should be noted, differ from epistemic statements. Categorical assertions are deemed 'epistemically non-modal', as they convey a speaker's strongest possible commitment to the factuality of an utterance while epistemic statements always involve some degree of qualification of the speaker's commitment to the veracity of the proposition being uttered (Lyons 1977, p. 763).

Finally, *perception* modality constitutes a sub-system of epistemic modality in that the level of the speaker's commitment to the veracity of a proposition is based upon a reference to human powers of perception, usually visual perception (see Perkins 1983, p. 81). It is conveyed through adjective plus 'BE ... THAT' and 'BE ... TO' constructions (e.g. *It is obvious that he is wrong*) and through their related modal adverbs (e.g. *Obviously, he is wrong*).

Having outlined the categories and accompanying characteristics of the four modal systems of English, it is necessary to move on to a consideration of how Simpson (1993) endeavours to overcome the problems associated with extant frameworks of point of view by developing a typology that engages fully with the intricacies of these modal systems.

A modal grammar of point of view in narrative

Simpson's development of a modal grammar of narrative viewpoint constitutes an attempt to extend Fowler's work and thereby offer a more nuanced framework that provides both accurate categorisation of point of view effects and a means of identifying the linguistic techniques that typify each of these categories. Simpson's modal grammar of point of view is based on the supposition that the four modal systems found in English are 'distributed unevenly across the point of view categories and that certain modalities are specific to, or at least dominant in, particular categories' (Simpson 1993, p. 51). Simpson begins by introducing the terms *category A* and *category B* narratives.

Category A narratives are defined as 'those which are narrated in the first person by a participating character within the story' (Simpson 1993, p. 55). As such they correspond with Genette's *homodiegetic* narrators as the narrator is a participant in the story he/she is narrating. *Category B* narratives are all related by a third-person narrator who is not a participant in the story; as such they can be equated with Genette's *heterodiegetic* narration (see Genette 1980, p. 248). Category B can be further broken down according to whether or not the narrator relates events through the internal consciousness of one of the story's characters. If events are related from *outside* a character's consciousness, it is category B in *narratorial mode*; if events are related from *inside* a character's consciousness, that is, they are *reflected* through a character's perspective, it is said to be category B in *reflector mode*. Both category A and category B narratives can be further subdivided on the basis of the type of modal shading in evidence, whether positive, negative or neutral. Identification of the type of modality employed will not only assist in identifying the mode of narration; it also provides a means of pinpointing the linguistic techniques involved in narrative point of view, something which preceding frameworks have largely failed to do.

Before delineating Simpson's modal grammar of viewpoint, it is best to first elaborate upon the concept of modal 'shading'. *Positive* shading is used to describe those narratives where the modal system employed renders a narrative more tangible or, in Simpsons' words, 'more co-operatively trained' towards the reader (1993, p. 56). In positively shaded narratives, the *deontic* and *boulomaic* systems of modality (particularly their high values) are foregrounded, resulting in a narrative which lays bare the psyche of the narrator and/or character(s) through the expression of their duties, obligations and desires. *Negative* modal shading, on the other hand, can result in a rather intangible narrative often characterised by a reader's uncertainty as to the 'facticity' of the events, actions or characters described. Appropriate use of (typically lower values of) *epistemic* and *perception* modality plays a pivotal role in the negative modal shading of a narrative. Finally, *neutral* modal shading is characterised by a complete absence of modality. As such, there is no psychological evaluation of actions, events or characters provided by narrator and/or character(s); rather, unmodalised categorical assertions are prevalent (see Simpson 1993, p. 56).

Category A narratives

This section will turn in full to Simpson's modal grammar of point of view and its attendant taxonomy of narrative types with a consideration of Category A narratives – that is, first-person narratives in which the narrator is a participant in the story-world. Simpson's *Category A Positive (A+ve)* can be considered 'virtually identical' to Fowler's Internal Type A (Simpson 1993, p. 56). The linguistic features integral to this type of narration are *verba sentiendi* and evaluative adjectives and adverbs; this is coupled with the employment of deontic and boulomaic modal indicators, while the more 'alienating' forms of epistemic and perception modality are absent. Simpson identifies Charlotte Brontë's *Jane Eyre* (1847) as being almost entirely in *A+ve* mode. The first-person narration of Esther Summerson in *Bleak House* (1853) also contains examples:

> Mrs. Rachael was too good to feel any emotion at parting, but I was not so good, and wept bitterly. I thought that *I ought to have* known her better after so many years and *ought to have* made myself enough of a favourite with her to make her sorry then. When she gave me one cold parting kiss upon my forehead, like a thaw-drop from the stone porch—it was a very frosty day—I felt so miserable and self-reproachful that I clung to her and told her it was my fault, I knew, that she could say good-bye so easily!
>
> *(Broadview edn., p. 79)*

Italicised in the above passage are the deontic modal indicators typical of this mode of narration; the use of *verba sentiendi* including 'thought', 'felt', 'wept', 'miserable' and 'self-reproachful', together with the certainty with which Esther castigates herself for Mrs. Rachael's coolness at their separation, are also noteworthy in this context. The overall effect is of a psychological 'closeness' to the events and actions occurring in the narrative, reflected as they are through a first-person participating narrator.

Category A Negative (A-ve) narratives are characterised by a proliferation of epistemic signifiers – such as modal auxiliaries, modal adverbs and modal lexical verbs – and perception modal markers such as *apparently* and *evidently*. In addition, as Simpson notes, there is 'a development of comparative structures which have some basis in human perception' – for example, *it seemed as if, it appeared to be, it looked as though* and so on (1993, p. 58). Because of its negative shading, this category is akin to Fowler's External Type D, although, unlike in Fowler's model, Simpson's category includes narratives which reflect a participating character's consciousness. The resultant narrative is characterised by a state of uncertainty, with events rendered less 'real' and hence potentially confusing to the reader. As Simpson notes, the position of the 'undermining' epistemic and perception markers in the narrative is fundamental to the resultant effect; foregrounding these markers results in the 'factuality' of what follows being immediately questioned, while placing them after the depiction of a certain event/thought results in readerly confusion as categorical assertions are effectively undermined. The following passage from F. Scott Fitzgerald's *The Great Gatsby* (1925) evidences the homodiegetic narrator's estrangement from his own thoughts and actions as foregrounded through the use of negative modality:

> But all this part of it *seemed* remote and unessential. I *found myself* on Gatsby's side, and alone. From the moment I telephoned news of the catastrophe to West Egg village, every surmise about him, and every practical question, was referred to me. At first I *was surprised* and *confused*; then, as he lay in his house and didn't move or breathe or speak hour upon hour it grew upon me that I was responsible, because no one else was interested – interested, I mean, with that intense personal interest to which every one has some vague right at the end.
>
> *(Penguin edn., pp. 155–56)*

Occurring as it does in the wake of Gatsby's murder, the 'surprise' and 'confusion' professed by the homodiegetic narrator of this passage act as a fitting juxtaposition to the confidence and self-assurance suggested by the levels of high modality identified by Fowler in the novel's opening passages (1996, pp. 171–72). While Fowler identified the novel as an archetypal Type A point of view, the addition of modal shading to the categorisation of narratorial mode enables an understanding of the nuances lent to a narrative through variations in modal shading. Overall, such use of the epistemic and perception modal systems can result in a 'destabilisation' of the 'facticity' of events and actions told by an *A-ve* narrator. As demonstrated above, such 'destabilisation' is particularly effective when carried out through a narrative transition from *A+ve* to *A-ve* mode; indeed, at the end of the above example there is a reversion to *A+ve* mode as the narrator becomes aware of his obligations to his dead friend.

The final Category A mode of narration, *Category A Neutral*, is typically devoid of any attempt at a psychological evaluation of the actions, events or characters which populate the narrative. Rather, the narrator tends to withhold their 'subjective' opinions, preferring to tell the story solely through categorical assertions. Eschewing psychological exposition, A neutral narratives are usually characterised by extended passages of physical description and whole texts in this mode are, unsurprisingly, rather rare. The following constitutes an example in a passage from William Faulkner's *As I Lay Dying* (1930):

> When we reach it I turn and follow the path which circles the house. Jewel, fifteen feet behind me, looking straight ahead, steps in a single stride through the window. Still staring straight ahead, his pale eyes like wood set into his wooden face, he crosses the floor in four strides with the rigid gravity of a cigar store Indian dressed in patched

overalls and endued with life from the hips down, and steps in a single stride through the opposite window and into the path again just as I come around the corner. In single file and five feet apart and Jewel now in front, we go on up the path toward the foot of the bluff.

(Vintage edn., p. 4)

It is important to note that, as evidenced in the Faulkner extract above, the purely physical description of events can nevertheless inform the psychological dimension of a narrative in multiple ways: for example, the physical distance between the brothers underscores their emotional estrangement; the apparent absence of immediate psychological evaluation – underscored by the temporal proximity accorded to the use of the present tense – reflects the numbness felt by the homodiegetic narrator now faced with his mother's imminent death; and the references to 'wood' and 'wooden face' anticipate the sight of their mother's coffin which awaits both boys in the passage that follows. Further examples of the 'flat, almost "journalistic" feel' of A neutral narratives are particularly prevalent in 'hard-boiled' detective novels, as Simpson notes (1993, p. 61).

Category B narratives

Category B narratives are more complex than their category A counterparts, though there are definite correspondences between the two. As noted above, category B narratives are all third-person *heterodiegetic* – that is, the narrator is not a participant in the story being told – and can be divided into two modes, depending on whether the narrator reflects the narrative action through the consciousness of a participating character (*reflector mode*) or not (*narratorial mode*). The resultant *narratorial* and *reflector* modes can be further categorised according to their positive, negative or neutral shading, in a manner which corresponds with the discussion of Category A narratives above.

Category B in *narratorial mode (B(N))* is characterised by a third-person heterodiegetic narrator relating a story from a '"floating" viewing position' (Simpson 1993, p. 55) outside of the consciousness of any character. In its foregrounded deontic and boulomaic modality, use of evaluative adjectives and adverbs and 'universal' statements, the first sub-category *B(N) positive (B(N)+ve)* corresponds closely with its category A counterpart, though a category B narrator does not participate in the narrative action. Examples can be found in the novels of Thomas Hardy, and they tend to suggest a merging of authorial with narratorial voice. The following example is drawn from *Far From The Madding Crowd* (1874):

> The wondrous power of flattery in *passados* at woman is a perception so universal as to be remarked upon by many people almost as automatically as they repeat a proverb, or say that they are Christians and the like, without thinking much of the enormous corollaries which spring from the proposition. Still less is it acted upon for the good of the complemental being alluded to. With the majority such an opinion is shelved with all those trite aphorisms which require some catastrophe to bring their tremendous meanings thoroughly home.
>
> *(Penguin edn., pp. 161–162)*

The positive modal shading of this passage – evidenced in the 'factuality' of its mode of narration and its use of generic assertions (e.g. 'so universal') which preclude the 'mitigating' presence of low value epistemic or perception modalities – plus the open access to the

185

narratorial psyche, together establish a distance between narrator and character which aligns appropriately with the relative 'objectivity' characteristic of third-person heterodiegetic narration. Degrees of shading can obviously vary, with the 'highly modalised' prose of D.H. Lawrence identified by Simpson as *B(N)+ve* in its most 'extreme' form (1993, p. 65).

B(N) negative (B(N)-ve) narratives have a similar 'feel' to their category A equivalents as epistemic and perception modalities are similarly foregrounded while deontic and boulomaic modal markers are suppressed. B(N) negative narratives are characterised by a negative modal shading which appears to destabilise the 'reality' of events and characters in the story world. This feature is further accentuated by the 'alienating or disquieting effects' (Simpson 1993, p. 66) caused by the absence of any report of characters' thoughts or feelings, and the employment of Fowler's 'words of estrangement'. In fact, this category corresponds closely with Fowler's External Type D narration. As Simpson notes, *B(N)-ve* narratorial mode is often used in the description of villains (1993, p. 67), with the supposition being that villains can be judged on their external appearance and actions alone, access to their psyches in such cases being deemed neither necessary nor desirable. The following description of the Dickensian villain Orlick in *Great Expectations* (1861) is a fitting example:

> He was a broadshouldered loose-limbed swarthy fellow of great strength, never in a hurry, and always slouching. He *never even seemed* to come to his work on purpose, but would slouch in *as if* by mere accident; and when he went to the Jolly Bargemen to eat his dinner, or went away at night, he would slouch out, like Cain or the Wandering Jew, *as if* he had no idea where he was going and no intention of ever coming back. […] On Sundays he mostly lay all day on the sluice-gates, or stood against ricks and barns. He always slouched, locomotively, with his eyes on the ground; and, when accosted or otherwise required to raise them, he looked up in a half-resentful, half-puzzled way, *as though* the only thought he ever had was, that it was rather an odd and injurious fact that he should never be thinking.
>
> *(Penguin edn., p. 30)*

The estrangement evidenced through use of non-factive verbs such as 'seemed' and repeated use of comparators such as 'as if' and 'as though' ensure a purposeful distance is maintained between the narrator and the villain's consciousness which is strengthened by the reservation of statements of 'facticity' – such as 'mostly' and 'always' – for descriptions of Orlick's external appearance, which, of course, bears the mark of his villainy.

B(N) neutral narratorial mode can be equated with Fowler's External Type C and Genette's 'external focalization', as well as what Rimmon-Kenan (1983) terms 'objective focalization'. It is also similar to A neutral, though obviously category B is rendered in the third-person. With no modal shading in evidence, and the story told from outside the consciousness of any narrative participants, B(N) neutral is perhaps the most impersonal, 'objective' form of narrative. As such, it is *ostensibly* the narrative mode of media broadcasting, although of course such an assertion is immediately problematised by the critical linguist's awareness that ideology can be encoded in language in many ways. Simpson points out that the characteristic 'flatness' of Hemingway's work may be explained by considering it an example of a B(N) neutral narrative, with its predominance of categorical assertions and corresponding absence of any narratorial modality (1993, p. 68).

The sub-categories within category B in *reflector mode (B(R))* are all characterised by a narratorial assumption of a degree of omniscience that facilitates entry into a character's consciousness and subsequent reflection of narrative events *through* their consciousness.

That character then becomes the *reflector* of fiction. Overall, the B(R) sub-categories all correspond closely both to their B(N) and their category A counterparts. B(R) positive (*B(R)+ve*), for example, displays the same type of modality as B(N)+ve and A+ve, with the primary difference being that in a B(R)+ve narrative, events are refracted by the third-person narrator through the consciousness of a participating character. B(R)+ve modes also employ similar linguistic techniques, such as *verba sentiendi*, evaluative adjectives and adverbs and deontic and boulomaic modal expressions. Speech and thought presentation is used to considerable effect in this narrative mode, particularly *free indirect discourse*. Novelist Henry James's technique of restricted or selective omniscience – or what Genette refers to as 'fixed' internal focalization (1980, p. 189) – effectively results in a B(R)+ve narrative mode.

Similarly, *B(R) negative* (*B(R)-ve*) narratives are akin to A-ve and B(N)-ve narratives, with a relatively high volume of 'words of estrangement' and negatively shaded epistemic and perception modal markers, the only difference being that in *B(R)-ve* narratives, the modality reflects that of a participating character rather than of the heterodiegetic narrator. Occurrences of *B(R)-ve* narratives often occur within *B(N)-ve* narratives, with temporary narratorial transitions into a character's consciousness taking place. The following extract from Kafka's *The Trial* (1925), cited by Simpson (1993, p. 72), constitutes an apt example, encapsulating in one brief passage the transition from *B(N)-ve* to *B(R)-ve* mode as Joseph K.'s perception of the 'old lady' is highlighted:

> K. waited for a little while longer, watching from his pillow the old lady opposite, who *seemed to be* peering at him with a curiosity unusual even for her …
>
> *(Penguin edn., p. 7)*

The final sub-category in the category B mode, *B(R) neutral*, is more complicated than its counterparts due to its neutrally shaded modality. In the absence of modality of any type, this narrative mode is comprised solely of categorical assertions, and the resultant 'objectivity' leads to confusion over whether the narrative remains in the reflector mode or has crossed over into narratorial mode. However, as Simpson notes, 'in either case, events and characters are viewed dispassionately and without recourse to the four available modalities' (1993, p. 73); as such, though with the same caveat applied as before, journalistic reportage is assumed to adopt the 'categorical, unmodalised discourse' typified by B(R) neutral narratives (1993, p. 74).

Simpson's modal grammar of point of view facilitates a more nuanced categorisation of narrative types than has been afforded by any of its predecessors, and in particular it enables identification of the linguistic devices integral to the narrative representation of point of view. While offering an extremely detailed, descriptive and all-encompassing framework of narrative viewpoint, Simpson's modal grammar is not, however, without its limitations. Short (2000), for example, raises questions as to the degree of internalisation that must be present in a narrative before a reflector effectively 'exists', while McIntyre (2006, p. 30) rightly suggests that Simpson's model cannot account for all the potential variations of narrative viewpoint. Furthermore, the boundaries between categories are rendered somewhat porous when fluctuations in the degree of modal commitment expressed in a narrative and the surrounding linguistic context of the utterance are taken into account. Moreover, most fiction narratives are comprised of more than one narratorial mode. Further refinement of Simpson's model is certainly necessary; nevertheless, as it stands this modal grammar of point of view offers an effective and viable framework by which to both identify and track alterations in the narratorial mode(s) adopted in a text, thereby facilitating a greater understanding of narrative processes such as characterisation.

Recommendations for practice

The degree to which narratives consistently adhere to a given narratorial mode can vary, particularly in terms of modal shading. However, it is the very 'slipperiness' of narratorial modes which confirms the usefulness of point of view categorisation as a tool of stylistic analysis. Consider the following passage from Hardy's *The Mayor of Casterbridge* (1886):

> They walked side by side in such a way as *to suggest afar off* the low, easy, confidential chat of people full of reciprocity; but *on closer view it could be discerned* that the man was reading, or pretending to read, a ballad sheet which he kept before his eyes with some difficulty by the hand that was passed through the basket strap.
> [...] That the man and woman were husband and wife, and the parents of the girl in arms *there could be little doubt.* No other than such relationship *would have accounted for* the atmosphere of stale familiarity which the trio carried along with them like a nimbus as they moved down the road.
>
> *(Penguin edn., pp. 69–70)*

As mentioned above, Hardy's novels are full of examples of B(N) positive narratorial mode. However, in the above example, though category B narratorial mode is maintained throughout, the 'authority' of the narratorial voice is undermined by the use of epistemic and perception modal markers (highlighted above) which compromise the facticity of events related in the passage and foreground the distance between author and narrator. In so doing the narratorial voice in this example aligns itself with the psychological viewing position of the reader; this is compounded through use of spatial deictic indicators such as 'afar' and 'on closer view' which place narrator and reader on a common spatial and psychological plane. Such shifts encourage complicity between narrator and reader and in securing the reader's cognitive investment they concomitantly encourage emotional and empathetic engagement with the narrative. As is the case with all stylistic shifts, any analysis of point of view should pay particular attention to the context in which such shifts take place, thereby facilitating investigation of their potential interpretive effect(s).

Future directions

Few attempts to resolve the issues attendant in both Simpson's framework and those of his 'predecessors' have resulted in the further development and/or categorisation of the relationship between point of view and modality. Instead, research into narrative viewpoint has expanded in other directions, though the Uspensky-Fowler and Simpson models remain of seminal importance. The cognitive turn in narrative viewpoint studies is particularly evident. In its attempt to at least partially account for viewpoint effects in readers by tracing such effects to their linguistic signifiers, Simpson's (1993) modal grammar and its Fowlerian antecedent may be considered harbingers of this 'turn'. McIntyre's (2006) extension of the discussion of point of view beyond the traditional generic boundaries of prose to drama, Sotirova's (2006) analysis of reader responses to narrative point of view, and Bosseaux's (2007) effective application of point of view theory to translated texts, together with the increasing use of Simpson's modal grammar of point of view by critical discourse analysts, all constitute some of the ways in which point of view studies continue to expand.

Related topics

Creative writing and stylistics, narratology, speech and thought presentation, stylistics and film, stylistics and performance

Further reading

Fowler, R., 1996. *Linguistic criticism,* 2nd edn. Oxford: Oxford University Press.

The second edition of this text further clarifies Fowler's pioneering contribution towards research in narrative point of view.

McIntyre, D., 2006. *Point of view in plays.* Amsterdam: John Benjamins.

In this text, McIntyre expands extant research on narrative point of view beyond the generic boundaries of prose, and in so doing, advocates a cognitive approach to research in this area.

Short, M., 1996. *Exploring the language of poems, plays and prose*. London: Longman.

Short's checklist of linguistic indicators of point of view, detailed in this text, is an excellent introduction to the myriad ways in which point of view can be expressed in a narrative.

Simpson, P., 1993. *Language, ideology and point of view*. London: Routledge.

Here, Simpson first develops and then applies his modal grammar of viewpoint to both literary and non-literary texts, using an array of stylistic and critical linguistic analytical tools.

Uspensky, B., 1973. *A poetics of composition*. V. Zavarin and S. Wittig, trans. Berkeley: University of California Press.

Uspensky's original framework of point of view is carefully delineated in this text, providing a foundation for subsequent theories and models of viewpoint.

References

Bosseaux, C., 2007. *How does it feel? Point of view in translation*. Amsterdam: Rodopi.
Brontë, C., [1847] 2006. *Jane Eyre*. London: Penguin.
Chatman, S., 1978. *Story and discourse: Narrative structure in fiction and film*. Ithaca: Cornell University Press.
Dickens, C., [1853] 2010. *Bleak house*. London: Broadview.
Dickens, C., [1861] 1999. *Great expectations*. London: Penguin.
Faulkner, W., [1930] 1991. *As I lay dying*. London: Vintage.
Fitzgerald, F. S., [1925] 2000. *The great Gatsby*. London: Penguin.
Fowler, R., 1986. *Linguistic criticism*. Oxford: Oxford University Press.
Fowler, R., 1996. *Linguistic criticism*. 2nd edn. Oxford: Oxford University Press.
Genette, G., 1980. *Narrative discourse*. New York: Cornell University Press.
Halliday, M. A. K., 1994. *An introduction to functional grammar*. 2nd edn. London: Edward Arnold.
Halliday, M. A. K. and Hasan, R., 1989. *Language, context and text: Aspects of language in a social-semiotic perspective*. 2nd edn. Oxford: Oxford University Press.
Hardy, T., [1874] 1994. *Far from the madding crowd*. London: Penguin.
Hardy, T., [1886] 2011. *The mayor of Casterbridge*. London: Penguin.
Herman, D., Jahn, M., & Ryan, M-L., eds. 2005. *Routedge encyclopedia of narrative theory*. London: Routledge.
Kafka, F., [1925] 1955. *The trial*. London: Penguin.
Lyons, J., 1977. *Semantics: Volume II*. Cambridge: Cambridge University Press.
McIntyre, D., 2006. *Point of view in plays*. Amsterdam: John Benjamins.
Perkins, M., 1983. *Modal expressions in English*. London: Frances Pinter.
Rimmon-Kenan, S., 1983. *Narrative fiction: Contemporary poetics*. London: Methuen.
Short, M., 1996. *Exploring the language of poems, plays and prose*. London: Longman.

Short, M., 2000. Graphological deviation, style variation and point of view in *Marabou Stork Nightmares* by Irvine Welsh. *Journal of Literary Studies,* 15 (3/4), 305–323.

Simpson, P., 1993. *Language, ideology and point of view*. London: Routledge.

Simpson, P., 2004. *Stylistics*. London: Routledge.

Sotirova, V., 2006. Reader responses to narrative point of view. *Poetics,* 34 (2), 108–133.

Uspensky, B., 1973. *A poetics of composition*. V. Zavarin and S. Wittig, trans. Berkeley: University of California Press.

Wales, K., 2011. *A dictionary of stylistics*. 3rd edn. London: Longman.

11

Stylistics and narratology

Dan Shen

Introduction

Although the coming into being of modern stylistics can be traced back to Charles Bally's *Traité de stylistique française* (1909), stylistics as a distinct academic discipline did not start enjoying a rapid development until the 1960s. In the 1960s, narratology, the systematic study of narrative as inspired by structuralism, came into existence in France and quickly spread to other countries. For the past half-century or so, stylistics and narratology have been developing side by side in the investigation of narrative fiction. Stylistics distinguishes between content and style and narratology between story and discourse. On the surface the two distinctions seem to match each other, with 'style' referring to how the content is presented and 'discourse' to how the story is told. In effect, however, 'style' in stylistics and 'discourse' in narratology differ drastically from each other, with only a limited amount of overlap between them. A clarification of the relation between 'style' and 'discourse' will enable us to gain a clearer picture of the respective limited coverage of the two closely related disciplines, and to see the complementarity between them.

A history of stylisticians' drawing on narratology

Roger Fowler's *Linguistics and the Novel* is one of the earliest stylistic attempts to draw on narratology. Fowler takes structuralist narratology to be a 'valid and important' enterprise in the study of the novel (1977, p. xi) and treats the narratological distinction between story and discourse as a general framework for his stylistic analysis. In *Style in Fiction* (1981), Geoffrey Leech and Mick Short also take narratology into account. In the section entitled 'the rendering of the fiction,' they draw on the narratological analogy between structures of narrative and structures of language and 'pursue the analogy between choices of rendering made on the fictional plane, and stylistic choices made on the linguistics plane.' They have singled out three elements of fictional technique to deal with, namely, point of view, sequencing, and descriptive focus. In *The Stylistics of Fiction* (1990) Michael Toolan draws on some narratological concepts or distinctions, such as 'extra-diegetic' (outside the story) versus 'intra-diegetic' (inside the story) narration by Genette (1980), covert narrator versus overt narrator by Chatman (1978), and focalization (a narratological term for point of view) by Genette and later by Bal (1985). A more extended effort to draw on narratology is made by Paul Simpson in *Language, Ideology and Point of View* (1993), where we find reference to the narratological distinction between story and discourse in various forms, to Genette's discussion of narrative time, as well as to the narratological models of focalization and narration (see Chapter 10 in this volume). In her *Feminist Stylistics* (1995),Sara Mills investigates the roles that female characters can fill, based on a modified version of the work by Propp, a forerunner of structuralist narratology. Mills also offers a detailed explication of the narratological concept of focalization in its various facets, which forms the technological basis for her ideological investigation of how supposedly neutral narration and point of view are in effect gendered (see also the chapter on feminist stylistics in this volume).

Short's (1999) analysis of Welsh's *Marabou Stork Nightmares* lays great weight on narratology. He first offers a discussion of the novel's complex narratological structuring and then goes on to explore the linguistic features of the text, especially those in the opening passage. Short's aim is to show how the novel's narratological innovation and stylistic invention interact with each other. A more radical attempt to draw on narratology is found in Simpson's recent book *Stylistics* (2004), which endeavours to extend stylistic investigation to cover quite fully narratological concerns. In the unit 'narrative stylistics' Simpson tries to incorporate narratology through three means: including narratological concepts or distinctions in stylistics literature, establishing a stylistic model of narrative structure, and applying narratological theory to practical analysis (see Shen 2005). In the second edition of *Style in Fiction* (2007), Leech and Short reflect on new developments in the stylistic analysis of prose fiction and discuss what, with hindsight, they would add to the book twenty-five years after its first appearance. More narratological elements, among other things, are what they would like to add to the book, since of the neighbouring areas of study 'which are important to stylistics,' narratology is 'probably the most notable for stylisticians interested in the study of prose fiction, as it has contributed much to the understanding of viewpoint, plot structure and fictional worlds, areas in which stylistics has long had an interest' (pp. 283–284).

The new century is marked by the thriving development of cognitive stylistics or cognitive poetics. What theoretically informs cognitive stylistics/poetics is, of course, primarily cognitive linguistics, but narratology is also adopted as one of the secondary theoretical frameworks. Commenting on cognitive poetics in Europe and Australia, Peter Stockwell (2002, p. 9) says that it 'sees the field as including issues of world-representation, reader interpretation and evaluation, and other concerns that are traditionally literary, such as in narratology and reception theory.' In his own cognitive investigation Stockwell draws on narratological concepts such as 'narratee' and 'extrafictional voice' (apparently adapted from Genette's extradiegetic voice), which form a framework for the cognitive stylistic exploration of deixis in literature. In *Cognitive Stylistics*, published in the same year, Catherine Emmott (2002) finds the studies by narratologists (e.g. Genette and Bal) of narrative levels and focalization helpful to her cognitive stylistic investigation on how language conveys 'split selves' in narratives.

These are some representative stylistic investigations that have drawn on narratology in various ways over the past three or four decades. The reason underlying the necessity for stylistics to draw on narratology or vice versa is that stylistics' 'style' and narratology's 'discourse' have very different coverage, a difference that is often hidden from view.

Difference and similarity: A general picture

Although some critics hold the monist view that form and content are inseparable, style 'is commonly seen as a CHOICE of form ("manner") to express content ("matter")' (Wales 2001, p. 158). Similarly, in narratology, 'discourse' (*histoire*) is regarded as the means (manner) used to present the story (matter). That is to say, 'style' and 'discourse' appear to be interchangeable, each covering fully the level of presentation in verbal narratives. Such an impression may be deepened by the following definitions offered by Michael Toolan in his *Language in Literature* (1998) and *Narrative* (2001):

> Stylistics is the study of **the language** *in* literature. (1998, p. viii, original italics and my boldface)

> Stylistics is crucially concerned with **excellence of technique**. (1998, p. ix, my boldface)

> ...*sjuzhet* or [narratology's] *discours* roughly denotes **all the techniques** that authors bring to bear in their varying manner of presentation of the basic story. (2001, p. 11, original italics and my boldface)

From these definitions, we may derive the following equation:

Style = Language = Technique = Discourse

Such an equation may also be found in the following observation by Fowler on the relation between stylistics' concern and narratology's concern:

> The French distinguish two levels of literary structure, which they call *histoire* [story] and *discours* [discourse], story and language. Story (or plot) and the other abstract elements of novel structure may be discussed in terms of categories given by the analogy of linguistic theory, but the *direct* concern of linguistics is surely with the study of *discours*.'
>
> *(1977, p. xi).*

Similarly, in Simpson's *Stylistics*, discoursal presentation is put on a par with language: 'Narrative discourse provides a way of recapitulating felt experience by matching up patterns of language to a connected series of events' (2004, p. 18). However, in effect, 'discourse' (*discours*) in narratology is to a large extent different from the 'language' or 'style' in stylistics. There is an implicit boundary separating the two, with a limited amount of overlap in between. Let's compare the following two observations made by Toolan in his *Language in Literature* and *Narrative* respectively:

(i) So one of the crucial things attempted by Stylistics is to put the discussion of *textual effects* and *techniques* on a public, shared, footing... The other chief feature of Stylistics is that it persists in the attempt to understand *technique*, or *the craft of writing*. If we agree that Hemingway's short story 'Indian Camp', and Yeats's poem 'Sailing to Byzantium', are both extraordinary literary achievements, what are some of *the linguistic components* of that excellence? Why *these word-choices, clause-patterns, rhythms, and intonations, contextual implications* [of conversation], *cohesive links* [among sentences], *choices of voice and perspective and transitivity* [of clause structure], etc. etc., and not any of the others imaginable?

(1998, p. ix, my italics)

(ii) That is to say, if we think of *histoire*/story as level 1 of analysis, then within *discourse* we have two further levels of organization, those of text and of narration. At the level of text, the teller decides upon and creates *a particular sequencing of events, the time/space spent presenting them, the sense of (changing) rhythm and pace in the discourse.* Additionally, choices are made as to *just how (in what detail, and in what order)* the particularity of the various characters is to be presented… At the level of narration, *the [structural] relations between the posited narrator and the narrative she tells are probed. …*

(2001, pp. 11–12, my italics)

It is not difficult to find that stylistics' 'techniques' (linguistic choices) in the first quotation are drastically different from narratology's 'techniques' (structural choices) in the second. Although the same term 'rhythm' appears in both quotations, it means entirely different things in the two different contexts. In the stylistic context, 'rhythm' means *verbal* movement resulting from the features of words (e.g. monosyllabic, disyllabic or polysyllabic words) and their combination (e.g. the sequence of stressed and unstressed syllables, alternation between long and short sentences, or different use of punctuation), whereas in the narratological context, 'rhythm' means, by contrast, *narrative* movement resulting from the different relations between textual duration and event duration (scenic presentation, brief summary, or ellipsis of events etc.). It is true that textual duration involves the number of words used, but whether to use two pages to narrate what happened during one hour or to use a few lines to summarise what happened during ten years is not a matter of linguistic choice but a matter of choosing the speed of narration.

Precisely because of the different coverage, we have the complementarity between style and discourse. In *Cognitive Poetics*, Stockwell observes:

This view of schema theory in a literary context points to three different fields in which schemas operate: **world schemas**, **text schemas**, and **language schemas**. World schemas cover those schemas considered so far that are to do with content; text schemas represent our expectations of the way that world schemas appear to us in terms of their sequencing and structural organisation; language schemas contain our idea of the appropriate forms of linguistic patterning and style in which we expect a subject to appear. Taking the last two together, disruptions in our expectations of textual structure or stylistic structure constitute **discourse deviation**, which offers the possibility for schema refreshment. … However, the headers and slots within schemas and the tracks through schemas can also be discussed in terms of their *stylistic* and *narratological* features.

(2002, pp. 80–2, original italics and boldface, my underlining)

In this tripartite distinction, we have one level concerned with content (world schemas) and two levels concerned with 'form' – text schemas (narratological features) and language schemas (stylistic features). Apparently, focusing only on stylistic techniques or narratological techniques will result in a partial picture of how the story is presented.

Difference and complementarity: Three specific areas

In this section, we shall examine three specific areas of investigation with different kinds of relation between stylistics and narratology: point of view/focalization, characterisation, and tense.

Point of view/focalization

Both stylistics and narraology have paid much attention to point of view or focalization, which forms one of the few overlapping areas of investigation between the two disciplines. However, even in such an overlapping area, the emphasis of investigation is still quite different. As suggested above, under the influence of narratology, Leech and Short (2007 [1981], pp. 139–141) have directed attention to 'fictional point of view,' that is, 'the slanting of the fictional world towards "reality" as apprehended by a particular participant, or set of participants, in the fiction.' However, their focus is on 'discoursal point of view,' where they investigate the author's choice of language in directly addressing the reader and the author's use of language in narration which, 'either in its sense or its connotations, expresses some element of value' (pp. 218–221).

In Leech and Short's and other stylisticians' discussions of point of view, linguistic choices such as value language, deixis, and modality take centre stage. By contrast, in narratological discussions of focalization, what figures prominently is the observer's (focalizer's) position vis-à-vis the story. While Leech and Short define 'discoursal point of view' – the stylistically 'more common' point of view – as 'the telling of the story through the words or thoughts of a particular person' (2007, p. 140), Genette starts his narratological discussion of focalization (1980, pp. 185–211) with the distinction between who speaks (voice) and who sees (eye), the former being a matter of narration, and only the latter falling within the scope of focalization. In first-person retrospective narration, this distinction enables narratologists to distinguish between two different perspectives pertaining to 'I': that of the experiencing self (the younger 'I' participating in the events), and that of the narrating self (the older 'I' recalling the past story). In Chapter 2 of Conrad's *Heart of Darkness*, the first-person narrator Marlow says:

(i) A long decaying building on the summit was half buried in the high grass. ... There was no enclosure or fence of any kind; but there had been one apparently, for near the house half-a-dozen slim posts remained in a row, roughly trimmed, and with their upper ends ornamented with round carved balls. The rails, or whatever there had been between, had disappeared.

(1973, p. 75).

Some pages later, these words appear:

(ii) You remember I told you I had been struck at the distance by certain attempts at ornamentation, rather remarkable in the ruinous aspect of the place. *Now* I had suddenly a nearer view, and its first result was to make me throw my head back as if before a blow. *Then* I went carefully from post to post with my glass, and I saw my mistake. ... They would have been even more impressive, those [human] heads on the stakes, if their faces had not been turned to the house.

(1973, p. 82, my italics)

Compare the first passage with:

> ... I saw half-a-dozen slim posts and thought they were what remained of a fence, but actually they were the posts used by Kurtz to hold human heads. ...

Here narration remains unchanged, but focalization shifts more than once. In the first passage, the retrospective narrator deliberately adopts the point of view of his younger self temporarily mistaking the heads of the killed African natives for ornamental balls. Since we at first believe that what are on top of the posts are ornamental balls, we experience a stronger shock effect when the real fact comes to light. Taking the two quoted passages together, we can distinguish three different points of view of 'I': a) the experiencing 'I' mistaking the heads for balls; b) the experiencing 'I' perceiving the heads as heads ('now,' 'suddenly'); c) the narrating 'I' perceiving the events in retrospect ('then'). According to narratological classification, a) and b) pertain to 'internal focalization' – the perceiver/focalizer is inside the narrated story – while c) is 'external focalization' – the retrospective 'I' is outside the narrated story. Moreover, in first-person narration, we can also distinguish between the point of view of 'I' as a protagonist (Dickens's *Great Expectations*) and that of 'I' as a mere observer of what happens to the protagonist (Anderson's 'Death in the Woods'). The former type is 'internal' focalization and the latter 'external' focalization ('I' as an observer is external to the protagonist's story).

The distinction between narration and focalization also enables us to see the similarity in focalization between the first-person narration where the viewpoint of the experiencing 'I' is adopted and the third-person narration where the viewpoint of an experiencing character is adopted. Compare:

(i) *Insoluble questions they were*, it seemed to her [Mrs Ramsay], standing there, holding James by the hand. He [Mr Tansley] had followed her into the drawing-room, that young man they laughed at; he *was standing* by the table, fidgeting with *something*, awkwardly, feeling himself out of things, as she knew without looking round. (Virginia Woolf, *To the Lighthouse*, Chapter 1, p.14, my italics)

(ii) *Insoluble questions they were*, it seemed to me, standing there, holding James by the hand. He had followed me into the drawing-room, that young man they laughed at; he *was standing* by the table, fidgeting with *something*, awkwardly, feeling himself out of things, as I knew without looking round.

Although the original version and the adapted version are respectively in third-person and first-person narration, the point of view or focalization remains very much the same. In both cases, we observe the fictional happening not through the eye of the narrator, but through that of the unmediated consciousness of the protagonist. The free indirect discourse 'Insoluble questions they were' (with spontaneity and immediacy), the progressive aspect 'was standing' (indicating the experiencing protagonist's immediate perception), and the vague referring expression 'something' (the experiencing protagonist's limited knowledge of what is happening behind) all indicate that the focalizer is the experiencing protagonist rather than the third-person or the first-person retrospective narrator. That is to say, in both cases, we have internal focalization. Genette (1980, pp. 189–90) distinguishes three kinds of internal focalization, a classification that is widely adopted in narrative studies: *fixed* (Henry James's *The Ambassadors*, where a character consistently functions as the focalizer), *variable* (Virginia Woolf's *To the Lighthouse*, where different characters focalize events alternately), and *multiple* (Robert Browning's narrative poem *The Ring and the Book*, where the same criminal case is perceived by different characters successively).

In the second edition of *Style in Fiction*, Leech and Short have added a section entitled 'Narratological aspects of viewpoint' (2007, pp. 299–301). They mention that in some novels the discourse structure may change quite a lot, and they take the 582-word prologue of Jane Gardam's *Bilgewater* as an example:

> This prologue begins, for the first 135 words, with a third-person narration combined with the fictional viewpoint of a prospective undergraduate being interviewed for a place at a Cambridge college. Then, in sentence 14, the narration slips into second-person mode, and by sentence 33, 137 words later (which include 63 words of free direct speech and free direct thought), the narrator has moved to the first-person and the tense of the narration has shifted from the past to the present (thus causing a possible ambiguity with free direct thought). Hence we begin with an apparently objective third-person narration, even though the narrator describes things from the prospective undergraduate's viewpoint, and are shifted in stages to a much more intimate and potentially limited and flawed viewpoint, a shift relatable to a tactic which leads to a surprise at the end of the novel.
>
> *(p. 300)*

Leech and Short ascribe relative objectivity of viewpoint to third-person narration, and relative subjectivity of viewpoint to second- and first-person narrations. By contrast, narratologists as represented by Genette distinguish focalization from narration. In third-person narration, we can have very subjective point of view as in many stream-of-consciousness novels (see the passage from *To the Lighthouse* quoted above). In the prologue in question, it is true that the point of view in the third-person narration is more objective, but the objectivity is to be attributed to the narrator's *not* having adopted the candidate's experiencing viewpoint for most of the time:

> 1. THE INTERVIEW seemed over. 2. The Principal of the college sat looking at the candidate. 3. The Principal's back was to the light and her stout, short outline was solid against the window, softened only by the fuzz of her ageing but rather pretty hair. [...] 4. I can't see her face against the light. 5. She's got a brooding shape. 6. She is a mass. 7. Beneath the fuzz a mass. [...] 8. Not a feeling, not an emotion, not a dizzy thought. 9. A formidable woman.
>
> *(Gardam 1976, pp. 9–10, my sentence numbering)*

Sentences 1 to 3 are in third-person narration, and 4 to 7 in first-person narration. In the former, the viewpoint unobtrusively shifts from the candidate to the narrator. In sentence 1 the narrator speaks but the candidate perceives, a limited perception as indicated by the epistemic link verb 'seem.' In sentence 3, however, the point of view shifts to the narrator who both speaks and sees. Since the narrator bears no grudge against the Principal, we get a quite objective picture of her. In sentences 6 to 9, however, we get a biased and subjective picture of the Principal from the viewpoint of the candidate. Notice the contrast between the quite neutral 'stout', 'ageing', 'pretty' and the biased 'mass', 'not a feeling', 'formidable'. Moreover, in contrast to the well-formed syntax of sentence 3, we have fragmentary and disjunctive syntax in sentences 6 and 7, which indicates the candidate's unmediated experiencing consciousness. The objectivity of the viewpoint in sentence 3 and the subjectivity of the viewpoint in sentences 4 to 7 would remain unchanged if sentence 3 were to appear in first-person narration and 4 to 7 in third-person narration ('She couldn't see the Principal's face against the light. The Principal had got a brooding shape. She was a mass. Beneath the fuzz a mass. [...] A formidable woman'). To gain a clearer picture, let us examine some other sentences in the prologue:

> 1. The candidate sat opposite wondering what to do [then]. 2. The chair had a soft seat but wooden arms. 3. She crossed her legs first one way and then the other – then wondered about crossing her legs at all. 4. She wondered whether to get up. [...] 5. But it's damp, old, cold, cold, cold. 6. Cold as home. 7. Shall I come here? 8. Would I like it at all?
>
> *(ibid., pp. 9–10, my sentence numbering)*

Compare an adapted version:

> 1. I sat opposite wondering what to do [then]. 2. The chair had a soft seat but wooden arms. 3. I crossed my legs first one way and then the other – then wondered about crossing my legs at all. 4. I wondered whether to get up. [...] 5. But it was damp, old, cold, cold, cold. 6. Cold as home. 7. Should she come here? 8. Would she like it at all?

No matter whether they are in first person or in third person, sentences 1 to 4 display a more objective viewpoint and sentences 5 to 8 a more subjective viewpoint. In the former case, we have indirect thought presentation (compare: What should she/I do now? Should she/I get up?). That is to say, we have the mediating viewpoint of the narrator (the omniscient narrator or the retrospective 'I') who somewhat summarises and edits the mental activity of the character ('she' or the experiencing 'I'). In sentences 5 to 8, however, we perceive the fictional world through the experiencing viewpoint of the character, an unmediated viewpoint in the form of free (in)direct discourse indicating spontaneity and immediacy. It should have become clear that the change from objectivity to subjectivity in the prologue is not due to the change in narration from third person to second or first person, but to the change in point of view from primarily that of the mediating narrator to that of the experiencing character.

In the second edition of *Style in Fiction*, Leech and Short (2007, pp. 300–301) mention what they would want to revisit and possibly change in terms of 'narratological aspects of point of view.' They notice that recently, narratological research on second-person narration has become more extensive compared with the situation in 1981. Therefore they 'would need to discuss second-person narration as well' in investigating 'discoursal viewpoint.' However, as shown above, what really deserves our attention is narratology's distinguishing point of view (who perceives) from narration (who speaks). With this distinction, we can come to a more accurate understanding of the change in point of view in texts like the prologue. In such cases, we can see the similarity in point of view between second-/first-person narration and third-person narration when an experiencing character functions as the focalizer (e.g. the first-person narration in the prologue and the adapted version in third-person narration, as shown above). Moreover, with this distinction, we may pay more attention to the different modes of point of view in first-person narration (e.g. the retrospective versus the experiencing viewpoint, or focalizer as observer versus focalizer as protagonist), as well as in third-person narration (e.g. the distinction among fixed, variable and multiple internal focalization).

Both stylistics and narratology have drawn on the Russian theoretician Boris Uspensky's discussion of point of view in *A Poetics of Composition* (1973), but there are notable differences between the two sides. On the stylistic side, Fowler (1986, pp. 127ff.) takes the lead in drawing on Uspensky and distinguishes among 'psychological' point of view, 'ideological' point of view, and 'spatial'/'temporal' point of view (see also Simpson 1993, which constitutes another influential attempt in this direction). Fowler starts with 'temporal' point of view, which 'refers to the impression which a reader gains of events moving rapidly or slowly, in a continuous chain or isolated segments,' among other kinds of movement. As for the 'spatial' dimension, the reader 'is led by the organization of the language to image them [the represented objects, people, landscapes etc.] as existing in certain spatial relationships to one another and to the viewing position which he feels himself to occupy.' Let us compare Fowler's discussion with Rimmon-Kenan's narratological discussion (2002, pp. 78–80) as based on Uspensky's model. The narratologist is not concerned with a reader's impression or imaging, but with the structural position of the focalizer. In spatial terms, the omniscient external focalization, for instance, is marked by a bird's-eye view, with the focalizer located at a point far above the objects, 'yielding either a panoramic view or a "simultaneous" focalization of things "happening" in different places.' In temporal terms, this type of focalization is 'panchronic' with the focalizer having 'at his disposal all the temporal dimensions of the story (past, present, and future),' which forms a contrast with an internal focalizer who is limited to the 'present' of the characters. The stylistic and narratological discussions of the temporal and spatial aspects are apparently complementary to each other.

As for the ideological point of view, Fowler defines it as 'the set of values, or belief system, communicated by the language of the text.' One example Fowler gives is Dickens's *Hard Times*, where 'various groups of characters represent and voice a number of different social theories' and '[t]hese points of view' constantly challenge and contradict each other (1986, pp. 131). Here we lose sight not only of the distinction between narration and point of view, but also of the distinction between characters' words and ways of seeing the fictional world. In her narratological discussion, Rimmon-Kenan is aware of this blurring of distinctions as she observes, 'A character may represent an ideological position through his way of seeing the world or his behaviour in it, but also—like Raskolnikov—through explicit discussion of his ideology. ... Thus, *in addition to its contribution to focalization*, ideology also plays a part in the story (characters), on the one hand, and in narration, on the other' (2002, p. 83, my italics). To have a clearer picture, we may confine ideological *point of view* to the focalizer's way(s) of seeing the world, and discuss how ideological point of view interacts with characters' spoken words and other elements to convey the total set of values of the text.

In terms of the 'psychological' point of view, Fowler observes that it 'concerns the question of who is presented as the observer of the events of a narrative, whether the author or a participating character' (1986, p. 134). However, Uspensky's definition is quite different: 'In those cases where the authorial point of view relies on an individual consciousness (or perception) we will speak about the psychological point of view' (Uspensky 1973, p. 81). In Uspensky's model, the psychological/subjective point of view is set in contrast with the author's (or rather, the authorial narrator's) objective point of view (p. 81ff.), a distinction that is carried over into Rimmon-Kenan's narratological discussion.

Uspensky makes a distinction between 'external' and 'internal' points of view depending on whether a character's outward behaviour (action, words etc.) or inner life (thoughts, sensory perceptions, feelings etc.) is observed, and Fowler has come up with subdivisions of the external and internal categories (1986, pp. 134–46). By contrast, narratologists would call the observation of a character's outward behaviour 'outside view' and that of a character's inner life 'inside view' on one hand, and, on the other, distinguish 'external focalization' and 'internal focalization' according to a different criterion: whether the focalizer is outside or inside the story (Rimmon-Kenan pp. 75–78). Let us take a look at the following passage taken from Jane Austen's *Pride and Prejudice*:

> [1] He was anxious to avoid the notice of his cousins, from a conviction that if they saw him depart, they could not fail to conjecture his design ... [2] His reception however was of the most flattering kind. [3] Miss Lucas perceived him from an upper window [4] as he walked towards the house, and [5] instantly set out to meet him accidentally in the lane.
>
> *(1980, pp. 109–110, my numbering)*

According to Uspensky's criterion, [1] and [3] would have internal point of view, and [2], [4] and [5] display external point of view. However, in [1] and [3] the characters' thoughts or perceptions only form the object of observation of the omniscient narrator – we perceive the characters' inner life as well as their outward behaviour through the eye of the narrator. According to the narratological distinction, the whole passage is in external focalization, but [1] and [3] give us 'inside view' of the characters and [2], [4] and [5] only 'outside view.' To gain a clearer picture, let us compare the following text from Thomas Hardy's *Tess of the d'Urberbvilles*.

> Tess still stood hesitating like a bather about to make his plunge, hardly knowing whether to retreat or to persevere, when *a figure* came forth from the dark triangular door of the tent. It was that of *a tall young man* ... his age *could not be* more than three- or four-and-twenty. Despite the touches of barbarism in his contours, there was a singular force in *the gentleman's* face, and in his bold rolling eye.
>
> *(2007, pp. 71, my italics)*

> [Paraphrase] Tess ... *saw* Mr d'Urberville come forth from the dark triangular door of the tent but she did not know who it was. She *noticed* that Mr d'Urberville was a tall young man. ... she *guessed* that Mr d'Urberville was no more than three- or four-and-twenty. Despite the touches of barbarism in his contours, Tess *sensed* a singular force in his face and his bold rolling eyes.

In Hardy's original version, the indefinite and vague referring expressions 'a figure,' 'a tall young man,' coupled with the epistemic modal auxiliary 'could' (in 'could not be') indicate that starting from 'when', the omniscient narrator, who knows the young man's identity and age, gives up his own perspective and is using instead Tess's limited viewpoint. In the paraphrase, although 'Tess saw,' 'she noticed,' 'she guessed' and 'she sensed' are used, the point of view is still the omniscient narrator's since only he knows that the man coming out of the tent is Mr d'Urberville. In other words, we are observing Tess and Mr d'Urberville through the omniscient narrator's perspective, rather than observing Mr d'Urberville through Tess's perspective. That is to say, Tess's mental processes only form the object of observation of the omniscient narrator, whose external focalization remains unchanged.

When discussing new developments in stylistics and what they would now change in *Style in Fiction*, Leech and Short (2007, p. 299) mention that they would like to draw on the model of point of view as established by Uspensky and advanced by other stylisticians. Apart from distinguishing among 'spatial,' 'temporal,' 'psychological' and 'ideological' kinds of viewpoint, Leech and Short would like to add a fifth kind of viewpoint, namely 'social viewpoint,' which 'expresses social relationships between the person whose viewpoint is being represented and other characters.' Moreover, they would like to extend the scope of ideological viewpoint to cover '*personal* attitudinal values (e.g. that a particular character "is horrible" or "looks kind"), as well as those associated with social or political groups' (*ibid.*). It is desirable to extend the coverage of point of view so long as we can maintain a clear distinction between point of view and narration and between the focalizer (observer) and the focalized (object of observation).

Characterisation

Although many stylistic analyses do not explicitly address characterisation, they 'could easily be re-cast as discussions of characterisation' (Leech and Short 2007, p. 296). Stylistic analyses are often concerned with how linguistic choices are used in depicting or presenting fictional characters. Some narratologists have also paid attention to characterisation, but their focus is on the classification of different structural modes. Rimmon-Kenan (2002, pp. 59–71) distinguishes three modes of characterisation. The first is 'direct definition,' that is, the authorial narrator's straightforward definition of a character's traits. A case in point is the very beginning of Jane Austen's *Emma*: 'Emma Woodhouse, handsome, clever, and rich, with a comfortable home and happy disposition.' Although a character may also comment on another character's traits, it cannot count as direct definition since only 'the most authoritative voice in the text' is in a position to offer direct definition. The second mode is 'indirect presentation,' which is the displaying, exemplifying, or implying of a character's traits through depicting a character's action, speech, external appearance, or environment. Rimmon-Kenan further classifies each of the four areas into sub-categories. Action, for instance, can be divided into one-time action and habitual action, both of which can be further categorised as 'act of commission' (actual performance), 'act of omission' (something which the character should, but does not do), and contemplated act (a planned/intended but unrealised act). External appearance is also classified into two categories: those external features beyond the character's control (e.g. height, colour of eyes) and those at least partly dependent on the character (e.g. hairstyle and clothes). The third mode of characterisation is 'reinforcement by analogy,' further classified into 'analogous names,' 'analogous landscape' and 'analogy between characters.'

In *Language and Characterization*, Jonathan Culpeper treats Rimmon-Kenan's classification as a 'valuable starting point' but finds it lacking specific detail and unconcerned with 'why particular features are chosen and others not' (2001, p. 163). Culpeper makes a distinction among 'explicit,' 'implicit,' and 'authorial' characterisation cues in texts, each of which is further classified into various sub-categories (2001, pp. 164–233). For instance, 'implicit' cues are divided according to conversational structure, conversational implicature, lexis, syntactic feature, accent and dialect, verse and prose, paralinguistic features, visual features, a character's company and setting. Through detailed stylistic analyses Culpeper shows the relevance of particular features for characterisation.

As distinct from stylisticians, narratologists in general are not interested in stylistic details themselves. Rather, they are concerned with the distinction and definition of various structural modes (e.g. what counts as 'direct definition'). To reveal how linguistic choices contribute to characterisation we need to carry out detailed stylistic analysis, but the narratological distinctions may help to form useful frameworks for stylistic investigation. The stylistic concern and the narratological concern are very much complementary to each other. In *Story Logic*, David Herman (2002, p.115ff.) effectively combines narratological approaches (especially Greimas' account of narrative actants) and linguistic theories (especially Halliday's transitivity model) in investigating the roles of and relations among characters.

Tense

In *A Dictionary of Narratology*, Gerald Prince (2003, p. 98) defines 'tense' in two different senses. The second is the common grammatical sense, a sense shared by stylistics and narratology, but most narratologists pay little attention to grammatical tense except when distinguishing different modes of speech/thought presentation. The first sense of 'tense' as defined by Prince is peculiar to narratology, which is 'the set of temporal relations – SPEED, ORDER, DISTANCE, etc. – between the situations and events recounted and their recounting.' When narratologists discuss tense or time in narrative, they tend to focus on this aspect. This sense of tense is highlighted in Genette's *Narrative Discourse*, which devotes three chapters out of five to it, respectively discussing narrative 'order,' 'duration,' and 'frequency.' In terms of 'order' (the relation between the chronological sequence of story events and the rearranged textual sequence of the events), the analysis is conducted both on the micro-structural and the macro-structural levels. At the micro level, the object of analysis is a short episode, which is classified into temporal sections according to the change of position in story time, such as from 'now' to 'once.' Genette's main concern is the macro level, at which Proust's *Recherche* is divided into a dozen temporal sections, some lasting for more than two hundred pages. In discussing narrative order, Genette focuses on various kinds of 'anachrony' – that is, discordance between the two orderings of story and discourse – such as analepsis (flashback) and prolepsis (flashforward).

As touched on above, under the influence of narratology, Leech and Short have paid attention to 'fictional sequencing' in *Style in Fiction* (1981, pp. 176–180 and 233–239). They offer a distinction among three kinds of sequencing: presentational, chronological, and psychological. An example of chronological sequencing is 'The lone ranger saddled his horse, mounted, and rode off into the sunset,' *versus* 'The lone ranger rode off into the sunset, mounted, and saddled his horse.' This is apparently a matter of syntactic ordering, forming a contrast with Genette's concern. As for psychological sequencing, the following is a case in point:

> Gabriel had not gone to the door with the others. … A woman was standing near the top of the first flight, in the shadow also. He could not see her face but he could see the terracotta and salmon-pink panels of her skirt which the shadow made appear black and white. It was his wife.
>
> *(James Joyce, 'The Dead', pp. 206–207)*

Here the readers 'seem to be with Gabriel, looking up the stairs towards a vague figure in the shadow, face hidden. … The effect [of the psychological sequencing] would have been nullified if Joyce had begun his third sentence: "His wife was standing..."' (Leech and Short 1981, pp. 177–178). This is essentially a matter of the author's choice of words in reflecting a particular point of view. It is worth noting that on the micro plane, the examples Leech and Short have chosen are usually in the mode of scenic presentation, with only one temporal position, 'now'. That is to say, these examples do not involve the structural reordering of the different temporal positions of past, present and future; rather, they involve different ways of using language to create different effects. That is to say, even in investigating 'fictional sequencing,' stylistic concern may differ drastically from narratological concern.

In discussing temporal arrangement in the strand 'narrative stylistics,' Simpson (2004, p. 19) offers the following syntactic example: 'John dropped the plates and Janet laughed suddenly.' Simpson points out that reversing the clauses to form 'Janet laughed suddenly and John dropped the plates' will invite an opposite interpretation in terms of the cause-effect relationship. Influenced by narratology, Simpson also mentions the structural 'flashback' and 'prevision,' which 'serve to disrupt the basic chronology of the narrative's plot' (*ibid.*, p. 20). The two kinds of sequencing are in effect quite different from each other. As regards the syntactic example in question, if John's accident caused Janet's laughter, the order of the two clauses cannot be reversed (other things being equal), otherwise a logical or temporal mistake would occur. By contrast, on the structural level, 'flashbacks' and 'flashforwards' do not bear on the actual logical or temporal relations of the story events, and they constitute artistic devices purposefully employed for producing desirable effects. As the term 'flashback' (from film studies) indicates, such techniques go beyond the verbal medium. Narratologists are typically concerned with structural techniques that often go beyond language, while stylisticians are characteristically concerned with aspects of language such as syntax.

The second aspect of Genette's 'tense' is 'duration' (narrative speed), which concerns the relationship between the actual duration of the events and textual length, such as detailed scenic presentation, summary, or ellipsis of events. In Proust's *Recherche*, the 'range of variations' goes from '150 pages for three hours to three lines for twelve years, viz. (very roughly), from a page for one minute to a page for one century' (Genette 1980, p. 92). To a narratologist, no matter what words describe an event, the narrative speed will remain unchanged as long as those words take up the same textual space. A stylistician, by contrast, will concentrate on what words are used to describe an event, while hardly paying attention to the larger narrative movement involved.

The last aspect of the narratological 'tense' is 'narrative frequency.' A narrative 'may tell once what happened once, *n* times what happened *n* times, *n* times what happened once, once what happened *n* times' (Genette 1980, p. 114).

It should have become clear that, in referring to the temporal structure in narrative, the linguistic term 'tense' is used only metaphorically. While grammatical tense normally goes with the natural temporal facts (e.g. past tense is used to describe past happenings), the narratological 'anachrony' ('flashback' or 'flashforward') concerns how the discourse deviates from the natural sequence of story events. In this sense, the relation between the narratological 'anachrony' and verbal tense change is essentially one of opposition rather than similarity. Absolutely no real similarity can be perceived between grammatical tense and 'duration' or 'frequency' as such.

Both the difference and the complementarity between narratological and stylistic approaches to 'tense' or narrative time are well reflected in Monika Fludernik's 'Chronology, Time, Tense and Experientiality in Narrative' (2003), where she uses several narratological frameworks (concerned with temporal arrangement, focalization and experientiality) for the detailed analysis of tense patterning in narratives, especially in Michael Ondaatje's *The English Patient*.

Recommendations for practice

It should have become clear that although stylistics' 'style' and narratology's 'discourse' appear to be interchangeable, stylistic techniques and narratological techniques differ greatly from each other, with only a limited amount of overlap. In order to interpret and appreciate more comprehensively the techniques of narrative fiction, we need to take advantage of the findings in both stylistics and narratology. Students interested in narrative art would ideally need to take both stylistic and narratological courses/modules and read books and essays in both fields. In writing stylistic papers, we may use narratological concepts and models as frameworks for detailed linguistic analysis. We may also follow Short (1999) in carrying out a parallel investigation of stylistic techniques and narratological techniques and see how they interact with each other in the text. In terms of theoretical discussions both in teaching and in research, it is necessary to give more specific definitions of stylistics' 'style' and narratology's 'discourse.' It needs to be pointed out that 'how the story is told' consists of two aspects, one verbal and the other organizational, with a certain amount of overlap in between. Thus, 'style' may be defined as the language aspect of how the story is presented, and 'discourse' as the structural aspect. It would be helpful to draw attention to the complementarity between the two disciplines whenever necessary.

Future directions

In Britain where stylistics has been thriving, the development of narratology has been much slower than in North America, despite the fact that the UK-based Poetics and Linguistics Association and its official journal *Language and Literature* have played an important role in promoting the interface of stylistics and narratology. As a result, some stylisticians treat narratology not as an independent discipline, but as part of stylistics. In recent years, some stylisticians such as Ruth Page have taken a keen interest in narratology, and Page's work (2006, 2010) on linguistic approaches to feminist narratology has contributed to the interface between stylistics and narratology. It is hoped that narratology will enjoy a swift development in Britain, and that more students and academics will become interested in the complementarity between and mutual promotion of stylistics and narratology. Narratologists have paid much attention to narratorial 'unreliability,' which is reflected in the narrator's verbal choices. This is an area where fruitful stylistic investigations can be carried out in the future.

In North America, during the last two decades of the twentieth century stylistics went on the decline due to combined pressure from deconstruction and cultural studies (which gives priority to context over text). In the new century, however, stylistics is gradually reviving in North America, where increasing importance is being attached to the text or to the relation between text and context. Narratologists in general have not paid much attention to stylistics, with the exception of some linguistically- or stylistically-informed narratologists as represented by Monika Fludernik and David Herman. There is a need to call for more attention to style and to the complementarity between narratology and stylistics. It is hoped that with a clearer awareness of the complementarity between narratological 'discourse' and 'style,' more conscious effort will be made towards combining the concerns of narratology and stylistics in narrative criticism.

Related topics

Feminist stylistics, formalist stylistics, point of view and modality, rhetoric and poetics, stylistics and film

Further reading

Phelan, J., 2005. *Living to tell about it*. Ithaca: Cornell University Press.

This book is an excellent discussion of the rhetorical effects of unreliability in character narration.

Shen, D., 2010. Unreliability. *In:* P. Huhn *et al.*, eds. *Living handbook of narratology*. Hamburg: Hamburg University Press. Online. Available at http://hup.sub.uni-hamburg.de/lhn/index.php/Unreliability (Accessed 30 June 2012).

This entry offers an overall picture of narratological investigations of unreliability.

Shen, D., 2011. Neo-Aristotelian rhetorical narrative study: Need for integrating style, context and intertext. *Style*, 45, 576–597.

This article shows the complementarity between narrative studies and stylistics, and argues for having an overall consideration of text, context, and intertext.

References

Austen, J., [1813] 1980. *Pride and Prejudice*. Oxford: Oxford University Press.
Austen, J., [1815] 2003. *Emma*. London: Penguin.
Bal, M., 1985. *Narratology*. C. van Boheemen, trans. Toronto: University of Toronto Press.
Bally, C., 1909. *Traité de stylistique française*. Heidelberg: Carl Winters.
Chatman, S., 1978. *Story and discourse*. Ithaca: Cornell University Press.
Conrad, J., [1899] 1973. *Heart of darkness*. Harmondsworth: Penguin.
Culpeper, J., 2001. *Language and characterization in plays and texts*. London: Longman.
Emmott, C., 2002. Split selves in fiction and in medical life stories: Cognitive linguistic theory and narrative practice. *In:* E. Semino and J. Culpeper, eds. *Cognitive stylistics*. Amsterdam: John Benjamins, 153–182.
Fludernik, M., 2003. Chronology, time, tense and experientiality in narrative. *Language and Literature*, 12, 117–134.
Fowler, R., 1977. *Linguistics and the novel*. London: Methuen.
Fowler, R., 1986. *Linguistic criticism*. Oxford: Oxford University Press.
Gardam, J., 1976. *Bilgewater*. London: Hamish Hamilton Children's Books Ltd.
Genette, G., 1980. *Narrative Discourse*. J. E. Lewin, trans. Ithaca: Cornell University Press.
Hardy, T., [1891] 2007. *Tess of the d'Urbervilles*. S. E. Maier, ed., 2nd edn. Peterborough: Broadview.
Herman, D., 2004. *Story Logic: Problems and Possibilities of a Narrative*. Lincoln, NE: University of Nebraska Press.
Joyce, J., [1914] 1956. The Dead. *In: Dubliners*, Harmondsworth: Penguin, 173–220.
Leech, G. and Short, M., [1981] 2007. *Style in fiction*. 2nd edn. Harlow: Pearson Education.
Mills, S., 1995. *Feminist stylistics*. London: Routledge.
Page, R., 2006. *Literary and linguistic approaches to feminist narratology*. New York: Palgrave MacMillan.
Page, R., 2010. Bridget Jones's diary and feminist narratology. *In:* M. Lambrou and P. Stockwell, eds. *Contemporary stylistics*. London: Continuum, 93–105.
Prince, G., 2003. *A dictionary of narratology*. revised edn. Lincoln: University of Nebraska Press.
Rimmon-Kenan, S., 2002. *Narrative fiction*. 2nd edn. London: Routledge.
Semino, E. and Culpeper, J., eds. 2002. *Cognitive stylistics*. Amsterdam: John Benjamins.
Shen, D, 2005. How stylisticians draw on narratology: Approaches, advantages, and disadvantages. *Style*, 39, 381–395.
Short, M., 1999. Graphological deviation, style variation and point of view in *Marabou Stork Nightmares* by Irvine Welsh. *Journal of Literary Studies*, 15, 305–323.
Simpson, P., 1993. *Language, ideology, and point of view*. London: Routledge.
Simpson, P., 2004. *Stylistics*. London: Routledge.
Stockwell, P., 2002. *Cognitive poetics*. London: Routledge.
Toolan, M. J., 1990. *The stylistics of fiction*. London: Routledge.
Toolan, M. J., 1998. *Language in literature*. London: Arnold.
Toolan, M. J., 2001. *Narrative*. 2nd edn. London: Routledge.
Uspensky, B., 1973. *A poetics of composition*. V. Zavarin and S. Wittig, trans. Berkeley: University of California Press.
Wales, K., 2001. *A dictionary of stylistics*. 2nd edn. Essex: Pearson Education Limited.
Woolf, V., [1927] 1977. *To the lighthouse*. London: Granada.

12

Metaphor and stylistics

Szilvia Csábi

Introduction

Figurative language has always been a key ingredient of literary works. Philosophers, linguists and stylisticians have continuously studied tropes, focusing primarily on metaphors, trying to understand the nature of figurative expressions such as those in Shakespeare's Sonnet 73:

> That time of year thou mayst in me behold
> When yellow leaves, or none, or few, do hang
> Upon those boughs which shake against the cold,
> Bare ruin'd choirs, where late the sweet birds sang.
> In me thou seest the twilight of such day
> As after sunset fadeth in the west,
> Which by and by black night doth take away,
> Death's second self, that seals up all in rest.
> In me thou see'st the glowing of such fire
> That on the ashes of his youth doth lie,
> As the death-bed whereon it must expire
> Consumed with that which it was nourish'd by.
>   This thou perceivest, which makes thy love more strong,
>   To love that well which thou must leave ere long.

Although here we read about parts of the day, light, darkness, fire and ashes, we can understand that the poem is about life, ageing, and death, and that Shakespeare meant to draw a parallel between the passing of a day, the fading of light, the extinguishing of fire on the one hand, and the passing of one's lifetime on the other. But how can we make sense of all this? The study of figurative language has offered several theories, conventional and novel, to answer this question.

The field of metaphor research has undergone considerable changes since the first attempts to define what tropes, or figures of speech, are. Until the 1980s metaphor and metonymy were considered to be major rhetorical devices that were used predominantly in literature. The cognitive turn in the 1980s, however, brought into focus the role of these figures of speech in human thought, understanding, and reasoning, manifested in both literary and non-literary language. Moving away from the historical view of metaphor and metonymy as decorative rhetorical devices, state-of-the-art cognitive research now concentrates on the embodied view of cognition in which metaphor and metonymy underlie human thought and language. The empirically grounded findings within the cognitive theory of metaphor contradict and surpass several claims of the conventional theories, as we will see in detail.

The following is by no means intended to be an exhaustive account of all the existing theories of metaphors and related figures of speech. Instead, it is meant to be an introduction from the stylistic point of view to the ideas of some major thinkers in the field of metaphor.

Conventional and novel views of metaphor

The most common views of metaphor are as follows (cf. Lakoff and Johnson 1980, Kövecses 2002/2010). First, metaphor is a linguistic phenomenon, a property of words. Thus, the metaphorical use of the word *angel* in an utterance such as *Sue is an angel* is a characteristic of the linguistic expression *angel*. Second, metaphor is based on a resemblance, a pre-existing similarity between the two entities that are compared and identified; it is a shortened comparison. Thus, Sue in *Sue is an angel* must share some essential features with an angel in order for us to be able to use the word *angel* as a metaphor for her. Third, metaphor is used for some artistic and rhetorical purpose, primarily in literary works. Fourth, since metaphor is a conscious and deliberate use of words, people must have a special talent to use it and to use it well. As a result, metaphor can be dominant in literary works only. Fifth, metaphor can be used for special effects, thus it is not an inevitable part of everyday human communication, thought or reasoning. Sixth, metaphor is often seen as the deviant, improper use of words because it is used instead of equivalent literal expressions. Finally, the dead metaphor view claims that metaphors have been conventionalised over the years and are not viewed as metaphors anymore, and we do not even know why they mean what they mean.

The above ways of thinking about metaphor also mean that metaphorical meaning is thought of as 'being created de novo, and [it] does not reflect pre-existing aspects of how people ordinarily conceptualise ideas and events in terms of pervasive metaphorical schemes' (Gibbs 2006a, p. 2). This is exactly what recent cognitive linguistic, philosophical and psychological studies now focus on, arguing for the potential that language, thought, and experience are fundamentally metaphorical.

Metaphor in a historical perspective

Since Aristotle, the term *metaphor* has been widely used as the basis and name of every trope, including metonymy and synecdoche. As Eco (1983, p. 217) puts it, '[t]o speak of metaphor, therefore, means to speak of rhetorical activity in all its complexity'. As Eco (1983, p. 218) argues,

> Every discourse on metaphor originates in a radical choice: either (a) language is by nature, and originally, metaphorical ... or (b) language (and every other semiotic system) is a rule-governed mechanism, ... a machine with regard to which the metaphor constitutes a breakdown, a malfunction, an unaccountable outcome, but at the same time the drive toward linguistic renewal.

Classical rhetoric generally favours the second option and considers the concepts of metaphor and metonymy as a matter of language alone, as opposed to the cognitive tradition which favours the first option, as we will see (for more on classical rhetoric and poetics see Chapter 1 in this volume).

Metaphor as transference

Metaphor for Aristotle in *Poetics* (Section 3, Part XXI) is 'the application of an alien name by transference', either:

- from genus to species: *There lies my ship* 'for lying at anchor is a species of lying',
- from species to genus: *Verily ten thousand noble deeds hath Odysseus wrought,* where ten thousand is used for a large number,
- from species to species: *With blade of bronze drew away the life* and *Cleft the water with the vessel of unyielding bronze* where *arusai,* 'to draw away' is used for *tamein,* 'to cleave,' and *tamein,* again for *arusai* – each being a species of taking away',
- by analogy or proportion: evening is *the old age of the day,* and old age is *the evening of life* as old age is to life as evening is to day.

In *Rhetoric* (Book III, Part 4), he adds that similes are also metaphors. The difference between the two is only in the form of expression: similes are explicit comparisons using the words *like* and *as* (resulting in longer and thus less attractive and less interesting phrases), whereas metaphors are implicit comparisons; they are rather straightforward identifications without explanation, and they can imply riddles. So *leapt on the foe as a lion* is a simile, whereas *the lion leapt* is a metaphor, both referring to the courageous Achilles.

In Aristotle's view, using metaphor, which is the mark of genius, provides freshness and liveliness to speech as it helps new ideas to be promptly grasped in novel ways, which attracts listeners. In *Rhetoric,* Aristotle claims that metaphor, which is a matter of words only and signals deviance in language, is a valuable device in poetry as well as prose, and appropriate and beautiful metaphors help to give 'style clearness, charm, and distinction' and thus persuade and please as well as decorate discourse. To this end, when giving names to nameless things with the help of metaphor, one should resort to kindred and similar (as opposed to remote) things to illustrate the kinship in order to help hearers perceive resemblances between the things mentioned.

Metaphor as the abuse of words

John Locke (1689/1836, pp. 372–373) calls the use of metaphors the abuse of words and figurative speech as the abuse of language. Locke claims that figurative speech is admitted largely because 'wit and fancy find easier entertainment in the world than dry truth and real knowledge', but if the goal of the speaker is not pleasure and delight but to 'speak of things as they are', we should be aware that the function of figurative speech is 'to insinuate wrong ideas, move the passions, and thereby mislead the judgment'. In this way, metaphors are seen by him as 'perfect cheats' only, belonging to 'the arts of fallacy' and promoting 'error and deceit', to be avoided at all costs if the speaker wants to inform or instruct in the discourse, and to be considered as a fault of the language or the speaker using them.

Metaphor as a fable in brief

In *The New Science,* Giambattista Vico (1725/1948, pp. 116–117) says that the most 'luminous', 'necessary and frequent' trope is metaphor, which can 'insensate' and animate things. He claims that 'every metaphor ... is a fable in brief'. Vico notes that the human body and its parts as well as human senses and passions often form phrases about inanimate things. His illustrative examples include, among many others, *head* for top or beginning, and *mouth* for any opening. He concludes that this is because 'man in his ignorance makes himself the rule of the universe, for in the examples cited he has made of himself an entire world'. Vico claims that all the tropes (including metaphor, metonymy, synecdoche and irony) are 'necessary modes of expression of all the first poetic nations' despite the fact that they had been seen as 'ingenious inventions of writers'.

Metaphor as the relation between tenor and vehicle

I.A. Richards, probably the most dominant figure of New Criticism, considered the study of metaphor vital in the study of language and laid out the basics of his metaphor theory in *The Philosophy of Rhetoric* (1936). Richards introduced new terms in metaphor scholarship: a metaphor is made up of a tenor (the underlying idea or principal subject that the vehicle refers to) and a vehicle (the imagery that is used to refer to the tenor). Their relationship is called the ground. The notion of tension refers to the literal incompatibility of the tenor and the vehicle.

Richards uses the word *metaphor* in a broad sense, including cases where a word, being grounded in some direct resemblance, compounds two ideas into one and we speak of one as if it were something else. He also uses it to refer to metaphoric processes 'in which we perceive or think of or feel about one thing in terms of another – as when looking at a building it seems to have a face and to confront us with a peculiar expression' (pp. 116–117). Indeed, he argues that everyday discourse is mostly metaphoric, as opposed to pure scientific language (p. 120). Richards' views were quite modern in the sense that he said that the dead vs. living metaphor distinction (which, he says, is itself 'a two-fold metaphor') has many disadvantages and needs 'a drastic re-examination' as dead metaphors such as *the leg of a table* come to life easily (p. 102). He also notes that words may be both literal and metaphorical at the same time, and they may even be used in several metaphors with different foci. This can be provisionally decided by considering 'whether, in the given instance, the word gives us two ideas or one; whether ... it presents both a tenor and a vehicle which co-operate in an inclusive meaning. If we cannot distinguish tenor from vehicle then we may provisionally take the word to be literal; if we can distinguish at least two co-operating uses, then we have metaphor' (pp. 118–119).

Richards gives a detailed discussion not only of the eighteenth-century comparison view of metaphor, but also mentions the technique used by then-contemporaries (such as André Breton in his poems) who favoured putting together two things that are very remote from one another. Here, Richards claims, the human mind tries to connect the two completely unrelated things despite all the tension created by confusion (which may nonetheless be resolved by the discourse or context) as '[i]n all interpretation we are filling in connections, and for poetry, of course, our freedom to fill in the absence of explicitly stated intermediate steps is a main source of its powers' (p. 125). Richards goes on to say that language 'is no mere signalling system. It is the instrument of all our distinctively human development, of everything in which we go beyond the other animals' (p. 131). Thus, Richards has pioneering ideas about combining the workings of the mind and the workings of language, and says that by learning more about one we can learn more about the other as well (p. 136).

Metaphor as focus and frame

Max Black developed his interaction theory of metaphor in seminal works from 1955, 1962 and 1979/1993, reaching back to I.A. Richards' ideas. Black's (1955) interaction theory differs from what he calls the substitution view, and its special case, the comparison view. In the substitution view, the meaning of the metaphorically used word or expression could have been expressed literally. Here, metaphor is a decorative device except when it is a catachresis ('the use of a word in some new sense in order to remedy a gap in the vocabulary' (p. 280)). In the comparison view, metaphor presents an underlying analogy or similarity. As opposed to interaction-metaphors, both substitution-metaphors and comparison-metaphors can be replaced by literal translations (with the possible exception of catachresis) without any loss of cognitive content although losing the vivacity of the original expression. The main theses of Black's theory are the following (quoted from Black 1993, pp. 27–28 unless otherwise indicated):

(1) A metaphorical statement, which is defined as a whole (set of) sentence(s) plus context/setting, has two distinct subjects, to be identified as the primary subject and the secondary one (cf. Black's (1955) terms: principal vs. subsidiary subjects). Metaphorical statements have a focus, which is the word(s) used nonliterally, and a surrounding literal frame. A metaphor-theme is 'an abstraction from the metaphorical statements in which it does/might occur' (p. 24).

(2) The secondary subject is to be regarded as a system rather than an individual thing.

(3) The metaphorical utterance works by projecting upon the primary subject a set of associated implications, comprised in the implicative complex (i.e. the common knowledge shared by the speakers of a language), which are predicable of the secondary subject.

(4) The maker of a metaphorical statement selects, emphasises, suppresses, and organises features of the primary subject by applying to it statements that are isomorphic with the members of the secondary subject's implicative complex.

(5) In the context of a particular metaphorical statement, the two subjects interact in the following ways: (a) the presence of the primary subject incites the hearer to select some of the secondary subject's properties; (b) it invites him to construct a parallel implication-complex that can fit the primary subject; and (c) it reciprocally induces parallel changes in the secondary subject.

In Black's view, metaphorical utterances can be more or less emphatic (depending on whether the metaphor can be substituted or paraphrased without losing its insight), and/or more or less resonant (having more or less possible interpretations). Strong (as opposed to weak) metaphors are both emphatic and resonant (pp. 25–26).

Black sees metaphors as having an important cognitive function, but he also touches upon the creativity/productivity of metaphors and says that metaphors as cognitive instruments can constitute new aspects of reality. His strong creativity thesis focuses on the possibility that metaphors create previously unrecognised connections between domains (1979/1993, pp. 37–38).

Metaphor based on similarity

In his famous 1956 essay on aphasia, a language disturbance, Roman Jakobson deals with the types of breakdowns in the communication of aphasic patients and claims that aphasic disturbances are 'the impairment, more or less severe, of the faculty either for selection and substitution or for combination and contexture' (1995, p. 129). The deterioration of metalinguistic operations, the suppression of similarity relations, and, as a result, the lack of metaphors characterise the former type of aphasia (similarity disorder), and the damaged capacity for maintaining the hierarchy of linguistic units, the suppression of the relation of contiguity, and, as a result, the lack of metonymy are typical of the latter type of aphasia (contiguity disorder). In the former case, patients can use the word *fork* for *knife* or *smoke* for *pipe* as these often co-occur as in expressions like *knife and fork* and *smoke a pipe*. In the latter case, patients speak with agrammatical simple sentences in telegraphic style. As such, they can use the word *spyglass* for *microscope*, or *fire* for *gaslight* (pp. 125–126).

Jakobson generalises the metaphor–metonymy dichotomy to include normal verbal behaviour as well, claiming that similarity/metaphor and contiguity/metonymy are continually operative, but one's culture, personality, verbal style and preference may determine which of the two processes are preferred in general. Jakobson adds that this is also true of any sign system, including verbal and other forms of art as well. In poetry, he says, metaphor prevails in Romanticism and Symbolism, whereas metonymy, including synecdoche, is central to Realism. Metaphor is considered to be a poetic device primarily available in poems, whereas prose usually favours the use of metonymy. Generally speaking, metaphor has always received more attention that metonymy; this is why, for example, the preponderance of metonymy in Realism can easily remain unnoticed (pp. 130–133).

Metaphor as foregrounded deviation in literature

Style, which according to Leech and Short (1981/2007) is 'the way in which language is used in a given context, by a given person, for a given purpose', can be translucent to various degrees: style can be relatively transparent/paraphrasable, or relatively opaque, where opacity means that text interpretation depends on the reader's creative imagination. Leech (2008) and van Peer (1986) consider both invented (i.e. novel) and dead metaphors as deviations from the norm and as such they are seen as a means of foregrounding. In general, the systematic norm violation of the standard is claimed to make poetry possible. Literary metaphors may not differ from other metaphors in kind, but more often than not they do differ in the degree of novelty and the fact that literature is designed to be re-read, re-interpreted, representing its own revisitable textual context. Still, literature does not deviate differently from the norm than other texts as it represents its own textual context, as opposed to other language uses which refer to extratextual context.

Metaphor in conversation

Searle (1979/1993) suggests that a clear distinction is needed between literal sentence meaning and speaker's utterance meaning. When using metaphorical utterances speakers mean something different from sentence meaning, so listeners may find the literal meaning of a sentence *Sam is a pig* odd and thus resort to finding an alternative, metaphorical meaning ('Sam is filthy, gluttonous, sloppy...') to make sense of the speaker's intended meaning. Metaphors are seen as not paraphrasable because loss of semantic content occurs in their literal paraphrases.

Grice (1975, p. 53) argues that metaphor, a case of particularised conversational implicature, flouts the maxim of quality (i.e. being truthful) since metaphorical utterances appear to be false when their meaning is taken literally. Metaphors, instances of speaking vaguely of something else, are considered to be deviant language use in context. Thus, *You are the cream in my coffee* characteristically involves categorial falsity, so the speaker refers to some ways of fanciful resemblance between the hearer and the coffee cream.

Reinterpreting Grice's work, relevance theory (Sperber and Wilson 1986/1995) claims that utterances are interpreted using the principle of relevance, trying to achieve maximal efficiency and cognitive effect while minimising processing efforts. Here, because metaphors are seen as instances of loose language use, they cannot be completely paraphrased, and lexicalised figurative meanings are seen as dead or frozen metaphors. However, processing efforts in literature are often not minimal, since savouring the shades of possible meaning contributes to literary appreciation: in this respect, stylistic analysis may point out differences in processing depth between conversational and literary uses of metaphors (for more on relevance theory see Chapter 9 in this volume).

Metaphor and usure

In his famous 1972 essay on metaphor, Jacques Derrida (1982) gives a critical deconstructive account of several theories of metaphor, including Aristotle's theory but also referring, among many other philosophers and linguists, to Nietzsche, and Hegel. Derrida focuses on the usage, or, to use his term, *usure,* of metaphor in philosophy and philosophical language. Words, he says, can be seen as coins with inscriptions on each side. Thus, words can have metaphorical inscriptions which can fade away with time, by *usure* ('the history and structure of the philosophical metaphor', the value of which corresponds to the opposition between actual/ effective/living and inactive/ineffective/dead metaphors – which, being unconscious, are of no interest in philosophy), just as in the case of exergues on the reverse of coins (p. 209, p. 225). Derrida says that metaphor simultaneously hides and is hidden by the original meaning, which has been so much used that it is worn away *(usé).* The original meaning equals the literal meaning and it only becomes a metaphor in philosophical discourse, after which it becomes forgotten and the unnoticed metaphor turns into the proper meaning. Thus, philosophy is the process of metaphorisation, which is thus 'a provisional loss of meaning... the circular reappropriation of literal, proper meaning' (p. 211, p. 270). Derrida concludes that '[m]etaphor, then, always carries its death within itself' (p. 271).

Metaphor as a contextual change of meaning

Paul Ricoeur largely agrees with Black's and Richards' theory in that he believes metaphors are more than substitutions for literal words, which could be paraphrased exhaustingly. However, Ricoeur takes the theory a step further to say that dead and novel metaphors should be treated within the same theory, without using the vague notion of associated commonplaces. Metaphor for him is a pair of contrasting traits, and a metaphorical sense both abolishes and preserves the literal sense in tension (1974, p. 154). Genuine novel metaphors, semantic innovations, can turn into dead metaphors having standard meaning if emergent meanings are adopted by a larger speech community (pp. 100–102).

In metaphorical propositions, the specific characters are attributed to the principal subject of a sentence (p. 97). Indeed, metaphor involves the dichotomy of sense ('what is said') and reference ('about what something is said'). Words only have potential meanings (dictionary meanings), and they get their actual meanings in sentences, within the framework of the discourse. Although the shift from literal to metaphorical meaning occurs on the level of words, it is words in specific contexts that can have metaphorical uses or nonliteral and novel meanings. Metaphorical use is only contextual, and therefore metaphor is 'a contextual change of meaning' (p. 99). Ricoeur (1978b) adds that 'the "place" of metaphor ... is neither the name, nor the sentence, nor even discourse, but the copula of the verb *to be*. The metaphorical 'is' at once signifies both 'is not' and 'is like'" (p. 7).

Ricoeur (1978a, p. 148) views imagination as the '*ability* to produce new kinds [of likeness relations] by assimilation and to produce them ... in spite of and through the differences'. Thus, metaphor, through insight, can change the way in which the world is perceived. Linguistic creations such as metaphor generally allow new worlds to emerge from poetry.

Turning from the linguistic to the cognitive view of metaphor

Some theories described above have already tried to avoid reducing the theory of metaphor to language alone and included the human mind and culture in their analysis. As Nerlich and Clarke (2001) add, some eighteenth- and nineteenth-century rhetoricians and philosophers such as B.H. Smart and Jean Paul can also be considered as forerunners of a cognitive view of metaphor since they refuted the claim that metaphor is purely a rhetorical device, and focused on the close link between body and mind as providing the basis for metaphor.

The cognitive linguistic theory of metaphor and other figures of speech, first described systematically in Lakoff and Johnson's (1980) seminal book *Metaphors We Live By,* runs counter to the comparison theory of metaphor since it claims that metaphor creates new realities, it does not just provide a passive comparison of pre-existing similarities, and it is not merely a linguistic or poetic device. They also state that their groundbreaking work is 'nothing radically new', being based on previous philosophical works including Wittgenstein's family-resemblance account of categorisation, among others (p. 182).

Current multidisciplinary metaphor research

Reuven Tsur coined the phrase *Cognitive Poetics* in the 1970s (Tsur 1992) to allude to his examination of literary aesthetics through cognitive psychology and neuroscience. His work is part of the movement which has become to be called the *cognitive turn,* a shift from the *linguistic turn* in arts, humanities, and social sciences, which places emphasis on the interaction between texts and readers. As Stockwell (2010, p. 169) notes, although this kind of cognitive stylistic study of literary reading is now becoming a 'genuinely multidisciplinary study' including linguistics, psychology, literary scholarship, critical theory, discourse analysis, social theory, anthropology, historical study, neuroscience, medical research, aesthetics, ethics, and philosophy, it relies heavily on the principles of cognitive science. Initially it drew on 'cognitive linguistics in focusing on the textual cues for literary reading', and more recently on 'cognitive psychology in order to explore issues of readerly effects and aesthetics'. In addition to using principles created by cognitive metaphor theory, conceptual integration and blending theory, a fundamental organising force in a large number of cognitive poetic studies is the cognitive claim that language is embodied, and the mind and the body cannot be separated. This can also explain the fact that communal readings are common in practice in addition to individual readings based on personal experience and the social circumstances of the reader (Stockwell 2010).

The human conceptual system plays a significant role in the interpretation of literature. Literary texts, which represent the workings of the conceptual system of writers, are good sources for linguistic examination. The thoughts represented in such texts are not direct reflections of reality – rather, they represent various construals and perspectives taken by the interpreter. As Margaret Freeman (2000, p. 253) also points out concerning literary texts and their interpretations, 'literary texts are the products of cognizing minds and their interpretations the products of other cognizing minds in the context of the physical and socio-cultural worlds in which they have been created and are read'.

Cognitive linguistic research has influenced cognitive poetic studies to a large extent. Cognitive linguistics, and primarily conceptual metaphor analysis as proposed by Lakoff and Johnson (1980) and Lakoff and Turner (1989), is helpful in studying the role of conceptual tools in literary texts. This framework offers a possibility to systematically analyse thought processes through language. Indeed, one of the most important claims of cognitive linguistics is that thought is largely – though not entirely – metaphorical, and our conceptual system makes use of metaphorical processes in the act of interpretation.

Conceptual metaphor theory

As we have seen above, traditional views of philosophy and language allow metaphor little space in the human understanding of the world because they consider metaphor to be a matter of peripheral interest in everyday language. Lakoff and Johnson (1980), however, argue against this theory of metaphor and focus on the significance of metaphor in language and thought. They claim that metaphor is a property of concepts, and not of words – this is why they primarily talk about conceptual metaphors. In their view, the most important role of metaphor is to help understand certain concepts better. Thus, metaphors are not merely created for some artistic or aesthetic purpose. A further claim is that metaphor is often *not* based on similarity. In addition, they show convincingly that metaphor is used without effort in everyday life by everyday people; moreover, it is a necessary process of human thought, reasoning, and imagination. It is pervasive in thought, experience, and everyday language.

The authors insist that conceptual metaphors play a central role in thought and language when people use concepts and expressions from one semantic area to think, understand and talk about others. The term *conceptual metaphor* refers to the process of understanding one concept or domain (i.e. any coherent segment of experience) in terms of another. Conceptual metaphors allow forms of reasoning and expressions from one domain to be used in another domain. For instance, people often talk and think unconsciously about love in terms of journeys. A short way of grasping this view of metaphor is CONCEPT A IS CONCEPT B, where CONCEPT A is the *target domain,* and CONCEPT B is the *source domain.* There is a set of systematic correspondences, *mappings,* between the source and target domains, so the constituent conceptual elements of the source domain correspond to constituent elements of the target. *Linguistic metaphorical expressions* are linguistic expressions from the terminology of the source concept used to understand the target. Thus, expressions related to LOVE which come from the domain of JOURNEY are linguistic metaphorical expressions (e.g. *They are at a crossroads in their relationship*), while the corresponding conceptual metaphor is LOVE IS A JOURNEY.

Conceptual metaphors can be classified according to their cognitive function into structural, orientational, and ontological metaphors. Structural metaphors project the structure of the source domain onto the structure of the target, and thereby speakers can understand one domain in terms of another. Orientational metaphors have an evaluative function. They make large groups of metaphors coherent with each other (e.g. metaphorical concepts that have an upward or downward orientation). Ontological metaphors provide an object/substance/container status to abstract targets, without specifying the exact nature of these. Personification, a type of ontological metaphor, is abundant in both poetic and everyday language. Death, for instance, is often personified as a reaper or a coachman in various works of art, which are motivated by the metaphors PEOPLE ARE PLANTS or DEATH IS DEPARTURE (Lakoff and Turner 1989).

Mappings between source and target domains are only partial since the source domain highlights only parts of aspects of the target and hides others, and therefore only a part of the source is mapped onto the target and only a part of the target is involved in the mappings from the source. Thus, in order to understand a target completely we need several source domains, since no single source domain can fully structure a target. Metaphorical entailments are cases when we map aspects of our rich knowledge about the source domain onto the target domain, thus structuring it in elaborate ways. The Invariance hypothesis, however, claims that each mapping has to be coherent with the image-schematic characteristics of the target domain and consistent with that of the source domain (Lakoff 1993).

Conceptual metaphors, as Lakoff and Turner (1989, p. 51) state, are 'part of the common conceptual apparatus shared by members of a culture'. Generally, metaphors are unconsciously and automatically used. Metaphorical linguistic expressions are usually highly conventionalised, and speakers can use them naturally and without effort for everyday purposes. Often, the metaphors that are claimed to be dead in the traditional approach appear to be the most active and vital in human life, since they are so deeply entrenched in our conceptual system that we use them effortlessly all the time. This is also made possible since metaphors are most often motivated by our common human experience in the world. As Kövecses (2002, p. 69) claims:

> …in addition to objective, preexisting similarity – conceptual metaphors are based on a variety of human experience, including correlations in experience, various kinds of non-objective similarity, biological and cultural roots shared by the two concepts, and possibly others. All of these may provide sufficient motivation for the selection of a source B_1 over B_2 or B_3 for the comprehension of a target A. Given such motivation, it makes sense to speakers of a language to use B_1, rather than, say, B_2 or B_3, to comprehend A. They consequently feel that the conceptual metaphors that they use are somehow natural.

Motivation is indeed a central phenomenon in cognition. However, motivation is not the same as prediction. It is not claimed that we can predict what the idiom *cheer up* means from the meanings of *cheer* and *up*. It is not claimed either that the meaning of these words is arbitrary. We can understand what *cheer up* means because of the conceptual metaphor HAPPY IS UP, which motivates its meaning.

In addition to conceptual metaphors, other cognitive mechanisms are also capable of providing possible motivations for meaning, such as conceptual metonymy of the CONCEPT A FOR CONCEPT B type (which provides mental access through one conceptual entity to another which is related to it within a single domain), conceptual blends (the conceptual integration of several domains/spaces into a new, blended mental space, used in accounting for metaphorical and non-metaphorical aspects of on-line understanding, where input spaces may be related to each other as source and target in the form of a conceptual metaphor), conventional knowledge (everyday knowledge shared by speakers of a linguistic community about particular domains), image schemas (e.g. the UP–DOWN schema, mapping only skeletal structure onto the target), and construals (different ways of structuring experience). On these phenomena, see Lakoff and Johnson (1980, 1999), Lakoff (1987), Langacker (1987), Fauconnier and Turner (2002) and Turner (1996).

Conceptual tools in literature – Implications for practice

So far we have focused on the ubiquity of conceptual tools in everyday language. However, conceptual tools are also ubiquitous in the arts and literature as well, besides many other areas of human activity. Lakoff and Turner (1989) focus on conceptual metaphors in literature. In *More Than Cool Reason,* the authors claim that the conceptual metaphors underlying unique, poetic linguistic expressions may be extremely common as poets and writers usually use a number of already existing metaphors at the conceptual level in various ways. They can call upon the readers' knowledge of specific conceptual metaphors and operate with these in extraordinary ways. They can arrange metaphors masterfully and in a conscious manner, and they can also produce novel, unconventional poetic language and images using everyday conceptual devices. Combining is the process of activating several metaphors at the same time, even compressed into a single sentence or clause. Composing is the use of several metaphors for a specific target. With the help of questioning, poets and writers call into question the appropriateness of everyday conceptual metaphors. By extension, a new conceptual element, and thus a new linguistic device, is used in the source domain. Elaborating on a source element in a unique way makes it possible to introduce a novel, unconventional way of understanding the existing source element. Poets and writers can also 'offer new modes of metaphorical thought or … make the use of our conventional basic metaphors less automatic by employing them in unusual ways' (Lakoff and Turner 1989, p. 51). Therefore, the majority of basic conceptual metaphors found in poetic language are based on conventionalised conceptual metaphors, and as such they also appear in and underlie everyday expressions. For instance, Shakespeare's poetic metaphor 'All the world's a stage, / And all the men and women merely players. / They have their exits and their entrances; / And one man in his time plays many parts.' (*As You Like It* 2.7) is a manifestation of the conventionalised conceptual metaphor LIFE IS A PLAY. Some examples of this metaphor from present-day English are the following: *It's curtains for him. She always wants to be in the spotlight. What's your part in this? He saved the show.* and *That's not in the script.* (Lakoff and Turner 1989, p. 20).

Image metaphors, including one-shot metaphors, can also be found in poetry. Lakoff and Turner's (1989) famous example of such a metaphor is André Breton's poem about his wife, which has the following image metaphor: 'My wife… whose waist is an hourglass', where the shape of the middle (and not the other parts) of an hourglass is mapped onto the shape of the waist of the poet's wife.

Most studies in cognitive linguistic metaphor analysis have mainly demonstrated how isolated linguistic metaphors taken from various literary texts can work. For instance, Lakoff and Turner (1989) illustrate the metaphor LIFE IS A JOURNEY with the following example: 'Two roads diverged in a wood, and I – / I took the one less travelled by, / And that has made all the difference' (Robert Frost: 'Stopping by Woods on a Snowy Evening'), and the metaphor LIFE IS A STORY by the following: 'Life is a tale told by an idiot' (from

Shakespeare's *Macbeth*). However, the cognitive perspective increasingly demands a search for larger patterns of metaphoric thought in texts, instead of single metaphor expression analysis.

Some studies have shown that there are organic texts in which one of the organising principles structuring the short story, novel or poem is the metaphorical 'undercurrent' that runs through the whole text and is realised in a series of various 'single' metaphors. Paul Werth (1994, p. 83) has already brought this problematic aspect to light through the analysis of *extended metaphors* where 'a metaphorical field extends through an entire discourse'. Werth analyses an extract from Dylan Thomas's *Under Milk Wood*, which is structured by the metaphors SLEEP IS DISABLEMENT, DISABLEMENT IS DEATH, which unify the text as connective forces.

Elaborating on the same basic idea, Donald Freeman (1995) uses the cognitive approach to analyse Shakespeare's *Macbeth* and the critical works on the play with respect to the dominant image schemas in the play, namely, the CONTAINER and PATH schemas. As Freeman (1995) argues, 'the PATH and CONTAINER image-schemata – skeletal structures of... "embodied human understanding" – constitute the terms in which we understand not only *Macbeth*'s language, but also its central characters, crucial aspects of its various settings, and the sequence and structure of its unitary plot' (1995, p. 691). The dominance of the two schemas also shows up in critical language about *Macbeth*, as Freeman suggests. *Macbeth* has recently been re-analysed by Peña Cervel (2011), whose analysis focuses on some idealised cognitive models, the DIVIDED SELF structural metaphor and further metaphors, metonymies and image-schemas including for instance EXCESS and VERTICALITY, which are at play.

Regarding the issue of metaphorisation in poetical thinking versus ordinary discourse, the systematic analysis of Emily Dickinson's poetry and conceptual universe shows that these are structured by the conceptual metaphor LIFE IS A VOYAGE IN SPACE, instead of the well-accepted metaphor of her contemporaries, LIFE IS A JOURNEY THROUGH TIME (Margaret Freeman 1995). As can also be seen in several poems, the poet's general state – Dickinson's physical, biological, mental, emotional condition or situation – influences her poems to a large extent. For instance, in the poem entitled 'I reckon–when I count it all', Dickinson makes use of her bodily condition of having impaired vision. In this way, unique personal experiences may also be the basis of embodied cognition. In addition, the choice of poetic images can also be motivated by context, especially the cultural context, including, for instance, the poets' belief systems, and the physical-cultural-social environment – as in the case of Sylvia Plath's poem 'Medusa', where the Greek mythological image of Medusa is used to think and talk about Plath's mother (Kövecses 2010).

Csábi (2000) analyses metaphors in Thomas Paine's *Common Sense* (1776/1986) and shows that the relationship metaphors combine with each other as well as with metonymies and blends in the text to provide a clear metaphorical undercurrent underlying Paine's argument for America's separation from Britain: the argument is that there is a specific time in every family's life when the child, America, has to start going his own way and has to separate from the parents, Britain, in order to start his/her individual life.

These cognitive analyses also suggest that creative people make use of conventional, everyday metaphors, and that their originality in fact derives from them. As Gibbs (1994, p. 119) also claims,

> much of our conceptualization of experience is metaphorical, which both motivates and constrains the way we think creatively. The idea that metaphor constrains creativity

might seem contrary to the widely held belief the metaphor somehow liberates the mind to engage in divergent thinking.

This suggests that metaphors not only set loose our imagination and allow a wide variety of expressions in language, but they also constrain our thinking and force it in a particular direction. The literary analyses outlined above also show that authors and poets make extensive use of metaphors and metonymies that constrain their thinking and are still active and forceful in present-day English.

The metaphor identification procedure

The only metaphor identification procedure in the cognitive linguistic framework that works with a defined list of criteria with which specific words in a text may or may not comply is the one outlined by the Pragglejaz Group. With the help of their method, linguistic metaphors can be identified reliably using precise, agreed criteria to avoid intuitions. Their metaphor identification procedure (MIP) consists of the following steps (Pragglejaz Group 2007, p. 3):

(1)   Read the entire text–discourse to establish a general understanding of the meaning.
(2)   Determine the lexical units in the text–discourse.
(3)   (a) For each lexical unit in the text, establish its meaning in context, that is, how it applies to an entity, relation, or attribute in the situation evoked by the text (contextual meaning). Take into account what comes before and after the lexical unit.
     (b) For each lexical unit, determine if it has a more basic contemporary meaning in other contexts than the one in the given context. For our purposes, basic meanings tend to be
       – more concrete; what they evoke is easier to imagine, see, hear, feel, smell, and taste,
       – related to bodily action,
       – more precise (as opposed to vague),
       – historically older.
      Basic meanings are not necessarily the most frequent meanings of the lexical unit.
     (c) If the lexical unit has a more basic current–contemporary meaning in other contexts than the given context, decide whether the contextual meaning contrasts with the basic meaning but can be understood in comparison with it.
(4)   If yes, mark the lexical unit as metaphorical.

Recommendations for practice

Within the framework of conceptual metaphor theory, the books and studies mentioned in the section on *Conceptual tools in literature – Implications for practice* provide great practical examples of the metaphor analyses of literary works, and they can be used as excellent guidelines to work from. Before exploring metaphors in specific literary texts, though, it may also be useful to take a close look at Kövecses (2002/2010) and Simpson (2004), which have several practically orientated activities that focus on, and exercise the analysis of, metaphors that occur in literary texts. A next step could be to read the specific works that the above books and studies deal with – starting with, for instance, Emily Dickinson's poems – and try to analyse the metaphors in them, applying the methods described in the related book or study – in the case of Dickinson's poems, Margaret Freeman's 1995 article – and compare the results. A further step could be to pick one's favourite poem or book, or any other piece of literature, and try to systematically identify the linguistic metaphors and the underlying conceptual metaphors in the text.

Future directions in the cognitive tradition

Lakoff and Johnson (1999) delineate a more complex version of metaphor theory, focusing on Johnson's theory of conflation, Grady's theory of primary metaphor, Narayanan's neural theory of metaphor, as well as Fauconnier and Turner's theory of conceptual blending. Conflation refers to the coactivation of the source and the target domains due to co-occurrence in experience, which are later on differentiated (e.g. SEEING–KNOWING). Primary metaphors such as PURPOSES ARE DESTINATIONS are metaphors that make up complex metaphors such as LOVE IS A JOURNEY. The neural theory of metaphor claims that conceptual mappings across domains correspond to neural connections in the brain since common sensory-motor experience provides the basis for the existence of the same conceptual metaphors in many languages. Blending theory deals with the integration of mental spaces through conceptual blending (for more on blending see Chapter 18 in this volume).

A growing number of cognitive studies deal with embodiment, the 'understanding [of] the role of an agent's own body in its everyday, situated cognition', which focuses on the close relationship between mind and body, and between thought, language, and bodily action (Gibbs 2006b). Gibbs et al. (2004, p. 1190), for instance, discuss the way Pablo Neruda talks about love and desire in his 'Love poem 11' in terms of the embodied experiences of hunger (e.g. 'I crave your mouth, hunger for your sleek laugh, I want to eat the fleeting shade, I pace around hungry') to illustrate that ordinary food (e.g. bread) cannot satisfy his metaphorical hunger. The meaning of the poem is basically grounded in people's ordinary body experiences like hunger and thirst. This kind of embodied grounding, which is rooted in people's ordinary, felt sensations of their bodies in action, is also true for several instances of poetic metaphor and conventional speech in general. Thus, the human body acts as a major source forming aspects of our cognition, as the most universal experience of humans is the way the human body is shaped.

Conclusion

From metaphors in literature to metaphors we live by, from rhetoric to cognition, the study of metaphor has had a rich history. Let us finally return to look at the Shakespeare sonnet quoted in the beginning of this chapter and analyse the text using the cognitive framework. The predominant metaphor that structures the meaning of the poem is A LIFETIME IS A DAY, which maps a day lasting from morning to night onto one's life from childhood to old age. Thus, morning corresponds to childhood, and night to death. Shakespeare also uses the metaphor LIFE IS LIGHT, where light maps onto life and darkness onto death. Due to the metaphor LIFE IS FIRE, we understand the cycle of life as a slow process lasting from heat and fire till complete coldness and total darkness. These metaphors are combined in the expressions used in the sonnet. The technique of composing is also utilised as more than one conventional metaphor is used for the target domain of life. Shakespeare thus masterfully uses the conceptual metaphors that we also often use in our everyday reasoning about our own lives.

Related topics

Blending, cognitive poetics, rhetoric and poetics, stylistics, emotion and neuroscience, text-world theory

Further reading

Ortony, A., ed. [1979] 1993. *Metaphor and thought.* Cambridge: Cambridge University Press.

The collection of essays on metaphor and thought written by key scholars in the field illustrates different theories on metaphor and metaphor understanding.

Gibbs, R. W. Jr., 1994. *The poetics of mind.* Cambridge: Cambridge University Press.

A great overview and discussion of different theories about metaphors and metaphor understanding can be found in Chapter 5: Understanding metaphorical expressions.

Simpson, P. 2004. *Stylistics: A resource book for students.* London: Routledge.

This book presents a detailed introductory reading for students of stylistics, which also discusses issues related to metaphor and metonymy research.

Stockwell, P., 2002. *Cognitive poetics: An introduction.* London: Routledge.

A solid introduction to the general precepts of cognitive poetics, with exercises at the end of each chapter to supplement the reader's learning.

References

Aristotle. *c.* 350 B.C. *Poetics.* S. H. Butcher, trans. Online. Available at http://classics.mit.edu/Aristotle/poetics.mb.txt (Accessed 15 August 2012).

Aristotle. *c.* 350 B.C. *Rhetoric.* W. R. Roberts, trans. Online. Available at: http://classics.mit.edu/Aristotle/rhetoric.mb.txt (Accessed 15 August 2012).

Black, M., 1955. Metaphor. *Proceedings of the Aristotelian society,* 55, 273–294.

Black, M., 1962. *Models and metaphors. Studies in language and philosophy,* Ithaca, New York: Cornell University Press.

Black, M., [1979] 1993. More about metaphor. *In:* A. Ortony, ed. *Metaphor and thought.* 2nd ed. Cambridge: Cambridge University Press, 19–41.

Csábi, S., 2000. 'The war of independence: A cognitive linguistic approach. A cognitive linguistic analysis of Thomas Paine's *Common Sense'.* Unpublished Thesis (MA). ELTE University, Budapest, Hungary.

Derrida, J., 1982. White mythology: Metaphor in the text of philosophy. *In: Margins of philosophy.* A. Bass, Trans. Chicago: University of Chicago Press, 207–272.

Eco, U., 1983. The scandal of metaphor: Metaphorology and semiotics. *Poetics Today,* 4 (2), 217–257.

Fauconnier, G. and Turner, M., 2002. *The way we think.* New York: Basic Books.

Freeman, D. C., 1995. 'Catch[ing] the nearest way': Macbeth and cognitive metaphor. *Journal of Pragmatics,* 24, 689–708.

Freeman, M. H., 1995. Metaphor making meaning: Dickinson's conceptual universe. *Journal of Pragmatics,* 24, 643–666.

Freeman, M. H., 2000. Poetry and the scope of metaphor: Toward a cognitive theory of literature. *In:* A. Barcelona, ed. *Metaphor and metonymy at the crossroads: A cognitive perspective.* Berlin: Mouton de Gruyter, 253–281.

Gibbs, R. W. Jr., 1994. *The poetics of mind.* Cambridge: Cambridge University Press.

Gibbs, R. W. Jr., 2006a. Cognitive linguistics and metaphor research: Past successes, skeptical questions, future challenges. *D.E.L.T.A.,* 22, 1–20.

Gibbs, R. W. Jr., 2006b. *Embodiment and cognitive science.* New York: Cambridge University Press.

Gibbs, R. W. Jr., Costa Lima, P. L. and Francozo, E., 2004. Metaphor is grounded in embodied experience. *Journal of Pragmatics,* 36, 1189–1210.

Grice, P., 1975. Logic and conversation. *In:* P. Cole and J. L. Morgan, eds. *Speech acts.* New York: Academic Press, 41–58.

Jakobson, R., 1995. *On language.* Cambridge, MA: Harvard University Press.

Kövecses, Z., [2002] 2010. *Metaphor: A practical introduction.* 2nd ed. Oxford, New York: Oxford University Press.

Kövecses, Z., 2010. A new look at metaphorical creativity in cognitive linguistics. *Cognitive Linguistics,* 21 (4), 655–689.

Lakoff, G., 1987. *Women, fire, and dangerous things: What categories reveal about the mind.* Chicago: The University of Chicago Press.

Lakoff, G., 1993. The contemporary theory of metaphor. *In:* A. Ortony (ed.) *Metaphor and thought.* 2nd edn. Cambridge: Cambridge University Press, 202–251.

Lakoff, G. and Johnson, M., 1980. *Metaphors we live by.* Chicago: University of Chicago.

Lakoff, G. and Johnson, M., 1999. *Philosophy in the flesh: The embodied mind and its challenge to Western thought.* New York: Basic Books.

Lakoff, G. and Turner, M., 1989. *More than cool reason: A field guide to poetic metaphor.* Chicago: University of Chicago Press.

Langacker, R., 1987. *Foundations of cognitive grammar,* Vols. 1 & 2. Stanford: Stanford University Press.

Leech, G., 2008. *Language in literature: Style and foregrounding.* London: Pearson.

Leech, G. and Short, M., [1981] 2007. *Style in fiction.* 2nd ed. London: Pearson.

Locke, J., [1689] 1836. *An essay concerning human understanding.* 27th edn. London: T. Tegg and Son.

Nerlich, B. and Clarke, D. D., 2001. Mind, meaning and metaphor: The philosophy and psychology of metaphor in 19th-century Germany. *History of the Human Sciences,* 14 (2), 39–61.

Paine, T., [1776] 1986. *Common sense.* New York: Penguin Books.

Peña Cervel, M. S., 2011. *Macbeth* revisited: A cognitive analysis. *Metaphor and Symbol,* 26, 1–22.

Pragglejaz Group, 2007. MIP: A method for identifying metaphorically used words in discourse. *Metaphor and Symbol,* 22 (1), 1–39.

Richards, I. A., 1936. *The philosophy of rhetoric.* Oxford: Oxford University Press.

Ricoeur, P., 1974. Metaphor and the main problem of hermeneutics. *New Literary History,* 6 (1), 95–110.

Ricoeur, P., 1978a. The metaphorical process as cognition, imagination, and feeling. *Critical Inquiry,* 5 (1), 143–59.

Ricoeur, P., 1978b. *The rule of metaphor.* London: Routledge & Kegan Paul.

Searle, J. R., [1979] 1993. Metaphor. *In:* A. Ortony, ed. *Metaphor and thought.* 2nd edn. Cambridge: Cambridge University Press, 83–111.

Simpson, P. 2004. *Stylistics: A resource book for students.* London: Routledge.

Sperber, D. and Wilson, D., [1986] 1995. *Relevance: Communication and cognition.* 2nd edn. Oxford: Blackwell.

Stockwell, P., 2010. Cognitive poetics. *In:* P. C. Hogan, ed. *Cambridge encyclopedia of the language sciences.* New York: Cambridge University Press: 169–171.

Tsur, R., 1992. *Toward a theory of cognitive poetics.* Amsterdam: Elsevier.

Turner, M., 1996. *The literary mind: The origins of thought and language.* New York: Oxford University Press.

van Peer, W., 1986. *Stylistics and psychology: Investigations of foregrounding.* London: Croom Helm.

Vico, G., [1725] 1948. *The new science of Vico Giambattista.* Trans. from 3rd edn. [1744] by T. G. Bergin and M. H. Fisch. Ithaca, New York: Cornell University Press.

Werth, P., 1994. Extended metaphor: A text-world account. *Language and Literature,* 3, 79–103.

13

Speech and thought presentation in stylistics

Joe Bray

Introduction

This chapter demonstrates the continuing importance of speech and thought presentation in the stylistic analysis of prose fiction. It focuses in particular on the category of free indirect thought, which has historically been of great interest to narratologists and literary critics. Recent attacks on the usefulness of the speech and thought presentation categories, for example by adherents of a 'theory of mind' approach, have singled out free indirect thought as being unrepresentative of the variety of mental functioning to be found in prose fiction. While supporting many of this group's insights concerning the importance of 'intermental thought' and 'the intermental mind' in the novel, this chapter argues that this does not mean that the traditional categories of speech and thought presentation should be disregarded altogether. With particular attention to one recent experimental novel, David Foster Wallace's posthumously-published *The Pale King* (2011), the chapter suggests that free indirect thought remains widespread in twenty-first century fiction, albeit in a different form to the most commonly studied examples of the style in the nineteenth- and twentieth-century novel. It demonstrates that free indirect thought can do more than represent a solitary individual consciousness in isolation, and that it is in fact ideally suited to the contemporary novel's depiction of the conflict between the individual and the vast impersonal and institutional forces of our current age.

Historical perspectives

The study of speech and thought presentation has always been central to the discipline of stylistics. Chapter 10 of the first edition of Geoffrey Leech and Michael Short's seminal *Style in Fiction* (1981) was the first stylistic treatment to bring a fully analytical approach to the topic, introducing a model that has proved influential over the subsequent three decades. In particular, Leech and Short's careful distinguishing of two separate, parallel scales of speech and thought presentation, with categories defined by both formal and contextual features, allowed stylisticians to investigate the varying effects of slight changes in point of view, and to analyse shifts in the degree of 'faithfulness' to the original thought or utterance precisely (1981, pp. 318–351). The original categories of speech and thought proposed by Leech and Short are represented in the following table:

Table 13.1 Leech and Short's original categories of speech and thought presentation

Speech	NRSA (Narrator's Representation of Speech Act)	IS (Indirect Speech)	FIS (Free Indirect Speech)	DS (Direct Speech)	FDS (Free Direct Speech)
Thought	NRTA (Narrator's Representation of Thought Act)	IT (Indirect Thought)	FIT (Free Indirect Thought)	DT (Direct Thought)	FDT (Free Direct Thought)

The narrator's degree of control or influence over the representation of the utterance or thought is greatest for those categories at the left-hand side of the table, and gradually diminishes with each step to the right. According to Leech and Short, the 'norms' for speech and thought presentation are at different points on each continuum; while the norm for speech is direct speech (DS), that for thought is indirect thought (IT). They assert that this explains the different effects of free indirect speech (FIS) and free indirect thought (FIT):

> FIS is a movement leftwards from the norm [...] and is therefore interpreted as a movement towards authorial intervention, whereas FIT is seen as a move to the right and hence away from the author's most directly interpretative control and into the active mind of the character.
>
> *(1981, p. 345)*

Discussions of discourse presentation have proliferated as stylistics has developed over the subsequent three decades, with an especially comprehensive example being Monika Fludernik's *The Fictions of Language and the Languages of Fiction* (1993). Noting that 'speech and thought representation in (fictional) narrative is clearly a crucial issue in narrative poetics', Fludernik observes that it is 'related to a number of macro-textual and interpretative aspects of the reading process in general' (1993, p. 7):

> Some of the contexts involved are more restrictedly literary, as for example the question of point of view, the narrative situation, mood or voice; others are of a more conceptual nature, involving, for instance, the reading conventions that trigger an interpretation in terms of speech or thought representation.
>
> *(1993, p. 7)*

Revisiting the topic for the second, expanded edition of *Style in Fiction*, Leech and Short draw particular attention to the findings of the Lancaster speech, writing and thought presentation research projects, which applied their original model not only to a corpus of written fictional and non-fictional narratives, but also to a corpus of spoken English (the work on the written corpus is usefully summarised in Semino and Short (2004); see also Short, Semino and Culpeper (1996) and Short (2003)). While mainly confirming the robust nature of the model, this work has also led to two significant additions, as Leech and Short note: firstly, a third parallel scale of writing presentation, which is especially relevant to the epistolary novel (see for example Bray (2010)), and secondly, a new category on the speech presentation scale which indicates that speech has taken place, without giving further information about the speech act(s) involved (this is named Narrator's Representation of Voice (NV)) (Leech and Short 2007, p. 303). Their revised model can therefore be represented as follows:

Table 13.2 Leech and Short's revised model of speech and thought presentation categories

Speech	NV	NRSA	IS	FIS	DS	FDS
Thought		NRTA	IT	FIT	DT	FDT
Writing		NRWA	IW	FIW	DW	FDW

Free indirect thought

Free indirect thought's ability to, in Leech and Short's words, provide insight 'into the active mind of the character' has led to it being of great interest to critics from a variety of disciplines. Following Charles Bally's identification of '*style indirect libre*' (1912a, b), literary critics and narratologists have used a variety of names for this technique of providing access to character consciousness. Jane Austen is often cited as the initiator of the style (see Pascal (1977), Lodge (1990)), and there has been a particular focus on the nineteenth- and early twentieth-century novel, with key treatments including Cohn (1978), Banfield (1982), and the above-mentioned Fludernik (1993). As a result of what Leech and Short call 'the concern that nineteenth- and twentieth-century novelists have had with portraying the internal drama of the minds of their characters' (2007, p. 277), the representation of character consciousness continues to be a very popular topic in studies of the novel, though critics often lack rigour in distinguishing between free indirect thought and related techniques such as interior monologue.

As a typical example of free indirect thought in the late nineteenth-century novel, consider the following example from Henry James's *The Portrait of a Lady* (1881), which comes just after the American heroine Isabel Archer has turned down her English suitor Lord Warburton:

(1) Isabel herself was upset, but she had not been affected as she would have imagined. What she felt was not a great responsibility, a great difficulty of choice; it appeared to her there had been no choice in the question. She couldn't marry Lord Warburton; the idea failed to support any enlightened prejudice in favour of the free exploration of life that she had hitherto entertained or was now capable of entertaining. She must write this to him, she must convince him, and that duty was comparatively simple. But what disturbed her, in the sense that it struck her with wonderment, was this very fact that it cost her so little to refuse a magnificent 'chance.' With whatever qualifications one would, Lord Warburton had offered her a great opportunity; the situation might have discomforts, might contain oppressive, might contain narrowing elements, might prove really but a stupefying anodyne; but she did her sex no injustice in believing that nineteen women out of twenty would have accommodated themselves to it without a pang. Why then upon her should it not irresistibly impose itself? Who was she, what was she, that she should hold herself superior? What view of life, what design upon fate, what conception of happiness, had she that pretended to be larger than these large, these fabulous occasions? If she wouldn't do such a thing as that then she must do great things, she must do something greater.

(1995 [1881], pp. 130–131)

The passage contains a number of the classic markers of free indirect thought which have been commonly identified in critical treatments. In particular, the entry into Isabel's consciousness from the third sentence onwards is signalled by cues such as a frequent use of modality ('She couldn't marry Lord Warburton'; 'She must write this to him, she must convince him'), coupled with lexical items which suggest a subjective point of view ('the situation might have discomforts, might contain oppressive, might contain narrowing elements, might prove really but a stupefying anodyne'), questions which she is asking herself ('Why then upon her also should it not irresistibly impose itself? Who was she, what was she, that she should hold herself superior?') and what Laurel Brinton identifies as the 'co-temporality of narrative past tense with present and future time deictics' (1980, p. 367) ('the idea failed to support any enlightened prejudice in favour of the free exploration of life that she had hitherto entertained or *was now* capable of entertaining'). The entry into Isabel Archer's consciousness through the technique of free indirect thought is marked by the characteristic combination, in Leech and Short's words, of 'the presence of third-person pronouns and past tense, which correspond with the form of narrative report and indicate indirectness, along with a number of features, both positive and negative, indicating freeness' (2007, p. 261) (see also Fludernik 1993, pp. 72–109).

This example is typical of those commonly found in discussions of free indirect thought. The style is usually associated with the exploration of an individual consciousness which extends over the course of an entire novel. Other frequently examined minds include those of the heroines of Austen's *Emma* (1816), Gustave Flaubert's *Madame Bovary* (1856) and Virginia Woolf's *Mrs Dalloway* (1925), Lambert Strether in James's *The Ambassadors* (1903) and Stephen Dedalus in James Joyce's *Portrait of the Artist as a Young Man* (1914). The investigation of how the hero's or heroine's mind is represented in free indirect thought often centres on the narrator's ironic exposure of early weaknesses and limitations, which are then gradually overcome in the course of his or her moral development. However, this focus on subjective experience, according to some critics, obscures the representation of other kinds of consciousness. The novel can do more, they claim, than represent the twists and turns of individual consciousness on a path of psychological awakening and growth.

Alan Palmer, for example, argues that what he calls *the speech category approach of classical narratology* 'does not do justice to the complexity of the types of evidence for the workings of fictional minds that are available in narrative discourse; it pays little attention to states of mind such as beliefs, intentions, purposes, and dispositions; and it does not analyze the whole of the social mind in action' (2004, p. 53). He identifies 'at least five problems with the use of speech categories to analyze presentations of fictional thought' (p. 57), and is particularly severe on the category of free indirect thought, describing the contestations surrounding it as 'a swamp that I had originally intended to avoid completely' (p. 56). According to Palmer, his 'embedded narrative approach' is an advance on 'the fragmentation of previous approaches' since it 'views characters' minds not just in terms of the presentation of passive, private inner speech in the modes of direct or free indirect thought, but in terms of the narrator's positive role in presenting characters' social mental functioning' (p. 185), and 'encourages a detailed, precise, functional, and inclusive approach toward the whole of a fictional mind' (p. 186). He claims that 'Currently, there is a hole in literary theory between the analysis of consciousness, characterization, and focalization. Oddly, as I hope to have shown, a good deal of fictional discourse is situated precisely within this analytical gap' (p. 186).

Palmer takes many of his examples from eighteenth-century novels, although at first sight much recent fiction would also seem to fit into this 'analytical gap'. The experimental novel in particular would seem to eschew the representation of private, individual consciousness which has long been a focus of critics of Austen, James, Woolf and others. However, in attending to one recent experimental novel, this chapter will argue that the traditional categories of speech and thought representation should not be discarded altogether. Indeed, they continue to be crucially valuable in the analysis of recent fiction. Focusing on the much-maligned category of free indirect thought, the chapter will show that this style is more flexible and adaptable than some of its critics, especially Palmer, imply, and that it is capable of representing more than simply the private, passive, solitary individual consciousness with which he associates it.

Current research: Speech and thought presentation in the contemporary experimental novel

Following David Foster Wallace's suicide in 2008, his widow and agent handed over to his editor, Michael Pietsch, an assortment of manuscripts and computer files for a book that Wallace had been working on since the publication of *Infinite Jest* in 1996. Pietsch put together the book that we now know as *The Pale King*, which was published in 2011. Pietsch acknowledges in his Editor's Note that in the absence of a draft outline, or any clear sense of how its various parts were supposed to fit together, 'assembling the best version of *The Pale King* that I could find' has been 'a challenge like none I have ever encountered' (2011, p. ix). However, on the basis of the notes he found, Pietsch suggests that Wallace 'did not intend for the novel to have a plot substantially beyond the chapters here', and that 'the novel's incompleteness is in fact intentional' (p. x).

Though it is hard to identify any kind of main narrative to the novel, with many chapters appearing self-contained and disconnected, one institution with which many of its characters have a link is the Internal Revenue Service (IRS), the US government agency responsible for tax collection and compliance. More specifically, it centres on a group of characters arriving, or already based, at the IRS Regional Examination Center in Peoria, Illinois in 1985, including an 'Author' figure who claims to have worked there at this time. Much of the novel is taken up with the day-to-day lives of those who work at the Center. As a result there is a lot of painstaking detail about the US tax system, which frequently leaves the reader baffled. See for example Chapter 34:

(2)

§34

IRM §781(d) AMT Formula for Corporations: (1) Taxable income before NOL deduction, plus or minus (2) All AMT adjustments excepting ACE adjustment, plus (3) Tax preferences, yields (4) Alternative Minimum Taxable Income before NOL deduction and/or ACE adjustment, plus or minus (5) ACE adjustment, if any, yields (6) AMTI before NOL deduction, if any, minus (7) NOL deduction, if any (Ceiling at 90%), yields (8) AMTI, minus (9) Exemptions, yields (10) AMT base, multiplied by (11) 20% AMT rate, yields (12) AMT prior to AMT Foreign Tax Credit, minus (13) AMT Foreign tax Credit, if any (Ceiling at 90% unless Exceptions 781 (d) (13–16) apply, in which case attach Memo 781–2432 and forward to Group Manager), yields (14) Tentative Alternative Minimum Tax, minus (15) Standard tax liability before credit minus standard Foreign tax Credit, yields (16) Alternative Minimum Tax.

(2011, p. 388)

The barrage of technical detail in chapters such as this connects *The Pale King* with Wallace's previous work. Pietsch observes that as he went through the notes Wallace had made on his new project, 'it became apparent as I read that David planned for the novel to have a structure akin to that of *Infinite Jest*, with large portions of apparently unconnected information presented to the reader before a main story line begins to make sense. In several notes to himself, David referred to the novel as "tornadic" or having a "tornado feeling" – suggesting pieces of story coming at the reader in a high-speed swirl' (2011, p. x). These 'pieces' are often, as in the case of Chapter 34, exceedingly dull. Like the reader, the characters in *The Pale King* struggle to deal with this mind-numbing swirl of complex tax-related data, and avoid its harmful effects. As one character puts it, 'Tedium is like stress but its own Category of Woe' (p. 17). Reflecting on his time at the IRS, 'The Author' asks 'Why we recoil from the dull':

(3) Maybe it's because dullness is intrinsically painful; maybe that's where phrases like 'deadly dull' or 'excruciatingly dull' come from. But there might be more to it. Maybe dullness is associated with psychic pain because something that's dull or opaque fails to provide enough stimulation to distract people from some other, deeper type of pain that is always there, if only in an ambient low-level way, and which most of us spend nearly all our time and energy trying to distract ourselves from feeling, or at least from feeling directly or with our full attention. […] This terror of silence with nothing diverting to do. I can't think anyone really believes that today's so-called 'information society' is just about information. Everyone knows it's about something else, way down.

(2011, p. 87)

The novel explores the myriad ways in which characters retreat into the 'information society' in order to try and escape from this 'psychic pain' of boredom and dullness. Like other recent novels, *The Pale King* is concerned with the constant bombarding of data which is often said to be typical of our contemporary 'information society'. Christian Fuchs notes that in what he calls 'transnational informational/network capitalism' technological advances have 'increased the speed of global flows of capital, commodities, power, communication, and information' (2008, p. 113). The result, he claims, is an 'emerging global space' consisting of 'global technological systems and transnational (economic, political, cultural) organizations and institutions that enable global flows of capital, power, and ideology that create and permanently re-create a new transnational regime of domination' (p. 113). Faced with this fast-moving, powerful flow of data, the individual consciousness can seem tiny and insignificant. Many contemporary novels are concerned with the struggle of the individual in the face of this 'transnational regime'; a recent example on this side of the Atlantic is John Lanchester's *Capital* (2012), set in pre- and post-credit crunch London. Like *The Pale King*, *Capital* documents the individual's apparent powerlessness at the hands of the often indiscriminate technological and economic forces of contemporary capitalism (see section 6). Yet as the individual consciousness becomes increasingly threatened and even subsumed in contemporary fiction, another kind of shared, group experience has come to the fore as a focus of novelistic experimentation.

In *The Pale King*, the collective consciousness of the workers at the IRS Examination Center is highlighted by a number of experiments with speech and thought presentation. Some chapters consist entirely of free direct speech, in which day-to-day office gossip is never attributed to particular individuals. For example, Chapter 29 opens as follows:

(4)
'I only have one real story about shit. But it's a doozy.'
'Why shit?'
'What is it about shit? We're repelled but fascinated.'

'I'm not fascinated, I can tell you that.'
'It's like watching a car wreck, impossible to tear the eyes away.'
'My fourth-grade teacher had no eyelashes. Mrs. Something.'
'I mean I'm bored, too, but why shit?'
'My earliest memory of shit is dog shit. Remember as a kid how potent a presence and threat dog shit was? It seemed to be all over. Every time you played outside, somebody was stepping in it, and then everything stopped and it was like, "OK, who stepped in it?" Everybody had to check their shoes, and sure enough somebody had it on their shoe.'

(2011, p. 349)

The conversation continues throughout the chapter, with no indications of who is speaking, or even how people are involved, though there are occasional narratorial interventions which reveal the office context: 'As much as two minutes elapsed between each remark, sometimes. It was 2:10 and even the agents' small personal movements were languid and underwater' (p. 351). The setting and tone of the conversation is more important than the identity of the individuals taking part; for the purposes of the chapter, all the reader needs to know is that they are tax agents.

An even more notable example of shared experience comes in Chapter 25, which shows the lowly employees of the Center, or the 'wigglers', at work, going through tax returns. Their collective consciousness is emphasised by the repetition of 'turns a page', which most of them do more than once; Ken Wax, for example, turns a total of thirteen pages in the course of the chapter. While his page-turning is not elaborated on, for others the activity is accompanied by more detail: 'R. Jarvis Brown uncrosses his legs and turns a page'; 'Ryne Hobratschk turns a page and then folds over the page of a computer printout that's lined up next to the original file he just turned a page of'. Furthermore, some of the characters are given humorous nicknames which suggest workplace banter designed to alleviate the tedium: '"Groovy" Bruce Channing'; 'Joe "The Bastard" Biron-Maint'. There are also narratorial comments which sometimes seem purely factual, and sometimes suggest the abstracted thoughts of the wigglers themselves: 'Jay Landauer feels absently at his face. Every love story is a ghost story'. The variation within repetition here is an example of what Leech and Short call 'internal deviation': 'features of language within [a] text may depart from the norms of the text itself: that is, they may "stand out" against the background of that the text has led us to expect' (2007, p. 44). The internal deviation here provides glimpses of individuality within the tightly constrained office routine, hinting perhaps at vivid imaginations and idiosyncratic subjectivities which cannot be expressed in the workplace.

At such moments, *The Pale King* would seem to present what Alan Palmer has called 'intermental thought'. For Palmer, 'such thinking is joint, group, shared, or collective, as opposed to intramental, individual, or private thought. It is also known as socially distributed, situated, or extended cognition, and as intersubjectivity' (2005, p. 427). In his view, 'it is a crucially important component of fictional narrative because much of the mental functioning that occurs in novels is done by large organizations, small groups, work colleagues, friends, families, couples, and other intermental units' (p. 427). He claims that 'this aspect of narrative has been neglected by traditional theoretical approaches such as focalization, characterization, story analysis, and the representation of speech and thought' (p. 428). For Palmer this is further evidence of the need to make use of what he calls 'the parallel discourses on real minds, such as cognitive science', since they 'contain a picture of consciousness very different from, for example, the kind provided by the traditional approach to the representation of speech and thought' (p. 429). 'In particular', he claims, 'the standard approach to fictional consciousness has given undue emphasis to private, solitary, and highly verbalized thought at the expense of all the other types of mental functioning because of its preoccupation with such concepts as free indirect discourse, stream of consciousness, and interior monologue. As a result, the social nature of fictional thought has been neglected. The dominant perspective on fictional minds has been an internalist one that stresses those aspects that are inner, passive, introspective, and individual. However […] an externalist perspective is required as well, one that stresses the outer, active, public, and social aspects of mental life' (pp. 429–430).

Certainly *The Pale King* is interested, like many other recent novels, in what Palmer calls 'the social nature of fictional thought'; in how mental life is displayed publicly, and in how institutions do, and do not, embody a collective consciousness. Yet this does not mean that all aspects of what Palmer calls 'the traditional theoretical approaches' should be automatically discarded. As the rest of this chapter will show, *The Pale King* in fact abounds in features that have been identified in stylistic accounts of the representation of speech and thought, especially the much-abused free indirect thought. One reason for its pervasiveness is the novel's concern with variations of point of view; specifically with how to select one train of thought from among many in a sometimes bewildering mental landscape.

The 'Author' writes that 'I learned, in my time with the Service, something about dullness, information, and irrelevant complexity. About negotiating boredom as one would a terrain, its levels and forests and endless wastes' (2011, p. 87). Negotiating this 'terrain' requires patience, diligence, and above all the selective focusing of 'attention'. This is a key word in the novel, another way of linking together the somewhat disparate chapters. Of one character who sweats profusely in embarrassing social situations we are told that 'It was in public high school that this boy learned the terrible power of attention and what you pay attention to' (p. 93). In Chapter 22, an extensive, often heavily digressive first-person narrative, one of the IRS 'wigglers' Chris Fogle describes what led him to change the directionless course of his life and apply for a job in the IRS, or 'the Service': 'It had something to do with paying attention and the ability to choose what I paid attention to, and to be aware of that choice, the fact that it's a choice' (p. 189). His words are echoed by another IRS employee, Claude Sylvanshine, who arrives at the Regional Examination Center at the start of the novel: 'It was true: The entire ball game, in terms of both the exam and life, was what you gave attention to vs. what you willed yourself to not' (p. 14). More than any other character in *The Pale King* Sylvanshine struggles with this effort of the will. He is described as a 'fact psychic', whose mind is continually afflicted with seemingly useless pieces of information, such as 'the middle name of the childhood friend of a stranger they pass in a hallway' (p. 120), or 'the number of blades of grass in the front lawn of one's mailman's home' (p. 121). The narrator reports that 'one reason Sylvanshine's gaze is always so intent and discomfiting is that he's trying to filter out all sorts of psychically intuited and intrusive facts' (p. 121).

The ability to pay careful attention, and the choice of what you pay attention to, is thus a key theme in the novel, a way of counteracting the boredom and discomfort which otherwise threatens to overwhelm all the IRS employees, and indeed the reader. How exactly the human mind chooses to pay attention to some things and not others has of course long been a major topic for investigation in the cognitive sciences, especially psychology. The so-called 'Father of Psychology', William James, devoted a chapter to 'Attention' in the first volume of his ground-breaking *Principles of Psychology* (1890), noting that 'millions of items of the outward order are present to my senses which never properly enter into my experience. Why? Because they have no *interest* for me. *My experience is what I agree to attend to.* Only those items which I *notice* shape my mind – without selective interest, experience is an utter chaos.

Interest alone gives accent and emphasis, light and shade, background and foreground – intelligible perspective, in a word' (1950, p. 402). James then explains further what this 'intelligible perspective' consists of:

> Every one knows what attention is. It is the taking possession by the mind, in clear and vivid form, of one out of what seem several simultaneously possible objects or trains of thought. Focalization, concentration, of consciousness are of its essence. It implies withdrawal from some things in order to deal effectively with others, and is a condition which has a real opposite in the confused, dazed, scatterbrained state which in French is called *distraction*, and *Zerstreutheit* in German.
>
> *(1950, pp. 403–404)*

James's claim that the 'essence' of attention, the mind's selection of 'one of what seem several simultaneously possible objects or trains of thought', is 'focalization, concentration, of consciousness' anticipates much recent work in narrative theory. Just over eight decades later, Gérard Genette noted a 'regrettable confusion' in the theoretical treatment of point of view, 'between what I call here *mood* and *voice*, a confusion between the question *who is the character whose point of view orients the narrative perspective?* and the very different question *who is the narrator?* – or, more simply, the question *who sees?* and the question *who speaks?*' (1980, p. 186). In order to avoid 'the too specifically visual connotations of the terms *vision, field*, and *point of view*' he settles on the term 'focalization' to assist with the first question, distinguishing between 'zero focalization', 'internal focalization' (which can be fixed, variable or multiple) and 'external focalization' (pp. 189–190). Like James, Genette associates focalization with readerly attention and concentration, observing that 'any single formula of focalization does not [...] always bear on an entire work, but rather on a definite narrative section, which can be very short', and that 'the distinction between different points of view is not always as clear as the consideration of pure types alone could lead one to believe' (p. 191). His main text for analysis in *Narrative Discourse*, Marcel Proust's *À la recherche du temps perdu*, is marked, he claims, by a complex 'polymodality', which involves a 'congruence of theoretically incompatible focalizations, which shakes the whole logic of narrative representation' (p. 211). The novel both encourages and complicates the reader's efforts to distinguish, in James's words, 'one out of what seem several simultaneously possible objects or trains of thought'.

The Pale King similarly challenges the reader with a complex and variable system of focalization, which requires attention, concentration, and the ability, in James's words, to '[withdraw] from some things in order to deal effectively with others.' 'Shifting p.o.v.s' are one of the features identified by 'The Author' in his Foreword (actually Chapter 9) as 'simply the modern literary analogs of "Once upon a time…" or "Far, far away, there once dwelt…" or any of the other traditional devices that signaled the reader that what was under way was fiction and should be processed accordingly' (2011, p. 74). However, as so often in the novel, 'The Author's' words are designed to mislead. The constantly shifting point of view in *The Pale King* is more than simply a 'literary analog'. Instead it subtly illuminates in itself the novel's central concerns. Take the opening to Chapter 33, which describes the dull working routine of another of the IRS 'wigglers':

> (5) Lane Dean Jr. [...] sat at his Tingle table in his Chalk's row in the Rotes Group's wiggle room and did two more returns, then another one, then flexed his buttocks and held to a count of ten and imagined a warm pretty beach with mellow surf as

instructed in the orientation the previous month. Then he did two more returns, checked the clock real quick, then two more, then bore down and did three in a row, then flexed and visualized and bore way down and did four without looking up once except to put the completed files and memos in the two Out trays side by side up in the top tier of trays where the cart boys could get them when they came by. After just an hour the beach was a winter beach, cold and gray and the dead kelp like the hair of the drowned, and it stayed that way despite all attempts. Then three more, including one 1040A where the deductions for AGI were added wrong and the Martinsburg printout hadn't caught it and had to be amended on one of the Form 020-Cs in the lower left tray and then a lot of the same information filled out on the regular 20 you still had to do even if it was just a correspondence audit and the file going to Joliet instead of the District, each code for which had to be looked up on the pull-out thing he had to scoot the chair awkwardly over to pull out all the way. Then another one, then a plummeting inside of him as the wall clock showed that what he'd thought was another hour had not been. Not even close. 17 May 1985. Lord Jesus Christ have mercy on me a poor sinner.

(2011, pp. 378–379)

The passage seems to start from an external, distanced perspective – an observation of Lane Dean Jr. at work, describing his behaviour quite mechanically, reflecting the repetitive, boring nature of his work. Even in the long second sentence there is a hint of his perspective and idiolect in 'checked the clock real quick'. The third sentence beginning 'After just an hour …' is nicely ambiguous. It could be the narrator's description of what has happened to the 'warm pretty beach' he imagined in the first sentence, or it could take us into Lane's imagining – in other words, his own impression of the beach. The simile 'dead kelp like the hair of the drowned' certainly suggests a subjective perspective, although there is a complication in that other workers may be imagining the beach too, 'as instructed in orientation the previous month.'

From this point on in the passage there is a subtle interweaving of Lane's individual perspective with both the collective focalization of his co-workers and that of the narrator. For example, the second person in the fourth sentence in 'you still had to do' seems to be a group 'you', referring to all the wigglers. There are hints of Lane's subjective perspective again in the vague term 'the pull-out thing', and when he looks up at the clock; 'Not even close' appears to be his despairing thought at the time, and presumably it is he who notices the date. The next sentence seems to represent his own silent prayer in the first person. Later in the chapter, as the representation of the humdrum work of Lane and his colleagues continues, there are further examples of intermental thought ('The joke this week was how was an IRS rote examiner like a mushroom? Both kept in the dark and fed horseshit'), coupled with more specific forms of reference ('his Chalk Leader'). Through the chapter, in other words, Lane Dean Jr.'s thoughts increasingly become subtly interfused with those of both the narrator and his fellow workers. At times it is very hard to untangle the different points of view of Lane, his co-workers, and the narrator, or even to discern any differences between them.

This passage represents a very different kind of free indirect thought to that found in, for example, passage **(1)** from *The Portrait of a Lady*, where the style is used to explore an individual consciousness in depth, and is signalled by such classic markers as the combination of third person and past tense with proximal spatial and temporal deixis. Here it is more subtle, more unobtrusive, veering between the individual and the collective, indicating both the individual's place within the collective and his or her struggle to be free of it.

Nevertheless, this *is* free indirect thought. Indeed, the ambiguity of detecting whether a shift into an alternative consciousness has taken place has always been part of the point, if not the main feature of the style. Monika Fludernik (a critic that Palmer would no doubt associate with the 'swamp' of debates surrounding free indirect discourse that he has tried to avoid) states in a key 1995 article that 'the position from which I am starting out sees FID as including material that syntactically allows itself to be read as FID although it lacks expressive features, with the impetus to a FID reading deriving from the *interpretation* of the passage' (1995, p. 92). According to Fludernik, all that is required for a reader to posit a 'discourse of alterity (that is, a notional discourse SELF different from that of the reportative SELF of the current narrator-speaker)', is a 'minimal set of syntactic features' (p. 95). This consists essentially of the alignment of referential expressions to the deictic centre of the reporting discourse, and the absence of subordinate clauses beginning with 'that'. Free indirect discourse *may* then be made more apparent by syntactic and lexical markers of 'explicitness', but equally it may not be; for Fludernik, 'If a passage contextually signifies discourse alterity and if it fits the minimal requirements for a prototypical FID form, then – in a flexible account of speech and thought representation – one can categorize it as FID' (p. 111). This 'flexible' approach, reliant to a large degree on the reader's interpretative role, explains why the style is so valuable to writers (of both fiction and non-fiction):

> The usefulness of this category lies precisely in its low profile (as only dimly recognizable by untrained speakers of the language), since that low profile has been exploited traditionally for the purposes of ambiguity, fast or imperceptible change of perspective, or apparent unmarkedness [...]
>
> *(1995, p. 111)*

As this chapter has shown, free indirect discourse, and free indirect thought in particular, can be low profile but pervasive, used to great effect in recent experimental novels as well as the more canonical examples. It is a more widespread and adaptable phenomenon, in other words, than critics such as Alan Palmer recognise. As passage **(5)** suggests, free indirect thought is often bubbling below the surface of *The Pale King*, ready to enter into the narrative at any time, or indeed it could be said to be subtly present all the time. Experimental writing such as this confirms that the style is flexible and adaptable, ideally suited to the contemporary novel's preoccupation with the struggles of the individual in the face of powerful institutions, and the overwhelming, 'tornadic' nature of our 'information society'.

Recommendations for practice

Read the following two passages from John Lanchester's *Capital* (2012) (passage **6**) and Dave Eggers's *A Hologram for the King* (2012) (passage **7**).Like *The Pale King*, both novels deal with the individual's place within contemporary global capitalist society. Consider how the main character's thoughts are represented in each passage. How is the use of Free Indirect Thought in each case similar and different to that in passage **(5)** from *The Pale King*? What does it reveal about the central character and his perspective on the world in which he finds himself?

> **(6)** Sitting on Roger's desk were three computer screens, one of them tracking departmental activity in real time, another being Roger's own PC, given over to

email and IM, another tracking trades in the foreign exchange department over the year. According to that they were showing a profit of about £75,000,000 on a turnover of £625,000,000 so far, which, although he said it himself, wasn't bad. Simple justice, looking at those numbers, would surely see him awarded a bonus of £1,000,000. But it had been a strange year in the markets ever since the collapse of Northern Rock a few months before. Basically, the Rock had destroyed itself with its own business model. Their credit had dried up, the Bank of England had been asleep, and the punters had panicked. Since then, credit had been more expensive, and people were twitchy. That was OK as far as Roger was concerned, because in the foreign exchange business, twitchy meant volatile, and volatile meant profitable. The FX world had seen a number of fairly self-evident one-way bets against high-interest currencies, the Argentinian peso for instance; some rival firms' FX departments had, he knew, made out like bandits. This was where the lack of transparency became a problem. The Politburo might be benchmarking him against some impossible standard of profitability based on some whizz-kid idiot, some boy racer who had pulled off a few crazy unhedged bets. There were certain numbers which couldn't be beaten without taking what the bank told him to think of as unacceptable risks. The way it worked, however, was that the risks tended to seem less unacceptable when they were making you spectacular amounts of money.

The other potential problem was that the bank might claim to be making less money overall this year, so that bonuses in general would be down on expectations – and indeed there were rumours that Pinker Lloyd were sitting on some big losses in its mortgage loan department. There had also been a well-publicised disappointment over their Swiss subsidiary, which had been outcompeted in a takeover fight and seen its stock price drop 30 per cent as a result. The Politburo might claim that 'times are hard' and 'the pain must be shared equally' and 'we're all giving a little blood this time' and (with a wink) 'next year in Jerusalem'. What a gigantic pain in the arse that would be.

(2012, pp. 16–18)

(7) Alan Clay woke up in Jeddah, Saudi Arabia. It was May 30, 2010. He had spent two days on planes to get there.

In Nairobi he had met a woman. They sat next to each other while they waited for their flights. She was tall, curvy, with tiny gold earrings. She had ruddy skin and a lilting voice. Alan liked her more than many of the people in his life, people he saw every day. She said she lived in upstate New York. Not that far away from his home in suburban Boston.

If he had courage he would have found a way to spend more time with her. But instead he got on his flight and he flew to Riyadh and then to Jeddah. A man picked him up at the airport and drove him to the Hilton.

With a click, Alan entered his room at the Hilton at 1:12 a.m. He quickly prepared to go to bed. He needed to sleep. He had to travel an hour north at seven for an eight o'clock arrival at the King Abdullah Economic City. There he and his team would set up a holographic tele-conference system and would wait to present it to King Abdullah himself. If Abdullah was impressed, he would award the IT contract for the entire city to Reliant, and Alan's commission, in the mid-six figures, would fix everything that ailed him.

So he needed to feel rested. To feel prepared. But instead he had spent four hours in bed not sleeping.

He thought of his daughter Kit, who was in college, a very good and expensive college. He did not have the money to pay her tuition for the fall. He could not pay her tuition because he had made a series of foolish decisions in his life. He had not planned well. He had not had courage when he needed it.

His decisions had been short sighted.
The decisions of his peers had been short sighted.
These decisions had been foolish and expedient.

But he hadn't known at the time that his decisions were short sighted, foolish or expedient. He and his peers did not know they were making decisions that would leave them, leave Alan, as he now was – virtually broke, nearly unemployed, the proprietor of a one-man consulting firm run out of his home office.

(2012, pp. 3–4)

Future directions

There is the potential for a great deal of further work on speech, thought and writing presentation in relation to the contemporary novel (both in its experimental and more realist forms). In addition to investigating further the persistence of the variety of unobtrusive, pervasive free indirect thought suggested in this chapter, other potentially fruitful topics include: the incorporation of different types of speech and dialect in free indirect speech, to reflect an increasingly globalised economy and culture; the presence or absence of a unifying narrative voice in the light of the contemporary novel's concern with fragmented identities; and the use of the categories of writing presentation in updated versions of the epistolary novel, such as those based on email, text, and Twitter exchanges. The argument of this chapter has been that traditional stylistic concepts can and should be combined with more cognitive approaches, such as those, in Palmer's words, that are concerned with 'the whole of the social mind in action.' The speech, thought and writing presentation categories can, given the chance, continue to be highly valuable in analysing how the novel represents its characters thinking, acting, and interacting.

Related topics

Cognitive poetics, corpus stylistics, narratology, point of view and modality

Further reading

Bray, J., 2010. Writing presentation, the epistolary novel and free indirect thought. *In:* D. McIntyre and B. Busse, eds. *Language and style*. Basingstoke: Palgrave Macmillan, 388–401.

This chapter applies the writing presentation scale to the epistolary novel, and suggests that the representation of writing and reading in the novel is one source for the development of free indirect thought.

Cohn, D., 1978. *Transparent minds: Narrative modes for presenting consciousness in fiction*. Princeton: Princeton University Press.

A classic account of thought representation in the novel, including a detailed account of narrated monologue (Cohn's term for free indirect thought).

Fludernik, M., 1993. *The fictions of language and the languages of fiction*. New York and London: Routledge.

An extensive treatment of all forms of discourse representation, which includes excellent summaries of previous approaches.

Leech, G. N. and Short, M. H., 2007. *Style in fiction: A linguistic introduction to English fictional prose*. Harlow: Pearson.

This is the most influential stylistic treatment of speech and thought representation, updated to incorporate developments in the field since the first edition of 1981.

References

Austen, J., [1816] 2008. *Emma*. Oxford: (Oxford World's Classics), Oxford University Press.

Bally, C., 1912a. Le style indirect libre en Français moderne I. *Germanisch-Romanische Monatsschrift*, 4, 549–556.

Bally, C., 1912b. Le style indirect libre en Français moderne I, *Germanisch-Romanische Monatsschrift*, 4, 597–606.

Banfield, A., 1982. *Unspeakable sentences*. London and New York: Routledge.

Bray, J., 2010. Writing presentation, the epistolary novel and free indirect thought. *In:* D. McIntyre and B. Busse, eds. *Language and style*. Basingstoke: Palgrave Macmillan, 388–401.

Brinton, L., 1980. Represented perception: A study in narrative style. *Poetics*, 9, 383–381.

Cohn, D., 1978. *Transparent minds: Narrative modes for presenting consciousness in fiction*. Princeton: Princeton University Press.

Eggers, D., 2012. *A hologram for the king*. San Francisco: McSweeney's Books.

Flaubert, G., [1856] 2008. *Madame Bovary*. Oxford: (Oxford World's Classics), Oxford University Press.

Fludernik, M., 1993. *The fictions of language and the languages of fiction*. New York and London: Routledge.

Fludernik, M., 1995. The linguistic illusion of alterity: The free indirect as a paradigm of discourse representation. *Diacritics*, 25 (4), 89–115.

Fuchs, C., 2008. *Internet and society: Social theory in the information age*. New York and London: Routledge.

Genette, G., [1972] 1980. *Narrative discourse*. Trans. J. E. Lewin, Ithaca and New York: Cornell University Press.

James, H. [1881] 1995. *The portrait of a lady*. ed. N. Bradbury. Oxford and New York: Oxford University Press.

James, H., [1903] 2008, *The ambassadors*. Oxford: (Oxford World's Classics) Oxford University Press.

James, W. [1890] 1950. *The principles of psychology*. Vol. I. New York: Dover Publications.

Joyce, J., [1914] 1992. *Portrait of the artist as a young man*. Ware, Hertfordshire: (Wordsworth Classics) Wordsworth Editions.

Lanchester, J., 2012. *Capital*. London: Faber and Faber.

Leech, G. N. and Short, M. H., 1981. *Style in fiction: A linguistic introduction to English fictional prose*. London and New York: Longman.

Leech, G. N. and Short, M. H., 2007. *Style in fiction: A linguistic introduction to English fictional prose*. Harlow: Pearson.

Lodge, D., 1990. *After Bakhtin: Essays on function and criticism*. London and New York: Routledge.

Palmer, A., 2004. *Fictional minds*. Lincoln and London: University of Nebraska Press.

Palmer, A., 2005. Intermental thought in the novel: The Middlemarch mind. *Style*, 39 (4), 427–442.

Pascal, R., 1977. *The dual voice*. Manchester: Manchester University Press.

Semino, E. and Short, M., 2004. *Corpus stylistics: Speech, writing and thought presentation in a corpus of English writing*. London and New York: Routledge.

Short, M., 2003. A corpus-based approach to speech, thought and writing presentation. *In:* A. Wilson, P. Rayson and T. McEnery, eds. *Corpus linguistics by the lune: A Festschrift for Geoffrey Leech,* Frankfurt/Main: Peter Lang, 242–271.

Short, M., Semino, E. and Culpeper, J., 1996. Using a corpus for stylistics research: Speech and thought presentation. *In:* J. A. Thomas and M. Short, *Using corpora for language research.* London and New York: Longman, 110–131.

Wallace, D. F., 2011. *The pale king.* ed. M. Pietsch. London: Penguin.

Woolf, V., [1925] 1996. *Mrs Dalloway.* Ware, Hertfordshire: (Wordsworth Classics), Wordsworth Editions.

Part III

Contemporary topics in stylistics

14

Pedagogical stylistics

Geoff Hall

Introduction

Stylistics has always claimed a close and privileged relation to pedagogy. Indeed, at times stylistics has been regarded by some outsiders as only or primarily a pedagogical activity rather than a field for research. *Language and Literature*, the leading international journal for stylistics, has had two special issues with pedagogical themes in recent years for example (Burke ed. 2010, Knights and Steadman-Jones eds. 2011). Many of the names appearing in the survey that follows, not coincidentally, are themselves acknowledged as unusually good teachers. Pedagogy has historically and conceptually always been close to the core of what stylistics is all about because it is an empirical discipline, testing ideas against texts and even generating ideas through textual interrogation. Such activities require students, classrooms and seminar rooms to engage in stylistic activity to keep advancing our understanding of how texts work, particularly as earlier more formalist stylistics moved towards a greater recognition of the role of readers in making meaning from texts. Thus stylistics research will often come out of classroom activity, or it will be immediately clear how an analysis or approach can offer productive affordances to teachers and learners.

Stylistics in a broad sense — careful linguistically-informed attention to language use in texts – may also be opposed to stylistics in more technical or specialist academic senses. Arguably, however, there is more of a continuum. Language study and language awareness at the lower end of a generously defined discipline of 'stylistics' is of more immediate interest to pedagogical stylistics than (say) some of today's more leading edge stylistics research into cognitive processes of reading, or the more rarefied reaches of speech and thought representation.

To begin this survey of pedagogical stylistics, then, our area of concern can be indicated as the use of stylistics in pedagogy. I will examine examples and concerns of this broadly defined stylistics (the close, systematic and linguistically informed study of language use and language choice) rather than what can be termed the narrower 'pedagogy of stylistics' (cf. Jeffries and McIntyre, 2010, 2011), which concerns itself with how better to teach stylistics as a pedagogical end in itself. Stylistics claims to have wider-ranging applied utility and relevance beyond the sphere of stylistics itself, in terms of applications, technologies and even an attitude to the gaining of knowledge and understanding.

The pedagogical value of stylistics

Practitioners have claimed that the study of style can be of value to a wide range of learning situations. Some key overlapping areas in which the value of stylistics to learning is claimed may be catalogued here:

- Stylistics can be used to teach literature, or at least to facilitate the study of literature or the study of linguistic creativity as it is more broadly understood
- Stylistics can support the study of texts in contexts and discourse more widely, in terms of genre, register, sociolinguistics and variation, as well as the grammar of standard spoken and written language through its fundamentally comparative method
- Stylistics is of value for foreign language or second language learning programmes, where attention to language use should facilitate language acquisition or where study of language use is valued
- Stylistics can be used to teach language use, language awareness and language arts as a resource for language users
- Stylistics is claimed to be of value in creative writing programmes, as well as in professional, academic or technical writing development
- Stylistics can be used to teach linguistics, an inductive way into a sometimes demanding subject area (involving 'bottom up' rather than 'top down' investigation) that teaches as much (or prompts as many questions) about 'language' as it does about 'literature'
- Stylistics may be used to teach empirical research skills, but also transferable intellectual and social skills and rhetoric (evidence-based argument, careful and systematic description and presentation, argumentation)
- Stylistics has recently been used in the study of readers and reading, to investigate questions of social and cognitive psychology and topics in psycholinguistics, particularly the study of cognition in reading, including topics such as 'noticing', attention, value and affect (Emmott 1997, Miall 2007, Stockwell 2002)
- Stylistics can be used to introduce and learn corpus stylistics and ICT skills, quantitative and qualitative learning and understanding
- In more recent multimodal stylistics, it is argued that film, cultural studies, the internet and complex multimodal texts more generally can be explored more precisely and systematically with the aid of stylistics (e.g. van Leeuwen 1999)

In short, then, stylistics is claimed to be of value wherever precise and articulated description and analysis of language and communication is felt to be of value in pedagogy. Stylistics offers both methods and a vocabulary for such analysis, and is claimed to be eminently teachable and to act as empirical groundwork and a training for more advanced analysis and argumentation. Stylistics is claimed to be of value at various levels of education and in varying contexts, whether L1 ('mother tongue' education) or L2 (foreign or second language education).

An expanding field of enquiry

In the broad understanding which I started out by proposing, stylistics is seen to deal with not only literature, canonical and non-canonical, which has been the historical focus of its main endeavour, but also features of style in newspapers, advertising and a whole broad range of more and less creative and expressive language use, to include sociolinguistic register, style and other variation study informed by linguistic awareness. In such an understanding the language of humour, of magazines, of sports commentary, or of media, comics, newspapers, ICT (see, for example, the range of titles in Routledge's 'Intertext' series) or interviews or instructions (Delin 2000) can all be seen as stylistic concerns with clear pedagogical relevance to the wider world of work within which our students need to function. Stylistics promotes the principled study of language use and a concentration on functional explanations for the forms found: why were those forms used in that sequence, presented like that? In this way stylistics can also be seen as intrinsic to discourse analysis more widely. The study of patterns, regularities, deviance and foregrounding will reveal much of how meaning is made in a given text, even though stylistics today also insists on the final importance of the reader for meaning making. The study of expressive uses of language, of language in the formation of identity (e.g. Coupland 2007), language in use, and language as text and discourse will all help us understand better the social world around us and how we can interact more successfully with it. Stylistics can offer ways into these complex areas.

The basic question and method of pedagogical stylistics is comparative: how are given texts (typically literary texts) different yet the same as other uses of language? In a prototypical stylistics class a poem may be juxtaposed with a non-poetic text on the 'same' topic or situation to investigate their linguistic differences and the effects of these. Intuitively we know the difference between a formal letter and a note on a fridge door, between a poetic elegy and an obituary notice in a newspaper. Stylistics claims it is valuable to be able to describe this difference explicitly and precisely in a way that will make sense to others, and even enable those who can do this to produce such texts more effectively for themselves in future. What features in a given instance, as well as across a range of instances, differentiate a specific text or type of text from others? '[T]exts must always be related to other texts' (McRae 1996, p. 26). Features of texts combine to make meaning. Meaning is made from a text by a reader both from features of the text itself and also by noticing these differences from other texts that have been known.

Pedagogically, it is of great importance to note that a stylistics approach is also typically transformative and hands-on (as advocated and exemplified *par excellence* by Pope 1995). Students are usually asked not just to contemplate differences abstractly, but to rewrite the sentence or a whole text in another style by changing syntax or to consider choice of lexis or other syntagmatic and paradigmatic choices, prompting attention to unusual or specific features of language use and so on to interpret activity in readers. What linguistic or textual changes prompt what changes in meaning for which readers? At what point and how does one genre transmute into another? If hybrid genres are the norm in communication today, how does an apparently chatty and friendly message from a stranger we have never met from our bank work (or not) to convince us to borrow more money we cannot afford? The most common word in advertising used to be 'new' (Leech 1972). Fairclough (2000) then showed it was the favourite word of Blair's 'new Labour' political spin in the UK. What does it tell us to learn about the greater importance of terms like 'natural' in today's advertising? Cook (2004) investigated what the satirical magazine 'Private Eye' has called 'green-wash', itself a stylistically interesting neologism. Students will be invited to contemplate the effects of given linguistic changes in terms of the meanings that can be achieved. This is a key method for raising language awareness, but it also feeds directly into areas such as creative or professional writing and other communication or rhetoric, developing a set of resources that students can be encouraged to develop in practical ways for their own ends. In this sense, hands-on, transformative stylistics ties back into the basic principles and precepts of classical pedagogical rhetoric as it was taught in antiquity (see Chapter 1 in this volume). The classic linguistic definition of style was Joos's (1961) formal-informal cline to describe levels of style. This is a basic level at which such pedagogic activities might take place – for example, among a class of foreign language learners, or 'translating' a text from written into spoken mode to highlight some characteristic differences. Indeed, translation itself inevitably raises stylistic issues in many educational contexts and is less frowned upon today than it has sometimes been in pedagogical circles (see Cook 2010).

Studies of social theory or even business studies arguably often leave the student as a spectator on the sidelines, at worst intimidated and diminished, perhaps at best understanding better but no more able to participate fully than they were when they started their course. Stylistic activities build confidence by offering systematic approaches (often even a 'toolkit', as in Short 1996), and so they can promote autonomy and empower. In this way stylistics can help to bridge the gap between school and university study of English, the world of study in general and the world of work. There is a growing conviction across many educational areas that 'doing' is at least as important as 'knowing', but also of course that such 'procedural knowledge', as the psychologists call 'doing', is actually linked to declarative knowledge. Being able to describe what you are doing for others means that it can be better analysed, discussed and even improved by sharing practices. We learn to teach by teaching; we learn to read by reading. However, the best readers and the best teachers are actually those who have also successfully discussed their teaching and their reading with others.

With the global expansion and extension of education at all levels, surprising gaps in the abilities and knowledge of students are widely reported by teachers who generally came from more privileged sectors of society, growing up at a time in the past when education was less widely available. In the UK, for example, 'false fluency' and even a misplaced confidence and assertiveness are often noted among students who have actually not fully mastered basic but essential lower level skills or knowledge in literacy or other communication skills. Literature professors complain of students who detect the workings of power and gender at every turn, but cannot point to a line in the text they are studying to support their arguments. Such students cannot describe the form and structure of a sonnet or define iambic pentameter, cannot identify Biblical allusions or hear the dactylic rhythm of 'The Charge of the Light Brigade'. They talk past each other in unproductive ways. At the same time, employers report dissatisfaction with graduates of English who cannot write a business letter, take notes at a meeting or answer a phone appropriately, even if they may be able to discuss the advantages and disadvantages of globalisation or decry the world's pollution. Of course, the solution to all this is not to 'return to basics' with prescriptive spelling bees and punctuation tests, as some simplistic politicians advocate. It is rather to 'teach the conflicts' as Graff (1993) once advocated, to help students understand why alternative spellings might exist and why they might matter more to some than others, to see gender and power in the workings of language not as abstractions that can or should be considered outside of concrete instances of human interaction. A feature such as a 'dactyl' has no value or interest in itself, but it is a way to direct attention to the workings of language in the service of communication and the intertextual workings of Tennyson's imagination and his appeal to (some) readers. To consider an author's or editor's choice of punctuation is not a question of deciding which version is 'right'; rather, the concern is to understand what different preferences might mean and why they might have become available. The transformation of a 'Times' newspaper report from the Crimean front into 'The Charge of the Light Brigade' is indeed a classroom activity as well as a scholarly enquiry that I have pursued myself across many different contexts and countries. In the same way, why not begin a classroom enquiry into gender by considering given names (John vs. Jenny) or a corpus enquiry into collocations of 'small' and 'little', rather than with a reading of Judith Butler? Butler's idea of speech acts comes out of linguistics and is best understood by starting with those linguistic origins. The subtle workings of power and resistance will be easier to approach through one of Rampton's (2006) classroom transcripts than through a reading of a postmodern philosopher like Foucault. Gender and the workings of power need to be understood and should be contested, globalisation is a complex process to be negotiated and pollution matters, but it is in the workings of everyday stylistic practices of language and communication that most individuals can best and most consistently make a difference. (See also Cameron 1995.)

Historical perspectives

Historically, in Britain and its empire from the late nineteenth century the new discipline of literature in schools, colleges and universities was in search of means to teach the effective reading of literature in classrooms. As the twentieth century wore on and literature became an established 'subject' in education, this search for pedagogically valid methods came to be combined with, or even eclipsed by, an increasing awareness of the problems of mediated reading of literature through cribs, secondary works of criticism and the like and proceeding to the use of internet sources today. The cry went up that students needed to read primary literary texts for themselves and with due respect for the exact uses of language and exact presentation (Atherton, 2005). Wider crises of literacy have also been raised, at least since we were all able to read them. (For critical accounts, see Graff 1987, Street 1985, through to Liu 2004.) Literary criticism did not ultimately offer sufficient pedagogical facilitation. Pedagogical stylistics would argue that this was because of its neglect of linguistic aspects of literary texts.

The new 'Schools of English' in British universities assumed that one's own language did not need to be studied, except perhaps historically (as with Anglo-Saxon philology at Oxford). Outside the Anglo-American world a balance of language and literature were usually required of all students in philology departments and in departments of English. Ironically, however, graduates of English, even some with named degrees in 'English language and literature', began to emerge from British universities in the twentieth century with little or no declarative or systematic knowledge of English or any other language or linguistics. Linguistic matters were taken to be obvious and to require no training or conscious study. Retrospectively the gap and the need for stylistics seems painfully clear, but at the time it was seen by very few (see Hall, 2014). Close examination of a text was held to be necessary, but it wasn't quite clear what exactly was being looked for, or how. Those who asked for more precision and clarity, as in the notorious exchanges between Bateson and Fowler (see Simpson, 2004, pp. 148–157), thereby only showed that they were not sensitive readers, so far as the literature professors were concerned. Calls for more objectivity, claimed professors like Bateson, threatened the pleasures of reading. This attitude can still be traced in Gower (1986) and beyond.

The 'close readings' of Practical Criticism arguably represent the beginnings of literary study as a replicable, teachable and testable subject (Atherton 2005), including the democratising urges or at least the expansion of (higher) education, however patrician and uninformed those efforts look now. Also, arguably in some ways stylistics was originally elaborated most fully as pedagogy, first to bring respectability and rigour to the study of literature in the second language classroom, but later extended (in principle) to all classrooms.

As the century advanced, however, phenomenology, structuralism, cultural studies, semiotics, and other social sciences, together forming a supposed 'linguistic turn' in the human sciences and more generally, insisted on the need to study the previously overlooked taken-for-granted everyday world around us. It became less possible to look through language and ever more necessary to look at it, whether in literary texts or elsewhere. Language use was no longer obvious and unproblematic. Literary language was to be demystified, not fetishised. To leave intellectual history for pedagogical practicalities, for example, like Joyce and Empson before them, many UK English graduates in the twentieth century found themselves at one stage or another teaching English in some way, often EFL (English as a Foreign Language), and they quickly realised that they knew nothing or little about their own language except intuitively, and certainly not compared to their own better-informed non-native speaking students.

Through the post-second world war period, with the strong growth of TEFL and enlightened and better trained teachers prompted by syllabuses or by their own desire to share their pleasure in the reading of literature, literary criticism in EFL contexts was necessarily succeeded by increasingly sophisticated stylistics in classrooms for EFL learners. By the end of the century in the UK, with English language A level and ever more 'non-traditional' learners coming into 'English' classrooms and increasingly for L1 learners at least up to school leaving levels, stylistics seemed a more convincing solution than traditional literary criticism. Thus, when the UK English school curriculum was being revised the UK government called in Widdowson and Carter to advise, even though ultimately neither could in conscience deliver the simplistic answers the governments of the time desired.

Stylistics in teaching today: EFL, ESL and L1

For many, however, pedagogical stylistics begins most decisively with Widdowson (1975), and then Carter, Short and colleagues publishing from the early 1980s onwards, and it has EFL/ESL education as its first priority. The collection edited by Brumfit and Carter (1986) showed how much pedagogical stylistics was already going on in TEFL by that time.

Henry Widdowson (EFL)

With decidedly traditionalist views of the nature of literature and literary value, views that are maintained to this day, Widdowson has always insisted that literary texts and non-literary texts can be shown to be quite different kinds of communication that work in different ways, and it is stylistics that will best enable students to see this. The contrast is more apparent than real with Carter, Simpson or others, who would maintain that literature is just one more use of language. However, all uses of language are special, so literature is or is not distinctive according to the emphasis we wish to give. The main difference between the views of Widdowson and others seems to lie in an insistence on the limited relevance of context, or a formalist notion of context. The context that matters for Widdowson is the one that the poem will make, rather than a context that a reader brings to it; literature is by nature a relatively decontextualised form of communication in this view. Widdowson insists on the importance of individual readers' agency and distinctiveness in meaning making, rather than considering the literary text as participating in social interaction – perhaps itself a pedagogic preference over more scholarly study of literature.

Widdowson argued that literary criticism is not opposed to stylistic analysis; rather, the two areas exist on a continuum (1975, p. 1). Stylistics was seen as particularly valuable as a preparation for literary study (1975, p. 106), but also as of value in itself for students of language use. Literature is of value as 'a use of language' (p. 124), 'a particular selection and arrangement of linguistic forms' (114). Widdowson particularly argued for literary texts as distinctive communicative uses of language in so far as literary language characteristically exceeds what simple 'referential' information exchange uses of language would call for. By looking at how language is used to make meaning in the literary text 'ordinary' language use can be learned, even as the wider expressive possibilities of the language are also noticed and understood. Widdowson insisted on the importance of 'precision of reference to the text in support of a particular interpretation' (1992, p. xii), and therefore on the value of stylistics in requiring student engagement with the primary text rather than with biographies, study notes or rehashing of a teacher's thoughts, the familiar bugbears of the literature teacher then as now. Interestingly, in 1992 Widdowson also insisted on the value of stylistics for what it could *not* explain as well as for what it could, the limits of our understanding and of our linguistics in the face of valued aesthetic experience. Widdowson spends more than half of his 1992 book giving detailed examples of techniques and strategies for the classroom of the kind that Duff and Maley (1990) or Carter and Long (1987) were already urging on teachers, particularly teachers of English as a foreign language, through their publications and their own teaching but also through more wide-ranging workshops and seminars overseas as well as in the UK, often supported or otherwise associated with the British Council. These were very influential activities and helped establish the reputation and knowledge of pedagogical stylistics across a generation of teachers and lecturers. The 'practical stylistics' that Widdowson so influentially advocated is pursued in 2004 and beyond: 'there is something distinctive about literature and this calls for a different mode of interpretation and a different kind of critical practice from those relevant to other kinds of language use' (Widdowson 2004, p. 161).

Cook in 1986, 1996 and elsewhere has also provocatively argued the distinctive literariness and the value of literature in the unfashionable, Widdowsonian mould. Nevertheless, Cook has provided a profound service to pedagogical stylistics by showing in detail how literature can be appreciated by students using stylistic approaches. Important wider stylistic work on advertising, promotional discourse and the importance of play in language learning followed (Cook 2000, 2001, 2004).

Carter, Short (EFL and L1)

What pedagogical stylistics deriving from the work of Widdowson, Carter and others offered students and teachers was a move from facts to skills, a move that is always of interest to literature teachers as well as language teachers, but also the teachability of such skills and the possibilities for assessment of demonstrable, specifiable abilities with unseen or other texts under exam conditions. In Carter's case this goes along with a conscious and often explicit awareness of the challenges from literary criticism and literary theory (Carter and Long 1991, Carter, Walker and Brumfit 1989) as well as deference to those with greater practical expertise in TEFL (Carter and McCarthy's exchanges with Prodromou, reprinted in Seidlhofer 2003, Section 2). Carter's position remains modest but firm: 'in pedagogic terms, the aim is to provide a systematic set of analytical tools, drawn from linguistics, that can foster insights into the patterning of literary texts in ways which allow those insights to be open, evidenced, and retrievable' (Carter 2010, p. 68).

For L1 teaching situations in the UK, A level English language as conceived from the 1990s was a natural outcome of experience and learning in earlier EFL applications of stylistics. Just as there is no essential difference between literary and non-literary texts, so the thinking went, there is no essential difference between so-called native speakers and non-native speakers. Indeed, with increasingly mixed international classes in most realms of education today, so it has proved in practice. The attempt was to move away from fine-sounding but generalised essays on literature towards the demonstration of ability to analyse specific texts in an informed, explicit and systematic way, and to communicate the analysis to others. Here, as in EFL pedagogical stylistics, Carter played a key role in the advocacy, spread and popularisation of the new ideas, including teacher training and higher education, workshops, book series and more. At the same time stylistics was also moving away from more formalist beginnings into more discourse-based understandings of how texts work (exemplified by Carter and Simpson 1989). McRae and Boardman (1984) also pointed to the importance of 'reading between the lines', a key idea for 'discourse' studies – 'considering what is absent or implicit in a text' (McRae and Clark, 2004, p. 333). The skilled reader of a text, literary or otherwise, needed to consider the meaning of what was and was not included and how this was done. In *Literature with a small 'l'*, McRae (1991) again stressed that there was no sharp linguistic dividing line between the literary text and the non-literary text. This approach is critically pursued in Wallace (2003, p. 3), arguing after Fairclough and others that ideology works 'by omission, imbalance and distortion', and readers must learn to look for these gaps and biases. Wallace further aligns her work with what I have identified as a loosely characterised 'stylistics' when she argues the importance of 'declarative, explicit knowledge' (2003, p. 21) and students learning to read intertextually, 'to focus on the interdependence between texts rather than their discreteness or uniqueness' if education is to encourage critical rather than compliant readers (Montgomery *et al.* 1992, quoted in Wallace 2003, p. 14). Similarly, Davies (1998) showed in a subtle but at the same time perfectly practical fashion how to use stylistics to help second language readers who are reading too literally and not seeing what lies between the lines: 'Non-native readers often miss the hidden discourse in a text' (p. 271). Davies introduced a precisely and fully reported set of useful exercises (including transformations) on modalisation, cliché and other language features, designed to raise L2 readers' awareness of the evasive and rather myopic character of Stevens in Ishiguro's *Remains of the Day*, to avoid his first-person narrative being taken at face value.

Also, from the 1980s Short co-taught and then led the large and successful (ongoing at time of writing) 'Language and Style' first-year course for literature and linguistics students of English at Lancaster University, resulting in a stream of valuable stylistics publications, most with more than half an eye toward pedagogy. Short (1989) is a good example of this borderland work of hands-on pedagogically-oriented research. In 1996 Short finally offered a set of tools or 'toolkit' based on his many years of teaching language and literature through a stylistics-inspired approach. An electronic version of the course itself went online in 2006 and is currently deliberately open access and free of charge. The 1996 textbook is exemplary in its clarity and organisation, including worked examples, extension activities, and above all in its no-nonsense 'checksheets' at the end of each chapter. This is stylistics at its most provocative and assertive, either reductive or emancipatory according to your perspective. Work through these headings with any text in this genre or topic, the checklists claim, and you will inevitably notice what you need to notice to get you up and started with the text, speaking or writing about it more convincingly than if you have merely found a crib on the internet the night before the seminar. These ideas have been promulgated by Short in many international contexts, including China, Japan and others, from as early as the 1980s. While many will feel the techniques need supplementation, there is no doubt of their effectiveness for many students and their teachers. An important idea in Short and many other of the pedagogical stylistics publications I have mentioned is to offer students scaffolding to help them deal with a particular text at hand, but also more generally to offer a transferable approach to their wider reading and to other interactions with and uses of language.

Later developments

Short's materials from his 'Language and Style' course went on line in 2006 and have been used across a range of countries and contexts (see, e.g. Crisp 2006 for Hong Kong applications). Elsewhere computers and software have been ever more commonly used for stylistic approaches to pedagogy, from Louw (1997, for example) to Mahlberg (2012) to Goddard (2011) or McIntyre (2012), to cite only a few strong studies. Stockwell, as editor of the series 'English Language Introductions' (Routledge), and Carter, as co-author of 'Working with Texts' (Routledge) and series editor of 'Intertexts', along with Goddard, herself a Chair of Examiners for English Language A level in the UK, were other important actors in propagating stylistic approaches to pedagogy beyond the narrow circles of stylistics or even applied linguistics specialists.

Clark and Zyngier (2003) in their own earlier survey article on pedagogical stylistics also raised the question I have asked in this piece: are L2 and L1 contexts so different? Their answer, like mine, is that probably the line, if it still exists, is ever more blurred in an increasingly interconnected world with education expanding globally and exponentially. Thus it is proposed that language awareness, empirical classroom research (including a growth of interest in the cognitive activities of readers), discourse processing in educational contexts, and meaning making in groups in institutions, as well as the growth of 'English' globally including language in UK schools and universities, and the expansion of (higher) education required 'to promote linguistically aware readers who can perceive the qualities of language which are manipulated for particular effects (including the aesthetic)', all augur a bright future for stylistic approaches to pedagogy (Clark and Zyngier 2003, p. 342).

In an impressive essay Badran (2007) shows how a stylistic approach can be used to investigate vocabulary use in discourse with students, rather than as isolated referential items in a 'vocab' book. The educator's concerns with memory, learning, proficiency and the ability to manipulate language to make one's own meanings are shown to result from engagement and interest, deep processing and more extended attention. This is the kind of study Paran (2008) calls for in critical comments I return to below in the section on 'Future Directions'.

Knights and Thurgar-Dawson (2006) arguably continue and develop Pope's (1995) valuable 'heuristic' transformative approach to pedagogy. In the more theoretical part of their book they deplore the lack of interest in language and indeed in the practicalities of teaching in many literature classrooms. 'It is a pedagogic tragedy that the theory revolution of the 1970s and 1980s was in general so temperamentally averse to empirical language study' (Knights and Thurgar-Dawson 2006, p. 11) The second more practically oriented part of the book goes on to look at what might be termed post-Pope interventions in English learning, particularly with reference to first-year undergraduates in the UK and to the teaching of creative writing. See also Scott (2012) on stylistics in the teaching of creative writing and Burke (2012) in the same volume on his 'systemic' approach to pedagogical stylistics, namely, (i) knowledge (rhetoric), followed by (ii) analysis (stylistics), followed by (iii) synthesis and creative production (creative writing).

Shen (2012) describes an impressive range of pedagogical work extending its influence through China, most of it published in Chinese, while Teranishi *et al.* (2012) describe the influence of such approaches in Japan. In both cases the influence can be seen to be moving beyond the stylistics of English language texts and English pedagogy to L1 texts in non-English language teaching. At the same time Paran (2006) includes examples of pedagogic stylistics in practice from Rosenkjar (2006) in Japan or Lin (2006) in Singapore in his valuable collection of case studies of literature in English language education. Carrioli (2008) writes on the teaching of modern foreign languages in Australia, particularly Italian, with some awareness of the relevance of Hallidayan systemic-functional stylistics, and Yáñez-Prieto (2010) reports on teaching grammar to US Spanish language learners through cognitive stylistics. For many years McRae has advocated and demonstrated the value of using 'world Englishes' texts in education (e.g. Watson and Zyngier 2007). An approach most strongly developed in the UK in the 1980s and 1990s, as we have seen, is demonstrably becoming ever more internationalised.

Finally, in the field of rhetoric, where paradoxically it all began, notable attempts to develop stylistic approaches to teaching may be found in Burke (2010, 2012) or Badran (2012). For example, cognitive poetics looks at foregrounding, metaphor, the importance of precise word choices in processing of discourse, including an increasing interest in emotional response to literary text reading, and a stress which must be of interest to educators on the experience of hypothesised 'ordinary readers' (Emmott 1997 or Stockwell 2002).

Future directions

In a perceptive article, Paran (2008), writing particularly from the perspective of EFL and L2 education, argues that pedagogical stylistics has been too much concerned with text and not enough with educational and methodological issues such as the dynamics of classrooms.

Paran (2006) is part of his own important effort to address this issue. I would also add the work of others, for example Badran (2007, 2012). Empirical work is beginning to be reported, but much more is undoubtedly needed in place of the speculation, assertion and counter-assertion which have tended to dominate too strongly in the past. What do stylistic approaches to texts do for language learning? We don't know enough about this, and the question is a complicated one. Perceived or argued limited relevance to classrooms has to be countered with empirical reports of actual classes and learning events and situations. There is a danger, too often courted, of 'linguistics applied' in Widdowson's terms (see e.g. Hall 2012) usurping language education.

What affordances do literary texts and stylistic investigations offer to learners? Why use literature? Why use stylistics? How best to use it for what purposes? What are the values of product or teacher-centred vs. process-oriented literary reading, with students exploring meanings for themselves? Carter and McRae raised such enquiries in 1996 and earlier, but the questions are not yet fully or well enough answered. Similarly, what of the charge that stylistics over-simplifies, reduces, and may be appropriate to lower secondary schooling but not tertiary education? Such charges are usually predictions made on the basis of looking at the method, but is there evidence of this in the work of students?

Claims from Carter and others for the value of pedagogical stylistics are in terms of language awareness and evidence of engagement. There has to date been pedagogical work on task design, reports on interesting lessons, materials and methodology, but little on what learning has actually been achieved, which is ultimately the key question for pedagogical stylistics to answer. Effects are assumed or asserted, not proven. We find advocacy rather than evidence; How is dealt with, rather than Why.

Also there is too much about 'English'. Even if we understood more about the pedagogical stylistics of English, this could not necessarily be generalised. More is needed on the stylistics and stylistic pedagogy of other languages and contexts. One promising direction is being pursued by the Brazilian research group REDES, associated with Zyngier, van Peer, and other members of IGEL, by Miall (2007), or Fialho from the next generation of researchers (Zyngier et al. 2002). Experimentalist research of this kind is open to criticism and certainly needs to be supplemented by more qualitative work (e.g. Swann and Allington 2009), but van Peer is right to suggest that at least such work has the virtue of opening up rather than closing down questions of the complexity of literature and literature reading: 'it is precisely because the world is so complex, that we cannot do without empirical research.' (van Peer, 2002, p. 23)

No doubt also more important work will come from researchers in rhetoric such as Burke and the PEDSIG group of PALA (the Poetics and Linguistics Association). Critical pedagogical research should also continue, such as Wallace (2003). Second language acquisition research should tell us more than it has done so far about the effects of intensive reading, but also about reading discussion groups. Reading behaviours of less fluent readers could be another area of interest, or social cognition and reading as a social and cultural practice. In the study of multimodality and visual and verbal design some ingenious frameworks for analysis have been proposed. However, what are the effects of using these in educational programmes?

Creativity has been an important buzz word in applied linguistics recently. This research can be related to learners' use of transformation and comparativist methodologies in pedagogical stylistics.

To conclude: "we [do] need stylisticians to engage less in conversation among themselves, and more with language teachers" (Paran 2008, p. 487). We need professional conversations between researchers and teachers at all levels and in a greater variety of contexts. We do need more educational research to investigate better the value and the possible problems of using stylistics in education. There is a need for longitudinal studies and case studies to investigate task parameters – all kinds of pedagogical research as advocated in Hall (2005). We note the vagueness (and modesty) of 'awareness' as aim and achievement of pedagogical stylistics. Even if 'awareness' can be shown, what might this translate into in terms of more tangible educational benefits?

My list of references grew ever longer as I wrote this piece, and newly published or forthcoming publications kept appearing to be added, and yet still I am aware that I omit too much valuable work and am probably unaware of much more. I return to my opening comment that stylistics and pedagogy are effectively inseparable. They feed off each other, and this symbiotic relationship is as strong and healthy today as it has ever been. To study or contribute to pedagogical stylistics is a central contribution to stylistics research more widely.

Related topics

Creative writing and stylistics, corpus stylistics, formalist stylistics, rhetoric and poetics.

Further reading

Brumfit, C. J. and Carter, R. A., eds. 1986. *Literature and language teaching.* Oxford: Oxford University Press.

The classic 'first wave' pedagogical stylistics collection. Still enormously stimulating today. Contains multiple examples as well as a discussion of principles and rationales.

Carter, R. and McRae, J., eds. 1996. *Language, literature and the learner.* Harlow: Addison Wesley Longman.

Ten years on from Brumfit and Carter (1986) and the good ideas were still flowing. A more confident collection in some ways, as pedagogical stylistics became less marginal and suspect and the L1/ L2 distinction less compelling.

Pope, R., 1995. *Textual intervention. Critical and creative strategies for literary studies.* London: Routledge.

Bold and stimulating ideas with examples for textual transformations in any classroom setting. Hands-on, defiantly showing how respect for literature and creative writing comes from doing it rather than contemplating it.

Short, M., 1996. *Exploring the language of poems, plays and prose.* Harlow: Longman.
Short, M., 2006. Online stylistics course 'Language and Style'. Available at http://www.lancs.ac.uk/fass/projects/stylistics/

A related classic textbook (1996) and online course (2006) in practical pedagogical stylistics, training users in what to look for and how across a very wide range of features, genres and text types. Explicit, replicable, systematic.

References

Atherton, C., 2005. *Defining literary criticism.* Basingstoke: Palgrave Macmillan.

Badran, D., 2007. Stylistics and language teaching: Deviant collocation in literature as a tool for vocabulary expansion. *In:* M. Lambrou and P. Stockwell, eds. *Contemporary stylistics.* London and NY: Continuum, 180–192.

Badran, D., 2012. Metaphor as argument: A stylistic genre-based approach. *Language and Literature,* 21 (2), 119–135.

Brumfit, C. J. and Carter, R. A., eds. 1986. *Literature and language teaching.* Oxford: Oxford University Press.

Burke, M., ed. 2010. Special issue: Pedagogical issues in stylistics. *Language and Literature,* 19 (1).

Burke, M., 2012. Systemic stylistics: An integrative, rhetorical method of teaching and learning in the stylistics classroom. *In:* M. Burke et al. eds. *Pedagogical stylistics: Current trends in language, literature and ELT.* London: Continuum, 77–95.

Burke, M., Csábi, S., Week L., and Zerkowitz, J., eds. 2012. *Pedagogical stylistics. Current trends in language, literature and ELT.* London: Continuum.

Cameron, D., 1995. *Verbal hygiene.* London: Routledge.

Carrioli, P., 2008. *Literature in second language education.* London: Continuum.

Carter, R., 2010. Methodologies for stylistic analysis: Practices and pedagogies. *In:* D. McIntyre and B. Busse *Language and style. In honour of Mick Short.* Basingstoke: Palgrave Macmillan, 55–68.

Carter, R. and Long, M. N., 1987. *The web of words: Exploring literature through language.* Cambridge: Cambridge University Press.

Carter, R. and Long, M. N., 1991. *Teaching literature.* Harlow: Longman.

Carter, R. and McRae, J., eds. 1996. *Language, literature and the learner.* Harlow: Addison Wesley Longman.

Carter, R. and Simpson, P., eds. 1989. *Language, discourse and literature.* London: Unwin Hyman.

Carter, R., Walker, R. and Brumfit, C., eds. 1989. *Literature and the learner. Methodological approaches. ELT documents 130.* London: Modern English Publications with the British Council.

Clark, U. and Zyngier, S., 2003. Toward a pedagogical stylistics. *Language & Literature,* 12 (4), 339–351.

Cook, G., 1986. Texts, extracts, and stylistic texture. *In:* C. J. Brumfit and R. A. Carter, eds. *Literature and language teaching.* Oxford: Oxford University Press, 150–166.

Cook, G., 1996. Making the subtle difference: Literature and non-literature in the classroom. *In:* R. Carter and J, McRae, eds. *Language, literature and the learner. Creative classroom practice.* London: Longman, 151–165.

Cook, G., 2000. *Language play and language learning.* Oxford: Oxford University Press.

Cook, G., 2001. *The discourse of advertising.* 2nd ed. London: Routledge.

Cook, G., 2004. *Genetically modified language.* London: Routledge.

Cook, G., 2010. *Translation in language teaching.* Oxford: Oxford University Press.

Coupland, N., 2007. *Style.* Cambridge: Cambridge University Press.

Crisp, P., 2006. E-learning and 'language and style' in Hong Kong. *Language & Literature,* 15 (3), 277–290.

Davies, D., 1998. Metadiscourse and the evasive narrator: A process-based approach to teaching Ishiguro's *Remains of the Day. Reading in a Foreign Language*, 12 (1), 271–279.

Delin, J., 2000. *The language of everyday life.* London: Sage.

Duff, A. and Maley, A., 1990. *Literature. Resource books for teachers.* Oxford: Oxford University Press.

Emmott, C., 1997. *Narrative comprehension.* Oxford: Clarendon Press

Fairclough, N., 2000. *New Labour, new language.* London: Routledge.

Goddard, A., 2011. Type you soon! A stylistic approach to language use in a virtual learning environment. *Language and Literature*, 20 (3), 184–200.

Gower, R., 1986. Can stylistic analysis help the EFL learner to read literature? *ELT Journal*, 40 (2), 125–130.

Graff, G., 1993. *Beyond the culture wars.* New York: Norton.

Graff, H.J., 1987. *The legacies of literacy.* Bloomington and Indianapolis: Indiana University Press.

Hall, G., 2005. *Literature in language education.* Basingstoke: Palgrave Macmillan.

Hall, G., 2012. *Revenons à nos moutons!* Metaphor and idiom in EFL and ESL teaching and learning. *In:* M. Burke et al., eds. *Pedagogical stylistics. Current trends in language, literature and ELT.* London: Continuum, 179–192.

Hall, G., 2014. Stylistics and literary criticism. *In:* P. Stockwell and S. Whiteley, eds. *Handbook of Stylistics.* Cambridge: Cambridge University Press.

Jeffries, L and McIntyre, D., 2010. *Stylistics.* Cambridge: Cambridge University Press.

Jeffries, L. and McIntyre, D., eds. 2011. *Teaching stylistics.* Basingstoke: Palgrave Macmillan.

Joos, M., 1961. *The five clocks.* New York: Harcourt, Brace, Jovanovich.

Knights, B. and Steadman-Jones, R., eds. 2011. Special issue: Stylistic analysis and pedagogic research. *Language and Literature*, 20 (3).

Knights, B. and Thurgar-Dawson, C., 2006. *Active reading. Transformative writing in literary studies.* London: Continuum.

Leech, G., 1972. *English in advertising. A linguistic study.* London: Longman.

Lin, B., 2006. Exploring the literary text through grammar and the (re-)integration of literature and language teaching. *In:* A. Paran, ed. *Literature in language teaching and learning.* Alexandria, VA: Teachers of English to Speakers of Other Languages (TESOL), 101–116.

Liu, A., 2004. *The laws of cool. The culture of information.* Chicago: University of Chicago Press.

Louw, B., 1997. The role of corpora in critical literary appreciation. *In:* A. Wichmann et al., eds. *Teaching and language corpora.* Harlow: Longman, 240–251.

McIntyre, D., 2012. Corpus stylistics in the classroom. *In:* M. Burke, et al., eds. *Pedagogical stylistics: Current trends in language, literature and ELT.* London: Continuum, 113–125.

McRae, J., 1991. *Literature with a small 'l'.* London: Macmillan.

McRae, J., 1996. Representational language learning. *In:* R. Carter and J. McRae, eds. *Language, literature and the learner.* Harlow: Addison Wesley Longman, 16–40.

McRae, J. and Boardman, R., 1984. *Reading between the lines.* Cambridge: Cambridge University Press.

McRae, J. and Clark, U., 2004. Stylistics. *In:* A. Davies and C. Elder, eds. *The Handbook of applied linguistics.* Oxford: Blackwell, 328–346.

Mahlberg, M., 2012. *Corpus stylistics and Dickens's fiction.* London: Routledge.

Miall, D., 2007. *Literary reading.* New York: Peter Lang.

Paran, A., ed. 2006. *Literature in language teaching and learning.* Alexandria, VA.: TESOL

Paran, A., 2008. The role of literature in instructed foreign language learning and teaching: An evidence-based survey. *Language Teaching*, 41 (4), 495–496

Pope, R., 1995. *Textual intervention. Critical and creative strategies for literary studies.* London: Routledge.

Rampton, B., 2006. *Language in late modernity.* Cambridge: Cambridge University Press.

Rosenkjar, P., 2006. Learning and teaching how a poem means: Literary stylistics for EFL undergraduates and language teachers in Japan. *In:* A. Paran, ed. *Literature in language teaching and learning.* Alexandria, VA.: TESOL, 117–131.

Scott, J., 2012. Creative writing: A stylistics approach. *In:* M. Burke et al., eds. *Pedagogical stylistics: Current trends in language, literature and ELT.* London: Continuum, 96–112.

Seidlhofer, B., ed. 2003. *Controversies in applied linguistics.* Oxford: Oxford University Press.

Shen, D., 2012. Stylistics in China in the new century. *Language and Literature*, 21 (1), 93–105.

Short, M., ed. 1989. *Reading, analysing and teaching literature*. Harlow: Longman.

Short, M., 1996. *Exploring the language of poems, plays and prose*. Harlow: Longman.

Short, M., 2006. Online stylistics course 'Language and Style'. Available at http://www.lancs.ac.uk/fass/projects/stylistics/

Simpson, P., 2004. *Stylistics. A resource book for students*. London: Routledge.

Stockwell, P., 2002. *Introduction to cognitive poetics*. London: Routledge.

Street, B., 1985. *Literacy in theory and practice*. Cambridge: Cambridge University Press.

Swann, J. and Allington, D., 2009. Reading groups and the language of literary texts. *Language and Literature*, 18 (3), 219–230.

Teranishi, M., Saito, A., Sakamoto, K., Nasu, M., 2012. The role of stylistics in Japan: A pedagogical perspective. *Language and Literature*, 21 (2), 226–244.

van Leeuwen, T., 1999. *Speech, music, sound*. London: Macmillan.

van Peer, W., 2002. Why we need empirical studies in literature. *In:* S. Zyngier et al., eds. *Fatos & Ficções*. Rio de Janeiro: Universidade Federal do Rio de Janeiro, 17–23.

Wallace, C., 2003. *Critical reading in language education*. Basingstoke: Macmillan

Watson, G. and Zyngier, S., eds. 2007. *Literature and stylistics for language learners: Theory and practice*. Basingstoke, Hants.: Palgrave Macmillan.

Widdowson, H. G., 1975. *Stylistics and the teaching of literature*. London: Longman.

Widdowson, H. G., 1992. *Practical stylistics*. Oxford: Oxford University Press.

Widdowson, H., 2004. Verbal art and social practice: A reply to Weber. *Language and Literature*, 11 (2), 161–167.

Yáñez-Prieto, M.C., 2010. Authentic instruction in literary worlds: Learning the stylistics of concept-based grammar. *Language and Literature*, 19 (1), 36–59.

Zyngier, S. et al., eds. 2002. *Fatos & Ficções*. Rio de Janeiro: Universidade Federal do Rio de Janeiro.

15

Stylistics, drama and performance

Andrea Macrae

Introduction

This chapter provides an overview of stylistic approaches to drama and performance, surveying methods of analysis of texts on the page and on the stage. The chapter begins by introducing past approaches taken to drama, particularly structuralist approaches to character and plot. The next section discusses two key critical issues in dramatic stylistics: the nature of communication and interpretation of dramatic discourse, and whether or not the performance of drama can and should be critically discussed beyond the (more stable) play text. This discussion is followed by an outline of current stylistic approaches to drama and performance, including socio-pragmatics, schema theory, deictic shift theory, historical and corpus stylistics, and research on multimodality. Socio-pragmatic and multimodal approaches are then employed in an illustrative analysis of an extract from Noel Coward's (1930) *Private Lives*. Though the focus is predominantly upon drama and dramatic performance, the chapter indicates the value and possibilities of stylistic analyses of other kinds of literary performance.

Historical approaches to drama

Drama has been described as 'the neglected child' of literature, as it has received relatively little attention from stylisticians and from literary critics in general (Culpeper, Short and Verdonk 1998, p. 3). Approaches to drama have historically been heavily influenced by Aristotle's *Poetics* and have focused predominantly upon character (i.e. the *dramatis personae*) and plot, these being considered the key means by which the audience's emotion is aroused (see Chapter 1 in this volume). Within some theoretical approaches, particularly structuralist and Russian Formalist models, character is subordinated to plot, with characters serving functional roles rather than being psychologically realistic representations of the individual. Propp (1968), using the folktale as his sample of narratives, distinguishes eight character types (hero, villain, etc.) according to their role in the moves of the plot (which he breaks down into thirty-one possible events), while Greimas (1983) distinguishes six 'actants' (helper, opponent, etc.) across three axes (desire, power, and transmission of knowledge), with the relationship between the actants across these axes determining the plot. (See Chapter 2 in this volume for more on this topic.) Literary critics have found value in transposing

Propp's and Greimas's models to a wide variety of forms and genres of literature. Some kinds of drama can be (and have been) fruitfully analysed through a conception of character as plot vehicle, most obviously early allegorical 'morality' plays, but such models are equally applicable to texts from early modern Shakespearian plays through to the drama of Anton Chekhov and Arthur Miller. However, many plays subordinate plot to character, creating more fully 'rounded' characters (in E. M. Forster's sense), or work against traditional notions of mimesis and so are less directly amenable to these models.

Similarly, literary criticism of dramatic plot has historically manifested the weight of Aristotle's heuristic and didactic division of drama into two distinct genres – comedy and tragedy – each with its own plot tendencies, character types/functions, and form of emotional catharsis. For example, Freytag (1983) proposes a triangular model mapping the relationships between the plot stages he identifies in traditional Greek and Shakespearian five-act tragedies (these stages being 'exposition', 'rising action', 'climax', 'falling action' and 'denouement/catastrophe/resolution'). However, it can be said that comedy and tragedy rely upon plot more heavily than other genres. As with theories of character, plot theories which focus on classical forms are less able to offer analytical insight to the many ways in which drama has developed in relation to and reaction against both past conventions and new cultural codes of meaning.

During the second half of the twentieth century, both the level of critical attention afforded to drama, and the kinds of critical approaches taken to it, began to change. Dramatic theory began to catch up with dramatic practice. Critical understanding of the relationship between a text and/or performance and its reader or audience in the construction of meaning evolved through linguistic and then cognitive turns in literary theory. Appreciation of the relationship between dramatic performance and other kinds of literary and non-literary discourse also began to change, along with, in turn, critical perceptions of the textual and performance aspects through which readers and audiences interpret meaning (c.f. Wells 1970, Knapp 2003). Furthermore, the scope of that which is considered dramatic performance started to expand, with dramatic criticism beginning to include not only film and television drama, but also other kinds of performance art and oral storytelling (Carlson 2004).

Stylistic approaches, informed by various sociolinguistic and cognitive models of communication and interpretation, have proven to have much to offer to developments in criticism of drama and dramatic performance, not least in the unique contribution stylistic theories can offer to some of the thornier issues that have arisen through these developments – issues such as the nature of communication and interpretation at work in dramatic performance, and the very possibility of critical discussion of performance, given the transience of the object of analysis. Some current stylistic perspectives on these issues are presented below, followed by an outline of the range of stylistic approaches currently applied to drama.

The play text and the performance

Literary criticism has tended to investigate the play text (the script) itself over and above the *performance* of a play text. Some branches of criticism of the drama and theatre of past centuries investigate historical evidence of the staging of, and the theatre culture around, particular productions, dramatic movements or eras (reviews, directorial notes, advertising leaflets, theatre company accounts etc.). However, criticism of the live performance features of contemporary productions has been seen as problematic, because not only do different productions of a play text vary, but each performance will also differ from the next, even if only slightly. Short argues that unless two critics have seen at least the same production (if not the same performance of that production) we meet the problem of not 'holding constant the object under critical discussion' (1998, p. 8). Short proposes that, in fact, 'in ontological terms, each production of a play would appear to be a play PLUS an interpretation of it' (capitalisation in the original) (p. 8). He also states that, often, rather than constituting very different interpretations of a play, 'many productions of plays are merely variations of the same interpretation' (p. 8) and suggests that each *performance* of a particular production 'in essence' constitutes an individual and distinct '*instantiation* of the same production' (italicisation in the original). (p. 8) The lack of variance in 'faithful' productions is, Short argues, due to the fact that performance features such as action (including gestures, facial expression and gaze direction), phonological and paralinguistic aspects of speech, and character appearance (including age and clothing) can be inferred from the play text, that is, from the dialogue and stage directions (1998, p. 12). He argues that analysing the text itself is sufficient, in that 'production and performance are based on, and constrained by, inferences drawn from a reading of the text' (Culpeper, Short and Verdonk 1998, p. 6). Contradicting Wells' (1970, p. ix) claim that 'the reading of a play [text] is a necessarily incomplete experience' (Short 1998, p. 6), Short argues that 'sensitive understandings of plays can be arrived at through "mere reading" and [...] that dramatic texts contain very rich indications as to how they should be performed' (p. 7).

Short's arguments are in some ways a logical continuation of a fundamental principle of stylistics – the assumption that readers of a text who share similar socio-cultural backgrounds will construct a largely shared interpretation of that text, and will generally be aware of, or be able to distinguish, aspects of their reading which are idiosyncratic (e.g. aspects related to particularly personal memory and associations). Short acknowledges that some directors stage radical interpretations of play texts, just as some literary critics propose radical interpretations of literary texts, but such interpretations, though not necessarily of less critical value, can often be said to result from the imposition of meaning onto the text, rather than a derivation of meaning directly from the text's own language (1998, pp. 7–8).

However, parts of Short's argument benefit from some exploration. For example, though a production of a play can be considered an interpretation, this in itself does not seem to be a reason to discount it as a valid object of study. Stylistics is the investigation of the ways in which the text prompts the analyst's interpretation, and thus the interpretation is itself as much an object of study as the text. Analysing a performance of a play text, rather than analysing the text itself, could be considered as simply analysing a different kind of text: the underlying printed play text is no longer directly relevant; the performance, as a literary work of multimodal discourse, is the object of study, via the analyst's interpretation (as audience member). Indeed, Short proposes that 'when you "see" a play while reading it, the "performance" is always perfect', (p. 9) suggesting that the reader's own interpretation is a performance, albeit an imagined one.

A key issue appears to be the nature of and relationship between a play text, a performance of the play text (via the theatre company's interpretation of it), and the reader's interpretation of both. Just as a novel doesn't describe every detail of its text world, working instead on the principle of minimal departure, so, too, a play text does not describe every detail of its text world. In the experience of reading a play the reader 'fleshes out' aspects of the text world based on his/her schematic knowledge, personal memory, etc. A play text may leave more space for this readerly fleshing out than a novel, as less narratorial detail is provided. In a production of a play text, however, more (though by no means all) of the text world is fleshed out by the director and the performance context, perhaps leaving less scope for variation in the audience's interpretation. The differences in one's reading of a play text and one's experience of watching a production of a play text are yet to be fully explored. Short's intuition that readers of play texts imagine that text in performance seems sound, though the nuances of the script format may make the processing experience quite different from that of reading a novel. Either way, the experience of a play text and the experience of a performance of a play text can be seen as two distinct things. However, it follows, then, that the stylistic analysis of a play text (or indeed of a printed story or poem) and the study of a performance of that play text (or story or poem) can be considered two distinct lines of enquiry, each of which can inform the other.

This stance can perhaps help to address the contentious issue of the place of multimodality in the analysis of the play text and the play performance. Short appears to suggest that performance features are not part of the reader's interpretation of a play text, that they can vary from production to production (if not from 'instantiation' to 'instantiation'), and (therefore) that they are transitory and thus cannot and should not be part of stylistic analysis of drama. However, some performance features are sometimes inscribed in the text (as specific direction, e.g., 'the table is laid ready for dinner', 'Arthur enters stage left', 'Sarah points to Michael', 'Anthony puts his head in his hands'), sometimes implied (e.g., by use of adverbs in parentheses, suggesting the manner in which the following speech should be expressed, e.g., '(*loudly*),' '(*happily*)'), and sometimes strongly inferable: although the play text does not explicitly describe the pace or nature of Antigonus' departure from the stage (and the world of the text) in Shakespeare's *The Winter's Tale*, the direction '*Exit pursued by a bear*' is likely to prompt little variation in different readers' interpretation of the speed of his exit. However, other performance features, such as facial expression, intonation, lighting, and blocking, are less often explicitly written into the text. McIntyre (2008) and Busse (2011) argue that the multimodal features inscribed and entailed in a play text, and *also* those which have been imposed or added in a performance, all warrant inclusion in any stylistic analysis of drama. McIntyre states that 'some performances of plays incorporate production elements that seem to add substantially to the original play script, and which arguably guide our interpretation of the play. In such cases, a stylistic analysis which ignores these production elements is arguably impoverished and incomplete' (2008, p. 309). He goes further to state that 'the multimodal elements of the production contribute to our interpretation of the play as much as the linguistic elements of the dramatic text'. Swann, in reference to oral storytelling performances, argues that 'the skill and artistry of the storyteller resides in their ability to orchestrate semiotic resources to construct the characters, places and events that make up the story and secure the audience's involvement in the story', semiotic resources which include gesture, movement, body language, intonation and more, beyond the verbal content of the story itself (2009, p. 188). McIntyre supports Short's contention that the transience of a performance creates a 'tension' in the analyst 'being methodologically rigorous', but nonetheless argues that 'a complete stylistic analysis of a play [...] takes into account production and performance elements' (2008, p. 309). Busse (2011, p. 153) likewise stresses 'the importance and interplay of drama as text and performance' and the need 'to enhance its systematic analysis by including the multimodality of (filmed or staged) drama as discourse'. She suggests that studying dramatic performance is itself, in its own way, a continuation of stylistic principles, in that 'a stylistic analysis of dramatic discourse takes as fundamental the interaction between action, speech and perception because stylistics focuses on how texts and (filmed or staged) performance mean what they do in context, how meaning is created and how language, interactional strategies and characterization interact' (p. 155).

The arguments in favour of the need for analysis of multimodal performance features in both play texts and productions are strong, but the issue of the transience of a performance still complicates the debate. In an article published in *Language and Literature*, McIntyre (2008, p. 311) proposes that the filmed and recorded, thus accessible and (re)viewable, nature of the dramatic performance he discusses offers 'one way to avoid the methodological issue that Short raises', as we *are* in fact able to 'hold [...] constant the object under discussion' (cf. Short 1998, p. 8). According to this argument, it seems that publication of a filmic recording legitimises the multimodal performance as an object of stylistic analysis. However, the reader of McIntyre's article does not need to return to the film itself to consider the rigour and convincingness of McIntyre's analysis. Though it may require more effort on the analyst's part, sections of performances can be relayed to the analyst's reader in great detail through close description of setting, lighting, costume and sound, through transcription of speech, and through the reporting of performance features such as facial expression, gesture, movement, the use of props and so on. These kinds of details, the performance 'data', as it were, can be presented objectively and systematically, just as a conversation being analysed by a sociolinguist can be presented objectively and systematically. Performance analysis can on this basis be as retrievable and replicable as it can be when the text in question is a printed poem or an extract from a novel, as is well illustrated by the detailed accounts (including illustrative camera shots, transcripts and description) provided in the strong, systematic and convincing multimodal performance analyses of McIntyre (2008) and Lwin (2010).

It seems both possible and fruitful, then, that the stylistician's attempt to be both rigorous and comprehensive should include in any analysis of a play text the multimodal performance features linguistically entailed in the stage directions (maintaining an awareness of the further multimodal features extrapolated within the analyst's interpretative imagined 'performance' of the play), and to include in any analysis of a production all the multimodal performance features (possibly, but not essentially, in relation to the play text). The influence of the performance features of a production of a play upon one's interpretation of the play script, and vice versa, also then becomes a further possible and valid object of stylistic enquiry.

The architecture of dramatic discourse

These issues have an interesting bearing on the matter of the nature of dramatic communication of meaning. Short proposes that the 'discourse architecture' of prototypical drama involves at least two levels of communication: that between the playwright and audience/reader, and that between the characters of the play, the 'message' (in a Jakobsonian sense: see Chapter 2 in this volume) between characters being embedded in and predominantly constituting the 'message' from playwright to audience/reader (Short 1996, p. 169), as follows:

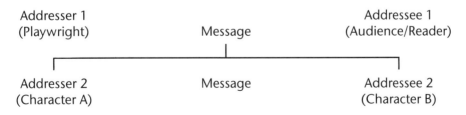

Addresser 1		Addressee 1
(Playwright)	Message	(Audience/Reader)
Addresser 2	Message	Addressee 2
(Character A)		(Character B)

This model of dramatic discourse usefully emphasises the double layer of communication in drama, i.e that characters' communication with each other is fundamentally designed to communicate meaning to the (conventionally) 'overhearing' audience. Hence, in cases of 'dramatic irony', words spoken by 'character A' can be interpreted as possessing one meaning and pragmatic function for 'character B', and another for the audience, who may know relevant further information that 'character B' is not privy to (which, for example, might expose the speech as a lie, or as designed to mislead, persuade etc.).

Contemporary cognitive and pragmatic approaches add to this model an appreciation of the contextual dependence of meaning as well as the role of the audience/reader in, and the significance of their background knowledge and schemata upon, the interpretation of meaning (or the construction of the 'message'), revising the conduit metaphor of communication (as a predetermined, finite form of meaning transference) implied by the unidirectionality of the 'message' at the playwright-audience/reader level.

Additionally, multimodal approaches stress the role of factors beyond character dialogue, such as gesture, movement, setting and lighting, in the construction and communication of meaning. The producer, director, actors and potentially other parts of the theatre company then become part of the discourse architecture, as both addressees of the playwright and addressers of the audience. McIntyre (2004, p. 143) finds Chatman's (1990) concepts 'slant' and 'filter' useful in distinguishing and discussing point of view in drama. He transposes the term slant (conventionally referring to attitudes expressed by the narrator) to the stage directions of the playwright, while filter refers to the attitudes of characters. Extra-textual performance features added by the director or actors may be considered as constituting a secondary kind of 'slant', or potentially multifarious (but ideally, supposedly, concordant) 'slants'. In this light, whether or not two different models of discourse architecture might be warranted and analytically useful, one for the play text, and one for the play production, and how far they might overlap, become interesting questions.

Theoretical insights on these issues continue to develop, alongside and enhanced by critically reflexive application of a range of key stylistic approaches to drama and performance. The following section presents brief outlines of current approaches and research within the stylistics of drama, including socio-pragmatics, schema theory, deictic shift theory, historical and corpus stylistics, and research on multimodality. Each of these stylistic approaches is explained more fully elsewhere in this book; this section focuses specifically on illustrating their particular applicability to the analysis of drama and performance.

Current stylistic approaches to drama and performance

Short (1996, p. 168) describes drama as 'the conversational genre', the form of literature which 'is most like naturally occurring conversation'. Though, as discussed, many semiotic tools contribute to plays and other kinds of literary performance, speech dominates drama. The socio-pragmatic theories of the 1970s still govern current discourse analysis, and remain invaluable in the analysis of dramatic discourse. These theories include conversation analysis, speech act theory, Grice's co-operative principle and maxims, and politeness.

Conversation analysis provides a useful framework for investigating dramatic dialogue (see Chapter 8 in this volume for more on this). The norms of conversational turn-taking, such as adjacency pairs and the three-part 'initiation-response-follow-up' turn-taking structure (as identified by Sacks, Schlegoff and Jefferson 1978 and Sinclair and Coulthard 1975), are often interestingly exploited within drama to communicate character relations to the audience.

The maxims of conversation identified by Grice (1975) are also meaningfully manipulated within dramatic discourse. Grice proposes that conversations occur through the tacit agreement of the co-operative principle (1975, p. 45): 'Make your conversational contribution such as is required at the stage at which it occurs, by the accepted purpose or direction of the talk exchange in which you are engaged.' He posits four conversational maxims that allow speakers to abide by the co-operative principle: the maxims of quality (say only what you believe to be true), quantity (say only as much as is required), relation (be relevant), and manner (avoid obscurity and ambiguity). Much of conversation operates through deliberate and overt 'flouting' (non-observance) of maxims, however, generating 'conversational implicature' in that the hearer expects that a communicative strategy underlies the speaker's flouting and so infers meaning from it. With the (at least) double-layered discourse architecture in mind, much of a play's meaningfulness can be communicated through the implicature derived from characters' flouting of maxims.

Speech act theory offers a further useful framework for the analysis of the interpretative significance of dramatic exchanges (see Chapter 7 in this volume for more on this). Searle's (1969, 1976, 1979) extension of Austin's theory (1962) distinguishes five types of speech acts: assertives and representatives, directives, commissives, expressives, and declaratives. As neo-Gricean pragmatic theory has illustrated, Grice's model doesn't easily accommodate some nuances of communication and conversational implicature, such as the possibility of speakers having divergent views on what constitutes co-operation within a particular conversational context. Divergent views on the aims of a conversation, for example, would most likely influence the actual perlocutionary effect of an utterance upon the hearer (the inferred meaning and consequence, as opposed to the speaker's intended perlocutionary effect), whatever its illocutionary force as one of the five acts. Speech act theory helps to facilitate understanding of the relationships between utterances and interpretation in drama (Short 2007).

Verbal politeness (and impoliteness) is often constituted by speakers' tactical use of turn-taking, strategic exploitation of the conversational maxims and so on. A speaker's 'positive face' (Brown and Levinson 1987) (i.e., the need for other people to share and support our personal desires and wants) may be threatened by a dispreferred response within the conventional adjacency pair of a greeting, for example, countering the speaker's implied belief in and want for a cordial relationship with the hearer. Likewise, a speaker's 'negative face' (i.e., the wish to be unimpeded by others) could be baldly threatened by interruption or by some sarcastic criticism suggested by a flouting of the maxim of quality, or vaguely threatened 'off-record' by indirect hints made through the flouting of the maxim of manner. The acts of tending to the positive face of a hearer, or mitigating face threatening acts, can equally be comprised of careful turn-taking and consideration of maxims: a speaker might cede the conversational floor to another, or redress a face threatening act by flouting the maxim of quantity by giving repeated apologies for the occurrence of something which contradicts the hearer's wishes. Other politeness strategies include the use of expressives to express empathy, the use of honorifics to acknowledge someone's status, other terms of address to express degrees of familiarity or endearment, and so on. Politeness theory provides a useful tool to analyse the social dynamics of conversational interaction.

To think of drama, or even specifically the play text, as *merely* 'the conversational genre', however, is to radically delimit analysis and appreciation of the discourse levels, and discourse forms, through which dramatic text and performance conveys meaning. A broad range of stylistic approaches can offer a wealth of insight into many kinds of performances – predominantly verbal or otherwise.

Schema plays a large part in our understanding of drama and performance (see Chapter 16 in this volume for more on this). As suggested earlier in this chapter, in interpreting a script a reader must flesh out a lot of the detail that is missing from the text based on his or her understanding and experience of the types of scenarios and interactions described. Culpeper (2001) extends schema theory (Schank and Abelson 1977) and the situation model (van Dijk and Kintsch 1983) to the reader's interpretation of a play text's characters. He delineates a model of the ways in which textual cues (of verbal and non-verbal behaviour) relating to a particular character evoke our culturally-specific schemata of characteristics and personality traits, and from this we build up a picture of that character as a rounded, sentient being. Theory of mind (Palmer 2004) offers a similar model of the ways in which we build up impressions of characters as psychologically real.

However, as Culpeper writes in relation to his approach to characterisation, 'it cannot be assumed that the schemata suggested by contemporary research necessarily apply in all cultures and all periods' (2001, p. 164). Historical stylistics (Busse 2007) has a lot to offer to the study of drama in its exploration of diachronic changes in the meaning and uses of particular words over time, changes in codes and performance of politeness, changes in perceptions of and production strategies relating to mimesis etc., as well as the period-specific interpretative significance of each of these factors and many more (see also Chapter 6 in this volume). Historical stylistics sometimes utilises the methods of corpus stylistics (Semino and Short 2004, Busse 2006) to examine the ways in which a particular word or phrase is used by a playwright in a single play or across the body of their work, for example, or how it is used in drama across any given period and how the meaning and uses of that term (and thus the audience's interpretation of it) may have changed over time. (Corpus stylistics cannot offer much assistance to the analysis of performance, however, beyond exploration of stage directions, directorial notes, etc.)

McIntyre (2006) analyses the establishment of point of view in drama, addressing in particular the role of deixis and deictic shifting in the construction and interpretation of the text worlds of plays. Deixis (Bühler 1934) is the language of 'pointing', including person deixis such as personal pronouns and demonstratives, spatial deixis such as 'here', 'there' 'near' and 'far', and temporal deixis such as 'now', 'then', 'tomorrow' and 'last year'. Deictic language establishes a relationship between the referent and the context of utterance, and only gains meaning in relation to the context of utterance (that is, the temporal instance referred to by the word 'now', for example, can only be interpreted in relation to the moment at which it is said). Deictic shift theory (Duchan, Bruder and Hewitt 1995, Stockwell 2002) proposes that in order to comprehend deictic terms, the reader (or audience member) has to conceptually shift to the context of the utterance (that is, to the deictic centre of the speaker). The reader or audience member may then be 'pushed' down to ontologically 'deeper' levels of the dramatic discourse architecture (such as when a speaking character refers to another character as 'you', and/or deictically refers to the spatial or temporal parameters of the text world in which they exist, such as referring to the 'now' or the 'tomorrow' of their text world context). Similarly the reader or audience member may be 'popped' upwards to 'higher' levels (by, for example, a chorus or narrator speaking from a deictic centre anchored outside the diegesis of the play's story).

The mechanics of deixis in performance contexts can work in tandem with multimodal semiotics of other kinds to construct (and confront) the parameters of text worlds and the relationships between characters and the viewer within and across these parameters. This is illustrated by McIntyre's (2008) analysis of the interrelationships between the language, staging and camera work (informed by Kress and van Leeuwen's (2001, 2006) visual grammar of features such as gaze vectors, and their distinction between represented participants (characters) and interactive participants (viewers) and their relative viewpoints).

More broadly, McIntyre and other multimodal theorists, drawing on film theory (e.g. Bordwell and Thompson 2001), stress the relevance of aspects of *mise-en-scène* to dramatic performance, such as setting, costume and make-up, lighting and staging (including movement). This recalls the first of Aristotle's six proposed constituents of drama – scenery and costume (spectacle) – to which we could add his second, an organised score of sound. Sound and movement can include communicative aspects of vocalisation (pausing, pace, intonation, emphasis) as well as the semiotics of body language and gesture, all of which can be systematically incorporated into a stylistics of performance of a variety of literary forms, such as children's storytelling (cf. Lwin 2010) and performance poetry.

This section has offered an overview of some of the most popular and productive stylistic approaches to drama. The next section briefly models a socio-pragmatic analysis of a play text employing and further illustrating some of these approaches, and follows this with a reflective discussion of the interpretative impact of the multimodal performance features of a 2001 production of the play upon my reading.

A socio-pragmatic and multimodal stylistic analysis of drama

Act one of Noël Coward's *Private Lives* (1930) begins with a scene in which two adjacent hotel suites open out downstage into terraces divided by a line of plant tubs. In the suite to the right a couple come out onto their terrace, on honeymoon, and while settling in, discuss the apparently appalling previous wife, 'Amanda', of the groom, 'Elyot' (the conversation led by the jealous questioning of the new bride, 'Sybil'). They go back into their room, and then a second couple come out onto the terrace on the left, also on honeymoon, and, addressing each other as 'Mandy' and Victor', discuss the apparently appalling previous husband, Elyot, of the new bride, Mandy. They then go back into their room, and Elyot comes back out onto his balcony and has a brief exchange with Sybil, who is inside. The text then gives us the following (2000, pp. 18–19):

> **Elyot** *saunters down the balustrade. He looks casually over on to the next terrace, and then out at the view. He looks up at the moon and sighs, then he sits down in a chair with his back towards the line of tubs, and lights a cigarette.* **Amanda** *steps gingerly on to her terrace carrying a tray with two champagne cocktails on it. She is wearing a charmingly simple evening gown [...]. She places the tray carefully on the table, puts her cloak over the back of a chair, and sits down with her back towards* **Elyot.** *She takes a small mirror from her handbag, and scrutinises her face in it. The orchestra downstairs strikes up a new melody. Both* **Elyot** *and* **Amanda** *give a little start. After a moment,* **Elyot** *pensively begins to hum the tune the band is playing. [...]* **Amanda** *hears him, and clutches at her throat suddenly as though she were suffocating. Then she jumps up noiselessly, and peers over the line of tubs.* **Elyot,** *with his back to her, continues to sing obliviously. She sits down again, relaxing with a gesture almost of despair. Then she looks anxiously over her shoulder at the window in case* **Victor** *should be listening, and then, with a little smile, she takes up the melody herself, clearly.* **Elyot** *stops dead and gives a gasp, then he jumps up, and stands looking at her. She continues to sing, pretending not to know that he is there. At the end of the song, she turns slowly, and faces him.*

Amanda Thoughtful of them to play that, wasn't it?

Elyot (*in a stifled voice*) What are you doing here?

Amanda I'm on honeymoon.

Elyot How interesting, so am I.

Amanda I hope you're enjoying it.

Elyot It hasn't started yet.

Amanda Neither has mine.

Elyot Oh, my God!

Amanda I can't help feeling that this is a little unfortunate.

Elyot Are you happy?

Amanda Perfectly.

Elyot Good. That's all right, then, isn't it?

Amanda Are you?

Elyot Ecstatically.

Amanda I'm delighted to hear it. We shall probably meet again sometime. Au revoir! (*She turns.*)

Elyot (*firmly*) Good-bye.

She goes without looking back. He stands gazing after her with an expression of horror on his face.

The long stretch of stage direction plays a large part in both the establishment of the play's farcical comedic tone, and in the construction of the characters of Amanda and Elyot. Dramatic irony is exploited to the full, with the audience seeing what Amanda and Elyot cannot: not only each other's presence, but also the partial symmetry of their behaviour. There is contrast within the symmetry, however, in the verbs and adverbs used to describe their similar movements: Elyot 'saunters', looks 'casually' around, and sits with a cigarette, while Amanda 'steps gingerly', places her cocktail tray 'carefully' on the table, and sits and 'scrutinises' her face in a mirror. Elyot is portrayed as relaxed, and Amanda as far more controlled. (Notably, this contrasting characterisation might be more overt to the reader of the play text than a member of the audience of a performance, given the greater difficulty of dramatically conveying the manner of movements as precisely as the lexis describes.) The contrasting impressions, and the play on dramatic irony, are further developed through Amanda's quicker realisation of Elyot's presence and the situation, and Elyot's continued 'obliviousness' while Amanda takes control of their encounter.

The comedic irony of Amanda's first utterance, 'Thoughtful of them to play that, wasn't it?', is conveyed through its flouting of the maxim of quality, in that the orchestra is unlikely to be aware of Elyot and Amanda's presence, or that the tune has sentimental value to them – and if it did, it wouldn't be thoughtful to play it in these circumstances. Far from being the simple, friendly, engaging remark its interrogative form might suggest, Amanda's utterance is wry sarcasm, primarily foregrounding the awkwardness of their situation. Furthermore, by opening the conversation this way, rather than with a greeting or a more direct acknowledgement of the problematic coincidence of their travels, Amanda's words simultaneously re-establish the familiarity of their relationship whilst drawing attention to the intimacy of its past.

The conversation proceeds in an overtly polite and formal manner. The turns are dominated by an initiation-response-feedback structure in which both characters offer polite comment on each other's replies: 'How interesting', 'Good' and 'I'm delighted to hear it'. There is further mirroring in both the syntax and the sense of their questions and responses, such as:

Amanda I'm on honeymoon.

Elyot How interesting, so am I.

Amanda I hope you're enjoying it.

Elyot It hasn't started yet.

Amanda Neither has mine.

[...]

Elyot Are you happy?

Amanda Perfectly.

Elyot Good. That's all right, then, isn't it?

Amanda Are you?

Elyot Ecstatically.

Amanda I'm delighted to hear it.

Elyot's tag question – 'isn't it?' – even neatly mirrors the tag question ending Amanda's opening turn – 'wasn't it?' There is also continued play on dramatic irony in the contrast between their cool formality and the reality of their emotional connection and feelings already revealed to the audience in Amanda's initial 'gesture almost of despair' and Elyot's 'gasp' and 'stifled voice'.

The comedy of the contrast between their pretended calmness and their real feelings is heightened by Elyot's single deviating expressive, 'Oh, my God!', in turn even more greatly foregrounding the contrasting controlled nature of Amanda's response: 'I can't help feeling that this is a little unfortunate'. In this way, Elyot's speech act arguably has far more communicative significance for the audience than for Amanda. The comedic understatement of her response perhaps marks the peak of the disparity between the cool politeness of the conversation and the emotion underlying it, and highlights its true nature: the expressions of interest and shared happiness for each other are not affirmations of each other's positive face, but rather protection of their own pride and self-esteem.

This pair of turns also perhaps marks the peak of the extract's exploitation of gender-related schema for comedic effect. It is Elyot whose emotions get the better of his cool facade, just as it is Elyot who is left 'gazing' after Amanda in 'horror' as she departs the terrace. As pointed out earlier, it is Amanda who initially takes control of their encounter while Elyot remains oblivious. It is Amanda whose movement, gestures and speech are predominantly proactive and deliberate, rather than reactive. It is also Amanda who controls the opening and closing of the conversation, and who maintains a calm and distant demeanour. Elyot's greater ignorance and emotional vulnerability, is further suggested by his asking the majority of the questions, wanting and needing answers from her. In turn, this might lead a reader to infer that his question 'That's all right, then, isn't it?' is potentially genuinely searching, rather than merely phatic, rhetorical feedback. The comedic emasculating of Elyot is extended within the next few pages, as he opts to lie and feign illness to Sybil rather than tell her the truth about their predicament (as Amanda does to Victor), and threatens to 'scream the place down' should Victor come near him. Elyot's protection of his positive face in his efforts at polite and formal responses to Amanda is radically undermined as the nature of their characters is increasingly revealed.

As Short predicts, many aspects of these pragmatic features are inferable from the play text, as are some of the performance features, such as the manner of movement in some instances, as discussed, and the occasional tone of voice (e.g., with the stage direction '(firmly)'). However, some performance features, such as the intonation of Amanda and Elyot's responses 'Perfectly', and 'Ecstatically', for example, and of his question 'That's all right, then, isn't it?', as well as their body language during the conversation, are not explicitly inscribed in the text, thus potentially leaving room for slight variation in interpretation. The director's and actors' choices around these features would necessarily further contribute to my interpretation of the characters, their communication, and their relationship when viewing a performance.

I am also aware that my own reading of the script and interpretative imagining of the play is highly coloured by the production of it I watched in 2001 (directed by Howard Davies), long before I read the play text, in which Amanda and Elyot were played by Lindsay Duncan and Alan Rickman. The ages of these actors deviate from those implied by the play text (which, early on, suggests Elyot is thirty years old). Amanda and Elyot aged in their forties or fifties come across as acting on their experiences of the ways of life and love, as well as on a seasoned sense of carpe diem, rather than as flighty, inconstant youths as they otherwise might. In addition, fixed in my memory is Duncan's particular performance of 'relaxing with a gesture almost of despair', with which she slumped in her chair, gawping slightly, legs and arms loose, as if a straw man. In reading the play text, this is what I imagine: a slightly unfeminine, entirely uncontrolled, deflated, deeply shocked response that starkly contrasts with the controlled demeanour adopted beforehand and resumed quickly afterwards. The depth of this remembered and re-imagined contrast significantly influences my understanding of the degree to which the polite formality of Amanda's character is a mirage.

This brief application of socio-pragmatic and multimodal approaches is indicative of their potential fruitfulness within the stylistics of drama and performance, and of the ways in which a combined attention to multimodality and socio-pragmatics can support an attempt to delineate the potential interrelationships between pragmatics and multimodality in the interpretation of performance features, both in relation to and independently of the play text.

Recommendations for practice

Drama cannot be considered as functioning solely at the diegetic level: it does not simply 'show' without 'telling'. Short's discourse architecture and McInytre's emphasis on the communication of the playwright's 'slant' within stage directions both illustrate this. Nor is it solely constructed through the pragmatics of character-to-character communication. Drama, like other kinds of performed literature such as storytelling and performance poetry, is constructed and interpreted through a variety of semiotic systems, and any stylistic analysis of drama and performance should endeavour to account for communicative features beyond the text and beyond language.

Current research suggests that a flexible, eclectic stylistic approach, sensitive to both the range and the particular nature of the modes through which the dramatic text or performance in question gains meaning, and drawing on, in particular, socio-pragmatic, historical and corpus stylistic, and deictic, schema and/or multimodal theories and models as appropriate in response, can best facilitate insightful analysis. Some playwrights to start with, whose texts might yield rich analyses, and whose plays remain widely produced, include William Shakespeare, Samuel Beckett, Oscar Wilde, Anton Chekhov, Sarah Kane, Brian Friel and David Mamet, although exploration beyond the canon of popular Western drama, and indeed beyond drama itself, is to be encouraged.

Future directions

Current developments in multimodal theory are opening the way for a more comprehensive, systematic account of performance features and their potential contribution to interpretation. For example, developments in sociolinguistics, so productive thus far, can be further incorporated into a multimodal stylistics of drama and performance in the areas of gesture and body language. The context-bound nature of meaningfulness can be explored in relation to the greater architecture of dramatic and performance discourse, with attention to the influence of the site and medium of the performance on the listening/viewing experience (as part of a live theatre audience, listening to a poetry podcast, watching a non-directed video recording of a theatre performance, watching a film of a screenplay, experiencing a literary installation in a gallery space, and so on). Film theory can inform stylistic approaches to recorded performance, enabling further incorporation of the semiotic significance of camera positioning, angles and focus, cuts and the like. Stylistics could also productively engage more directly with the disparate, interdisciplinary field of performance theory itself. Continued advances in cognitive and empirical poetics can offer avenues of investigation into medium-specific differences in interpretative processing of drama and performance (e.g., differences between a reader's interpretative processing of play text, an audience member's interpretative processing of a live performance, and a viewer's interpretative processing of a filmed screenplay). Through these kinds of enquiry, we can move towards a better understanding of the relationships between text, performance and interpretation, and a more systematic, comprehensive and theoretically coherent stylistic approach to drama and performance.

Related topics

Conversation analysis and the cooperative principle, corpus stylistics, formalist stylistics, literary pragmatics, multimodality, (new) historical stylistics, point of view and modality, speech acts and (im)politeness theory, stylistics and film,

Andrea Macrae

Further reading

Culpeper, J., Short, M. and Verdonk, P., eds. 1998. *Exploring the language of drama: From text to context*. London: Routledge.

This edited volume offers a wide range of chapters by leading authors in the stylistics of drama, explaining and illustrating approaches from conversation analysis to cognitive metaphor theory. Its opening chapter also presents Short's argument in favour of the analysis of play texts over performance.

McIntyre, D., 2006. *Point of view in plays: A cognitive stylistic approach to viewpoint in drama and other text types*. Amsterdam: John Benjamins.

McIntyre's text presents a systematic cognitive approach to point of view in plays, including a sophisticated development and application of deictic shift theory.

McIntyre, D., 2008. Integrating multimodal analysis and the stylistics of drama: A multimodal perspective on Ian McKellen's *Richard III*, *Language and Literature*, 17 (4), 309–334.

This ground-breaking article is the first of its kind to integrate socio-pragmatics, multimodal theory and film theory in the analysis of a screenplay.

Short, M., 1996. *Exploring the language of poems, plays and prose*. London: Pearson.

Short's textbook provides an accessible overview of socio-pragmatic approaches to play texts and a clear outline of his views on the discourse architecture of drama.

References

Austin, J.L., 1962. *How to do things with words*. Oxford: The Clarendon Press.
Bordwell, D. and Thompson, K., 2001. *Film art: An introduction*. 6th edn. New York: McGraw-Hill.
Brown, P. and Levinson, S., 1987. *Politeness*. Cambridge: Cambridge University Press.
Brown, G. and Yule, G., 1983. *Discourse analysis*. Cambridge: Cambridge University Press.
Bühler, K., 1934. *Sprachtheorie: Die darstellungsfunktion der sprache*. Stuttgart and New York: Fischer.
Busse, B., 2006. *Vocative constructions in the language of Shakespeare*. Amsterdam and Philadelphia: John Benjamins.
Busse, B., 2007. The stylistics of drama: *The reign of King Edward III*. In: M. Lambrou and P. Stockwell, eds. *Contemporary stylistics*. London and New York: Continuum, 232–243.
Busse, B., 2011. Teaching the stylistics of drama. In: L. Jeffries and D. McIntyre, eds. *Teaching stylistics*. London: Palgrave Macmillan, 152–177.
Carlson, M., 2004. *Performance: A critical introduction*. New York and London: Routledge.
Chatman, S., 1990. *Coming to terms: The rhetoric of narrative fiction and film*. Ithaca, New York: Cornell University Press.
Coward, N., 2000. *Private Lives*. London: Methuen Publishing.
Culpeper, J., 2001. *Language and characterisation: People in plays and other texts*. London: Pearson Education.
Culpeper, J., Short, M. and Verdonk, P., eds., 1998. *Exploring the language of drama: From text to context*. London: Routledge.
Duchan, J. F., Bruder, G. A. and Hewitt, L. E., eds., 1995. *Deixis in narrative: A cognitive science perspective*. Hillsdale, New Jersey: Lawrence Erlbaum.
Freytag, G., [1863] 1983. *Die technik des dramas*. Stuttgart: Reclam.
Greimas, A.J., 1983. *Structural semantics: An attempt at a method*. D. McDowell, R. Schleifer and A. Velie, trans. Lincoln, Nebraska: University of Nebraska Press.
Grice, H. P., 1975. Logic and conversation. In: P. Cole and J.L. Morgan, eds. *Syntax and semantics 3: Speech acts*. New York: Academic Press, 41–58.
Jeffries, L. and McIntyre, D., eds., 2011. *Teaching stylistics*. London: Palgrave MacMillan.
Knapp, J. V., 2003. Talking the walk in cognitive stylistics. *Style*, 37 (1), 104–112.
Kress, G. and van Leeuwen, T., 2001. *Multimodal discourse: The modes and media of contemporary communication*. London: Arnold.

Kress, G. and van Leeuwen, T., 2006. *Reading images: The grammar of visual design*. 2nd edn. London: Routledge.

Lambrou, M. and Stockwell, P., eds., 2007. *Contemporary stylistics*. London and New York: Continuum.

Lwin, S. M., 2010. Capturing the dynamics of narrative development in an oral storytelling performance: A multimodal perspective. *Language and Literature*, 19 (4), 357–377.

McIntyre, D., 2004. Point of view: A socio-pragmatic analysis of Dennis Potter's *Brimstone and Treacle*. *Language and Literature*, 13 (2), 139–160.

McIntyre, D., 2006. *Point of view in plays: A cognitive stylistic approach to viewpoint in drama and other text-types*. Amsterdam: John Benjamins.

McIntyre, D., 2008. Integrating multimodal analysis and the stylistics of drama: A multimodal perspective on Ian McKellen's *Richard III'*. *Language and Literature*, 17 (4), 309–334.

Palmer, A., 2004. *Fictional minds*. Lincoln, Nebraska: University of Nebraska Press.

Propp, V., [1928] 1968. *Morphology of the folktale*. L. Scott, trans. Austin: University of Texas Press.

Richardson, K., 2010. *Television dramatic dialogue: A sociolinguistic study*. New York: Oxford University Press.

Sacks, H., Schegloff, E.A. and Jefferson, G., 1978. A simplest systematic for the organization of turn-taking in conversation. *Language*, 50, 696–735.

Schank, R. C. and Abelson, R. P., 1977. *Scripts, plans, goals, and understanding: An inquiry into human knowledge structures*. Hillsdale, New Jersey: Lawrence Erlbaum.

Searle, J. R., 1969. *Speech acts: An essay in the philosophy of language*. Cambridge: Cambridge University Press.

Searle, J. R., 1976. A classification of illocutionary acts. *Language in Society*, 5, 1–23.

Searle, J. R., 1979. *Expression and meaning: Studies in the theory of speech acts*. Cambridge: Cambridge University Press.

Semino, E. and Short, M., 2004. *Corpus stylistics: Speech, writing and thought presentation in a corpus of English narratives*. London: Routledge.

Short, M., 1996. *Exploring the language of poems, plays and prose*. London: Pearson.

Short, M., 1998. From dramatic text to dramatic performance. *In:* J. Culpeper, M. Short and P. Verdonk, eds. *Exploring the language of drama: From text to context*. London: Routledge, 6–18.

Short, M., 2007. How to make a drama out of a speech act: The speech act of apology in the film *A Fish Called Wanda. In:* D. Hoover and S. Lattig, eds. *Stylistics: Retrospect and prospect*. Amsterdam: Rodopi, 169–189.

Shakespeare, W., 1996. *The winter's tale*. S. Orgal, ed. Oxford: Oxford University Press.

Sinclair, J. M. and Coulthard, M., 1975. *Toward an analysis of discourse: The English used by teachers and pupils*. Oxford: Oxford University Press.

Stockwell, P., 2002. *Cognitive poetics: An introduction*. London: Routledge.

Swann, J. and Haggarty, B., 2009. Stories in performance. *In:* J. Swann, R. Pope and R. Carter, eds. *Creativity in language and literature*. London: Palgrave Macmillan, 184–188.

Swann, J., Pope, R. and Carter, R., eds., 2009. *Creativity in language and literature*. London: Palgrave Macmillan.

van Dijk, T. A. and Kintsch, W., 1983. *Strategies of discourse comprehension*. London: Academic Press.

Wells, S., 1970. *Literature and drama*. London: Routledge and Kegan Paul.

16

Schema theory in stylistics

Catherine Emmott, Marc Alexander, and Agnes Marszalek

Introduction

Schema theory is a key idea within cognitive stylistics which derives primarily from psychology and artificial intelligence. A *schema* (plural 'schemata') is a cognitive structure which provides information about our understanding of generic entities, events and situations, and in so doing helps to scaffold our mental understanding of the world. A schema (sometimes known as a 'frame,' 'script' or 'scenario') contains common default information which aids comprehension by allowing a reader to extrapolate details which are either not mentioned at all in a text or which are not fully specified. Authors stipulate only some elements, and readers easily comprehend such texts by uniting these elements with their appropriate generic knowledge from schemata. These elements therefore provide cognitive support for the default inferences readers make when they process language, and enable a reader to fill 'gaps' in the information given in a text.

Schema theory is important not only because it explains a central mechanism by which all reading takes place, but also because 'special effects' can be created by an author through the subversion, exploitation, alteration, or violation of a reader's schema knowledge. This article outlines the background to schema theory in psychology and artificial intelligence and explains some of the key areas in which it has been used in stylistics and related disciplines, followed by a range of representative examples and an indication of directions for future research.

Background: Psychology and artificial intelligence

Some of the earliest proponents of the ideas underlying schema theory were gestalt psychologists in studies of perception and child development (e.g. Piaget 1925, Köhler 1930, Koffka 1935). The term 'schema' was introduced into general psychology by Bartlett (1932) to describe a speaker's unknowing gap-filling in the process of retelling stories. It was the distortion of such retellings which led Bartlett to describe the process of 'remembering' as one which drew on the teller's schematic generic experience.

The concept of a schema was not widely taken up by psychologists until the 1970s, at which point artificial intelligence researchers became interested in the necessary knowledge structures that were required for a computer to understand texts. Any such comprehension would require structured computational knowledge bases which would reflect a normal reader's schemata. Minsky (1975) developed a theory of *frames* which contain *slots* corresponding to relevant attributes (e.g. in a bedroom frame, the slots would correspond to various attributes of the bedroom) which could be filled by the text or by the frame's default values. Researchers then began to describe, categorise and attempt to explicate such schemata in order to advance the study of computational linguistic comprehension and the general study of reading. Rumelhart (1975, 1980, also Rumelhart and Norman 1978) took Minsky's computational insights and applied them to cognitive psychology. In particular, Rumelhart and Norman (1978) described the three processes by which these schemata can change: *accretion* (adding new information), *tuning* (slightly altering existing information) and *restructuring* (creating new schemata, e.g. by the division, combination or radical alteration of existing ones).

Around this time, Schank and Abelson (1977) produced their key book *Scripts, Plans, Goals and Understanding*, which is the foundational text of modern schema theory. They supplement the general term 'schema' with more specific terminology. In their model, a general restaurant schema would contain information about the entities present there, but would also contain temporally-ordered information in the form of a *script*, which focuses on goal-oriented sequences that 'define a well-known situation' (1977, p. 422). A script for a restaurant scene would contain information about the sequence and prerequisites for structured activities such as paying a bill, ordering food and drink, and so forth. In addition to event sequences, many scripts contain *slots*, within which are placed the various *roles* that people fulfil (customers, sommeliers, waiters, chefs), the *props* that are used (menus, tables, cutlery, food, cash, credit cards), the *entry conditions* which define prerequisites (the customer wants food, the restaurant is open) and the end *results* (the customer no longer desires food, the restaurant has less food, the restaurant has more money). Scripts can have different *tracks* through which an event can pass, so that the same generic restaurant script will have, for example, a fine-dining track with different slots to, say, a greasy-spoon track (such as the clothing and appearance of staff in the roles slot, the range and cost of the items in the menu prop slot, the presence or absence of alcohol in the drink prop slot, and so forth). Beyond scripts, where non-stereotypical events occur, a highly-generic *plan* can structure events by providing knowledge which links actions taking place with the goals to be satisfied by the actors in the event.

Later, Schank (1982) extended this concept by breaking scripts into their component parts (such as the individual acts of ordering an item or paying a bill), which he termed *memory organisation packets* (MOPs). Sets of MOPs can then each be organised into a script, removing the necessity to argue that discrete schemata encode similar shared elements repeatedly. For example, multiple scripts can use the MOP which encodes the sequence required for the payment of a bill, be it a restaurant bill, a supplier's invoice, or a tax demand. Scripts and their other elements are, in this approach, constructed from MOPs and configured dynamically according to the demands of the discourse event.

The term *scenario* is used by Sanford and Garrod to describe situation-specific knowledge used for interpreting a text (1981, 1998, see also Sanford and Emmott 2012). Sanford and Garrod argue that knowledge is made available when a scenario is initially set up and so is readily available for a reader to use to interpret subsequent text, rather than being called up as a result of encountering gaps in the text. This account has been extensively empirically tested and shown to be psychologically valid. Sanford and Garrod also make a useful distinction between different types of character, distinguishing between minor *scenario-*

dependent characters (e.g. waiters in restaurants), who are normally expected to appear specifically in episodes relating to their relevant situation, and principal characters, who are more likely to be referred to in the text generally.

In addition to studies of how everyday schema knowledge is drawn on to interpret texts, psychologists have suggested that readers have knowledge of the overall structure of stories, termed *story schemata* (e.g. Rumelhart 1975, Mandler and Johnson 1977, Mandler 1984). However, other psychologists (e.g. Black and Wilensky 1979) have argued that general reasoning might account for knowledge of typical stories rather than these special cognitive structures.

Core uses of schema theory in stylistics and related areas

Stylisticians (and researchers in related disciplines such as narratology and critical discourse analysis) have used these findings from psychology and artificial intelligence in many different ways. In this section, we explore some of the core research applications of schema theory in these areas.

Schemata in relation to narratives, text structures, genres and intertextuality

Schemata have been used in explaining the nature of narrative. Narratives are usually seen as consisting of strings of events. Schema theory neatly shows how inferences can be made to link these events, providing extra information about what is unstated and also allowing further interpretation of what is stated. The need for supplementing textually presented information with the reader's knowledge has long been recognised in literary studies. In particular, Ingarden (1931) refers to 'spots of indeterminacy.' In addition to connecting events, inference-making enables readers to build a model of the world of a narrative, including adding details about characters and contexts. (See Sanford and Emmott (2012) for a discussion of psychological work on inferencing.)

Although events are generally seen as a key defining feature of narrative, Fludernik (1996) challenges this idea, suggesting instead that the crucial identifying factor is the requirement to draw on schemata reflecting human experience. Another approach is Herman's (2002, pp. 85–86) use of scripts to distinguish between narratives and non-narratives. He argues that it is gaps in the text which cannot be filled by standard inferences that prompt interest and thereby lead to storytelling (see also Hühn's (2010) study of 'eventfulness').

Important research has also been conducted on the overall shape of stories and other texts. Story schemata, as discussed in the previous section, offered an early psychological version of this type of work, but have been heavily criticised for not reflecting the complexity of different narratives (e.g. Toolan 1990). Hoey (2001) has suggested a more flexible approach which involves identifying *culturally popular patterns* in texts generally. This includes common patterns such as the problem-solution pattern. Knowledge of certain structures has also been linked to knowledge of specific genres (e.g. Fludernik 1996 and Herman 2002 on narrative, and Corbett 2006 on other texts).

Sometimes the relevant schema knowledge is not of stories in general but of a specific well-known story. Hence, texts such as myths and fairy stories become part of a culture's repertoire. *Intertextual schemata* provide readers with the knowledge to make links with well-known texts when reading (e.g. Eco 1984).

Incongruity: Humour studies

One highly productive stylistic application of schema theory has been in the study of *incongruous scripts*. Although incongruity may have different functions, this has been a particularly prominent approach for suggesting the mechanisms involved in the production and comprehension of humorous language (for reviews, see Raskin 1985, pp. 30–40 and Ermida 2008, pp. 14–25). Raskin's notion of 'script opposition' in verbal jokes is that a joke is a text which is compatible with two different scripts (Raskin 1985, p. 99), one which 'describes a certain 'real' situation and evokes another 'unreal' situation which does not take place and which is fully or partially incompatible with the former' (p. 108).

Within stylistics, Semino discusses the ways in which 'switches between schemata' can lead to amusement in the comprehension of jokes and sketches (1997, pp. 229–330), an idea similar to Coulson's psycholinguistic concept of 'frame-shifting' in one-line joke processing (2001, p. 49). The notion of incongruity has been central to the development of a number of linguistic models of humour (e.g. Attardo and Raskin's (1991) General Theory of Verbal Humour). Incongruity models have been applied to humorous texts in a range of genres, including narrative humour (e.g. Hidalgo Downing 2000, Ermida 2008, Marszalek 2013); drama (e.g. McIntyre and Culpeper 2010), and satirical magazines (Simpson 2003).

Other minds

A key use of schema theory in stylistics has been in studying *mind style* (Fowler 1996), which generally involves examining the style of the thought representations of characters who perceive the world differently from ordinary modern-day adult humans. Examples include Neanderthals, children, animals, insane people or those with limited intelligence (see Semino 2006 for a summary). In such cases, the writing style is sufficiently unusual to signify the way of thinking. One key technique is to under-specify descriptions of items in the perceiving character's context to reflect a lack of understanding (Halliday 1971, Fowler 1996, Leech and Short 2007; see also Emmott 2006). In such cases, readers usually need to draw on their own schemata to interpret what the character is actually perceiving, but this is only possible if the text gives sufficient clues to make such an interpretation possible. Such texts therefore need to provide enough unusual language to make the mind style plausible, but not so much as to make it unreadable and uninterpretable (unless the writer specifically wants to make interpretation difficult or impossible).

The term 'mind style' tends to be used particularly for deviant thinking styles rather than thinking styles in general. Nevertheless, schemata are also relevant to a wide range of types of thought presentation, some not so unusual. Fludernik (1996) argues for schemata which allow readers to experience other minds in narrative, and Palmer (2004) suggests that readers need 'continuing-consciousness frames' which enable readers to construct a sense of continuity of mental processing from the diverse mentions of a character's thoughts throughout a story.

Other worlds

All fictional worlds depart in some respect from our knowledge of the real world, but some are more radically different than others. Ryan (1991) has developed the 'principle of minimal departure' to account for how readers use their general knowledge as a default for constructing worlds unless differences are overtly identified. For radically different worlds (e.g. science

271

fiction, fantasy texts and absurdist texts), readers may need to replace or supplement existing schemata (e.g. Hidalgo Downing 2000, Stockwell 2003). Research in neuroscience suggests that readers rapidly adjust their conceptions and make inferences appropriate to counterfactual worlds (e.g. Nieuwland and van Berkum 2006, Ferguson and Sanford, 2008, Filik and Leuthold 2008, Sanford and Emmott 2012). Nevertheless, real world schemata still need to be drawn on to interpret many aspects of these worlds. Stockwell (2003, 2010) provides useful discussion of the stylistic strategies that authors use to present radical alterations to the nature of those schemata, presenting the new information either explicitly or as presupposed, and integrating it with readers' existing knowledge.

Socio-cultural schemata and reader variability

Schemata are often assumed to relate to knowledge which readers have in common, but social and cultural groups may have very different types of knowledge. *Socio-cultural* schemata take account of factors such as gender, race, class, age and social roles. Useful theoretical discussions are provided by van Dijk (e.g. 1998) from a critical discourse analysis perspective, and in Culpeper's (2001) summary of relevant work from social psychology. Two rather different areas of study in socio-cultural studies are the way in which a text is constructed and the reader's response to a text.

In the construction of texts, the use of *stereotypes* has been studied, particularly in relation to gender and race (e.g. Mills 1995, Pickering 2001, Montoro 2007, Schweinitz 2010). Stereotypes are usually regarded as imposing simplistic, ignorant and/or inflexible schemata on reality which are prejudicial to the individuals or entities depicted (see Pickering 2001 for debates on this topic). Culpeper (2001) also uses schema theory to examine more complex characters and to study how they change throughout a text. Culpeper's (2001) work on Shakespeare also shows how schemata may change diachronically, potentially leading to modern and Elizabethan audiences having different interpretations (see also Hühn (2010) for a more general discussion of diachronic factors in relation to schema theory).

Empirical studies of readers from different socio-cultural groups go beyond studying the texts themselves, examining how real readers of different types respond. Observations of different cultural schemata in psychology date back as far as Bartlett (1932), whose studies showed how Native American stories were misremembered when given to British readers because those readers lacked the same socio-cultural schemata. Schema theory has also been influential in second language teaching, where reading is viewed as the interaction between 'top-down' socio-cultural schemata guiding reading and 'bottom-up' signals from the text, and where varying schemata can explain misunderstandings by readers of different cultures (e.g. see Carrell and Eisterhold 1988 for a seminal discussion). László (1999, 2008) provides a discussion of empirical work on how different cultures read literature. A major new area within stylistics is the study of reading groups, which explores cultural differences in reading responses in these groups (e.g. Swann and Allington 2009).

Sensory and motor schemata, and the role of emotions

Due to the influence of artificial intelligence approaches to knowledge-engineering, schema theorists have traditionally focused on how cognitive inferences are made using knowledge stores. However, reading is not just a matter of processing facts: to feel a real sense of experiencing the world of a text, readers need to relate to the text as embodied beings. Recent work in neuroscience has focused attention on the importance of the senses, basic physical movements and the emotions in language understanding (e.g. Burke 2011, Sanford and Emmott 2012). There is now substantial evidence that, as we read, brain areas which would be activated for real physical and emotional responses in the real world are activated for their imaginary equivalents in stories. We need to postulate *sensory schemata* to explain our awareness of what is involved in basic sensory perception such as vision, hearing, smell, touch and taste. *Motor schemata* explain physical movements such as how we move our own bodies, how we grasp objects in our environment and how we understand the movement of others. (For applications to literary reading, see Burke 2011, Kuzmičova 2012, Sanford and Emmott 2012.)

Another important area is the role of emotions (see Miall 1989, Burke 2011). We need an *affective component to schema theory* to explain how we interpret emotions in characters (e.g. shaking may (or may not) signal fear) and also how readers' emotions are activated by the texts that they read (e.g. how readers respond to suspense). In addition, findings from social psychology and critical discourse analysis suggest that *attitude schemata* organise common stereotyping positive and negative emotional responses (see van Dijk 1998, pp. 60–64 for relevant theory; and Culpeper 2001 and Montoro 2007 for stylistic applications).

Literariness: Schema refreshment

A related concept is the use of schema theory to identify 'literariness'. Guy Cook links this concept to what he calls *discourse deviation*, where a narrative gains literary status if it can 'bring about a change in the schemata of a reader' (1994, p. 182). This means that literary discourse is *schema refreshing*, where the reading experience causes readers to update, change, or transform their existing schemata, whereas non-literary discourse is simply *schema reinforcing* or *schema preserving*. Such a claim is controversial for a range of reasons. First, non-literary texts, such as texts which aim to inform or argue, will necessary bring about changes to schemata (e.g. scientific texts or philosophy books), and second, literary texts, as Semino (1997, p. 175) argues, can often confirm some existing schemata while disrupting others. Moreover, Jeffries (2001) suggests that there may be value in texts which simply offer readers the chance to recognise socio-cultural experiences similar to their own, even if such texts do not offer a radically new perspective.

The recognition of the common role of literary texts as schema refreshing is useful if not taken too prescriptively. For example, Lang (2009) uses readers' feedback on Andrea Levy's *Small Island* to suggest that the novel (which discusses ethnicity, colonialism and slavery) provides an opportunity for engaging with themes that some British readers find difficult, and that its discomfiting elements can challenge the readers' beliefs about Britain's relationship with its colonies.

Beyond schemata: Text world theory and personal experience

Schema theory needs to be viewed in relation to other types of mental representation. General knowledge needs to be supplemented with information accumulated from the text itself. Emmott (1997) calls this 'text-specific knowledge', arguing that readers will normally build, develop and utilise large mental stores of information about characters and contexts (termed 'character constructs' and 'contextual frames'). Text world theory (Werth 1999, see also Gavins 2007) offers a similar view (for more on this see Chapter 17 in this volume). Schemata also need to be supplemented by knowledge structures containing rich stores of individual personal knowledge (e.g. Culpeper 2009, p. 136).

Practical examples of the use of schema theory in stylistics

There are many different ways in which schema theory can be used in stylistics. The examples below are intended to give representative indications of some practical applications to the analysis of literary texts and popular fiction, but they are not intended to be exhaustive.

Filling gaps: Schema knowledge and standard inferences

The significance of using schema knowledge to supplement the text was described earlier. Here we illustrate some specific ways in which it can be used in inference-making.

(1a) She grabbed a cigarette to try and keep [her hands] from shaking. Cigarette ash tumbled on to her black and purple shell suit.

(Danziger 1997, p. 14)

(1b) The waitress took their orders

(Shriver 2008, p. 22)

(1c) Their sashimi platters arrived

(Shriver 2008, p. 24)

(1d) They walked back to A&E. [...] 'They've had to sedate him,' she said.

(Rankin 2000, p. 13)

In (1a), readers can use their schema knowledge of smoking to infer that the character has lit and smoked the cigarette. Hence links can be made between stated actions. In (1b) the definite article (rather than an indefinite article) is used for the first mention of a waitress because the presence of serving staff is assumed by the restaurant script. In (1c), the waitress's role in bringing the plates is elided but can again be assumed. In (1d) the underlined pronoun is used without a previous antecedent (i.e. a prior name or role label), but the mention of A&E (Accident and Emergency) implies that 'they' must be doctors or nurses.

These examples show standard inferences, which are extremely common and crucial to basic sense-making when reading.

Jumping to conclusions – Characters' assumption-making

By relying on readers to make inferences, writers can reveal the assumption-making processes by which characters come to recognise states of affairs, hence mimicking their thought processes. Rather than inferences simply providing the backdrop to reading about certain events (as in 1a–d), the focus shifts to the process of inference-making in itself.

Example (2) illustrates a character's correct assumption making. In this example, from Audrey Niffenegger's *The Time Traveler's Wife*, a woman is observing the following items in the bathroom of the man she has been sleeping with:

(2) And then I notice that there are two toothbrushes in the white porcelain toothbrush holder.

I open the medicine cabinet. Razors, shaving cream, Listerine, Tylenol, aftershave, a blue marble, a toothpick, deodorant on the top shelf. Hand lotion, tampons, a diaphragm case, deodorant, lipstick, a bottle of multivitamins, a tube of spermicide on the bottom shelf. The lipstick is a very dark red.

I stand there, holding the lipstick. I feel a little sick. I wonder what <u>she</u> looks like, <u>what her name is</u>. I wonder how long they've been going out.

(Niffenegger 2005, p. 21)

The list clearly includes certain items, such as the tampons, the diaphragm case, and the lipstick, which break schema expectations about the contents of a man's bathroom cabinet. Both the character and the reader can draw on schema knowledge about women's pharmaceutical items to allow the assumption of another female presence and, moreover, to infer a relationship involving sexual intimacy. World knowledge therefore enables readers to draw conclusions. Only if the inference is made can the reader make sense of the character's emotional reaction to the lipstick. In addition, the use of the pronoun 'she,' without an antecedent name or other reference to the female character, only makes sense if the writer assumes that this is a natural conclusion. The lack of explicitness here enables the reader to make the same discovery as the character. (See also Emmott, Sanford and Alexander (2010) for discussion of cases where the reader is cued to make false assumptions.)

Creating an alien mind style:
Under-specification to reflect a character's lack of understanding

Example (2) above showed the thinking style of a character, reflecting the process of realisation. Fowler's term 'mind style' is used for the presentation of thoughts, but, as discussed above, it tends to be used for very unusual thinking styles, such as the representation of the alien in the example below. In the most extreme cases, characters often lack the schemata for any ordinary inference-making, replacing this with their own highly idiosyncratic worldview. In example (3), from Douglas Adams's *Dirk Gently's Holistic Detective Agency*, the main character, an 'electric Monk', is an alien entity who does not have any standard schema knowledge of police.

(3)   As he approached the petrol station he noticed a car parked there at <u>an arrogant angle</u>. The angle made it quite clear that the car was not there for anything so mundane as to have petrol put into it, and was <u>much too important to park itself neatly out of the way</u>. Any other car that arrived for petrol would just have to manoeuvre around it as best it could. <u>The car was white with stripes and badges and important looking lights</u>.

Arriving at the forecourt the Monk dismounted and tethered his horse to a pump. He walked towards the small shop building and saw that inside it there was a man with his back to him wearing <u>a dark blue uniform and a peaked cap</u>. [...]

The Monk watched in transfixed awe. The man, he believed with an instant effortlessness which would have impressed even a Scientologist, must be a God of some kind to arouse such fervour. He waited with bated breath to worship him. [...]

The Monk realised that the God must be waiting for him to make an act of worship [...]

His God stared at him for a moment, <u>caught hold of him, twisted him round, slammed him forward spreadeagled over the car and frisked him for weapons.</u>

(Adams 1988, p. 180)

This passage uses the very common device of representing alternative mind styles by under-specifying, i.e. by not using obvious lexical items such as 'police car' and 'policeman', but providing enough clues for readers to guess these entities from their schema knowledge. The Monk's misinterpretation is also characteristic of mind style presentations since he sees the world through his own perspective, believing the policeman to be a God. He also misinterprets the car being parked hurriedly to deal with a police emergency as being a sign of importance rather than speed.

Another common feature of such mind styles is that the presentation format is not consistent. The Monk is portrayed as not knowing about the police, but he does know what a petrol station is. Moreover, the word 'frisked' in the final sentence is highly specific to a police scene (in contrast to the previous under-specifications) and this mix of registers may reflect the presence of a knowing narrator.

Making murderers invisible and creating narrative interest: Low and high prominence

In detective and mystery stories, writers can detract attention from the key characters and vital clues by making descriptions heavily schema consistent. The most obvious use of this is in hiding a murderer by presenting the individual in the role of a scenario-dependent character. If a character only behaves according to a standard script, the other characters and the reader are unlikely to attach much importance to that character. This is a common strategy in Agatha Christie's work and her novel *Death in the Clouds* (1935) provides an example (see also Emmott and Alexander 2010 and Emmott, Sanford and Alexander 2010 for similar examples). During the period leading up to the murder, stewards on an airplane are mentioned intermittently by purely scenario-dependent actions, such as the following.

(4a) The steward, very deferential, very quick and efficient, disappeared again.

(Christie 1935, p. 15)

(4b) He said to the steward who hovered at his side with the menu, 'I'll have cold tongue.'

(Christie 1935, p. 16)

(4c) The steward said, 'Excuse me, ladies, no smoking.'

(Christie 1935, p. 16)

(4d) A steward placed coffee in front of her.

(Christie 1935, p. 17)

Later we find that the murder has been committed by one of the main characters whilst dressed as a steward (he leaves his seat and changes in and out of the uniform in the toilet). The near-invisibility of stewards in their standard role enables Christie to claim that this has enabled him to approach the woman he murders and subsequently to go unnoticed by his fellow passengers.

(4e) *'Nobody notices a steward particularly.'*

(Christie 1935, p. 187, Christie's italics)

The invisibility of scenario-dependent characters in their standard roles has also been shown in empirical work (Emmott, Sanford and Smith 2008). Participants in the experiment were asked to read short passages and then write their own continuations. Two sample passages are shown below.

(5a) [Passage supplied by experimenter] Craig wanted to buy a new bicycle for his teenage son's birthday. At the bicycle shop, he saw the assistant putting a mountain bike in the window.
[Participant's continuation] However, he saw the price tag and it was too expensive. He kept on walking.

(5b) [Passage supplied by experimenter] Craig wanted to buy a new bicycle for his teenage son's birthday. At the bicycle shop, he saw the assistant running out of the shop and shouting.
[Participant's continuation] The previous customer had simply got on a bike and kept cycling out of the store! His confidence had totally fooled the poor shop assistant.

In (5a) a participant reads a passage where the assistant performs a standard action and the participant simply ignores the assistant completely in the continuation and focuses on the more interesting aspect of the scene – the bicycle. By contrast, in (5b) the assistant behaves out of the standard role and this prompts an explanation of events in the continuation (generating the beginnings of a story) and the assistant is not only mentioned but an evaluative expression ('poor shop assistant') is used. The results overall (for thirty-two participants reading fifty-six passages each) showed a statistically significant difference in the continuation in terms of whether the scenario-dependent character continued to be mentioned and whether there was extra description and/or emotion.

Re-telling traditional tales in the twenty-first century: Incongruity, humour, intertextual knowledge and cultural specificity

As discussed earlier, incongruity underlies much humour. The following example, from Hans Christian Asboson's *The ASBO Fairy Tales*, illustrates this incongruity in a parody of a well-known fairy story. The text requires the reader to draw on two quite different types of knowledge, the intertextual knowledge of Hans Christian Anderson's *Little Red Riding Hood* and highly specific cultural knowledge of modern-day Britain (as will be explained shortly). This use of culturally-specific knowledge can have significant appeal within the relevant community, but inevitably it may also exclude readers who are unable to make full sense of the allusions (see Simpson 2003, p. viii).

(6) Little Red Riding Hoodie

Once upon a time there lived a little girl who was loved by everyone who met her; but most of all by her grandmother, who adored her so much she gave her a hooded tunic of red velvet. It suited the girl so well that she would never wear anything else – even in the market at Bluewater, where hooded tunics were forbidden – so she was called 'Little Red Riding Hoodie'.

> One day her mother said to her, 'Come, Little Red Riding Hoodie, here are some chips and a flagon of Thunderfist cider: take them across the park to your grandmother for she is ill and weak and not strong at thirty-two years of age.
>
> 'Whatever,' said Little Red Riding Hoodie.
>
> 'Don't stray off the path,' shrieked her mother. [...]
>
> Grandmother lived on the other side of the park, a one-league BMX ride away and, just as Little Red Riding Hoodie passed the first burned-out litter bin, she was greeted by a wolf.
>
> *(Asboson 2008, pp. 23–24)*

The inter-textual allusion is clearly signalled by the mention of fairy tales in the book title, the play on the name of the author (Hans Christian Asboson) and the character (Little Red Riding Hoodie), as well as assumed familiarity with the overall content of the story. In terms of style, the traditional opening of the fairy story is used ('Once upon a time') and there are also words such as 'market,' 'tunic' and 'flagon' which might be viewed as particularly appropriate to this genre.

By contrast, the cultural allusion to modern-day Britain is cued by the book title. Most British readers are likely to be aware that 'ASBO' stands for 'anti-social behaviour order', a type of penalty given to out-of-control children and teenagers who are too young to be prosecuted. This sets up a disjunction between a fairy tale world and the reality of modern Britain. 'Hoodie' relates to casual clothing where a top has an integrated hood. Within the British news media, the term is also used for young people who wear this type of clothing. The term generally has strong negative affect in the news media, since there is a stereotype of young people wearing hoods to hide their faces when they are gathering in potentially threatening groups. The text alludes very specifically in the opening paragraph to a particular news story in which hoodies were banned from Bluewater shopping centre in London. The forbidding of Little Red Riding Hoodie from the market of the same name potentially critiques this stereotyping reaction.

The rest of the example (and the story as a whole) keys into the absurd contrast between the traditional fairy story and the reality of modern-day Britain in terms of poverty and violence, plus further references to stereotypes of youth culture. The grandmother is only thirty-two but her illness is indicative of health problems in the poorer areas of Britain, and the chips and alcohol provide a stereotype of a diet lacking in nutrition. The grandmother's young age may be significant since the British media is highly critical of teenage pregnancies which are under the legal age. The distance to the grandmother's house is measured according to a BMX bike ride (bicycles used by some British teenagers), and the scenery is marred by 'the first' burnt-out litter bin (implying others), which sometimes result from youth vandalism.

The humour of this passage comes from its absurd incongruity, but it also makes a social comment. For those who understand the allusions, there is the possibility of schema recognition as they see aspects of Britain which they are familiar with, either in real life or through media portrayals.

Dystopian perspectives on gender and culture:
Cross-cultural schemata, political allegory, and schema refreshment

So far we have seen schema knowledge used for standard processing (examples 1a–d) and for various special effects (examples 2–6), but texts may also draw on schemata in ways which have the potential to radically change the way that a reader thinks. Political allegory is one type of text that may prompt schema refreshment for some readers. Margaret Atwood's *The Handmaid's Tale* is a story which might have this effect. The 'I-narrator' (unnamed at this point in the novel) lives in an alternative world in which she is kept as a sexual slave, denied access to literacy, and is required to wear a long red outfit which covers her body and a winged structure around the face. In example (7) she and her companion spot a group of tourists who are dressed quite differently.

(7) [The tourists] look around, bright-eyed, cocking their heads to one side like robins, their very cheerfulness aggressive, and I can't help staring. It's been a long time since I've seen skirts that short on women. The skirts reach just below the knee and the legs come out from beneath them, nearly naked in their thin stockings, blatant, the high-heeled shoes with their straps attached to the feet like delicate instruments of torture. The women teeter on their spiked feet as if on stilts, but off balance; their backs arch at the waist, thrusting the buttocks out. Their heads are uncovered and their hair too is exposed, in all its darkness and sexuality. They wear lipstick, red, outlining the dark cavities of their mouths, like scrawls on a washroom wall, of the time below.

I stop walking. Ofglen stops beside me and I know that she cannot take her eyes off these women. We are fascinated but also repelled. They seem undressed. It has taken so little time to change our minds, about things like this.

Then I think: I used to dress like that. That was freedom.

Westernized, they used to call it.

(Atwood 1996, pp. 38–39, Atwood's italics)

To understand this passage we need to use schema knowledge of Western female attire, which is defamiliarised through the focalization of the I-narrator's alternative perspective. The outfits as described (below-knee-length skirt, stockings, high heels and red lipstick) do not seem to be unusual or particularly revealing from a Western stance, but these clothes are viewed as shocking and laden with negative affect (e.g. 'aggressive,' 'naked,' 'blatant,' 'delicate instruments of torture,' 'repelled,' 'dark cavities,' 'scrawls,' 'undressed'). This episode is nevertheless somewhat ambivalent, providing a complex mix of perspectives which is typical of literary texts (e.g. 'fascinated but also repelled' and the positive affect in 'freedom'). Later in the episode (after this extract), Atwood defamiliarises further by focusing on how the I-narrator is 'mesmerized' by the women's feet, using basic sensory schemata to convey memories of the I-narrator's past life evoked by the smell of nail polish on the toenails, and the feel of the stockings and the shoes on the feet, plus a motor schema (relating to the process of applying the nail varnish) (p. 39).

The description in example (7) has particular resonance in this alternative text world (e.g. the theme of red (including the reference to robins), the mention of torture and the reference to low-level literacy in 'scrawls on a washroom wall'). Nevertheless, this text also has the potential to provide schema refreshment as a political allegory, and may offer readers insights into oppressive regimes where women are treated in this way (see, for example, Hammill 2005 for a discussion of possible real-life antecedents for this story).

Future directions

Schema theory is a core theory in stylistics since it has been used to explain a broad range of phenomena including the essential elements of text processing, genre distinctions, fictional world construction, and an extensive list of special effects including defamiliarisation. The main way that schema theory is likely to be used in the future in stylistics is in its continuing application to the analysis of specific texts, as illustrated in the examples above. In addition, there needs to be a more systematic study of the inter-relation between schemata and other types of knowledge, notably text-specific knowledge and personal knowledge. Stylisticians also have a significant opportunity to utilise current and future scientific findings, since brain imaging provides a key to understanding the neural mechanisms underlying how readers respond to expected and unexpected events. Such work also shows how general knowledge is used in the construction of fictional worlds, how specific effects are created (e.g. why incongruity may be both humorous and non-humorous on different occasions) and how sensory details activate our imaginations. Moreover, schema theory provides extremely productive ways of engaging with varying socio-cultural readings of texts, such as in studies of different genders and ethnic groups. Overall, schema theory has a significant history as a foundational topic in stylistics and promises a major contribution to our understanding of all texts, ranging from the most ordinary to the most extraordinary.

Related topics

Cognitive poetics, linguistic levels of foregrounding, narrative fiction, stylistics and real readers, stylistics, emotion and neuroscience, text world theory

Further reading

Cook, G., 1994. *Discourse and literature: The interplay of form and mind*. Oxford: Oxford University Press.

    This work is the key text on schema refreshment, an idea which has been particularly influential in discussions of literariness.

Sanford, A. J. and Emmott, C., 2012. *Mind, brain and narrative*. Cambridge: Cambridge University Press.

    This book discusses psychological work on inference-making and scenarios, plus relevant neuroscience work on counterfactual worlds and how readers respond to sensory, motor and emotional cues in texts.

Schank, R. C. and Abelson, R. P., 1977. *Scripts, plans, goals and understanding*. Hillsdale: Lawrence Erlbaum.

    This classic work is one of the key texts in the study of schema theory and hence it is indispensable for any study of this area.

Semino, E., 1997. *Language and world creation in poems and other texts*. London: Longman.

    This book gives a broad-ranging summary of key aspects of schema theory and its application in stylistics.

Stockwell, P., 2006. Schema theory: Stylistic applications. *In:* K. Brown, ed. *Encyclopedia of Language and Linguistics*, Volume 11, Oxford: Elsevier, 8–13.

    This encyclopaedia article offers a useful summary of schema theory's historical background and stylistic applications.

References

Adams, D., 1988. *Dirk Gently's holistic detective agency*. London: Pan.

Asboson, H.C. (a.k.a. Pilbeam, C.), 2008. Little Red Riding Hoodie. *In: The ASBO fairy tales*. London: Michael O'Mara Books.

Attardo, S. and Raskin, V., 1991. Script theory revis(it)ed: Joke similarity and joke representation model. *Humor: The International Journal of Humor Research*, 4 (3–4), 293–348.

Atwood, M., 1996. *The Handmaid's Tale*. London: Vintage.

Bartlett, F.C., 1932. *Remembering: A study in experimental and social psychology*. Cambridge: Cambridge University Press.

Black, J.B. and Wilensky, R., 1979. An evaluation of story grammars. *Cognitive Science*, 3 (2), 213–230.

Burke, M., 2011. *Literary reading, cognition and emotion: An exploration of the oceanic mind*. New York: Routledge.

Carrell, P. L. and Eisterhold, J. C., 1988. Schema theory and ESL pedagogy. *In:* P. L. Carrell, J. Devine and D. E. Eskey, eds. *Interactive approaches to second language reading*. Cambridge: Cambridge University Press, 73–92.

Christie, A., 1935. *Death in the clouds*. Glasgow: Fontana.

Cook, G., 1994. *Discourse and literature: The interplay of form and mind*. Oxford: Oxford University Press.

Corbett, J., 2006. Genre and genre analysis. *In:* K. Brown, ed. *Encyclopedia of Language and Linguistics*, Volume 5. Oxford: Elsevier, 26–32.

Coulson, S., 2001. *Semantic leaps*. Cambridge: Cambridge University Press.

Culpeper, J., 2001. *Language and characterisation: People in plays and other texts*. Harlow: Pearson.

Culpeper, J., 2009. Reflections on a cognitive stylistic approach to characterisation. *In:* G. Brône and J. Vandaele, eds. *Cognitive poetics: Goals, gains and gaps*. Berlin: Mouton de Gruyter, 125–159.

Danziger, N., 1997. *Danziger's Britain: A journey to the edge*. London: Flamingo.

Eco, U., 1984. *The role of the reader: Explorations in the semiotics of texts*. Bloomington: Indiana University Press.

Emmott, C., 1997. *Narrative comprehension: A discourse perspective*. Oxford: Oxford University Press.

Emmott, C., 2006. Reference: Stylistic aspects. *In:* K. Brown, ed. *Encyclopedia of Language and Linguistics*, Volume 10. Oxford: Elsevier, 441–450.

Emmott, C. and Alexander, M., 2010. Detective fiction, plot construction, and reader manipulation: Rhetorical control and cognitive misdirection in Agatha Christie's *Sparkling Cyanide*. *In:* D. McIntyre and B. Busse, eds. *Language and Style: In Honour of Mick Short*. Houndmills: Palgrave MacMillan, 328–346.

Emmott, C., Sanford, A.J. and Alexander, M., 2010. Scenarios, role assumptions, and character status: Readers' expectations and the manipulation of attention in narrative texts. *In:* F. Jannedis, R. Schneider and J. Eder, eds. *Characters in fictional worlds: Understanding imaginary beings in literature, film and other media*. Berlin: de Gruyter, 377–399.

Emmott, C., Sanford, A.J. and Smith, F., 2008. 'Then somebody appeared': Scenarios, character under-specification and narrative interest. Paper presented at the meeting of the Society for the Empirical Study of Literature and Media (IGEL), Memphis: University of Memphis.

Ermida, I., 2008. *The language of comic narratives: Humor construction in short stories*. Berlin: Mouton de Gruyter.

Ferguson, H. J. and Sanford, A. J., 2008. Anomalies in real and counterfactual worlds: An eye-movement investigation. *Journal of Memory and Language*, 58, 609–626.

Filik, R. and Leuthold, H., 2008. Processing local pragmatic anomalies in fictional Contexts: Evidence from the N400. *Psychophysiology*, 45 (4), 554–558.

Fludernik, M., 1996. *Towards a 'natural' narratology*. London: Routledge.

Fowler, R., 1996. *Linguistic criticism*. Oxford: Oxford University Press.

Gavins, J., 2007. *Text world theory: An introduction*. Edinburgh: Edinburgh University Press.

Halliday, M. A. K., 1971. Linguistic function and literary style: An inquiry into the language of William Golding's *The Inheritors*. *In:* S. Chatman, ed. *Literary style: A symposium*. New York: Oxford University Press, 330–365.

Hammill, F., 2005. Margaret Atwood: *The Handmaid's Tale. In:* D. Seed, ed. *A companion to science fiction.* London: Blackwell, 522–533.

Herman, D., 2002. *Story logic: Problems and possibilities of narrative,* Lincoln: University of Nebraska Press.

Hidalgo Downing, L., 2000. *Negation, text worlds, and discourse: The pragmatics of fiction.* Stamford: Ablex.

Hoey, M., 2001. *Textual interaction: An introduction to written discourse analysis.* London: Routledge.

Hühn, P., 2010. *Eventfulness in British fiction.* Berlin: de Gruyter.

Ingarden, R., [1931] 1973. *The literary work of art: An investigation on the borderlines of ontology, logic and theory of literature.* Evanston: Northwestern University Press.

Jeffries, L., 2001. Schema theory and white asparagus: Cultural multilingualism among readers of texts. *Language and Literature,* 10 (4), 325–343.

Koffka, K., 1935. *Principles of gestalt psychology.* London: Kegan Paul, Trench, Trubner.

Köhler, W., 1930. *Gestalt psychology.* London: Bell.

Kuzmičova, A., 2012. Presence in the reading of literary narrative: A case for motor enactment. *Semiotica,* 189 (1/4), 23–48.

Lang, A., 2009. Reading race in *Small Island*: Discourse deviation, schemata and the textual encounter. *Language and Literature,* 18 (3), 316–330.

László, J., 1999. *Cognition and representation in literature: The psychology of literary narratives.* Budapest: Akadémiai Kiadó.

László, J., 2008. *The science of stories: An introduction to narrative psychology.* Hove: Routledge.

Leech, G. and Short, M., [1981] 2007. *Style in fiction: A linguistic introduction to English fictional prose.* London: Longman.

Mandler, J. M., 1984. *Scripts, stories and scenes: Aspects of schema theory.* Hillsdale: Lawrence Erlbaum.

Mandler, J. M. and Johnson, N. S., 1977. Remembrance of things parsed: Story structure and recall. *Cognitive Psychology,* 9, 111–151.

Marszalek, A., 2013. 'It's not funny out of context!': A cognitive stylistic approach to humorous narratives. *In:* M. Dynel, ed. *Developments in linguistic humour theory.* Amsterdam: Benjamins, 393–421.

McIntyre, D. and Culpeper, J., 2010. Activity types, incongruity and humour in dramatic discourse. *In:* D. McIntyre and B. Busse, eds. *Language and Style.* Basingstoke: Palgrave Macmillan, 204–222.

Miall, D., 1989. Beyond the schema given: Affective comprehension of literary narratives. *Cognition and Emotion,* 3 (1), 55–78.

Mills, S., 1995. *Feminist stylistics.* London: Routledge.

Minsky, M., 1975. A framework for representing knowledge. *In:* P. H. Winston, ed. *The psychology of computer vision.* New York: McGraw-Hill, 211–277.

Montoro, R., 2007. Stylistics of cappuccino fiction: A socio-cognitive perspective. *In:* M. Lambrou and P. Stockwell, eds. *Contemporary stylistics.* London: Continuum, 68–80.

Nieuwland, M.S. and van Berkum, J.J.A., 2006. When peanuts fall in love: N400 evidence for the power of discourse. *Journal of Cognitive Neuroscience,* 18, 1098–1111.

Niffenegger, A., 2005. *The time traveler's wife.* London: Vintage.

Palmer, A., 2004. *Fictional minds.* Lincoln: Nebraska University Press.

Piaget, J., [1925] 1960. *The language and thought of the child.* London: Routledge.

Pickering, M., 2001. *Stereotyping: The politics of representation.* Houndmills: Palgrave.

Rankin, I., 2000. *The hanging garden.* London: Orion.

Raskin, V., 1985. *Semantic mechanisms of humor.* Dordrecht: D. Reidel Publishing.

Rumelhart, D.E., 1975. Notes on a schema for stories. *In:* D. G. Bobrow and A. Collins, eds. *Representation and understanding: Studies in cognitive science.* New York: Academic Press, 211–236.

Rumelhart, D.E., 1980. Schemata: The building blocks of cognition. *In:* R. Spiro, B. Bruce and W. Brewer, eds. *Theoretical issues in reading comprehension.* Hillsdale: Lawrence Erlbaum, 33–58.

Rumelhart, D.E. and Norman, D.A., 1978. Accretion, tuning and restructuring: Three modes of learning. *In:* J.W. Cotton and R. Klatzky, eds. *Semantic factors in cognition.* Hillsdale: Lawrence Erlbaum, 37–53.

Ryan, M.-L., 1991. *Possible worlds, Artificial intelligence and narrative theory.* Bloomington: Indiana University Press.

Sanford, A. J. and Emmott, C., 2012. *Mind, brain and narrative.* Cambridge: Cambridge University Press.

Sanford, A. J. and Garrod, S. C., 1981. *Understanding written language: Explorations in comprehension beyond the sentence*. Chichester: Wiley.

Sanford, A. J. and Garrod, S. C., 1998. The role of scenario mapping in text comprehension. *Discourse Processes*, 26, 159–190.

Schank, R. C., 1982. *Dynamic memory: A theory of reminding and learning*. Cambridge: Cambridge University Press.

Schank, R. C. and Abelson, R. P., 1977. *Scripts, plans, goals and understanding*. Hillsdale: Lawrence Erlbaum.

Schweinitz, J., 2010. Stereotypes and the narratological analysis of film characters. *In:* J. Eder, F. Jannidis and R. Schneider, eds. *Characters in fictional worlds: Understanding imaginary beings in literature, film and other media*. Berlin: de Gruyter, 276–289.

Semino, E., 1997. *Language and world creation in poems and other texts*. London: Longman.

Semino, E., 2006. Mind style. *In:* K. Brown, ed. *Encyclopedia of Language and Linguistics*, Volume 10, Oxford: Elsevier, 142–148.

Shriver, L., 2008. *The post-birthday world*. London: Harper.

Simpson, P., 2003. *On the discourse of satire*. Amsterdam: John Benjamins.

Stockwell, P., 2003. Schema poetics and speculative cosmology. *Language and Literature*, 12 (3), 252–271.

Stockwell, P., 2010. The eleventh checksheet of the Apocalypse. *In:* D. McIntyre and B. Busse, eds. *Language and Style*. Basingstoke: Palgrave Macmillan, 419–432.

Swann, J. and Allington, D., eds. 2009. *Literary reading as a social practice*. Special issue of *Language and Literature*, 18 (3).

Toolan, M., 1990. *The stylistics of fiction: A literary linguistic approach*. London: Routledge.

van Dijk, T. A., 1998. *Ideology: A multidisciplinary approach*. London: Sage.

Werth, P., 1999. *Text worlds: Representing conceptual space in discourse*. London: Longman.

17

Stylistics and text world theory

Ernestine Lahey

Introduction

Text world theory is a cognitive linguistic theory of discourse processing proposed in its initial form by Paul Werth (Werth 1995a, Werth 1995b, Werth 1999). The foundations of the theory were first set out in a series of articles published during the 1980s and 1990s. Werth's work on the theory was cut short by his death in 1995. However, Werth was nearing completion of a manuscript for a monograph on text world theory at the time of his death, and this manuscript was seen to be of such significance to the scholarly community that the work of preparing it for publication was taken on by Werth's colleague and fellow linguist Mick Short (Gavins 2007, Werth 1999, pp. viii–ix). The monograph, posthumously published in 1999 under the title *Text Worlds: Representing Conceptual Space in Discourse*, contains Werth's fullest explication of his text world theory (Werth 1999).

Since the publication of *Text Worlds*, text world theory (hereafter TWT) has enjoyed a sustained level of attention, scrutiny, and development thanks to the work of other scholars (see for instance Gavins 2007, Gibbons 2011, Hidalgo-Downing 2000, Lahey 2006, Semino 2010, Whiteley 2010). The interest that TWT has generated over the past two decades has not only ensured the survival of the theory following the loss of its creator, but has furthermore seen TWT become a canonical stylistic-analytical framework, especially under the rubrics of 'cognitive stylistics' or 'cognitive poetics' (which, in line with most other stylisticians, I treat here as largely overlapping if not wholly synonymous terms; see e.g. Nørgaard *et al.* 2010, Semino and Culpeper 2002. See also Chapter 19 in this volume for more on this). The extent to which TWT has become integrated within the standard (cognitive-)stylistic 'toolkit' is demonstrated by its inclusion in several recent collections providing overviews of the field (Brône and Vandaele 2009, Lambrou and Stockwell 2007, McIntyre and Busse 2010).

Historical perspectives

Three main strands of influence can be traced in the early development of TWT. The first of these is Werth's dissatisfaction with mainstream generative linguistics. Most closely associated with the early work of Noam Chomsky, the generative approach dominated the field during the latter half of the twentieth century to the extent that 'linguistics' was often regarded as synonymous with the Chomskyan generative programme (Chomsky 1964, Chomsky 1965, Kenneally 2007, Trask and Stockwell 2007, p. 157). However, like many of his contemporaries in cognitive linguistics, Werth would eventually become dissatisfied with generative linguistics' objectivist stance and its attendant neglect of the subjective and experiential aspects of language use (Werth 1999, p. 20).

The ultimate aim of generativist grammars is to establish 'rules' which can account for and/or generate an increasingly wide range of 'well-formed' sentences, the sentence being the linguistic unit which comprises the starting point for generativist analysis (Chomsky 1964, p. 13). This focus on the abstract sentence level is completely consistent with the discipline's rejection of context since a sentence is essentially a context-less utterance, an utterance being the 'real' unit of naturally-occurring language to which the abstracted sentence typically corresponds (Werth 1999, p. 1). However, Werth (1999) echoes the thinking of many of his contemporaries when he proposes: '[l]et us assume that it is preferable to derive theoretical units from phenomena which actually *occur* (or, at least, which we *perceive* as occurring)' (Werth 1999, p. 1, emphasis in original).

Werth's assumption that it is preferable to derive theoretical units from naturally-occurring phenomena is central to his cognitive discourse grammar. He opens his (1999) monograph with the following:

> A **text** is to a **sentence** as a **discourse** is to an **utterance**. That is to say, a text, like a sentence, is somewhat of an abstraction which is made for the purposes of analysis. What it is abstracted from is its **context**.
>
> *(Werth 1999, p. 1, emphasis in original)*

For Werth, the starting point for linguistic analyses should not be the sentence or the text, but the *discourse*. A discourse will always have text as one of its components, but a complete picture of discourse must include some understanding of the context in which that text is produced and received. Context is, of course, a notoriously difficult and complex phenomenon to try to investigate, a fact acknowledged by Werth. However, Werth asserts that we cannot afford to ignore context if we claim to be interested in a 'more human' linguistics, one which treats language as a non-autonomous component of human experience (Werth 1999, pp. 3–7, 19).

The second strand of influence on TWT comes from the possible worlds theories of modal logic associated with the work of Saul Kripke, David Lewis, and Nicholas Rescher and ultimately derived from the eighteenth-century theological philosophy of Gottfried Willhelm Leibniz (Kripke 1972, Lewis 1986, Liebniz 1985, Rescher 1975). Possible worlds theories have proved useful in solving certain long-standing philosophical problems relating to truth and reference. From the point of view of linguistics, they have served as a corrective to certain limitations with truth-conditional models of semantics, such as that proposed by Davidson (1984) (for an overview see Lycan 2000).

Truth-conditional semantics assumes that the meaning of any given sentence is exactly equivalent to that sentence's truth value. This perspective on linguistic meaning is problematic for a number of reasons, not least because it fails to account for the full range of sentences that any ordinary language user would be likely to identify as meaningful. The much-cited example 'the present King of France is bald' demonstrates this point. This proposition cannot be said to be true or false in the actual world since there is no present King of France in the actual world (Gavins 2001, p. 22, Russell 1905). Possible worlds semantics solves this problem by specifying that the sentence refers into an unactualised possible world in which there exists a present King of France who may or may not be bald. The advantage of a possible worlds approach, then, is that it provides a framework by which we may talk about the various ways in which things might have been otherwise, a capacity that is not found in traditional logic (Lewis 1986, pp. 1–3).

While TWT borrows some of its basic architecture from possible worlds theories – most notably, the concept of a 'world' as a representation of a particular state of affairs – it departs from these theories considerably in its own treatment of meaning. As an experientialist, usage-based approach in which linguistic meaning is derived in part from extra-linguistic local and cognitive contexts, TWT assumes a rich but highly indeterminate structure for the worlds resulting from any particular use of language. Possible worlds, by contrast, are rigidly specified, minimalistic worlds, which contain only as much information as is needed to solve the particular logical problem for which the worlds have been constructed, and nothing more. In the case of the proposition 'the present King of France is bald', for instance, the possible world that is constructed to solve this logical paradox contains only the knowledge that there exists a King of France and that he either is or is not bald. Any contextual information that might be relevant – a hearer's attitude toward monarchies or his or her knowledge of French history, for instance – is not accounted for in the possible worlds approach.

Werth argues that possible worlds theories' lack of sensitivity to context means that possible worlds are both over-specific (because they are tailor-made in response to a single proposition) and underspecified (because they lack the complexity of anything language users would recognise as a world) (Werth 1999, p. 70). For Werth, possible worlds theories are insufficient to account for language in use because what is needed for such an account is not a world that is defined by what it *must minimally contain* in order for some logical equation to come out right, but a world which is defined by what it *might potentially contain* taking into account all the possible textual and contextual variables which impinge upon its construction.

In spite of the limitations which Werth identifies with the possible worlds approach, possible worlds theories have nevertheless been adapted by a number of other scholars who have found the notion fruitful, particularly for analyses of literary texts (Bell 2010, Doležel 1998, Maître 1983, Pavel 1975, Ronen 1994, Ryan 1991, Semino 1997). Of these, the most influential has been a possible-worlds-based theory of narrative proposed by Ryan (1991). While there are a great many similarities between Ryan's possible worlds approach and TWT, Ryan's approach differs from text world theory primarily in that the former is not explicitly cognitive-experientialist. While Ryan acknowledges a debt to cognitive psychology, mainly because of what she borrows from research in artificial intelligence, and, in her later work, from the research of Richard Gerrig (Gerrig 1993), the philosophical underpinnings of Ryan's work are more closely tied to a post-structuralist American literary critical tradition than to the cognitive experientialism of either the European or the American schools of cognitive linguistics and poetics (Stockwell 2006, Stockwell 2008, p. 591). While Werth takes issue with certain well-established principles of the cognitive linguistics enterprise (see for instance his critique of the theory of conceptual metaphor popularised by Lakoff and colleagues), his theory remains firmly grounded in the same foundational assumptions (Lakoff and Johnson 1980, Lakoff and Turner 1989, Werth 1999, p. 317).

The differences in lineage and alignment between possible worlds theories like Ryan's possible worlds approach and Werth's TWT are not without importance in terms of what these differences mean for the perceived relevance of the research programmes which employ the two theories. At a time when increasing pressure is being exerted within academia to produce research which is seen to be relevant to a wider non-academic community, the 'cognitive turn' that has taken place within the humanities and social sciences has been instrumental in triggering a shift away from literary critical approaches which have often tended to produce yet more (and increasingly abstruse) readings of 'classic' (often Anglo-European, male-authored) texts (Gavins and Steen 2003b, Stockwell 2009, p. 11, Whiteley 2011a). Within stylistics, the move toward usage-based analytical approaches is just the most recent in a continued democratisation of literary study already evident in the discipline's valuing of 'popular' texts on a level with canonical literature (Carter and Stockwell 2008, p. 300).

The third and final major influence on the development of TWT has been alluded to in the course of the preceding discussion and concerns developments in the sub-discipline of linguistics known as cognitive linguistics. As noted above, TWT, while departing in a number of ways from the cognitive linguistics that was contemporaneous with its development, is nevertheless strongly grounded in the basic principles of cognitive linguistics. This is not only evident in Werth's explicit commitment to a usage-based, cognitivist-experientialist viewpoint; it is also apparent in TWT's adoption of a wide variety of mechanisms from other cognitive theories including schema theory (Schank and Abelson 1977), mental spaces theory (Fauconnier 1994), frame semantics (Fillmore 1982), conceptual metaphor theory (Lakoff and Johnson 1980, Lakoff and Turner 1989), and prototype theory (Lakoff 1987, Rosch 1978), to name but a handful. While these theories have been applied independently in text analysis, often to good effect, TWT has an advantage over an independent application of any of these other theories because it incorporates the central insights from each into its own architecture. TWT therefore has more explanatory power for the discourse stylistician, who must address all of the cognitive processes described by the above theories.

Text world theory basics

The basic premise of TWT is that whenever we participate in a discourse (defined simply as a combination of a text and its relevant context) we build up a networked configuration of conceptual spaces or 'worlds' which correspond to distinct ontological layers of the discourse. The 'outside' or macro-level of this layered configuration is known as the 'discourse world' and it is a representation of the immediate context in which the discourse takes place. As a conceptualisation of the discourse context, the discourse world necessarily contains at least two discourse participants and a naturally-occurring language event (i.e. discourse). It also contains everything that is perceivable by the discourse participants in their immediate surroundings, as well as the full range of cognitive resources – attitudes, emotions, knowledge, experiences, hopes, beliefs, expectations etc. – that humans have at their disposal and which discourse participants are assumed to bring to and activate during the discourse process (Werth 1999, p. 85).

The presence of participants in the discourse situation is not just important, but mandatory. The discourse world constitutes a type of situation, which Werth defines as a particular kind of state of affairs holding in a particular location (l) and at a particular time (t), containing various entities, including at least one sentient entity (i.e. a human being) and the various interrelationships between these (Werth 1999, pp. 80–84). For Werth, a situation cannot exist without some conceptualisation of it as such – i.e. a situation must be conceived, with 'conceived' here including directly perceived, remembered, or imagined (Werth 1999, pp. 83–84). Werth's experientialist understanding of what constitutes a situation is in contrast to the view of situations espoused by possible worlds semantics, which allows for situations which do not necessarily contain sentient entities but which may instead be 'mere collections of entities at a certain place and time' (Werth 1995a, 50; Werth 1999, p. 83).

For Werth, the prototypical (i.e. the most basic and most frequent) language event-type is face-to-face conversation, in which the discourse world represents the 'here and now' of the discourse participants (Werth 1999, p. 85, Werth 1995a, p. 51). Participants in face-to-face conversations, because they share the same spatio-temporal context, may make direct reference to mutually perceivable entities or events in their discourse world; indeed, the discourse that happens in the discourse world of face-to-face conversation may even be *about* the discourse world, or something in it. More usually, however, even in face-to-face interactions, the discourse will represent a state of affairs which is remote in some way from the 'here and now' context of the discourse world (Werth 1999, p. 86).

By contrast to the discourse worlds of spoken communication, the discourse worlds of written communication are typically 'split'. This is because in the vast majority of cases the time and place in which a text is read is different to the time and place in which it was written. For Werth, since writers and readers typically do not have access to a shared spatio-temporal context, the immediate situations of writing and reading will be less important to the discourse process than the shared cultural assumptions, general knowledge and other shared cognitive contexts that surround and inform the discourse (Werth 1995a, p. 55).

In line with Werth's treatment of face-to-face conversation as the default discourse model, he borrows two key notions from pragmatics. The first is the concept of 'negotiation' (manifested in face-to-face communication as conversational turn-taking, for example), which Werth extends to all types of discourse including written discourses (Werth 1999, pp. 85, 103). For Werth, participants enter into a discourse with a certain amount of knowledge, 'the propositions constituting his/her knowledge base', only some of which will be relevant to the current discourse (Werth 1999, p. 47). However, traditionally there has been a problem of understanding how discourse participants go about determining *which* propositions will be relevant since the knowledge of any individual is too vast for all of it to be deployed each time a person participates in a discourse (Werth 1999, p. 103). In answer to this problem Werth suggests that the discourse process is *text-driven*, which is to say that language input determines exactly which areas of knowledge will be retrieved by the recipient (Werth 1999, p. 103).

'Negotiation' as it is used in TWT, then, refers in part to the text-driven process through which only relevant areas of knowledge become activated in discourse, as prompted by the mechanism of the text. The text facilitates the negotiation of discourse in written communication by acting as a guide for the conceptualisations built up in the minds of the spatio-temporally displaced writer and reader. Thus, although the process of negotiation that takes place during written communication may be more hidden and private than the turn-taking of face-to-face conversation, written communication is treated in TWT as no less a joint endeavour (Werth 1999, p. 48).

Werth also borrows from work in pragmatics the idea that communication is regulated by a set of discourse 'meta-principles', similar to the well-known maxims for communication proposed by Grice (1975). Werth argues that we normally expect discourses to be: (1) communicative (informative, purposeful and efficient); (2) coherent (consisting of propositions which are relevant and non-superfluous); and (3) cooperative (the participants in the discourse adhere to the first two principles and are responsible and authoritative) (Werth 1999, pp. 49–50). Therefore, 'negotiation' in TWT concerns not only the text-driven mechanism through which knowledge is prompted and retrieved, as described above; it also subsumes the assumptions of purposefulness which underlie our interactions in discourse.

The discourse that takes place in a discourse world prompts the construction of the next layer in the TWT system – the text world. The text world is a conceptualisation of the 'story' of the discourse, or what the discourse is about. In the prototypical case of spoken conversation the text world represents the topic of conversation. As noted above, the process of text world construction is text-driven, meaning that the textual portion of a discourse guides the establishment and ongoing elaboration of the resulting text world.

The text contributes two distinct types of information which direct the construction of the text world. First, the text establishes the *situational variables* of the text world: its time, place, entities (characters and objects) and certain entity properties and relationships. Such deictic and referential information is known as 'world-building' because it provides the basic scaffolding of the situation against which the events of the discourse unfold. Werth notes that 'in normal cases', where the text world represents a situation distinct from the discourse situation, the situational variables mentioned above are set out explicitly by the text at the beginning of a new discourse, 'though in the case of time, this may simply be by means of the tense used' (Werth 1999, p. 187).

The second type of textual information which informs the ongoing construction of the text world comes via what are known as function-advancing propositions. Function-advancing propositions are those propositions which fulfil the function (i.e. aim) of the discourse as determined by the discourse's register-type (e.g. narrative: advance the plot; discursive: argue a point, etc.) (Werth 1995, p. 59). Function-advancing propositions therefore represent the foreground of the text world, serving to propel the plot (the description, the argument and so forth) of the discourse forward. There are two types of function-advancers: path expressions and modifications. Path-expressions encompass actions or processes, while modifications include states, circumstances and metonymies (Werth 1999, pp. 197–199).

The third and final level of discourse proposed by Werth is the sub-world. Sub-worlds originate from within the text world and represent some kind of perceived shift away from the parameters of the text world. These shifts may be prompted by the discourse participants or by characters in the text world, and according to Werth (1999) they may be of three types: deictic (representing some spatial or temporal shift, as in the case of flashbacks, for instance), attitudinal (prompted by expressions of desire, belief or intention), or epistemic (prompted by expressions of modality) (Werth 1999, pp. 210–258).

Following Gavins' (Gavins 2001, Gavins 2007) modifications to the sub-world level of the TWT framework, intended to bring Werth's treatment of epistemic contexts in line with accepted theories of modality (e.g. Simpson 1993), most theorists have now dispensed with Werth's terminology, preferring to distinguish between two broad categories of world: *world-switches* (subsuming spatial, temporal, and spatio-temporal shifts) and *modal worlds* (accommodating deontic, boulomaic and epistemic modal contexts) (see Gavins 2007). For ease of reference I will nevertheless continue to employ the term 'sub-worlds' as a general label for these types of worlds throughout what follows.

Sub-worlds, according to Werth, have different 'privileges of access' associated with them, this privilege of access being determined by who is responsible for creating the sub-world. While the text world for any discourse can only be created by discourse participants, sub-worlds differ in this respect, since sub-world creation can also be cued by characters in a text world. Werth therefore refers to the sub-worlds built by participants and characters as participant- and character-accessible sub-worlds respectively.

Participant-accessible sub-worlds, as the term suggests, are associated with privilege of access for participants. 'Accessibility' here refers to the reliability a recipient may give to the content of a speaker's propositions (Werth 1995a, p. 61). Participants, says Werth, are bound by principles of cooperativeness, coherence and communicativeness (see above), such that co-participants will be expected to place a high degree of confidence in the truth of each other's contributions. Following from the assumption that the propositions of participants in a discourse are reliable is the assumption that any sub-worlds resulting from those propositions are likewise reliable (i.e. 'accessible').

However, characters in a text world, while they are treated by TWT as fully psychologised (i.e. they are assumed to have the same cognitive capacities as 'real' people), are nevertheless constructs born of the discourse. They therefore do not come to the discourse with the same wilfulness as discourse participants, and they are therefore not bound by the same discourse principles (Gavins 2007, p. 76). This makes it impossible for participants to verify the truth of propositions expressed by characters. Therefore, any character-initiated sub-worlds are deemed inaccessible from the participant perspective. The issue of accessibility is just one of a number of aspects of TWT to have undergone modification in later scholars' work with TWT. We will therefore return to the issue of accessibility below, where these developments as well as current trends in TWT scholarship will be considered.

Developments and current research

Since the publication of *Text Worlds*, further work with TWT has led to a number of augmentations to the parameters of the framework as first set out by Werth. While Werth claimed that TWT was capable of accounting for all discourse types, his own analyses using the theory were heavily focused on nineteenth- and early twentieth-century realist narrative fiction. As such, some of the earliest developments to TWT were the result of attempts to test the boundaries of the theory against other discourse types.

Joanna Gavins' work on TWT and absurdist fiction has led to a number of important changes to the theory which have subsequently been adopted by most TWT scholars. First, as noted above, Gavins (2001, 2007) brings TWT's treatment of modality in line with current thinking by disposing of Werth's distinction between attitudinal and epistemic sub-worlds. In Gavins' alternative approach, all modalised expressions, including those signalling want-, belief- and desire-class contexts (classified by Werth as attitudinal worlds, as distinct from epistemic worlds) fall under her new 'modal world' category.

Related to this, and as also alluded to in the preceding discussion, Gavins also drops the 'sub' prefix when referring to the sub-world level of the system, since she argues that the prefix suggests a subsidiary relationship which does not always hold. In many discourses the sub-world level may turn out to be more important for the discourse than the text world level. Where fixed focalization occurs in narrative, for instance, the events of the narrative are filtered through the stable viewing point of a single character. The resulting world – because it is a product of a character's mind – would be treated by Werth as a sub-world despite the fact that it is the only world which continues to be updated throughout the discourse, the text world having been relegated to the status of an 'empty' background element (Gavins 2007, pp. 133–134, Lahey 2004, p. 26).

A number of further changes to TWT have been made by Gavins in response to insights from other scholars. For instance, Gavins' use of the term 'enactors' (which she borrows from the work of Catherine Emmott) is a response to interest in readerly immersion as explained in terms of cross-world projection and self-implication (Emmott 1997, pp. 180–181, Kuiken *et al.* 2004, Lahey 2005). The notion of 'world-repair', also proposed by Emmott, is also incorporated into TWT by Gavins as a means of accounting for situations in which readers are forced to go back to a previously constructed world and modify it in the light of new information (e.g. we find out at the end of a book that our narrator has been dead since the start of the narrative) (Emmott 1997, Gavins 2007). Finally, Gavins has also suggested ways in which conceptual integration theory (or 'blending theory') might be integrated into TWT (Fauconnier and Turner 2002, Gavins 2007).

To date, Gavins has provided the most extensive augmentation to TWT. However, the work of several other scholars has also contributed to the ongoing development of Werth's framework. Lahey's contributions to the development of the theory have been alluded to above and include: early work on self-implication and emotion, including the introduction of the concept of the 'empty' text world; an extended explication of certain problems with Werth's treatment of world-building and function-advancing propositions; and an account of the role of megametaphor in the representation of cultural identity in literature (Lahey 2004, Lahey 2006, Lahey 2007). An article by Cruickshank and Lahey is also the first of its kind in suggesting how TWT can be adjusted to account for drama and performance (Cruickshank and Lahey 2010).

Further work on TWT and forms of self-implication and emotion has also been done by Peter Stockwell and Sara Whiteley (Stockwell 2009, Whiteley 2011b). Whiteley's work is particularly notable for its use of feedback from real readers in a reading group environment. Stockwell's work also relies on input from real readers, albeit less heavily and in a less structured way; his (2009) monograph *Texture* makes occasional use of commentary provided by readers on book-related internet forums (Stockwell 2009, see e.g. p. 80). Both of these attempts to integrate the feedback of real readers into the TWT framework reveal the extent to which the boundaries and uses of TWT are currently being reinterpreted in light of current trends in the field of cognitive stylistics/poetics.

A focus on the experiences of ordinary non-professional readers (i.e. readers with little or no academic training in literary reading or text analysis) is a growing trend in cognitive stylistics (see also Chapter 27 in this volume). While there are debates about the way in which reader responses should be collected, with some scholars preferring an experimental approach (see e.g. Miall 2006) and others a sociolinguistic-interactional approach (usually employing reading groups) (Swann and Allington 2009, Whiteley 2010, Whiteley 2011a), many agree that a move toward studying the responses of real readers is an essential step forward in any account of literary reading (Gavins and Steen 2003a, Miall 2006, Stockwell 2005). While many distinct problems are raised by analyses which incorporate reader feedback, a fact generally acknowledged by those who choose reader-response methodologies (see e.g. Whiteley's discussion of the limitations of working with real readers in her 2010 unpublished PhD thesis), it is probably true that much future development in TWT will reflect the growing interest in cognitivist reader-response-type research.

Another recent trend in cognitive stylistics which has made its mark in TWT research concerns analyses of multimodal discourses. Recent interest in multimodality has not only resulted in the application of TWT to new discourse types, such as film, but also in proposed changes to TWT architecture (Gibbons 2011, Montoro 2006). Alison Gibbons' work on multimodal experimental literature has led her to suggest the addition of a new world type to the TWT system which she calls a 'figured trans-world'. This new world type is proposed in order to account for texts which demand that their readers enact some kind of performative engagement with a text at the discourse world level; in the texts Gibbons discusses, this performative engagement emulates corresponding actions in the text world (e.g. books which must be rotated in order that the text may be read, mimicking a character's manoeuvring of an object at the text world level) (Gibbons 2011). (For more on the topics of multimodality and film, see Chapters 28 and 29 in this volume).

While Gibbons' focus in her monograph is on experimental multimodal texts, this work could easily be extended to account for the multimodal and more broadly paratextual aspects of *all* written discourses, including more traditional forms (Genette 1997). As I have argued elsewhere, one of the drawbacks of current TWT is that its principle of 'text-drivenness' – in many ways one of the theory's great strengths (because it enables rigorous, replicable, and retrievable 'steam stylistic' analyses; see e.g. Gavins and Stockwell 2012, p. 40) – means that the theory has more trouble accounting for multimodal texts than some alternative theories which rely less on textual input (such as conceptual integration theory) (Lahey 2012). This is a problem for a theory of discourse, and one that requires attention in future TWT work.

Recommendations for practice

TWT is intended as a practical tool in the analysis of discourses. Therefore the best way to develop an understanding of how the theory works is to apply it in analysis. This section provides two recommendations regarding the application of TWT in analysis. The first is a general recommendation regarding the usefulness of diagramming in TWT analysis. The second is a recommendation for the analysis of a specific text, intended to guide the beginning student of TWT in a practice application of the theory.

General

TWT conventionally employs a set of diagrams for the representation of the various worlds that can be constructed (for examples of this see Gavins 2007). One method that can be helpful to beginning students of TWT is to sketch out the world structure of the texts under analysis using these diagrams. Doing this will result in a concrete visual overview of the types of worlds evoked by a text, as well as a 'map' through which the origins of each world – and the relationships between worlds – can be traced. Such a map can be helpful in the analysis of characterisation for instance, since the diagrams will clearly indicate the type and arrangement of worlds associated with different characters in the text.

Suggestions for practice analysis

Below is a short extract from *Angels and Demons* by the American novelist Dan Brown. Read the extract and complete the suggestions for analysis which follow.

> His stomach dropping, Langdon gazed farther into the distance. His eyes found the crumbling ruins of the Roman Coliseum. The Coliseum, Langdon had always thought, was one of history's greatest ironies. Now a dignified symbol for the rise of human culture and civilization, the stadium had been built to host centuries of barbaric events – hungry lions shredding prisoners, armies of slaves battling to the death, gang rapes of exotic women captured from far-off lands, as well as public beheadings and castrations. It was ironic, Langdon thought, or perhaps fitting, that the Coliseum had served as the architectural blueprint for Harvard's Soldier Field – the football stadium where the ancient traditions of savagery were reenacted every fall ... crazed fans screaming for bloodshed as Harvard battled Yale.
>
> *(Brown 2000, pp. 142–143)*

- This extract is a description of Rome's Coliseum, as focalized through the mind of the novel's protagonist, Robert Langdon. The extract prompts the construction of a number of participant-accessible epistemic modal sub-worlds which are attributed to Langdon. These epistemic sub-worlds contain details about the history of the Coliseum. Consider why these details have been provided in this way. What does this strategy contribute to our understanding of Langdon's character?

- The extract also prompts a number of *embedded* sub-worlds: sub-worlds which originate not from within the main text world, but from within an already existing sub-world. Draw a diagram which shows these embedded worlds and their relation to other worlds in the discourse, and notice the physical distance between these embedded worlds and the main text world. What is the effect of this embedding on your interpretation of the text?
- Werth defines descriptive texts as those which 'characterise a static scene' (Werth 1999, p. 180). To what extent does your analysis of the above extract support this definition?

Future directions

A few directions for future TWT work have already been alluded to in the preceding discussion. These include continued efforts to combine TWT with reader-response type methodologies, as well as extensions to the theory which increase its capability for dealing with multimodal texts and for paratextual phenomena generally. In addition to these, a number of additional concerns merit attention in future applications of the theory.

To date the vast majority of TWT scholarship has focused on examining the products of discourse at the text- and sub-world levels. The result is that while we know a great deal about the kinds of text- and sub-worlds that result from certain types of discourse, we know comparatively little about the nature of the discourse worlds which surround them and how these might also be influenced by our engagements in discourse. How might participant knowledge be not only *activated* in world-building, but also *accreted* through it, for instance? In what other ways might the cognitive resources of participants be modified via the upward influence of text- and sub-worlds on the discourse world cognitive environments that give rise to them?

One important area of future development for TWT, then, concerns a shift in focus away from examining how text worlds unfold in discourse to considering how elements in the discourse world – and in particular the cognitive resources of discourse participants – are themselves changed by the process of world-building that takes place within them. Cognitive psychologists have already begun to attend to the question of how literary reading influences human cognition (Kuiken *et al.* 2004, Oatley 2011). In keeping with TWT's tradition of drawing on such insights from the cognitive sciences, a consideration of how this research pertains to TWT is a priority for future work. A beginning has already been made by Stockwell, whose cognitive theory of literary aesthetics uses TWT to account for the ethical positioning of authors and readers. Stockwell's work suggests how analyses of literary texts have the potential to shed light on the ethical perspectives of those who engage with them and thus to reveal something not only about the worlds which result from such discourses, but also about the minds that create them (Stockwell 2009).

Another area where more work remains to be done is in treatments of drama and performance. To date, only one explication of how TWT might be adapted to a drama and performance context has been published (Cruickshank and Lahey 2010). However, this study focused primarily on the processing of stage directions versus dialogue in dramatic play-texts; it did not account for performance. Further work is therefore needed to equip TWT with the mechanisms needed to account for the performative context(s) of dramatic play-texts, an area which has often been neglected in stylistic accounts of drama generally (McIntyre 2006, Short 1981, Short 1988; Short 1989).

A final area of potentially very fruitful development for TWT would be in the devising of a 'pedagogical text world theory'. TWT is particularly good at making evident the distinct ontological layers in discourse, as well schematising, through the use of a series of conventionalised diagrams (see Werth 1999 and Gavins 2007), the distance between the various worlds in a discourse. This ability makes TWT a potentially excellent tool for teaching students of stylistics about the discourse structures of poetry, prose and drama, and for comparing the discourse structures of different individual discourses (Giovanelli 2010). As such TWT would make a good supplement to models of discourse structure provided in existing stylistics textbooks.

Further reading

Werth, P., 1999. *Text worlds: Representing conceptual space in discourse*. London: Longman.

> This monograph (unfortunately no longer in print) provides the most complete account of Werthian TWT.

Gavins, J., 2007b. *Text world theory: An introduction*. Edinburgh University Press.

> Gavins' introductory textbook provides a good overview of TWT's basic principles, including augmentations made following the publication of Werth's *Text Worlds*, but its status as a textbook means that it lacks the depth that more advanced undergraduate and postgraduate students would be likely to require.

Gavins, J., *Text World Theory*, http://www.textworldtheory.net/Welcome.html, last accessed July 10, 2012.

> In addition to her scholarly research on TWT, Joanna Gavins is also founder of the text world theory website and the director of a text world theory special collection housed at the University of Sheffield (more information about this is available via the above website). A downloadable bibliography of items in the collection is available in the 'special collection' section of the website.

Related topics

Blending, cognitive poetics, multimodality, point of view and modality, stylistics and real readers, stylistics, emotion and neuroscience.

References

Bell, A., 2010. *The possible worlds of hypertext fiction*. Basingstoke: Palgrave Macmillan.
Brône, G. and Vandaele, J., 2009. *Cognitive poetics: Goals, gains and gaps*. Berlin and New York: Mouton de Gruyter.
Brown, D., 2000. *Angels and demons*. London: Corgi.
Carter, R. and Stockwell, P., 2008. Stylistics: Retrospect and prospect. *In:* R. Carter and P. Stockwell, eds. *The language and literature reader*. London and New York: Routledge, 291–302.
Chomsky, N., 1964. *Syntactic structures*. The Hague: Mouton.
Chomsky, N., 1965. *Aspects of the theory of syntax*. Cambridge, Massachusetts: The MIT Press.
Cruickshank, T. and Lahey, E., 2010. Building the stages of drama: Towards a text world theory account of dramatic play-texts. *Journal of Literary Semantics*, 39 (1), 67–91.
Davidson, D., 1984. *Inquiries into truth and interpretation*. Oxford: Clarendon Press.
Doležel, L., 1998. Possible worlds of fiction and history. *New Literary History*, 29 (4), 785–809.
Emmott, C., 1997. *Narrative comprehension: A discourse perspective*. Oxford: Clarendon.
Fauconnier, G., 1994. *Mental spaces*. Cambridge: Cambridge University Press.
Fauconnier, G. and Turner, M., 2002. *The way we think: Conceptual blending and the mind's hidden complexity*. New York: Basic Books.
Fillmore, C., 1982. Frame semantics. *In:* T.L.S.O. Korea, ed. *Linguistics in the morning calm*. Seoul: Hanshin Publishing, 111–137.

Gavins, J., 2001. *Text world theory: A critical exposition and development in relation to absurd prose fiction*. Unpublished PhD thesis. Sheffield Hallam University.

Gavins, J., 2007. *Text world theory: An introduction*. Edinburgh University Press.

Gavins, J., *Text World Theory*, http://www.textworldtheory.net/Welcome.html, last accessed July 10, 2012.

Gavins, J. and Steen, G., 2003a. *Cognitive poetics in practice*. London and New York: Routledge.

Gavins, J. and Steen, G., 2003b. Contextualising cognitive poetics. *In:* J. Gavins and G. Steen, eds. *Cognitive poetics in practice*. London and New York: Routledge, 1–12.

Gavins, J. and Stockwell, P., 2012. About the heart, where it hurt exactly, and how often. *Language and Literature*, 21 (1), 33–50.

Genette, G., 1997. *Paratexts: Thresholds of interpretation*. Trans. J.E. Lewin, Cambridge: Cambridge University Press.

Gerrig, R. J., 1993. *Experiencing narrative worlds: On the psychological activities of reading*. New Haven and London: Yale University Press.

Gibbons, A., 2011. *Multimodality, cognition, and experimental literature*. London: Routledge.

Giovanelli, M., 2010. Pedagogical stylistics: A text world theory approach to the teaching of poetry. *English in Education*, 44 (3), 214–231.

Grice, H. P., 1975. *Logic in conversation*. New York: Academic Press.

Hidalgo-Downing, L., 2000. *Negation, text worlds, and discourse: The pragmatics of fiction*. Stamford, Connecticut: Ablex Publishing Corporation.

Kenneally, C., 2007. *The first word: The search for the origins of language*. New York: Penguin.

Kripke, S. A., 1972. *Naming and necessity*. Oxford: Blackwell.

Kuiken, D. et al., 2004. Forms of self-implication in literary reading. *Poetics Today*, 25 (2), 171–203.

Lahey, E., 2004. All the world's a subworld: Direct speech and subworld creation in 'after' by Norman Maccaig. *Nottingham Linguistic Circular*, 18, 21–28.

Lahey, E., 2005. *Text-world landscapes and English-Canadian national identity in the poetry of Al Purdy, Milton Acorn and Alden Nowlan*. Unpublished PhD Thesis. University of Nottingham.

Lahey, E., 2006. (Re)thinking world-building: Locating the text-worlds of Canadian lyric poetry. *Journal of Literary Semantics*, 35 (2), 145–164.

Lahey, E., 2007. Megametaphorical mappings and the landscapes of Canadian poetry. *In:* M. Lambrou and P. Stockwell, eds. *Contemporary stylistics*. London: Continuum, 157–167.

Lahey, E., 2012. Blended discourses: Reading the multimodal north in Al Purdy's 'North of Summer'. *In:* D. Zetu, ed. *Contemporary Canadian literature: European approaches*. Iasi, Romania: Al. I. Cuza University Press, 68–99.

Lakoff, G., 1987. *Women, fire and dangerous things: What categories reveal about the mind*. Chicago: University of Chicago Press.

Lakoff, G. and Johnson, M., 1980. *Metaphors we live by*. Chicago: University of Chicago Press.

Lakoff, G. and Turner, M., 1989. *More than cool reason: A field guide to poetic metaphor*. Chicago: Chicago University Press.

Lambrou, M. and Stockwell, P., 2007. *Contemporary stylistics*. London: Continuum.

Lewis, D., 1986. *On the plurality of worlds*. Oxford: Blackwell.

Liebniz, G., 1985. *The monadology and other philosophical writings*. New York: Garland.

Lycan, W. G., 2000. *Philosophy of language: A contemporary introduction*. London and New York: Routledge.

Maître, D., 1983. *Literature and possible worlds*. London: Middlesex Polytechnic Press.

McIntyre, D., 2006. *Point of view in plays: A cognitive stylistic approach to viewpoint in drama and other text-types*. Amsterdam: John Benjamins.

McIntyre, D. and Busse, B., 2010. *Language and style: In: honour of Mick Short*. Basingstoke: Palgrave Macmillan.

Miall, D., 2006. Empirical approaches to studying literary readers: The state of the discipline. *Book History*, 9, 291–311.

Montoro, R., 2006. Text-world theory and cinematic discourse. Annual Conference of the Poetics and Linguistics Association (PALA), Joensuu, Finland.

Nørgaard, N. et al., 2010. *Key terms in stylistics*. London: Continuum.

Oatley, K., 2011. *Such stuff as dreams: The psychology of fiction*. Oxford: Wiley-Blackwell.

Pavel, T. G., 1975. Possible worlds in literary semantics. *Journal of Aesthetics and Art Criticism*, 34 (2), 165–176.

Rescher, N., 1975. *A theory of possibility*. Pittsburgh: Pittsburgh University Press.

Ronen, R., 1994. *Possible worlds in literary theory*. Cambridge: Cambridge University Press.

Rosch, E., 1978. Principles of categorization. *In:* E. Rosch and B. B. Lloyd, eds. *Cognition and categorization*. Hillsdale, NJ: Lawrence Erlbaum, 27–48.

Russell, B., 1905. On Denoting. *Mind,* 14, 479–493.

Ryan, M-L., 1991. *Possible worlds, Artificial intelligence, and narrative theory*. Indiana University Press.

Schank, R. C. and Abelson, R., 1977. *Scripts, plans, goals and understanding*. Hillsdale, NJ: Lawrence Erlbaum.

Semino, E., 1997. *Language and world creation in poems and other texts*. London: Longman.

Semino, E., 2010. Text worlds in poetry. *In:* D. McIntyre and B. Busse, ed. *Language and style*. Houndsmills, Basingstoke: Palgrave Macmillan, 116–132.

Semino, E. and Culpeper, J., 2002. *Cognitive stylistics: Language and cognition in text analysis*. Amsterdam: John Benjamins.

Short, M., 1981. Discourse analysis and the analysis of drama. *Applied Linguistics,* 11 (2), 180–202.

Short, M., 1988. From dramatic text to dramatic performance. *In:* J. Culpeper, M. Short and P. Verdonk, eds. *Exploring the language of drama*. London: Routledge, 6–18.

Short, M., 1989. Discourse analysis and the analysis of drama. *In:* R. Carter and P. Simpson, eds. *Language, discourse and literature*. London: Unwin Hyman, 139–186.

Simpson, P., 1993. *Language, ideology, and point of view*. London: Routledge.

Stockwell, P., 2005. Texture and identification. *European Journal of English Studies,* 9 (2), 143–153.

Stockwell, P., 2006. On cognitive poetics and stylistics. *In:* H. Veivo, B. Pettersen and M. Polvinen, eds. *Cognition and literary interpretation in practice*. Helsinki: University of Helsinki Press, 267–282.

Stockwell, P., 2008. Cartographies of cognitive poetics. *Pragmatics and Cognition,* 16 (3), 587–598.

Stockwell, P., 2009. *Texture: A cognitive aesthetics of reading*. Edinburgh: Edinburgh University Press.

Swann, J. and Allington, D., 2009. Reading groups and the language of literary texts: A case study in social reading. *Language and Literature,* 18 (3), 247–264.

Trask, R. L. and Stockwell, P., 2007. *Language and linguistics: The key concepts*. Abingdon, Oxon: Routledge.

Werth, P., 1995a. How to build a world (in a lot less than six days and using only what's in your head). *In:* K. Green, ed. *New essays on deixis: Discourse, narrative, literature*. Amsterdam: Rodopi, 49–80.

Werth, P., 1995b. 'World enough and time': Deictic space and the interpretation of prose. *In:* P. Verdonk and J.J. Weber, eds, *Twentieth century fiction: From text to context*. London: Routledge, 181–205.

Werth, P., 1999. *Text worlds: Representing conceptual space in discourse*. London: Longman.

Whiteley, S., 2010. *Text world theory and the emotional experience of literary discourse*. Unpublished PhD Thesis. The University of Sheffield.

Whiteley, S., 2011a. Talking about 'An Accommodation': The implications of discussion group data for community engagement and pedagogy. *Language and Literature,* 20 (3), 236–256.

Whiteley, S., 2011b. Text world theory, real readers and emotional responses to *The Remains of the Day*. *Language and Literature,* 20 (1), 23–42.

18

Stylistics and blending

Barbara Dancygier

Introduction: The concept of a blend

In an article on today's environmentalism, published in the *Orion Magazine* (Jan/Feb 2012), Paul Kingsnorth comments on the recently emerged version of environmentalism which is connected very closely to the capitalist economy. He refers to this new form as *the catalytic converter on the silver SUV of the global economy*. This innovative phrase is a perfect example of how existing linguistic structures are used creatively to construct previously unavailable meanings. In terms of recent theories of language and cognition, this expression would quickly be identified as representing a *blend*.

The notion of *conceptual integration*, or *blending*, has emerged as the next link in a chain of frameworks which connects the study of language with the study of cognition (e.g. cognitive grammar and the theory of conceptual metaphor). The common assumption of these approaches, shared by the broader field of cognitive linguistics, is that meanings are not neatly packaged into words, but that they emerge in the process of meaning construction. While cognitive linguists study form/meaning pairings at both the grammatical and the lexical level, they also uncover processes which lead to the emergence of the actual interpretation of linguistic expressions of varying length and complexity. This theoretical view makes cognitive theories very useful in the study of a variety of texts, including literary texts. The assumption that meaning is constructed rather than uncovered allows the analysts to focus on the *process* rather than the *product* of reading. Additionally, it leaves the question of the actual interpretation open, so that it is naturally accepted that various readers may arrive at different interpretations while relying on the same textual prompts. This does not make meaning indeterminate, but it does allow for some variety in the deployment of comprehension strategies.

Blending, as a process of meaning emergence, has been talked about in terms of its stages and components. The description usually starts with the recognition of two or more *inputs* – conceptual packets structured by frames (knowledge structures linked to vocabulary items, cf. Fillmore 1985, 2006) or mental spaces (Fauconnier 1994/85, 1997, Fauconnier and Sweetser 1996, Oakley and Hougaard 2008). Typically, the inputs are signaled by the choice of wording and the meaning of the expression. The inputs are brought into the blend to contribute aspects of meaning, but there is also a higher level at which they are seen as correlated – this is known as the *generic space*. For example, in the expression quoted above, the wording suggests a blend of the structure of a car and the structure of global economy. The two inputs have seemingly very little in common, but the assumption that both are complex structures, with various parts performing specific functions, allows us to view them both against a generic understanding of complex mechanisms and the role their parts play in smooth functioning.

The two inputs are internally structured in terms of components and features. The expression, interpreted as a blend, allows the person interpreting the phrase to construe specific *cross-mappings*, linking the inputs in a coherent way. For example, the global economy is not viewed here in terms of financial markets or even production; instead it is talked about as a complex mechanism. Its inner workings are construed in terms of those of a car, whose function is to allow people to reach their destinations (spatial or otherwise); consequently, the goal of economic activity can also be viewed as a destination to be reached. The kind of car selected in the expression, *the (silver) SUV*, is framed as a luxury object, very powerful and elegant, but not necessarily efficient in its use of fuel, and it is thus clear that the global economy is presented here as looking attractive, but using more materials and power than it should. These central cross-mapped features of the structure are *selectively projected* into the blend – a new conceptual structure, called an *emergent structure*, in which the economy is thought of in terms of the features of a car. The new structure created in the blend is fully cohesive, so that we can reason further, thinking about the global economy in automotive terms. This is called the *running of the blend*. Once the structure is established we can not only see Kingsnorth's point, but we can also think through further inferences of the set-up, such as the lack of correlation between the appealing aesthetic values and actual engineering soundness, the habits of consumers, who might ignore harmful effects and opt for the status symbol instead, and so on. In the conceptualisation emerging from the expression, the effects of excessive fuel consumption are moderated not by a re-design of the engine (which would be equivalent to the very core of economic decisions), but by preventing all the harmful emissions from being spewed into the environment (installing a converter). Kingsnorth's article claims that environmentalism today is equivalent to just such a converter – it is not really interested in preserving the environment by reducing the excessive use of materials and power (and SUVs are heavy cars, often described as 'gas-guzzlers'), or simply relying less on dirty technology (e.g. riding a bicycle or walking instead of covering more terrain with paved roads). Rather, it focuses instead on reducing carbon emissions. The role assigned to the current shape of environmentalism in the blend presents it as spurious and inefficient, deeply immersed as it is in promoting technological advances, rather than environmental protection. This view of environmentalism emerges only in the blend, as all the inferences we draw from it would not be available outside it.

Blends also play a role in grammar. Kingsnorth's expression is a good example of what Fauconnier and Turner call the 'XYZ construction' (Fauconnier and Turner 2002). Their argument is that some grammatical constructions are specifically designed to represent a category of blends which construct meaning similarly, in spite of varied lexical material. In their simplest form, XYZ blends are represented by expressions such as *Melissa is the mother of Bill*, which represent two pairs of cross-mappings: Melissa is linked to the concept *mother*, while Bill is linked to the concept *child*. However, the Bill-as-child link is not explicitly expressed, and is read into the meaning of the phrase through the converse of the 'mother' concept. So an expression modeled by the *X is the Y of Z* formula actually profiles the link between X and Y (*Melissa-mother*) and completes the required role for Bill (that of *child*) via the process of blending. Blending is an appropriate description of the meaning emergence here, since two relations (Melissa as mother and Bill as child) are blended into one coherent understanding of how the four entities are related. A blending network like this has been described as a simplex network, in which there are no clashes between the inputs.

Such blends are commonly very creative, and often leave much of the meaning of the phrase unresolved. For example, when the poet Wisława Szymborska was given the Nobel Prize for Literature in 1986, the Swedish press described her as *the Greta Garbo of poetry*. The assumption seemed to be that the position Greta Garbo held in the realm of movie acting was parallel to the position of Szymborska in the realm of poetry. The readers were expected to run the blend and so see the expression as the ultimate praise Swedish critics could give to an artist (also considering that Garbo was Swedish). However, the exact meaning of the phrase could not be predicted outside the frame of Garbo's fame, and it did not have to be identical for every reader. Reading the connection between *the catalytic converter on the silver SUV of the global economy* and environmentalism also requires the completion of the implied relations, as well as fusing entities in the blend with new roles assigned to them. First, the reader needs to construe the global economy as an SUV, and then within that blend they must see the role of environmentalism as analogous to the converter.

Blending is a relatively recent theory, formed in the 1990s and given its complete expression in Fauconnier and Turner (2002). In its early form it built on the claims of conceptual metaphor theory. However, it argued that not all expressions similar to metaphorical ones are strictly unidirectional, but instead that all domains evoked can contribute to the emergent meaning. In other words, conceptual metaphor theory argues that a mapping links two domains, the source and the target, in such a way that conceptual structure from the source is unidirectionally projected into the target (so that features of the concept 'journey' are projected into the abstract concept such as a long-term relationship). Blending also recognises such patterns (as single-scope blends), but argues that other types of patterns of projection are also available (described as mirror and double scope blends). In all the blending patterns, regardless of the amount of structure actually taken from either one of the inputs, the projection of conceptual structure targets the newly set-up concept, the blend.

Early formulations of blending (mostly published in the early nineties; see http://markturner.org/blending.html) were criticised for imposing very few limitations on what kind of structure can emerge in the blend – its usefulness was seen as a sufficient explanation. In response to these comments, in their 2002 book Fauconnier and Turner have imposed *optimality constraints* on blending, arguing that aspects of blending such as the degree and tightness of integration of the new structure, the global impact of the new meaning, or the ability of the expression to present complex problems in ways appropriate to human scale are all constraints guiding the establishment of new blends. John Fitzgerald Kennedy's famous *We choose to go to the moon* speech (delivered in September 1962 at Rice University) establishes the conquest of outer space as a national US strategy; in the speech, the role of human scale is indeed crucial to the portrayal of the situation:

> No man can fully grasp how far and how fast we have come, but condense, if you will, the fifty thousand years of man's recorded history in a time span of but a half-century. Stated in these terms, we know very little about the first forty years, except at the end of them advanced man had learned to use the skins of animals to cover them. Then about ten years ago, under this standard, man emerged from his caves to construct other kinds of shelter. Only five years ago man learned to write and use a cart with wheels. Christianity began less than two years ago. The printing press came this year, and then less than two months ago, during this whole fifty-year span of human history, the steam engine

provided a new source of power. Newton explored the meaning of gravity. Last month electric lights and telephones and automobiles and airplanes became available. Only last week did we develop penicillin and television and nuclear power, and now if America's new spacecraft succeeds in reaching Venus, we will have literally reached the stars before midnight tonight.

The fragment achieves the intended human scale and global insight by relying heavily on the primary mechanism of blending, called *compression*. The concept refers to the observation that when elements from the inputs get fused in the blend (environmentalism = catalytic converter) the conceptual distance between them is reduced or eliminated, so that we no longer focus on how different the concepts really are. In the JFK speech the rhetorical device is to very deliberately compress the time over which human civilisations developed, so that the pace of change and the vision of the future could be clearly seen in human scale. Importantly, the whole blend leads the audience into perceiving the goal of space exploration as near and feasible, rather than distant and hard. Indeed, this shows the extraordinary power of blending in bringing a new perspective to familiar objects and situations.

The rhetorical goals of this part of the speech are also well-supported with the compression it outlines. Out of the 'fifty years' construal, the first forty years of overall cultural progress are withdrawn from consideration, so that the speech can then focus on recent technological advances. Since the exploration of outer space will require much fast progress in this area, it is rhetorically useful to show that the required pace is in fact nothing miraculous, since over the last ten years of the compressed time so many new ideas have already been implemented. The accessibility of the technology required is thus construed through extreme time compression in the blend.

The crucial compression in the speech is that of time. However, compressions may rely on other *vital relations*, as Fauconnier and Turner call them, such as causality, analogy, disanalogy, role-value mapping, part-whole, change, identity and so on. For example, the relation of analogy underlies the compression in the converter/environmentalism blend above. The role that the converter plays with respect to the car is used to set up an analogous relationship between environmentalism and the global economy. The analogy is based on the understanding that the addition of a mechanism which only alleviates detrimental results does not change the harmful core of the mechanism, and that such a change should be the goal.

Blending analysts also talk about a process which reverses natural compression – unsurprisingly called *decompression*. This is a common feature of ordinary linguistic choices, such as when a speaker decompresses her identity through expressions such as *I'm not myself today*, suggesting that the speaker sees her identity as split between her ordinary sense of self and an unusual one that day. A variety of decompression, termed *decompression for viewpoint*, appears to play an important role in written discourse, as it allows the writer to construe the situation depicted from more than one viewpoint at a time. Dancygier (2005, 2012a) illustrates the concept with numerous excerpts from travel texts and literature; for example, travel writer Jonathan Raban describes meeting his father after many years by saying *There were two men in my father's chair*. The context makes it clear that the description targets two different perceptions of the father's personality, the one established in the writer's childhood and the other just forming in view of the changes that have occurred. The father is thus conceptually decompressed into two different personas, and the consistent narrative viewpoint of the writer can now be enriched with a perspective independent of the current narrative, which nevertheless narrates the emerging new conceptualisation. To sum up, decompression for viewpoint is a narrative device which functions to construe narrative situations from multiple viewpoints.

Blending has been formulated broadly as a theory of meaning emergence. It has been introduced in the linguistic context in the special issues of the journals *Cognitive Linguistics* (Coulson and Oakley 2000) and *Journal of Pragmatics* (Coulson and Oakley 2005). Numerous articles apply blending to areas of language use, including grammar, but also visual art, film, and various creative forms (see Sweetser 2000, 2004, 2006, Coulson 2001, 2006, Coulson and Oakley 2005, Rubba 2009, Turner 2006). It has also recently been discussed with respect to viewpoint phenomena in various communicative modalities, including narratives (Dancygier and Sweetser 2012). Although questions are still raised about the psychological reality of blending and there have also been calls for more work on experimental confirmation of the theoretical claims, blending is gaining popularity in various areas of study as a productive interpretive framework.

Recently, blending has also been fruitfully applied to works of literature. It has become a stylistic tool, and has been applied to a broad range of genres and texts. It has been introduced to the stylistics community in the special issue of *Language and Literature*, guest-edited by Dancygier (2006a and 2006b). A comparison between blending and other text world theories is proposed in Semino (2009). One of the earliest books to apply blending to a literary category is Turner's *The Literary Mind* (1996), where the concept of narrativity is discussed from the point of view of metaphor and blending. Work on narratives (from a blending perspective) has been done by Dancygier (2005, 2007, 2012b), Semino (2006, 2010), Copland (2008, 2012) and Harding (2007, 2012); also, Dancygier's recent book (2012a) proposes a new model for narrative analysis, built on the blending concept of viewpoint compression. Finally, blending and narrative are treated in a collection of articles in the volume on *Blending and the Study of Narrative*, edited by Schneider and Hartner (2012). As regards poetry, interesting contributions to blending have been published, among others, by Canning (2008), Borkent (2010), Turner (2004) and Cánovas (2011). Cook (2007, 2010) is applying blending to the study of theatre and performance. Blending is thus finding applications in all areas of creativity, but it is also enriched with the concepts brought in by the disciplines in question. It has certainly profited from stylistic applications, in that the study of textual phenomena helps in developing new blending tools (see, for example, Dancygier 2012a).

In what follows, I will illustrate the way in which a blending analysis of a text can be conducted. I will focus on the ways in which the approach helps to specify the correlations between linguistic and interpretive choices.

Blending analysis of a poem

In this section I will consider in detail a blending analysis of a poem – Wilfred Owen's 'Parable of the Old Man and the Young' (cf. Stallworthy 1994). Owen is widely known as a poet of the shell shock generation – young men who were psychologically scarred by the Great War, often being victims of it (Owen died in action in 1918). Indeed, poets like Owen or Siegfried Sassoon presented an image of the war from the perspective of a soldier, rather than from the point of view of a patriot or a politician. The texts are thus often focused on the horrors of trench warfare, rather than assuming a broad perspective of a country. It is therefore interesting to see what Owen does in one of his few poems addressing the overall situation of Europe in the context of First World War:

Parable of the Old Man and the Young

So Abram rose, and clave the wood, and went,
And took the fire with him, and a knife.
And as they sojourned both of them together,
Isaac the first-born spake and said, My Father,
Behold the preparations, fire and iron,
But where the lamb, for this burnt-offering?
Then Abram bound the youth with belts and straps,
and builded parapets and trenches there,
And stretchèd forth the knife to slay his son.
When lo! an Angel called him out of heaven,
Saying, Lay not thy hand upon the lad,
Neither do anything to him, thy son.
Behold! Caught in a thicket by its horns,
A Ram. Offer the Ram of Pride instead.

But the old man would not so, but slew his son,
And half the seed of Europe, one by one.

The immediately noticeable linguistic feature of the poem is its stylised reference to Jacobean English. The purpose of these choices is to remind the reader of one of the best known Biblical stories, Genesis 22, as rendered in the King James Bible. There are very striking similarities between Owen's poem and Genesis 22, both in the story itself and in its vocabulary. First God speaks to Abraham:

> 2 *And he said, Take now thy son, thine only son Isaac, whom thou lovest, and get thee into the land of Mori'ah; and offer him there for a burnt offering upon one of the mountains which I will tell thee of.*

Abraham resolves to follow the Lord's will:

> 6 *And Abraham took the wood of the burnt offering, and laid it upon Isaac his son; and he took the fire in his hand, and a knife; and they went both of them together.*
> 7 *And Isaac spake unto Abraham his father, and said, My father: and he said, Here am I, my son. And he said, Behold the fire and the wood: but where is the lamb for a burnt offering?*
> 9 *And they came to the place which God had told him of; and Abraham built an altar there, and laid the wood in order, and bound Isaac his son, and laid him on the altar upon the wood.*
> 10 *And Abraham stretched forth his hand, and took the knife to slay his son.*
> 11 *And the angel of the LORD called unto him out of heaven, and said, Abraham, Abraham: and he said, Here am I.*
> 12 *And he said, Lay not thine hand upon the lad, neither do thou any thing unto him: for now I know that thou fearest God, seeing thou hast not withheld thy son, thine only son, from me.*
> 13 *And Abraham lifted up his eyes, and looked, and behold behind him a ram caught in a thicket by his horns: and Abraham went and took the ram, and offered him up for a burnt offering in the stead of his son.*

Abraham's obedience to the Lord is then rewarded, as all his people are blessed:

> 18   *and in thy seed shall all the nations of the earth be blessed because thou hast obeyed my voice.*

If we consider the linguistic choices, Owen's text repeats many of the KJB's forms (*spake, behold, builded, thy* etc.), but also uses vocabulary which prompts some frames characteristic of WWI warfare: *belts, straps, trenches, parapets*. In fact the poem quotes whole expressions from KJB, such as *But where the lamb for this burnt-offering?*, or *caught in a thicket by (his/its) horns.* Through its vocabulary choices the text thus signals the blending of two widely divergent narratives: the Biblical story of Genesis 22 and the trench warfare reality of WWI. The blending is also quite striking at the genre level. The poem tells a story in a way closely resembling a parable (hence the title), but it maintains the structure and form of a short poetic piece. Importantly, the stylistic choices are quite obvious, so that 'the seams are showing', as in the contrast between *building an altar* and *building parapets and trenches*, which is clearly a poetic choice rather than simply a case of crafting the text based on a stylised Biblical format. It appears that the Genesis text is essentially re-told in poetic form, with only some minor vocabulary changes, in order to highlight its unexpected deviation from the Genesis story in the final two lines –which are additionally foregrounded by being the only ones which rhyme (*son/one*). The obviousness of the blend is thus precisely what triggers the reading of the poem based on comparing the original Genesis story and its moral message with the presented ethical view of the events of WWI.

In what follows, I will go over the blend prompted by the text of the poem and show how the structure of the blend yields the unstated message – the claim that the political leaders who made the decision to engage in war have in fact committed an immoral act and violated the ethical standards of Christianity. The blend represented by the poem is a complex one, which would be described technically as a double-scope blend –where the inputs are not fully compatible and the projection involves resolution of the ways in which the inputs differ from each other. In the discussion I will follow the stages in the construction of the blend, from the generic space, through inputs, to the backward projection.

Generic space

The poem builds on a generic space containing a very important and culturally salient frame, also clearly signaled in the title of the poem – that of a *family*, especially with regard to relations between *ancestors* (or those who are family elders) and *descendants* (or those who are younger and dependent). Both roles involve frame-specific obligations: fathers have a duty to protect their sons, while sons have a duty to obey their fathers. I will be using the terms *father* and *son* as names for the roles in the frame (not necessarily as kinship terms), since it is common to use these terms to signify the type of relationship, rather than specifically family ties (as in addressing priests and seniors as *father*, or in the somewhat dated colloquial form *my son*, used by older men to address much younger ones). Furthermore, the poem also builds on the *sovereign/subjects* frame, which involves some of the same kinds of relations. For example, a sovereign is required to protect his subjects, while they owe him or her their loyalty and obedience. In fact, Owen evokes a whole range of frames built on the concept of seniority (age difference, social status, ruler versus subjects, deity versus believers), focusing on the reciprocal obligations which the two sides have rather than on the particular nature of the relationship. In order not to complicate the interpretation too much, I will refer to the *father/son* frame as a broad depiction of the relationships involving similar framing.

It is common to represent blends through diagrams detailing all the spaces and inputs. Since the blend represented by Owen's poem is quite complex, I will illustrate the stages in the emergence of the blend through three independent figures. Figure 18.1 is a skeletal representation of the composition of the generic space. The roles available there are then projected onto the elements of the inputs.

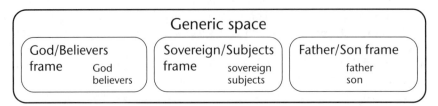

Figure 18.1 Generic space

Inputs

Being so close to the Genesis story, the poem relies heavily on Judeo-Christian tradition. In fact there are three inputs emerging from that tradition: God as the father of the people of Israel (*input 1*), God and his son Jesus (*input 2*), and Genesis 22 (*input 3*). The first frame comes from the Old Testament, and presents God as the father (protector) of the people of Israel. What the poem then takes from this frame is the idea that an elder (king or sovereign) is responsible for the well-being of the nation in his care, while the nation is treated as a descendant or the son. All that is asked of the son in exchange is trust and obedience.

The second frame, from the New Testament, is crucial to the meaning of Owen's poem. It is an instance of the father/son frame, but it also introduces the second frame central to the poem, the frame of *sacrifice*. The sacrifice frame profiles two primary roles: the *offerer* (the person performing the sacrifice) and the *offering* (the entity offered). The third role is that of the entity who desires or will appreciate the sacrifice and give something in exchange. In the case of the traditional view of sacrifice, something of value (such as an animal) is destroyed (killed) and the value of the life so destroyed is given, in a ritual form, to a supreme being whose favour is asked for. The offerer is thus giving away something of value and expects to *gain* something in exchange. The expected gain, even if not material, is what makes sacrificial killing different from simple killing.

God, as the father of Jesus, sacrifices his son's life for the greater gain of redeeming the sins of humanity. Within the family frame, God violates his fatherly duty of protecting his descendants, but the greater moral gain resulting from the application of the sacrifice frame outweighs the diminishment of the fatherly role. Crucially to the meaning of the poem, the Biblical frame supports the belief that a father's duty to protect can be overridden by a higher duty. Also, it suggests that the concept of sacrifice requires that the offering be highly valuable to the offerer. In fact, the moral gain from the sacrifice increases with the value of the offering.

It is interesting to consider the frame of sacrifice in the context of the Moral Accounting metaphor, discussed in Johnson (1994) and Lakoff and Johnson (1999). The metaphor represents the common belief that good deeds earn us some credit in society's books, while trespasses against others constitute moral debt and need to be paid for. It is good to have as many good deeds in your 'moral account' as you can because the society then 'owes you' something, for example respect or recognition. Sacrifice seems to be an older frame representing similar logic – the more you give to your god, the more moral credit you earn and the more protection you can expect. The Biblical story, in which an offering is typically a lamb, can then be translated into a more modern situation wherein people sacrifice their desires and feelings (such as pride) to please those who judge their morals and to earn the reputation of moral men.

There is an interesting correlation between *input 2* and the Genesis story recounted in Owen's poem. In both cases the father (God or Abraham) is prepared to sacrifice his son, but for different reasons. Abraham puts his duties as a son (obedience and trust) ahead of his duties as a father (protection of his own son), while God sacrifices his son to protect his people, as God is not expected to be obedient to any higher moral authority (and the son is resurrected as well). The various meanings of these kinds of obligations are exploited in the poem.

The next input is the Genesis 22 story itself (*input 3*). In the parable, Abraham is at the same time a father (and so he owes protection to Isaac) and a son (and so he owes obedience to God, even if God requires the ultimate sacrifice). He has to choose between the moral duties resulting from these two types of roles. Throughout the story it is clear that obedience and trust in God's justice and wisdom override Abraham's fatherly duties – he is prepared to sacrifice his son. However, his trust is rewarded right away, since seeing his unhesitant readiness, God tells him not to kill Isaac. The solemn intention of performing the sacrifice is equivalent to the deed itself. The story in this version makes it clear that trust in and obedience to God are higher values which guarantee increased protection, so that as a result the whole tribe is blessed and thrives. The conclusion is that a just father requires obedience, but does not also require that important moral values be abandoned. The moral gain in Abraham's story is indeed great, as he performs all his duties and remains a moral man.

These three inputs are often viewed jointly and form a cultural blend (the God/father blend – *Blend 1*) in which God, who has sacrificed his own son, can demand the ultimate sacrifice from his people – and in this blend Abraham stands for all those who are in God's care but who also owe obedience to him. They also have to trust in God's protection. The Genesis story makes it clear that God does offer this protection, even if he is asking for an ultimate sacrifice in return.

It is important to note that the Genesis story relies also on several implied counterfactual scenarios. In the eyes of most people, sacrificing his son is a demand that a father might choose to refuse. The consequences are also clear – he would continue protecting his son (which is a frame-related obligation), but he would disobey God. As Genesis 22 suggests, then, the choice Abraham makes brings more gain – saving the son and gaining God's love and trust. Therefore, the two scenarios the story profiles (Abraham obeys/does not obey) are alternatives, but it is also clear that he might refuse to obey the command to kill, while it would be nonsensical for him to refuse to obey the second command – to let his son live and sacrifice a ram instead. Nevertheless, this is the alternative that Owen explores in the poem.

Dancygier and Sweetser (2005) argue that the concept of alternativity is in fact crucial to the meaning of all counterfactual constructions, so that all sentences such as *If he had tried, he would have won* rely on two alternative scenarios – in one, the man tries and wins (the counterfactual scenario), in the other the man does not try and does not win. The verb forms in the construction are signals of the alternativity. In Owen's poem there are no grammatical signals of alternativity, but it emerges out of the blend constructed – we can easily propose appropriate sentences, such as *If Abraham had not respected God's will, he would have refuse to kill Isaac*. The diagram in Figure 18.2 thus shows the interaction between the three inputs, enriched by the sacrifice frame, and the two alternative scenarios (the counterfactual one and the 'real' one) profiled in *Blend 1*.

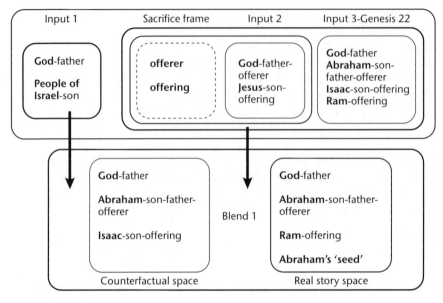

Figure 18.2 Blend 1

The final input is the story of WWI (*input 4*). The leaders of the warring nations are framed as 'fathers', and thus they are expected to offer protection to the younger men, even though they can also ask for obedience in return. However, the input also evokes concepts such as patriotism, loyalty to one's country, and the demands made on people when the country is in danger as a result of being engaged in a war. These aspects of the WWI input are not actually projected into the final blend, which shows that the *selective projection* that every blend relies on is restricted to the aspects of the frame which are relevant to the blend. Because the poem's goal is to totally re-frame the moral obligation inherent to the 'war' frame, much of the structure of the input is not projected. Even though this input provides very little new framing to the blend, it is at the same time the one which is being elaborated through the blend.

The final blend

Blend 1 and *input 4* form the final blend of the poem. Two primary father/son participants are projected from *input 4* (leaders of warring countries, soldiers), while God/the father is projected from *Blend 1*. Since in *Blend 1* God is framed as demanding sacrifices, the sacrifice frame is projected into the final blend. Thus leaders are also framed as 'offerers', and young soldiers are the 'offering'. This framing presents the plight of WWI soldiers not as a patriotic duty, but instead sees them as sacrificial lambs at the mercy of those who owe them protection.

Crucially, in the poem, when offered an opportunity to preserve their moral strength intact, the leaders refuse to give obedience to God and at the same time withdraw their protection of the young men. They are condemned, and the nations they are responsible for suffer.

There are multiple *cross-mappings* linking the inputs, with respect to both frames present in the generic space. All the *father* roles in the four inputs are linked: God (*inputs 1, 2* and *3*), Abraham (*input 3*), and political leaders (*input 4*). Similarly, all the *son* roles are cross-mapped too (Jesus, people of Israel, Isaac, and WWI soldiers). Within the sacrifice frame, the *offerer* roles are connected: God (*input 2*), Abraham, and the political leaders. The assignment of the role of the *offering* is in fact more complex. In *input 3*, Isaac is the offering God requires of Abraham at first, but in the end it is the ram that is sacrificed after God spares Isaac's life. In *input 4*, by comparison, young soldiers are the offering, and even though the *Ram of Pride* is suggested as a satisfactory offering, the sons are sacrificed in the end.

The final blend, like *input 3* which it takes the most from, inherits the alternative option of Abraham disobeying God. However, while in Genesis the alternative usually considered is disobeying the first command (to kill the son), in the final blend the alternative is disobeying the second command. The leaders of Europe's countries feel obliged to sacrifice the soldiers in the name of victory, but now the blend gives them a choice by which they do not have in *input 4* – they can sacrifice their pride instead. That choice is not available in *input 3*, as Abraham's pride is not an issue at all – he shows he has none when he decides to obey. The final blend is based on the vital relation of disanalogy – WWI leaders choose the option which preserves their self-esteem, rather than trusting the commands of the moral authority. Crucially, in the final blend the decisions are based on choosing one value over another, while in Genesis Abraham follows the same value – obedience.

The two offerings in *inputs 3* and *4* (Isaac and the ram, soldiers and the Ram of Pride) are the crux of the blend the poem creates. Human sacrifice is quite naturally considered extreme in any cultural context, and ancient cultures that practiced it typically sacrificed slaves or captured soldiers of their enemies. The sacrifice of a son is even more extreme, and thus serves as a good test for the father's obedience. A ram as an offering is the expected norm, but the Ram of Pride is a different category. It links the traditional offering with a more contemporary understanding of sacrifice, where no killing is expected. People can sacrifice one value for another (a career for the family's well-being or vice versa, dietary preferences for health and so on), but the contemporary concept of sacrifice relies primarily on the idea of giving up on something desirable to protect something else, rather than to appeal to a supreme being's grace. Owen's juxtaposition of the two values that political leaders might cherish (pride versus the life of the descendants/prosperity of the nation) makes it clear that the choice should have been easy – the safety of one's 'seed' (whether understood as descendants or the nation in one's care) is obviously of higher value than one's own sense of pride. Suffering a humiliation is clearly a more acceptable choice, especially in view of the fact that within the religious frames evoked, pride is also one of the seven deadly sins. The Biblical story of Abraham suggests that the moral choice is to trust God, as this is the only way not to err into judging the world by one's own desires. In the blend, the leaders of WWI countries make a different choice, as they trust their own egos more than they trust the love God offers. Their choice and its moral consequences exist only in the blend, not in any of the inputs alone. The contributions of all the inputs and the two scenarios they yield are represented in Figure 18.3.

There is also the question of the gain resulting from a sacrifice. Again, the emergent structure frames military leaders as making a decision which represents no moral gain. This

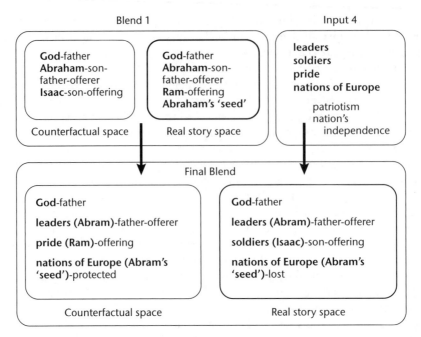

Figure 18.3 Final blend

is directly available in the blend, where Abraham's choices are compared to the WWI choices. Outside of the blend, the protection of one's country's integrity is an ultimate patriotic gain, but in the blend that value is not profiled. The gain in Abraham's story comes from his total trust in a judgement other than his own, and the loss in the WWI story is a result of trusting one's own judgement, which is necessarily marred by one's ego. This, again, is created in the running of the blend.

Backward projection

The structure of the blend and the new conceptualisation it yields also has the goal of shedding more light on at least one of the inputs. In the case of Owen's poem, the input which is put in different light is *input 4* – WWI. The poem re-evaluates the common wisdom about the inevitability of military response and refocuses the war frame away from the patriotic angle, to consider the humanistic and ethical aspects instead. However, it does not simply deplore the brutality of trench warfare, which has been acknowledged in numerous historical analyses and in literature. Rather, the poem puts the issue on the moral plane and questions the ethical value of the political decision to enter a worldwide military conflict. By applying the clear and transparent values of the Genesis frame to a complex political issue, Owen changes the reader's perception entirely.

Style and the structure of the blend

More specific aspects of the blend also participate in the construction of the meaning. This is especially true for vocabulary items which are solely responsible for prompting the WWI frame: *belts and straps, parapets and trenches.* In Genesis 22 Abraham binds his son; in the poem he uses typical items of soldier's gear – belts and straps. While this may simply evoke the image of equipment worn by a soldier, it also sheds a different light on the idea of a military uniform as a tool of restricting a man's freedom. Just as Isaac is bound so he cannot avoid his horrible fate, a soldier is equipped with a uniform which marks him as a victim of sacrifice and in effect already extracts him from the world of civilians and takes away his free will. Crucially, those who give orders have a choice which an 'offering' does not have, but they use their choice to send young men to death against their will.

Similarly, where Abraham in Genesis 22 builds an altar – a sacred place, which turns the planned killing into a moral act of sacrifice – the Abram of the poem builds parapets and trenches. A possible reading of this is to view military installations as places where death of young men is morally justified. However, while an altar, as a sacred place where sacrifice has meaning, evokes the presence of God, the trenches seem to be the kind of altar where victims are offered to a godless concept of war.

Importantly, as noted above, the majority of the vocabulary of the poem comes from the language of Genesis 22, even though Abraham's name is changed to a shorter form, 'Abram'. However, the usage discussed in the preceding paragraphs prompts a total reframing of that vocabulary, so that it now evokes the Great War. Naturally, the name of the author also participates in the reframing, as Owen is perhaps the best known poet of the WWI era. However, one can also argue that the poem has a broader impact, and that it is universally applicable to any situation where young men are sent to a war against their will, to satisfy political ambitions. One can easily imagine the poem appealing to someone who considers the Vietnam War to have been a senseless and unnecessary conflict. Thus the WWI frame can easily be generalised to any 'war' frame.

It is also worth pointing to the compressions in the blend. Quite clearly, the blend compresses the conceptual distance between the time in which the poet lived and the distant and mythical conception of Biblical times. There are also space compressions (Biblical lands and WWI theatre of operations), as well as numerous identity compressions (political leaders are fused with Abram, young soldiers with Isaac, the people of Israel with the nations of Europe, and so on). However, there are also interesting frame-internal compressions. For example, the specific father/son relation in Genesis 22 is re-construed as a broadly viewed difference in age and seniority in the context of WWI. Compressing these conceptual differences also creates an unusual view of the obligations of political leaders– they are responsible not only for the overall well-being and preservation of nations, but they should also be expected to care for younger men as they would for their own sons.

Owen's poem is an interesting example of blending as a poetic tool. It is not uncommon to find poems in which an obvious blending of culturally, historically or linguistically different mental spaces yields interesting effects (see the poem discussed in Semino (2009), where contemporary gender values are highlighted through an evocation of the fate of the wives of famous men from various mythical and historical stories). Owen's poem is similar to these in that it uses an older and culturally salient frame to comment on contemporary issues, but his message is made much more specific and revealing through his careful construction of the blend. It is blending theory as an analytic stylistic tool that has allowed us to explore these hidden meanings in Owen's poem, bringing them into focus and explaining the conceptual and cultural intricacies involved.

Recommendations for practice

Not all examples of blends are as striking as those in the poem discussed above, but examples of blending can be found both in poetry and prose. Depending on the period, it might take different forms – for example, there are clear genre and stylistic differences between medieval allegories, the novels of Virginia Woolf and contemporary poetry. Even so, since blending is not necessarily connected to specific formal choices and is more reliant on striking conceptual clashes evoked by vocabulary choices or discourse forms, practically any text can be fruitfully analysed with blending tools. In any case in which frames evoked through vocabulary are re-construed in the context of a text, blending is a helpful and effective stylistic tool. Its most important asset is the high level of accuracy we can achieve in untangling stylistic complexities and accounting for multiple readings.

Future directions

Blending is a general thought process, and uncovering its functioning leads to very clear and accurate descriptions of emerging meanings. With respect to this, blending is gaining popularity in analyses of various creative genres – visual, textual, cinematic, or theatrical. It has also proven very useful in the study of contemporary multimodal forms, such as graphic novels and comics (see Chapter 30 in this volume). It is therefore likely that blending will continue to develop as a tool for the interpretation of a variety of creative artifacts, both literary and non-literary. At the same time, it is asking important questions about the psychological or neural underpinnings of human creative thought, and so it will continue to prompt experimental research. Its strength, however, will most likely remain in the design of interpretive tools which will give deeper insights into how meanings emerge in a range of culturally salient artifacts.

Related topics

Cognitive poetics, emotion and neuroscience, metaphor and metonymy, text world theory, stylistics and comics.

Further reading

Coulson, S. and Oakley, T., eds. 2000. *Conceptual blending*. Special issue of *Cognitive Linguistics* 11 (3–4).

> An excellent introduction to blending basics. The collection includes articles spelling out the principles of blending, but also illustrating its applications in a broader context of language and culture.

Dancygier, B., ed. 2006b. *Blending and literature*. Special issue of *Language and Literature* 15 (5).

> A collection of articles introducing blending methodology to stylisticians, and presenting applications of the theory in various areas of stylistics (poetry, prose, film, drama, rhyme, etc.).

Dancygier, B., 2012a. *The language of stories: A cognitive approach*. Cambridge: Cambridge University Press.

> The first full-scale genre application, developing blending tools for the specific purposes of the study of the narrative. Chapters show example analyses, relying on a variety of fiction texts including prose, poetry, and drama.

Fauconnier, G. and Turner, M., 2002. *The way we think: Conceptual blending and the mind's hidden complexities*. New York: Basic Books.

A full theoretical introduction to blending, clarifying all the concepts and explaining the cognitive underpinnings of blending processes. Examples come from various areas of usage, illustrating all the terms which are now in broader use.

Schneider, R. and Hartner, M., eds. 2012. *Blending and the study of narrative: Approaches and applications*. Berlin: de Gruyter.

A recent selection of articles illustrating applications of blending in all narrative artifacts, including novels, drama and film. Clearly shows the potential of the theory for stylistic analysis of various textual phenomena and the resulting meanings.

References

Borkent, M., 2010. Illusions of simplicity: A cognitive approach to visual poetry. *In:* B. Dancygier and J. Sanders, eds. *Textual choices and discourse genres: Creating meaning through form*. Special issue of *English Text Construction* 3 (2), 145–164.

Canning, P., 2008. 'The bodie and the letters both': 'Blending' the rules of early modern religion. *Language and Literature*, 17, 187–203.

Cánovas, C. P., 2011. 'The genesis of the arrows of love': Diachronic conceptual integration in Greek mythology. *American Journal of Philology*, 132 (4), 553–579.

Cook, A., 2007. Interplay: The method and potential of a cognitive approach to theatre. *Theatre Journal* 59 (4), 579–594.

Cook, A., 2010. *Shakespearean neuroplay: Reinvigorating the study of dramatic texts and performance through cognitive science*. New York: Palgrave Macmillan.

Copland, S., 2008. Reading in the blend: Collaborative conceptual blending in the *Silent Traveller* narratives. *Narrative*, 16 (2), 140–162.

Copland, S., 2012. Conceptual blending in *The Waves*: 'A mind thinking'. *In:* R. Schneider and M. Hartner, eds. *Blending and the study of narrative*. New York: de Gruyter, 253–278.

Coulson, S., 2001. *Semantic leaps: Frame shifting and conceptual blending in meaning construction*. Cambridge: Cambridge University Press.

Coulson, S., 2006. Conceptual blending in thought, rhetoric, and ideology. *In:* G. Kristiansen, M. Achard, R. Dirven and F. R. de Mendoza Ibáñez, eds. *Cognitive linguistics: Current applications and future perspectives*. New York: de Gruyter, 187–210.

Coulson, S. and Oakley, T., eds. 2000. *Conceptual blending*. Special issue of *Cognitive Linguistics* 11 (3–4).

Coulson, S. and Oakley, T., eds. 2005. *Conceptual blending theory*. Special issue of *Journal of Pragmatics*, 37.

Dancygier, B., 2005. Blending and narrative viewpoint: Jonathan Raban's travels through mental spaces. *Language and Literature*, 14 (2), 99–127.

Dancygier, B., 2006a. What can blending do for you?' *In:* B. Dancygier, ed. *Conceptual blending*. Special issue of *Language and Literature*, 15, 5–15.

Dancygier, B., ed. 2006b. *Blending and literature*. Special issue of *Language and Literature*, 15 (5).

Dancygier, B., 2007. Narrative anchors and the processes of story construction: The case of Margaret Atwood's *The Blind Assassin*. *Style* 41 (2), 133–152.

Dancygier, B., 2012a. *The language of stories: A cognitive approach*. Cambridge: Cambridge University Press.

Dancygier, B., 2012b. Narrative time, sequence, and memory: A blending analysis. *In:* R. Schneider and M. Hartner, eds. *Blending and the study of narrative*. New York: de Gruyter, 31–56.

Dancygier, B. and Sweetser, E., eds. 2005. *Mental spaces in grammar: Conditional constructions*. Cambridge: Cambridge University Press.

Dancygier, B. and Sweetser, E., eds. 2012. *Viewpoint in language: A multimodal approach*. Cambridge: Cambridge University Press.

Fauconnier, G., [1985] 1994. *Mental spaces: Aspects of meaning construction in natural language*. Cambridge: Cambridge University Press.

Fauconnier, G., 1997. *Mappings in thought and language*. Cambridge: Cambridge University Press.

Fauconnier, G. and Sweetser, E., eds. 1996. *Spaces, worlds, and grammar*. Chicago: University of Chicago Press.

Fauconnier, G. and Turner, M., 2002. *The way we think: Conceptual blending and the mind's hidden complexities*. New York: Basic Books.

Fillmore, C., 1985. Frames and the semantics of understanding. *Quaderni di Semantica* 6, 222–254.

Fillmore, C., 2006. Frame semantics. *In:* D. Geererts, ed. *Cognitive linguistics: Basic readings*. Berlin: de Gruyter, 373–400.

Harding, J., 2007. Evaluative stance and counterfactuals in language and literature. *Language and Literature*, 16 (3), 263–280.

Harding, J., 2012. Metaphor, narrative frames and cognitive distance in Charles Chesnutt's 'Dave's Neckliss'. *In:* R. Schneider and M. Hartner. Eds. *Blending and the Study of Narrative*. New York: de Gruyter, 229–252.

Johnson, M., 1994. *Moral imagination: Implications of cognitive science for ethics*. Chicago University Press.

Kingsnorth, P., 2012. Confessions of a recovering environmentalist. *Orion Magazine*, Jan/Feb.

Lakoff, G. and Johnson, M., 1999. *Philosophy in the flesh: The embodied mind and its challenge to western thought*. New York: Basic Books.

Oakley, T. and Houggard, A., eds. 2008. *Mental spaces in discourse and Interaction*. Amsterdam and Philadelphia: John Benjamins.

Rubba, J., 2009. The dream as blend in David Lynch's *Muholland Drive*. *In:* V. Evans and S. Pourcel, eds. *New directions in cognitive linguistics*. Amsterdam: John Benjamins, 465–498.

Schneider, R. and Hartner, M., eds. 2012. *Blending and the study of narrative: Approaches and applications*. Berlin: de Gruyter.

Semino, E., 2006. Blending and characters' mental functioning in Virginia Woolf's *Lappin and Lapinova*. *Language and Literature*, 15 (1), 55–72.

Semino, E., 2009. Text worlds. *In:* G. Brône and J. Vandaele, eds. *Cognitive poetics: Goals, gains, and gaps*. New York: de Gruyter, 33–72.

Semino, E., 2010. Unrealistic scenarios, metaphorical blends, and rhetorical strategies across genres. *English Text Construction*, 3 (2), 250–274.

Stallworthy, J., ed. 1994. *Wilfred Owen: The war poems*. Chatto and Windus.

Sweetser, E., 2000. Blended spaces and performativity. *Cognitive Linguistics*, 11 (3–4), 305–334.

Sweetser, E., 2004. 'The suburbs of your good pleasure': Cognition, culture, and the bases of metaphoric structure. *The Shakespearean International Yearbook*, 4, 24–55.

Sweetser, E., 2006. Whose rhyme is whose reason? Sound and sense in Cyrano de Bergerac. *Language and Literature*, 15 (1), 29–54.

Turner, M., 1996. *The literary mind: The origins of thought and language*. New York: Oxford University Press.

Turner, M., 2004. The ghost of anyone's father. *In:* G. Bradshaw, T. Bishop and M. Turner, eds. *The Shakespearean international yearbook 4*. Aldershot: Ashgate Publishing, 72–97.

Turner, M., ed. 2006. *The artful mind: Cognitive science and the riddle of human creativity*. Oxford: Oxford University Press.

19

Cognitive poetics

Margaret H. Freeman

Introduction

'What is cognitive poetics?' This is a question I am invariably asked when I have to say what I do. It is a difficult question to answer because it means different things to different people. In its narrowest sense, *poetics* literally refers to the study of poetry. For example, Tsur's theory of cognitive poetics (1992 and 2008) focuses on ways in which human cognitive processing constrains and shapes both the language and aesthetic form of poetry and readers' responses to them. In a more general sense *poetics* (from the Greek term *poesis*, 'making') refers to the study of all the arts. Within this broader definition, further discriminations are made. For example, Semino (10 July 2012) focuses on linguistic creativity and interpretation:

> Cognitive poetics combines the detailed analysis of linguistic choices and patterns in texts with a systematic consideration of the mental processes and representations that are involved in the process of interpretation. Within Cognitive poetics, literary reading is assumed to involve the same mental processes and representations that are involved in comprehension generally. However, special attention is paid to linguistic creativity and its interpretation, since creativity is a central part of the literary experience (even though it is not an exclusively literary phenomenon).

If *poetics* may be understood in several ways, the same is true for *cognitive*. Traditionally, the term *cognitive* refers to the rationalising, conceptual processes of the human mind that are based in logic and true/false dichotomies. However, with the rise of the cognitive sciences and especially cognitive psychology, researchers increasingly recognise that the human mind/brain/body interface involves much more than conceptual reasoning; conceptual reasoning itself can be seen to be both motivated and affected by processes and phenomena that include bodily sensations, emotions, feelings, memory, attention, imagery, metaphor, and analogous thinking. Spolsky (16 July 2012) focuses on cognition in her description of cognitive approaches to the arts as:

> an anti-idealist, anti-Platonist enterprise that entails the following assumptions: 1) the embodiment of the mind-brain both enables and constrains what humans can think,

know, believe, do; 2) human works, including works of art, are attempts to extend the boundaries of what can be controlled, known, understood by imaginative re-representations in many media; 3) any study of cognitive issues in a specific work of art must be historically sensitive to the contexts of its creation and reception.

The role of cognition in the literary arts long precedes the rise of the cognitive sciences, especially in philosophy, from Aristotle's *Poetics* and *The Art of Rhetoric* to aesthetic theories in the eighteenth century (see Chapter 1 in this volume for more on this). In the twentieth century, Ingarden (1973, p. 4) addresses two questions: '1) How is the object of cognition – the literary work of art – structured? and 2) What is the procedure which will lead to knowledge of the literary work; that is, how does the cognition of the work of art come about and to what does or can it lead?'. Both questions combine a literary critical focus on product with a scientific focus on process. This combination has led to a more general approach than is captured in terms like poetics, stylistics, or rhetoric, reflected in the title *Cognitive Literary Studies* (Jaén and Simon 2012).

Another focus of cognitive poetics resides in its emphasis on the aesthetic effects of human creativity on human cognition, so that it may be defined as a theory of the aesthetic that, while its primary focus concerns the literary arts, it explores links common to all art forms. My own research attempts to explain the subliminal cognitive processes by which we experience a poem through its imagery, language and prosody. These processes are not merely or even primarily conceptual: the aesthetic elements of sensations and emotions that we articulate as feelings enable us to experience poetry (and for that matter all art forms) as *the semblance of felt life through forms symbolic of human feeling*. As Abram (1996) has noted, we in the Western tradition have suppressed the fact that we are part of sensible nature, have divorced ourselves from our ancient sensuous and emotional connections to the material life-world. It is noticeable that story and song figure prominently in Abram's accounts of pre-literate societies. The arts provide the means whereby without losing sight of the many achievements of scientific methodologies, we can reconnect with the subliminal, precategorial, and primordial interactions with the larger life-world of which we are a part. Studies of the arts thus illuminate these aspects of human cognition. At its best, cognitive poetics is Janus-faced, looking toward both the aesthetic text and the embodied mind. In so doing, it offers the possibilities of contributing toward both a cognitive theory of the arts and a theory of the embodied mind.

Historical perspectives

Cognitive poetics is a fairly recent development in studies of cognition and literature. The term has a somewhat complex history. Tsur (1992) outlined a theoretical approach to prosody based solidly in a wide range of interdisciplinary fields, including Gestalt psychology, Russian Formalism, New Criticism, literary criticism in general, linguistics, and neuroscience. A separate strand was meanwhile developing in the mid 1990s. Unaware of Tsur's use of the term, I began to use 'cognitive poetics' to describe my own interdisciplinary approach to poetry, following Tabakowska's (1993) seminal application of cognitive linguistics to literature (Freeman 1998, 2007b, 2008). Another theoretical strand arising from conceptual metaphor studies in cognitive linguistics gave rise to Lakoff and Turner's (1989) *More than Cool Reason: A Field Guide to Poetic Metaphor.* This strand broadened into further studies as a result of Fauconnier and Turner's (2002) work in conceptual integration theory, or 'blending' (see Chapter 18 in this volume). This cognitive linguistic emphasis is reflected in

Semino and Culpeper (2002) and in Stockwell's (2002) textbook, with its companion volume by Gavins and Steen (2003). The cognitive linguistics approach has thus tended to dominate as a description of the term, as evidenced by my survey in *The Cognitive Linguistics Handbook* (Freeman 2007a). More recently, Brône and Vandaele (2009) specifically explore the interface between cognitive linguistics and cognitive poetics.

Yet another strand emerged from a more general interest in the relation of cognition, reflected in the multidisciplinary approaches of cognitive science to literary studies (Crane 2000, Crane and Richardson 1999, Hogan 2003, Spolsky 1993), along with work in cognitive psychology (Gardner 1982, Holland 1988, 2009), cognitive rhetoric (Oakley 1997, Turner 1987), cognitive narratology (Emmott 1997, Fludernik 1993), text-world theory (Gavins 2007, Werth 1999), cognitive stylistics (Burke 2011, Semino and Culpeper 2002), cognitive archaeology (Mithen 1996), evolutionary psychology (Boyd 2009, 2012), and cognitive neuroscience (Dehaene 2009). Such explorations have expanded the role of cognitive poetics to include other theoretical perspectives and all literary texts.

Critical issues and topics

The question arises from this history as to whether cognitive poetics in its current state is a general movement, a clearly delineated field of study, or, as Tsur's title suggests, a theory. Tsur (2008) attempts to characterise what cognitive poetics is (or might be), and how it is similar to, or differs from, other cognitive approaches to literature. He shows, quite persuasively, how Lakoff's theory of conceptual metaphor cannot adequately account for the literary use of metaphor. He challenges Stockwell's adoption of the term *cognitive poetics* by focusing on what is meant by 'cognitive'. Tsur notes that the *products* of human cognitive processes are not themselves cognitive. In practising cognitive poetics, Tsur argues, one needs to explore the cognitive processes or mechanisms by which writers create and readers respond to literary texts, and to show how they illuminate poetic effects.

Tsur (2008, p. 623) acknowledges that 'Cognitive poetics is not a homogeneous enterprise'. The differences among the various approaches lie in the kinds of questions one asks, and the ways in which one explores the cognitive processes at work in experiencing literature. One major difference is whether the focus is primarily on interpretation or experience. Sweetser's (2006) study of versification in *Cyrano de Bergerac*, Tsur argues, is meaning-oriented as opposed to his own gestalt-oriented approach that considers the play's versification from the perspective of the perceptual qualities it generates. In his conclusion, Tsur makes the important point that his theoretical framework does away with the form-content distinction that underlies Sweetser's study. Like Sweetser, Hiraga (2005) also maintains this distinction in her work on metaphor and iconicity. In my own work, I propose a theory of poetic iconicity that does not depend on a form-content dichotomy.

By focusing on the ways in which research in the cognitive sciences can contribute to the study of literature, Tsur's approach demands a consideration of literary critical approaches in helping to distinguish artistic expressions from everyday discourse. Whereas cognitive science research in general focuses on features common to all human cognition, cognitive poetics is concerned with what differentiates literary from conventional creativity. It highlights those aspects of cognitive processing that the cognitive sciences need to consider in understanding the full scope of human cognition.

Bergs (2009) has identified ten areas in cognitive poetics that need theoretical development from a cognitive linguistic perspective. These include: the different expectations common readers and literary experts have in responding to literary as opposed to conventional texts;

empirical studies that go beyond statistical data; literature's aesthetic qualities and its openness to variable meanings; the importance of contextual grounding, as in historical and genre studies; the various effects of linguistic and cognitive elements influencing memory in the processing of replicable written texts as opposed to spoken utterances; and the development of integrative theories that move beyond simply recognising correspondences between findings in the cognitive sciences and literary studies. Already interdisciplinary as these agendas are, they overlap with various approaches in psychology, neuroscience, empirical literary research and historical/genre studies, among others. Studies in evolutionary psychology, for example, raise important theoretical questions as to the role of the arts in the development of the human mind; research in the neurosciences explores imaginative creativity in brain function; empirical/experimental studies provide evidence for theoretical hypotheses on literary reading; studies of metalinguistic effects of prosody focus on the affective aspects of the sensuous and the emotional in human cognitive processing; research in the cognitive sciences and the humanities explores integrative links between them. The challenge for cognitive poetics is how to incorporate these questions and issues into an aesthetic theory for literature that also links to an overall aesthetic theory of the arts in general.

Current contributions and research

Given the many areas that fall under the scope of cognitive poetics, I have selected seven categories that reflect current research from various perspectives, all of which develop theories that integrate research in human cognitive processing and literature and the arts.

Literary creativity in the evolution of the human mind

Theorists of human cognitive development commonly assume that the arts are by-products of the human mind, emerging after the more direct needs for tool-making, social communication, and survival have been satisfied. Boyd (2009), for example, who calls his speciality 'evolutionary literary criticism', or 'evocriticism' for short, does not see creativity as necessary for evolution, but rather the development of 'cognitive play', and considers both art and science as 'unnatural' adaptations. For Boyd, apparently, 'creativity' is equivalent to 'originality' or 'novelty'. In his latest work (2012, p. 14), he describes the specific ability to play with language patterning in non-narrative lyrics as not needing 'extra cognitive design' that would trigger adaptation. Such assumptions are challenged by other cognitive research. Turner (1996) establishes, through close analysis of the principles of story, projection, and parable, that these mechanisms of mind not only preceded human language but were necessary for its development. Whereas Boyd focuses on art as *product*, which encourages the idea of its emergence as post-cognitive, Turner focuses on the creativity of art as cognitive *process* that is needed for human thought to emerge at all.

The distinction between Boyd's and Turner's approaches is reflected in Benedetto Croce's argument that the *products* of art are not the *works* of art: 'If we take an aesthetic production, say a recognised work of art, we generally mean by expression the translation of the artist's vision into physical phenomena – colours, shapes, or sounds. ... The works of art are the aesthetic activity. The true artistic expression is never anything physical, on the contrary it is the aesthetic mental synthesis, and it is independent of outward translation, however necessary this translation may be for its communication' (quoted in Carr 1917, p. 162). Miall (2006, pp. 190–191) makes a similar point in contrasting content-directed approaches to the evolutionary significance of the arts with functional approaches of aesthetic activity such as dehabituation through foregrounding.

Arguing that the 'literary mind is the fundamental mind', Turner (1996, p. v) claims that 'the central issues for cognitive science are in fact the issues of the literary mind'. These issues are further explored in Turner (2006), with essays written by researchers in linguistics, semiotics, psychology, and the neurosciences that reflect just some of the extensive work being done in exploring the cognitive bases of human thought and creativity.

Mithen (1996, p. 194) provides forensic evidence from archaeological discoveries to reconstruct the evolution of the modern human mind, arguing that art emerged as the product of a cognitive fluidity in the human brain that occurred in a cultural explosion beginning at different times in different populations between sixty thousand and thirty thousand years ago. Although 'the three cognitive processes critical to making art – mental conception of an image, intentional communication and the attribution of meaning – were all present in the Early Human mind', it was not until these isolated cognitive processes began to function together that the modern human mind emerged (p. 162). Mithen's argument for the emergence of cognitive fluidity through a generalised intelligence that integrated the earlier specialised but isolated intelligences provides independent evidence for Turner's (1996, p. 57) argument that the modern human mind emerged as the result of projection of story in parable, the 'complex operations of projection, binding, linking, blending, and integration over multiple spaces' that enable human creativity to occur.

Mithen's and Turner's perspectives suggest that aesthetic cognition is by no means a luxury or afterthought in human cognitive development. Mithen's cognitive fluidity thesis provides a means whereby the imaginative faculty can be seen as a crucial and critical element not only for the arts, but for the development of language, the sciences, and religion. In its explorations of the cognitive processes engaged in producing and responding to the arts, cognitive poetics is in a position to provide further illumination into these aspects of the human mind.

Literature and neuroscience

Mithen's cognitive fluidity thesis is supported by recent neuroscientific research into brain processes. Although the origins of conscious awareness are still little understood, research on the neural workings of the brain illuminates the nature of the literary skills we possess. For example, the emergence of cognitive fluidity in the brain may have enabled the transposing of sensory perceptions into visual forms. As Abram (1996, p. 138) notes, 'iconic writing systems – those that employ pictographic, ideographic, and/or rebuslike characters – necessarily rely, to some extent, upon our original sensory participation with the enveloping natural field'. Alphabetical writing systems depend upon tight neurological connections in the brain between the senses of sound and sight. Dehaene (2009, pp. 318–319) describes modern research experiments by both psychologists and neuroscientists that identify specific regions of the brain that are specialised for letter identification and interpretation. Learning to read enables the brain to develop multiple neural pathways among these regions to link visual recognition with oral pronunciation and semantic, lexical meanings. These pathways do not work in linear fashion, but rather act in recycling simultaneity of network activation in the enlarged prefrontal cortex of the human brain. Holland (2009) explores the ways in which these multiple pathways interconnect across both hemispheres of the brain in literary reading. He provides extensive evidence from a wide variety of research in psychology and neuroscience to establish the role of the right hemisphere in integrating the processing of prosodic features, emotions and literary devices with the recognition and decoding capacities of the left hemisphere. Kane (2004, p. 22) suggests that 'the degree of right-hemispheric involvement in language is what differentiates "poetic" or "literary" from "referential" or "technical" speech and texts'. These studies provide important justification for the role of the arts in developing human brain capacity. Holland (2009, p. 359) notes that

> when our brains work in special ways to create or re-create a literary work, we can freshly sense our selves and our world, relish our language, and confront our feelings toward one another. Fully engaged with and thinking through works of literature and the arts, we uncover our own individuality. We open ourselves to the largest truth of who we are, who we have been, and who finally we will be. In the last analysis, understanding a literary work means understanding our own humanity.

Cognition and poetics: Integration or exchange?

Relations between the sciences and the arts and humanities have suffered from several factors, among them the Cartesian confidence in scientific methodology as the only route to true knowledge, and the strict division between the natural world and the world of human affairs. What I call the Cartesian factor, for example, has led to two recent publications whose titles imply science's superiority to its weaker, subservient cousins: Slingerland (2008) and van Peer *et al.* (2012). A consilience workshop in 2008 attempted to counteract this one-way tendency, resulting in an edited volume by Slingerland and Collard (2012), which includes a section on approaches to literature. In a revealing afterword to this book, Harpham points out that it was only with the demise of philology, known as the 'Queen of the Sciences', in the twentieth century that literary studies took an anti-scientific turn. Meanwhile, Bruhn (2011, p. 447) takes a different approach to the relation between the sciences and arts/humanities, in which contributors explore, not integration, but 'a set of topics that are of central importance to both literary and cognitive research: affective, embodied, and distributed cognition; agency and intentionality; creativity and fictivity; genre; and metaphor ... to illustrate a genuinely two-way exchange of considerable value – both immediate and indicative – for poetics and, even more so, for cognitive science'. In urging non-consilience, Harpham concludes his afterword by describing an empirical study that was designed to discover, with EEG and fMRI technology, whether literary language forced the brain out of its customary routines to negotiate new pathways. This experiment, Harpham reports, discovered 'a new way of thinking about literary language, as the purest form of consciousness itself, "the best model brain science has to work from, if it is to capture the spontaneous living complexity of the human brain"' (Slingerland and Collard 2012, p. 430). Such studies are perfect examples of cognitive poetics' Janus-faced role, illuminating both literary language and human cognitive processing.

Empirical/experimental studies

Miall (2006) adds a new dimension to cognitive poetics in developing several methodologies for empirical research into the way readers respond to literary texts. Combining theoretical and experimental approaches, Miall describes several empirical strategies for exploring how readers read, as well as a methodology for identifying and modeling phonemic contrasts. Rejecting the simplistic notion that phonemes have intrinsic meaning, Miall's methodology nevertheless shows that systematic contrasts between phonemes in certain contexts trigger affective responses in readers that can motivate meaning. Claassen (2012) reports on empirical studies of how common readers construct images of authors in their reading. Recognising the distortions that result from reader-response tests in a laboratory environment, Burke (2011) emphasises the need to design experiments that reflect readers' emotional responses in the kind of environment in which they choose to read for pleasure. Burke (2011, pp. 254–255) focuses on three questions that arise from a reader's commitment to engage with a literary work: 'i) what role does emotion play in a cognitive event like literary text processing?, ii) which kinds of bottom-up and top-down inputs are most prominently involved in literary reading, and how do they interact in meaning-making?, and iii) what happens in the minds and bodies of readers when they experience intense or heightened emotions at literary closure?'. All three studies rely on quantifiable measures for determining readers' responses to literary texts, and focus on ordinary as opposed to expert readers. A different empirical strategy was employed in my qualitative study of the kinds of cognitive mapping strategies participants employed in a web-based forum during their readings of a Dickinson poem (Freeman 2002). These strategies, I discovered, partially depended on participants' level of education, their profession, and their experiential background.

Cognitive linguistic approaches

Most writers on literature from a cognitive linguistics perspective who self-identify as practising cognitive poetics employ theoretical research in such areas as cognitive grammar, schema theory, conceptual metaphor and blending in their analyses, thus overlapping with cognitive stylistics approaches discussed in other chapters in this volume. The problems involved in differentiating cognitive poetics as a separate, independent research paradigm from these other approaches are outlined in Brône and Vandaele (2009), in which respondents to each article critically examine the work presented. The most recent contribution to cognitive poetics in this area is Wójcik-Leese (2010). In the first full-length cognitive poetics study of a single poet, Wójcik-Leese identifies a complex structuring metaphor, MENTAL LIFE/POETIC CREATIVITY IS AN EXPLORATION OF A VISUAL FIELD, in order to chart the movements of the poet's mind thinking. In reaching toward the cognitive processes that motivate the various drafts Bishop created as she worked on her poems, Wójcik-Leese (2010, p. 22) achieves the objectives of a cognitive poetics that relies on 'our awareness of the embodied mind, the cognitive unconscious, metaphorical thought, radial categories centred round prototypes, polysemy as a form of categorization, conceptual semantics and the encyclopedic nature of linguistic meaning'.

Affective studies

Missing from Wójcik-Leese's list is emotional affect. As Oatley (2003 p. 168) notes: 'Emotions have become the most interesting of current topics in psychology, cognitive science, and neuroscience. In the same way, in cognitive poetics there was a relative neglect of emotions, but this phase too is passing.' Oatley's 'relative' is, I believe, a nod in the direction of Tsur's focus on the affective qualities of prosody. Tsur's primary aim in his extensive research spanning almost fifty years is based on the principle set out at the beginning of his seminal work (1992, p. 1):

> Cognitive Poetics … offers cognitive theories that systematically account for the relationship between the structure of literary texts and their perceived effects. By the

same token, it discriminates which reported effects *may* legitimately be related to the structures in question, and which may not.

Tsur (2003, p. 37) identifies one assumption that underlies cognitive poetics: poetic texts display emotional qualities that are *perceived* by the reader; that is, these qualities are aesthetic, in that they display 'some structural resemblance between the sound patterns and emotions'. One central problem Tsur (2003, p. 116) addresses is 'how poetic language – which, like all language, is conceptual and linear – is able to convey experiences that are nonconceptual and non-linear'. This problem is related to the question of how the complex semiotic systems of poetry capture felt qualities through an indefinite number of verbal strategies when there is no one-to-one correspondence between them.

Tsur (1992, 2008) addresses these questions by distinguishing between convergent style, characterised by strong, articulated and stable shapes, and a divergent style that is more diffuse in expressing undifferentiated gestalts. These are linked, respectively, to high and low categorisation, which enable either rapid or delayed conceptualisation, and, in metaphor, to split and integrated focus. These cognitive processes shape and constrain language at every level: semantic, phonological, syntactic and prosodic. Literary styles can be identified by the extent to which they converge or diverge from high versus low categorisation, as can critical styles adopted by readers' preferences for either rapid or delayed conceptualisation. Delayed conceptualisation, with its propensity for open-ended possibilities, is the preferred strategy for appreciating the aesthetics of a literary text.

Aesthetic theory

The term *aesthetics* was coined in the eighteenth century by Alexander Gottlieb Baumgarten to describe a science of sensory perception that includes the arts (Freeman 2011). From the outset, aesthetics is associated with phenomenology, our sensory experiences of the external world, especially as characterised in the work of Merleau-Ponty. As Abram (1996, p. 124) notes: 'Merleau-Ponty's careful phenomenology of perceptual experience had begun to disclose, underneath our literate abstractions, a deeply participatory relation to things and to the earth, a felt reciprocity curiously analogous to the animistic awareness of indigenous, oral persons'. Art reflects this attachment through the activity of *poesis*. Croce (1953 [1909], p. 10) identifies artists not by a special kind of intuitive faculty, but by the fact that they are able to capture the qualities of sensation and impression: 'The painter is a painter, because he sees what others only feel or catch a glimpse of, but do not see. We think we see a smile, but in reality we have only a vague impression of it, we do not perceive all the characteristic traits of which it is the sum, as the painter discovers them after he has worked upon them and is thus able to fix them on the canvas.' Croce's description suggests that it is the activity of making that leads to aesthetic discovery of the nature of reality. From the perspective of cognitive aesthetics, I situate cognitive poetics as a subset that focuses in particular on the literary arts, and I am developing a theory of poetic iconicity that attempts to capture the essence of aesthetic experience.

Not all poetry is iconic. It becomes iconic for the reader when the reader responds emotionally to the forms of the poem (its metres, rhythms, sound patterns, structures, semantic networks of meaning) that carry the essence of its intentionality, purpose, motivation. When the term *iconicity* is used in cognitive linguistics, it usually refers to elements in language (semantic, phonetic, or syntactic) that reflect what is meant; that is, a semiotic intentional sign. Alexander Pope's line 'And ten low words oft creep in one dull line' is iconic because it contains ten words which are all monosyllables ('low') and eight of which carry heavy stress which weighs the line down and makes it monotonous ('dull'), so that the line is doing what it is saying.

This semiotic sense of iconicity occurs also in my theory of poetic iconicity. The difference is that in semiotics, any image is understood to be iconic. However, the popular use of the word *iconic* (and it crops up every day in newspapers, magazines, and books) refers to something special, which is emotionally meaningful to a person or group. Yellow chequered taxicabs are said to be iconic of New York, the Eiffel tower of Paris, and so on. In this usage, something usually becomes iconic when it is meaningful to a community or nation, so that anything can become iconic. Bryson (2008) includes articles written by contributors who describe some element of England (places, people, or things) that they find represents the essence of Englishness to them.

My theory draws from both semiotics and popular usage, as well as from phenomenology and aesthetics. It provides a model for identifying those forms in a poem that make it iconic, not just in the senses described above, but also to the extent that it makes immediate the essence of experienced reality. According to my theory, poetic iconicity is not purely subjective, in that any poem can become iconic if the reader thinks it is. The forms of the poem have to physically embody the impetus that led the poet to conceive the poem in just that way. Wallace Stevens' poem 'Of Mere Being' reflects the phenomenological sense of iconicity in this respect (Freeman 2007b).

Main research methods and recommendations for practice

What differentiates cognitive poetics from other stylistics approaches, I suggest, is its focus on exploring the ways in which human cognitive processes constrain aesthetic creativity in all its forms, and the ways in which aesthetic creativity can illuminate the workings of human cognition. In my own work on poetry I employ a range of strategies depending on the scope of my focus and the poetry under consideration. For example, I found conceptual metaphor theory especially useful in identifying a structuring metaphor that characterised Dickinson's conceptual universe throughout her poetic corpus (Freeman 1995). Blending theory helped my analysis of Sylvia Plath's poem 'The Applicant' (Freeman 2005). Focus on prosodic effects inevitably results in exploration of the ways feeling (emotion and sensation) motivate expression. As I began to develop my theory of poetic iconicity, I incorporated methodologies drawn from Peircean semiotics Hoopes 1991), Merleau-Ponty's (1962[1945]) phenomenology, and Langer's (1953, 1967) theory of art, as well as tools developed by other cognitive researchers. On a practical level, in attempting a cognitive analysis, I first take the following steps (not necessarily in the order presented here and always cycling among them) before reaching an understanding of what a poem might be doing. It is important to note that the steps reflect one's experience of the poem's effects, not an interpretation of its meaning. To show how they work, I present a very brief analysis of a Dickinson poem (Franklin 1981, #1328).

1 To make Routine
2 a Stimulus
3 Remember it
4 can cease -
5 Capacity to
6 terminate
7 Is a specific

8   Grace -
9   Of Retrospect
10   the Arrow
11   That power to
12   repair
13   Departed with
14   the torment
15   Become, Alas,
16   more fair -

Intuiting aesthetic emotion

First readings provide an immediate response of engagement or otherwise. A poem's tone has emotional resonance, and is the preliminary indicator for cognitive creativity in understanding the poem. Like many of Dickinson's short poems, this one is not transparent on a first reading. The first eight lines seem straightforward enough, but the final eight lines puzzle. However, I intuitively feel a sense of consolation and reassurance, even in the face of language that suggests otherwise.

Looking closely at the language of the text

Because the medium of poetry is language, linguistic analysis is a necessary subpart of a cognitive approach. Often, different readings of a Dickinson text result from resolving ambiguous syntax in only one way. However, recognising possible ambiguities can also allow the reader to hold more than one reading at the same time. So first I look at the poem's structure. On a macro level, the poem divides into two parts, both comprised of eight lines. Immediately, I am led to consider the second part an elaboration or commentary on the first part, with Dickinson following the characteristic format of a Biblical passage (Berlin 1985).

In the first four lines, the speaker apostrophises an addressee with the admonition 'Remember'. The opening phrase, 'To make', can be understood either as 'if you want to make' or 'in order to make'. Is 'Routine' something to be appreciated or deprecated? Why should the thought of routine ending turn it into a stimulus? The use of a noun phrase in the second line presents a possible ambiguity: a stimulus for what? To make routine something other than it is? Or to make routine itself stimulating? Is 'Capacity to / terminate' an example of the middle voice, in the sense that routine itself is capable of ceasing, or does the phrase refer to the fact that we can end routine whenever we want? Why grace?

As if these eight lines don't present problems enough, the next eight are worse. Does the phrase 'of Retrospect' belong to 'Grace' or does it start a new thought? What is/are the subject(s) of the verbs *departed* and *become*? Is *departed* a past participle or the simple past tense of a main verb? Is *that* in line 11 a demonstrative or a relative pronoun? Why should something 'more fair' be regretted in that parenthetical 'Alas'? How did an arrow get into this poem?

I could run through all the possible syntactic readings one could give to these last eight lines, including attaching them syntactically to the end of the first part. Such linguistic analysis reveals why readers come up with different meanings. However, a linguistic analysis in itself cannot determine which formulations cohere in the poem's total gestalt. Instead, I turn to other language strategies. Overall, a certain symmetry occurs across the two parts of the poem. I note the three infinitives: *to make, to terminate, to repair*; the appearance of *terminate* and *repair* on lines of their own, making the word *to* appear twice at line end; the parallelism of *capacity to* and *power to*, *can cease* and *terminate*, *remember* and *retrospect*. I note that the noun phrases *a stimulus*, *the arrow*, *the torment* also appear on separate lines, as do the end rhymes *can cease*, *Grace* and *repair*, *more fair*. Endings and aftermaths seem to dominate as themes.

Identifying prosodic features

The emotional weight of a poem lies in its prosody. Multiple worksheets are helpful here, as they enable study of individual features like metre, rhythm, enjambment, phonetic patterning, parallelism, and so on. This is the most extensive and elaborate part of my process. Without presenting all the details of my analysis, here is a list that reveals how sound patterning supports the poem's overall symmetry:

- [p] and [m] never occur in the same line.
- [m] drops out after *terminate* in line 6 and doesn't reappear until *torment* in line 14 (note the same pattern of [t-m-t], with no [k] or [s] or [p] in the paired lines).
- The only lines in which only one of the sounds [t, k, s, m, p] occur are line 8, *grace*, line 12, *repair*, and line 16, *more fair*. Note that these do not include [t] or [k].
- [p] occurs with [s] three times in the first part (ll. 5–9) and three times in the second without [s] (ll. 11–13).
- [m] occurs only in the first three lines and the last three lines, except for line 6 on *terminate*.
- [k] and [s] predominate in the first part; they disappear altogether in the second part until line 15 when their order [k, s] chiasmically mirrors the [s, k] of line 9, linking *of retroSpeKt* with *beKome, alaS*. (Note also the disappearance of [t] from the second of these two lines.)
- l. 10, *the arrow*, is sore-thumbed: it sticks out by being the only line in the entire poem that contains none of the sounds [t, k, s, m, p]. Is this the eye of the poem?

The rhymes of 'cease' and 'grace' serve to link the idea of ending as something desired, while the rhyming of 'repair' and 'more fair –' that bring the poem to its ending strikes the more positive note that may have contributed to my initial feelings of consolation and reassurance.

Recognising cognitive import

The interrelation of prosody and language reveals the underlying forces that capture the 'minding' that the poet creates and the reader re-creates in bringing a text to life. We have already seen how sounds appear and disappear, how they interplay with each other as the poem proceeds, how they link lexical items with each other. Images of departure and termination, of memory and retrospect, of pain and reparation are reinforced by such sound patterning. To cite just one example, note how the sound [r] appearing at word onset in *routine* in the first line occurs in word middle in the sore-thumbed line 10 (*arrow*), and then repeats on the last two lines of the poem at word end (*more fair*). In brief, my cognitive reading notes that the whole poem after the first two lines is commenting on what happens if routine ceases. Although engaging in routine may seem torturous, the fact that it is continuous means that it has the power of restoration. Once it's gone, in retrospect it seems 'more fair'. The central four lines serve to divide the first six from the last six lines, so that I now see more clearly how the line 'Of Retrospect' reflects both the preceding 'specific / Grace' and the ensuing 'Arrow'. The poem strikes a cautionary note: we need to think of routine as a stimulus because otherwise we will lose the advantages it provides.

I suggest that a cognitive reading is not simply another literary analysis. Rather, it provides the grounding for literary interpretation. For example, one could generalise the themes of this poem by elaborating the roles of memory or regret, or by linking it to other Dickinson poems with similar semantic networks, such as 'routine' and 'round'.

Evaluating a poem's success

For me, a poem's success lies in its ability to create a shiver up my spine. That occurs when I perceive how all its elements cohere to create poetic iconicity, the power to create a feeling of presence in the present moment enacted by the poem doing what it is saying. A poem 'works' when its reader is drawn into emotional engagement with the world of the text and through it, the world of the poet. Dickinson's poem works for me because it 'makes real' its statements about routine and reparation, retrospect and regret through its prosodic structure. Cognitive analysis enables me to explain my intuitive feelings on first reading. Abram (1996, pp. 158–159) gives me a clue to the poem's cognitive effect in his description of Apache *'agodzaahi* ('that which has happened') stories, which always begin and end where the events in the story actually occurred ('It happened at...'):

> The telling of any such tale today is always prompted by a misdeed committed by someone in the community; the *'agodzaahi* story, precisely told, acts as a remedial response to that misdeed. Thus, when an Apache person offends the community by a certain action, one of his or her elders will wait for an appropriate moment – perhaps at a community gathering – and will then "shoot" the person by recounting an appropriate *'agodzaahi* story. Although the offender is not identified or named aloud, he or she will know, if the "arrow" (the tale) has been well chosen and well aimed, that he is the target; he will feel the story penetrate deep beneath his skin and sap his strength, making him feel ill and weak. Then the story will begin to work on him from within, making him want to change his ways, to "replace himself," to live right. And so his behavior will change. Yet the story will stay with him. For he will continually encounter the place in the land where it all happened.

I don't know if Dickinson would have learned of such a thing, or anything like it, but even the language of Abram's description resonates with her Routine poem (remediation, deep within, working from within, replacement, continuity, encounter). Read in the light of an *'agodzaahi* story, the poem makes perfect sense. The topography of Dickinson's poem is the mind. The arrow (telling the story reminding one of the possibility that routine can end) has the capacity to terminate one's attitude about routine and the power to repair one's feeling of torment as we endure routine. Remembering that routine can cease transforms it into something stimulating, and thus can change our minds about it, causing the torment to depart. But if it does, our retrospective thoughts about routine will become 'Alas, / more fair –' (thus explaining the alas), and we will regret the ending of routine by recollecting that it is a good thing which will thus restore (repair) our attitude toward it.

Future directions

So, then, how do I respond to the question, 'What is cognitive poetics?' Cognitive poetics is a way of looking at poetry as the product of an artistic process that utilises all subliminal regions of the brain: conceptual, emotive, and sensuous. By focusing on all aspects of poetic art, readers can come to understand a poem's wellsprings in the primordial, precategorial recesses of the brain/mind/body's self-identification with the life-world of which we are a part. The painter Peter London (2003) puts it well in his deliberately double-meaninged phrase: drawing closer to nature draws us closer to ourselves.

Although I have concentrated on poetry, I believe that iconicity functions in all the arts. As Abram (1996, p. 120) notes:

> Stories, like rhymed poems or songs, readily incorporate themselves into our felt experience; the shifts of action echo and resonate with our own encounters – in hearing or telling the story we vicariously *live* it, and the travails of the characters embed themselves into our own flesh. ... And the more lively the story – the more vital or stirring the encounters within it – the more readily it will be in-corporated.

As cognitive poetics continues to develop, I see it emerging as a more clearly defined field that relates artistic activity to human cognition. Along these lines, Oxford University Press has inaugurated a book series on 'Cognition and Poetics' that seeks to further high quality interdisciplinary research at the intersection of cognitive sciences and the arts.

Related topics

Blending, emotion and neuroscience, metaphor and metonymy, rhetoric and poetics, text world theory

Further reading

Gibbs, R. W., Jr., ed. 2008. *The Cambridge handbook of metaphor and thought*. Cambridge: Cambridge University Press.

A useful compendium of articles that describe some of the key developments in contemporary metaphor research, detailing the contribution of metaphor to human cognition, communication, and culture.

Harbus, A., 2012. *Cognitive approaches to old English poetry*. Woodbridge, UK: D.S. Brewer.

This book offers a new approach to the study of Old English poetry by adopting key ideas from cognitive literary/cultural studies, cognitive poetics, and conceptual metaphor theory in conjunction with more familiar models derived from literary analysis, stylistics, and historical linguistics.

Hogan, P. C., 2011. *What literature teaches us about emotion*. Cambridge: Cambridge University Press.

This book integrates literary insights with work from neuroscience, psychology and philosophy, among other disciplines, in order to contribute to current interdisciplinary emotion research.

Johnson, M., 2007. *The meaning of the body: Aesthetics of human understanding*. Chicago and London: The University of Chicago Press.

A major contribution to research into aspects of embodied meaning and cognition that involve qualities, feelings, emotions, and temporal processes, this book argues for the arts as giving form, significance, and value to our lives.

Robinson, J., 2005. *Deeper than reason: Emotion and its role in literature, music, and art*. Oxford: Oxford University Press.

This book takes the insights of modern psychological and neuroscientific research on the emotions and brings them to bear on questions about our emotional involvement with the arts.

References

Abram, D., 1996. *The spell of the sensuous*. New York: Random House.

Bergs, A., 2009. 10 theses on literature, language, and the cognitive enterprise. Osnabrück: Unpublished ms.

Berlin, A., 1985. *The dynamics of biblical parallelism*. Bloomington: Indiana University Press.

Boyd, B., 2009. *On the origin of stories: Evolution, cognition, and fiction*. Cambridge, MA and London: The Belknap Press of Harvard University Press.

Boyd, B., 2012. *Why lyrics last: Evolution, cognition, and Shakespeare's sonnets*. Cambridge, MA and London: Harvard University Press.

Brône, G. and Vandaele, J., eds. 2009. *Cognitive poetics: Goals, gains, and gaps*. Berlin: Mouton de Gruyter.

Bruhn, M., 2011. Introduction: Exchange values and cognitive science. *Poetics Today*, 32 (3–4), 403–460.

Bryson, B., ed. 2008. *Icons of England*. London: Think Publishing.

Burke, M., 2011. *Literary reading, cognition and emotion: An exploration of the oceanic mind*. London and New York: Routledge.

Carr, H.W., 1917. *The philosophy of Benedetto Croce: The problem of art and history*. London: Macmillan.

Claassen, E., 2012. *Author representations in literary reading*. Amsterdam and Philadelphia: John Benjamins.

Crane, M.T., 2000. *Shakespeare and the brain*. Princeton, NJ: Princeton University Press.

Crane, M.T. and Richardson, A., 1999. Literary studies and cognitive science: Toward a new interdisciplinarity. *Mosaic*, 32 (2), 123–140.

Croce, B., [1909] 1953. *Aesthetic: As science of expression and general linguistic*. Douglas Ainslie, trans. New York: The Noonday Press.

Dehaene, S., 2009. *Reading in the brain: The science and evolution of a human invention*. New York: Viking.

Emmott, C., 1997. *Narrative comprehension: A discourse perspective*. Oxford: Oxford University Press.

Fauconnier, G. and Turner, M., 2002. *The way we think: Conceptual blending and the mind's hidden complexities*. New York: Basic Books.

Fludernik, M., 1993. *The fictions of language and the languages of fiction*. Washington, D.C.: Taylor and Francis.

Franklin, R. W., ed. 1981. *The manuscript books of Emily Dickinson*. 2 vols. Cambridge, MA: The Belknap Press of Harvard University Press.

Freeman, M. H., 1995. Metaphor making meaning: Emily Dickinson's conceptual universe, *Journal of Pragmatics*, 24, 643–666.

Freeman, M. H., 1998. Poetry and the scope of metaphor: Toward a theory of cognitive poetics. *In:* A. Barcelona, ed. *Metaphor and metonymy at the crossroads*. The Hague: Mouton de Gruyter, 253–281.

Freeman, M. H., 2002. Cognitive mapping in literary analysis. *Style*, 36 (3), 466–483.

Freeman, M. H., 2005. The poem as complex blend: Conceptual mappings of metaphor in Sylvia Plath's 'The Applicant'. *Language and Literature*, 14 (1), 25–44.

Freeman, M. H., 2007a. Cognitive linguistic approaches to literary studies: State of the art in cognitive poetics. *In:* D. Geeraerts and H. Cuyckens, eds. *The Oxford handbook of cognitive linguistics*. Oxford University Press, 1821–1866.

Freeman, M. H., 2007b. Poetic iconicity. *In:* W. Chlopicki, A. Pawelec, and A. Pojoska, eds. *Cognition in language: Volume in honour of Professor Elzbieta Tabakowska*. Kraków: Tertium, 472–501.

Freeman, M. H., 2008. Reading readers reading a poem: From conceptual to cognitive integration. *Cognitive Semiotics*, 2, 102–128.

Freeman, M. H., 2011. The aesthetics of human experience: Minding, metaphor, and icon in poetic expression. *Poetics Today*, 32 (4), 717–752.

Gardner, H., 1982. *Art, mind and brain: A cognitive approach to creativity*. New York: Basic Books.

Gavins, J., 2007. *Text world theory: An introduction*. Edinburgh: University of Edinburgh Press.

Gavins, J. and Steen, G., eds. 2003. *Cognitive poetics in practice*. London and New York: Routledge.

Gibbs, R. W., Jr., ed. 2008. *The Cambridge handbook of metaphor and thought*. Cambridge: Cambridge University Press.

Harbus, A., 2012. *Cognitive approaches to old English poetry*. Woodbridge, UK: D.S. Brewer.

Hiraga, M., 2005. *Metaphor and iconicity: A cognitive approach to analysing texts*. Houndsmill, Basingstoke and New York: Palgrave Macmillan.

Hogan, P. C., 2003. *Cognitive science, literature, and the arts*. New York: Routledge.

Hogan, P. C., 2011. *What literature teaches us about emotion*. Cambridge: Cambridge University Press.

Holland, N., 1988. *The brain of Robert Frost: A cognitive approach to literature*. New York and London: Routledge, Chapman, and Hall.

Holland, N., 2009. *Literature and the brain*. Gainesville, FL: The PsyArt Foundation.

Hoopes, J., ed. 1991. *Peirce on Signs: Writings on Semiotic by Charles Sanders Peirce.* Chapel Hill and London: The University of North Carolina Press.

Ingarden, R., 1973. *The cognition of the literary work of art.* R. A. Crowley and K. R. Olson, trans. Evanston, IL: Northwestern University Press.

Jaén, I. and Simon, J., eds. 2012. *Cognitive literary studies: Current themes and new directions*. Austin: University of Texas Press.

Johnson, M., 2007. *The meaning of the body: Aesthetics of human understanding*. Chicago and London: The University of Chicago Press.

Kane, J., 2004. Poetry as right-hemispheric language. *Journal of Consciousness Studies*, 11 (5–6), 21–59.

Lakoff, G. and Turner, M., 1989. *More than cool reason: A field guide to poetic metaphor*. Chicago and London: The University of Chicago Press.

Langer, S. K. 1953. *Feeling and form: A theory of art*. New York: Charles Scribner's.

Langer, S. K. 1967. *Mind: An essay on human feeling.* Baltimore: The Johns Hopkins Press.

London, P., 2003. *Drawing closer to nature: Making art in dialogue with the natural world*. Boston and London: Shambhala.

Merleau-Ponty, M. [1945] 1962. *Phenomenology of perception.* Charles Smith, tr. London: Routledge and Keagan Paul. Miall, D. S., 2006. *Literary reading: Empirical and theoretical studies*. New York: Peter Lang.

Mithen, S., 1996. *The prehistory of mind: The cognitive origins of art and science*. London: Thames and Hudson.

Oakley, T. V., 1997. The new rhetoric and the construction of value: Presence, the universal audience, and Beckett's 'Three Dialogues'. *Rhetoric Society Quarterly*, 27 (1), 47–88.

Oatley, K., 2003. 'Writingandreading: The future of cognitive poetics. *In:* J. Gavins and G. Steen, eds. *Cognitive poetics in practice*. London and New York: Routledge, 161–173.

Robinson, J., 2005. *Deeper than reason: Emotion and its role in literature, music, and art*. Oxford: Oxford University Press.

Semino, E., 2012. Definition of cognitive poetics. E-mail (10 July 2012).

Semino, E. and Culpeper J., 2002. *Cognitive stylistics: Language and cognition in text analysis*. Amsterdam: John Benjamins.

Slingerland, E., 2008. *What science offers the humanities: Integrating body and culture*. Cambridge: Cambridge University Press.

Slingerland, E. and Collard, M., eds. 2012. *Creating consilience: Integrating the sciences and the humanities*. Oxford and New York: Oxford University Press.

Spolsky, E., 1993. *Gaps in nature: Literary interpretation and the modular mind*. Albany: State University of New York Press.

Spolsky, E., 2012. Definition of cognitive poetics. E-mail (16 July 2012).

Stockwell, P., 2002. *Cognitive poetics: An introduction*. New York and London: Routledge.

Sweetser, E., 2006. Whose rhyme is whose reason?: Sound and sense in *Cyrano de Bergerac. Language and Literature*, 15 (1), 29–54.

Tabakowska, E., 1993. *Cognitive linguistics and poetics of translation*. Tübingen: Gunter Narr Verlag.

Tsur, R., 1992. *Toward a theory of cognitive poetics*. Amsterdam: North Holland.

Tsur, R., 2003. *On the shore of nothingness: A study in cognitive poetics*. Exeter, UK: Imprint Academic.

Tsur, R., 2008. *Toward a theory of cognitive poetics*. 2nd expanded and updated edn. Brighton and Portland, OR: Sussex Academic Press.

Turner, M., 1987. *Death is the mother of beauty: Mind, metaphor, criticism*. Chicago and London: The University of Chicago Press.

Turner, M., 1996. *The literary mind*. Chicago and London: The University of Chicago Press.

Turner, M., ed. 2006. *The artful mind: Cognitive science and the riddle of human creativity*. Oxford: Oxford University Press.

van Peer, W., Hakemulder F., and Zyngier S., eds. 2012. *Scientific methods for the humanities*. Amsterdam and Philadelphia: John Benjamins.

Werth, P., 1999. *Text worlds: Representing conceptual space in discourse*. London: Longman.

Wójcik-Leese, E., 2010. *Cognitive poetic readings in Elizabeth Bishop: Portrait of a mind thinking*. Berlin and New York: De Gruyter Mouton.

20

Quantitative methodological approaches to stylistics

Olivia Fialho and Sonia Zyngier

Introduction

Stylistics, understood as the study of the language of literary texts (Halliday 1967) and a method for textual analysis (Carter 2007, Verdonk 2002), is a product of the twentieth century formalists' concern for the systematising of literary interpretation (see Jeffries and McIntyre 2010, p. 1). However, since the institutionalisation of literature around the end of the nineteenth century, literary scholars have tended to keep borders between language and literature very clear-cut and have resisted methods that could bear resemblance to those used in natural sciences. Most still hold the view that 'the humanities deal in what is deep down, really humane, benign, mild, open-minded and understanding, the quintessence of what is taken to be human, while the sciences would fail such a perspective' (van Peer 2008, p. 5). More recently, Sklar (2013, pp. 166–167) has stressed that 'In literary studies, there is a tendency for some scholars to reject the inclusion of psychological, philosophical, and, especially, scientific content in support of literary aims or theories,' and he adds that they are 'ill-equipped to speculate on issues that lie outside of their areas of specialty. Yet, they frequently make assertions or raise questions that literary scholarship, as a discipline, seems incapable of answering.'

In this chapter, we show that literary scholars may now have access to thinking and methods that may bring them closer to scientists in other areas. Indeed, we may be approaching the third culture that C.P. Snow envisioned in 1959, when he proposed that it was time that natural scientists should become conversant with humanists and when humanists could understand the methods used in the natural sciences. During Snow's lifetime, literary scholars were not ready to understand the scope of his assertions or willing to become literate in quantitative methods. This picture has now changed. There are quite a few journals that publish quantitative studies (e.g. *Literary and Linguistic Computing*, *Computers and the Humanities*, *Journal of Literary Semantics*, *Language and Literature*, *The Scientific Study of Literature*). New technological advances have also helped change this setting. In this chapter we will see what quantitative research can do and how it has been impacting on literary studies and stylistics. Here we show that by actually adapting methods familiar to natural scientists and making good use of advances in computer technology, literary studies can be enriched. This change in attitude will allow us to arrive at new knowledge that could not have been obtained otherwise. However, stylisticians have not been as radical as literary scholars in avoiding quantitative approaches, as the next section shows.

Historical perspectives

Interest in quantitative approaches to stylistics has been on the rise since the advent of personal computers, mainly in the form of studies in which measurement and comparison of linguistic items can be checked electronically. Still, there was life before the computer. Stylistics as a method that studies the forms, norms and usage of language dates from early twentieth century. Thus, quantitative methods in stylistics are not new, and neither are they few.

Roughly speaking, we can distinguish two main historical branches in stylistics and quantitative research. The first one, stylostatistics (terminology varies here and includes statistical stylistics, stylometry, or stylometrics) is concerned with the investigation of quantitative features of style and has its roots in Saussurean linguistics. As such, stylostatistics owes much to Charles Bally's (1909) study of expressive language on the emotional, social, and individual planes but not exclusively in literary texts. Stylostatisticians are mostly concerned with the distribution of language phenomena, such as word frequency, or the distribution of grammar forms to check whether certain stylistic uses result from chance or from choice. Also interested in the attribution of authorship, stylostatistics relies on quantitative data to look for countable features that may stand as indications of a possible style. Clark (2011, p. 13) attributes an earlier date to stylometric authorship analysis when he explains that in the mid-1800s 'these early analysts would simply choose 'style markers' according to little-to-no rational basis for the selection of these markers, and then, based on observed similarities or differences between texts (which some analysts count mathematically and some do not), the analyst would announce a conclusion.' According to Schaalje *et al.* (2012, p. 28), stylometrics dates back to '1851, when mathematician Augustus de Morgan proposed using average word length to numerically characterise authorship style.' And they explain:

> By identifying the word-use patterns in a text of unknown or questioned authorship and then comparing and contrasting those patterns to the patterns in texts of known authorship, the similarities and dissimilarities between the textual patterns can provide supporting evidence for or contradicting evidence against an assertion of authorship.

Stylostatistics (stylometrics or stylometry) finds application in forensic authorship analysis, which looks for legal evidence for authorship attribution (see Smith 1989). Forensic stylometry has also been quite useful in detecting genuine confessions, in spotting plagiarism and even authors of computer viruses. At present, stylostatistical works can be said to share two interdependent issues (Tulsa 2004, p. 141) in textual investigation: a) from the standpoint of individual or functional styles; b) with a view of author identification, particularly in the case of disputed or anonymous authorship (e.g. Hoover 2001).

Quantitative studies in stylistics (especially corpus stylistics), however, may claim a different background. Beginning in the early twentieth century, they follow the efforts of Russian formalists, particularly those of the Moscow Linguistic Circle in the 1920s (see Durant and Fabb 1990, p. 32 for a summary), whose main concern was how textual patterning worked in literary-aesthetic communication. In this sense, they go beyond linguistic analysis by combining other fields such as psychology and sociology. In fact, a specific date can be attributed to the birth of stylistics as a method of investigation of poetic language: Roman Jakobson's seminal paper delivered at a conference in Indiana in 1958 and published later in Sebeok (1960, pp. 350–377), in which he defined 'poetic language' as communicative language that, differently from other communicative acts, focuses on the message for its own sake. Jakobson's paper has been widely accepted as the first manifesto for the linguistic study of literary texts. It must be pointed out, however, that these early studies were restricted to single poems or short texts. This focus would be expanded later.

The history of stylistics stems not only from the Russian formalists' interest in the scientific study of literary texts, taken up by the Prague Linguistic Circle established in 1926 (Mukařovský 1964) in the aftermath of the Russian Revolution. It also owes much to the reaction against Anglo-American literary criticism. More precisely, stylisticians reacted against Practical Criticism (Richards 1929) and New Criticism (Wimsatt and Beardsley 1954), by arguing that intuition was necessary but not sufficient in literary studies. Although Spitzer (1948) contributed to defining the scope of stylistics by pinning its objective to the study of choice and effect in the literary text, it was the social-cultural dimension that Halliday (1978) contributed later that distanced stylistics from other approaches to style. As most theories develop from previous efforts, functional-systemic linguists such as M. Halliday and J. McH. Sinclair are in fact considered to be neo-Firthians for owing much to John Rupert Firth (1957), who, in his turn, was influenced by the studies of ethnomethodologist Malinowski (1922). Firth's (1957, p. 11) axiom 'You shall know a word by the company it keeps' became a motto to corpus stylistics. (For more corpus approaches to stylistics see Chapter 23 in this volume.)

Although we can say that there has been more than a century of stylistic studies, the area really gained momentum after the development of functional systemic linguistics. Stockwell (2006, p. 745) states that:

> advances in pragmatics, sociolinguistics and discourse analysis in the 1970s allowed stylistics to move beyond the analysis of short texts and sentence-level phenomena. Studies involving speech act theory, norms of spoken interaction, politeness, appropriacy of register choice, dialectal variation, cohesion and coherence, deictic projection, turn-taking and floor-holding all allowed stylistics the opportunity of exploring text-level features and the interpersonal dimension of literature, especially in prose fiction and dramatic texts.

We must admit, however, that in spite of all its vast production, quantitative research in stylistics remains under-represented in comparison with qualitative approaches. Statistical stylistics (stylometrics or whichever other denomination it may take) has kept a constant pace and has been quite productive, but its focus is rather limited, as pointed out above (Tulsa 2004). In the next section we will discuss some of the quantitative studies that have been developing lately.

Critical issues and topics

The kind of stylistics analysis undertaken depends on the research question as well as on the researcher's assumptions about the nature of textual meaning – whether the focus is placed on the reader or on the text. Jeffries and McIntyre (2010) suggest the following sub-division of current stylistics methods of research: (a) the qualitative analysis of literary texts (pp. 176–181); (b) corpus stylistics (pp. 181–185); and (c) responses to texts (pp. 185–188). This section does not aim to cover all methods used, but rather to focus on the directions that quantitative studies have been taking. To ground our claims in empirical data, we collected the papers published in *Language and Literature* over the last five years (2007 to 2011) to see what kind of methods are being used. *Language and Literature* is one of the major international publications in stylistics, and its articles cover a very broad range of approaches and methodologies. Our analysis brings out the main critical issues and topics with which research in the area has recently been concerned. We will also support the analysis with reference to works published elsewhere, where applicable.

From the *Language and Literature* (hereafter *L&L*) issues dated 2007 to 2011, excluding brief introductions and responses in special issues but including book reviews and review articles, ninety-five articles were collected. In only twenty-five of them some form of quantitative approach was used, as Figure 20.1 illustrates:

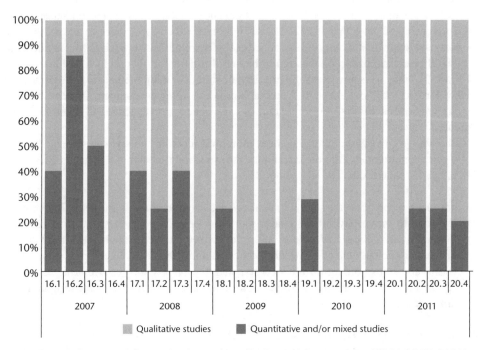

Figure 20.1 Percentage of quantitative and qualitative articles compared (*L&L* 2007–2011)

From simple descriptive statistics (frequency, median, mode, histograms, etc.) to more sophisticated statistical inference tests, the twenty-five quantitative studies analysed have relied on computerised programs and/or statistics to bring out the structure and the nature of literary texts. From a Popperian perspective, they are valuable not only for confirming general theories, but also for falsifying some of them. This section shows how quantitative studies can lead to insights about literary texts and their environment. Besides strong manifestations of validity, the critical issues and topics that these studies have developed concentrate on the different planes of meaning of or about literary texts, arguing for more evidence-based interpretations.

In order to obtain an overall picture, the studies were categorised in terms of their scope and objectives. The segmentation about to be offered, however, is not discrete since much overlapping occurs. For practical reasons, the studies have been grouped in terms of what they prioritise. It must be stressed, however, that due to the scope of this chapter, the categories have been drawn exclusively from the corpus collected. We are aware that they may be limited and may not reflect the wider richness of the area. However, they serve the purpose of illustrating quantitative studies in stylistics. Where applicable, we also make references to studies that have not necessarily been published in these issues of *L&L* but which may stand as support for the argument.

Textual level

As discussed above, most studies in stylistics are of a qualitative nature and concentrate on text as discourse, looking at the formal and functional aspects of both literary and non-literary language (Jeffries and McIntyre 2010, p. 173), but quantitative contributions have also been thriving. Indeed, stylistics grew from the need to make literary interpretations more precise, but its techniques of analysis have now extended much further, ranging from spoken discourse to advertising, film productions, political speeches and so on. This freedom is reflected in Swann and Allington's (*L&L* 2009, pp. 247–264) study, which analyses discourse produced by reading group discussions. In order to contrast observational approaches to literary reading with experimental approaches, they prepared a dataset of around three hundred thousand words of text and submitted this corpus to thematic analysis, using Atlas-ti software for coding. They divided the transcripts into episodes that were tagged according to categories drawn from several code sets. Their thematic analysis allowed them to notice, for instance, that where participants referred to their subjective responses, they would present their evaluations in mitigated form. This software-assisted qualitative sociolinguistic analysis of reading group discussion as a cultural, interactional and interpersonal activity illustrates how stylistic analysis can go beyond the world of literary texts.

As regards purely quantitative studies, the corpus contained few but significant contributions, such as Abbott and Forceville's (*L&L* 2011, pp. 91–112), which look at visual representation of emotion in *manga*. For the sake of categorisation, we organise the studies in the corpus collected in terms of the levels and units of language analysis on which they focus. It must be stressed that these levels, however, are not discrete and that overlapping may occur.

Prosody and phonology

The main concern of the studies on this level of language is the meaning potential of sound patterning (see Duffel 2008, pp. 5–20). Another example is Shen and Aisenman's study (*L&L* 2008, pp. 107–121) of synaesthetic metaphors. In these studies, empirical support for the claims made is provided.

Lexical patterns

Word choice, their meaning, and their use in context are the focus of the studies collected here and which belong to the area of lexicology and semantics. The search for meaningful lexical patterns is where corpus linguistics has been most effective. It points out the environment of certain lexical items as used by an author and allows insights that can be demonstrable (Mahlberg 2007b, Louw 1993, 1997, Viana *et al.*, 2008). The computer may help us to assess literary texts in ways that have not been available so far, thus providing more substantiation to intuitive interpretations and to decisions on literary evaluation (Carter 1999, Zyngier 2008). This method of investigation may help to contradict statements about texts that have been taken for granted, and based on the observation of language in use they can determine to a large extent the literary quality of the text (for a fuller account of corpus stylistics and its methods, see Chapter 23 in this volume).

Syntax

The ways in which words combine to form phrases and sentences come under the label of syntax. One of the studies in the corpus collected, the stylistic distinctiveness in the use of *ed* clauses in parts of Milton's poem *Paradise Lost* (Twose *L&L* 2008, pp.77–96), illustrates the concern for colligation (Sinclair 1991) in literary texts. Other studies that focus on syntax can be illustrated by research in discourse markers, such as connectives in English children's literature (Oku 2007).

Discourse

Above sentence level, a few studies in the corpus analysed look at discourse, 'a much more open-ended term used to encompass aspects of communication that lie beyond the organisation of sentences' (Simpson 2004, p. 7). The quantitative studies we noticed on this level examine functional and pragmatic structures such as ways in which speech and thought are presented in literary texts. For instance, Mahlberg and Smith (2012) offer a computer-assisted approach to the study of character discourse in Dickens. In fact, interest in the computational study of speech and thought presentation resulted in a special issue (*Language and Literature* 2006). Further examples can be found in Zimmer's (2011) review in which he argues against the claims that modern fiction (particularly American fiction) is free from stylistic artistries. Corpus linguistics studies have shown that, in fact, some words and collocations are much more frequent in these fictions than in spoken discourse and other genres. He noticed, for example, that past-tense verbs such as 'grimaced,' 'scowled,' 'grunted,' 'wiggled' and 'gritted' show up more frequently in fiction than in academic prose. He also refers to a study conducted by Hargraves, encompassing about two billion words of twenty-first-century English and using the Oxford English Corpus, which revealed peculiar patterns more frequently found in fiction.

Nowadays, computational linguistic analyses transcend the selective attention of an individual observer and go beyond readers' reactions to a single work. They can demonstrate how some collocations are typically and recursively *literary*. Such developments indicate that quantitative studies on the discourse level have been thriving and will bring new insights to stylistic studies.

Culture and context

The quantitative research in the corpus examined also extends beyond textual discourse, such as research on how and when humour occurs (e.g. Partington 1995). They provide evidence that its distribution is not random (Corduas, Attardo and Eggleston, *L&L* 2008, pp. 253–270). Others may be better seen as cross-cultural studies, looking at the extent to which the meeting of different cultures may affect literature (Albakry and Hancock, *L&L* 2008, pp. 221–234).

Response and reading practices

Stemming from reader response theories, most studies in the corpus concentrate on empirical approaches for investigating how readers read the world of the text (van Peer 1986, Miall and Kuiken 1994, Hakemulder 2000, Bortolussi and Dixon 2003). They explore the role of foregrounding (see the special issue of *Language and Literature* 2007), articulate how literariness comes about in the process of reading, and discuss how to locate emotional engagement in the process of reading. They also study how cognitive poetics and emotion theories help to understand the ways that readers experience literary texts (see Emmott 1997, Toolan 2009, Fialho 2012, Campbell 2012, among others).

Education

Compared to the other areas of study, pedagogical stylistics remains rather dormant. However, interest in the area is growing, as evidenced in van Peer *et al.* (2010) and in the special issue of *Language and Literature* published in 2010. In the preface to this issue, Burke provides a strong ethical argument for why pedagogical stylistic research is needed. In his words, 'doing [stylistics] for the sake of our students is a commendable necessity' as we would be preparing 'a better citizen in order to serve the democratic process' (2010, p. 11). However, only two of the articles in that volume carry out quantification.

Besides classroom strategies and practices, some studies have looked into what characterises learners' writing about literature (Zyngier and Shepherd 2003) and the role of emotion in the classroom (Fialho *et al.*, 2011a, b, 2012).

Some considerations

Although much overlapping does occur, what we can say about current quantitative studies in stylistics is that the past five years may be characterised as the golden period of corpus stylistics, with studies covering all levels of language. According to Carter (2012, p. 108), '*Corpus methods have emerged as a major methodological feature of the present and future landscape for the discipline of stylistics and have created the strongest platform yet for both detailed synchronic and diachronic stylistic studies*' (italics in the original). There has also been a growth of empirical studies in reader response and in the contexts where literary texts circulate and make their mark.

It is a basic principle of stylistic analysis that others need to be able to see how an interpretive account has been reached. This means making the account retrievable and recoverable, allowing others to agree or disagree, and making it possible for different interpretations to be compared transparently and objectively in the sense defined by Wales (2001), who holds that '[s]tylistics is only 'objective' (and the scare quotes are significant) in the sense of being methodical, systematic, empirical, analytical, coherent, accessible, retrievable and consensual' (p. 373).

Current research and methods

Having discussed main current critical issues, we now look at the way in which those central research topics and questions have been addressed; that is, how the different 'elements' – the samples or groups, measures, treatments, and methods of assignment – work together to provide a coherent structure for each study. To this purpose, we will focus on the types of research design that have been used. As we illustrate this chapter with studies from *Language and Literature*, and due to copyright issues, we will not reproduce the graphs and tables in the studies mentioned. We only refer the reader to them.

There are three main types of quantitative research design: explorative/descriptive, explanatory, and computer-driven analysis. It is important to stress that despite the differences, quantitative studies share the principle of rigour, which is obtained by means of reliability, and validity (van Peer *et al.* 2012). Both reliability and validity have to do with the quality of measurement and they are two interrelated concepts. In its everyday sense, reliability is the 'consistency' or 'repeatability' of the measures used. Validity means that the measures, samples and designs used should lead to valid inferences and conclusions. Ideally, measures should be both reliable and valid.

Stylistics studies all kinds of texts, written or verbal, from a linguistic perspective, and in fact most of the current contributions that use a quantitative approach are hybrid, combining aspects of both qualitative and quantitative research. As a result of being by nature plurimethodological, the prospect of describing the main quantitative methods in stylistics is rather daunting. We therefore propose that the methods are set on a cline, the two poles being quantitative and qualitative approaches. Most of the studies analysed here fall within these two poles. Since we will be focusing on the more quantitative end, it is useful to keep in mind that the starting point of any quantitative study is counting things. In stylistics research we can count feature(s) of a single text or of many texts. With the help of the computer, studies can now take into account the complexities of working with ever larger quantities of data.

Explorative and/or descriptive research

Roughly one third of the studies that use some form of quantitative approach in the corpus observed are either explorative or descriptive. Explorative studies look for new areas where hypotheses have not been formulated in a systematic way yet. One of the aims of this type of research is to formulate hypotheses that can be subsequently tested by means of explanatory research (e.g. Fialho *L&L* 2007, pp. 105–123 and Ji, *L&L* 2009, 61–73). Their primary goal is to describe the object or phenomenon of investigation, an end in itself (e.g. Albakry and Hancock, *L&L* 2008, 221–234; Abbott and Forceville, *L&L* 2011, 91–112). The statistical method used to explore or describe the basic features of data and therefore the phenomena investigated is *univariate descriptive statistics*. The ways that some of the research published in *Language and Literature* over the past five years has used this statistical method is discussed next.

Univariate descriptive statistics

Descriptive statistics organises a mass of quantitative data in a manageable form by providing simple summaries about the sample and the measures. Therefore, together with simple graphics analysis, these summaries form the basis of virtually every quantitative analysis of data. In investigating a large number of people or things on a single measure we use univariate analysis, which examines one single variable at a time across different cases. There are three major characteristics (or measures) for each single variable: the distribution (a summary of the frequency of individual values or ranges of values for a given variable), the central tendency (the mean, median and mode), and the dispersion (the range, standard deviation and variance). In this section, we will be focusing on one of them, namely distribution, since it is used in all the explorative and/or descriptive research in the corpus observed.

One of the studies that uses univariate analysis is Abbott and Forceville's (*L&L* 2011, p. 91–112) study of visual representation of emotion in manga. The researchers focus on a single corpus and on one arguably unusual marked stylistic choice of emotion expression (or single variable), namely 'hand loss' (HL). In their descriptive study, they first analyse the occurrences of HL in the 1257 panels of the volume and categorise the varied ways in which it occurred, described by the authors as follows: (1) *"No HV/HL"*: cases where a character is visually present in the panel, but her hands (or absence-of-hands) are hidden from view (i.e. outside the frame, or invisible behind an object or text balloon'; (2) *"HV + HL"*: 'hands visible' and 'hand loss' cases combined'; (3) *"HV"*: all 'hands visible"; (4) *"HL"*: hand loss' (p. 98). In analysing the narrative use of each of these four variables, their occurrences were counted separately across different cases (characters). To further their analyses, the authors describe the different types of HL in six characters. In the tables they provide, they show the simplest distribution since they list every value of a variable and the number of occurrences (or the frequency) of each variable per character. Thus, they use one of the most common ways to describe a single variable: frequency distribution (either simple or percentual). Their analyses allow the authors to conclude that 'hand loss' is a marked stylistic choice to suggest that a character is affected by loss of (emotional) control (p. 98). Part of their findings '(1) show how non-facial information helps express emotion in manga', and '(2) demonstrate how hand loss contributes to the characterization of Azuma's heroines' (p. 91).

In reporting descriptive research, the data gathered must be presented in a clear way so that patterns found can be observed. In most write-ups, it is of great value to represent data not merely through numbers, but also visually. For example, frequency distributions may be displayed by using absolute numbers or percentages, and they can be carefully organised into summary tables such as those provided by Abbott and Forceville (see Table 1, p. 98 and Table 2, p. 99), or into graphs (e.g. Graph 1 above) that only display the most relevant information.

Some of the most widely used graphs that can be used to depict descriptive statistics graphically are, for example, the bar chart, the line graph, and the scattergram. An example of a bar chart can be seen in Albakry and Hancock's (*L&L* 2008, pp. 221–234; see Figure 2, on p. 232) examination of the phenomenon of code switching in *The Map of Love* (1999) by the Egyptian-British writer Ahdaf Soueif. Here, the researchers describe the frequency distribution of one single variable – the use of Arabic words (vertical column) per chapter (horizontal column). They demonstrate that following a tradition of postcolonial writers, Soueif uses code switching or a hybrid English as a means to represent different aspects of the linguistic and cultural norms of Egyptian society and preserve her cultural identity (p. 233).

Line charts are better suited to trace the development of a measure over time. In her study of the stylistic differences between two modern Chinese translations of Cervantes' *Don Quijote* (*L&L* 2009, pp. 61–73), for example, Ji uses a line chart to organise her numerical data (see Figure 1, p. 65). The chart not only enables us to visualise the distribution of the use of archaisms in the protagonist's speeches throughout a proposed ten subdivisions of the text, but also gives us some idea of the major (dis)similarities between the source and target texts.

So far we have examined the numeric methods used to organise, summarise and describe single variables at a time. Frequently, the aim of the stylistician is to go beyond investigations of the characteristics of a single variable at a time and study the relation between two variables. Relationships (or linear associations) between variables are measured by correlation, which is another common and extremely useful measure in statistics. Correlational techniques might be used in explorative studies, to describe data and to determine whether a relationship exists, and in hypothesis-testing studies, to test a hypothesis about a particular relationship (Munro 2005, p. 239). In Ji's (*L&L* 2009, pp. 61–73) study, the author aimed at verifying whether relationships existed between the three variables observed (see Figure 1, p. 65). In other words, she wanted to verify whether the patterns revealed by the line graph (Figure 1, p. 65) could be corroborated by correlation. To this purpose, the researcher used the Pearson product moment test (see Table 4, p. 65).

To interpret correlation coefficients, one must know how the variables are measured. A positive sign indicates that individuals or things (in the case of her study, texts) that score highly on one of the variables tend to score high on the other and vice versa. In Table 4 (p. 65), Ji shows that there is a positive correlation ($r=0.685$) between Liu's Chinese version and the original *Don Quixote*. There is also a positive correlation ($r=0.630$) between Yang's Chinese version and the original *Don Quixote*. This means that the higher the use of archaisms in Don Quixote, the higher the use of archaisms in both Chinese versions of the text.

To judge the strength of the relationship, one must consider the actual value of the correlation coefficient and also its associated p value. Table 4 (p. 65) shows that the correlation of 0.685 (between Liu and *Don Quixote*) was significant at the .05 level, but the correlation of 0.630 (between Yang and *Don Quixote*) was not. The researcher concludes that in Liu's recent rendition of *Don Quijote* (Part I), the Chinese translator has drawn on the phraseological strategy as devised by his predecessor. However, when dealing with the Castilian archaism in the original text, Yang's translation has been shown to be more distant from the original (p. 66).

Correlation concerns a relation that can be measured mathematically. A correlation that shows that two variables are related does not mean that one variable caused the other. In other words, one cannot infer causation from correlation alone. Therefore, it is important to keep in mind that although a relationship may exist, other factors also may affect the variables under study.

Many other measures of description and relationship are available, such as factor analysis, regression analysis and partial, semipartial or multiple correlations, among others. It is important to stress that the present chapter is introductory and refers to the measures used in the research published in *Language and Literature* (2007 to 2011) to illustrate quantitative approaches to stylistics. Therefore, it mentions only a few of the measures available. For more exploratory and descriptive studies, see Bray (*L&L* 2007, pp. 37–52), Fialho (*L&L* 2007, pp. 105–123), Mandala (*L&L* 2007, pp. 53–73), and Zyngier and Fialho (*L&L* 2010, pp. 13–33). For a detailed description of other quantitative methods and a step-by-step explanation, see van *Peer et al.* (2012).

In sum, descriptive statistics provide a powerful summary of the characteristics of a single case. If the researcher is interested in knowing whether the observations obtained can be replicated or whether generalisations to other cases can be made, inferential statistics must come into play. The next section moves from description to explanatory research and shows how the nature of research questions differs when inferential statistics are used.

Explanatory research

When the research objective is to extend beyond the immediate data alone and verify whether the patterns obtained also apply to other informants and/or cases, inferential statistics are needed. Inferential statistics enable the testing of models and hypotheses so as to allow a generalisation of the observations of a given sample to its population. Several statistical techniques are available depending on the research question. In this section we will discuss some of the techniques that are appropriate to stylistics research and that are used in the studies reported in *Language and Literature* (2007 to 2011).

A useful distinction is between *parametric* and *non-parametric* tests. Statistical tests such as the t-test, analysis of variance (ANOVA), and the general linear model (GLM) are examples of the former, whereas the Wilcoxon, Chi-square, and Mann-Whitney tests are examples of the latter. A basic presupposition of parametric tests is that the data are normally distributed (for a useful flowchart to aid the decision about which test to select for a given research, see van Peer *et al.* 2012, p. 231).

Perhaps one of the simplest (and yet most powerful) ways to use inferential statistics is to compare the average performance of two groups on a single measure to see if there is a difference between them. In this case, a t-test is conducted. The statistical question asks whether there are differences between the two groups. To answer this question, the t-test involves an evaluation of the means and distributions of each group. It allows the researcher to verify (a) if the means of the two groups differ and (b) if this difference really occurs, either revealing an important difference between the two groups or showing that it may be due to chance alone.

In their exploration of the structure of synaesthetic metaphors, Shen and Aisenman (*L&L* 2008, pp. 107–121) developed a series of studies to test a cognitive account of the 'lower-to-higher', according to which 'this lower-to-higher mapping reflects a cognitively simpler and more basic directionality than the inverse one' (p. 107). Here, the authors tested three hypotheses using three psychological measures, namely 'recall,' 'difficulty in context generation,' and 'naturalness judgments' (p. 107). To investigate the hypothesis that the lower-to-higher structure would be judged by readers as more natural than the inverse using the third measure (p. 113), the authors compiled twenty novel pairs of synaesthetic expressions and controlled for conventionality. Each pair consisted of 'a lower-to-higher synaesthesia, (e.g. 'perfumed rustle') and a corresponding higher-to-lower synaesthesia (e.g. 'rustling perfume')' (p. 114). Participants were given booklets with ten pairs each and were asked to choose the expression in each pair that seemed more natural to them. A significant difference was found between responses to the two groups of synaesthetic expressions. Participants significantly preferred the lower-to-higher expressions. This significance was found for both participant analysis ($p < .015$) and for item analysis ($p < .02$) (p. 115), thus confirming the hypothesis that participants judged the lower-to-higher structure as representing a more natural structure than its inverse. They also conducted two other similar experiments testing recall and difficulty. T-tests indicated that the lower-to-higher structure was also better recalled and judged to be easier to construct a context for, thus confirming the cognitive account of the robust pattern of synasthetic metaphors (pp. 107, 118–119). Here we see how, in writing up their results, Shen and Aisenman (*L&L* 2008, pp. 107–121) followed the common practice of linking each of the inferential analyses to specific research questions or hypotheses.

Another type of t-test can be used, namely the correlated or paired t-test, if the two groups compared are matched or paired on some basis – for example, when the same participants are tested at two points in time. Since chances are that the differences between these two 'paired' groups will not be as large as when they are mutually exclusive, the correlated t-test makes a correction that has the effect of increasing the measure *t*, thus making it more likely to find a significant difference if there is one (Munro 2005, pp. 145–146). For an exemplary study, see Hakemulder (*L&L* 2007, 125–139), who, in aiming to trace the emergent effects of foregrounding in responses to film, collects responses of two groups of participants at two points in time: before and after a screening of one scene from two Shakespeare film adaptations, either low or high in foregrounded elements.

When a study aims to compare two or more groups on a particular measure, the most appropriate technique is the analysis of variance (ANOVA). While the basic t-test compares two means in relation to the distribution of the differences between pairs of means drawn from a random sample, the ANOVA enables the examination of the differences among several groups through an analysis that considers the variation across all groups at once. In the case of comparison between two groups, both the t-test and the ANOVA are appropriate. Although the mathematics behind the two tests differs, the results should be the same. The statistical question using ANOVA is based on the null hypothesis: all groups are equal and drawn from the same population. Any difference comes from a random sampling difference. The ANOVA shows if group means differ from each other. ANOVA can be used with one categorical independent variable (with two or more levels) and one continuous dependent variable (this analysis is called One-Way ANOVA). It can also be used with more than one independent variable and more than one dependent variable (such an analysis is usually called multivariate analysis of variance – MANOVA). MANOVA allows the researcher to look for relationships among dependent and independent variables (see, for example, van Peer et al. 2007). Studies that have used inferential statistics are Corduas et al. (*L&L* 2008, pp. 253–270), Duffell (*L&L* 2008, pp. 5–20), Twose (*L&L* 2008, pp.77–96), Sopcák (2007), Martindale (*L&L* 2007, pp. 141–153), and Shen (*L&L* 2007, pp. 169–181).

It is beyond the scope of this chapter to offer a detailed description of all the possibilities currently available. Some user-friendly statistical packages are available for running the aforementioned tests, such as SPSS and R. A course on statistics, however, would be strongly recommended if the researcher wants to be in a better position to understand what each test can do. In terms of corpus stylistics, we refer to Viana *et al.* 2011 for collected views from major corpus linguists and Mahlberg (Chapter 23 in this volume) for an extensive overview.

Recommendations for practice

Using the statistical techniques here discussed is not as hard as it may seem at first. A step-by-step introduction has been offered by van Peer *et al.* (2012), useful exercises have been provided by Jeffries and McIntyre (2010, pp. 188–189), and resources have been reviewed by Wynne (2005). Here are just a few suggestions for topics that can be treated quantitatively:

1. Following work in stylometrics, select a novelist (Dickens, for instance), get a corpus of his works and compare it to a corpus of works by his contemporaries to find out what is stylistically relevant.
2. On the lexical level of language, use WordSmith tools to look at the use of specific words in the works of an author (e.g. love and death in Shakespeare's plays). You will be quite surprised to see what happens in *Richard III*, for instance, as compared to *Romeo and Juliet*.
3. In terms of reader response, if you want to conduct research to see if reading literature in a foreign language influences readers' emotions, compare the reactions of EFL students reading a literary passage in English and its translation in their mother tongue. Check if and how emotion variables are affected.
4. Select a statement from an acknowledged literary scholar and look for evidence of his or her claim by conducting a quantitative analysis to see if the claims find empirical evidence for support.
5. Compare detective fiction written by female and male writers and compare aspects of language use such as their transitivity choices. Are the protagonists represented differently? You can also compare representations of women detectives in fiction written by female writers in the first and the second half of last century. How do they differ in terms of the way the detectives are represented?

Future directions

Indeed, stylistics is becoming increasingly multidisciplinary. Stylisticians have been dialoguing with sociologists, psychologists, cognitive linguists, cultural historians, corpus linguists, literary critics and many other researchers who contribute to provide a more kaleidoscopic view of the area. These cross-fertilisations have broadened the range of research questions and the options for methodological approaches. As more and more researchers engage in joint projects they bring together different fields of study, different epistemologies, and the methodologies often associated with them.

In fact, we have been witnessing the proliferation of plurimethodological studies (cf. Slingerland 2008, van Peer *et al.* 2012, pp. 53–55) or the use of 'mixed methodologies' (Angouri 2010, p. 29) and, with them, the advent of Snow's 'third culture' (see above). A closer examination of research in stylistics indicates that a larger number of the methodologies showcase the blurring of the boundaries between qualitative and quantitative procedures. Examples are not only the growing development of cognitive stylistics with their plurimethodological apparatuses, but also the emergence of new methodologies such as 'Lexical Basis for Numerically Aided Phenomenology' (LEX-NAP, Fialho 2012). Interdisciplinary in nature, LEX-NAP results from insights from literary studies, phenomenology, psychology, neuroscience, and stylistics. An adaptation of previously described procedures (Kuiken and Miall 2001), LEX-NAP is a hybrid of qualitative and quantitative procedures, and is based on lexical repetition and theme modification. The method is demonstrably effective in allowing for dynamic descriptions of readers' embodied repositionings as their reading of a short story unfolds, resulting in a typology of reading experiences.

Moreover, with the continuing development of new media and the invention of new technology, stylistics will necessarily branch out into multimodal and multimedia semiotics all aiming at rigour (see, for instance, the discourses of television drama [Richardson 2010a, b] and DVD advertising [Bednarek 2010]). Future directions might also include the need to keep up with the developments in evolutionary literature so that we know the where, the why and the how of literature from a diachronic perspective (Carroll 2004). This seems to be the direction some stylometrics research is taking. Hughes *et al.* (2012), for example, have conducted the first large-scale temporal stylometric study of literature by using the Project Gutenberg Digital Library corpus. They have found evidence for stylistic coherence with a given literary topic among different authors in a certain time and offer quantitative support to the notion of temporally localised styles, or, in other words, to the notion of a literary 'style of a time' (p. 7682).

In short, what the future holds for research in stylistics is the proliferation of hybridism, of multidisciplinary projects, of multimethod designs, and of new ways of doing research, which will further our understanding of the area. Challenges also lie ahead. While crossing disciplinary and methodological boundaries, novice and experienced stylisticians will necessarily need to acquire new competences and skills, not only in both quantitative and qualitative research, but also in performing in multidisciplinary and multi-cultural research groups.

Related topics

Corpus stylistics, formalist stylistics, linguistic levels of foregrounding, multimodality, pedagogical stylistics, reader response criticism, stylistics and comics, stylistics, emotion and neuroscience.

Further reading

Jeffries, L. and McIntyre, D., 2010. *Stylistics*. Cambridge: Cambridge University Press.

An introductory book aimed at newcomers to stylistics, it is quite helpful in its description of methodologies for stylistic analysis, which includes quantitative approaches. The volume also offers an updated bibliography that indicates the areas where stylistics is thriving.

Sinclair, J. M. H., 1991. *Corpus, concordance, collocation*. Oxford: Oxford University Press.

Despite its date of publication, this book is an indispensable introduction to corpus linguistics and demonstrates how a truly empirical approach to language can lead to evidence-based theories. A small but powerful volume, it has helped shape quantitative methods in modern linguistics.

Stubbs, M., 2005. Conrad in the computer: Examples of quantitative stylistics methods. *Language and Literature*, 14 (1), 5–24.

An exemplary description of how quantitative methods may help to find significant linguistic features which literary critics tend to overlook.

van Peer, W., Hakemulder, F. and Zyngier, S., 2012. *Scientific methods for the humanities*. Amsterdam: John Benjamins Publishing Company.

Offering a wide variety of examples, exercises and illustrative studies, as well as help for self-instruction, this book also brings out the misconceptions about the use of scientific methods in humanities fields and shows that scientific procedures should be included in the methodological toolkit of those who deal with the humanities.

Zyngier, S., Bortolussi, M., Chenokova, A. and Auracher, J., eds. 2008. *Directions in empirical literary studies*. Amsterdam: John Benjamins Publishing Company.

This volume widens the scope of empirical studies and looks at them from an intercultural perspective. It brings together renowned scholars from the fields of philosophy, sociology, psychology, linguistics and literature, all focusing on how empirical studies have impacted these different areas, showing the relation between empirical studies and new technology.

References

Abbott, M. and Forceville, C., 2011. Visual representation of emotion in manga: Loss of control is loss of hands in Azumanga Daioh Volume 4. *Language and Literature*, 20 (2), 91–112.

Albakry, M. and Hancock, P.H., 2008. Code switching in Ahdaf Soueif's *The Map of Love*. *Language and Literature*, 17 (3), 221–234.

Angouri, J., 2010. Quantitative, qualitative or both? Combining methods in linguistic Research. *In:* L. Litosseliti, ed. *Research methods in linguistics*. London: Continuum International Publishing Group, 29–45.

Bally, C., [1909] 2010. *Traité de Stylistique Française*. Paris: Librairie C. Klinscksiec.

Bednarek, M., 2010. *The language of fictional television: Drama and identity*. London: Continuum.

Bortolussi, M. and Dixon, P., 2003. *Psychonarratology: Foundations for the empirical study of literary response*. Cambridge, New York: Cambridge University Press.

Bray, J., 2007. The 'dual voice' of free indirect discourse: A reading experiment. *Language and Literature*, 16 (1), 37–52.

Burke, M., 2010. Why care about pedagagoical stylistics? *Language and Literature*, 19 (1), 7–11.

Campbell, P., 2012. A bridge from artificial places: An empirical phenomenology of mystical reading in Rilke and Eliot. Unpublished PhD Thesis. University of Alberta.

Carroll, J., 2004. *Literary Darwinism: Evolution, human nature, and literature*. New York and London: Routledge.

Carter, R., 1999. Common language: Corpus, creativity and cognition. *Language and Literature*, 8 (3), 195–216.

Carter, R., 2007. Literature and language teaching 1986–2006: A review. *International Journal of Applied Linguistics*, 17 (1), 3–13.

Carter, R., 2012. Coda: Some rubber bullet points. *Language and Literature*, 21 (1), 106–114.

Clark, A. M. S., 2011. *Forensic stylometric authorship analysis under the Daubert standard*, Washington, D.C.: University of the District of Columbia. Online. Available at: http://ssrn.com/abstract=2039824 or http://dx.doi.org/10.2139/ssrn.2039824 (accessed 28 August 2012).

Corduas, M., Attardo, S. and Eggleston, A., 2008. The distribution of humour in literary texts is not random: A statistical analysis. *Language and Literature*, 17 (3), 253–270.

Duffel, M.J., 2008. Some observations on English binary metres. *Language and Literature*, 17 (1), 5–20.

Durant, A. and Fabb, N., 1990. *Literary studies in action.* London & New York: Routledge.

Emmott, C., 1997. *Narrative comprehension: A discourse perspective.* Oxford: Clarendon Press; New York: Oxford University Press.

Fialho, O., 2007. Foregrounding and refamiliarization: Understanding readers' response to literary texts. *Language and Literature*, 16 (2), 105–123.

Fialho, O., 2012. Self-modifying experiences in literary reading: A model for reader response. Unpublished PhD Thesis. University of Alberta.

Fialho, O., Miall, D. S. and Zyngier, S., 2012. Experiencing or interpreting literature: Wording instructions. *In:* M. Burke et al., eds. *Pedagogical stylistics: Current trends in language, literature and ELT.* London, New York: Continuum, 58–74.

Fialho, O., Zyngier, S. and Miall, D. S., 2011a. Interpretation and experience: Two pedagogical interventions observed. *English in Education*, 45 (3), 236–253.

Fialho, O., Zyngier, S. and Miall, D. S., 2011b. Pedagogische strategieën voor literaire educatie: Een empirische studie. *In:* F. Hakemulder, ed. *De stralende-lezer: Wetenschappelijk onderzoek naar de invloed van het lezen.* Delft: Eburon, 246–266.

Firth, J. R., 1957. *Papers in linguistics 1934–1951.* London: Oxford University Press.

Hakemulder, F., 2000. *The moral laboratory: Experiments examining the effects of reading literature on social perception and moral self-concept.* Amsterdam: John Benjamins Publishing Company.

Hakemulder, F., 2007. Tracing foregrounding in responses to film. *Language and Literature*, 16 (2), 125–139.

Halliday, M. A. K., 1967. The linguistic study of literary texts. *In:* S. Chatman and S. R. Levin, eds. *Essays on the language of literature.* New York: Houghton Mifflin, 325–360.

Halliday, M. A. K., 1978. *Language as social semiotic: The social interpretation of language and meaning.* Maryland: University Park Press.

Hoover, D., 2001. Statistical stylistics and authorship attribution: An empirical Investigation. *Literary and Linguistic Computing*, 16, 421–444.

Hughes, J. M. et al., 2012. Quantitative patterns of stylistic influence in the evolution of Literature. *PNAS*, 109 (20), 7682–7686.

Jakobson, R., 1960. Closing statement: Linguistics and poetics. *In:* T.A. Sebeok, ed. *Style in language.* Cambridge, Massachusetts: MIT Press, 350–377.

Jeffries, L. and McIntyre, D., 2010. *Stylistics.* Cambridge: Cambridge University Press.

Ji, M., 2009. Corpus stylistics in translation studies: Two modern Chinese translations of *Don Quijote. Language and Literature*, 18 (1), 61–73.

Kuiken, D. and Miall, D. S., 2001. Numerically-aided phenomenology: Procedures for investigating categories of experience. *Forum Qualitative Sozialforschung/Forum: Qualitative Social Research*, 2.1.

Louw, W., 1993. Irony in the text or insincerity in the writer? The diagnostic potential of semantic prosodies. *In:* M. Baker, G. Francis and E. Tognini-Bonelli, eds. *Text and technology.* Amsterdam: John Benjamins Publishing Company, 157–176.

Louw, W., 1997. The role of corpora in critical literary appreciation. *In:* A. Wichman, S. Fligelstone, T. McEnery and G. Knowles, eds. *Teaching and language corpora.* Harlow: Addison Wesley Longman, 240–251.

Mahlberg, M., 2007a. Corpus stylistics: Bridging the gap between linguistic and literary studies. *In:* M. Hoey, M. Mahlberg, M. Stubbs and W. Teubert, eds. *Text, discourse and corpora.* London: Continuum, 219–246.

Mahlberg, M., 2007b. Review of M. Hori. 2004. Investigating Dickens' style: A collocational analysis' *Language and Literature*, 16 (1), 93–96.

Mahlberg, M. and Smith, C., 2012. Dickens, the suspended quotation and the corpus. *Language and Literature*, 21 (1), 51–65.

Malinowski, B., 1922. *Argonauts of the Western Pacific: An account of native enterprise and adventure in the archipelagos of Melanesian New Guinea.* London: Routledge & Kegan Paul.

Mandala, S., 2007. Solidarity and the scoobies: An analysis of the -y suffix in the television series Buffy the Vampire Slayer. *Language and Literature*, 16 (1), 53–73.

Martindale, C., 2007. Deformation forms the course of literary history. *Language and Literature*, 16 (2), 141–153.

Miall, D. S. and Kuiken, D., 1994. Foregrounding, defamiliarization, and affect: Response to literary stories. *Poetics*, 22, 389–407.

Mukařovský, J., 1964. Standard language and poetic language. *In:* P. L. Garvin, ed. A *Prague School reader on esthetics, literary structure and style*. WashingtonD.C.: Georgetown University Press, 17–30.

Munro, B. H., 2005. *Statistical methods for health care research*. 5th ed. Philadelphia: Lippincott Williams & Wilkins.

Oku, S., Connectives in children's literature. Paper presented at PALA Conference, Kansai Gaidai University, July–August 2007.

Partington, A., 1995. Kicking the habit: The exploitation of collocation in literature and Humor. *In:* J. Payne, ed. *Linguistic approaches to literature*. Birmingham: University of Birmingham, 35–44.

Richards, I. A., 1929. *Practical criticism: A study of literary judgment*. London: Kegan Paul.

Richardson, K., 2010a. Multimodality and the study of popular drama. *Language and Literature*, 19 (4), 378–395.

Richardson, K., 2010b. *Television dramatic discourse: A sociolinguistic study*. Oxford: Oxford University Press.

Schaalje, G. B., Roper, M. and Fields, P., 2012. Stylometric analyses of the Book of Mormon: A short history. *Journal of the Book of Mormon and Other Restoration Scripture*, 21 (1), 28–45.

Shen, Y. and Aisenman, R., 2008. Heard melodies are sweet, but those unheard are sweeter: Synaesthetic metaphors and cognition. *Language and Literature*, 17 (2) 107–121.

Shen, Y., 2007. Foregrounding in poetic discourse: Between deviation and cognitive Constraints. *Language and Literature*, 16 (2), 169–181.

Short, M., Busse, B. and Plummer, P. 2006. Special issue on e-learning and stylistics. *Language and Literature*, 15 (3).

Simpson, P., 2004. *Stylistics: A resource book for students*. London and New York: Routledge.

Sinclair, J., 1991. *Corpus, concordance, collocation*. Oxford: Oxford University Press.

Sklar, H., 2013. *The art of sympathy: Forms of moral and emotional persuasion in fiction*. Amsterdam: John Benjamins Publishing Company.

Slingerland, F., 2008. *What science offers the humanities*. Cambridge: Cambridge University Press.

Smith, M. W. A., 1989. Forensic stylometry: A theoretical basis for further developments of practical methods. *Journal of the Forensic Science Society*, 29 (1), 5–33.

Snow, C. P., 1959. *The two cultures and the scientific revolution*. New York: Cambridge University Press.

Sopcák, P., 2007. 'Creation from nothing': A foregrounding study of James Joyce's drafts for *Ulysses*. *Language and Literature*, 16 (2), 183–196.

Spitzer, L., 1948. *Linguistic and literary history: Essays in stylistics*. NJ: Princeton University Press.

Stockwell, P., 2006. Language and literature: Stylistics. *In:* B. Aarts and A. McMahon eds. *The handbook of English linguistics*. Oxford: Blackwell, 742–758.

Stubbs, M., 2005. Conrad in the computer: Examples of quantitative stylistics methods. *Language and Literature*, 14 (1), 5–24.

Swann, J. and Allington, D., 2009. Reading groups and the language of literary texts: A case study in social reading. *Language and Literature*. 18 (3), 247–264.

Toolan, M. J., 2009. Textual signalling of immersion and emotion in the reading of stories: Can reader responses and corpus methods converge?' Paper presented at PALA Conference, Middelburg, July–August 2009.

Tulsa, J., 2004. The development of statistical stylistics: A survey. *Journal of Quantitative Linguistics*, 11 (1–2), 141–151.

Twose, G., 2008. What's in a clause? Milton's participial style revisited. *Language and Literature,* 17 (1), 77–96.

van Peer, W., 1986. *Stylistics and psychology: Investigations of foregrounding*. London, Sydney, Wolfeboro: Croom Helm.

van Peer, W., ed. 2007. Special issue on foregrounding. *Language and Literature*, 16 (2).

van Peer, W. 2008. Introduction: The inhumanity of the humanities. *In:* J. Auracher and W. van Peer, eds. *New beginnings in literary studies*. Newcastle: Cambridge Scholars Publishing, 1–22.

van Peer, W., Hakemulder, F. and Zyngier, S., 2007. Lines on feeling: Foregrounding, aesthetics and meaning. *Language and Literature*, 16 (2), 197–213.

van Peer, W., Hakemulder, F. and Zyngier, S., 2012. *Scientific methods for the humanities*. Amsterdam: John Benjamins Publishing Company.

van Peer, W., Zyngier, S. and Viana, V., eds. 2010. *Literary education and digital learning: Methods and technologies for humanities studies*. Hershey, New York: Information Science Reference.

Verdonk, P., 2002. *Stylistics*. Oxford: Oxford University Press.

Viana, V., Silveira, N. and Zyngier, S., 2008. Empirical evaluation: Towards an automated index of lexical variety. *In:* S. Zyngier et al., eds. *Directions in empirical literary studies*. Amsterdam and Philadelphia: John Benjamins Publishing Company, 271–282.

Viana, V., Zyngier, S. and Barnbrook. G., 2011. *Perspectives on corpus linguistics*. Amsterdam: John Benjamins Publishing Company.

Wales, K., 2001. *A dictionary of stylistics*. 2nd ed, Harlow: Pearson Education Limited.

Wimsatt, W. K. J. and Beardsley, M. C., 1949. The affective fallacy. *The Sewanee Review*, 57 (1), 31–55.

Wynne, M., 2005. *Stylistics: Corpus approaches*, Oxford: Oxford University. Online. Available at: http://www.pala.ac.uk/resources/sigs/corpus-style/Corpora_stylistics.pdf (accessed 28 August 2012).

Zimmer, B, 2011. The mechanic muse. The jargon of the novel computed. *Sunday Book Review. New York Times*. Online. Available at: http://www.nytimes.com/2011/07/31/books/review/the-mechanic-muse-the-jargon-of-the-novel-computed.html?_r=0 (Accessed 4 June 2012).

Zyngier, S., 2008. *Macbeth* through the computer: Literary evaluation and pedagogical Implications. *In* W. van Peer, ed. *The Quality of Literature*. Amsterdam: John Benjamins Publishing Company, 169–190.

Zyngier, S., Bortolussi, M., Chenokova, A. and Auracher, J., eds. 2008. *Directions in empirical literary studies*. Amsterdam: John Benjamins Publishing Company.

Zyngier, S. and Fialho, O., 2010. Pedagogical stylistics, literary awareness and empowerment: A critical perspective. *Language and Literature*, 19 (1), 13–33.

Zyngier, S. and Shepherd, T., 2003. What is literature, really? A corpus-driven study of students' texts. *Style*, 37 (1), 15–26.

21

Feminist stylistics

Rocío Montoro

Introduction

Feminist stylistics can be defined as the sub-branch of stylistics which aims to account for the way in which gender concerns are linguistically encoded in texts, and which attempts to do so by employing some of the frameworks and models pertaining in the stylistics tool-kit. However, the phrase 'gender concerns' can encompass a plurality of meanings which has given rise to the multifaceted perspectives from which the notion of gender has been approached. One of those perspectives is offered by feminist stylistic analyses which, along with other approaches to the study of language and gender on the one hand and feminism on the other, conceive of gender in a rather fluid and adaptable way. Feminist stylisticians' contribution to the study of gender has traditionally illustrated how the interface of gender issues and language materialises in literary texts, but such a focus should not be understood as exclusive. This chapter presents an overview of the way gender matters have been dealt with and discussed within stylistics. In order to achieve that aim, I start by presenting a general overview of language and gender so that feminist stylistic concerns are diachronically and thematically contextualised in relation to other linguistic treatments of gender and feminism. I then illustrate the way gender issues are investigated by revisiting some of the now classical stylistic analyses that have openly espoused a feminist perspective, as well as more recent case studies. Finally, this chapter also hints at ways in which future work can be undertaken.

Dating from the early work produced in the 1960s, stylisticians have not only been bent on providing interpretations of textual meaning based on potentially replicable analyses, but have also proudly embraced the 'interdisciplinary' and 'multimethodological' labels, which has resulted in a constant re-evaluation, further augmentation and subsequent betterment of the items that compose the prototypical stylistics tool-kit. Feminist stylistics also exhibits the same urge to come up with easily observable, potentially replicable analyses for the explanation of how gender issues materialise linguistically. Moreover, feminist stylistics is also subject to the same kind of re-assessment in relation to which models of analysis might be of better service to cater for how gender issues are encoded in texts (see, for instance, the chapter on Corpus Stylistics in this volume). Interestingly, this openness to new methodological possibilities has also helped us to understand more fully the evolving nature of the notion of gender. In relation to the linguistic devices that have been identified as prototypically capable of gender-inscription, feminist stylistics has investigated the grammatical and/or lexical aspects of literary and non-literary texts on the one hand, and supra-sentential, discoursal devices on the other. Additionally, non-verbal, multimodal aspects are also being identified as potential gender-encoders. With regard to the notion of gender itself, feminist stylistics also looks at how linguistic (verbal or multimodal) devices are capable of signalling the shift from a primarily dichotomous understanding of the notions of maleness and femaleness, to a more encompassing definition of the idea of 'genders' as non-discerning, because these genders do not form homogenous groups to begin with. In sum, feminist stylisticians are keen to emphasise that the notion of gender still needs much more evaluation and that feminist issues are far from being resolved, although they might be formulated in ways other than those originally proposed in the 1960s or 1970s. It is through the systematic and methodical investigations characteristically defining stylistics that these new challenges can be properly investigated and discussed.

Historical perspectives

The label 'feminist stylistics' should be properly credited to Mills (1995) because, although she was not the first stylistician to implement a feminist stylistics perspective, she was nonetheless the one who coined the term and described more fully the practices of this sub-branch. Mills had previously used a slightly different version of the label, namely 'Marxist feminist stylistics' (1992), but because of the overt, extra ideological load of the term I do not discuss the Marxist components of that earlier version in this chapter. Mills (1995) originally defines feminist stylistics as a particular 'form of analysis':

> Both the 'feminist' and the 'stylistics' parts of this phrase are complex and may have different meanings for readers. Nevertheless, the phrase itself is one which best sums up my concern first and foremost with an analysis which identifies itself as feminist and which uses linguistic or language analysis to examine texts [...]. Thus, feminist stylistic analysis is concerned not only to describe sexism in a text, but also to analyse the way that point of view, agency, metaphor, or transitivity are unexpectedly closely related to matters of gender, to discover whether women's writing practices can be described, and so on.
>
> *(Mills 1995, p. 1)*

Despite the multiplicity of meanings associated with stylistics and feminism, Mills (1995) advocates that a collaborative merger of the two in terms of their tenets and principles can bring particularly fruitful results. These positive outcomes can come about, she argues, when a description of gender's linguistic encoding is undertaken by utilising some of the devices discussed in stylistics, such as 'point of view, agency, metaphor or transitivity' (nowadays perhaps in a rather less 'unexpected' way than was the case when the above assessment was made). Mills goes on to underscore that paying attention to aspects of text production will not suffice to evaluate fully the way gender meanings are created, so the way readers process those meanings needs to be borne in mind too, especially because 'when we read we do not always read suspiciously; we are used to certain types of messages and they often do not strike us as necessarily oppressive or pernicious' (Mills 1995, p. 1). Subsequent reformulations by Mills concerning the role that readers play in the creation of gendered meanings highlight that the readership does not necessarily always remain completely oblivious to some of those gendered significations; instead, readers are capable of detecting those meanings that stand out as being 'oppressive and pernicious' and they may, consequently, resist or react to them:

> Rather than assuming that notions of gender are simply a question of discriminatory messages about sex difference embedded in texts, feminist stylistics is concerned with unravelling the complex messages which may be deduced from texts and also with analyzing the way that readers piece together or resist these messages.
>
> *(Mills 2006, p. 221)*

The aim of feminist stylistics, then, is twofold: on the one hand, analysts investigate the way text producers employ linguistic features which specifically project male or female values; but also, stylisticians consider the way readers (or, indeed, advertising, cinema or radio audiences, and many other types of discourse participants, for that matter) advertently or inadvertently identify specific gendered meanings in texts. In order to understand the dual aim which characterises feminist stylistic approaches, it is helpful to first pay attention to the way general theoretical approaches to language and gender studies on the one hand, and linguistic feminism, on the other, have evolved and have come to influence feminist stylistic work.

Language and gender studies

This brief survey on the development of general issues on language and gender studies and linguistic feminism needs to begin by clarifying that the concerns which characterise practices related to the former should not, by default, be seen as similar to investigations pertaining to the latter:

> It is important to point out [...] that language and gender studies do not *have* to be feminist in orientation. [...] Leading language and gender researcher Deborah Cameron (2006) has pointed out that non-feminist studies will present descriptive linguistic accounts of gender and language, often detailing processes of language shift or change [...] or present descriptions of how women and men use language in specific locations at particular points in time [...]. The key difference between this knowledge-gathering research and 'feminist' research is that the latter has a specific political purpose by focusing on gender as a social, political and ideological category.
>
> *(Mills and Mullany 2011, p. 2)*

Whereas studies on the interface of language and gender usually highlight differences of language use as employed by men and women (despite the fact that those linguistic variations are not always necessarily proven to be based exclusively on the gender variable), feminist linguistics identifies a political and ideological component which might not be the main focus for the former. Analyses of women's language in literary texts, such as those I summarise below, have mostly opted for underscoring some kind of politically-motivated slant; furthermore, they have predominantly (at least in early feminist stylistics work) highlighted through linguistic means issues concerning the general position of powerlessness attributed to female characters (in contrast to the dominance of male protagonists in many cases), as the now classic example by Burton (1982) illustrates. Feminist stylistics, therefore, originally sat comfortably in the feminist linguistics camp although recent developments have suggested that the actual boundaries between those two approaches should be best understood as fluid and malleable, just like the notion of gender.

As far as language and gender research is concerned, the most influential scholarly work of the past has generally centred around three major axes (because of space constraints, I am restricting my discussion to work published in the latter half of the twentieth century onwards), each one representing a particular standpoint concerning the discrepancies between men and women's linguistic practices: the *deficit* theory, the *dominance* theory and the *difference* theory. The deficit theory illustrates the earliest stance regarding women's linguistic characteristics; it is mainly associated with the work of Robin Lakoff (1973) and her description of prototypical women's language as being ineffective and 'lacking' when compared to that of men. Lakoff's work also highlights a specific correspondence between women's linguistic features and their situation of powerlessness in society, especially when seen in relation to males. Lakoff (1973) identifies linguistic traits such as the use of lexical hedges or fillers (e.g. *you know, sort of, well, you see*), 'empty' adjectives (e.g. *divine, charming, cute*), or precise colour terms (e.g. *magenta, aquamarine*) as prototypically female and, thus, potentially discerning.

The second major axis came about as a kind of rebuttal to the deficit theory and it should be credited to the investigations of Barrie Thorne and Nancy Henley (1975). Thorne and Henley, far from accepting certain lacks in the linguistic characteristics that identify females, emphasise that it is societal constraints and patriarchal values that actually determine the way women are viewed, discussed and conceptualised. In general, those values result in an unfair treatment of females in personal as well as professional scenarios, mainly because the rules that govern such scenarios have been written out and dominated by men. It would follow, thus, that such an unfair treatment would also have linguistic repercussions since this is one way in which the imbalance of power can be not only established but, more importantly, maintained. The third axis is exemplified by work published in the 1980s and 1990s, especially that of Daniel Maltz and Ruth Borker (1982), and Deborah Tannen (1990, 1994). These and other scholars advocate that there are differing linguistic practices between genders, but they eschew claiming antagonistic dimensions between males and females simply because they might make use of distinct linguistic devices. Instead they emphasise that those differences need to be understood as merely linguistic and, for the most part, apolitical. Finally, the proponents of the difference tenets claim that acknowledging a separation between what is considered linguistic and what is viewed as ideologically loaded should enable researchers to focus on investigating which role those differing linguistic practices actually fulfil both for men and women.

Each position has attracted its own supporters, opponents and subsequent counterstatements. For instance, the currency of Lakoff's conclusions was soon lost when it became clear that the set of linguistic variables which she identified as prototypically female was drawn up on the back of research which included only the linguistic features of white, middle-class, American female informants. On the other hand, the difference theory has also been berated for failing to acknowledge that those linguistic discrepancies that they claim are for the most part apolitical do not occur in a vacuum, but rather within particular societies where all sorts of overt or covert dominance practices operate, and consequently they are hardly free from political or ideological influence. Nowadays, most of the research on language and gender has relocated its focus from essentialist positions to more fluid conceptualisations of the notions of maleness, femaleness and gender, so that no linguistic variable should be identified as intrinsically male or female. As Freed (2003) states:

> These data demonstrate in vivid detail that the amount of talk, the structure of narratives, the use of questions, the availability of cooperative and competitive speech styles, the

employment of prestige speech forms, the use of intimate friendly talk, the occurrence of various phonological and prosodic patterns sometimes representative of linguistic change, the occurrence of vernacular speech forms, lexical choices, the use of silence, interruption, aggravated forms of address, and forms of politeness – these do not correlate in any consistent pattern with either sex or gender.

(Freed 2003, p. 705)

Linguistic feminism

All of the above has developed alongside considerations of linguistic feminism, from Second Wave feminist positions to more recent Third Wave perspectives (because of space constraints, I am not dealing with First Wave feminism). As mentioned above, linguistic feminism has traditionally placed special emphasis, in a more overt and compromised way, on the political significance of language research. As Mills and Mullany (2011) put it:

We feel it is politically important to continue to use the term feminism overtly within the field of language and gender research and beyond. We do the research we do in order to change the way that women and men think about the language that they use and the way that others represent women and men in language; [...] Overall, we define the specific political purpose of feminist linguistic studies as producing work which investigates the role that language plays in creating, sustaining and/or perpetuating unequal gender relations and discrimination against women and gay, lesbian and transgendered people.

(Mills and Mullany 2011, p. 3)

Scholars who specifically underscore the need to maintain proactive and engaged positions regarding the denouncement and subsequent reproval of gender inequalities tend to frame their work within broader social concerns so that 'a focus on language has to be a focus on gender inequality in general' (Mills and Mullany 2011, p. 3). Nonetheless, this focus has also been witness to significant changes, from those more belligerent positions concerning women's inequalities that characterised Second Wave feminism research to the new Third Wave feminist perspectives that vouch for non-essentialist descriptions of gender instead. Thus, whereas Second Wave feminism achieved significant developments with regard to the social, labour and personal situations of women, critics have pointed out that those accomplishments have only emphasised a false sense of homogeneity with regard to the female gender in general. Second Wave feminism treated females as if they were part of a unified and subjugated group, which consequently also made all men part of some kind of consolidated, stable and dominant group. Third Wave feminism has rightly pointed out that such characterisation is rather reductive as it conceives of different groups of women as equally powerless or different groups of men as always powerful, as if belonging in one gender category was enough to determine the question of power, for instance:

In contrast, in Third Wave feminism, these large scale categories are now questioned, so that rather than gender being seen as a stable unified variable, to be considered in addition to race or class, gender is now considered as a variable constrained and constituted by them and in turn defining them in the context of local conditions.

(Mills 2002)

Consequently, Third Wave feminism observes the linguistic practices of both men and women as they assume specific gendered identities, whether these are prototypically masculine or feminine (including all their multifarious variations, that is, lesbian, gay, or transgendered). Thus, professional career women working in male-dominated environments can, and often do, assume linguistic practices which the dominance theorists might have identified as masculine, proving that gender is not the social variable determining linguistic choices in that particular case. Conversely, male counsellors might adopt the kind of 'rapport talk' which Tannen (1990) associates with the empathetic and cooperative style of women in their professional treatment of patients. Third Wave feminism, in sum, defines gender in terms of the plurality of identities that both men and women can take on in response to situational or societal constraints and/or expectations. Nevertheless, the new practices identified by Third Wave feminists do not appear to be totally free from controversy either. As Mills (2002) highlights:

> It seems that within this type of analysis sexism becomes difficult to analyse or challenge, and this I suggest that rather than seeing Second and Third Wave feminist linguistics as chronological, they need to be seen more as approaches which may be more or less appropriate depending on the context and social situation. In the case of sexism, for certain types of sedimented sexism a Second Wave feminist approach is more applicable, whereas in others a more locally-oriented and context-specific Third Wave approach is preferable. Thus Second Wave feminism needs to be integrated into Third Wave feminist linguistics, so that both local and global issues can be addressed.
>
> *(Mills 2002)*

So, although Third Wave feminism advocates a shift away from deterministic language differences between genders, this might have unfortunately resulted in less immediate ways to underscore the very aim of feminist research which ultimately attempts to draw attention to inequality issues:

> Sexism has been a key concern of feminist linguists, but it has become more and more difficult to pin down what sexism consists of and to agree that certain words or phrases are unequivocally sexist (Dunant 1994). While feminist linguists still concern themselves with the type of vocabulary which is used to describe female characters in texts, there is a sense in which they have moved to describe a wider range of features which contribute to certain messages being constructed about women. Furthermore, they have recognized that there are forms of indirect sexism which draw on irony and humor which are more difficult to identify than the direct sexism which was the focus of second-wave feminist analysis.
>
> *(Mills 2006, p. 221)*

If this is the case, Third Wave feminism could be failing to address concerns which were at the forefront of Second Wave feminism simply because sexist instances have been masked as comedic or ironic. Furthermore, women might not want to be seen as 'puritanical and lacking a sense of humour, [so] there is little possibility of contesting these ways of presenting sexist ideas, even though sexism is still kept in play by these means' (Mills 2002). In sum, Third Wave feminism might be running some risks that feminist scholars are keen to flag up and also address.

This brief historical outline of the ways that issues on language and gender (on the one hand) and linguistic feminism (on the other) operate also needs to include some reference to post-feminist concerns and preoccupations. The interdisciplinary nature of stylistics makes it especially receptive to influences emanating from literary as well as linguistic criticism (among many other sources), so the way post-feminism has been defined in both fields merits special attention. Attempting to understand the scope of the term immediately highlights its multiplicity of meanings, especially as post-feminism is a label prolifically bandied around in popular culture writing and the media, more often than not loaded with negative assessments of the whole issue of feminism itself. This might have contributed to subsequent unfavourable evaluations of the term on the part of some scholars. For instance, Mills and Mullany (2011, p. 10; see Mills (1998) for a slightly different standpoint regarding the term 'post-feminism') argue that the post-feminism label would encode 'the passing of or the alleged end of feminism, since it is argued that it is no longer needed'; the prefix 'post-', therefore, could be seen to indicate that the ideological content of the noun feminism is somehow passé and unnecessary. Having said that, Mills and Mullany stress that 'the broader political landscape, including sites of resistance, of which 'post-feminism' is a prime example, needs to be analysed and critiqued' (Mills and Mullany 2011, p. 10). Taken in its most extreme version, therefore, post-feminism might seem to vouch for an invalidation of all the claims that the feminist movement had made over the years; for some those aspirations would now be a reality, and hence the demands would automatically become obsolete. Viewed from this reductive perspective, post-feminism could actually be doing a rather damaging disservice to feminist concerns. However, other scholars argue for a rather different version of this notion. For instance, Brooks (1997) states that 'post-feminism':

> [...] is about the conceptual shift within feminism from debates around equality to a focus on debates around difference. It is fundamentally about, not a depoliticisation of feminism, but a political shift in feminism's conceptual and theoretical agenda. Postfeminism is about a critical engagement with earlier feminist political and theoretical concepts and strategies as a result of its engagement with other social movements for change. Postfeminism [...] represents a dynamic movement capable of challenging modernist, patriarchal and imperialist frameworks.
>
> *(Brooks 1997, p. 4)*

Far from embracing a total nullification of feminist demands, Brooks suggests that post-feminism needs to re-evaluate some of those demands and engage with 'other social movements for change'; in fact, according to Brooks, post-feminism has managed to draw attention to the fact that some feminist claims (especially those associated with Second Wave feminism) were not about women's rights in general but became exclusively concerned with the members of those developed societies and communities of practice that most feminists were writing in and about: 'The collapse of consensus from within feminism formed around issues of theorising. Concepts such as "oppression", "patriarchy", "sexuality, identity and difference" as used by white middle-class feminists were increasingly challenged' (Brooks 1997, p. 5). Therefore post-feminism does not imply the end of feminist claims, but points instead at the need for an otherwise healthy re-evaluation of those claims so that their effectiveness can become more inclusive of a plurality of females. Despite the common aims highlighted by Third Wave feminism and post-feminism, there are still terminological discrepancies; as Mills (2002) states:

> Whilst the term Second Wave feminism is fairly uncontentious, referring to the largely liberal and radical feminism of the 1960s onwards which argued for the equality of

women, the term Third Wave feminism is more contentious. […] Third Wave feminism is a preferable term to postfeminism (which assumes implicitly that the aims of feminism have been achieved and that therefore feminism is largely irrelevant).

(Mills 2002)

Feminist linguists, on the whole, seem more inclined to ditch the term post-feminism in favour of Third Wave feminism to avoid any suggestion that the principles of feminism have become obsolete. Nevertheless, and as will be seen below, post-feminism as a label has been employed in some stylistic analyses, so for some scholars the term is still a useful way of describing how earlier feminist positions have subsequently developed.

Critical issues and topics

In what follows, I illustrate certain critical issues and topics raised in some feminist stylistic analyses. For instance, feminist stylisticians have tended to favour analyses that display an engaged and political standpoint in their linguistic description of certain texts, so they have been particularly successful at pointing out the depiction of female characters as powerless and ineffective, especially when compared to their male counterparts. One of the most often quoted feminist stylistic studies highlighting a political perspective is that of Burton (1982), who argues that 'stylistic analysis is not just a question of discussing "effects" in language and text, but a powerful method for understanding the ways in which all sorts of "realities" are constructed through language'(1982, p. 201). More specifically, she formulates her investigation within a committed feminist framework in which the 'personal is political' (1982, p. 201) and exemplifies it with the analysis of clinical depression as described in Sylvia Plath's novel *The Bell Jar* ([1963] 2005):

We want to understand the relationships between severe and crippling depression that many women experience and the contradictory and disenabling images of self available for women in models of literature, the media, education, folk-notions of the family, motherhood, daughterhood, work, and so on.

(Burton 1982, p. 201)

Burton uses the transitivity framework described in systemic functional linguistics (Halliday 1968, Berry 1975, see Halliday and Matthiessen 2004 for a more updated version) as this model aims to account for the way in which experience is encoded in language. In particular, Burton focuses on the way experiential meaning becomes encoded in the 'processes' of a clause– that is, the clause components projecting (mainly, though not exclusively) actions and linguistically realised by verbs. These processes rely on the presence of certain entities called 'participants' (linguistically expressed as noun phrases) which enact them. Finally, the processes which those participants endowed with an agentive function activate sometimes also affect further participants in the clause. In sum, Burton looks at the issue of 'who does what to whom' (1982, p. 200) in a short paragraph of *The Bell Jar* in which the female protagonist is subjected to electric shock treatment to heal her mental problems. The paragraph under scrutiny is analysed in terms of the various processes ('material', 'mental' and 'relational', as well as their sub-categories) followed by a classification of which participants are primarily endowed with an agentive and proactive role and which others are, instead, mainly affected by the actions undertaken by others (for further examples on the use of the transitivity model see Halliday 1971, Jeffries 2007, Kennedy 1982, Mills 1994, and Nørgaard

2003). Burton concludes that the transitivity framework can assist the analyst in spelling out, in a clear but refined way, how a specific disenabling situation, such as the one the novel's protagonist is enduring because of her mental instability, is linguistically encoded. Despite the fact that the incident is clearly focalized via the female protagonist's consciousness, her actual role in the paragraph is decided by how other characters' actions impinge upon her body and mind which results in virtually all traces of volition being taken away from her. For instance, even the electrical current administered to her temples during electric shock treatment is permitted to have a more participatory, non-affected linguistic role than the female protagonist herself. Burton argues, therefore, that it is possible for the analyst to tease out socially-constructed meanings from language (in this case, a stigmatised vision of female depression) via the application of frameworks such as transitivity. Admittedly, Burton also highlights that 'if I have given the impression that there is any simple set of relationships between language, thought and socially constructed reality, it was an unintentional and artificial contingency' (1982, 211). Nevertheless, the absence of a necessary connection between linguistic structures and specific significations does not mean that such a connection between form and meaning cannot otherwise exist.

Other frameworks of analysis

The general gender and feminist concerns which a transitivity framework allows us to shed light on have been echoed in many other feminist stylistic analyses; moreover, other feminist stylisticians have subsequently picked up the 'powerlessness and disenabling' gauntlet to also bring to the fore the way in which passive heroines recurrently take centre stage in some genres or literary discourses. Ryder (1999), for instance, combines some of the principles of transitivity with further semantic and cognitive tenets to account for gender representation in a prototypically female narrative form, romance novels, with a special focus on one of Barbara Cartland's historical romances. She investigates the actions/inactions of both male and female characters in an attempt to resolve what she identifies as one of romantic novels' paradoxes whereby the female protagonist is, virtually without exception, typified as a passive agent who lacks initiative and engages in very few real activities despite the fact that 'the plot of the typical popular novel of any genre consists of a series of actions, most of which are initiated by the main character' (Ryder 1999, p. 1067). She analyses the way in which the plotline of romances perpetuates the image of the passive heroine despite popular narratives being, generally speaking, inclusive of lots of activities and happenings, as opposed to passages of internalised mental activities, for instance. To investigate this apparent contradiction she combines elements from the transitivity framework briefly referred to above, but she extends some of the aspects described there to include the notion of 'event structure' (Langacker 1991) which she summarises as:

> **Features of a prototypical event:**
> 1. a volitional
> 2. self-moving
> 3. concrete
> 4. entity$_1$
> 5. produces a discernible change in
> 6. another concrete entity$_2$
> 7. by means of a discernible action with definable boundaries.
>
> *(Ryder 1999, p. 1069)*

By looking at the event structure of her chosen passage, Ryder aims at monitoring which entities are given an agentive function (entity$_1$) by being involved in actions which enforce discernible changes in further concrete creatures (entity$_2$). Her interests, thus, run parallel to those of Burton insofar as both aim at eliciting agentivity and affectivity (that is, initialising actions or receiving the direct effect of the action initiated by the agent). Events, however, are not always prototypical, nor are all discerning actions by default conceived of as affecting other entities. Ryder argues that when an event does not fulfil all the criteria above (for instance, because there is no entity$_2$ to affect, nor is there clear volition on the part of entity$_1$) we should not speak of full events but of what she describes as 'quasi-events' (Ryder 1999, p. 1069). In this way, the question Burton addresses above concerning 'who does what to whom' can be more thoroughly and comprehensively investigated.

What seems relevant is the fact that Ryder, like Burton, underscores that looking at the processes, participants and events of texts can help illustrate the way experiential and also socially-constructed significations are linguistically encoded. In romances, Ryder argues, not only are certain textual identities allowed a more participatory and engaged role than others, mainly the male characters in contrast to the more passive female protagonists, but also the latter mainly feature in what Ryder calls 'upgrade strategies of events' (1999, p. 1071), by means of which they are falsely involved in events which suggest action by the narration of a constant rush of activity which, effectively, has little or no consequences for other characters or even themselves. For instance, if these heroines embark on some sort of activity, they might 'struggle, get to her feet, walk, [...] tiptoe, creep, [...] cover[ed] her face in her hands, [...] giv[ing] a little involuntary cry' (Ryder 1999, pp. 1071, 1072), but these activities do not guarantee that criterion five above ('produce a discernible change') is fulfilled; as a result, their actual 'doing' in the novel consists of actions which do not seem to help the plotline move forward. Conversely, the rest of the characters become involved in what Ryder calls 'downgrading strategies' which aim at boosting the apparent protagonism of females by making males' involvement in the actual actions that help advance the plotline appear less prominent. Examples include: 'he seized her by the ankle, he made her a prisoner, [...] she felt herself being lifted up by strong arms and flung violently, [...] she felt herself being carried away' (Ryder 1999, pp. 1073, 1074). These examples also illustrate that the agentive presence of the male automatically places the heroine as 'entity$_2$', who is directly affected by the discernible change that entity$_1$ puts into effect. In sum, Ryder concludes that Cartland uses a variety of strategies aimed at diminishing the impression of the heroine as a mere non-participatory passive entity.

The aims and interests so far defined in this chapter are also present in Wales's *Feminist Linguistics and Literary Criticism* (1994) (this volume was actually published before Mills's *Feminist Stylistics* (1995), although the label 'feminist stylistics' itself is not as fully exploited as in Mills's work). This collection of essays highlights the need for investigating the political and social dimensions of gender issues, and argues for the application of linguistic methodologies 'in order to address directly questions and ideas that have been raised in feminist literary theory, criticism and linguistics about gender and style' (Wales 1994, p. vii). According to the editor, the result is 'a kind of feminist stylistics, a field which [...] has considerable potential in the future' (Wales 1994, p. vii); it seems fair to confirm that, at the time of writing this chapter, almost two decades after that statement was made, such a potential has not only been realised but is constantly being further challenged. However, the eclectic nature of the collection means that the core aim is practically realised in a variety of ways – so, for instance, whereas Jeffries (1994) looks at 'apposition' in contemporary female poetry, Wareing (1994) and Mills (1994) concern themselves with representations of femaleness in popular culture, and Calvo (1994) focuses on the discourse tactics used by the character Celia in Shakespeare's *As You Like It*. Interestingly, this collection also proves that the remit of feminist stylistics goes beyond discourses which are intrinsically literary; for instance, by mirroring Burton's use of the transitivity framework (1982), Mills investigates the 'who does what to whom' paradigm in popular songs and suggests that the socially-constructed meanings that can be deduced from the application of a transitivity analysis need to be properly contextualised and should not be understood as a univocal relationship between linguistic form and function. Feminist stylisticians, therefore, are keen to constantly problematise both the gender issue and the tools, models and frameworks employed to bring to the fore the linguistic encoding of gender. Below, I illustrate this duality by summarising some of the current contributions and research striving to fulfil this endeavour.

Current contribution and research

The feminist stylistics work published in the aftermath of Second Wave Feminism or, more recently, amid Third Wave Feminist influences seems to have drawn some core conclusions from the work of the past. Most recent contributions to the feminist stylistics cause (as already suggested in Mills (1998), especially in relation to the transitivity framework) tend to converge in their abandonment of any claims of linguistic essentialism, so most of the analyses on gender emphasise that there is no way to successfully identify different genders by considering the linguistic choices of a particular language user. As Livia (2003) explains, this lack of linguistic essentialism applies equally to literary discourse:

> We have seen that although many prominent writers have set out to discover the differences between men's and women's sentences, following in the footsteps of Virginia Woolf at the beginning of the twentieth century, no convincing linguistic evidence has yet been provided to indicate the stylistic characteristics of each. Instead, we have found that there are conventions of masculine and feminine style which any sophisticated writer, whether male or female, can follow.
>
> *(Livia 2003, p. 156)*

The outcomes of past research, therefore, have enabled current investigators to avoid claims of univocal correspondences between linguistic forms and notions of maleness and femaleness. However, eschewing linguistic determinism is not the only way in which feminist stylistics has evolved from positions of the past; current research also tends to focus on the multiplicity of values included in the notion of gender which is understood in a rather more fluid way than was the case in the past. Finally, recent feminist stylistic research has also incorporated non-verbal, multimodal markers as linguistic indices of gender manifestation.

One of the more recent ways in which feminist stylistics is branching out into territories that might have been slightly less populated in the past is in what has been termed 'feminist narratology': 'In recent decades, both narratology and feminist studies have become established as highly influential fields of study. One area that combines insights from both is the development of feminist narratology' (Page 2003, p, 43). Although narratology is a firmly established and amply researched discipline whose general interests are distinct from those of stylistics, it is also true that there exist a number of overlapping concerns which seem to become highlighted when these interests are also combined with gender and feminist matters. Cross-fertilisation from either discipline onto the other should bear fruit which could also shed light on gender matters. For instance, in the same way as feminist linguists and feminist stylisticians currently discard linguistic determinism, Page (2003) also claims that assigning a certain degree of 'narrativity' to a text and correlating that degree with a specific gender (as may have been done in past accounts regarding the narrative structure of texts) may be controversial and also misleading: 'any given text may be considered as having weaker or stronger narrativity than another. What is striking about this in relation to feminist analyses of plot types is that there seems to be a correlation between degrees of narrativity and the stereotypical gendering of plot where the "male" and "female" plots exhibit strong and weak narrativity respectively' (Page 2003, p. 45). There is no space here to develop fully the notion of narrativity, but Page summarises it as follows:

> A complex relationship between linguistic features 'in' the text, such as the marking of narrative coherence through chronology, characterization and evaluation often combined as culturally recognizable patterns of organization [...]; and extra-linguistic factors 'outside' the text, such as the reader's world knowledge that may be shaped by specific cultural contexts in various ways.
>
> *(Page 2003, p. 45)*

As mentioned above, although stylistics and narratology are customarily understood to have distinct aims (the former perhaps endorsing a stronger linguistic slant over other concerns), there are nonetheless plenty of linguistic devices which both narratologists and stylisticians exploit to account for meaning creation in texts. Devices such as deictic temporal markers to indicate chronology, characterisation signalled by specific idiolects or evaluation signposted in particular adjectival structures, for instance, are also recognised as being part of the stylistics tool-kit. It seems that findings emanating from feminist narratology in relation to the narrative structure of texts and their potentiality for gender inscription can easily be incorporated as part of feminist stylistics research. Moreover, the current tendency in feminist narratological work to cast doubts on whether a particular degree of narrativity should be unequivocally conceived within a 'binary model which relates narrative form to gender' (2003, p. 54) also suggests a similar move away from the linguistic (and narrative) determinism developed in feminist stylistics research.

Recent additions to the set of feminist stylistic interests include research concerned with the analysis of gender in multimodal, non-exclusively verbal discourses as well as in some genres which could be considered outside the prototypically female spectrum, such as children's fiction. Sunderland (2011), for instance, investigates 'the fiction young children read (at home and school), the language of that fiction, and the way female and male characters, and gender relations, are represented in the language of that fiction' (2011, p. 1). Sunderland openly assumes a 'feminist, critical approach but also draws broadly on the insights of stylistics' (2011, p. 18) which confirms that the combination of the tenets subsumed in either discipline can be multifariously put to the test to research a variety of discourses and genres. Sunderland concludes that the gender balance regarding the representation of male and female characters in the sample of children's fiction she investigates has improved, at least in relation to the ratio of male/female characters and the roles they are assigned; but she also acknowledges that finding a kind of 'gender equilibrium' is a much more complex issue than simply increasing the number of female characters in children's texts. Feminist stylisticians have also started to point out that gender matters need investigating in contexts other than the exclusively verbal. For example, Koller (2008) focuses on the use of the colour pink as a marker of gender and sexuality. Using both social semiotics and cognitive semantic principles and tools, Koller argues that the use of the colour pink has evolved in a way that has recently become linked to certain values that stand close to post-feminist formulations. As she explains:

> There seems to be a tendency to reclaim pink and redefine it as the colour of women who regard themselves as having achieved equality in social and economic terms and are therefore able to embrace pink as a marker of their femininity. While such post-feminist thinking rests on false premises – even a cursory glance [...] shows that women have not yet achieved socio-economic equality – it nevertheless constructs a new brand of femininity; the 'fun fearless female' [...]. And she comes clad in pink. In this framework, pink is used to communicate fun and independence, financial and professional power without conforming to masculine norms, as well as femininity and self-confidence.
>
> *(Koller 2008, pp. 415–416)*

Koller's evaluation of the kind of significations that a non-verbal marker is capable of encoding clearly demonstrates that issues of gender can no longer be exclusively analysed from the perspective of verbal, mono-modal language. Furthermore, Koller's work also appears to rekindle the contentious use of the term 'post-feminism', as discussed above. However, whether analysts prefer to substitute Third Wave feminism for post-feminism, or whether the latter term is embraced fully, seems less relevant than the acknowledgement that current feminist positions have undoubtedly evolved from those of the past, and have therefore incorporated aspects which may not have been addressed previously simply because they might not have been an issue at earlier stages of the development of feminism.

Finally, in my own work on *Chick Lit* (Montoro 2012) I analyse the multimodal components of a corpus of *Chick Lit* book covers and argue that the engendering of meaning that feminist stylisticians have prototypically identified in the verbal components of texts must be extended to non-verbal aspects too. For instance, I combine an analysis of two main semiotic resources, typography and colour, to highlight the way that values associated with a very specific group of females (white, middle-class, in their thirties, and prototypically urbanite) are recurrently realised on the book (and back) covers of these novels, suggesting that feminist stylistics should pay urgent heed to the way multimodal concerns can also help the feminist cause.

Recommendations for practice

There is no shortage of examples to implement a feminist stylistics analysis, so the suggestions below are intended simply as a way of prompting students to identify gendered practices by themselves in a variety of genres:

1. Popular fiction is peppered with examples of novels and short stories written by and for (mainly, although not exclusively) women. The most often quoted genre is, of course, romantic fiction. Using a romance novel of your choice, try to identify the 'who does what to whom' paradigm described above by using a transitivity analysis (you will need to do sample analysis). Consider whether this methodology is as effective as previous scholars have claimed at bringing gendered messages to the fore. You should also bear in mind the fact that most of these novels are authored by women themselves. Can female authorship be reconciled with possible examples of overtly anti-feminist messages?

2. Romantic fiction, however, is also often described as a particularly 'sentimental' narrative genre, an aspect which is prototypically associated with fiction aimed at women. Using

a corpus stylistics methodology (see the related chapter in this volume), try to ascertain whether sentimentality is, indeed, specifically marked in a corpus of romantic novels; you should also consider the way that sentimentality is linguistically realised, that is, whether female characters are made to 'feel', whether they 'love', whether they 'ache' or 'suffer', etc. The analysis of semantic categories has proven especially useful for this task, but feel free to explore any other avenues that can help you confirm whether the sentimentality claimed by scholars is, indeed, a major component of romantic fiction.

3. Because of new technological advances (the internet, for instance), advertisers have had to consider new ways of targeting their products at the appropriate audience. Having said that, the female body is still repeatedly exploited to advertise all sorts of products. Compile a corpus of adverts which utilise printed images of male and female bodies and consider whether male representation is as explicitly employed nowadays as female, and for which purposes. Consider the implications of this extension in light of linguistic feminist concerns, especially those discussed in Third Wave feminism.

Future directions

As we have seen, feminist stylisticians are keen to highlight the fluidity of the term feminism itself, its practices, its linguistic (verbal and non-verbal) manifestations, its analyses, constructions and interpretations. This chapter has explored the various nuances that current research on language and gender on the one hand and feminism on the other have already brought to the fore in relation to the understanding of past and current forms of feminism. Nevertheless, the investigation of feminist concerns in literary (and other) forms still needs to delve deeper into issues perhaps not so clearly described, such as feminism and fictionality, the stylistic and linguistic representation of femininity as opposed to femaleness, as well as questions related to femaleness and gendered authorship (that is, the representation of femaleness by female and male authors), all of which would seem to indicate that there is still ample scope for further research in this field.

Related topics

Corpus stylistics, critical stylistics, point of view and modality, multimodality

Further reading

Coates, J. and Pichler, P., eds. 2011. *Language and gender: A reader*. 2nd edn. Malden and Oxford: Wiley and Blackwell.

> The second edition of *Language and Gender* is not simply a revamped version of the original but a much more enriched overview of gender and language issues. The initial thirty-two chapters have been extended to forty-three, including both practical and theoretical considerations on language and gender. This volume can help students gain an insight into the ample array of approaches and varied contexts of use in which the interface of language and gender is being investigated.

Jeffries, L, 2000. Point of view and the reader in the poetry of Carol Ann Duffy. *In:* L. Jeffries and P. Sampson, eds. *Contemporary poems: Some critical approaches*. Huddersfield: Smith/Doorstop Press, 54–68.

> There is very little work which combines an interest in poetry and feminist concerns. Jeffries's chapter is one of the very few stylistic analyses of contemporary poetry from a feminist perspective. Jeffries examines Duffy's poems by utilising some prototypical stylistics devices, such as point of view, but interestingly she also considers the effect of point of view manipulation on the reader.

Opas, L. L. and Tweedie, F. J., 1999. The magic carpet ride: Reader involvement in romantic fiction. *Literary and Linguistic Computing*, 14 (1), 89–101.

This chapter uses a computational methodology to explore reader involvement in romantic fiction novels. By looking at markers of stance, the authors investigate the way in which readers are strategically 'pulled' into the storyworld of the novels. This chapter is a good example of how computational tools and corpus analysis can effectively support the analysis of feminist issues in texts.

Thornborrow, J., 1998. Playing hard to get: Metaphor and representation in the discourse of car advertisements. *Language and Literature*, 7 (3), 254–272.

From the very beginning feminist stylistics has been concerned with discourses other than the literary. In this article, Thornborrow looks at the way car advertisements exploit male and female bodies as metaphors to encode advertising messages. As such, on the one hand this article provides a critical stylistic/feminist perspective, and on the other it also underscores the importance of considering the non-verbal components of texts.

Warner, C., 2009. Speaking from experience: Narrative schemas, deixis, and authenticity effects in Verena Stefan's feminist confession *Shedding*. *Language and Literature*, 18 (1), 7–23.

Warner anchors her analysis of autobiographical novels in cognitive stylistics. She utilises the concepts of narrative schemas and deixis to investigate autobiographical and confessional writing, and demonstrates how deictic shifts, for instance, allow the reader a particular sense of involvement with the narrative by making some narrative parameters more prominent than others.

References

Berry, M., 1975. *An introduction to systemic linguistics*. London and Sydney: B.T. Batsford, Ltd.

Brooks, A., 1997. *Postfeminisms: Feminism, cultural theory, and cultural forms*. London: Routledge.

Burton, D., 1982. Through glass darkly: Through dark glasses. *In:* R. Carter, ed. *Language and literature. An introductory reader in stylistics*. London: George Allen and Unwin, 195–214.

Calvo, C., 1994. In defence of Celia: Discourse analysis and women's discourse in *As You Like It*. *In:* K. Wales, ed. *Feminist linguistics in literary criticism*. Woodbridge, England: Boydell and Brewer, 91–116.

Cameron, D., 2006. *Language and sexual politics*. London: Routledge.

Coates, J. and Pichler, P., eds. 2011. *Language and gender: A reader*. 2nd edn. Malden and Oxford: Wiley and Blackwell.

Dunant, S., ed. 1994. *The war of the words: The political correctness debate*. London: Virago.

Freed, A., 2003. Epilogue: Reflections on language and gender research. *In:* J. Holmes and M. Meyerhoff, eds. *The handbook of language and gender*. Oxford: Blackwell, 699–721.

Halliday, M. A. K., 1968. Notes on transitivity and theme in English, Part 3. *Journal of Linguistics*, 4, 179–215; reprinted in J. Webster, ed. 2005. *Studies in English language*. London, New York: Continuum, 110–153.

Halliday, M. A. K., 1971. Linguistic function and literary style: An inquiry into the language of William Golding's *The Inheritors*. *In:* D. C. Freeman, ed. 1981. *Essays in modern stylistics*. London and New York: Methuen, 325–360.

Halliday, M. A. K. and Matthiessen, C. M. I. M., 2004. *An introduction to functional grammar*. 3rd edn. London: Hodder Arnold.

Jeffries, L., 1994. Language in common: Apposition in contemporary poetry by women. *In:* K. Wales, ed. *Feminist linguistics in literary criticism*. Woodbridge, England: Boydell and Brewer, 21–50.

Jeffries, L, 2000. Point of view and the reader in the poetry of Carol Ann Duffy. *In:* L. Jeffries and P. Sampson, eds. *Contemporary poems: Some critical approaches*. Huddersfield: Smith/Doorstop Press, 54–68.

Jeffries, L., 2007. *Textual construction of the female body. A critical discourse approach*. Houndmills, Basingstoke: Palgrave Macmillan.

Kennedy, C., 1982. Systemic grammar and its use in literary analysis. *In:* R. Carter ed. *Language and literature: An introductory reader in stylistics*. London: George Allen and Unwin, 83–99.

Koller, V., 2008. Not just a colour: Pink as a gender and sexuality marker in visual communication. *Visual Communication*, 7 (4), 395–423.

Lakoff, R., 1973. Language and woman's place. *Language in Society*, 2 (1), 45–80.

Langacker, R., 1991. *Foundations of cognitive grammar II*. Stanford, California: Stanford University Press.

Livia, A., 2003. One man in two is a woman: Linguistic approaches to gender in literary texts. *In:* J. Holmes and M. Meyerhoff, eds. *The handbook of language and gender*. Oxford: Blackwell Publishing, 142–158.

Maltz, D. N. and Borker, R. A., 1982. A cultural approach to male-female miscommunication. *In:* J. J. Gumperz, ed. *Language and social identity*, Cambridge: Cambridge University Press, 196–216.

Mills, S., 1992. Knowing your place: A Marxist feminist stylistic analysis. *In:* M. Toolan, ed. *Language, text and context: Essays in stylistics*. London: Routledge, 182–205.

Mills, S., 1994. Close encounters of a feminist kind: Transitivity analysis and pop lyrics. *In:* K. Wales, ed. *Feminist linguistics in literary criticism*. Woodbridge, England: Boydell and Brewer, 137–156.

Mills, S., 1995. *Feminist stylistics*. London: Routledge.

Mills, S., 1998. Post-feminist text analysis. *Language and Literature*, 7 (3), 235–252.

Mills, S., 2002. Third wave feminism and the analysis of sexism. *Discourse Analysis Online*, available at http://extra.shu.ac.uk/daol/articles/open/2003/001/mills2003001.html [Accessed 28th August 2012].

Mills, S., 2006. Feminist stylistics. *In:* K. Brown, ed. *Encyclopaedia of language and linguistics*. Amsterdam: Elsevier Science, 221–223.

Mills, S. and Mullany, L., 2011. *Language, gender and feminism. Theory, methodology and practice*. London and New York: Routledge.

Montoro, R., 2012. *Chick lit: The stylistics of cappuccino fiction*. London: Continuum.

Nørgaard, N., 2003. *Systemic functional linguistics and literary analysis. A Hallidayan approach to Joyce – a Joycean approach to Halliday*. Odense, Denmark: University Press of Southern Denmark.

Opas, L. L. and Tweedie, F. J., 1999. The magic carpet ride: Reader involvement in romantic fiction. *Literary and Linguistic Computing*, 14 (1), 89–101.

Page, R., 2003. Feminist narratology? Literary and linguistic perspectives on gender and narrativity. *Language and Literature*, 12 (1), 43–56.

Plath, S., [1963] 2005. *The bell jar*. London: Faber and Faber.

Ryder, M. E., 1999. Smoke and mirrors. Event patterns in the discourse structure of a romance novel. *Journal of Pragmatics*, 31 (8), 1067–1080.

Sunderland, J., 2011. *Language, gender and children's fiction*. London: Continuum.

Tannen, D., 1990. *You just don't understand: Women and men in conversation*. New York: William Morrow.

Tannen, D., 1994. *Gender and discourse*. New York: Oxford University Press.

Thornborrow, J., 1998. Playing hard to get: Metaphor and representation in the discourse of car advertisements. *Language and Literature*, 7 (3), 254–272.

Thorne, B. and Henley, N., eds. 1975. *Language and sex: Difference and dominance*. Rowley, MA: Newbury House.

Wales, K., ed. 1994. *Feminist linguistics in literary criticism*. Woodbridge, England: Boydell and Brewer.

Wareing, S., 1994. And then he kissed her: The reclamation of female characters to submissive roles in contemporary fiction. *In:* K. Wales, ed. *Feminist linguistics in literary criticism*. Cambridge: D. S. Brewer, 117–136.

Warner, C., 2009. Speaking from experience: Narrative schemas, deixis, and authenticity effects in Verena Stefan's feminist confession *Shedding*. *Language and Literature*, 18 (1), 7–23.

22

Literary pragmatics and stylistics

Chantelle Warner

Introduction

News Item
Men seldom make passes
At girls who wear glasses.

At first glance, the reader whose eyes fall upon this page may wonder at the short bit of text presented above. The words 'News Item' might seem to suggest a blurb in a periodical of some sort, whereas the format of the text – in particular the line breaks – might lead some to speculate whether this is an aphorism or even a poem. Given that this is a chapter bearing the title 'Literary Pragmatics and Stylistics' in a handbook on stylistics, you are likely to try to infer what I, the author, hope to convey through this example. If you had instead encountered this same text in a different context – for example, in the sidebar of a women's magazine or in the collection of writings from author and humorist Dorothy Parker, in which I found it – the effect might have been somewhat different. The area of study that focuses on exactly these communicative dimensions of literary encounters is called literary pragmatics; how the interactions between producer, recipient and text are manoeuvred in various ways through linguistic choice is the matter of a closely related field, pragmatic stylistics.

Pragmatics, in its broadest definition, is the area of linguistic study that investigates relationships between language, its users, and its contexts of use. Both the name and the initial focus of the subfield originate in the semiotic theories of Charles Morris (1938) who described signs as governed by three types of relations that have come to define modern linguistics: the syntactic, the semantic, and the pragmatic. However, it was philosophers like J. L. Austin, Paul Grice and John Searle in the 1950s and 1960s who popularised the basic principles of pragmatic analysis for a number of language-based fields by showing that language users do not simply communicate through their words, but implicate and perform particular acts and effects.

Literary pragmatics and pragmatic stylistics have emerged out of work within this field and share these same concerns with regard to literary texts. While various theories and scholars devote varying degrees of attention to the formal features of literary works, pragmatic approaches share in common an understanding of language, including literary language, as most importantly a form of symbolic social action. From a pragmatic viewpoint, considerations of literary style are inextricable from questions of context, including speakers' and readers' identities, intentions, beliefs and frames of relevance.

The emergence and evolution of pragmatic stylistics

Because it developed out of a sense that textual meaning ought to be disassociated from formal features of language, pragmatics research found itself turning to literary language early on in its disciplinary history. Linguist Jacob L. Mey edited the first issue of the *Journal of Pragmatics*, the first scholarly periodical devoted to the field, in 1977, the same year as Mary Louise Pratt, a comparatist by training, published her book *Towards a Speech Act Theory of Literary Discourse*. Many of the earliest scholars in this burgeoning field shared the opinion of Roger Sell, who wrote in 1985 that the first aim of a literary pragmaticist is to 'demythologise the concept of literature' as an agentless conveyor of truths and ideas and to reveal the processes of discourse between writer and recipient. The two earliest introductory volumes on pragmatics, Stephen Levinson's *Pragmatics* and Geoffrey Leech's *Principles of Pragmatics* (both published in 1983) each mention literary language and poetics at least in passing, which evidences the attention paid to poetic phenomena such as metaphor in the then nascent field. In fact, Leech's interest in literary linguistics and stylistics predates his work in pragmatics – one of his earliest monographs was *A Linguistic Guide to English Poetry* (1969), he was one of the founding members of the *Poetics and Linguistics Association* in 1980 and co-author of a seminal work in the field of stylistics, *Style in Fiction: A Linguistic Introduction to English Fictional Prose* with Mick Short in 1981.

Leech's work points to the close relationship that literary pragmatics and stylistics have shared since at least the early 1970s, as stylistics began to expand into an ever more interdisciplinary field. Many have noted correlates between core pragmatic principles and foundational theories within stylistics such as Mikhail Bakhtin's sociological poetics and Roger Fowler's account of literature as social discourse. Pragmatics scholar Leo Hickey has argued that the two fields have been moving closer together and suggests that pragmatics is in some sense inherent in stylistic research, in that 'a student of style will be interested primarily in those features or aspects of a text, written or spoken, which are not imposed by the grammar of the language or by the semantic content, that is, by the information to be conveyed, but are selected by the speaker (and we use the term speaker to include writer) for other reasons' (Hickey 1993, p. 573). One of the guiding questions of stylistics thus ought to be what 'other reasons' drive stylistic choices, in terms of desired effects, communicative qualities, and the context or situation of the speaker and reader.

More recent calls for contextualised stylistics research and movements towards more ecological frameworks that locate meaning making in the combined efforts of texts, readers, and environmental factors can be understood as a continuing evolution of the pragmatically attuned stylistics that Hickey envisions, but importantly these calls also point to the fact that the juncture between these two fields has not always been a perfect fit. Stylistics is defined by its orientation toward textual effects. Although the field has expanded to include a wide array of texts (spoken and written) and effects, a particular attention towards literary works has traditionally characterised stylistic inquiry. For this reason, research in stylistics, like other textually-oriented fields, has expanded the field of pragmatics by pushing scholars to account for relatively long and complex acts of verbal communication. At the same time, stylistic theories have often relegated contextual factors to the margins of analysis, and thus a pragmatic perspective might help scholars to understand how style intersects with contexts of use and interactants' perceptions thereof.

The emphasis in this chapter will be on literary pragmatic research conducted within or closely adjacent to the field of stylistics. Some researchers have attempted to delineate this area of research by providing it with subdisciplinary labels such as 'pragmatic stylistics' (Black 2006) or 'pragmastylistics' (Hickey 1993). Such headers give credence to what is without a doubt a vibrant body of work taking place at the intersection between these two fields; however, the boundaries around such a field are fluid and permeable, and indeed this might be one of the great advantages of such interdisciplinary work. One possible way of understanding the relationship between pragmatic stylistics and other areas of literary pragmatics scholarship is along a continuum from relatively more 'text-focused' to more 'world-focused' emphases. Whereas the former aims to provide fairly detailed accounts of linguistic features, the latter also includes work that is more oriented towards the context or reader-reception. However, this is by no means a rigid distinction and indeed principles from pragmatics have been foundational for a great deal of stylistics research focusing on cognitive or formal aspects of style, which does not explicitly characterise itself as pragmatic. The emphasis in this chapter is on theories and analyses that attempt to wed principles of pragmatic and stylistic scholarship in some way, and on concepts and frameworks that have served as common ground between the two. For this reason I have not been overly cautious about devoting this chapter strictly to work that neatly fits one label or another, although it should be noted that both stylistics and literary pragmatics are broad field, which extend beyond the spaces where they converge.

Critical issues

In spite of the many changes that literary pragmatics and its sister disciplines – linguistics, stylistics, and literary studies – have undergone over the past few decades, the basic schema of the field was anticipated by linguist Teun van Dijk in an early article titled 'The Pragmatics of Literary Communication' (1977). The key questions and problems identified by van Dijk are as follows:

1. What kind(s) of action are accomplished by the production of literary texts?
2. What are the appropriateness conditions of these actions?
3. What is the structure of the context in terms of which the appropriateness is defined?
4. How are 'literary actions' and their context related to structures of literary text?
5. In which respect are these actions, contexts and textual manifestations similar to and/or different from those in other types of communication, both verbal and non-verbal?
6. Which extant problems of both poetics and the actual functioning of literature in society can be (re)formulated in terms of pragmatic theory?
7. Which extant problems of both poetics and the actual functioning of literature in society can be (re)formulated in terms of a pragmatic theory?

And finally:

8. What is the cognitive (emotive, etc) basis of the pragmatic notions?
9. What is the social and cultural basis of the pragmatic notions mentioned above? Which conventions, norms, values, and which societal structures link the appropriateness of 'literary' action with the actual processes of acceptance, rejection, etc., of literary texts?

Van Dijk wrote this treatise from a position within the burgeoning fields of European text linguistics and discourse analysis in the 1960s and 1970s – two fields which created the possibility for the pragmatic and stylistic subfields that developed shortly thereafter. Van Dijk's intellectual wish list for literary pragmatics highlights a couple of key concerns that were on the scholarly horizon at that time and which have shaped the landscape of linguistic and literary studies in the years since: namely an understanding that the primary unit of language is the *text*, as opposed to word-, phrase-, or sentence-level structures, and an emergent awareness of *language as discourse*, that is, a contextually- and situationally-embedded social phenomenon. For this reason, the guiding questions for the study of literary texts posed by van Dijk coincide with the preoccupations of researchers within literary pragmatics and the theoreticians whose ideas have informed their work. Although some of the issues cited by van Dijk are arguably less text-focused in the vein of literary pragmatics, many explicitly invoke structural and poetic aspects of literature solidly within the purview of stylistic inquiry.

Van Dijk's list (especially queries 1 to 7) thus ought to echo in the back of the reader's head as we move into the following section, which outlines the main perspectives from pragmatics that have influenced the study of literary style in turn: speech act theory as theorised by Austin and Searle, Gricean implicature, Sperber and Wilson's relevance theory, and interactionist notions of facework and politeness (for more on these topics see Chapters 7, 8 and 9 in this volume). One of Van Dijk's final two questions, number 8, which pertains to the cognitive dimension of literary pragmatics, has received increasing attention in recent work and will be picked up again towards the end of this chapter in the section titled 'Future Directions.'

Speech act theory

Speech act theory, as you have read in depth elsewhere in this volume (Chapter 7), aims to explain the kinds of action performed through the utterance of certain words or the use of certain styles and the appropriateness conditions within which they are recognised as successful acts of communication. The concept of a *speech act* can be traced back to language philosopher J. L. Austin's 1962 book *How to do Things with Words*, a collected culmination of lectures that he delivered at Harvard University. Speech act theory was further developed by philosopher John Searle, most notably in his 1969 book *Speech Acts*. More so than the other theoretical perspectives that are introduced in this chapter, the notion of the speech act has had a lasting influence on the study of language and literature across a variety of fields. The most central insight of speech act theory is that language is not only form, but also social process, i.e. that speaking is an act through which we – as Austin says – *do things with words*. The notion of the speech act has become an undisputed underpinning in many areas of literary linguistic analysis and has inspired a number of influential scholars in the humanities fields, from Mary Louise Pratt's *Speech act theory of literary discourse* (1977) to Judith Butler's *Excitable speech* (1997). Speech act theory has also brought to the fore questions that have continued to define contemporary stylistics concerning the kinds of action accomplished through the production of literary works and the role of linguistic style in their performance.

Austin's motivation behind speech act theory arose through his identification of what he dubbed performative utterances, linguistic expressions that not only passively describe a given reality, but actively change the social reality that they are describing. To borrow one of Austin's oft cited examples, uttering the words 'I do' in a standard Anglo-American wedding ceremony performs a double action in that the soon-to-be newlywed does not merely describe what he or she is doing at that moment, but also performs the act of marrying. Performative utterances such as 'I do' are not evaluable under truth conditions, although they are subject to what Austin called *felicity conditions*. The felicity conditions of the performative 'I do' might, depending on cultural context, include the presence of a religious or governmental representative invested with the power to pronounce a couple married, or the location in a sanctioned space, or that neither member of the couple is currently married. If one of the individuals ends up being a serial polygamist, this might render the marriage invalid and the speech act, in Austin's words, *unhappy* or *infelicitous*, but it does not reveal the performative to be untrue. (In fact, the resulting legal consequences that one could imagine are, if anything, evidence that a marriage has in some sense taken place, albeit one that is likely to be unhappy on multiple levels.)

Although Austin began with explicit speech acts like the example cited above, he quickly recognised that performatives can also be implicit – or, in Searle's vocabulary, *indirect*. Thus, the comment 'It's hot in here' may describe the propositional reality of the room, but it might at the same time be a request that someone open a window. Speech act theory accounts for this through a distinction between the *locutionary act* and the *illocutionary act*. The locutionary act is the physical enunciation, whereas the illocutionary act is a socially codified act of communication, i.e. a request, a promise, a declaration, or an oath. An illocutionary act is direct if it corresponds to its illocutionary force – for example, the locution 'I now declare this couple man and wife.' It is indirect when there is a disjuncture between the illocutionary act and its force, as in the previously cited request to open a window. Austin notes that 'the performance of an illocutionary act involves the securing of *uptake*' (1962, p. 116). In other words, the interlocutor must recognise the intended speech act. Austin also identified a third act, the perlocutionary act, the resulting effect on the receiver – e.g. someone in the room stands up and pushes the window open. There has been some dispute as to whether the perlocutionary effect properly belongs to the speech act. In any case, it is hard to dispute the centrality of its anticipation in speakers' formulation and performance of speech acts, i.e. their intentionality.

Neither Austin nor Searle wholly neglects literature in their writings on speech act theory, but by and large they do reject literary works from their model of normal speech acts. When speech acts appear in works of fiction such as novels and plays, they are considered by speech act theory to be 'parasitic,' which means that they pretend to be serious speech acts but they do not intend for us to believe in them in the same way that we would their normal equivalents. When the Queen of Hearts points to Alice and shouts 'Off with their heads!' in Lewis Carroll's famous tale, we know that no real heads will actually roll. By dismissing literature as nonserious, Austin is able to get on to what he sees as the real business of his work, which is the investigation of sincere speech acts. It is important to note that Austin only discusses represented speech acts in literature, e.g. a promise made by one character to another character in a novel or play, and he does not seem to consider the literary utterance itself as an act. Searle does nod towards the notion that the authors of literary works might be performing special kinds of illocutionary acts such as 'telling a story' or 'writing a novel,' but he immediately rejects this idea on the grounds that this would imply that speech acts appearing in a work of fiction have a different sense than they would otherwise have. Despite the careful attention that they give to the role of convention, for both Austin and Searle intentionality is central to speech acts' ability to function, and this is the primary criterion used to discriminate between normal and parasitic discourse. In fiction, they maintain, the author does not intend to perform but merely to pretend an illocutionary act.

Austin and Searle's reliance on speaker intention for the classification of speech acts has been a source of frustration for a number of literary scholars. The so-called 'intentional fallacy,' a literary critical notion posited by Wimsatt and Beardsley that 'the design or intention of the author is neither available nor desirable as a standard for judging the success of a work of literary art' (1954, p. 3), had been influential in Anglo-American literary criticism and many literary scholars objected to a theory of language so grounded in intentionality. Literary studies' discomfort with speech act theory was heightened through the poststructuralists, most vocally Jacques Derrida. In fact, the debate that ensued between Derrida and Searle around this issue sowed scepticism among many literary scholars about the potential of pragmatics as a legitimate approach to literary study (see Derrida 1988; Searle 1977). The failure of early pragmatic theories, such as those espoused by Austin and Searle, to include literature in their conceptions of language was perceived by mainstream literary studies as evidence that pragmatics was too positivist to deal with the complexities of literary interpretation.

Another potential limitation of speech act theory for the study of literature is that it is restricted to sentence structures and is thus unsuited to deal with discourse on the level of the text. However, many scholars have viewed this as a surmountable problem, and have nevertheless found the framework productive as a way of disassociating 'literariness' from formal properties of texts and grounding poetics in a social theory of the utterance. Richard Ohmann writes, 'Our readiness to discover and dwell on the implicit meanings in literary works – and to judge them important – is a consequence of our knowing them to *be* literary works, rather than that which tells us they are such' (1971, p. 6). A pragmatics of literature might focus on such institutional aspects, including the felicity conditions for an *appropriate* literary text, for example its being written by a *literary* author, having been published in a *literary* publishing house or exhibiting a *literary* style. Speech act theory points to the fact that extralinguistic cultural conditions are involved in readers' perceptions of a work as 'literary' or not.

Sandy Petrey convincingly uses the case of Salman Rushdie's *The Satanic Verses* in order to repudiate Austin's assertions that literature is unserious. Rushdie's novel was inspired in part by the life of Mohammed and by a group of mythic Quranic verses. After its publication in 1988 the Ayatollah Khomeini placed a death sentence on the author declaring that Rushdie's book was a sin against God. These two speech acts – the literary utterance and the death sentence from the Iranian religious leader – which stand in a cause–effect relationship to one another, demonstrate clearly that 'words do things on which life and death depend' (Petrey 1990, p. 54). Furthermore, this example shows that the illocutionary force derived by literary texts varies across communities and their socially specific circumstances.

While speech act theory may provide useful models for contextualising literary utterances, it does not, as some scholars within stylistics have been quick to point out, yield many insights into specific literary effects or how they might contribute to the felicity of a particular speech act. This is an area where stylistic and pragmatic theory can be mutually enriching. For example, the distinctions laid out in speech act theory between illocutionary effects and perlocutionary acts might help scholars in stylistics to contemplate the connections between the poetic effects experienced by an individual in the process of reading and the various forms of social action in which reading can be embedded.

Conversational implicature

As discussed elsewhere in this volume (see especially Chapter 8), the theoretical notion of implicature originates in the philosophical linguistic work of H. P. Grice, whose conversational maxims have had a deep and prolonged effect on pragmatics scholarship, including work within literary pragmatics. At its outset, the notion of implicature provided a theoretical solution to the linguistic reality that there can be and often are discrepancies between sentence-meaning and speaker-meaning, which allow language to imply or express more than it explicitly entails. Because one of the most agreed-upon features of literary language is that it conveys meanings beyond what is actually said, the theoretical notion of implicature has been embraced by many scholars within stylistics and literary linguistics in order to describe how writers manipulate language to varying readerly effects.

His recognition that language so readily conveys unqualified, unstated meanings led Grice to also ponder how it is that we are in actuality able to communicate so effectively most of the time. Grice posited that our conversational behaviour must be governed by what he called a *Cooperative Principle*. As phrased by Grice, interactants tend to heed the following: 'Make your contribution such as it is required, at the stage at which it occurs, by the accepted purpose or direction of the talk exchange in which you are engaged' (1975 [1957], p. 45). This assumption serves as the basis for the Cooperative Principle, which consists of four sub-principles or 'maxims':

Maxim of quality *or truth*

- Do not say what you believe to be false.
- Do not say that for which you lack adequate evidence.

Maxim of quantity *or information*

- Make your contribution as informative as is required for the current purposes of the exchange.
- Do not make your contribution more informative than is required.

Maxim of relation *or relevance*

- Make your contribution relevant.

Maxim of manner *or clarity*

- Avoid obscurity of expression.
- Avoid ambiguity.
- Be brief ("avoid unnecessary prolixity").
- Be orderly.

These maxims are, according to Grice, shared expectations held by members of society and consequently they can also be 'flouted' by speakers in order to signal that the interlocutor should infer an intended meaning that is not directly expressed in what was said. Scholars within stylistics have seen a correlation between this aspect of Grice's theories and the concept of foregrounding, linguistic means of shifting interactants' attention to aspects of the speech. In literary works, deviant conversational behaviour can become a salient part of characterisation and plot development.

For example, in Swiss author Friedrich Dürrenmatt's tragicomedy *The Visit* (*Der Besuch der alten Dame* in the original), the figure Claire Zachanassian returns to her hometown of Güllen in order to seek revenge on her childhood sweetheart, Alfred Ill, who deserted her in their youth when she became pregnant. After years of hardship and debauchery and several strategic marriages, Zachanassian is now in possession of a great fortune, which she agrees to share with the impoverished and war-torn town on one condition – that someone kill Ill. This announcement ends the first act of the play, and the second act finds the villagers struggling with their consciences. Ill, feeling increasingly threatened, approaches three of the most influential members of the society (the mayor, the police chief, and the preacher) to seek help. In each of these scenes, it is his interlocutor's continual flouting of conversational maxims that tips off Ill (and the reader) that something insidious is underway. For example, when Ill tells the preacher the he is afraid of the villagers, the preacher replies, 'One should not fear men, but God. Not the death of the body, but the soul.' While this response is relevant, in that it addresses Ill's fear for his life, it in insufficient with regard to quantity, because the information that Ill seeks, namely confirmation as to whether or not he has cause to fear, is not given. For this reason, it also lacks clarity. Does the preacher mean to say that Ill's life is indeed in danger, but that he need not worry about it? The obscurity of the answer allows the preacher to evade breaking with the maxim of truth, since he neither expressly confirms nor denies Ill is under threat.

Grice's pragmatic theories emphasise the interactional functions of language and have proven useful for analysing conversation in literary texts, in particular in those genres in which dialogue is predominant. However, the move from analysing conversational maxims in the text to explaining the maxims that hold between the narrator/author/text and the reader has proven somewhat more problematic for scholars of literary pragmatics. Roger Sell has suggested that authors of written texts, including literary works, might flout conversational maxims 'in order to make a conversational implicature, perhaps for some special and striking effect' (Sell 2001, p. 52) in ways very similar to speakers in face-to-face communication (Sell 2001, p. 58). In cases of unreliable narration, for example, it can be very telling when an authorial or character narrator seems to flout certain maxims. For instance, in the opening pages of Monika Maron's 1996 novel *Animal Triste*, the narrator seems to flout the maxims of quality, quantity and possibly even relevance by telling a personal narrative for which she seems to lack even the most basic information such as her age and how she found herself living alone. As the story proceeds, it is revealed that the narrator decided to withdraw from society and not add 'any more episodes to her life', after being left by her lover, so that she could relive the final encounter with him over and over again. In Gricean terms it could be said that readerly expectations regarding the maxims of quality and quantity are at first flouted in order to establish a paradigm for what is truly relevant to this tale, namely the details that enable her to continue to worship this lost love.

Grice's maxims and the notion of implicature have helped stylisticians to describe and explain how conversational norms become resources for meaning-making upon which authors draw in the design of represented dialogue and narrative. However, as critics including John Searle have pointed out, Grice's model largely ignores the role of convention and therefore fails to differentiate among the various effects that might be created through the performance of an utterance. Mary Louise Pratt has criticised Grice's treatment of certain ways of speaking as neutral and unmarked and others, notably many of those central to literary works, as troublesome and uncooperative. Nevertheless, Grice's insight that utterances always bear a surplus of unstated, implicated meanings helped to lay a foundation for theories of literary communication, since literary texts, almost by definition, rely upon indirect inferred meanings. Grice's work has also served as an inspiration for a number of influential models within the field of pragmatics, including the approach discussed in the next section of this chapter – relevance theory.

Relevance theory

Relevance theory was developed by Dan Sperber and Deirdre Wilson as an alternative to Gricean accounts of inferential language use (see also Chapter 9 in this volume). As the name indicates, a central claim of the theory is that relevance is the single principle guiding effective communication, and that this principle, when suitably theorised, can handle the full range of data that Grice sought to explicate. Sperber and Wilson's account is also an attempt to rectify what they see as a fault in Gricean notions of implicature, which assume that interlocutors have a common purpose or set of purposes. In relevance theory, successful communication requires only that the speaker make her intention to convey particular meanings manifest to both herself and her interlocutors. In this way, Sperber and Wilson circumvent a logical conclusion of Grice's maxim of quality, which seems to imply that utterances which are more interpretively opaque are necessarily uncooperative, by acknowledging that readers often feel that more extensive effort is warranted by literary texts in order to convey complex thoughts and expressions. For this reason, relevance theory deals more expressly with instances of metaphoric and poetic language than either Gricean models of implicature or speech act theory, and scholars with an interest in literary pragmatics have found it well-suited for describing how poetic effects are created and perceived.

An underlying assumption of relevance theory is that in processing any utterance, people work to draw out as many cognitive effects as possible for the least amount of effort. The hearer or reader is guided by the presumption that their interlocutor's speech is 'optimally relevant,' i.e. that the effects yielded are worth the processing efforts (see Sperber and Wilson 1995, p. 270; Wilson and Sperber 2002, pp. 256–257). The implicatures suggested by a given utterance can be either *strong(er)* or *weak(er)*. Implicated meanings that the interlocutor is relatively certain were purposefully communicated can be said to be *strong implicatures*. Those which the reader is driven to explore with less certainty about whether they are intentionally expressed are *weak implicatures*. For Sperber and Wilson, metaphor is a prime example of the kinds of effects that weaker implicatures can have. Although it might take greater effort to process a metaphor, the exploration of a range of weaker implicatures might also yield pleasurable effects that make this worthwhile. Sperber and Wilson also note that in some cases, the effects may not satisfy the hearer or reader's presumption of relevance. What is most encouraging here for the student of stylistics is that 'literariness' is not simply treated as unserious speech that violates pre-established conventions or maxims, but is rather an effect of the interpretive principles of communication. Relevance theory thus views linguistic form as an important stimulus in literary communication, but it ultimately locates poetic effects in situated cognitive events rather than in text structures.

Relevance theory is a pragmatic theory of verbal communication grounded securely in a theory of cognition. For Sperber and Wilson the principle of relevance is not a maxim in Grice's sense – communicators do not choose whether or not to follow it – but it is an indispensible aspect of linguistic processing. The cognitive orientation of relevance theory also leads to a view of context that is different from speech act theory, at least in its earliest instantiations. Whereas speech act theory primarily treats context in terms of pre-existing felicity conditions that are or are not fulfilled in the performance of an utterance, in relevance theory the context is dynamically accessed and constructed in the process of inferencing. This allows relevance theory to depart from the conventionalised utterance types emphasised in speech act theory and Gricean models of implicature and better account for creative, one-off expressions such as may be found in prized works of literature. For example, when I first encountered the Dorothy Parker text with which I began this chapter, I construed the rhyme 'passes' and 'glasses' as ostensively meaningful. The rhyme, combined with the line breaks after each of these words, strengthens the creative opposition implied by the short poem, which suggests to me a number of weak implicatures about how intelligent or bookish women are perceived in a society that sees smart as antithetical to sexy.

Wilson and Sperber also introduce a concept that has been embraced by many researchers within stylistics – that of echoic discourse. Echoic discourse is the interpretive use of an utterance to (meta)represent another utterance or thought that it can be assumed to resemble (2002, p. 272). In this way, the speaker tacitly expresses an attitude towards someone else's viewpoint. This also requires that the interlocutor is able to recognise that the speaker's thoughts are not on the world, but on speech or thoughts that she attributes to someone else. Sperber and Wilson's characterisation of echoic discourse is similar to Mikhail Bakhtin's notion of double-voiced discourse, the use of another's speech in another's language to express authorial perspectives, a use which he associates with novelistic genres. Sperber and Wilson use the idea of echoic discourse in order to explain phenomena such as parody and irony. Returning again to Dorothy Parker's 'News Item,' for example, my familiarity with Parker's wit and what I perceive to be the kitschiness of the little rhyme led me to interpret the proclamation that 'Men seldom make passes, at girls who wear glasses' as an ironic echo of the kind of mentor (a mother or older female) who might offer this advice.

Although relevance theory has found much endorsement from stylisticians, it has not escaped criticism. Jonathan Culpeper (1994) has argued that relevance theory leaves many pertinent pragmatic questions unanswered. For example, given a wide array of weak implicatures leading to poetic effects, how do hearers and readers establish an order of preference between possible meanings? This encompasses aspects of the context that are outside of the theoretical purview of relevance theory. Culpeper also contends that the cognitive view of communication taken in relevance theory neglects social factors of power and authority that might affect the listeners' or readers' willingness to invest cognitive efforts in speech that is stylistically more complex or obtuse. This final point pertains to the participation of literary utterances in systems of face and politeness, which will be the focus on the next section.

Facework and politeness

The pragmatics theories that I have discussed thus far examine how interactants implicate and infer meaning from utterances, what kinds of effects arise, and what kinds of acts are performed. A further area of pragmatics research attempts to account for the more relational dimensions of illocution – how social actors negotiate, maintain, or contest relationships with their fellow participants in the course of interaction. This body of scholarship acknowledges that utterances – including literary utterances – are performed within relations of relative power, status, and social distance. This pertains to phenomena that scholars and laymen alike have described under rubrics of *politeness* and *face* (see Chapter 7 in this volume for more on *face*).

As a theoretical concept, *face* originates from the theories of Erving Goffman. Face, according to Goffman, is defined as 'the positive social value a person effectively claims for himself by the line others assume he has taken for himself during a particular contact' (1967, p. 5. Through facework individuals try to conduct themselves so as to maintain their own face, but this is a relational process, because face is only claimed insofar as it is acknowledged by others. For this reason, social actors must also work to preserve the face of other interactants, sometimes even sacrificing aspects of their own self-image to achieve this purpose, so that their other purposes might be fulfilled. Penelope Brown and Stephen

Levinson were the first to connect Goffman's concept of face with a theoretical model of politeness in their much-cited book *Politeness: Some Universals in Language Use* (1978). Politeness, according to Brown and Levinson, comprises the rituals through which we protect face. Brown and Levinson introduce a distinction between two types of face: negative and positive. Whereas positive face refers to the self-image or personality claimed by an individual, and one's desire to have this self-image recognised, appreciated and approved of, negative face involves the individual's right to not be imposed upon, to act freely, and to claim their own space (both figuratively and literally).

Geoffrey Leech (1983) offers an alternate model of politeness that builds on Grice's 'Cooperative Principle.' According to Leech, most interactions are governed not only by cooperation, but also by what is considered to be 'polite social behaviour' within a certain community. There is, in short, a 'Politeness Principle', which allows conversation partners to engage in relative harmony most of the time. Leech proposes six politeness maxims to supplement Grice's framework:

- Maxim of tact: minimise cost to other; [maximise benefit to other]
- Maxim of generosity: minimise benefit to self; [maximise cost to self]
- Maxim of approbation: minimise dispraise of other; [maximise praise of other]
- Maxim of modesty: minimise praise of self; [maximise dispraise of self]
- Maxim of agreement: minimise disagreement between self and other; [maximise agreement between self and other]
- Maxim of sympathy: minimise antipathy between self and other; [maximise sympathy between self and other]

The bracketed portion of each of the maxims, which Leech called sub-maxims, corresponds to positive politeness, which aims at 'maximizing the politeness of polite illocutions' (1983, pp. 83–84), while the first imperative corresponds to negative politeness, which aims at 'minimizing the impoliteness of impolite illocution.' For Leech politeness that is focused more strongly on the other than on the self is more powerful, which means that negative politeness is 'a more weighty consideration than positive politeness' (Leech 1983, p. 133). For this same reason, not all of the maxims are valued the same. For instance, tact typically influences what we say more powerfully than generosity, while approbation is in general more important than modesty.

The theories of facework and politeness proposed by Brown and Levinson and by Leech have received their share of criticism within pragmatics, mainly for their focus on cooperation (to the exclusion of aggressive face or impoliteness) and for a tendency to stress individualistic aspects of face work (rather than interactional and relational aspects). Nevertheless, the detailed, language-based models developed by Brown and Levinson and by Leech have proven productive for many scholars who wish to identify conventions of linguistic politeness. This is of the utmost importance for literary pragmatics, since literary works are more or less exclusively linguistic expressions. Politeness principles have been used within stylistics in order to help explain the interactions between literary and dramatic figures and how this contributes to characterisation. For example, Derek Bousfield (2010) builds on the pragmatic models of Goffman, Brown and Levinson and Leech in order to describe the use of impoliteness and banter in Shakespeare's Henry V. Through a careful analysis of how impoliteness disguised as banter establishes the character of Hal as witty and linguistically deft, Bousfield demonstrates how politeness theory can help stylisticians to identify characterisation threads in works of literature.

Petrey's example of Salman Rushdie's novel and the ensuing death threats demonstrates well that literary works also engage with facework and politeness as utterances in their own right. Roger Sell has even suggested the written literary work might be conceived as a particularly long turn. Long turns, like those taken in normal conversation when a participant launches into spontaneous narrative, require special participation from their interlocutors. Like speakers in face-to-face communication, authors must attract and keep their listener's attention in order to gain the right to continue speaking. In the case of a written text, this need to justify one's turn is all the more dire since the speaker cannot redress any boredom, offense, or apathy experiences by the reader in the midst of conversation and must anticipate and plan well for such possible responses. What requires further consideration from scholars within fields of literary pragmatics and pragmatic stylistics is how to conceptualise literary discourse, with its complex participant structures and its ability to communicate across multiple time scales, as relational. The development of working models for literary interaction will also enable scholars within stylistics to consider the role of the stylistic domain in the analysis of interactional manoeuvres related to facework and politeness.

Pragmatic stylistics: Doing things with poetic effects

As the examples that have been cited in this chapter have indicated, the application of pragmatic models can emphasise either the analysis of represented communicative acts in literary works or the analysis of the literary text as an utterance in its own right. What unites the various theoretical perspectives described above is a concern with 'the kinds of effects that authors, as text producers, set out to obtain, using the resources of language in their efforts to establish a 'working cooperation' with their audiences, the consumers of the texts' (Mey 1999, p. 12). Stylistics, as a field of study devoted to understanding the relationship between textual features and readerly effects, is in some sense necessarily pragmatic. Nevertheless, pragmatic theories can help stylisticians to move towards a more rigorous engagement with context by linking the readers' experiences and evaluations of style to the conventions, norms and values of the societies in which texts as produced and received (see van Dijk's point of enquiry number 9 above). Pragmatic theory can also provide a critical vocabulary through which to examine the ways in which style influences the social processes of acceptance, rejection, exaltation or dismissal that shape literary institutions and cultural practices of publishing and reception. In short, a pragmatic stylistics grounded in the wealth of theoretical insights available from both of these fields might push those of us who study literature to consider how we do things not only with words, but perhaps more exactly with poetic effects.

Recommendtions for practice

Elsewhere in this volume you have been given the opportunity to apply some of the concepts that are central to this chapter, including speech act theory, Grice's conversational maxims, relevance and implicature, facework and politeness (see especially Chapters 6, 7 and 8). A recurring theme in this chapter on the intersections between literary pragmatic and stylistics has been the relationship between the stylistic effects of literary works and their social existence as acts – or as Teun van Dijk expresses it, the actual functioning of literature in society. The questions that follow ask you to explore this pragmatic dimension of literary style, while building on the concepts that you have encountered.

1. Many readers will recognise the following poem from Francis Scott Key, as it now
    serves as the national anthem for the United States of America.

    > 'The Star Spangled Banner'
    > O say can you see by the dawn's early light,
    > What so proudly we hailed at the twilight's last gleaming,
    > Whose broad stripes and bright stars through the perilous fight,
    > O'er the ramparts we watched, were so gallantly streaming?
    > And the rockets' red glare, the bombs bursting in air,
    > Gave proof through the night that our flag was still there;
    > O say does that star-spangled banner yet wave,
    > O'er the land of the free and the home of the brave?

    This text was originally written as a poem to capture the bombardment of Fort McHenry
    by British Royal Navy ships during the Battle of Fort McHenry in the War of 1812. It
    was quickly set to the tune of a popular British song, 'The Anacreontic Song', and was
    adopted as the American national anthem in 1931. How would you describe this text as
    a kind of literary speech act? Is it possible to categorise the illocutionary act that this text
    performs as a poem? As a patriotic song? As a national anthem? It might be helpful to
    remember the Petrey quote cited above in the section 'Speech acts': 'words do things
    upon which life and death depend.'

2. To echo one of Teun van Dijk's questions, 'What are the appropriateness conditions of
    the social actions performed by this text in its function as a national anthem?' In addition
    to the structure of the context mentioned explicitly by van Dijk, which stylistic features
    might contribute to the poem's success as a national anthem? Although the 'felicity'
    conditions of speech acts such as this may be far less conventional than those associated
    with the kinds of performative utterances described by Austin and Searle, we can look to
    relevance theory to consider what aspects of this poem suggest strong implicatures,
    which might encourage us to read the poem as a National Anthem performing the kinds
    of social action that you described in response to question 1. (Note that the relevance
    theoretic perspective also pushes us to see the 'appropriateness conditions' in a more
    dynamic way than speech act theory envisions.)

3. Finally, the text begins and ends with a second-person address, each marked by the
    opening two words, 'Oh, say...' Returning to the section on conversational implicatures,
    consider the degrees to which this text ostensibly follows or flouts the maxims suggested
    by Grice. Now do the same with Leech's politeness maxims, which are listed under
    'Facework and Politeness'. Both Grice's and Leech's sets of maxims draw our attention
    to the ways in which stylistic choices mark relations between interactants even in literary
    acts of communication. Now consider the kinds of facework – 'the positive social value
    a person effectively claims for himself by the line others assume he has taken for himself
    during a particular contact' – potentially involved in the utterance of the national anthem
    'The Star Spangled Banner.' (Note: context may be important here, e.g. the original
    situation of the War of 1812 versus an international sports event such as the Olympics or
    a more local event such as a high school baseball game.) In your estimate, which aspects
    of the text's style seem to contribute most ostensively to the facework taken up through
    the utterance of this song/poem?

Future directions

Cognitive pragmatics

In *The Stylistics Reader* (1996) Jean Jacques Weber points to a shift which has taken place within stylistics, away from the formalist study of texts towards a perspective which views linguistic acts as not only action (pragmatic) but also involving mental processes (cognition). The fact that the pragmatic turn and the cognitive turn entered stylistics so closely together makes sense on some level; both frameworks attempt to move the study of language and literature beyond the structure of the text. Underlying key pragmatic concepts such as inference and implicature are also assumptions about cognitive processing that were nevertheless left unaddressed because of pragmatics' roots in the philosophy of language. In recent years, cognitive pragmatics has emerged as an interdisciplinary field of research studying the cognitive principles and processes involved in the construal of meaning-in-context.

One of the areas in which cognitive-pragmatic approaches to stylistics have been most influential in recent years is in the study of mind style and characterisation. Our ability to attribute personalities to figures that are constructed in literary and dramatic works requires that we infer characters' goals, attitudes, and desires from their speech and represented thoughts. This in turn relies on our ability to recognise patterns in a character's communicative behaviour, such as the repeated flouting of a maxim, as corresponding to or diverging from our conceptual schemas of normal linguistic behaviours. This is, of course, only one example of how pragmatic and cognitive processes intersect in readers' experience of style. As cognitive-pragmatic research continues to expand, stylisticians will continue to benefit from the new models that emerge from this interdisciplinary field as they attempt to develop more ecological approaches to stylistic inquiry.

Pedagogical applications

As a field stylistics has always maintained an awareness of its applicability to the teaching and learning of language and literature, and it is thus hardly surprising that pragmatic stylistics has also found its way into the classroom. For example, Clark and Owtram (2012) describe how they have effectively implemented pragmatic stylistics in the teaching of writing and composition in order to raise students' awareness of how readers think. By giving students a basic understanding of how inference works within pragmatic models such as relevance theory, college students at the advanced levels of two BA programmes learned to anticipate the likely effects of particular linguistic forms on their audience. The instructors also provided targeted feedback that brought students' attention to the kinds of meanings that their words might convey, as the students learned to constrain inferences made by the reader at key moments in the text and to better convey the meanings they intend.

Pragmatic perspectives have also been used to conceptualise the experience of foreign language learners when encountering literary discourse. For example, Gramling and Warner (2012) encourage instructors to take what they call a 'contact pragmatics' stance to the teaching of texts in second and foreign language contexts, which they see as an alternative to the common approaches that ask students to project themselves into the perspective of an imagined native speaker other based on cultural schemas conveyed by the teacher. Instead Gramling and Warner suggest that instructors begin with the students' experiences of the literary work and the text's most salient stylistic features for them. Students can then explore published readerly reactions from other readers in order to conduct their own comparative pragmatic study of the kinds of responses the text has elicited from other readers, including native speakers and contemporaries of the literary work. This allows students to become aware of the range of effects that the author's stylistic designs can have, while also increasing their awareness of any tendencies that obtain in other pragmatic contexts.

The two examples cited here point to the need for future research into how pragmatic perspectives might be brought to bear in the teaching of L1 and L2 texts. In particular, there are to date few empirical studies comparing the inferences made by learners – be they L1 or L2 – and those made by expert or professional readers, or documenting the effectiveness of the explicit teaching of pragmatic principles. Nevertheless these studies demonstrate the potential of pragmatic stylistics for sensitising students to stylistic effects in varying contexts, ranging from the register shifts experienced in academic writing to the cultural differences encountered by foreign language learners.

Related topics

Conversation analysis and the cooperative principle, reader response criticism, relevance theory, speech acts and (im)politeness theory, speech and thought representation, stylistics, drama and performance

Further reading

Black, E., 2006. *Pragmatic stylistics*. Edinburgh: Edinburgh Press.

Black's book provides a thorough introduction to areas of pragmatic theory that are of interest to scholars and students of stylistics.

Mey, J., 1998. *When voices clash: A study in literary pragmatics*. Berlin: Mouton de Gruyter.

The central focus of Mey's book is those instances of narrative discourse when the words that literary characters speak do not fit with how they are otherwise portrayed, and in this sense 'clash.' The first chapters of the book provide a more general introduction to literary pragmatics.

Pilkington, A., 2000. *Poetic effects*. Amsterdam/Philadelphia: John Benjamins.

Pilkington's book offers a relevance theory perspective on the poetic effects in the aesthetic experience, and includes an introductory look at this pragmatic model for scholars with an interest in stylistics and poetics.

Sell, R., ed., 1991a. *Literary pragmatics*. London: Routledge.

This volume, edited by Roger Sell, contains a number of essays on literary pragmatics from a variety of perspectives, providing readers with an overview of the kinds of research represented in this field.

Warner, C., 2012. *The pragmatics of literary testimony*. London/New York: Routledge.

In her analysis of key works of German-language autobiographical literature and the authenticity effects experienced by many readers when encountering them, Warner develops a cognitive-pragmatic approach grounded in contemporary stylistic theory.

References

Austin, J.L., 1962. *How to do things with words*. Oxford: Clarendon.

Black, E., 2006. *Pragmatic stylistics*. Edinburgh: Edinburgh Press.

Bousfield, D., 2007. Never a truer word said in jest: A pragmalinguistic analysis of impoliteness as banter in Shakespeare's *Henry IV, Part I*. In: M. Lambrou and P. Stockwell, eds. *Contemporary stylistics*. London: Continuum.

Brown, P, and Levinson, S., 1987. *Politeness: Some universals in language use*. Cambridge: Cambridge University Press.

Butler, J., 1997. *Excitable speech*. New York: Routledge.

Clark, B. and Owtram, N., 2012. Imagined inference: Teaching writers to think like readers. *In:* M. Burke, S. Csábi, L. Week and J. Zerkowitz, eds. *Pedagogical stylistics: Current trends in language, literature and ELT*. Continuum: London, 126–141.

Culpeper, J., 1994. Why relevance theory does not explain the relevance of reformulations. *Language and Literature*, 3 (1), 43–48.

Culpeper, J., 2011. *Impoliteness: Using language to cause offence*: Cambridge: Cambridge University Press.

Derrida, J., 1988. *Limited Inc.* Evanston: Northwestern University Press.

Dijk, T. van., 1980. The pragmatics of literary communication. *In:* E. Forastieri-Braschi, G. Guinness and H. Lopez-Morales, eds. *On text and context*. Rio Piedras, Puerto Rico: Editorial Universitaria, 3–16.

Dürrenmatt, F., 1962. *The visit*. P. Bowles, trans. London: Jonathan Cape.

Goffman, E., 1967. On face-work: An analysis of ritual elements in social interaction. *In:* E. Goffman, *Interaction ritual: Essays on face to face behaviour*. New York: Pantheon, 5–46.

Gramling, D. and Warner, C., 2012. Toward a contact pragmatics of literature: Habitus, text, and the advanced L2 classroom. *In:* G. S. Levine and A. Phipps, eds. *Critical and intercultural theory and language pedagogy*. Boston: Cengage Heinle, 57–75.

Grice, J. P., 1957. Meaning. *The Philosophical Review*, 66 (3), 377–388.

Grice, J. P., 1975. Logic and conversation. *In:* P. Cole and J.L. Morgan, eds. *Syntax and semantics 3: Speech acts*. New York: Academic Press, 41–58.

Hickey, L., 1993. Stylistics, pragmatics and pragmastylistics. *Revue Belge de Philologie et d'Histoire*, 71 (3), 573–586.

Leech, G., 1969. *A linguistic guide to English poetry*. London: Longman.

Leech, G., 1983. *Principles of pragmatics*. London: Longman.

Leech, G. and Short, M., 1981. *Style in fiction*. London: Longman.

Levinson, S., 1983. *Pragmatics*. Cambridge: Cambridge University Press.

Maron, M., 1996. *Animal triste*. Frankfurt a.M.: Fischer.

Mey, J., 1999. *When voices clash: A study in literary pragmatics*. Berlin: Mouton de Gruyter.

Morris, C., 1938. *Foundations of the theory of signs*. Chicago: University of Chicago Press.

Ohmann, R., 1971. Speech, action and style. *In:* S. Chatman, ed. *Literary style*. London: Oxford University Press, 241–254.

Petrey, S., 1990. *Speech acts and literary theory*. New York and London: Routledge.

Pilkington, A., 1991. Poetic effects: A relevance theory perspective. *In:* R. Sell, ed. *Literary pragmatics*. London: Routledge, 44–61.

Pilkington, A., 2000. *Poetic effects*. Amsterdam/Philadelphia: John Benjamins.

Pratt, M. L., 1977. *Towards a speech act theory of literary discourse*. Bloomington: Indiana University Press.

Rushdie, S., 1988. *The satanic verses*. New York: Viking.

Searle, J., 1969. *Speech acts: An essay in the philosophy of language*. Cambridge: Cambridge University Press.

Searle, J., 1977. Reiterating the differences: A reply to Derrida. *Glyph*, 1, 198–208

Sell, R., 1985. Tellability and politeness in 'The Miller's Tale': First steps in literary pragmatics. *English Studies*, 66 (6), 496–512.

Sell, R., ed., 1991a. *Literary pragmatics*. London: Routledge.

Sell, R., 1991b. The politeness of literary texts. *In:* R. Sell, ed. *Literary pragmatics*. London: Routledge, 208–224.

Sell, R., 2001. *Literature as communication: The foundations of mediating criticism*. Amsterdam: John Benjamins.

Semino, E., 2007. Mind Style 25 Years On. *Style*, 41 (2), 153–173.

Sperber, D. and Wilson, D., 1995. *Relevance: Communication and cognition*. 2nd ed, London: Blackwell.

Sperber, D. and Wilson, D., 2002, Pragmatics, modularity and mindreading. *Mind and Language*, 17, 3–23.

Warner, C., 2012. *The pragmatics of literary testimony*. London/New York: Routledge.

Weber, J. J., 1996. *The stylistics reader*. London: Arnold.

Wilson, D. and Sperber, D., 2002. Relevance theory. *UCL Working Papers in Linguistics*, 13, 249–287.

Wimsatt, W. K. and Beardsley, M. C., 1946. The intentional fallacy. *Sewanee Review*, 54, 468–488.

23

Corpus stylistics

Michaela Mahlberg

Introduction

Corpus stylistic research applies corpus methods to the analysis of literary texts, giving particular emphasis to the relationship between linguistic description and literary appreciation (Mahlberg 2013). Corpus stylistics is part of the much wider interdisciplinary field of digital humanities which is concerned with the preservation, study and accessibility of physical artefacts and archives as well as born-digital data. The term 'corpus stylistics' has become popular over the past decade, with Leech and Short (2007, p. 286) noting a 'corpus turn' in stylistics. Biber (2011, p. 20) points out that the use of the term 'corpus stylistics' may put a particular spin on the historical development of the field it refers to, so that the emphasis is on 'the more rhetorical concerns of recent studies' (Biber 2011, p. 20), whereas earlier work in computational and statistical stylistics might receive less attention under the umbrella of corpus stylistics. Biber (2011) makes an important point when he draws attention to the potential that is still to be realised by integrating the statistical approaches of earlier research with the more recent qualitative concerns of corpus stylistics. However, not every time that the term 'corpus stylistics' is used, theoretical implications about the range of principles and approaches and the development of a field will be consciously evoked. Part of the popularity of the term seems to be simply due to the fact that corpus linguists are increasingly taking the opportunity to look at literary texts as data – not least because of the ever-growing number of electronically available texts. Equally, stylisticians seem to profit from the increasing availability of easy-to-use off-the-shelf corpus tools. As part of this development, handbooks on or introductions to corpus linguistics include sections on the study of literary texts (e.g. Chapelle 2012, Flowerdew 2012, Lindquist 2009, O'Keeffe and McCarthy 2010) and textbooks or reference works on stylistics take account of corpus approaches and methodology (e.g. Jeffries and McIntyre 2010, Leech and Short 2007, McIntyre and Busse 2010, or the present volume, for that matter).

While it may not be true that every study that refers to itself as 'corpus stylistic' research does so because of an explicit theoretical foundation, I think there is still value in considering whether corpus stylistics is just a fashionable term or whether it can be usefully associated with a set of underlying principles that will yield a particular kind of research result. A crucial aspect of corpus stylistics is the fact that it combines methods and principles from both corpus linguistics and literary stylistics. The kind of literary stylistics that it draws on emphasises the focus on the literary effects that a particular text creates. Leech and Short (2007) illustrate this relevance of literary appreciation in stylistics through Spitzer's (1948) concept of the philological circle: we approach a text both as an example of language and as a work of art. Hence, linguistic description and literary appreciation are at work together in a stylistic analysis. In a corpus stylistic approach, the linguistic description can take innovative forms through the corpus methods that make it possible to investigate linguistic phenomena in new – quantitative – ways. The corpus stylistic circle (Mahlberg 2013) captures this relationship between linguistic description and literary appreciation with the added corpus linguistic perspective. Carter (2010, p. 67) describes this approach to the study of literary texts in the following way: 'Corpus stylistic analysis is a relatively objective methodological procedure that at its best is guided by a relatively subjective process of interpretation'. While the notion of the corpus stylistic circle might appear at first sight simply to be a re-labelling of basic methodological principles, it highlights the tension between the individual example of the literary text and the more general description of the language that a corpus linguistic approach can help to provide. It is also this tension that accounts for both the similarities with and differences from statistical stylistics, which has a more widely recognised tradition within the digital humanities.

When Hockey (2004) traces the history of humanities computing, she clearly pinpoints a crucial starting point in the work of Father Roberto Busa. In 1949, this Italian Jesuit priest began work on an *index verborum* of all the words in the work of St. Thomas Aquinas and related authors, amounting to about eleven million words of medieval Latin. Busa explored the possibilities of how computers could help his project, which resulted in the use of texts on punched cards and the writing of a concordance program. Busa's project illustrates that an important aspect of humanities computing is the data management that computers can support. Generally, the interest in concordances also shows the interest in the works of a particular writer. This emphasis on identifying the characteristics of writings of specific authors is still a crucial concern in computational stylistics, focusing on techniques for authorship attribution. Burrows (1997, p. 186) defines 'style' as 'whatever marks the distinct identity of an author or a school, a set of loosely consistent features'. These features include phenomena that can be classified and counted and hence may be captured by stylometric techniques. Such techniques typically focus on the most common words. Hoover (2007: 176) points out that '[s]tylometric techniques assume that word frequencies are largely outside the author's conscious control because they result from habits that are stable enough to create a verbal fingerprint'. Word frequencies can be used to measure textual differences or group sets of texts together that appear to be most similar on the basis of the patterns among their most frequent words. Such techniques can identify groups of texts by the same author, they can determine the likely authorship of a particular text, they can help to trace the stylistic development of an author over time, or they can indicate groups of stylistically similar or different works by the same author (cf. e.g. Hoover 2007, Tabata 2002). An important contribution to computational stylistics was Burrow's (1987) study of works by Jane Austen, which, for instance, showed differences between narrative and dialogue as well as features of the intermediate form 'free indirect style'.

Burrows (2004) sees a key contribution of computational stylistics in the fact that it becomes possible to classify and characterise texts through comparison. In this way it is different from approaches to literature that focus on a single work in order to discuss the distinguishing qualities of this work. However, Burrows (2004, p. 345) also points out that even research that focuses on a single work is ultimately contrastive, drawing on reference data gathered through the individual analyst's reading experience. In contrast, computational statistics provides comparative data through quantitative information based on actual texts. The comparative element that is key to computational statistics is highlighted by Hoover (2013, p. 518), who emphasises that in the analysis of texts 'the unusual and the characteristic must be validated by counting and comparison'.

Counting and comparing is also important to corpus stylistic work, which puts greater emphasis on a qualitative dimension than computational stylistics does. It is exactly the counting and comparing that contributes the additional systematicity to literary stylistics which seems to make corpus stylistics such an attractive undertaking (cf. Stubbs 2005, O'Halloran 2007). To see how corpus stylistics – as a combination of corpus linguistics and literary stylistics – might differ from computational stylistics it is useful to begin with some basic methodological principles of corpus linguistics. The chapter will then focus in particular on how corpus methods are employed for the study of literary texts, before some corpus linguistic concepts are discussed that can add new linguistic categories for the analysis of texts. The chapter will then focus on practical aspects of corpus stylistics, before concluding by considering some challenges for the future development of corpus stylistic research.

Corpus linguistics

Corpus linguistics studies linguistic phenomena on the basis of electronically stored samples of naturally occurring language. When such samples are collected and stored in a principled way, we talk about a 'corpus'. There are corpora of written language containing, for instance, newspaper articles, leaflets, examples of academic essays, or spoken corpora that include transcriptions of spoken language, e.g. from conversations, classroom discourse, interviews or TV shows. A crucial quality of corpus data is that texts in a corpus are real texts – they have been used by people to communicate and interact. The fact that corpora are stored electronically makes it possible to process the texts with the help of computer tools. Hence the texts can be searched and displayed in a number of ways, and the computer can generate a range of quantitative information. A very basic but nonetheless important aspect of the quantitative dimension of corpus data is the observation of repetitions. Repeated patterns of words are associated with different meanings of words. The ability to identify such relationships between patterns and meanings has had significant impact on the way in which dictionaries are compiled. Especially very frequent words occur in a range of patterns, and data from corpora can help to structure dictionary entries according to the most frequent and therefore presumably the most useful patterns (cf. e.g. Sinclair 1987).

Figure 23.1 presents a sample of thirty-five concordance lines for the word *shoulder.* This sample was retrieved with the tool *WebCorp Live* that accesses the web as a corpus. The search was restricted to sites of UK broadsheets. A concordance is a display format that shows a 'node' word in the centre with a specified amount of context on either side. The sample in Figure 23.1 is sorted according to the first word on the left of the node *shoulder.* Repetitions of the same words around *shoulder*, i.e. the 'collocations' of *shoulder*, illustrate different meanings of the word. The collocation *cold shoulder* in lines 2 to 6 shows a metaphorical meaning of the word, in lines 13 and 14 *shoulder* occurs in the combination *hard shoulder* referring to an area of the motorway, while other collocations include *lamb/ pork/roast/roasted shoulder* indicating a type of meat. The instances where *shoulder* refers to a part of the human body also illustrate patterns of meanings. They mainly refer to injuries or problems, as reflected in the collocations *shoulder injury* (lines 32 to 34) or *shoulder problem* (lines 31 and 35), as well as *dislocated/injured shoulder* (line 8, 9, 17 and the related line 10). Shoulder problems are also referred to in line 1 *shoulder scare*, line 27 *salsa shoulder* or line 16 *iPad shoulder*. Also line 30 *shoulder specialist* indicates that this part of the human body is often mentioned when there is a problem that may need treatment or affects progress (often in the case of sports people). Additionally, the newspapers make reference to the shoulder in the context of fashion (lines 11 and 12). While most examples are nouns, there are also two lines illustrating the verb meaning: *rich countries shoulder 'responsibility'* (line 7) or *UK taxpayers shoulder 'subsidised stagnation'* (line 29).

The examples in Figure 23.1 were not retrieved following some principled criteria, but they are mainly included to illustrate how a random sample from a sufficiently large corpus will always illustrate patterns for a word that are associated with particular meanings. Still, the fact that the search was restricted to UK broadsheets is also visible in the results. Newspapers typically include reports of accidents or other kinds of bad news, in particular accidents that happen to celebrities such as sports people or actors. The pattern *get/give the cold shoulder* also fits this picture as it refers to some form of confrontation. Additionally, the references to the types of meat fit with the fact that newspapers include recipes or sections that deal with food and drink. The patterns in the concordance reflect to some extent properties of the kinds of texts they come from.

The relationship between patterns of words and types of texts is not only relevant to corpus research that works with concordance samples, but it also applies to other quantitative methods that look at distributions of word frequencies or compare the frequencies of

```
 1  aldo given all clear for Portugal after shoulder scare • Real Madrid forward passed
 2  The Times Subscribe now Author gets cold shoulder from SNP after English 'colonists'
 3  Scottish Premier League give Celtic cold shoulder over Champions League fixture sche
 4   shop Kate Moss gives Leon Max the cold shoulder at London store opening Supermodel
 5   Ice cool Peter Sagan gives rivals cold shoulder • Slovakian outfoxes Fabian Cancel
 6  ichie McCaw ready to give ice baths cold shoulder after All Blacks's Twickenham Test
 7  oha climate talks: should rich countries shoulder 'responsibility' for carbon cuts?
 8  do Vaz Tê opts for surgery on dislocated shoulder for long-term fix • West Ham forwa
 9  man': 6ft 4in thug left with dislocated shoulder after attacking ex-boxing champion
10  st two months of 2012 after dislocating shoulder snowboarding Paul Casey's hopes of
11  n Previous | Next | Index How to dress: shoulder robing This style has been around
12  disclosed that the Queen wears an extra shoulder pad on one side to disguise a sli
13  » Road and rail transport Miles of hard shoulder opened to cut jams Hard-shoulders
14  ailed over 'hero' PC's death on M1 hard shoulder The widow of a policeman killed wh
15  nced yoga exercises like the headstand, shoulder stand and plough could be dangerou
16  pp Reviews Home» Technology» Apple iPad shoulder becomes the latest modern life aff
17      Sport > Tennis Nadal to rest injured shoulder Friday 30 December 2011 Tweet Prin
18       Food and Drink» Recipes Roast lamb shoulder with summer and autumn vegetables
19        Yotam Ottolenghi's recipes for lamb shoulder with broad beans and herbs, plus
20  ood and Drink» Recipes Slow-cooked lamb shoulder with sweetcorn and
21   Sport Athletics Yamilé Aldama: Hope my shoulder will be OK for 2012 Olympic trials
22  nnis Djokovic feels hand of history on shoulder ahead of battle with Nadal Paul
23  bs Life & style Barbecue Barbecue pork shoulder, Carolina style: recipe Barbecue
24   Cafédirect recipes: Slow-roasted pork shoulder with spiced apple relish Share
25  s» Christmas food and drink Slow roast shoulder of pork recipe Margot Henderson's
26  rs Jobs Life & style Meat Slow roasted shoulder of lamb recipe Shoulder tends not
27  ng: Lisa Riley is suffering from 'salsa shoulder' Albertina Lloyd Thursday 13
28  t St. George's Day recipe: slow-braised shoulder of mutton On chilly days when the
29  Construction and Property UK taxpayers shoulder 'subsidised stagnation' in housing
30  season after Wales openside referred to shoulder specialist Sam Warburton's hopes o
31   for Wales as Ryan Jones sent home with shoulder problem • Ospreys back-row forward
32  ngs ruled out of South Africa tour with shoulder injury England's dismay at losing
33  cs: Ben Swift out of Giro d'Italia with shoulder injury as he suffers Games blow B
34  t of autumn Test against Argentina with shoulder injury Wales back-rower Ryan Jones
35  an Jones will miss Argentina match with shoulder problem • We took the decision out
```

Figure 23.1 Concordance sample for *shoulder* retrieved with *WebCorp Live*

particular phenomena across texts. Corpus linguists might be interested, for instance, in how frequencies of progressive forms have changed over time, or whether men and women make use of different types of vagueness expressions.

Corpus methods and stylistics

Literary stylistics is concerned with the artistic function of a text and the impressions the text creates in the mind of the reader. Its focus is on specific uses of language. Such specific configurations of forms and meanings are best studied within a single text or even a text extract (Leech and Short 2007, p. 11) so that literary stylistics in this sense is essentially linked to close reading (Carter 2012, p. 107). Concordance tools can support the analysis of text-specific meanings by retrieving all the occurrences of a form to trace a meaning or the development of meanings throughout the text.

Figure 23.2 shows a concordance for *shoulder* in the Dickens novel *Nicholas Nickleby*, where the noun appears forty times. Highlighted in bold are the two main patterns that become apparent through repetition. The pattern *looking/looked over ... shoulder* mainly

```
 1  ad to see the cloth laid. 'We have but a shoulder of mutton with onion sauce,'
 2   Kate, throwing herself on her brother's shoulder, 'do not say so. My dear broth
 3  eman, laying his hand upon his brother's shoulder, 'that I came to you in mercy.
 4  followed by Smike with the bundle on his shoulder (he carried it about with him
 5   Smike once again with the bundle on his shoulder trudging patiently by his side
 6  as, as the brown bonnet went down on his shoulder again, 'this is more serious t
 7  who had been looking anxiously over his shoulder, 'can this be really the case?
 8   He had turned away, and looked over his shoulder to make this last reply. The e
 9  o legs nearest Nicholas, looked over his shoulder in breathless anxiety. Brother
10  observed the coachman, looking over his shoulder at Nicholas with no very pleas
11  ay with great alacrity; looking over his shoulder every instant, to make quite c
12  a blind man; and looking often over his shoulder while he hurried away, as thou
13  ntomime collection, and pointed over his shoulder. 'You don't mean the infant ph
14   on his feet, and a bugle slung over his shoulder like the guard of a long stage
15  er, retired; looking stealthily over his shoulder at Ralph as he limped slowly o
16  n. 'He broke a leg or an arm, or put his shoulder out, or fractured his collar-b
17  the old man, and laying her arm upon his shoulder; 'I do not mean to be angry an
18   friend. Nicholas laid his hand upon his shoulder. 'I can't do it,' said the dej
19   said Nicholas, laying his hand upon his shoulder: 'it was the wrong servant too
20  oined Nicholas, laying his hand upon his shoulder; 'and if I did, I have neither
21  rother Charles, laying his hand upon his shoulder, bade him walk with him, or Ni
22   said Nicholas, laying his hand upon his shoulder. 'Be a man; you are nearly one
23  oes it not?' Kate sunk her head upon his shoulder, and sobbed out 'Yes.' 'And he
24  t cloak, worn theatrically over his left shoulder, stood by, in the attitude of
25  s as though in armour; and over his left shoulder he wore a short dusky cloak, w
26  ings of a mother, and fell upon the left shoulder of Mr Kenwigs dissolved in tea
27  id Nicholas, laying his hand on Newman's shoulder. 'Before I would make an effor
28   a green veil attached, on Mr Nickleby's shoulder. 'This foolish faintness!' 'Do
29  this compliment, but looked over Ralph's shoulder for an instant, (he was adjust
30  , or the green gauze scarf worn over one shoulder and under the other; or any of
31  d, and under the leg, and over the right shoulder, and over the left; and when t
32  d Nicholas, grasping him heartily by the shoulder, 'shall never be said by me, f
33  embracer's laying his or her chin on the shoulder of the object of affection, an
34  lapping the capitalist familiarly on the shoulder. 'By- the-bye, what a VERY rem
35  said the old man, laying his hand on the shoulder of Nicholas, and walking him u
36  hilly), walked in, and tapped her on the shoulder. 'Well, my Slider,' said Mr Sq
37  oy,' retorted Noggs, clapping him on the shoulder. 'I HAVE seen her. You shall s
38  aid this gentleman, smiting Ralph on the shoulder. 'Not yet,' said Ralph, sarcas
39  r, he thrust in his arm nearly up to the shoulder, and slowly drew forth this gr
40  that she actually laid her hand upon the shoulder of the manageress for support.
```

Figure 23.2 All forty occurrences of *shoulder* in *Nicholas Nickleby* (e-text from Project Gutenberg, www.gutenberg.org)

expresses how fictional characters are positioned in relation to one another. They look over their shoulders as they move or turn away from others. If no-one else is around, a look over one's shoulder can indicate that a character rushes away hastily as if being followed. Additionally, characters do not always look over their own shoulder but sometimes over someone else's – as in line 8, for instance, where Tim Linkinwater looks over the shoulder of Nicholas when he first begins writing into the books of Cheeryble Brothers. The pattern *laid/ laying his hand (up)on ... shoulder* seems to be associated even more clearly with a particular meaning. In most cases it is Nicholas who puts his hand upon someone's shoulder and in all cases the pattern reflects the friendship and closeness of a group of people around Nicholas. This friendship is in contrast to the coldness of Ralph Nickleby (Mahlberg 2013, p. 177f). The exception is line 40, where the pattern refers to physical support.

The example analysis of *shoulder* in *Nicholas Nickleby* illustrates how a concordance shows repetitions and hence patterns of meanings that occur across stretches of text. Because of the distance between the individual occurrences of the search word, readers might not easily notice such links between different sections of a text. Words have to be sufficiently frequent so that a concordance for a specific text will provide any patterns at all. One of the questions is how the words are best identified for which a concordance analysis provides useful insights – especially if their patterns are not particularly striking. I will return to the word *shoulder* below. Here, I first want to mention a use of concordances for stylistic analysis that Louw (1993, 1997) links to the concept of the 'semantic prosody'.

The semantic prosody of a lexical item refers to some kind of evaluative or attitudinal meaning associated with the item. It is not necessarily realised through the verbatim repetition of forms that would constitute collocations. Instead, it can be expressed through formally diverse patterns in a concordance that nevertheless show some positive, negative or otherwise evaluative meaning associated with the node. Sinclair (2004) defines the semantic prosody as the obligatory component of a lexical item that accounts for the function of the item in context. Louw (1993, 1997) argues that the concept of semantic prosody adds a useful tool to stylistic analysis because it can help to explain creative or unusual uses of words that then create specific literary effects. The use of a word in a textual example can be analysed by relating its meaning in the example under investigation to the typical patterns in a large general corpus where a word's semantic prosody can be identified. This kind of comparison is what Louw (1993) refers to as 'matching texts against corpora' (Louw 1993, p. 161). Among his examples is an analysis of Larkin's poem 'Days', which Louw (1993) analyses with the help of the semantic prosody of the collocation *days are*. He finds that *days are* is typically followed by words such as *gone, over* and *past*, so that *days are* is associated with a feeling of melancholia.

Although using different terminology in the context of his theory of lexical priming, Hoey (2007) illustrates a similar method of comparing particular uses in textual examples with more general patterns in reference corpora. The approach of 'matching texts against corpora' is in line with Hoover's (2013) emphasis on the need to contextualise unusual uses 'by counting and comparison' (see above). However, in the case of concordance analyses the focus is on contextual and functional patterns rather than statistical accounts of word frequencies. The background information on typical uses that a large reference corpus provides can to some extent be seen as an approximation of the linguistic experience that readers might bring to a text. However, with regard to any such corpus comparison, Dillon (2006) points out that quantitative information can only help to assess how common or typical a particular use of a word is. The comparison as such cannot say anything about how 'adept' the usage is in the given context. This assessment will have to be made by the reader.

To identify words as starting points for concordance analyses there are basically two main options. A manual stylistic analysis can highlight words that might benefit from further corpus stylistic analysis. In this sense, corpus data can provide complementary evidence to support notions of foregrounding. If the focus is not on striking words or patterns, corpus methods can help to identify potentially relevant words. One such corpus method is the key words procedure. Key words are words that are significantly more frequent in one text compared to another text or reference corpus (such words may or may not be perceived as foregrounded). The 'significance' of the difference in frequency between the text and the reference corpus is assessed through statistical measures. Key words tend to be proper names or content words that provide an indication of what the text is about. Additionally, function words can come up as key. Function words are typically high frequency items, and the 'keyness' of such items relates to their usefulness in approaches to authorship attribution that focus on the behaviour of the most common words as features for the stylistic characterisation of texts (see above).

Corpus stylistic studies that begin with the generation of key words need criteria for the selection of those key items that will then be studied in more detail. An initial step can be to identify groups of key words by focusing on semantic categories or semantic fields, as illustrated by Fischer-Starcke (2009). For corpus stylistic studies that seek links between literary and linguistic concerns the classification of key words can also be guided by the search for links with literary critical arguments. For the example of Austen's *Pride and Prejudice*, Mahlberg and Smith (2010) illustrate how key words can be linked to thematic concerns. They study the key word *civility* that relates to observations by literary critics as well as to corpus linguistic findings on patterns of body language. Toolan (2009) illustrates how key words can be interpreted in terms of the roles they play in the creation of texture. Focusing on short stories, Toolan (2009) investigates how the top key words can provide a method for story-abridgement. He finds that the top key words and the sentences in which they occur are more relevant to the story and more cohesive and coherent than other parts of the text. Toolan's (2009) study shows how top key word sentences are one of the elements that signal textual progression. A 'keyness' comparison is not only limited to key words, but can also be applied to other units such as clusters (cf. e.g. Mahlberg 2007, Bednarek 2010).

Similar to the generation of key words is the retrieval of key semantic domains. Key semantic domains can be identified with the tool *WMatrix* (Rayson 2008). This tool begins by assigning a semantic tag to each word in the text. Examples of semantic domains (that each have subcategories) are 'general and abstract terms', 'numbers and measurements' or 'social actions, states and processes' (for details on the semantic tagset see http://ucrel.lancs. ac.uk/usas/, accessed January 2013). The key comparison focuses on differences in the frequencies of tags and so identifies semantic domains that occur relatively more frequently in the text under investigation than in the reference corpus. Culpeper (2009) illustrates how information on key semantic domains can complement a key word analysis of Shakespeare's *Romeo and Juliet* that compares the speech of individual characters. Further examples of corpus stylistic studies that investigate key words and key semantic domains include Archer and Bousfield (2010), who study character speech in *King Lear*, or McIntyre (2010) who investigates character distinctions in the screenplay *Reservoir Dogs*.

As Toolan's (2009) study of signals of textual progression shows, the value of a key comparison can go beyond selecting words for more detailed analysis. The nature of key words and key semantic domains also raises further questions about the theoretical status of key items and fundamental properties of lexical patterns in literary texts. For Ian Fleming's *Casino Royale*, Mahlberg and McIntyre (2011) begin to outline a general classification of key words that distinguishes between 'fictional world' key words and 'thematic signals'. Fictional world key words function as world-building elements and are more concrete than thematic signals, which are open to a range of interpretations or tend to have evaluative or metaphorical meanings. Because of the interpretative effort that thematic signals trigger, Mahlberg and McIntyre (2011) refer to them as 'reader-centred' key words, whereas the 'text-centred' fictional world key words are interpreted in terms of their references to characters, concrete objects and places in the fictional world.

Simpson (2004) points out that a stylistic analysis can draw on every linguistic resource available. Theoretically, this is also the case for corpus stylistics. However, some textual features are easier to quantify than others. The work on speech, writing and thought presentation by Semino and Short (2004) shows that for some questions that are relevant to literary stylistics there are no ready-made tools that can easily be employed. Semino and Short (2004) were interested in comparing the frequency of speech, thought and writing categories across different types of texts. They had to work with corpora where categories such as indirect thought, free indirect speech and so on were manually annotated because there is no existing algorithm that could count all these phenomena automatically. In addition to their findings on the distribution of categories, Semino and Short (2004) observed another type of contribution that a corpus stylistic approach can make. The annotation of a large amount of data entails a critical engagement with the existing categories, and Semino and Short (2004) found that new subcategories had to be added in order to account for the data. Building on the model of Semino and Short (2004), Busse (2010) studied categories of speech, thought and writing presentation in a corpus of nineteenth century fiction. She also points out that the rigorous process of annotation requires explicit definitions of categories. Additionally, Busse (2010) suggests that the repetitive patterns that are found with discourse presentation categories could go some way towards an algorithm for automatic annotation.

Corpus linguistic concepts and stylistics

In addition to providing quantitative data for linguistic categories, corpus linguistic research has also added new categories for the description of linguistic phenomena such as collocation, semantic prosody or key words. Another concept that has been employed in the study of literary texts is the 'cluster', i.e. a repeatedly occurring sequence of words. Clusters are also referred to as 'n-grams' where n specifies the number of words that occur repeatedly. Starcke (2006) studies 3-grams (or 3-word clusters) in Jane Austen's *Persuasion*, focusing on the two most frequent 3-grams *she could not* and *she had been.* Starcke (2006) also looks at 3-frames, i.e. 3-grams with a variable slot indicated by the wild card *, as in the 3-frame *the * of.* Starcke's (2006) findings include patterns that relate to the atmosphere of the novel or reflect relationships between characters.

Related to the concept of the cluster are 'lexical bundles' (Biber *et al.* 1999). Lexical bundles also refer to repeated sequences of words, but additionally focus on sequences that occur with high frequencies (for a detailed discussion of these concepts see Mahlberg 2013). The frequency with which lexical bundles occur is a reflection of the textual functions that they fulfil in texts. Drawing on the functional categories suggested by Biber *et al.* (2004), Viana *et al.* (2007) compare two literary texts with regard to the lexical bundles they contain. Viana *et al.* (2007) are interested in real readers' preferences for canonical and non-canonical texts and compare Dan Brown's *O Código Da Vinci* and *Dom Casmurro* by Machado de Assis. Viana *et al.* (2007) find more diversity in the use of lexical bundles in *Dom Casmurro*, whereas the usage of lexical bundles in *O Código Da Vinci* appears relatively repetitive. The authors interpret the more repetitive patterns as less creative language use that is easier to follow, which might be one of the factors contributing to the popularity of Dan Brown's novel. However, the interpretation of the findings also has to take account of the fact that *O Código Da Vinci* is a Brazilian Portuguese translation of a text originally written in English.

Another corpus linguistic concept that can usefully be related to literary stylistic concerns is the concept of 'local textual functions'. Local textual functions capture the meanings of lexical items in texts. They are local because the functions they describe only relate to specific items in specific texts (Mahlberg 2005, 2007, 2013). With a focus on Dickens's fiction, I have illustrated how clusters can be interpreted in terms of textual building blocks. The local textual functions that are associated with clusters contribute to a description of meanings in fictional worlds. The functional areas that are accounted for by the 5-word clusters in Dickens refer to the labelling of characters and themes, the interaction between characters through speech, body language, narrator comment and time and place references. Going back to the example in Figure 23.2 above, the concordance includes examples of the 5-word clusters *his hand upon his shoulder* and *laying his hand upon his*. These clusters belong to one of the two main patterns illustrated by the concordance for *shoulder* in *Nicholas Nickleby*: *laid/laying his hand (up)on ... shoulder.* Although this pattern is not automatically realised by a cluster, it is in most of the cases.

A study of 5-word clusters in Dickens shows that there is a set of clusters that refer to body language. The functions associated with these clusters can be further described in terms of 'highlighting' and 'contextualising' functions. Highlighting functions give particular emphasis to the description of body language and tend to refer to body language that is habitual or so striking that it is an identifying feature of a specific fictional character. An example is the cluster *and his nose came down* that highlights a feature of Rigaud in *Little Dorrit*. The pattern *laid/laying his hand (up)on ... shoulder* in *Nicholas Nickleby* functions more in a contextualising than a highlighting way. Patterns with contextualising functions may occur with more than one character in a novel. They also often accompany other information in the text such as character speech. The *–ing* form *laying* reflects this accompanying function of the body language pattern. Although contextualising functions might not contribute to the clear identification of character features, they still contribute character information and illustrate authenticating effects of body language presentation. It seems that readers might be less consciously aware of contextualising patterns, in contrast to patterns with highlighting functions that are more striking. Hence, the corpus linguistic method of retrieving clusters makes an important contribution to a text-driven account of body language presentation in literature (Mahlberg 2013). Returning to the question raised above concerning how useful items for concordance analyses are found, the example of body language also illustrates how clusters can first be used to identify functionally relevant groups of items, before a concordance analysis of words that occur in such a cluster can help to add detail to patterns associated with local textual functions.

Practical considerations

A necessary requirement for the applicability of corpus methods is the availability of electronic texts. Useful resources are, for instance, the Oxford Text Archive (OTA) or Project Gutenberg. Project Gutenberg provides free e-books which have been digitised with the help of volunteers. The texts are available in different formats. The plain text versions in particular provide a useful resource for the creation of literary corpora. The OTA collects and distributes corpora as well as texts that can be used to compile corpora. The TEI texts held by the OTA are created following the guidelines of the Text Encoding Initiative. Some of these texts are

TEI versions of Project Gutenberg texts. Although a full review of the currently available corpus tools is beyond the scope of this paper, it is worthwhile mentioning a few examples. A very easy-to-use concordance software package is *WordSmith Tools* (Scott 2012). Among its main features are a word list tool, a concordance tool and a tool for the generation of key word lists. An alternative, free option with similar functionalities is *AntConc* (Anthony 2011). Currently the main tool for the analysis of key semantic domains is *WMatrix* (Rayson 2008). Freely accessible reference corpora for the kind of 'matching of texts against corpora' as suggested by Louw (1993), are, for instance, the *British National Corpus* accessed through *BNCweb* or the *Corpus of Contemporary American English* (*COCA*) that comes with its own web interface. *WebCorp Live*, as illustrated with the example of *shoulder* above, can be used to retrieve corpus data from the web.

The main advantage of employing corpus methods in the study of literary text is that a degree of quantification can be achieved that is not easily possible in a manual analysis. At the same time, it is important to note that not every text is amenable to the same kind of quantitative approach. A short story may not yield a sufficient number of 5-word clusters for a useful analysis, or a word that appears interesting in a text extract from a novel may be insufficiently frequent to show patterns in the form of a concordance. Even if there were a reasonable number of key words for a text, the analysis of these key words might not provide observations that have much to contribute to the literary stylistic analysis. If and how corpus methods are applicable to the analysis of a literary text depends on the text under analysis. The fact that corpus studies require a certain critical mass of data to be able to retrieve useful findings is also reflected by studies that focus on several texts by the same author, e.g. Hori (2004), Hardy (2007), Fischer-Starcke (2010).

While there are a number of standard concordance packages, a challenge for the development of corpus stylistics will be to address research questions for which there are no default tools available yet. Mahlberg and Smith (2010, 2012) provide an example with their study of 'suspensions', i.e. stretches of narration that interrupt the speech (or thought, or writing) of characters as in the example below, where the suspension appears in italics. (As the example is taken from an e-text from Project Gutenberg no page references are provided.)

> 'Uncle,' *he said gaily, laying his hand upon the old man's shoulder*, 'what shall I send you home from Barbados?'
>
> *(Charles Dickens, Our Mutual Friend)*

A suspension, or 'suspended quotation', is initially defined in purely formal terms, following the criteria set out by Lambert (1981) which require that the interrupting narration contains at least five words. A definition that focuses on features on the textual surface makes it possible to automatically annotate and search texts with the help of corpus tools, as illustrated by Mahlberg and Smith (2010, 2012) with their tool CLiC (Corpus Linguistics in Cheshire). Patterns that become observable in this way can then help to identify functional categories. In the example above, the suspension contains an instance of the *laid/laying his hand (up)on ... shoulder* pattern. Suspensions can create an impression of simultaneity in the description of body language and speech in a fictional text. In this way an authenticating effect can be achieved, since in real life speech and body language typically occur together. Suspensions add a further dimension to corpus stylistic approaches as they stress the relevance of linguistic units that are defined through their position in the text (cf. also Mahlberg *et al.* 2013). For the definition of such textual units punctuation plays a crucial role, which is also illustrated by the work of González-Díaz (2012) that focuses on round brackets.

Recommendations for practice

Before embarking on any kind of corpus stylistic analysis, it is useful to get some basic experience with using corpus tools and analysing corpus data; see the textbooks in the 'Further Reading' section to get some pointers in this direction.

Crucial to corpus stylistic analysis is to compare a particular pattern or a particular text with reference data. In a corpus of Dickens's novels, the following two come up among the 5-word clusters: *his hand to his forehead* and *his hands in his pockets*. To analyse how these clusters can contribute to the creation of fictional characters, progress through the following steps:

1. Begin by studying the clusters in a corpus of Dickens's novels. You can easily compile such a corpus by downloading texts from the Project Gutenberg website. Use for instance *WordSmith Tools* or *Antconc* to run concordances for the clusters. Try sorting the concordances in a useful way, but also take into account the distribution of the clusters across the different novels in the corpus. Can you identify examples where the clusters have contextualising functions and examples where the clusters have highlighting functions?

2. Once you have an idea of how the clusters function in Dickens, study them in a reference corpus of novels by other authors. Again, use Project Gutenberg to compile such a reference corpus. When you compare frequencies across the two corpora, take into account that the corpora may be of different size, so you need to work with normalised frequencies (see also 'Further Reading').

3. Finally, use *WebCorp Live* to retrieve examples of the clusters in UK broadsheets. Use the 'Advanced Options' function in *WebCorp Live* to focus on UK broadsheets. You will find it useful to only select one concordance line per web page.

4. Having looked at the clusters, now broaden your analysis to patterns of the body part nouns that occur in the clusters: *hand, hands* (look at the singular and plural forms separately) and *forehead*. What other patterns can you find around these nouns? Are there any differences across the three corpora from your steps 1) to 3)?

Future directions

Corpus stylistics can add both methods and descriptive concepts to a variety of research in literary stylistics, thus situating the field within the wider context of the digital humanities. Corpus stylistic methods are closely related to the techniques applied in stylometry and quantitative statistics, but corpus stylistics gives extra emphasis to qualitative concerns to guide the analysis and interpret the results. Corpus stylistics highlights the relationship between linguistic analysis and literary appreciation. Basic corpus methods that rely on comparison and quantification are applicable to literary texts to various degrees. Not in each case will the necessary critical mass of data be available to draw meaningful conclusions to answer a specific research question. Therefore it is crucial that corpus stylistic research is not in the first instance motivated by the availability of off-the-shelf corpus software. Running a concordance or generating key words is not in itself a useful research method if it is not applied to address a particular research question. The application of corpus procedures without searching for theoretically grounded links to interpretative concerns bears the danger of uninsightful and naive observations on a text. One of the challenges for the future of corpus stylistics is therefore to identify research questions that can be usefully addressed with corpus methods so that the method provides innovative insights that go beyond what the human analyst would be able to achieve. Such research questions might be shaped by the descriptive concepts that corpus linguistics has started to add to the inventory of linguistic description, such as collocations, semantic prosodies or local textual functions. At the same time, questions in literary stylistics will trigger the development of new methodological procedures and corpus stylistic tools that are tailored to properties of literary texts. In this area there is also plenty of opportunity for the incorporation of methods and procedures of quantitative stylistics.

A major aspect of the potential of corpus stylistic research is that quantitative data can highlight linguistic phenomena that readers may not be aware of. Patterns may be present in a text and affect the readers' overall reaction to the text, but it might be difficult for readers to pinpoint what features contribute to which effect. Research in both stylometry and corpus linguistics focusing on frequent patterns of frequent words has provided a range of insights in this regard. For corpus stylistics, the investigation of subliminal textual patterns suggests far-reaching links with cognitive poetics. Cognitive approaches in stylistics highlight the readers' role in the creation of meaning, where the impressions that readers create in their minds are triggered by features in the text. Corpus stylistics can provide innovative ways of approaching the principle of text-drivenness. This area of research can also usefully benefit from links with psycholinguistic research to investigate how readers actually read the patterns retrieved with the help of corpus methods. Overall, it seems that corpus stylistics has a lot to offer to mixed methods approaches to the study of literature.

Related topics

Cognitive poetics, linguistic levels of foregrounding in stylistics, (new) historical stylistics, quantitative methodological approaches to stylistics, stylistics and real readers, text world theory

Further reading

Biber, D., Conrad, S. and Reppen, R., 1998. *Corpus linguistics: Investigating language structure and use*. Cambridge: Cambridge University Press.

An introduction to essential research methods with a focus on the study of register variation. The final part of the book includes very useful methodology boxes covering topics such as normalisation.

Hoey M., Mahlberg, M. Stubbs, M. and Teubert, W., 2007. *Text, discourse and corpora: Theory and analysis*. London: Continuum.

This book highlights that corpus linguistics has not only methodological but also theoretical relevance. Two of the chapters illustrate analyses of literary texts.

Mahlberg, M., 2012. Corpus analysis of literary texts. *In:* C. A. Chapelle, ed. *The encyclopedia of applied linguistics*. Blackwell. Online. DOI: 10.1002/9781405198431.wbeal0249 [Accessed January 2013].

An overview article that illustrates principles and approaches in corpus stylistics.

Sinclair, J., 2003. *Reading concordances. An introduction*. Harlow: Pearson.

The book is an extremely useful and very practical introduction to the method of concordance analysis. Each chapter consists of a task together with an extensive key so that the reader can practise the analysis of concordance data.

Wynne, M., 2006. Stylistics: Corpus approaches. *In:* K. Brown, ed. *The encyclopedia of language and linguistics*. Oxford: Elsevier, 223–226.

This is a useful article to see how corpus stylistics has developed. It mainly emphasises the potential of corpus stylistic work while later overview articles, such as Mahlberg (2012), can already draw on more examples in the field.

Resources and tools

AntConc

Anthony, L. 2011. *AntConc (Version 3.2.4m)* [Computer Software], Tokyo, Japan: Waseda University. Available from http://www.antlab.sci.waseda.ac.jp/ [Accessed January 2013].

BNCweb

http://bncweb.lancs.ac.uk/bncwebSignup/user/login.php [Accessed January 2013]

The Corpus of Contemporary American English (COCA)

http://corpus.byu.edu/coca/ [Accessed January 2013]

The Oxford Text Archive

http://ota.ahds.ac.uk/ [Accessed January 2013]

Project Gutenberg

http://www.gutenberg.org/ [Accessed January 2013]

WMatrix

Rayson, P. 2008. 'From key words to key semantic domains', *International Journal of Corpus Linguistics, 13*(4): 519–549.

Wmatrix is available from http://ucrel.lancs.ac.uk/wmatrix/ [Accessed January 2013]

WebCorp Live

Research and Development Unit for English Studies (1999–2013), Birmingham City University. Available from http://www.webcorp.org.uk/live/ [Accessed January 2013]

WordSmith Tools

Scott, M. 2012. *WordSmith Tools version 6*, Liverpool: Lexical Analysis Software. Available from http://www.lexically.net/wordsmith/ [Accessed January 2013]

References

Archer, D. and Bousfield, D., 2010. 'See better, Lear'? See Lear better! A corpus-based pragma-stylistic investigation of Shakespeare's *King Lear. In:* B. Busse and D. McIntyre, eds. *Language and style.* London: Routledge, 183–203.

Bednarek, M., 2010. *The language of fictional television: Drama and identity*. London: Continuum.

Biber, D., 2011. Corpus linguistics and the scientific study of literature: Back to the future? *Scientific Study of Literature,* 1 (1), 15–23.

Biber, D., Conrad, S. and Cortes, V., 2004. *If you look at...*: Lexical bundles in university teaching and textbooks. *Applied Linguistics,* 25 (3), 371–405.

Biber, D., Conrad, S., Finegan, E., Leech, G. and Johansson, S., 1999. *Longman grammar of spoken and written English*. Harlow: Longman.

Biber, D., Conrad, S. and Reppen, R., 1998. *Corpus linguistics: Investigating language structure and use*. Cambridge: Cambridge University Press.

Burrows, J., 1987. *Computation into criticism: A study of Jane Austen's novels and an experiment in method*. Oxford: Clarendon.

Burrows, J., 1997. Style. *In:* E. Copeland and J. McMaster, ed. *The Cambridge companion to Jane Austen*. Cambridge: Cambridge University Press, 1997, 170–188. Cambridge Collections Online, Cambridge University Press, DOI:10.1017/CCOL0521495172 [Accessed 5 January 2013]

Burrows, J., 2004. Textual analysis. *In:* S. Schreibman, R. Siemens and J. Unsworth, eds. *A companion to digital humanities*. Oxford: Blackwell, 323–348.

Busse, B., 2010. *Speech, writing and thought presentation in a corpus of nineteenth-century English narrative fiction*. University of Bern.

Carter, R., 2010. Methodologies for stylistic analysis: Practices and pedagogies. *In:* B. Busse and D. McIntyre, eds. *Language and style*. Basingstoke: Palgrave, 55–68.

Carter, R., 2012. Coda: Some rubber bullet points. *Language and Literature*, 12 (1), 106–114.

Chapelle, C.A., ed. 2012. *The encyclopedia of applied linguistics*. Blackwell. DOI:10.1002/9781405198431.

Culpeper, J., 2009. Keyness: Words, parts-of-speech and semantic categories in the character-talk of Shakespeare's *Romeo and Juliet*. *International Journal of Corpus Linguistics*, 14 (1), 29–59.

Dillon, L. G., 2006. Corpus, creativity, and cliché: Where statistics meet aesthetics. *Journal of Literary Semantics*, 35, 97–103.

Fischer-Starcke, B., 2009. Keywords and frequent phrases of Jane Austen's *Pride and Prejudice*. *International Journal of Corpus Linguistics*, 14 (4), 492–523.

Fischer-Starcke, B., 2010. *Corpus linguistics in literary analysis: Jane Austen and her contemporaries*. London: Continuum.

Flowerdew, L., 2012. *Corpora and language education*. Basingstoke: Palgrave Macmillan.

González-Díaz, V., 2012. Round brackets in Jane Austen. *English Text Construction*, 5 (2), 174–207.

Hardy, D. E., 2007. *The body in Flannery O'Connor's fiction. Computational technique and linguistic voice*. Columbia: University of South Carolina Press.

Hockey, S., 2004. The history of humanities computing. *In:* S. Schreibman, R. Siemens and J. Unsworth, eds. *A companion to digital humanities*. Oxford: Blackwell, 3–19.

Hoey. M., 2007. Lexical priming and literary creativity. *In:* M. Hoey, M. Mahlberg, M. Stubbs and W. Teubert, *Text, discourse and corpora. Theory and analysis*. London: Continuum, 7–29.

Hoey M., Mahlberg, M. Stubbs, M. and Teubert, W., 2007. *Text, discourse and corpora: Theory and analysis*. London: Continuum.

Hoover, D., 2007. Corpus stylistics, stylometry, and the styles of Henry James. *Style*, 41 (2), 174–255.

Hoover, D., 2013. Quantitative analysis and literary studies. *In:* R. Siemens and S. Schreibman, eds. *A companion to digital literary studies*. Oxford: Blackwell, 517–533.

Hori, M., 2004. *Investigating Dickens' style: A collocational analysis*. Basingstoke: Palgrave Macmillan.

Jeffries, L. and McIntyre, D., 2010. *Stylistics*. Cambridge: Cambridge University Press.

Lambert, M., 1981. *Dickens and the suspended quotation*. New Haven and London: Yale University Press.

Leech, G. and Short, M., [1981] 2007. *Style in fiction. A linguistic introduction to English fictional prose*. Harlow: Pearson Education.

Lindquist, H., 2009. *Corpus linguistics and the description of English*. Edinburgh: Edinburgh University Press.

Louw, W. E., 1993. Irony in the text or insincerity in the writer? The diagnostic potential of semantic prosodies. *In:* M. Baker, G. Francis and E. Tognini-Bonelli, eds. *Text and technology: In honour of John Sinclair*. Amsterdam: John Benjamins, 157–174.

Louw, W. E., 1997. The role of corpora in critical literary appreciation. *In:* A. Wichman, S. Fligelstone, T. McEnery and G. Knowles, eds. *Teaching and language corpora*. Harlow: AddisonWesley Longman, 240–251.

Mahlberg, M., 2005. *English general nouns: A corpus theoretical approach*. Amsterdam: John Benjamins.

Mahlberg, M., 2007. Clusters, key clusters and local textual functions in Dickens. *Corpora*, 2 (1), 1–31.

Mahlberg, M., 2012. Corpus analysis of literary texts. *In:* C. A. Chapelle, ed. *The encyclopedia of applied linguistics*. Blackwell. Online. DOI: 10.1002/9781405198431.wbeal0249 [Accessed January 2013].

Mahlberg, M., 2013. *Corpus stylistics and Dickens's fiction*. New York and London: Routledge.

Mahlberg, M. and McIntyre, D., 2011. A case for corpus stylistics: Ian Fleming's *Casino Royale*. *English Text Construction*, 4 (2), 204–227.

Mahlberg, M. and Smith, C., 2010. Corpus approaches to prose fiction: Civility and body language in *Pride and Prejudice*. *In:* D. McIntyre and B. Busse, eds. *Language and style*. Basingstoke: Palgrave Macmillan, 449–467.

Mahlberg, M. and Smith, C., 2012. Dickens, the suspended quotation and the corpus. *Language and Literature*, 21 (1), 51–65.

Mahlberg, M., Smith, C. and Preston, S., 2013. Phrases in literary contexts: Patterns and distributions of suspensions in Dickens's novels. *International Journal of Corpus Linguistics,* 18 (1), 35–56.

McIntyre, D., 2010. Dialogue and characterization in Quentin Tarantino's *Reservoir Dogs*: A corpus stylistic analysis. *In:* D. McIntyre and B. Busse, eds. *Language and style*. Basingstoke: Palgrave Macmillan, 162–182.

McIntyre, D. and Busse, B., eds. 2010. *Language and style*. Basingstoke: Palgrave Macmillan.

O'Halloran, K., 2007. The subconscious in James Joyce's 'Eveline': A corpus stylistic analysis that chews on the 'Fish hook'. *Language and Literature*, 16 (3), 227–244.

O'Keeffe, A. and McCarthy, M., eds. *The Routledge handbook of corpus linguistics*. Abingdon: Routledge.

Rayson, P. (2008) 'From key words to key semantic domains', *International Journal of Corpus Linguistics, 13*(4): 519–549.

Semino, E. and Short, M., 2004. *Corpus stylistics: Speech, writing and thought presentation in a corpus of English writing*. London: Routledge.

Simpson, P., 2004. *Stylistics. A resource book for students*, London: Routledge.

Sinclair, J., ed. 1987. *Looking up. An account of the COBUILD project in lexical computing*. London: HarperCollins.

Sinclair, J., 2003. *Reading concordances. An introduction*. Harlow: Pearson.

Sinclair, J., 2004. *Trust the text. Language, corpus and discourse*. London: Routledge.

Spitzer, L., 1948. *Linguistics and literary history*. Princeton: Princeton University Press.

Starcke, B., 2006. The phraseology of Jane Austen's *Persuasion*: Phraseological units as carriers of meaning. *ICAME Journal, 30, 87–104.*

Stubbs, M., 2005. Conrad in the computer: Examples of quantitative stylistics Methods. *Language and Literature*, 14 (1), 5–24.

Tabata, T., 2002. Investigating stylistic variation in Dickens through correspondence analysis of word-class distribution. *In:* T. Saito, J. Nakamura and S. Yamazaki eds. *English corpus linguistics in Japan*. Amsterdam: Rodopi, 165–182.

Toolan, M., 2009. *Narrative progression in the short story: A corpus stylistic approach*. Amsterdam: John Benjamins.

Viana, V., Fausto, F. and Zyngier, S., 2007. Corpus linguistics and literature: A contrastive analysis of Dan Brown and Machado de Assis. *In:* S. Zyngier, V. Viana and J. Jandre, eds. *Textos e leituras: Estudos empíricos de língua e literature*. Rio de Janeiro: Publit, 233–256.

Wynne, M., 2006. Stylistics: Corpus approaches. *In:* K. Brown, ed. *The encyclopedia of language and linguistics*. Oxford: Elsevier, 223–226.

24

Stylistics and translation

Jean Boase-Beier

Introduction

It is easy to see why stylistics might potentially have close links with translation: both are concerned with the fine linguistic detail of a text and how it can be seen as a reflection of a writer's textual choices and as the source of effects on readers. Yet until recently these links have only sporadically been explored in depth. Before considering some of the historical fluctuations in their interaction, it seems important to explore why translation studies remains incomplete without stylistics. A good place to begin this exploration is with the various possible views about what is or is not an instance of translation. While most readers would agree that Don Paterson's rendering of Rilke's *Sonette an Orpheus* (2006) as the English *Orpheus* is a translation (even if he himself calls it a 'version'), opinions would differ as to whether every act of speaking could be considered a translation, in that it puts thoughts into words. Barnstone (1993, p. 20) says that it could, but this is not a generally accepted view (see Boase-Beier 2011b, pp. 3–6). And can a rendering of *Beowulf* or a poem in Yorkshire dialect into standard modern English be called a translation? Jakobson, whose publications from the 1920s onwards show him to be one of the first modern theoreticians to link the study of style explicitly with the study of translations, called this 'intralingual translation' ([1960] 2008, p. 139), but whether it is seen as intra- or interlingual (what Jakobson calls 'translation proper') depends on what is considered to be a language and what is considered to be a dialect.

What almost everyone agrees on, though, is that translation involves a transfer from one language (or dialect) to another. Besides the question of what constitutes a language, the area of most disagreement among translation scholars is probably regarding what it is that is transferred. A traditional view is that it is the meaning of a word, expression or text. However, such an apparently straightforward view gives rise to two further questions: Can meaning be transferred, or does it change when rendered in another language? And what constitutes the meaning of a text? To a very large extent the answer to both questions is tied up with the concept of style. Stylisticians would generally agree that style cannot be completely separated from meaning; as Leech and Short (2007, p. 22) point out, this fact poses a problem for the simple view of translation as the transfer of meaning or content. Some writers on translation also make this point clearly (e.g. Hatim and Munday 2004, p. 65), but many others do not

393

mention style at all. Yet this question – is style separate from meaning? – lies at the heart of both stylistics and translation. Furthermore, the view that style is more difficult to separate from meaning in poetry than in prose, and in literary prose more difficult than in non-literary texts, suggests a distinction between literary and non-literary texts. It is a distinction that has been the subject of much discussion in translation studies, too.

Some writers on translation have assumed that the differences between the translation of literary and non-literary texts depend upon the different functions of such translations (see Nord 1997, pp. 80–103), but this simply raises the further question of whether literary texts have a function. Most translation scholars who suggest the difference is connected to style (e.g. Gutt 2000, p. 130) argue that a literary translation (or the translation of a literary text) will be particularly concerned to maintain a close stylistic link with the source text, whereas a non-literary translation can opt simply to report the content or reproduce the function (as in the translation of a tourist brochure). Thus the difference between literary and non-literary translation seems to depend crucially upon the role of style.

One of the essential issues for an examination of the different roles of style in literary and non-literary translation is the extent to which style is considered to embody a set of choices made by the author, and thus to provide clues to such elusive elements as attitude or ideology or a character's or narrator's point of view. One way that features of style such as metaphors or ambiguous expressions are characterised in recent works on stylistics and translation is as 'weak implicatures' (see Boase-Beier 2011b, p. 9). These are aspects of the meaning of a text not made explicit but left open to the reader's interpretation. Such openness to interpretation has often been regarded as one of the main characteristics of literary writing (cf. Attridge 2004, p. 111). The weaker the implicatures in the text, the more the reader will need to engage with the text. This will mean that the style of a poem which allows several interpretations will need to be treated differently from the style of a newspaper article in which the ironical position of the writer is made clear. In the latter case, the style will matter more to the translator than in the translation of a road sign, where, it could be argued, the attitude of the writer or the stylistic effects on the reader do not play any role at all.

In any case, then, translation is concerned with reflecting not only what is said but how it is said, and both the translation scholar and the translator herself need to consider the style of the text. However, it is also the case that, as recent works such as Parks (2007) or Boase-Beier (2011a) have suggested, studying what happens when texts are translated can offer important insights to stylisticians because the study of translation is concerned with many of the same issues: the form-meaning interaction, questions of authorship, voice and the reader's role.

Historical perspectives

If, then, for all the reasons just given, stylistics and translation are not merely mutually beneficial but interdependent, it is interesting to consider why their interaction has not always been a straightforward matter.

Though style has often been mentioned in writing about translation, it is only in recent years (e.g. Boase-Beier 2006) that its role in and effects on translation, and those of translation on the study of style, have been systematically studied. One reason for this is that most translation scholars are not stylisticians. They might focus on the linguistic differences between languages and the role of culture and ideology (Hatim and Munday 2004), or the translation of particular genres (Barnstone 1993), but often they only mention style in passing, and then as though it were clear what we mean by it. The term 'stylistics', too, if it is mentioned at all in recent studies of translation, is often used without explanation (e.g. Munday 2012).

According to Wales (2001, p. 269), it is only since the 1960s that stylistics has become an established discipline, so we would not expect studies of translation before this time to mention stylistics, although they may mention style. Some of the earliest writings on translation to mention style are those of Cicero and Horace; both writers were concerned that translation should preserve the 'style and effect' (Qvale 1998, p. 9) of the original text, rather than attempting a word-for-word closeness. Many writers on translation in the following centuries discussed style in translation either in terms of the linguistic particularity of different languages, e.g. Dolet in 1540 (Qvale 1998, p. 11) or in terms of the writer's personal style, e.g. Dryden in 1680 (Qvale 1998, p. 13), usually demanding a close reading of the original text. Because modern stylistics is particularly concerned with reading (cf. Stockwell 2002, pp. 1–11), and with an analysis of the textual features that engender particular readings, it is able, when used as part of the study of translation, to provide a more concrete and verifiable analysis of the sort of thing these earlier writers called upon translation to preserve.

The modern discipline of translation studies is generally considered also to date from the 1960s, with the writings of James Holmes (see e.g. Holmes 2005). It is therefore not surprising that the beginning of the engagement between stylistics and translation can be dated to around this time. A particularly good example (even though it names neither discipline) is Jakobson's discussion of types of translation, mentioned above, which first appeared in a 1960 article. Because Jakobson was concerned with language, poetry, linguistics, psychology, style and translation, he touched on many issues – the difference between a masculine figure of death in German and a feminine figure in Russian, for example – that continue to interest those working in the stylistics of translation today. Several other stylisticians of the 1960s and 1970s, such as Riffaterre, who continued to work in a structuralist stylistic context, showed an interest in translation; Riffaterre later wrote explicitly about the translation of style (see e.g. 1992). A 1958 French work by Vinay and Darbelnet, *Stylistique comparée du français et de l'anglais*, translated into English in 1995, had been one of the first books to explicitly link stylistics and translation: the authors described translation as 'a practical application of comparative stylistics' (1995, p. 4), and said that translation and stylistics could not be separated. Several collections of articles in the 1980s with a broad stylistics focus included articles on translation. A 1981 issue of the journal *Poetics Today*, for example, whose editorial board included Banfield, Fowler and Riffaterre, was devoted exclusively to translation. Also, d'Haen in the introduction to his 1986 book *Linguistics and the Study of Literature* includes studies by early translation theorists such as Lefevère, noting that these, like stylistics, developed from the work of the Russian formalists and Prague structuralists. Early functionalist views of translation such as Reiss and Vermeer (1984) were also strongly influenced by the Prague structuralists. Yet in spite of these common origins, the interaction of stylistics and translation has only recently become more commonly recognised. It is not only that most translation theorists have no background in stylistics; many stylisticians are reluctant to consider translation issues because they only speak one language. Furthermore, many important works were not immediately translated into other languages: Vinay and Darbelnet's book, for example, did not appear in English for nearly forty years.

One of the problems with many of these earlier approaches to stylistics and translation was that their structuralist origins made them seem, to many translation scholars, excessively focused on the detail of the text, and on minute linguistic differences between source and target text. If one problem for translators in integrating stylistics has generally been its monolingual focus, it could be argued that the problem of such comparative structuralist studies was in fact their detailed bilingual focus. Because they tended to concentrate on the stylistic distinction between, say, 'to speak French' and 'parler bien le français' (that is, to speak it well), it could be hard to see how such observations could be generalised to apply to translations between Icelandic and Arabic, or Yiddish and Spanish. This is an issue that persists today, though judicious use of glosses or back translations (as in the second edition of Parks' book) makes discussion more generally accessible. Moreover, from the early 1980s, studies such as those by Vinay and Darbelnet, Riffaterre or Jakobson no longer fulfilled the needs of a translation studies trying to keep pace with post-structuralist views of literature, which questioned the determinability of meaning and the suggestion that it could be separated from form, as well as placing emphasis on context and interpretation. While stylistics after structuralism continued to develop an increased concern with context, translation studies, having generally become disaffected both with early structuralist studies and with early generative linguistic approaches such as that of Nida (1964), tended to turn instead to considerations of the ethics of translation (Venuti 2008, first published in 1995) or the various issues of identity, politics or culture. Thus for several years after the linguistically-orientated translation studies of the 1960s and the functionalist and comparative views of the 1970s and 1980s, there was very little work on the stylistics of translation. One still sometimes hears stylistics equated with structuralist linguistics or stylistics by translation scholars (and by literary scholars) who are unaware of the recent developments in stylistics, and indeed linguistics, that an enhanced pragmatics (e.g. Sperber and Wilson 1995) has made possible. Such lack of knowledge can lead to fears that a stylistically-based translation studies is narrow and focuses on the text to the exclusion of issues of context, creativity and interpretation. Given such possible fears, the development of cognitive poetics seems particularly useful for the stylistics of translation because of its dual concern with explaining the way that choices embodied in the style of a text can be reconstructed by readers and also with the effects of the text on its readers. In translation the situation is complicated because there are always two writers and two groups of readers to consider. Cognitive poetic studies of translation can thus account for the style of the source text as an embodiment of the source text author's choices, the style of the source text as it affects readers (including the translator), the style of the target text as an embodiment of the translator's choices, or the style of the target text as it affects the readers of the translation. Earlier studies of style and translation, such as Vinay and Darbelnet's, tended to speak of a 'spontaneously generated' (1995, p. 4) source text and to locate style in the languages compared, which embodied different world views, whether in literary or non-literary texts. A clear distinction is made between a writer and a translator; the translator is advised not to 'stray from literalness' too much (1995, pp. 288–289). The translator is clearly not assumed to have an interpretative or creative role. However, views based on cognitive poetics (such as Boase-Beier 2006) are concerned much more than earlier studies with what goes beyond the most obvious textual meaning: with connotations, suggestions, ambiguities and gaps in the text. Cognitive poetics, with its concern with what such features suggest about attitude, world view, or ideology, can give a much more nuanced view of stylistic choice and effect, and thus explain changes between source and target text as a result of different choices made by source author and translator.

Cognitive poetic views of translation are also concerned with the differing cognitive contexts of original and target readers, who may be separated not only by language but also by geography and history, resulting in large discrepancies in their background knowledge. Consider for example the English readers of Nobel prize-winning German-Romanian writer Herta Müller. They are extremely unlikely to understand the extent to which the author's irony and use of free indirect thought relates to the inherent repressiveness of German communities in Romania, and are more likely to relate such stylistic features (where the translation recreates them) only to what is known in England about the communist regime there. Unless a translator takes account of the different cognitive context of the new readers, the style of the target text can seem merely odd, in that it is divorced from other aspects of the text.

The fact that recent cognitive poetic analyses of translation are concerned to explain such differences between the author's and the translator's background or that of readers of the original and the translation is not only a result of developments in stylistics to include a wider view of context; it results also from an increased sense, within translation studies, of the writerly activity of the translator. If Vinay and Darbelnet's view, in 1958, was that the translator should not pretend to be a writer, recent scholars working in a variety of traditions (e.g. Venuti 2008, Boase-Beier 2011b) assume that the translator is by definition a writer, and that translation is a creative act. This means that differences between source and target text, once seen as translation 'losses', or, more neutrally, as 'shifts' (Toury 1995, p. 11) have recently come to be viewed much more as conscious choices for reasons of stylistic coherence or stylistic effect. Thus stylistic studies of the target text are now more likely to focus on the voice of the translator, and to what extent the translator is distinguishable from the narrator or characters in the text, as translated texts have come to be treated as texts in their own right and not just as incomplete substitutes for originals.

Understanding translation through stylistics

Since the beginning of this century there has been a renewed interest among translation scholars in the study of style. In part, this has to do with the development of university courses, especially at postgraduate level (such as those at the University of East Anglia (UEA) in Norwich and the University of Leicester, both in the UK) which consider literary translation as something which goes far beyond linguistic difference in a narrow sense.

In part the rise of such studies can also be linked with the increased broadening and contextualisation of stylistics, which allows for consideration of background knowledge and effect. Recent studies that focus on how the style of a text has been translated can be roughly divided into three types:

(i)   Studies of the translation of particular stylistic features, such as ambiguity (Boase-Beier 2004) or transitivity (Marco 2004);

(ii) Studies that compare examples of texts or passages with their originals to discover what stylistic changes result from translation (e.g. Malmkjaer 2004, Boase-Beier 2011a); and

(iii) Studies that undertake stylistic analyses of different translations of the same text, in order to explain their different effects (e.g. Millán-Varela 2004, Jones 2011, pp. 110–172).

Studies of the first type use a stylistics framework to describe what is meant by the feature in question. For example, in order to understand how one of the most common stylistic features of poetry, ambiguity, has been translated, we must first understand exactly what it is. Thus a stylistic study of the use of 'wenn' (if/when) in German Holocaust poetry enables an examination of the differences that arise in an English translation, where no correspondingly ambiguous lexical item is possible (cf. Boase-Beier 2010b). Such differences may involve a change from the uncertainty of 'if and when' in German to the certain future suggested by 'when' in English, or they may involve a loss of poetic rhythm when a translator feels obliged to spell out 'wenn' in its English translation as 'if and when' (Boland 2004, p. 23).

Most studies focusing on the translation of style are of the second type, comparing passages in original and translation. These were of particular importance to a group of Tel Aviv and Leuven scholars including Toury, Even-Zohar and Lambert, who argued for a view of literature in which the translated text has a place in the literary 'polysystem'; the 1981 issue of *Poetics Today*, mentioned above, includes their work. The focus here is less on what can be translated than on reconstructing the reasons behind particular ways of translating, a shift in focus which requires stylistics (though it is usually not called this) in order to analyse textual detail. Many such studies, for example Toury's examination of Shlonsky's (1946) translation of Hamlet's 'To be or not to be' monologue (Toury 1995, Chapter 10) go into great detail in discussing the minute requirements of 'stylistic acceptability' in the target text. Toury is concerned with the adaptation of Shakespeare's metrical scheme to Hebrew, and the resulting Hebrew text, when minutely compared with the original, is seen to be subject to the stylistic expectations of the target-language literature, even to the extent of becoming independent of its connection to Shakespeare's stylistic usages.

Many later studies have compared source text and target text, though rarely with such emphasis on target-text norms. For example, Boase-Beier (2013) considers the effects of the loss of metaphor in the English version *The Passport*, a translation by Martin Chalmers (2009) of a novel by Herta Müller. A miller, seeking to leave the country, observes a nightwatchman's dog, and the miller's thoughts are recorded in the original (narrated in the present) in free indirect mode as 'Seine weißen Zähne sind ein Biß' (Müller 2009, p. 7), literally 'his white teeth are a bite'. This is a particularly odd metaphor because it compares an object (teeth) with an action (bite), suggesting a threat. The translation 'its white teeth set wide' (Chalmers 2009, p. 8) not only fails to suggest a threat by losing the metaphor, but with its lack of a verb it is not free indirect thought, merely narrative description. In a novel set in totalitarian Romania, reading thoughts appears to be of particular significance, and thus the stylistic deployment of free indirect thought can be seen to echo the thought-reading everyone fears. The consequences of changing both the metaphor and the free indirect thought are thus to make the English version much less threatening.

The 1991 study by Gutt (2000) mentioned above used relevance theory as its basis to undertake several comparative close readings of the second type, with a view to drawing conclusions about the 'mental faculties' concerned (2000, p. 206).

Taking style to be a direct result of a writer's choices, Gutt argues that relevance theory can explain the differences between these choices and those made by the translator. For Gutt, stylistic features in translation should thus not be seen as important for their intrinsic value, but for the fact that they are 'communicative clues' which guide the audience to the interpretation intended by the communicator (2000, p. 134), who, in the case of translation, is not the original writer but the translator.

Gutt has sometimes been interpreted as suggesting that there is a specific 'message' to be found by following stylistic clues that might have to be different in the target text in order to provide similar guidance to the target reader, a view that would be at odds with the open-ended meaning assumed by both modern literary criticism and stylistics. However, he states clearly that poetic effects depend upon the freedom of the audience to 'consider a wide range of implicatures ... which taken together create an "impression" resulting from the style of the text' (2000, p. 164).

The third type of stylistic translation study, in which several translations of the same source text are compared, can only be undertaken in cases where multiple translations of a text into the same language exist. This is often the case for well-known poets such as Baudelaire or Rilke translated into English, or novelists such as Joyce translated into other languages (see

Millán-Varela 2004). As an example of this sort of study one might compare translations by Michael Hamburger (2007) and John Felstiner (2001) of Celan's poem 'Stumme Herbstgerüche'. The second and third lines read: 'Die / Sternblume, ungeknickt, ging', literally 'The / star-flower, un-bent, went'. Hamburger translates this as 'The / marguerite, unbroken, passed' while Felstiner has 'The / aster, unbent, passed'. There are many observations that can be made about these different translations. 'Sternblume' recalls the stars Jews were made to wear, whereas 'marguerite' recalls Goethe's heroine Margareta, who is mentioned in other poems by Celan. 'Aster' is closer to 'Sternblume' because it actually comes from the Greek word for star, and usually 'Sternblume' refers to a species of aster. However, the aster in English is unlikely to carry connotations of stars for most readers, in spite of its etymology. Of course, such studies are usually carried out upon longer passages or whole texts; conclusions can be drawn about the translator's intentions, the translator's interpretation of the original author's intentions, the reception of the translation, and so on.

Some studies of this type (such as Jones 2011, pp. 110–172) use the translator's own work to provide alternative versions. In keeping with the generally non-evaluative tenor of most modern stylistics, such studies generally avoid saying that the writer's own version is an improvement on the others, and instead simply explain what the differences are, what choices they result from, and what different effects they have.

Several studies of all three types have pointed to the need for translations to conform to the stylistic expectations of the target culture's literary system. Theorists like Venuti argue that the danger in this is that there can be an expectation of 'invisibility' (2008). Against this he advocates that texts should be stylistically and culturally 'foreignised', that is, marked as translations, either by closeness to the original or by other means of undermining expectations of fluency in the target literary language. Whether or not translators feel free to foreignise will partly depend upon publishers' wishes and partly on the type of work. An audience buying a popular novel is less likely to be tolerant of a foreignised style than is the audience of a bilingual poetry collection such as Hamburger's Celan (2007), where the facing-page presentation encourages the reader to read the English version as a translation.

However, it is also possible to understand the style of a translated text not merely as the result of market forces or text-type, nor of an ideologically-based strategy of foreignisation or domestication, but at least in part as exhibiting characteristics peculiar to a particular translator. Michael Hamburger's Celan translations, for example, exhibit the asyndetic co-ordination that is so typical of both his original poetry and his other translations (see Boase-Beier 2011b, pp. 63–65), and that can thus be seen as a marker of Hamburger's personal style.

Understanding style through translation

It is inevitable that the interaction of stylistics and translation studies will be more heavily weighted towards the integration of the former into the latter: anyone who studies translation will at least potentially be able to do stylistics, but you need at least two languages to be able to investigate the effects of translation upon stylistics. Moreover, a superficial knowledge will often not be enough: you need to have in both languages the fine detailed understanding of how a text works that makes stylistics possible. However, while most of the examples looked at up to now illustrate how stylistics might help us to understand what happens when we translate, there are a number of studies that ask a different question: how can translation help understand the style of the original? This is a question which studies based on the target-orientated models of Toury (e.g. 1995) or its forerunners in the 1981 *Poetics Today* issue did not ask, being concerned instead to understand the target text in its own cultural and linguistic situation, whereby its relation to its source text is reconstructed from the translation itself, just as is the process which produced it (1995, p. 35). However, a few of these early target-orientated views (notably that of Lefevère 1981) suggest a link between translation and textual analysis which was later to become important in translation studies.

For Lefevère (1981, p. 49) it was the translator, rather than the translation scholar, who performed an act which could be seen as a 'scientific endeavour in the field of literary studies'. However, Parks' 1998 book (Parks 2007) showed how analysis performed by the translation critic could help in understanding the original. His method was to compare passages of novels by writers such as Lawrence, Joyce or Woolf with their Italian translations, in order to give 'new insights into the English original' (2007, unnumbered page). These insights are often quite detailed and allow Parks to identify characteristics of a specific author, by analysing passages where the target text deviates significantly from the source text. Thus he shows that the Italian translation of *Women in Love* weakens the reader's sense of disorientation, and this allows him to argue that a sense of disorientation is a significant effect arising from Lawrence's style. His descriptions are written largely from the point of view of a particularly sensitive literary critic; although their focus is on style, they do not use the methods or vocabulary of stylistics. However, they provided an important starting-point for later studies from a similar perspective.

Especially when fuller stylistic analyses of source text and translation are undertaken, it is possible to develop Parks' notion that noticeable shifts between source and target illuminate the style of the original author in interesting ways. This is often because such points of divergence between target and source represent what Riffaterre (1959) called 'convergences', or points at which a large number of stylistic features come together in the source text; they are consequently difficult to translate. The discussion of several English poems alongside their German translations (Boase-Beier 2011b, pp. 139–142) demonstrates how such comparison can shed light on the original. Consider the ambiguity of the pronoun 'it' in the poem 'Agnus Dei' by R. S. Thomas. This may not be particularly noticeable in the original: an initial interpretation of 'On what altar does one sacrifice an idea? / It gave its life / for the world?' might simply assume that 'it' refers to 'an idea'. However, the German translation has 'Es gab sein Leben / für die Welt?', and because in German 'it' varies according to gender, 'es' can only refer to the earlier noun phrase 'the lamb', which appears in the first line (and title) of the poem. On comparing the German translation with its original, it becomes clear that the original poem contains an ambiguity – did the lamb or the idea give its life for the world? – not reproduced in the German. This realisation in turn leads one to speculate on the reason for the ambiguity in Thomas' poem, and to consider whether the first two lines 'No longer the lamb / but the idea of it' are expressing what Thomas regards as a fundamental ambiguity in his faith: how to reconcile the physical and the spiritual. A comparison like this illustrates what Benjamin (1992, pp. 72–73), in an influential essay first published in 1923, had meant by saying translation signals the 'afterlife' of a text within and beyond a particular culture. For Benjamin a text's afterlife depended upon a quality of 'translatability' inherent in the text itself, irrespective of its actual translations. What comparisons such as this suggest is that this quality depends upon a particular stylistic complexity, which lends the text the ability to be interpreted in a multitude of different ways.

Theory and practice

Up to now I have been treating stylistics and translation studies as two academic disciplines which are mutually beneficial. However, this is not the full picture. Translation studies is not only the study of how we read translated texts, or of how we understand the translation process, or of how a translator might read the source text. Implicit in translation studies is an act of creative writing: almost all translation scholars are also themselves translators. Those working in the area of stylistics and translation are therefore always obliged to consider the links between theory and practice. In fact it has been argued that a 'stylistically-aware' (Boase-Beier 2006, p. 113) reading of the source text can lead to better translation. While the trend in translation studies, as described above, has since the 1980s been towards examining how translation has been done rather than evaluating it, many scholars would consider that stylistics also has an important role to play as a tool to aid translation. Toury, in formulating his 'Descriptive Translation Studies', is careful to argue that it is not the job of the theorist to 'effect changes in the world of our experience' (1995, p. 17), a view that accords well with contemporary stylistics. However, one of the ways in which the place of stylistics in pedagogy is understood is that in learning more about how we read, we can become more sensitive as readers (cf. Carter 2010, p. 119).

A stylistically-aware reading of the source text is one which takes account of the possibilities of its translation. As an example, consider two stanzas from a poem by Paul Celan (Hamburger 2007, p. 124):

Heimkehr

Schneefall,	dichter	und	dichter,			
snow-fall	thicker	and	thicker			
taubenfarben,	wie	gestern,				
dove-coloured	like	yesterday				
Schneefall,	als	schliefst	du	auch	jetzt	noch.
snow-fall	as	slept(subj)	you	also	now	still

Weithin	gelagertes	Weiß.	
far-to	layered	white	
Drüberhin,	endlos,		
over-to	endless		
die	Schlittenspur	des	Verlorenen.
the	sledge-trace	of-the	lost

As in all Celan's poems, there is a great deal of repetition of sound ('Schnee-', 'schliefst', 'Schlittenspur'), as well as ambiguity ('dichter' means both 'thicker' and 'poet', and 'taub(e)' means both 'dove' and 'deaf'), and so the poem demands careful reading. There is evidence that bilingual readers (as translators always are) and especially those reading with the specific intention of translation, read differently from monolingual readers (see Boase-Beier 2006, pp. 21–24); reading a literary text for translation therefore involves both reading it in the understanding that it is literary (and thus demands the reader's engagement) and with an awareness of how one's target language might render the text. That is, one reads it both as a text in German and as a potential English text, and one is aware of the sort of stylistic differences documented by Toury (1995), or Parks (2007). Of course, the two meanings of 'dichter' or 'taub(e)' will be available to a monolingual German reader, but the fact that there are no similar ambiguities in English will make them doubly striking to the reader who aims to translate. A similar process to those described by Toury and Parks will thus happen during the preparation for translation as the style of an imagined target text ('thicker', 'dove-coloured') compared with the original ('dichter', 'taubenfarben') will render the style of the source text more visible. Its ambiguities will be highlighted, its repetition made more noticeable, its connotations ('Lager', the noun from which 'gelagert' derives, is a camp) more obvious.

A stylistically-aware reading for translation cannot happen if the translator subscribes to a view of translation as the simple transference of meaning. As an illustration one might consider a poem by Ingeborg Bachmann and its translation by Eavan Boland (2004). A comparative stylistic analysis of the two poems (see Boase-Beier 2010a) sheds light on the importance of iconicity in Bachmann's first line: 'Aus der leichenwarmen Vorhalle des Himmels tritt die Sonne' (literally 'Out of the corpse-warm entrance-hall to the heavens steps the sun'). Boland's translation splits the line into two: 'Out steps the sun / out of the corpse-warmed entrance hall to the sky' (Boland 2004, pp. 94–95). The difference shows clearly how the original poem, in the awkward rhythm of this first line, echoes the movement of the sun emerging uncertainly. Though target-orientated studies such as that by Toury (1995) suggest there is no reason why the target text should replicate such stylistic features, for the relationship between target and source texts is a non-evaluative *a posteriori* one, it could be argued that a lack of stylistic awareness has led, in Boland's case, to a simplified image of the relationship between translation and source. Her view that translations should be 'windows' on to the source text and 'as faithful as possible' (2004, p. 11) ignores the cognitive element of style and assumes that stylistic faithfulness is the same as linguistic faithfulness. In fact, Boland's translations are inevitably both linguistically and stylistically different from the originals, as the above example illustrates. However, if a translator assumes that style is not merely a set of formal features but a set of textual elements which represent the attitude or state of mind of the reconstructed figure of the author, narrator or character, then she can read the source text through the eyes of the stylistician, and make informed decisions about both the sort of stylistic choices behind it and the stylistic choices available to a recreation of the text in the target language.

Recommendations for practice

You do not need to be absolutely competent in two or more languages in order to see how translation and stylistics interact. The following analyses can be done with differing degrees of competence. Start by finding a bilingual text where the target language is your native language or the one in which you feel most at home. There are many translated poems and prose texts on the internet, and most published books of translated poetry are produced bilingually. You can use the same text for each exercise or find different ones (perhaps different passages or poems from a longer work).

1.   Start with a translated text (the target text). Mark everything you consider to be stylistically interesting or foregrounded, such as repetition, ambiguity, iconicity, syntactic deviations, and so on. There are several examples earlier in this chapter and throughout the book, if you are unsure. Now mark the corresponding passages in the original (source) text, and compare the marked passages in the two texts. What has changed, and why? Do these changes make the target text less stylistically interesting, or more so? Would you translate differently, and, if so, why? If your language skills are not good enough for such detailed comparison, start by marking passages in the target text, as above. Do they sound translated? What does 'sound translated' mean? Adjust their style so they no longer sound translated. What has the text now lost in stylistic terms?

2. Again, start with a translated text. Mark stylistically salient or unusual elements, then mark them in the source text and compare the differences, as in exercise 1. Now consider what these differences tell you about the source text. What has the translator left untranslated? Can you work out the significance of these particular elements for the source text? Using these elements as a starting point, do a stylistic analysis of the source text. Has the comparison with the translation told you things about the style of the source text you would not otherwise have seen? If you are not confident in analysing the source text, start with the target text again, focusing on repetition. Mark instances of repeated words and phrases, repeated syntactic structures, or, if it is a poem, rhyme, alliteration, and other types of repetition. Can you see whether the source text exhibits the same patterns? Has the translation changed the rhyme scheme, or the distance between repeated elements? Does it matter? Should translation preserve repetition? If so, why? Think about the difference between preserving repetition *per se* and preserving it in the same places.

3. This time, start with the source text. Do a detailed stylistic analysis. Now translate the passage yourself, using the existing translation to help with comprehension where necessary. Translate with particular attention to your stylistic analysis of the text. What have you done differently compared to the existing translation? Does a prior stylistic analysis help you translate? Are there stylistic features the translator has missed? If your language skills aren't up to doing a stylistic analysis of the source text, try suggestion 4 instead.

4. You do not need a second language for this. Find a text that has two or more translations and compare the translations with one another. How do they differ stylistically? What do these differences suggest about the original text (and language)? Can the differences be explained because the texts have been translated at different times, or by translators of different genders? How do the translations differ in terms of likely effects on the reader? In what sense do the different translations represent the same text?

Future directions

Recent developments in the areas where translation studies and stylistics interact have to some extent, not surprisingly, followed developments in each of the separate disciplines. Many come from within stylistics, following the way it changes as views of language and literature change and develop. If Jakobson, in the middle years of last century, was working with a code-view of language and translation, and a broadly structuralist view of literature, today's and tomorrow's translational stylistics is likely to be largely cognitive, if only because it has followed the movement from text to context to mind that all stylistics (whether calling itself 'cognitive' or not) has followed.

One way in which this development has specifically affected translation research is in the area of what Jones (2011, p. 13) calls a 'family of approaches ... [which] ... stresses ... the social context of action'. While many of these approaches were formulated with neither translation nor stylistics in mind, Jones for the first time brings together what are often called 'cognitive processing' models of translation (*ibid.*), involving translators recording what they are thinking at each stage of the translation task, with the broad field of cognitive poetics, in order to understand the various factors – social, political, ideological, poetic, linguistic – which result in the translation of poetic texts. This is a very good example of the way insights

403

from cognitive poetics can be used to enhance descriptions of what translators do with the style of a text.

Further developments in the interaction of cognitive poetics and translation could involve new ways of looking at translation itself. As St André (2010, pp. 1–16) explains, previous ways ranged from metaphors of bridges, ships and cross-dressing to various attempts to describe it without metaphor using taxonomies such as that of Vinay and Darbelnet (1995) or diagrams such as that given by Nord (1997, p. 83). St André notes a tension in studies of translation metaphors between views that see metaphor as potentially limiting and those that stress its ability to lead to new ways of thinking. Yet in fact metaphors have the potential for both effects. Metaphors of translation have sometimes been limiting (as in the 'window' metaphor given in the previous section) and have had a negative impact on practice. However, they can also lead to new ways of explaining translation. One such possibility comes from blending theory: the metaphor of a translation as a conceptual blend. Assuming blends to be the result of cognitive processes which bring together elements of separate cognitive domains into a blended domain, it is possible to use this concept as a metaphor for a translated text, thus providing a cognitive poetic model for the many earlier views of translations as hybrids, or as texts that would have been produced by a hypothetical author-figure who could actually write in the target language. Some possible consequences of such a view are given in Boase-Beier (2011b, pp. 67–72), but this is an area still to be explored.

The notion of a conceptual blend can also be used to explain the differences between an original and a translated text. It could be argued that many texts arising from traumatic situations, such as Holocaust poetry, work by suggesting failed blends between what was and what might have been: the familiar 'dislocation' or 'fragmentation' of such work. Translation, then, in order to allow similar effects on the target reader, would need both to suggest such possible blends and to show them to be impossible. See Boase-Beier (2011a) for an example.

Recent developments in narratology, for some thirty years an important area of stylistics (cf. Leech and Short 2007, p. 284) are beginning to be used in the study of translation, especially to examine changes to narrative structure. Narratological devices such as transitivity (see Marco 2004) or shifts in point of view, discussed by Bosseaux (2007), are less easy to detect in a text by the translator unfamiliar with stylistics than are features such as rhyme or other repetitive patterns. The likelihood of unwanted shifts during the process of translation is thus greater. If we consider the case of Romanian-German novelist Herta Müller, mentioned above, it would appear that a further issue is the difference between free indirect thought and free indirect speech (see Leech and Short 2007, p. 270). It is always possible to report a speech, but it is not possible to report thought unless one has the power to read minds or to invent them (like the novelist does). Thus, to do what the novelist does is to act out a metaphor for the behaviour of the repressive regime under which Müller was writing. Shifts in speech and thought representation that occur during translation will thus change not only the style of the text but also potentially its politics. Narratology and translation is still a fairly new area of research but it is developing rapidly.

What unwanted shifts in translation show is the need for stylistics to be an important component of both translation research and the teaching of translation practice. In fact the use of stylistics in translation pedagogy is, with a few exceptions, not yet well-established. It is to be hoped that more work will appear in this area.

Other recent developments come from within translation studies rather than stylistics. Translation theorists such as Tymoczko (2006) have started to argue for a broader definition of translation and a broader understanding of translation theory, and this argument has had the effect of encouraging researchers in translation studies to be less narrow, less concerned with simple definitions and with Western approaches. There are two ways in which translation and its description could be broadened further with respect to stylistics. The first is by taking views from other disciplines or areas and using insights from them in translation. Thus the use of stylistics to understand translation, as outlined above, could be seen as part of a general trend towards adopting a multidisciplinary model, and one which is likely to persist and grow in importance. Stylistics, in this model, is one of a number of approaches, including actor-network theory (as used by Jones 2011) or relevance theory (Gutt 2000), which, taken together, will lead to a greater understanding of translation.

The second way is by considering other cultures and their views of the relationship between stylistics and translation. This is a project only just beginning to be undertaken in the English-speaking world. However, it seems especially important that the international and global concerns inherent in translation, which are used by writers such as Tymoczko as the basis for an internationalising of translation theory, should be extended to all its various aspects. It makes little sense to call for an understanding in the West of Chinese or Arabic translation theory while not wanting to know about Chinese or Arabic stylistics. It is to be hoped that future studies of stylistics and translation will increasingly consider other views of both areas.

Finally, the reading of translation *as* translation is a growing area of concern. It is a concern that arose from studies such as Venuti's call in 1995 (see Venuti 2008) to resist the invisibility of translation. Now that this concern is almost universally understood (if not always accepted, especially in the publishing world), attention has started to turn more and more to a view of translation as a particular type of writing with its own characteristics. Gutt (2000, p. 211) argued that a translated text was merely functionally different from a non-translated text. However, it could equally well be argued that it demands a more complex involvement of the reader, or even that it is stylistically different; some studies suggest that at least in other languages this is the case. For example, Yoshihiro (2005) shows that in Japanese the need to domesticate and erase traces of the process of translation has historically not been felt to the same degree, and so translated texts often incorporate elements of the original. New studies based on English texts are needed which go beyond discussion of a negatively-perceived 'translationese' to examine whether there are in fact any common stylistic properties of translated texts which mark them out as belonging to a particular type of literature.

Related topics

Blending, cognitive poetics, creative writing and stylistics, formalist stylistics, narratology, pedagogical stylistics, relevance theory.

Further reading

Boase-Beier, J., 2006. *Stylistic approaches to translation*. Manchester: St Jerome Publishing.

This book is a study of the role of style and stylistics in translation theory. It looks at the way style has been written about by translation theorists and discusses the importance of stylistic awareness for translators and translation scholars.

Boase-Beier, J., 2011. Translating Celan's poetics of silence. *Target*, 23 (2), 165–177.

This article examines a poem by German-Romanian poet Paul Celan from the perspective of stylistics. It shows how conceptual blending helps the translator to understand the poem and therefore to decide how best to translate it.

Boase-Beier, J., 2011. *A critical introduction to translation studies*. London: Continuum.

This is an introductory work that uses a cognitive poetics basis to emphasise the importance of style and stylistics both for the practising translator and for anyone studying translation or writing about translated texts.

Bosseaux, C., 2007. *How does it feel? Point of view in translation*. Amsterdam: Rodopi.

This book deals specifically with narratives and the changes in narrative structure that come about when texts are translated. It shows very clearly how point of view can be quite different in the translated text.

Malmkjaer, K., 2004. Translational stylistics: Dulcken's translations of Hans Christian Andersen. *Language and Literature*, 13 (1), 13–24.

This article suggests the need for a 'stylistics of translation' which analyses a translated text with specific reference to the source text, and the stylistic changes the translator has made. Other articles in this issue of the journal also address aspects of stylistics and translation.

Munday, J., 2012. *Introducing translation studies: Theories and applications*. 3rd edn. London: Routledge.

Though this book only mentions style and stylistics in passing, it is a very useful introduction to translation issues and the theories that describe them.

References

Attridge, D., 2004. *The singularity of literature*. London: Routledge.

Barnstone, W., 1993. *The poetics of translation: History, theory, practice*. New Haven and London: Yale University Press.

Benjamin, W. 1992. The task of the translator.. H. Zohn, trans. *In:* J. Biguenet and R. Schulte, eds. *Theories of translation: An anthology of essays from Dryden to Derrida*. Chicago: University of Chicago Press, 71–82.

Boase-Beier, J., 2004. Knowing and not knowing: Style, intention and the translation of a holocaust poem. *Language and Literature*, 13 (1), 25–35.

Boase-Beier, J., 2006. *Stylistic approaches to translation*. Manchester: St Jerome Publishing.

Boase-Beier, J., 2010a. Who needs theory? *In:* A. Fawcett, K. Guadarrama and R. Hyde Parker, eds. *Theory and practice in dialogue*. London: Continuum, 71–82.

Boase-Beier, J., 2010b. Translation and timelessness. *Journal of Literary Semantics*, 38 (2), 101–114.

Boase-Beier, J., 2011a. Translating Celan's poetics of silence. *Target*, 23 (2), 165–177.

Boase-Beier, J., 2011b. *A critical introduction to translation studies*. London: Continuum.

Boase-Beier, J., 2013. Herta Müller in translation. *In:* B. Haines and L. Marven, eds. *Herta Müller*. Oxford: Oxford University Press, 190–203.

Boland, E., trans., 2004. *After every war: Twentieth-century women poets*. Princeton: Princeton University Press.

Bosseaux, C., 2007. *How does it feel? Point of view in translation*. Amsterdam: Rodopi.

Carter, R., 2010. Issues in pedagogical stylistics: A coda. *Language and Literature*, 19 (1), 115–122.

Chalmers, M., trans., 2009. *Herta Müller: The passport*. London: Serpent's Tail.

d'Haen, T., ed., 1986. *Linguistics and the study of literature*. Amsterdam: Rodopi.

Felstiner, J., trans., 2001. *Selected poems and prose of Paul Celan*. New York: Norton.

Gutt, E.-A., 2000. *Translation and relevance*. 2nd edn. Manchester: St. Jerome Publishing.

Hamburger, M., trans., 2007. *Poems of Paul Celan*, London: Anvil.

Hatim, B. and Munday, J., 2004. *Translation: An advanced resource book*. London and New York: Routledge.

Holmes, J., 2005 *Translated! Papers on literary translation and translation studies*. 2nd edn. Amsterdam: Rodopi.

Jakobson, R., 1960. Closing statement: Linguistics and poetics. *In:* T. A, Sebeok ed. *Style in language*. Cambridge, MA: The MIT Press. Reprinted in D. Lodge and N. Wood, eds., 2008. *Modern criticism and theory: A reader*. 3rd edn., London: Pearson, 141–164.

Jones, F., 2011. *Poetry translating as expert action*. Amsterdam: John Benjamins.

Leech, G. and M. Short, [1981] 2007. *Style in fiction: A linguistic introduction to English fictional prose*. London: Pearson.

Lefevère, A., 1981. Programmatic second thoughts on 'literary' and 'translation' or 'where do we go from here'. *Poetics Today*, 2 (4), 39–50.

Marco, J., 2004. Translating style and styles of translating: Henry James and Edgar Allan Poe in Catalan. *Language and Literature*, 13 (1), 73–90.

Malmkjaer, K., 2004. Translational stylistics: Dulcken's translations of Hans Christian Andersen. *Language and Literature* 13, (1), 13–24.

Millán-Varela, C., 2004. Hearing voices: James Joyce, narrative voice and minority translation. *Language and Literature*, 13 (1), 37–54.

Müller, H., 2009. *Der Mensch ist ein großer Fasan auf der Welt*. Frankfurt am Main: Fischer.

Munday, J., 2012. *Introducing translation studies: Theories and applications*. 3rd edn. London: Routledge.

Nida, E., 1964. *Toward a science of translating*. Leiden: Brill.

Nord, C., 1997. *Translating as a purposeful activity: Functionalist approaches explained*. Manchester: St Jerome Publishing.

Parks, T., 2007. *Translating Style*. 2nd edn. Manchester: St Jerome Publishing.

Paterson, D., trans., 2006. *Rilke: Orpheus*. London: Faber and Faber.

Qvale, P., 1998. *From St Jerome to hypertext: Translation in theory and practice*. Manchester: St Jerome Publishing.

Reiss, K. and Vermeer, H. J., 1984. *Grundlegung einer allgemeinen Translationstheorie*. Tübingen: Niemeyer.

Riffaterre, M., 1959. Criteria for style analysis. *Word* 15, 154–174.

Riffaterre, M., 1992. Transposing presuppositions on the semiotics of literary translation. *In:* R. Schulte and J. Biguenet, eds. *Theories of translation*. Chicago: University of Chicago Press, 204–217.

Shlonsky, A. T. F., 1946. *Hamlet, Prince of Denmark*. Tel Aviv: Habimah Theatre Productions.

Sperber, D. and Wilson, D., 1995. *Relevance: Communication and cognition*. Oxford: Blackwell.

St. André, J., ed., 2010. *Thinking through translation with metaphors*. Manchester: St Jerome Publishing.

Stockwell, P., 2002. *Cognitive poetics: An introduction*. London: Routledge.

Toury, G., 1995. *Descriptive translation studies and beyond*. Amsterdam and Philadelphia: John Benjamins.

Tymoczko, M., 2006. *Enlarging translation, empowering translators*. Manchester: St Jerome Publishing.

Venuti, L., 2008. *The translator's invisibility: A history of translation*. 2nd edn. London: Routledge.

Vinay, J.-P. and Darbelnet, J., 1958. Stylistique compare du français et du l'anglais. J. Sager, and M.-J. Hamel, trans., 1995. *Comparative studies of French and English: A methodology for translation*. Amsterdam and Philadelphia: John Benjamins.

Wales, K., 2001. *A dictionary of stylistics*. 2nd edn. London: Longman.

Yoshihiro, O., 2005. Amalgamation of literariness: Translations as a means of introducing European literary techniques to modern Japan. *In:* E. Hung and J. Wakabayashi, eds. *Asian translation traditions*. Manchester: St Jerome Publishing, 135–154.

25

Critical stylistics

Lesley Jeffries

Introduction

Critical stylistics developed in reaction to the rise of critical discourse analysis as an increasingly influential approach to ideology in language. While the origins of critical discourse analysis are close to stylistics, with Roger Fowler an influential stylistician as well as one of the founders of critical discourse analysis, the two have grown increasingly distant from each other in the intervening decades. As Jeffries and McIntyre (2010, p. 15) state, 'the unavoidable basis of all stylistics remains the text itself'. My intention in developing a strand of stylistics which was concerned with ideology was to keep that principle intact while demonstrating that stylistic analysis was as useful and insightful when the data was non-fiction as when it was literary in nature. Indeed, the development of a specifically ideological or 'critical' stylistics has led me to the conclusion that the tools of analysis that we need to perform all kinds of text analysis are the same. In other words, texts make meaning in fundamentally the same way, whether they are poems, novels, newspapers or political manifestoes. This chapter, then, will introduce a framework which places stylistic analysis at the heart of the endeavour to see the power in language. The tools of analysis can be used for non-critical (i.e. literary or aesthetic) stylistics too, but here I will focus mainly on the ideological aspects of the linguistic features to be found in texts.

Critical discourse analysis

Before I begin to introduce the framework of critical stylistics, I would like to acknowledge a debt to critical discourse analysis as well as distinguishing my approach from theirs. The early stirrings of what is now widely called critical discourse analysis, but which has also been called critical linguistics in the past, influenced my thoughts about the uses and functions of stylistic analysis. However, the fact that the main protagonists of critical discourse analysis largely adhere to a particular form of Marxist/socialist politics made me wonder whether I wished to also abandon some of linguistics' hard-won scientific credibility by giving up on all attempts at objectivity, rigour and replicability. I was not – and am not – convinced that the gains achieved by abandoning the aim of rationality and scientific methods for a more discursive and open-ended approach were worthwhile. Indeed, the inherent lack of clarity that arises once all individual variation (in producer, recipient and analyst) are accounted for makes the attempt seem to squander the undeniable insights of a century of linguistic research and scholarship.

Textual construction of meaning

At the heart of critical stylistics is the idea that there is a level of meaning which sits somewhere between the systematic (coded) meaning of what Saussure called the '*langue*' and the contextual and relatively variable meaning of language in use, which Saussure called '*parole*'. At this level, the text (or utterance) will use the resources of the language to present a particular view of the world – or in the case of literature, of a fictional world. At this level, the analyst needs to work out what the text is doing – how it is presenting the text world. The main tools of analysis of critical stylistics are known as 'textual-conceptual functions'. This rather clumsy description is intended to capture the fact that texts can create specific types of meaning in a number of different ways. As in the underlying system, in the textual production of meaning there is no single relationship between a linguistic form and its function (or meaning). The textual-conceptual functions will be introduced below as a vital part of the stylistic approach to critical language study. The idea of textual-conceptual functions in general is that they try to capture what a text is doing conceptually in presenting the world (or a fictional world in the case of literature) in a particular way. In doing so, they also explain how the resources of the linguistic system are being used to produce this conceptual meaning – this is the textual part of the process and is what defines this approach as essentially stylistic. Thus, for example, linguistic features of texts 'name' items in the text world in certain ways or 'hypothesise' about the world being presented, and they do so through a variety of naming mechanisms in the first case (including, for example, the use of nominalisation) and through a variety of modal and other structures in the second case.

Ideational metafunction

The nature of the textual meaning which is proposed by critical stylistics is that it draws on all the fundamental structures and systems of the language (*langue*) and is subject to all the contextual influences and individual responses of the situation (*parole*) but that it is an identifiable level of meaning between these two which it is useful to explore in its own right. The best way to set this textual meaning in context is to base it in Halliday's (1994) idea of the three metafunctions of language (ideational, interpersonal and textual) as a general model of linguistic meaning. However, I want to take Halliday's notion of 'ideational' meaning out of the underlying system of the language and link it with the use of language in context (specifically co-text). The ideation, then, is activated when the language system is put to work. Some of the problems of critical (e.g. feminist) approaches to language are made less intractable by seeing that it is not the language itself that is producing, for example, sexist meanings; rather, it is the *use* of that language in texts that can do so. I am not the first to point this out, but critical stylistics is an attempt to put this particular notion of textual meaning at the centre of our theory of language.

Critical

Before I continue with the background to critical stylistics, I would like to add a few words on the question of what is meant by 'critical' in this context. I have only recently been made aware (by an anonymous reviewer) that the 'critical' in 'critical discourse analysis' is intended to denote a specifically socialist (and probably Marxist) view of the analysis of language. While I have a great deal of political sympathy with this outlook on life, I cannot conceive of a linguistic approach which takes a narrowly political view as axiomatic. It is simply not credible that the things we left-wing people might want to criticise in texts might not also be the same things that others would criticise in ours. Of course, the argument runs that it is the dominance of capitalist, right-wing views that means we need to critique the press and other privileged opinion-makers. This is absolutely my view too, but I do not see it as part of the textual level of meaning that concerns me here. Instead, I would offer critical stylistics as a method of finding the ideology in any text, whether or not you agree with it. The rest is personal choice.

Historical perspectives

Systemic functional linguistics (SFL)

The founding principles of much work in the 'critical' tradition are, in many cases, drawn from Halliday's work in functional linguistics and the wide-ranging developments of his insights within the tradition of systemic-functional linguistics (SFL). Halliday's work has taken the idea that language is a 'social semiotic' and made this the centre of his model of human communication. Underlying this concept is the notion that the function of language is more important or more central to language than anything formal or structural. For example, Halliday produced a model of meaning based on verb choice called transitivity, which has been taken up and used very widely by those who are concerned with how language actually works in the real world, as opposed to theoretical and descriptive linguists whose concern is mainly with the identifiable units and structures of languages, linked to meaning in many cases but not linked to use. The answers that Halliday and others in the SFL tradition have come up with to the question of how form-function pairings work in human language have been adopted widely in stylistics, and critical stylistics is no exception.

Critical discourse analysis

Critical linguistics, followed by critical discourse analysis, was partly a reaction to the scientific claims of linguistics in its modern phase of development, arising out of the frustration of those who wanted to make their research relevant to their political and social outlook. This is understandable, but it led to the assumption that since absolute objectivity, rigour and replicability were unattainable, they should not be pursued and instead the work should progress from a point of view of avowed Marxist ideology and socialist aims. I part company from critical discourse analysis at this point, despite sharing many of the political assessments of its practitioners and admiring some of its output. I do not agree that since absolute objectivity is unattainable, we should abandon its pursuit. Developing critical stylistics was the answer to feelings of frustration in the face of critical discourse analysis's deliberate lack of methodology or framework and its apparent abandonment of many of the achievements of linguistics in its scientific phase of development.

Critical stylistics

Where critical stylistics fits into the picture, then, is as an attempt to bring the text back into discussions of discourse meaning, while acknowledging that much of the discussion of context over the last twenty years has been productive and insightful. However, the notion that the language system at the centre of human communication is of little relevance to the meanings being conveyed has taken too strong a hold, and I propose the model which follows in the spirit of adding to, not replacing, the insights into contextual features of ideological meaning arising from critical discourse analysis.

Critical issues and topics

The place of textual meaning in a linguistic theory

The question of where textual meaning fits into our overall understanding of human language goes beyond the scope of this chapter, and yet it is of vital importance that stylisticians themselves understand and accept the centrality of text in linguistic theory more generally. Stylistics has long been seen as peripheral to the main business of linguistics – as just one of the many ways in which linguistics is 'applied' to real world issues, because of its historical link to literary analysis. However, it ought to be central to general linguistics, since it concerns the way that language works beyond the systematic operations of the fundamental units and structures. Once we go beyond text to include context of situation and background as well as language in context, then linguistics quite rightly becomes linked to other disciplines including sociology, history, cultural and literary studies, political science, psychology and so on. What stylistics does is to bridge the gap between the de-contextual and the fully contextual with a model explaining the presentation of ideas by texts. Once stylistics is extended beyond the interpretation of literary language, the central importance of its concerns is clearer.

If we see textual meaning as intermediate between *langue* and *parole*, we can draw a parallel for this kind of meaning with the locution-illocution-perlocution of speech act theory (Austin), which comes under what Halliday's model might see as the 'interpersonal' metafunction of language. For speech act theory, the basic systems and structures of language are 'locution' and are seen as underlying a producer's meaning (illocutionary force) which has an effect in the actual situation (perlocutionary effect). Whilst some utterances may not distinguish between locution and illocution in an obvious way, many demonstrate a difference between their superficial meaning ('What time is it?') and their illocutionary force (nagging = you're late again). Many analysts would question the extent to which the illocutionary force of Austin's model is intended to invoke conscious intention, but the three-way distinction is a useful one, whether or not intention is construed. In the case of ideational as opposed to interpersonal meaning, it is also useful to distinguish between the basic units and structures that are realised in a text (equivalent to locution in speech act theory) and the intended (or naturalised) meaning (equivalent to illocutionary force). A sentence such as 'Boris Johnson has no serious experience or track record of managing substantial budgets' is superficially nothing more than a statement of fact, but Nahajec (2012) demonstrates how the text projects the expectation of a Mayor of London that s/he should have such experience. This is more than implicature, whereby the very commenting on such a lack in the candidate could be construed as flouting the maxim of quantity. Nahajec's work shows that the negation itself produces a conceptualisation of the positive version of the proposition (i.e. that Boris Johnson does have serious experience or a track record of managing substantial budgets) and this mental image of the reverse of the sentence's proposition is held at the same time as the negative version, thereby producing the implicature that the candidate for Mayor of London (as he was then) is not what he ought to be. This demonstrates textual meaning in action, where the text itself produces expectations about the world (whether real or fictional) and the reader/recipient has a choice (though not always a completely free one) to accept or reject the expectations produced in this way. This latter part of the process, the recipient's response to the textual meaning, is equivalent to the perlocutionary effect in Austin's model of speech acts.

How textual meaning interfaces with producer/recipient meaning

I would like to avoid giving the impression that critical stylistics is returning to a model of textual meaning whereby the text has a single, inflexible and authoritative meaning which arises automatically from the words spoken or on the page. This is not the case at all with textual meaning of this kind, which is triggered by the text but interacts in complex ways with interpersonal and basic linguistic meaning, as well as the context of situation and all the background features which discourse analysis often focuses upon. The producer of textual meaning may or may not intend the ideational content that arises in a text. Some of it will be so naturalised as to be unnoticed, although other aspects of it will be semi-consciously or self-consciously embedded in the text. Similarly, the reader may respond consciously or not to the ideologies that underpin the ideational meaning of the text. This ideation is not always and only ideological in the tabloid sense of being suspicious and negatively valued. Much of the production of ideation in texts will be world-building (see text world theory) and could be the basis of literary stylistic interpretation (see Jeffries 2014) as well as a clue to ideological content.

The nature and number of textual-conceptual functions

Critical stylistics differs from critical discourse analysis also in having a framework to guide its practice which draws together insights from a number of models, but is unified at the broadest level of metafunctions. Thus, all of the textual-conceptual functions that are the basis of critical stylistic analysis are part of the ideational function of language in that they create a particular view of the world (or text world). The textual-conceptual functions are each described in a little more detail in the next section, but here I will try to explain their nature and the links they have to the basic linguistic units and structures of the langue.

The first thing to note about textual-conceptual functions is that they are, as the name suggests, a combination of textual features (triggers) and ideational function. Many of them have a prototypical form which always carries the conceptual effect, and a set of more or less peripheral forms which also carry the conceptual effect, although sometimes not consistently or not so obviously. The shading from prototype to periphery is sometimes so extensive that it is difficult to complete an enumeration of all of the ways in which that particular concept can be delivered textually. This can be illustrated by the function of 'Negating' where the prototypical forms *no* and *not* are surrounded by other relatively central forms such as the morphological negators (*un-, dis-, non-* etc.); grammatical items with strong negative semantic content (*never, nowhere*) and the slightly more peripheral lexical items with incidental semantic negativity (*lack, fail*). Even here it is difficult to trace all the negative lexical items, and not all negation is carried purely linguistically either, so that a shrug or a shake of the head can negate an ostensibly positive sentence.

The second general point to be made about textual-conceptual functions is that the list may not be complete and possibly not able to be complete. There is the potential for different languages and cultures to have a different (sub-)set of textual-conceptual functions to English, or to prioritise their use differently to English-speaking communities. It is also possible that there are a small number of additional functions that have not yet been identified or perhaps new ones may arise over time, though I doubt that they are fashionable categories which change frequently. There is work to be done on comparing the ways in which different languages create textual meaning of this kind. In the meantime, the textual-conceptual functions which follow can be seen as a provisionally complete list.

The textual-conceptual functions

This section will briefly introduce the textual-conceptual functions as they currently stand. Many of them will be familiar to people working in stylistics or linguistics more generally as they have been developed as part of other linguistic models. Here, I am re-contextualising them within an overall framework of textual meaning.

Naming and describing

The most obvious thing that texts do is to name – and describe – the animate, inanimate and abstract 'things' that the projected world of the text contains. While this function might seem rather banal, it goes well beyond the question of whether you choose to call a politically-motivated producer of violence a *terrorist* or a *freedom-fighter*. Of course, there are choices to be made between denotatively equivalent words and phrases which differ connotatively, often along formal to informal clines, such as the words for 'toilet' which include the formal and euphemistic *powder room* and slightly less formal *ladies* as well as the neutral *loo* and more taboo terms like *bog*. However, more interesting, usually, is the way in which noun phrases are put together and what is included within them. Thus, the adjectives preceding the head noun may be evaluative (e.g. *the important review of taxation*) although the recipient is not really in a position to question the applicability of this evaluation, embedded as it is in the noun phrase. Similarly, the postmodification of the head noun may also place some ideologically sensitive material in a prepositional phrase (e.g. *the TV presenter with a dubious background*) or relative clause (e.g. *the privatisation of the railways which was such a disaster*). The other interesting feature of naming is the use of nominalised verbs (e.g. *interruption* as opposed to *interrupt*) which reify processes and remove any sign of Agents or Actors so that attributing actions (e.g. *the degradation of family life*) becomes difficult on the evidence of the text.

Representing actions/events/states

The representation of processes, Halliday's 'transitivity' (1994), which is normally the preserve of the verbal element of the structure, has the power to make events, actions and states more or less connected to particular participants and create the impression of much (or little) activity; more talking than acting; a static scene with little going on; events beyond human intervention – or accidental actions. The choice of main verb in a clause can alter the potential perception of the process by recipients of the utterance/text. For example, the same occurrence (someone telephoning the police) can be described in a number of ways which emphasise different aspects of the process without changing the essential information:

> *John informed the police* (Material Action Intentional)
> *John spoke to the police* (Verbalisation)
> *John was a police informer.* (Relational Intensive)
> *John let the cat out of the bag to the police.* (Supervention)

Of course, some of the details have to change a little when different verbs are chosen, but the point is that text producers do have choices about how to tell their stories and these choices have (sometimes ideological) consequences.

Simpson (1993) is a good place to read about transitivity in relation to the presentation of the producer's (or narrator's) point-of-view. Simpson produces a clear and usable framework for the analysis of transitivity patterns in texts, though the labels he (and others) use are really idealised points of reference rather than categorisations. Thus, it is often the case that a verb's transitivity can be debated – particularly in context of use – and sometimes it is tempting to use two labels together. Thus, for example, we might want to comment on a sentence like *John informed the police* which I have labelled as an intentional material action above, but where the so-called 'action' is clearly carried out using language and is therefore also a verbalisation process, albeit one in which the actual words used are not reproduced.

Equating and contrasting

I first noticed the potential for texts to make non-conventional synonyms and opposites when I saw texts like the following in an election poster campaign run by the Conservative Party in the UK:

> Labour says he's black.
> Tories say he's British.

These sentences were placed below a photo of an Afro-Caribbean man in one case and an Asian man in another case. The parallel structures with conventional opposites (Labour/Tory) in the subject position set up an expectation in the reader that the two object complements (black/ British) will also be opposites. Of course, the right wing of the Tory (Conservative) Party would indeed see black and British as opposites, so they would be reassured by the implicit racist ideology of the text. At the same time, the superficial meaning of the text, that the Tories are 'colour blind' – and therefore not racist – is presumably designed to appeal to the more liberal potential voters who would be flattered by the suggestion that 'their' party is not racist, though Labour is. This textual-conceptual function was incorporated into the critical stylistic framework in Jeffries (2010a) following its development in Jeffries (2010b). The range of textual 'triggers' which can cause opposition to be created contextually is explored further in Davies (2012) and its ideological power can be seen in Davies (2010) and Jeffries (2010b).

Exemplifying and enumerating

The ubiquitous three-part list has long been known to symbolise completeness without being a 'real' list, and to be an important part of the rhetorical armoury for politicians (see Atkinson 1984). What is less often mentioned is the range of meaning that can be covered between the extreme case of an itemised list, which demonstrates how texts enumerate members of categories, and the other extreme, where items are explicitly used to exemplify a category without any claim to being comprehensive. Between these extremes there are many examples which are less easy to categorise as either enumerating or exemplifying, but which nevertheless demonstrate the text presenting a particular world view. Jeffries (2010a) explores the subtleties of exemplifying and enumerating in more detail, and Jeffries (2007) shows the potential ideological consequences of listing choices in relation to the textual construction of the female body in women's magazines.

Prioritising

The positioning of information in main or subordinate structures is a feature of textual meaning that sits clearly at the juncture of decontextual systematic language structure and its use in context. While the technicalities of subordination are accounted for by the conventional syntactic mechanisms, the resulting description of levels of subordination is enlightening when we consider which bits of information are backgrounded by being subordinate and which foregrounded by being in the main clause. For example, the following two sentences place a different emphasis on the same information by swapping round which part is subordinated:

> Though the Government is split down the middle, Ministers are not admitting there's a problem.

> Though Ministers are not admitting there's a problem, the Government is split down the middle.

There is a propositional difference between these sentences that means the first (subordinate) clause is presupposed to be true, whilst the main clause contains the proposition. However, the issue of prioritising is more than this issue of presupposition. It also tells the recipient what the values or opinions of the producer are. Thus, the first example above is more interested in the behaviour of Ministers and the second is more interested in the health of the coalition Government. Jeffries (2010a) explores prioritisation in more detail and any basic textbook on grammar will assist in identifying subordination.

Implying and assuming

The textual-conceptual functions of implying and assuming relate to what is technically known as implicature in pragmatics and presupposition in semantics respectively (see Chapters 8 and 22 in this volume). There is not space here to explore these types of textual meaning in detail, but a couple of examples will demonstrate that as with other textual-conceptual functions, these also sit between the decontextual and the fully contextual.

Presupposition is ubiquitous and is a useful shorthand way to make meaning more economically, but it also has the potential to be ideologically significant. Presupposition overlaps to some extent with naming because definite noun phrases tend to presuppose the existence of the referent (e.g. *the incompetent Home Secretary*) but there is also a long list (Levinson 1983) of triggers of logical presuppositions, including factive verbs which presuppose the truth of their complementary subordinate clauses (e.g. *The President regretted that he had made the situation worse*).

Implicature, belonging as it does to the domain of pragmatics, might be expected to 'belong' under the interpersonal metafunction, but its textual nature and the real world similarity between 'assuming' and 'implying' make it at least partly an ideational function. Like the other textual-conceptual functions in the critical stylistics framework, it produces a view of the world (or text world) which reflects the opinion of the producer (or narrator) and is therefore less interpersonal than, for example, a speech act, though it may be used to produce one. Though implicature was developed as part of a theory of interaction, there is scope, as Simpson (1993) noted, for it to be applied to the written language (or other one-way communication) as well, so that the Gricean maxims can be invoked when a politician, for example, says too much or too little on a topic and can be accused as a result of protesting too much – or covering up the truth. Implicature is one of the tools of analysis deriving from Grice's (1975) work on the co-operative principle and can also be read about in Levinson (1983) and is part of Simpson's (1993) model of point-of-view (see also Chapter 10 in this volume).

Negating

We saw earlier that negating has the effect of producing mental images of both the negated and the positive proposition. This means that negating can have a significant ideological effect if the producer of a text is attempting to influence the reader towards imagining the positive version (e.g. *The Prime Minister is not an incompetent fool out of touch with the electorate*). The more detailed the negated version, the more a positive version is likely to be imagined by the recipient. Nahajec's work (2009, 2012) demonstrates the power of negating in texts and shows that its occurrence is unlimited by text type or genre. She also demonstrates (2012) that negated meaning works at the textual level, walking a fine line between semantic and pragmatic meaning – or between the system and its use.

Hypothesising

The Hallidayan system of modality is often seen by followers of SFL as an interpersonal system, because it clearly presents the view of the producer (e.g. *No one should deny the importance of controlling government spending*). However, since all of the textual-conceptual functions in the critical stylistics model are also seen as promoting the world view of the producer, modality is clearly part of this textual production of meaning and fits perfectly well as an ideational phenomenon. Modality is a typical textual-conceptual function in having a clear prototypical form, the modal verb, while also having a large number of increasingly peripheral forms to the extent that some forms of modality are not even linguistic (e.g. a shrug). The ideological importance of modality is that it allows producers to suggest things that are not certain without being accused of over-stating them (e.g. *Climate change could be unfounded*). Simpson (1993) develops an excellent model of modality which serves the purpose of critical stylistics very well. (See also Chapters 3 and 10 in this volume.)

Presenting others' speech and thoughts

Another feature of meaning which clearly operates at the textual level is the quoting of others' speech and thoughts. While there has long been a recognition of the mechanics of indirect and direct quotation, Short (2012) was the first to point out in detail the subtle effects of a much wider range of possibilities from the general indication that speech (or writing) has occurred at one end (e.g. *They talked for hours*), through a number of more or less 'free' versions of the verbatim speech (e.g. *She was certain that he wouldn't have let her down like this*) to the other extreme of direct speech, where the claim of faithfulness is strongest (e.g. *She said 'I am certain that he wouldn't have let me down like this'*). The ideological potential for this textual-conceptual function, of course, is that words and thoughts can be implicitly attributed to people without the risk of being sued for libel, particularly if modality is also introduced (e.g. *He seemed to think that Europe was the problem and not the solution*). Semino and Short (2004) explore the textual presentation of others' words and thoughts in a range of text types, confirming that, as with other textual-conceptual functions, speech and thought presentation works across genres and at the textual level of meaning (see Chapter 13 in this volume).

Representing time, space and society

There is not space here to do justice to the broad range of ways in which deixis plays a part in producing the ideational landscape of a text. The basic principle of deixis is linked not to ideation but to interaction, as deictic words and phrases primarily function to 'point to' things in the real world through references to time (*then, now*), space (*here, there*) or social structures (*Sir*). The adaptation of the deictic facilities of language to decontextual texts, including written texts, means that human beings have developed the ability to negotiate an unknown 'world' created entirely by the text. This can be fictional, mythological or some kind of representation of the actual world. The ideological implications of this facility are extensive, as the ability to create 'text worlds' which reflect political realities (e.g. *Here we are in recession again*) can also reflect political dogmas (e.g. *People from elsewhere are taking our jobs*). The development of text world theory (see Gavins 2007 for an introduction, and Chapter 17 in this volume) and the application of deictic shift theory to literary texts (McIntyre 2006) demonstrate the textual nature of this meaning creation. The ideological potential of the creation of text-based worlds is significant and is explored in Jeffries (2007) and (2010a).

Current contributions and research

Critical stylistics is a new field of stylistics, related to critical discourse analysis as well as to stylistics itself. It has the aim of bringing the rigour and textual focus of stylistics to the analysis of non-literary texts with a view to identifying the ideological underpinnings of such texts. The discussion above has demonstrated just how reliant critical stylistics is on the work of other linguists. In this section, I would simply point to one major inspiration for my framework, namely the work of Simpson (1993), and introduce my own work a little before mentioning the continuing work of two of my research students in this field.

Simpson's (1993) book, though aiming to consider point-of-view and ideology as part of an approach to literary analysis, nevertheless strays into the non-literary field in its choice of texts to illustrate a number of features. This book confirmed for me that there was something missing in the practice of stylistics that I needed if I was to extend its insights to consider non-literary texts. Simpson showed how existing frameworks such as modality, transitivity, presupposition and implicature could be brought together to deliver a broad understanding of the attitudes behind a text, whether these were seen as the attitudes of the producer (the author) or the narrator. I found this book also filled a hole in the practice of critical discourse analysis which I was trying to teach at the time and which seemed to me to lack tools of analysis. I used Simpson's book as a critical discourse analysis textbook for a number of years, while I developed a slightly broader framework that I called critical stylistics.

My work in this field has been piecemeal and exploratory, but is now beginning to build into a framework which this chapter attempts to explain in broad terms. I worked on the textual construction of opposition (Jeffries 2010b) long before I tried to bring it into a model of how texts make meaning, but it was the impetus for the notion of textual-conceptual functions as it was so clearly an example of meaning created within texts but unavoidably reliant on an understanding of de-contextual opposition as well as being interpretable only in (situational) context. Alongside the work on opposition, I was trying to bring together such tools of analysis as critical discourse analysis practitioners had used in the context of my work on the textual construction of the female body (Jeffries 2007). It was here that I realised that opposition might sit alongside more recognised linguistic systems such as modality and transitivity in a coherent framework of textual meaning. At this point I had developed my ideas to the stage where they could be taught to undergraduate students as an approach to critical discourse analysis, and from this teaching I produced a textbook (Jeffries 2010a).

The framework of critical stylistics is now being used in different ways by a number of research students, and two of them, having completed their theses, have made one of the textual-conceptual functions their own. Davies (2012) has produced an extensive analysis of the textual triggers that produce opposition as well as demonstrating the ideological potential of this textual practice (2010). Nahajec, who first alerted me to the relevance of negation to my framework, has investigated thoroughly the status of text-based negation in both literary and non-literary works (2009, 2012).

Main research methods and recommendations for practice

The research methods of critical stylistics, like stylistics more generally, are broad and varied. The researcher should determine their research questions early on as well as deciding at the outset what the balance will be between inductive and deductive research. The former may well be quite open-ended (what are the ideologies identifiable in this set of texts?) whereas the latter might be closely focused on a series of hypotheses about the expected ideological nature of the data, which can then be tested.

The other decision that all researchers in this field have to make is whether the project is wholly or partly quantitative. If there is an intention to characterise a set of data in general, there may be scope for integrating the approach with a corpus linguistic methodology in order to capture backgrounded features or organise the data for later (qualitative) analysis. Baker and McEnery (2005) and Baker et al. (2008) demonstrate the integration of corpus methodologies within a critical discourse analysis approach (see also Chapter 23 in this volume). Jeffries and Walker (2012) similarly use corpus methods to organise data in a critical stylistic approach. The difficult question for researchers working with a lot of data is how to use the textual-conceptual functions in the qualitative phase of the work, since some of them are much more time-consuming than others to analyse comprehensively.

This problem is also relevant to researchers carrying out purely qualitative analysis using the critical stylistic framework. Even with small quantities of data, the comprehensive analysis of transitivity or naming, since they occur in every clause in a text, can be overwhelming. One approach, as with conventional literary stylistics, is to identify foregrounded and deviant features by other means (e.g. initial impressions or informant-testing) and then analyse them thoroughly. The other approach is to select extracts or limit the tools of analysis by not employing all the textual-conceptual functions in the process, focusing on, for example, negating and modality as they tend to work together in presenting hypothetical ideational worlds.

The stylistic principles of aiming for objectivity by being rigorous in applying the tools of analysis and making the process and results of the project as clear as possible to make it replicable apply here too. The focus should be on linking the textual features, through the analysis of textual-conceptual functions, to the ideological landscape of the text. This will include surface meanings, but it is likely to focus mainly on those which are backgrounded stylistically as a result of being naturalised (i.e. seen as common-sense) either for society in general (e.g. *little children should not be sent out to work*) or in the particular text (e.g. *gay marriage is right/wrong*).

This section has assumed so far that the researcher will have questions about the text(s) (e.g. do the Tories still use opposition construction politically? How does Labour represent its attitude to immigration? What does a women's magazine see as the 'natural' place of women in society?). However, there is also more work to be done on each of the textual-conceptual functions themselves and this could be the focus and aim of some research projects. The more familiar tools of analysis (e.g. transitivity, modality, speech and thought presentation) have less to offer in this regard, though their appearance within this new framework may lead to new questions being asked about their nature. There are other textual-conceptual functions, however, such as enumerating and exemplifying or prioritising, where there is some basic groundwork that is missing.

Future directions

Many projects in critical stylistics, I anticipate, will attempt to answer questions about a particular body of data and also contribute to the development of the framework. Future work in this field requires the development of a full model of textual meaning as a stylistic theory, or even a theory of language, and not just a critical approach to texts. Jeffries (2014) makes some tentative steps in the direction of using the framework as a stepping stone to understanding more about textual interpretation, but this is just the start.

As I suggested above, there is work to be done on describing those textual-conceptual functions which are not already fully developed. There is also the question of what would constitute a full list of textual-conceptual functions, which may not be answered definitively but ought to be addressed. One possible approach to this question is to ask whether these functions appear to be universal and if not, whether there are core functions which all languages use, and peripheral functions used by only some languages. Two other areas of development of critical stylistics include the use of the model across all text types and genres, to see whether, despite the apparent uniformity discovered so far, there are variations of practice or differing stylistic tendencies among different types of texts. Finally, one useful practical development would be the refinement of a method for using critical stylistic insights in conjunction with corpus linguistic methodologies.

Related topics

Feminist stylistics, point of view and modality, speech and thought presentation, text world theory.

Further reading

Davies, M., 2012. *Oppositions and ideology in news discourse*. London: Continuum

This volume details the ways in which texts construct new opposition and demonstrates the effects of these oppositional meanings on ideological content.

Jeffries, L., 2010a. *Critical stylistics*. Basingstoke: Palgrave Macmillan.

This textbook takes the student through each of the textual-conceptual functions in turn (they are called 'tools of analysis' here) and demonstrates their importance in ascertaining the ideological underpinnings of texts.

Jeffries, L., 2010b. *Opposition in discourse*. London: Continuum.

This monograph sets out a theory of opposition in texts and links it to both literary and non-literary stylistic analysis.

Simpson, P., 1993. *Language, ideology and point of view*. London: Routledge

> While not labelled as 'critical stylistics', I identify Simpson's excellent book as the beginning of my journey towards an integrated model of textual meaning-making.

References

Atkinson, M., 1984. *Our masters' voices: Language and body language of politics*. London: Routledge.

Baker, P. and McEnery, T., 2005. A corpus-based approach to discourses of refugees and asylum seekers in UN and newspaper texts. *Language and Politics*, 4 (2), 197–226.

Baker, P., Gabrielatos, C., Khosravinik, M., Krzyzanowski, M., McEnery, T. and Wodak, R., 2008. A useful methodological synergy? Combining critical discourse analysis and corpus linguistics to examine discourses of refugees and asylum seekers in the UK press. *Discourse and Society*, 19 (3), 273–306.

Davies, M., 2007. The attraction of opposites: The ideological function of conventional and created oppositions in the construction of in-groups and out-groups in news texts. *In:* D. Bousfield, L. Jeffries and D. McIntyre, eds. *Stylistics and social cognition*. Amsterdam: Rodopi, 71–100.

Davies, M., 2010. A new approach to oppositions in discourse: The role of syntactic frames in the triggering of non-canonical oppositions. *Journal of English Linguistics*, 40 (1), 47–73.

Davies, M., 2012. *Oppositions and ideology in news discourse*. London: Bloomsbury.

Fowler, R., 1991. *Language in the news*. London: Routledge.

Gavins, J., 2007. *Text world theory: An introduction*. Edinburgh: Edinburgh University Press.

Grice, H. P., 1975. Logic and conversation. *In:* P. Cole and J. L. Morgan, eds. *Syntax and semantics 3: Speech acts*. New York: Academic Press, 41–58.

Halliday, M. A. K., 1994. *An introduction to functional grammar*. London: Edward Arnold.

Jeffries, L., 2007. *Textual construction of the female body*. Basingstoke: Palgrave Macmillan.

Jeffries, L., 2010a. *Critical stylistics*. Basingstoke: Palgrave Macmillan.

Jeffries, L., 2010b. *Opposition in discourse*. London: Continuum.

Jeffries, L., 2014. Interpretation. *In:* P. Stockwell and S. Whiteley, eds. *The handbook of stylistics*. Cambridge: Cambridge University Press, 469–486.

Jeffries, L. and McIntyre, D., 2010. *Stylistics*. Cambridge: Cambridge University Press.

Jeffries, L. and Walker, B., 2012. Key words in the press: A critical corpus-driven analysis of ideology in the Blair years (1998–2007). *English Text Construction*, 5 (2), 208–229.

Levinson, S. C., 1983. *Pragmatics*. Cambridge: Cambridge University Press.

McIntyre, D., 2006. *Point of view in plays: A cognitive stylistic approach to viewpoint in drama and other text-types*. Amsterdam: John Benjamins.

Nahajec, L., 2009. Negation and the creation of implicit meaning in poetry. *Language and Literature*, 18 (2), 109–127.

Nahajec, L., 2012. Evoking the possibility of presence: Textual and ideological effects of linguistic negation in written discourse. Unpublished PhD Thesis. University of Huddersfield.

Semino, E. and Short, M., 2004. *Corpus stylistics: Speech, writing and thought presentation in a corpus of English writing*. London: Routledge.

Short, M., 2012. Discourse presentation and speech (and writing, but not thought) summary. *Language and Literature*, 21 (1), 18–32.

Simpson, P., 1993. *Language, ideology and point of view*. London: Routledge.

Part IV
Emerging and future trends in stylistics

26

Creative writing and stylistics

Jeremy Scott

Introduction

To write is to be a linguist.

This opening statement might seem either highly debatable or downright obvious, depending on the point at which the reader is positioned along the prevailing language-literature cline. However, I make no apologies for opening a chapter on interfaces between stylistics and creative writing with this assertion. The reasons why I make it should become clear in the course of the following. To summarise as succinctly as possible: to write is to engage, inexorably, with the mechanics of language, and stylistics, in its assuming of the mantle previously drawn around the field known as poetics, is the academic discipline best suited to the study of the mechanics of language in literature. This chapter will explore a selection of the many potential interfaces between stylistics and creative writing, and will proceed from the premise that these interfaces have been underexplored to date. It is important to note at the outset that the observations which follow are intended to relate not just to the pedagogy of the two disciplines within the academy; they should also be of interest to the creative practitioners, i.e. they relate directly to the act of writing 'at the coalface'.

As a summarising justification for the approaching of creative practice through stylistics (and, ultimately, linguistics in general), it will be useful to turn to Toolan (1998, p. ix):

> [One of the] chief feature[s] of stylistics is that it persists in the attempt *to understand technique, or the craft of writing*. ... Why these word-choices, clause-patterns, rhythms and intonations, contextual implications, cohesive links, choices of voice and perspective and transitivity etc. etc., and not any of the others imaginable? Conversely, can we locate the linguistic bases of some aspects of weak writing, bad poetry, the confusing and the banal?
>
> Stylistics asserts we should be able to, particularly by bringing to the close examination of the linguistic particularities of a text an understanding of the anatomy and functions of the language. ... Stylistics is crucially concerned with excellence of technique. [My emphasis]

Toolan's remarks are related to what he terms, in a paraphrase of Socrates, the 'examined text' – the usual application of what is often called 'the stylistics toolkit'. For our purposes I would like to substitute 'text' with 'practice', and reverse the usual paradigm. What applications might the stylistics toolkit have in the *production* of the literary text, not just in its analysis by academic critics 'post-event'? Of course, the most obvious answer to that question is: during the editorial phase of the creative process, i.e. during re-reading and re-writing. The stylistics toolkit, as Toolan suggests, can help identify and, crucially, account for moments of 'excellence' as well as parts of the work which are less successful (leaving aside for the moment the vexed question of qualitative evaluation). However, I would like to suggest that the stylistics toolkit and the insights it provides into literary process can become an integral part of creative practice itself. Stylistics also has the potential to complement and augment current creative writing pedagogy in the academy (and beyond) by providing a detailed and rigorous critical taxonomy with which to describe the key issues of both craft and readerly reception that come up for discussion time and time again in creative writing workshops. I have lost count of the number of times I have taken part in or led writing workshops, or been a part of reading groups, to find that a particular technical or reading issue comes up which participants struggle to articulate clearly. I find myself thinking, 'Stylistics has a word for this...'.

A note of caution, though: it is in no way the intention of this chapter to suggest that creative practitioners *must* engage with stylistics. Such a proposition would be patently absurd. You do not need to understand stylistics to be a good writer. My hope, though, is to point to the various ways in which a practical exploration of stylistics through writing rather than just reading can benefit both the creative writer and the student of stylistics, or anyone with an interest in the mechanics of language; indeed, as the opening sentence of the chapter demonstrates, I would venture that anyone with a desire to write creatively must have, by definition, an interest in these things. Rather than showing the only way to write well, combining stylistics and creative writing provides opportunities to explore how you *can* write, how to avoid certain common pitfalls of the beginning writer, and, at the very least, to consider in depth the question posed by Toolan above: why *these* words, and not others?

Historical perspectives

The notion of approaching the act of literary writing from the perspective of its mechanics (or craft) has a long history. I have identified here three broad areas of poetics which all to a greater or lesser extent pre-date the appearance and development of stylistics and contribute to the state of the discipline today: classical poetics and rhetoric, formalism, and narratology.

Classical poetics

The discussion of poetry and the representative arts in general which makes up much of Plato's *Republic* Books III and X is, arguably, the first theorisation of the function and purpose of literary discourse. The theme of the dialogues in Book X is representational poetry and its processes of *mimesis*: the depiction, or imitation, of reality, an activity Socrates sees as superfluous to his utopian society. It reproduces, rather than creates, and imitation is a game or sport; it is play. Plato ignores craft and focuses on inspiration, anticipating Wordsworth's Romantic ideal of the 'spontaneous overflow of emotion':

The poet is an airy thing, winged and holy, and he is not able to make poetry until he becomes inspired and goes out of his mind.

(Leitch et al. 2001, p. 35)

Crucially, in Book III Plato distinguishes between mimesis and *diegesis*, seeing the latter as representation of actions in the poet's own voice and the former as the representation of action in the imitated voices of characters. He uses Homer as an example, citing the opening scene of *The Iliad* where the Trojan Chryses asks Menelaus and Agamemnon to release his daughter for a ransom. The exchange is 'imitated' initially by the narrator (hence, diegesis) and then mimetically via the direct speech of the characters concerned. To illustrate his point even more clearly, and prefiguring one aspect of practice to be discussed in this chapter, Plato goes so far as to intervene in the text (Pope 1995) and rewrites the scene diegetically, in the voice of the authorial narrator, transposing all direct speech into indirect speech. As will be seen in a later section, this distinction between mimesis and diegesis is of great use to the writer.

Building on Plato's slightly haughty discourse on literary mimesis and poetic inspiration, Aristotle's *Poetics* constitutes the first rigorous categorisation of literary discourse. *Poetics* is a scientific anatomisation, just as can be found in Aristotle's work on classifications of the natural world, and as such anticipates the ambition of stylistics to provide rigorous accounts of the form of literary discourse. During the Renaissance it was treated as rulebook or manual for literary composition, and it can be seen as the first work of true literary criticism, putting down the roots which grew into neoclassicism, formalism and new criticism. Note, then, that at the dawn of the discipline we find an interest in the processes of *composition*, not textual analysis. *Poetics* is a technical manual.

Aristotle makes a distinction between objects which are 'natural' and those which are 'man-made'; for example, a tree and a chair. Poetry is made from language as a chair is made of wood. Thus poetry, *poiēsis*, is based on the verb 'to make'. Aristotle treats poetry as a *craft*, distinguishing himself from Plato. Alongside his well-known definition of tragedy he spends a great deal of time discussing plot and its structures, anticipating the key concerns of story narratology. Central to this, again, is mimesis; the best plots must be plausible, and imitate life (bringing to mind Henry James's appeal for 'solidity of specification').

To summarise: *The Republic* and *Poetics* pre-echo the paradigm set up in the introduction to this chapter, between the way a text works (the mechanics of craft) and the way it is received in context by readers and by the culture at large (the mechanics of reading). In addition, Plato and Aristotle begin the debate which still rages in and around the subject of creative writing in the academy: is it a craft with a set of rules (or guidelines) which can be taught, or is it primarily the result of personal creativity and, dare I say it, inspiration? (For more on this see Chapter 1 in this volume on rhetoric and poetics, 'the classical heritage of stylistics').

Russian formalism

Poetics was influential, almost two thousand years later, in the development of Russian formalism in the late nineteenth and early twentieth centuries, another forerunner of both stylistics in general and of an interest in textual mechanics, with a focus on the nature of poetic language. Roman Jakobson, associated with this school, theorised a *poetic function* of language (Jakobson 1960, p. 356), defining it as discourse which highlights (or foregrounds) the linguistic form of the message. In short, poetic language calls attention to itself as 'performance'.

The set towards the MESSAGE as such, focus on the message for its own sake, is the POETIC function of language. This function cannot be productively studied out of touch with the general problems of language, and, on the other hand, the scrutiny of language requires a thorough consideration of its poetic function. Any attempt to reduce the sphere of poetic function to poetry or to confine poetry to poetic function would be a delusive over simplification.

(1960, p. 356)

Note that Jakobson, in contrast to Aristotle and in common with modern stylistics, makes no distinction between literary discourse and 'quotidian' language, seeing the poetic function as an attribute of all language. As we will see in the next section, this point is of key relevance to the writer. (For more on this see Chapter 2 in this volume).

Another theorist who was strongly influenced by formalism is Mikhail Bakhtin. Bakhtin's work has much to say which is of relevance to the creative writer. He sees discourse as 'caught' between speaker and listener.

The word in language is half someone else's ... every word is directed towards an *answer* and cannot escape the profound influence of the answering word that it anticipates.

(2001, p. 280)

Thus, meaning occurs as a struggle between speaker and listener, a process Bakhtin termed *dialogic*. In literary terms, dialogism happens on several planes: between writer and reader in the wider discourse situation, between narrator and character in the story world, and between character and character. As writers, we anticipate reader response (as we do in everyday dialogue), and this of course has an effect on narrative voice.

Bakhtin also asserted that fiction was more vibrant and significant than poetry because it contained not just one voice but many. He referred to these 'many languages' as *heteroglossia* (2001, pp. 291–292), which the novelist manipulates for artistic and creative effect. In short, the writer is a ventriloquist, speaking in voices which are not his or her own. The more authentically these other voices are realised, the more effective is the writer's voice (Boulter 2007, p. 67). Thus, the voice of fiction is a double-voiced discourse, mimicking and echoing other voices and holding on to the 'taste' of the ways in which those words have been used before (another dialogic effect: between past and present utterances). All words are 'populated by intentions', argues Bakhtin (2001, p. 239), and there is dialogic conflict between voices, between meanings, and between 'tastes in the mouth' of characters. A writer's unique style (stylistic fingerprint) lies in the way he or she manipulates this conflict between discourses for artistic effect. The lesson for the writer is clear: he or she should revel in the heterogeneity and riotous variety of language in all its glory – in 'dialogised heteroglossia'. As Boulter puts it: 'The writer should use the diversity of language to express the singularity of their creative intention' (2007, p. 68).

Narratology

The final part of this discussion of historical perspectives must look to narratology, a discipline which has myriad applications to creative practice and which was influenced by both classical poetics and Russian formalism. Stylistics has many interconnections with narratology (Shen 2007), and together they give an intricate account of narrative function and effect on two levels: that of *story* and of *discourse*, corresponding to the formalist distinction between *fabula* and *syuzhet* (Propp 1968 and Shklovsky 1965). From the first, we gain insight into plot structure (e.g. the simple linear plot of exposition, complication, climax, resolution) and simple versus complex structures (the ways in which the time of the discourse need not correspond to the time of the story it mediates; more on this shortly). The second level explores, like Bakhtin, the complex interrelationships between authorial voice, narrator voice and character voice, the various methods of representing discourse (speech, thought, writing), and also the essential distinction between point of view (who tells) and focalization (who sees).

Initially narratology was associated with structuralism (due to its attempt to model the underlying patterns of narrative universally), but it has now become more 'catholic' in its ambitions, having applications to disciplines as diverse as psychology (e.g. the study of memory), anthropology (e.g. the evolution of folk traditions) and even philosophy (especially ethics). Narratologists such as Propp (1928), Todorov (1977), Genette (1980) and Greimas (1983) deconstructed the machinery of narrative with a view to putting together a narrative 'grammar' which would be as rigorous and universal as, say, accounts of syntax in linguistics. However, some modern theorists have argued that this formal grammar of narrative now seems a little 'clunky' and 'unnecessarily scientific' (van Loon 2007, p. 19).

One of the most important narratological works, and perhaps the most relevant for our purposes here, is Genette's *Narrative Discourse: an Essay in Method* (1980). Again, it is interesting to note the use of the word 'method' in this context; Genette's work has an ambition to be more than purely descriptive. Genette identified several salient features of narrative drawing on grammatical terms to classify them: order, frequency, duration, voice and mood. Three of these (at least) have great relevance to the writer.

Order concerns structure at the level of story. For example, imagine the structure of a murder mystery. First, the clues of a murder are discovered by a private investigator (call this Event A). Then, what actually happened – the circumstances of the murder – is revealed (Event B). Finally, the private investigator identifies the murderer and brings him or her to justice (Event C). Now, we can give each of these events a number corresponding to the *order* in which they are actually presented to the reader (or viewer, or listener) during the act of narration (or representation). Say the story is to be narrated chronologically (in the order that the events 'happened' in the story world). We could notate this as follows: B1, A2, C3. First comes the murder, then its discovery, then the revelation of the murder's identity. However, in the 'text' as described above, the order is as follows: A2 (discovery), B1 (flashback), C3 (resolution). The disjunction between story (what happened) and discourse (how it is represented) is full of creative potential, heightening suspense, causing the reader to ask questions and to want to read on. It is helpful to the writer, then, to envisage a separation between narrative discourse itself and the story (or fabula) being mediated by that discourse. This is a common device, often found in film (see Quentin Tarantino's *Pulp Fiction* for an extreme example).

There are other creative possibilities here. It follows from the above that there must be a discourse time and a story (or fabula) time. Genette called the relationship between these two times *duration* (1980, p. 86). 'Twenty years passed' is a long time in story terms, but is a short piece of discourse which takes only a second to write or read. Conversely, James Joyce's *Ulysses* is set in a relatively short story period of one day; however, it takes a great deal longer than that to read. In short, it has a long discourse time. Again, duration can be exploited by writers to great effect in terms of creating suspense, ironic distance, and in summarising lengthy information which is important in plot terms but need not be represented in detail by the discourse. Martin Amis's novel *Time's Arrow* (1992) famously has the discourse time and the story time running in opposition to one another.

Genette's term *voice* (1980, p. 212) is concerned with who narrates, and from what perspective. First, where the narration 'comes from': *intradiegetic* (inside the story world, as is the case with the individual pilgrims in Chaucer's *Canterbury Tales* or the character of Marlow in Joseph Conrad's *Heart of Darkness*) or *extradiegetic* (outside the story world, as is the case with most 'standard' third-person narration). The second aspect Genette defines is whether or not the narrator functions also as a character in the story, hence *heterodiegetic* (the narrator is not a character in the story, again as is common in third-person narration) or *homodiegetic* (the narrator is also a character, as in J.D. Salinger's *The Catcher in the Rye* or Mark Twain's *Huckleberry Finn*). He also deals with *focalization*, describing who 'sees' particular narrative events. This may or may not be the same as who 'tells' (the narrator). For example, a heterodiegetic narrator (in the third-person) can occupy different character perspectives at different points in the story (see Simpson 2004, pp. 27–29 for an excellent illustration of this concept).

What drives narrative? What makes reading compelling? How can we as writers apply the insights of narratology to the act of creating narrative fiction (and, indeed, poetry)? As Evenson (2010) writes with reference to understanding the effect of narrative technique:

> Elements and techniques are better understood not in relation to intuitive expressivist standards but in relation to their function in bringing about certain effects in the work as a whole. Intuition is not an end point but an initial response to be tested with the tools of narrative theory and the idea of means-ends relations between techniques and effects – so that we can offer clearer reasons for our intuitions or come to a new evaluation.
>
> *(p. 72)*

We will be returning to the applications of narratology in more detail in the 'Suggestions for Practice' section.

Critical issues and topics

The justifications for approaching creative writing through stylistics can be divided into two principle categories, which correspond to the distinction set out at the 'dawn' of poetics by Plato and Aristotle between the latter's explicit interest in craft and Plato's in 'poetry's' effects on readers. In other words, stylistics has much of interest to say about both literary technique *and* the mechanics of reading. The majority of what follows relates to the first category; the second is ripe for further exploration and development, as we will see.

Our brief discussion of historical perspectives on this topic brought to the fore two essential themes which bear further definition: the interaction between mimesis and diegesis and the cline between so-called 'standard' language and (again, so-called) 'literary' language. These two themes constitute the essential paradigms of this chapter. Both can be brought together under the umbrella of Carter and Nash's (1990) description of the styles of English writing as mediums for 'seeing through language'. The interaction between the mimetic and diegetic functions of discourse on one hand allows writers to create worlds from language, and on the other allows readers to see through language into those worlds. It will always benefit the creative writer to take account of this ineluctable fact: to be aware not only of *what* the reader is seeing but also *how* they are seeing it. The writer, in almost all cases, should be an enabler, not an obfuscator.

There is an artificiality and brittleness to the division between mimesis and diegesis as proposed by Plato, and, as Lodge (1990, p. 28) points out, it is not straightforward; neither is it a simple matter to distinguish between the two effects. Broadly, however, the terms map usefully onto the 'showing-telling' dichotomy beloved of the modern creative writing class, with mimesis corresponding to 'showing' and diegesis to 'telling'. To recap: for Plato, diegesis is representation of action 'in the poet's voice', while mimesis is representation of action in the 'voice(s) of characters'. However, as we shall see, the taxonomy which stylistics proposes to categorise literary representation of discourse is more complex, ranging from the Narrator's Representation of Action, pure diegesis ('She opened the door and walked into the room, seeing him standing by the window') to Direct Discourse, as close to a pure mimesis as written language can get ('Here she comes', he said). Thus, stylistics addresses Lodge's valid objection, mapping the distinction between mimesis and diegesis, and thus between showing and telling, more rigorously. This can only be of benefit to creative practice, allowing the writer to explore the extent to which mimetic process can enter into the diegetic narrative voice, so that the writer can 'show' as much as possible at the expense of 'telling'. For example, instead of 'He lost his temper', we prefer 'He left the room, slamming the door behind him.' Why? The second mediation of the story event is closer to the 'psychic space' of the character. There is no external voice of mysterious provenance explaining what the character is feeling on his behalf. Rather, the character's actions 'speak for themselves'. To be glib for a moment: actions speak louder than words. The description of a character's behaviour leaves space for the reader to interpret it, as he or she would in the 'real' world, based on the everyday familiarity with the kinds of mood that slamming a door indicates (in cognitive terms, the reader has a 'losing one's temper' schema which is activated by the slamming of the door). Straight diegetic description bypasses that space, enervating the reader's visualisation of the events of the text. Rather than seeing *through* language, the reader is *looking at* the narrative voice. In short, as cognitive approaches can demonstrate (see section below), the narrative discourse should aim for proximity to the sphere of character rather than narrator (although as always, there will be exceptions to this general rule). We can also argue here for a connection to connotative as opposed to denotative functions of discourse; mimesis corresponds to the former, while diegesis draws upon the latter.

This leads on to the second theme: the question of how (or whether) we can define literary language as having certain universal characteristics. This debate has been well-rehearsed elsewhere (a useful summary can be found in Jeffries and McIntyre (2010, pp. 61–62) and in Carter and Nash (1990, pp. 30–34)), and stylisticians have generally agreed that there is no linguistic feature which can be definitively categorised as belonging to literary language and never found elsewhere. As we have seen, however, a universal characteristic of literary language (although not, of course, exclusive to it) can be found in its function of creating worlds through mimesis and diegesis. These worlds are created through the interaction of two distinct (but inextricably linked) aspects of narrative (and I include poetry here): the discourse and the fabula. The discourse exploits mimetic and diegetic aspects of narrative discourse the more effectively to represent, or mediate, the fabula. In doing so, it sets up a second important cline which is related to the 'ease' with which the reader 'sees through' this discourse to the fabula beyond: i.e. between the transparency or otherwise of the discourse, and thus between the covertness or overtness of the narrator.

Another indicator of the position of literary discourse along the transparency-opacity cline is linguistic deviation (language that draws attention to itself by varying from the perceived norm). Carter and Nash (1990, p. 31) summarise the concept as follows:

According to deviation theory literariness or poeticality inheres in the degrees to which language use departs or deviates from expected configurations and normal patterns of language, and thus defamiliarises the reader. Language use in literature is therefore different because it makes strange, disturbs, upsets our routinized normal view of things, and thus generates new or renewed perceptions.

Carter and Nash cite Dylan Thomas's use of the phrase 'a grief ago' as an example of this; it departs from normal semantic selection restrictions, with the result that grief becomes seen as process connected with time (as in the standard 'a month ago'). They also draw attention to the ways in which this notion can help the practitioner during composition (not just in editorial analysis), prefiguring the goals of this chapter:

> We have been looking at stylistics from the outside, as it were, pointing as observers to features of language, structure, contextual function and general orientation of texts. This is a useful occupation, indeed a necessary one if we are to 'see through' language in the dual sense, or perceiving a message with the help of a medium and at the same time perceiving the ways in which the medium may obscure, distort or condition the message. Now, however, it is time to admit that we are not wholly and exclusively observers of texts. We are also in some measure creators of texts.
>
> *(p. 174)*

To summarise: I have suggested here that it is helpful for the writer, drawing on stylistics, to picture two clines present in literary discourse: from mimesis to diegesis, and from transparency to opacity. I would like to combine the two, and propose a concept of *stylistic balance* which combines the insights of both to give concrete guidance to the creative practitioner relevant to the writing of both fiction and poetry. We will discuss and illustrate stylistic balance in more detail in the next section.

Recommedations for practice

The practical applications of these are ideas are, of course, numerous, and the interested reader is referred to a forthcoming book (Scott 2013) for a much more detailed account. However, for the purposes of this overview I would like to provide some questions for further reflection and discussion, and also some concrete examples and exercises for use in creative practice. I will focus in turn on four areas: figurative language, point of view, representing speech and thought, and metaphor.

Figurative language

Stylistics furnishes us with a detailed knowledge of the workings and potentialities of language at its various levels: phoneme, morpheme, lexeme, clause, sentence, paragraph, text. It also examines the way these linguistic elements are chained together, and the way alterations in these patterns can affect meaning – including meaning which occurs above and beyond the purely semantic. In this sense, stylistics gives writers a greater understanding of the ways in which meaning becomes a product of linguistic form as well as of semantic content. The concepts of linguistic deviation and foregrounding in the effect of literary discourse on its readers (Leech 1969, p. 57, Stockwell 2002, pp. 13–26) are again key here. They draw attention to the ways in which writers can manipulate language so that its use in that instance is foregrounded against the 'background' of 'standard' usage.

There is danger lurking here too, however. As Gardner (2001, p. 127) points out:

About style, the less said the better. Nothing leads to fraudulence more quickly than the conscious pursuit of stylistic uniqueness.

Thus, the other side of the equation leads to a different problem: the dangers of stylistic inventiveness for its own sake. Take a look at some of the writing of particularly strident stylists such as Will Self and Martin Amis, for example. Both of these writers make use of various types of deviation, including discoursal, semantic and grammatical (see Amis's *Money* (1984) or Self's *How the Dead Live* (2009)), non-standard Englishes (even fabricated languages, as in the 'Mocknee' of Self's *The Book of Dave* (2007)) and unusual lexis/ neologisms to creative effect. However, it could be argued that the very stridency of these narrative voices detracts from their overall effect. To return to an earlier analogy: the reader ends up staring at the voice, bewildered, rather than seeing through it. The stylistic balance is upset, and discourse takes precedence over fabula. There may well be some creative projects where this is desirable, but I would argue that they are rare; nevertheless, it is true that linguistic deviation can be a source of great poetic invention.

We should return now to the concept of stylistic balance, and our two clines: between transparency and opacity, and between mimesis and diegesis. Stylistic balance can be usefully envisaged using the metaphor of a see-saw. Style is the pivot under the plank of the see-saw; on one side is the 'story world' (the world we see through language) and on the other side is the 'discourse-world (the world we write or read). The see-saw must compensate for emphasis on one side by lessening emphasis on the other (to mix the metaphor for a moment, the 'canvas' of a piece of imaginative writing is of a fixed size). Putting more weight on one side of the see-saw (for example, through a strident style) leads to a change in the nature of the other side (the imaginative world as 'seen' by the reader). A further question is implicit here: does emphasis on one lead to *detraction* from the other? The relationship between mimesis and diegesis is also part of stylistic balance, and thus the metaphor of the see-saw applies here too. Overemphasis on diegesis detracts from mimesis. As Aristotle argued, creative writing methodology must inevitably, respond to and/or correlate with specific visions of the world; perhaps the stylistic balance should not draw undue attention to itself (over-emphasising diegetic process?), but should focus attention on the imagined world (mimesis?). Does this apply if the emphasis is the other way round? There is a fundamental choice for the writer to make here, which stylistics can illustrate: between style that calls attention to itself, and style that calls attention to the imagined world.

There are other issues to be considered here. For the writer of fiction, does a lack of deviation correspond to narrative transparency (or narratorial covertness), and thus to mimesis? For the poet, is the presence of deviation and figurative language sufficient as a definition of 'the poetic'? Should poetic discourse always draw attention to itself? In thinking about these questions, it will be useful to revisit the concept of connotative versus denotative functions of language. Figurative language (or poetic discourse in general?) relies, surely, on the former capacity of language, and lays the ground for a richer, more textured and nuanced interaction between reader and text. Instead of following 'well-worn' paths in language, the writer can aim to 'make fresh', and thus to create expressions that are more vivid, and more effective. When figurative language follows well-trodden paths the effect ceases to be inventive, and instead becomes denotative (or diegetic).

Practice

1. Write two stanzas of overtly 'poetic' poetry, putting in as many linguistically deviant features as practicable. Examine the results, concentrating on linguistic features that

seem expressly 'poetic' in nature. Now re-write the piece, aiming to 'smooth away' those aspects deemed to be excessive, alongside rigorous consideration of why they should be deemed so. What happens if the poem is re-written in as 'standard' a discourse as possible? Further: what judgements have been brought into play to decide whether language is standard or not? How does an awareness of these judgements question the existence of a standard language?

2. Take some examples of narrative voices that you consider to be explicitly deviant (look at Amis's *Money* or Self's *The Book of Dave* for examples if you like). Rewrite some passages in a 'standard', normalised discourse. Is anything gained in terms of effectiveness? Is anything lost?

3. Consider the suggestion that the very 'effervescence' of some styles can divert attention away from the story world and lead to undue focus on the discourse-world. Is this more of an issue in fiction than in poetry? Is the reader more accepting of deviation in poetry than in fiction? If so, why?

Point of view

Point of view is one of the essential methodological choices that any writer makes in the act of sitting down to a new project: who tells, and (often) who sees (see Chapter 10 in this volume for a more detailed account). Too often (and in literary criticism in general), the term 'point of view' is used as a catch-all phrase; it is beneficial to the writer to be able to identify that who *sees* what is happening in a scene may or may not be the same as who *tells* the reader what is happening. Stylistics, drawing on narratology, can help to make this distinction clearer. We can distinguish between 'who tells/speaks', which we can define as *point of view* (signalled, for instance, by grammatical features such as first- or third-person verbs), and 'who sees', defined as *focalization* (signalled by the presence of deictic language and the discernible presence of a deictic *origo*). We should draw here on Genette's narratology to distinguish between differing types of point of view: *heterodiegetic, homodiegetic* and so on.

A connection can also be made between the use of the term *diegesis* to describe the 'universe' of the narrative, and to differentiations set out in cognitive stylistics (see Werth 1999 and Gavins 2007) between a text-world (or diegetic universe, inhabited perhaps by a homodiegetic narrator) and further sub-worlds (which may be set up, for example, by subsequent *intradiegetic* narration or by flashback). It is very useful for the writer to envisage their narrator in relation to this universe: within it or without it, integral to the story or removed from it and so on (see Chapter 17 in this volume for more on text world theory and Chapter 11 for more on narratology).

Focalization can be defined as the perspective from which the diegetic universe (or text world) is perceived at any given moment of the narrative; this may or may not be the same as the point of view, and may or may not vary throughout the progress of the narrative (i.e. *fixed focalization* versus *variable focalization*). The aim is to define the wide range of options available to the writer and the creative possibilities and tensions which can be exploited.

Practice

1. These exercises are based on textual intervention, or creative re-writing. Choose a short extract from either Kazuo Ishiguro's novel *The Remains of the Day* or Carol Ann Duffy's poem cycle *The World's Wife* (depending on your interest and/or intended focus) and re-

write it from a heterodiegetic perspective. Now examine what you have written and consider the interrelationships between style and representational process. What grammatical and syntactical changes are necessitated? What is lost (in expressive terms, and in terms of the reader's experience of the narrative) and what is gained? How is it possible to transform a character idiolect into a narrative voice?

2. Re-write either the famous 'brown stocking' scene (as discussed by Auerbach 2003) from Virginia Woolf's *To the Lighthouse* (1977, p. 78), which makes use of multiple focalizations, from Mr Ramsay's point of view only, either in homodiegetic of heterodiegetic form, or Susan Howe's poem 'The Liberties', which also makes use of different focalizations and points of view. Consider the same questions, with a view to contrasting the expressive potentialities of limited perspective versus 'omniscient' ways of seeing, with reference, again, to the tension between mimesis and diegesis.

Representing speech and thought

Speech and thought presentation is a broad complex area, and it is beyond the scope of this overview to consider it in the detail it deserves (see Chapter 13 in this volume for a more detailed account). There are various methods available to the writer for representing the speech and thought of characters and narrators, and stylistics has evolved a useful and relatively precise taxonomy to describe them (Short 2007). It is important, however, to consider too the extent to which and by what method spoken discourse and internal discourse can be 'simulated' through written language. Interesting technical responses to this question can be found in novels such as Graham Swift's *Last Orders* (1996) and James Kelman's *How Late It Was, How Late* (1994) and in the demotic poetry of Patience Agbabi, Moqpai Selassie and Sue Brown, all of whom attempt to represent both the voices of characters and narrators through a textual representation of the oral demotic – in Kelman's case, at times, phonetically. The issue of how the sound, intonation and 'texture' of, say, a local dialect or the authentic idiolect can be best represented is also a central issue (Scott 2009).

Kelman's novel illustrates an interesting resolution of a common fictional dilemma: the ways in which an author's voice will often have a tendency to ride roughshod over those of his or her characters ('literary' language versus the demotic). Kelman evolves a technique whereby the heterodiegetic narrator and the protagonist speak on the same level, and in the same voice (Scott 2009, pp. 92–94). These techniques shed further light on stylistic balance: the tension between the sometimes-competing demands of mimesis and diegesis, and between 'literary' and 'non-literary' discourses.

The following terms are important (Short 2007): *free direct discourse, direct discourse, free indirect discourse, indirect discourse, narrator's representation of speech/thought* and *narrator's representation of action* (see Figure 26.1). The writer should pay attention to the way in which the 'tug of war' between narrator and character, between diegesis and mimesis, shifts along the cline (with discourse under control of *character* at the start – in free direct discourse – and under the control of the *narrator* at the end).

Perhaps the most intriguing of these methods occurs at the mid-point along the cline: free indirect discourse (FID) allows the voices of character and narrator to coexist simultaneously. In FID the narrative discourse gains an enlivening flexibility; the character is allowed to 'own' the words at times, but the limitations of a pure homodiegetic perspective are avoided (Rimmon-Kenan 1983 pp. 109–110, Bray 2007). Crucially, the reader can engage with the story via both the narrator's *and* the character's discourse, with, as it were, a dual empathy.

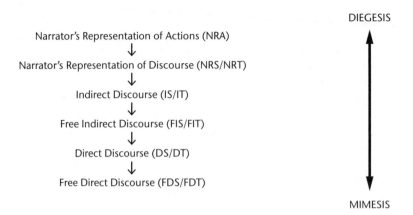

Figure 26.1 Representing speech and thought

It is also interesting to consider the complex issue of the extent to which 'thought' corresponds to language, as exploited in stream-of-consciousness writing and internal monologue (a technique very much in vogue in High Modernist works such as Virginia's Woolf's *To the Lighthouse* and in Joyce's *Ulysses*). It could be argued that the experiments of the modernists (and others) in representing thought to some extent led them up a methodological blind alley (Scott 2009, p. 32). The writer would be well advised to see representations of speech and thought as *simulations*, not as attempts at transcript; they should aim to capture the 'flavour' of real discourse, not its full content.

Practice

1. The following exercise explores the workings of dialogue by re-writing direct speech as indirect speech and vice versa. You should focus on *showing* the manner of speech rather than describing it (preferring mimesis over diegesis), and avoid using any narrator's representation of action whatsoever. Convert the following from indirect speech to free direct speech:
    a. The driver addressed me abruptly, asking if I was from Kent.
    b. David queried the meaning of the word 'discourse'.
    c. As he opened the door, he told her to move over.
    d. Roughly, Carl said she should stop being so stupid.
    Convert the following from direct speech to indirect.
    a. "So he says," Mrs Peters gossiped, "'Annie wouldn't have done that,' he says, so I says, 'Blast, and she would.' And so she would."
    b. He insisted on putting the car into the barn for me, so I got out and directed him into the narrow space.
    Which representation works best in each case? Why?
2. Take a section of *The Canterbury Tales* (the opening of 'The Pardoner's Tale', for example) and rewrite it in a modern English demotic (drawing on your own background for the language). What stylistic changes are necessitated? What happens when the poem is read aloud by the author rather than read 'silently'? What is lost in the transition from oral to written, and vice versa? What is gained?

3. Think about the difference between these five representations in terms of the 'distance' between narrator and character. Why include these examples in a section on speech and thought representation?
   a. It was the winter of the year 1953. A large man stepped out of a doorway.
   b. Henry Warburton had never cared much for snowstorms.
   c. Henry hated snowstorms.
   d. God how he hated these damn snowstorms.
   e. Snow. Under your collar, down inside your shoes, freezing and plugging up your miserable soul…

Metaphor

One of the great contributions of stylistics to the practice of literature is in its rigorous deconstruction of the function and effect of metaphor, and here I mean 'metaphor' in its broadest sense, embracing metonymy, synecdoche and simile (see Chapter 12 in this volume for a more detailed account). It is important to grasp how fundamental metaphor is to communication, as Jakobson (1960) demonstrated. Mark Haddon's novel *The Curious Incident of the Dog in the Night-time* (2004) is a wonderful exploration of this concept. The narrator of this novel, Christopher, suffers from a form of Asperger's Syndrome which means that he cannot process or understand metaphorical constructions; for him, 'skeletons in cupboards' are not secrets, but hidden corpses. For Christopher, metaphors are just 'lies'.

Investigations within cognitive linguistics and psychology generally have proposed models for the function of metaphor, and introduced terminology such as *grounds*, *target* and *source* (or variations on these) to illustrate the ways in which meaning is 'carried over' from one term to another (from 'rose' to 'love', say, with 'rose' as source, 'love' as target, and the grounds being, for instance, the intense colour of the rose, its propensity to hide thorns, the fact that it is mutable and impermanent yet beautiful, and so on), in the process combining two senses to produce a third, distinct (in the best examples, unique) sense (Lakoff and Johnson 1981, Steen 1994). More recently, applications of blending theory (see Chapter 18 in this volume) have come up with exciting new ways of understanding the function of metaphor as a blending of two conceptual spaces in the mind of the reader (Fauconnier and Turner 2002). An understanding of these concepts allows the writer to pinpoint and develop effective metaphor and to understand the ways they work on the reader, and also to avoid some of the common problems of metaphor writing: the mixed, or incompatible, metaphor and the danger of cliché.

The central idea to grasp is the way in which sophisticated use of metaphor leads to a more active process of world building in the mind of the reader by virtue of the fact that the process of semantic cognition 'travels further' in the act of arriving at interpretation. By forcing the reader's mind to arrive at meaning via new routes (for example, in the transfer of meaning from target to source, from 'rose' to 'love'), a text will prove more stimulating, and the reading experience become more vivid. Understanding this process has a role to play, like that of figurative language, in the avoidance of cliché (interestingly, 'rose' as 'love' is now a cliché), where the reading brain trundles along frequently-travelled routes. Also intriguing in this connection is Lakoff and Johnson's (1981) anatomisation of different types of archetypal metaphor, which are seen to be integral and paradigmatic to the human mind's methods of interfacing with the world, for example: *purposes are destinations, states are locations, time moves, life is a journey, death is sleep* and so on. Are these archetypes by necessity the building blocks of all metaphor, or are there ways of forging new connections between targets and sources?

435

Practice

1. Write metaphors from the following prompts: 'Your eyes are…' 'I cried…', 'Love is…', 'That autumn was…', 'The journey was…'. The challenge is to avoid cliché at all costs. Once you've done this, add another line, making sure that the metaphor isn't mixed (i.e. that your two sources come from the same conceptual domain; a rose and a garden, say, in a metaphor about love). You should then aim to refine and distil the results so that the metaphor is one line long, thinking again about the interaction of diegesis and mimesis.

2. Think of a hobby or pastime that you are familiar with (e.g. photography, playing or watching sports, video gaming, etc.). Use the lexical field associated with that hobby to create an extended metaphor from prompt nouns taken from Lakoff above. 'Love' combined with 'football'? 'Time' with 'role playing games'? 'Death' with 'graffiti art'? The more disparate the two, the more interesting the exercise. Is it true to say that the more disparate the target and source, the more effective the expressive results? If so, why?

Future directions

Three different strands for further research, investigation and development have emerged during the course of my work on this topic. The first can be found in the relationship, referred to on a number of occasions throughout this chapter but not yet explored in the detail it deserves, of creative practice to cognitive poetics, especially in terms of the latter's interest in the processes of reading. Cognitive poetics draws on both cognitive linguistics and 'traditional' poetics, and its ambition is to provide a rigorous account of the mechanics of reading (see Chapter 19 in this volume for more on this). The field makes use of cognitive concepts such as Gestalt psychology (figures and grounds) and schema theory to develop rigorous models of what happens when we read literary texts (Stockwell 2002, Gavins and Steen 2005). One of the most useful and relevant branches of cognitive poetics in terms of creative practice is text-world theory (Werth 1999, Gavins 2007). In its delineation of the various conceptual spaces which a reader creates as he or she engages with a literary text as well as the myriad ways in which these spaces (text-worlds) interact, text-world theory gives the writer the tools to devise an invaluable conceptual map, depicting both the ways in which his or her text might be read (or, more precisely, *imagined and envisaged*) and, from the point of view of craft, the position of a narrative or poetic voice in relation to this text-world: within it or without it, integral to the story or removed from it and so on, thus keeping the writer attuned to the epistemological status of that voice. This status will impact upon the kinds of knowledge a character/narrator will/will not (or should/should not) have access to and, crucially, the kinds of *language* that he or she will or will not have access to.

A second area deserving of further exploration is that of the text in performance. Plenty of work has been done on the stylistics of play texts (see also Chapter 15 in this volume), especially on how they create character (Culpeper 2001) and in terms of the use of pragmatics-based frameworks to analyse dialogue (Short 1996), but little from the perspective of the playwright. To what extent could an understanding of pragmatics (for example, politeness frameworks and conversational maxims) aid and inform the writing of authentic-sounding dialogue, rather than just its analysis? Also of potential relevance here are the ways in which modern stylistics, and, indeed, studies of linguistic creativity in general, are embracing analysis of non-textual media, for example film, TV, plays and poetry in performance (Swann *et al.* 2011). This could certainly inform creative practice, for example in devised approaches to theatre and in other forms of improvisation, such as informed the writing of Patience Agbabi's performance poem 'Word' (see Swann *et al.* 2010, pp. 36–37).

Thirdly, and perhaps most speculatively, it would be interesting to investigate what stylistics, especially its cognitive branches, has to say about the process of 'poetic inspiration' (returning once more to Plato's side of the equation) – or perhaps, to put it less contentiously, about the relationships between language and creativity. It has long been my ambition to inculcate stylistic awareness into creative practice, not as a post-composition editorial facility but as part of the process of writing. The most promising route for this investigation would appear to be through research into language and creativity. One example can be found in the process referred to by Keith Oatley (Gavins and Steen 2005, p. 161) as *writingandreading*. When reading a text, we perform it, and thus we mentally 'write' it. In what ways can this experience of writingandreading be mined for insights into the processes involved in creating texts? Another avenue of enquiry lies in looking at creativity as arising from within language, not from external sources; in other words, from the act of writing itself. As Carter and Nash (1990, p. 176) make clear, a lot can be learned about the relationships between language and creativity through writing games, wherein language itself provides the creative stimulus which might normally be expected to come from an extra-linguistic source (as it were, from the fabula rather than the discourse). Creativeness, it must be agreed, is directly accessible *through* language, and thus to everyone.

> Creativity is a pervasive feature of spoken language exchanges as well as a key component in interpersonal communication, and … it is a property actively possessed by all speakers and listeners; it is not simply the domain of a few creatively gifted individuals.
>
> *(Carter 2004, p. 6)*

This chapter can only ever be a cursory overview of the subject, and thus there is an ever-present danger of a lack of depth and, indeed, a certain over-simplification, especially for the scholar approaching the topic from an interest in stylistics as an academic discipline rather than in creative writing *per se*. Nevertheless, it is hoped that the series of ideas and suggestions for practice here could be useful ways of exploring stylistics from a different 'angle' (from that of producing our own texts rather than analysing those written by others) and as a springboard for a different kind of appreciation of certain aspects of the stylistics toolkit.

For the creative practitioner, it is hoped that this stylistic toolkit could form the basis of a heightened critical awareness of the mechanics of literary discourse, most obviously during the editorial phase of the writing process (and during re-writing), but also during the act of writing itself. Thus, stylistics stands as a means of exemplifying the two persons of the writer as defined, famously, by Dorothea Brande:

> Think of yourself as two-persons-in-one. There will be a prosaic, everyday, practical person to bear the brunt of the day's encounters. It will have plenty of virtues to offset its stolidity; it must learn to be intelligently critical, detached, tolerant, while at the same time remembering that its first function is to provide suitable conditions for the artist self. The other half of your dual nature may then be as sensitive, enthusiastic, and partisan as you like; only it will not drag those traits out into the workaday world.
>
> *(1983, pp. 48–49)*

Indeed, considerations of craft are becoming more and more a feature of creative writing teaching across the academy, and stylistics seems ideally placed to provide a workable critical taxonomy for describing the various aspects of craft in all their glorious complexity. Once again: this is not to suggest that we can talk about a 'right way to write'; however, it is surely reasonable to offer up a series of precepts and themes to act as a bowstring against which the individual creative voice can pull.

Related topics

Cognitive poetics, drama and performance, linguistic levels of foregrounding, metaphor and metonymy, narrative fiction, point of view and modality, real readers, rhetoric and poetics, speech and thought presentation, text world theory.

Further reading

Boulter, A., 2007. *Writing fiction: Creative and critical approaches*. London: Palgrave Macmillan.

A discussion of creative writing from the perspective of critical literary theory.

Carter, R. and Nash, W., 1990. *Seeing through language: A guide to styles of English writing*. Oxford: Basil Blackwell.

An overview of style from the perspective of creativity.

Scott, J., 2013, *Creative Writing and Stylistics*. London: Palgrave Macmillan.

More detailed and wide-ranging explortion of the issues discussed in this chapter, including suggestions for practice.

Swann, J., Pope, R., and Carter, R., eds., 2010. *Creativity in language and literature: The state of the art*. London: Palgrave Macmillan.

An anthology of current research on linguistic creativity.

Wood, J., 2008. *How fiction works*. London: Jonathan Cape.

An excellent discussion of narrative craft from the perspective of a literary critic.

References

Amis, M., 1984. *Money: A suicide note*. London: Vintage.
Amis, M., 1992. *Time's arrow*. London: Faber and Faber.
Attridge, D., 1995. *Poetic rhythm: An introduction*. Cambridge: Cambridge University Press.
Auerbach, E., [1953] 2003. *Mimesis: The representation of reality in Western literature*. Princeton: Princeton University Press.
Bakhtin, M., 2001. *The dialogic imagination: Four essays*. Austin: University of Texas Press.
Boulter, A., 2007. *Writing fiction: Creative and critical approaches*. London: Palgrave Macmillan.
Brande, D., 1983. *Becoming a writer*. London: Macmillan.
Bray, J., 2007. Free indirect discourse: Empathy revisited. *In:* M. Lambrou and P. Stockwell. eds. *Contemporary stylistics*. London: Continuum, 81–99.
Carter, R., 2004. *Language and creativity: The art of common talk*. London: Routledge.
Carter, R. and Nash, W., 1990. *Seeing through language: A guide to styles of English writing*. Oxford: Basil Blackwell.
Culpeper, J., 2001. *Language and characterisation: People in plays and other texts*. London: Routledge.
Eliot, T.S., 1975. *Selected prose of T.S. Eliot*. Orlando: Harcourt Inc.
Evenson, B., 2010. Across the curriculum: Creative writing. *In:* D. Herman, B. McHale and J. Phelan, eds. *Teaching narrative theory*. Modern Language Association of America, 70–78.
Fabb, N., 2005. Linguistics in a department of literature. *English Subject Centre Newsletter*, Issue 8, 2005.

Fauconnier, G. and Turner, M., 2002. *The way we think: Conceptual blending and the mind's hidden complexities*. New York: Basic Books.

Gardner, J., 2001. *The art of fiction*. London: Vintage.

Gavins, J., 2007. *Text world theory: An introduction*. Edinburgh: Edinburgh University Press.

Gavins, J. and Steen, G., eds., 2003. *Cognitive poetics in practice*. London: Routledge.

Genette, G., 1980. *Narrative discourse: An essay in method*. New York: Cornell.

Goldberg, N., 1986. *Writing down the bones*. Boston, MA: Shambhala.

Greimas, A. J., 1983. *Structural semantics: An attempt at a method*. D. McDowell, R. Schleifer and A. Velie, trans. Lincoln, Nebraska: University of Nebraska Press.

Haddon, M., 2004. *The curious incident of the dog in the night-time*. London: Vintage.

Jakobson, R., 1960. Concluding statement: Linguistics and poetics. *In:* T. A. Sebeok, ed. *Style in language*. New York: John Wiley and Sons, 350–377.

Jeffries, L. and McIntyre, D., 2010. *Stylistics*. Cambridge: Cambridge University Press.

Joyce, J., [1922] 1986. *Ulysses*. London: The Bodley Head/Penguin Books.

Kelman, J., 1994. *How late it was, how late*. London: Secker and Warburg.

Lakoff, G. and Johnson, M., 1981. *Metaphors we live by*. Chicago: University of Chicago Press.

Leech, G., 1969. *A linguistic guide to English poetry*. London: Longman.

Leitch, V. B., Cain, W. E., Finke, L., Johnson, B., McGowan, J. and Williamsn, J. J., 2001. *The Norton anthology of theory and criticism*. New York: W. W. Norton and Co.

Lodge, D., 1990. *After Bakhtin: Essays on fiction and criticism*. London: Routledge.

Patterson, D., 2007. The lyric principle. *Poetry Review* 97 (2), 56–72.

Pope, R., 1995. *Textual intervention: Critical and creative strategies for literary studies*. London: Routledge.

Propp, V., [1928] 1968. *The morphology of the folktale*. Austin: University of Texas Press.

Rimmon-Kenan, S., 1983. *Narrative fiction: Contemporary poetics*. London: Routledge.

Scott, J., 2009. *The demotic voice in contemporary British fiction*. London: Palgrave Macmillan.

Scott, J., 2012. Creative writing: A stylistics approach. *In:* M. Burke *et al.*, eds. *Pedagogical Stylistics: Current trends in language, literature and ELT*. London: Continuum, 96–112.

Scott, J., 2013. *Creative writing and stylistics*. London: Palgrave Macmillan.

Self, W., 2007. *The book of Dave*. London: Penguin.

Self, W., 2009. *How the dead live*. London: Penguin.

Shen, D., 2007. What stylistics and narratology can do for each other. *In:* J. Phelan and R. J. Rabinowitz, eds. *A companion to narrative theory*. London: Blackwell, 136–149.

Shklovsky, V., [1965] 1917. Art as technique. *In:* L. Lemon and M. Reis, eds. *Russian formalist criticism: Four essays*. Lincoln, Nebraska: University of Nebraska Press, 3–24.

Short, M., 1996. *Exploring the language of poetry, prose and plays*. London: Longman Pearson.

Short, M., 2007. Thought presentation twenty-five years on. *Style*, 41 (2), 227–241.

Simpson, P., 2004. *Stylistics: A resource book for students*. London: Routledge.

Steen, G., 1994. *Understanding metaphor in literature: An empirical approach*. London: Longman.

Stockwell, P., 2002. *Cognitive poetics: An introduction*. London: Routledge.

Swann, J., Pope, R. and Carter, R., 2011. *Creativity in language and literature: The state of the art*. London: Palgrave Macmillan.

Swift, G., 1996. *Last orders*. London: Picador.

Todorov, T., 1977. *The poetics of prose*. London: Wiley-Blackwell.

Toolan, M., 1998. *Language in literature: An introduction to stylistics*. London: Arnold.

Van Loon, J., 2007. Narrative theory/narrative fiction. *New Writing*, 4 (1), 18–25.

Werth, P., 1999. *Text worlds: Representing conceptual space in discourse*. London: Longman.

Wood, J., 2008. *How fiction works*. London: Jonathan Cape.

Woolf, V., 1977. *To the lighthouse*. London: Grafton Books.

27

Stylistics and real readers

David Peplow and Ronald Carter

Introduction

Stylistics has long claimed to be an empirical method of literary analysis. One aspect of this empiricism is stylistics' commitment to studying the effect of texts on readers. Short (1996, p. 6) emphasises the reader-centred nature of stylistics, stating that researchers in the field are 'profoundly interested in the *rules and procedures* which we, as readers, intuitively know and apply in order to understand what we read'. In reality, however, stylisticians have tended to focus more on textual analysis than on the reader (Hall 2009, p. 331; see also Allington and Swann 2009), and generally the 'reader' has remained a theoretical construct, similar to the ideal reader in much literary reader-response criticism (see Culler 2002, Iser 1978, Fish 1980). However, there is a growing body of research within stylistics that is centrally interested in considering how readers find meaning in literary texts and testing whether the assumptions and frameworks of stylistic analysis are supported by evidence from real readers.

In this chapter we give a selective overview of literary linguistic research into real readers, focusing on two aspects: experimental approaches to foregrounding and its effect on readers, and recent research undertaken by stylisticians into natural reading environments such as the book group. We conclude by suggesting some future directions for research in this exciting and burgeoning field of stylistics. Before that, in the Historical Perspectives section we discuss the theoretical background of real reader research in stylistics. We consider reader-response criticism within literary studies more generally, and then introduce the two broad approaches to real reader research within stylistics: the empirical study of literature (ESL) and the naturalistic study of readers (NSR).

Historical perspectives

In the last seventy years of literary criticism there has been a movement away from conceiving of literary meaning as residing in the author or in the structural features of the text, and a subsequent movement towards considering the reader as the principal meaning-maker. This shift began in the work of Wimsatt and Beardsley (1946), was extended by Barthes (1977), and in more recent years has led to the establishment and growth of 'reader-response' criticism within literary departments, most famously associated with Culler (2002), Fish

(1980), and Iser (1978). However, research into readers within literary criticism has a longer history than this would suggest, as I. A. Richards's (1929) study into his students' responses to poetry demonstrates.

A general difference between Richards's empirical study and the work of reader-response critics, however, is that the latter has not generally been particularly interested in looking at the actual responses of real readers to literary texts. Indeed, reader-response scholars frequently emphasise the incongruity between their 'readers' and flesh-and-blood readers. For instance, Culler warned against taking 'too seriously the actual and doubtless idiosyncratic performance of individual readers' (2002, p. 300); Iser was interested in a highly theoretical implied reader that 'in no way should be identified with any real reader' (1978, p. 34); and Fish's concept of interpretive communities – groups of like-minded readers 'who share interpretive strategies' (1980, p. 171) – was left as a theoretical model for those in empirical literary study to test and expand (e.g. Dorfman 1996). Indeed, Fish did not actually draw on his interpretive communities model in his own literary criticism (Mailloux 1982, Pratt 1982). This lack of engagement with the reading practices of real readers means that the distinction between reader response criticism and other forms of literary criticism 'is more a matter of presentation than of methodology' (Allington and Swann 2009, p. 221), with reading idealised and the natural performance errors of real readings 'considered to be irrelevant' (Short and van Peer 1989, p. 26). By contrast, Richards's (1929) famous study used real reader response as the primary object of inquiry. He presented each of his students with a poem and asked them to offer a written response to the poem. Richards concluded that the reactions of his participants were highly variable and idiosyncratic. Although Richards's study is arguably a little crudely designed by modern standards and his interpretation of his empirical data may be questionable (see Martindale and Dailey 1995), his study is a rare thing within literary criticism – an engagement with the reactions of real readers.

Although relatively little research has been conducted into real readers in traditional literary criticism, this research has been carried out in two fields closely related to stylistics: the empirical study of literature (ESL) and the naturalistic study of reading (NSR). These two approaches differ greatly in terms of methodology. While ESL favours experimental methods, with researchers carrying out reading tests with participants in quasi-laboratory conditions, NSR considers readers in more natural habitats such as book groups. Both of these approaches have advanced our understanding of the cognitive and the social processes underlying reading, and in their different ways both can help stylisticians to ground their 'armchair analyses of texts' in 'concrete readers' reactions' (van Peer 2001, p. 337). Having said this, both approaches have shortcomings and it is important that researchers are aware of these when designing their studies. In the following section we discuss the two approaches in more detail, considering the areas of interest to the different methods.

Critical issues and topics

ESL has encouraged collaborations between literature specialists and psychologists in order to investigate the processes underlying real reading. For a comprehensive overview of the history of ESL, see Miall (2006). The vast majority of work in this field is experimental in nature. In devising these experiments, the researchers strive to eliminate all extraneous variables so that, as much as it can be, the cognitive processes of reading can be isolated and studied as independently as possible. ESL is a broad and varied field, but following Dixon and Bortolussi (2008, p. 76) we can distinguish three strands of research that scholars in this field are interested in studying: the effects of specific formal textual features on readers, the importance of reader background on the reading process, and the effect of contextual factors on reading. Studies looking at reader background might consider the effects of literary training, or literary 'competence' (Culler 2002), on readers' evaluations of particular literary passages (for examples of this, see Bortolussi and Dixon [1996], Fiahlo [2007], and van Peer [1986]). ESL researchers considering contextual factors have looked at issues such as reader goals and the effects these have on reading. For instance, Cupchik, Oatley and Vorderer (1998) asked participants to adopt a particular perspective when reading. Some participants were asked to read as spectators sympathising with the protagonist, while others were asked to identify with the protagonist. Cupchik *et al.* (1998) considered how these particular goals affected the emotions that the readers experienced. Although reader background and contextual factors may be of indirect interest to those in stylistics, ESL studies that focus on the 'formal features of texts and their influence on readers' (Miall 2006, p. 293) that are particularly pertinent to literary linguists. Within this strand, ESL researchers have been specifically interested in how real readers process literary metaphor, narrative perspective, and foregrounded passages in literary texts. In the next section we concentrate on some studies from ESL into foregrounding.

Rather than carrying out experiments on readers, those working within NSR advocate studying literary interpretations that emerge from 'habitual processes of reading' (Swann and Allington 2009, p. 248). This means studying real readers using a broadly ethnographic approach (defined on p. 447) rather than an experimental one, taking the data provided by readers 'as it comes' rather than searching for specific phenomena or creating research situations that are unusual for the participants. Studies within NSR tend to be qualitative, as opposed to the more quantitative ESL tradition. To date, much of this research has focused on the book club as a site of 'natural' reading (e.g. Benwell 2009, Hartley 2001, Swann and Allington 2009, Peplow 2011), with researchers typically observing, recording and transcribing groups' meetings. A potential drawback with this ethnographic approach is that researchers cannot control their data in the way that they might like. Researchers may have certain interests and specific research questions in mind when they approach the data, but for Swann and Allington these must be 'let go' if the readers do not attend to this in their talk (2009, p. 249). Research in the naturalistic tradition should be conducted in a bottom-up fashion, which may mean that researchers find themselves considering elements of the qualitative data that are highly salient for the readers, but were not necessarily of interest to the researcher(s) from the outset.

In the following section, we provide examples of studies from the two areas just outlined. We then consider some of the associated problems with research in these fields, before moving on to recommendations for conducting real reader studies and then the future directions of research into stylistics and real readers.

Current contributions and research

The concept of foregrounding has long been a central concern for those working in stylistics. In her ever-useful *Dictionary of Stylistics*, Wales (2001, p. 157) defines foregrounding as the 'throwing into relief of the linguistic sign against the background of the norms of ordinary language' which, in a literary text, means that certain linguistic features will be 'made prominent' against the rest of the text. Formalists of the Czech and Russian schools were the first to stress the importance of foregrounding to literary texts. Indeed, for the Czech critic Mukařovsky who coined the term (a translation from *aktualisace*), foregrounding is the feature that distinguishes literary texts from everyday language. For Mukařovsky, everyday language is 'automatised' so that effective communication can take place. Literary language is defined in contrast to this, functioning to draw attention to itself: 'In poetic language foregrounding achieves maximum intensity to the extent of pushing communication into the background as the objective of expression and of being used for its own sake' (Mukařovsky 1964, p. 19).

Although making an absolute distinction between 'everyday' language and 'literary' language is problematic, hiding the extent to which everyday language can be extraordinarily creative (Carter 2004, Swann, Pope and Carter 2011), foregrounding remains central to stylistic analysis and to notions of literariness within stylistics and cognitive poetics (Simpson 2004, Short 1996, Stockwell 2002). As foregrounding has been so important to stylistic analysis, there are a number of studies within ESL that have focused on this area. As Miall and Kuiken (1994, p. 405) argue, foregrounding is a feature that is 'amenable to careful and systematic empirical study', which also explains the popularity of foregrounding reader experiments in ESL. We now describe four influential studies into foregrounding: van Peer (1986), Miall and Kuiken (1994), Emmott *et al.* (2006), and Zyngier, van Peer and Hakemulder (2007). For each study we will describe the methods used and the conclusions drawn. Of course, the summaries offered here are selective and we stress the need for readers to directly engage with these studies.

In his pioneering study van Peer (1986) instructed participants to read six poems by six different poets, marking the lines that they found to be the most striking. Before eliciting reader response, van Peer had performed his own stylistic analysis of the poems (1986, pp. 57–96). Following Mukařovsky's work (1964), van Peer analysed the degree of foregrounding in the poems on three levels: phonological, grammatical and semantic. For each poem he ranked the lines from 'most foregrounded' to 'least foregrounded', and then proceeded to compare his own rankings with those of the readers. Although the participants in the study had differing degrees of literary training, van Peer found significant agreement between the readers in terms of the lines of the poems they found most striking. In addition, the readers largely agreed with van Peer's ranking of foregrounding in the poems, assessing the strikingness of the lines in a similar fashion. From this, van Peer concluded that foregrounding is an observable feature of literary texts regardless of training, thus supporting the claim from many stylisticians that this feature is a defining literary quality.

In another important study in the field, Miall and Kuiken (1994) made similar findings to those of van Peer (1986). In addition to focusing on readers' judgements of foregrounding, Miall and Kuiken's study was also interested in the effect of foregrounded sections of text on the participants' reading times. Miall and Kuiken predicted that sections of text containing a high degree of foregrounding would be read more slowly, with the readers paying more attention to these sections of text. They selected three short stories for participants to read: *The Trout* by Sean O'Faolain, *The Wrong House* by Katherine Mansfield, and *A Summing Up* by Virginia Woolf. Each story was split up into roughly equal segments using phrase and sentence divisions so that the number of segments per story ranged from 77 to 86. Three 'judges', comprising of two English graduates and the first author (Miall), analysed each of the segments across the three stories in terms of foregrounding. Like van Peer (1986), Miall and Kuiken considered the phonological, grammatical and semantic foregrounding in the stories (1994, p. 396–397).

Miall and Kuiken (1994) conducted four studies, with each study using a different story and/or reader participants with different levels of literary training. In all four studies, however, the readers were asked to read the chosen story twice on a computer screen. On the first reading the story was presented one segment at a time, with the readers clicking through a segment when they had finished reading it. On this first reading the participants' reading time was assessed. On the second reading the participants were shown each story segment in the context of the two preceding and succeeding segments. During this rereading the participants were instructed to rate the strikingness or 'affect' of each segment on a scale of 1 to 5.

Miall and Kuiken's study (1994) corroborated van Peer's results (1986), finding agreement between the readers and the judges on the foregrounded sections of literary text. On the first reading, reading times were greater during heavily foregrounded segments of the stories, while on the second reading the readers' judgements of strikingness and affect were higher for the foregrounded sections (Miall and Kuiken 1994, p. 404). These findings suggest that the readers paid more attention to the foregrounded elements of the stories and were more moved by these particular sections. Similar to van Peer (1986), these results were true for the readers regardless of their expertise and experience of reading literature, which for Miall and Kuiken 'provides evidence that foregrounding is indeed ... an intrinsically literary quality' (1994, p. 405).

It is worth noting, however, that other ESL studies have reached very different conclusions on the effect of literary training on the identification and perception of foregrounding. For example, Dixon, Bortolussi, Twilley and Leung (1993), Hakemulder (2004) and Zyngier et al. (2007 – described in more detail below) found that the participants' degree of exposure to literary texts was a predictor of their acknowledgement and appreciation of foregrounding. These studies used similar rereading tasks to those described in Miall and Kuiken (1994), so they are directly comparable. Due to this lack of consensus, the relationship between literary training and the appreciation of foregrounding is still very much a fruitful area of future research.

Emmott et al. (2006) also considered foregrounding, but focused on a particular issue within foregrounding studies, approaching this using a rather different method to those outlined above. In this study the authors were specifically interested in how text fragmentation affected the attention of readers. In other words, this study was focused on whether short and stand-alone sentences and mini-paragraphs were identified as foregrounded. Emmott et al. defined sentence fragments as 'words, phrases or clauses that cannot be classed as syntactically full sentences, but are nevertheless punctuated graphically as sentences' (2006, p. 2). As an example, Emmott et al. provide the final two noun phrases from the following extract, taken from Brick Lane (Ali 2004, p. 19): 'It was only dinner. One dinner. One guest.' The second form of text fragmentation considered is the mini-paragraph. This is defined as a very short paragraph, comprised of a single short sentence or a single sentence fragment (for examples, see Emmott et al. 2006, pp. 3–4).

Having defined their terms, Emmott et al. (2006) moved on to offering a stylistic account of the possible functions of text fragmentation. The authors regarded text fragmentation as typically occurring at 'key plot moments' (2006, pp. 6–8), often serving to grab the attention of the reader and alerting them to important information that might otherwise have been overlooked. For Emmott et al., therefore, text fragmentation is an important form of foregrounding in literary texts. The empirical investigation attempted to test the extent to which real readers' processing of these phenomena supports these stylistic assumptions.

Emmott et al. (2006) constructed an experiment using the text change detection method and involving twenty-four undergraduate students from the University of Glasgow. In the text change detection procedure participants initially read through a text. They are then given either an identical text (roughly half of the time) or given a slightly altered text with one word changed (the remaining percentage – roughly half). The assumption was that 'if readers were attending to a particular word in detail, they would recognize that a change had occurred more often than if they were not attending' (Emmott *et al.* 2006, p. 20). As the authors were interested in text fragmentation, the altered sections of text occurred at places in the text where this occurred (for examples, see Emmott *et al.* 2006, p. 21).

Emmott *et al.* (2006) created thirty-six short passages, each of which appeared in three forms. These three forms differed in terms of where the critical, altered element of the story was placed. The 'critical region' was either assimilated into an earlier sentence (condition 1), presented as a separate sentence fragment (condition 2), or occurred on its own as a mini-paragraph (condition 3). Given their assumption that text fragmentation leads to foregrounding, the authors hypothesised that the readers who were given the altered texts on second reading would be likely to notice the change if they had been given the condition 2 or condition 3 texts. By contrast, readers who had been presented with the texts in condition 1 would be unlikely to notice the change due to the lack of text fragmentation in these examples.

The results confirmed Emmott *et al.*'s hypothesis for one type of text fragmentation but not for the other type. The authors found evidence that changes were frequently detected in condition 2 (sentence fragmentation) but were not so readily attended to in condition 3 (mini-paragraphs). However, the results led the authors to conclude that 'more careful, deeper, processing is occurring for short stand-alone items, just as we have generally been assuming in the stylistic analysis' (Emmott *et al.* 2006, p. 23). To an extent, these results therefore confirm the legitimacy of stylistic claims about graphological and syntactic foregrounding. However, it is perhaps of greater interest that the supposedly more foregrounded form of text fragmentation – the mini-paragraph – did not confirm this assumption, thus making this a fascinating area for future research.

The final ESL study into foregrounding discussed in the present chapter is Zyngier *et al.*'s (2007) account of the relationship between foregrounding and textual complexity. Like Miall and Kuiken (1994) and Emmott *et al.* (2006), this study used a rereading method in order to test whether texts with a greater degree of foregrounding were evaluated higher on a second reading. Zyngier *et al.*'s assumption was that texts that contained more foregrounding are interpreted as more complex and will therefore 'prolong the reader's experience' (2007, p. 660).

In this study three extracts from longer published works were selected. The extracts were taken from Lee Stafford's *When Love Awakes* (a Mills and Boon romance novel – Text 1), Jane Austen's *Pride and Prejudice* (Text 2) and *Mrs Dalloway* by Virginia Woolf (Text 3). The three extracts were picked on the basis that they shared a particular narratological feature: free indirect discourse. As in Miall and Kuiken (1994), the three extracts were assessed in terms of foregrounding, with the Mills and Boon novel *When Love Awakes* judged to contain the least foregrounding and *Mrs Dalloway* the most foregrounding.

Zyngier *et al.* (2007) enlisted 115 participants from 'three different cultures' (2007, p. 668). The first group was comprised of students and teachers of English from a Brazilian university; the second group was made up of undergraduate English students from an Egyptian university; and the third group consisted of students taking a literary theory course at a Dutch university. The participants were initially asked to read each extract once and then fill out a questionnaire, which comprised of three general questions regarding their reaction to the story (Zyngier *et al.* 2007, pp. 667). Participants were also asked to rate each story on a variety of features: boring; complex; deep; intense; powerful; rich; senseless; striking; tiresome; trivial; unimportant; weak (Zyngier *et al.* 2007, p. 668). Having read the extracts and submitted their questionnaires, the readers were asked to reread the passages and complete the same questionnaire again.

The results of this study found that the readers agreed with the researchers on the perceived complexity of the three texts, consistently rating *Mrs Dalloway* as the most complex and *When Love Awakes* as the least complex (Zyngier *et al.* 2007, p. 669). However, contrary to the researchers' predictions the results from the readers in the Brazilian and Egyptian groups showed no significant differences between first and second readings for any of the texts. By contrast, the Dutch group did report an increased appreciation after the second reading of the texts with greater foregrounding. In sum, only the Dutch group supported the 'central hypotheses of foregrounding theory: readers will evaluate more highly the texts which offer more complex patterning on different levels, especially on a second reading' (Zyngier *et al.* 2007, p. 673).

Zyngier *et al.* (2007, pp. 674–677) posit several possible explanations as to why they found differences between the three groups in terms of their appreciation of foregrounding. One reason suggested was the Dutch students' greater proficiency in English, another the failure of rereading as a universal method of testing, while a third reason offered was the perceived cultural differences between the three groups. This third explanation was the one that received the most attention, with Zyngier *et al.* focusing on the 'reading culture' of the Netherlands in comparison to the relative lack of such a culture in either Brazil or Egypt (2007, p. 675). The Dutch group reported spending a far greater proportion of their leisure time reading than either the Brazilian group or the Egyptian group, even though all these groups consisted of students or teachers of English (2007, p. 676).

These conclusions may be a little speculative and perhaps over-generalise cultural differences, but they do make two interesting contributions to the field of ESL research into foregrounding. Firstly, the raw findings suggest that appreciation of textual complexity and foregrounding are 'in the eye of the beholder' (Zyngier *et al.* 2007). While other studies into foregrounding have tended to focus on real readers' awareness of foregrounded elements of literary texts, this study also considers readers' appreciation of foregrounded features, and the findings suggest that this appreciation is not universal amongst readers, even if awareness of foregrounding is generally shared between readers. Secondly, Zyngier *et al.*'s conclusion is interesting because it is fairly unusual for researchers in an ESL experiment to seek to explain findings in terms of contextual differences (in this case, national and cultural differences between the participants). In the Future Directions section below we suggest that a combination of socio-cultural and experimental methods, as touched on by Zyngier *et al.* (2007), is one potentially fruitful way that stylistic research into real readers can progress.

Although ESL studies with their experimental designs have tended to dominate stylistic research into real readers, this approach is not free from criticism. We outline some of these criticisms, which have tended to come from researchers advocating more natural methods of reader data collection. Outlining these criticisms of ESL therefore offers a neat segue to the alternative approach offered by NSR.

In a paper discussing research conducted within ESL, Hall (2008) criticises the reliance on highly experimental methods within the field. For Hall, studies such as those described above suffer from three fundamental problems: focusing too much on sentence processing at the expense of discourse processing, relying too heavily on researcher-produced narrative passages (disparagingly referred to as 'textoids' by Graesser, Millis and Zwaan [1997]) or on short and decontextualised extracts taken from longer literary works, and forcing the participants to read the text under atypical conditions. As a result of these problems, Hall argues that the experimental studies that typify ESL inhabit a 'frustratingly parallel research universe', often failing to adequately address 'the phenomenon it purports to tell the researcher and the readers of that research about' (2008, p. 31). These criticisms of the experimental paradigm are echoed by Allington and Swann (2009), who argue that reader studies conducted in ESL remove the act of reading so far from its natural context of experience that 'it may be better to treat such practices as indicative of the competencies on which particular groups or individuals *are able to draw when pressed* than of how reading 'normally' proceeds' (2009, p. 224 – emphasis in original).

Due to these perceived shortcomings of the ESL field and questions over the validity of the findings of individual studies, the Naturalistic Study of Reading field (NSR) has developed in recent years as an alternative approach to real reader data. The studies in this field take a broadly ethnographic approach. Leeds-Hurwitz (2005, p. 327) defines ethnography as 'a method used to describe everyday human behavior, relying heavily on participant observation in natural settings ... [T]he researcher documents what occurs in some way, through taking fieldnotes, photographs, audiotapes, and/or videotapes, as part of the effort to learn the meanings the behavior holds for participants'. Leeds-Hurwitz's definition of ethnography refers to the use of the term in anthropology. Like other linguists, NSR researchers tend to adopt an 'ethnographic perspective' (Green and Bloome 1995), moving outside the university and/or laboratory setting and engaging with readers in their natural habitat.

To date, much of this NSR research has concentrated on the book group as a source of real reader data. As collectives 'who meet on a regular basis to discuss books' (Hartley 2001, p. 20), book groups have become immensely popular in the last fifteen years. As a result, book groups have become a site of study in their own right (e.g. Hartley 2001), a data source for the discussion of taste and cultural authority in reading (e.g. Allington 2011), and a prism through which to examine reading as a social practice (e.g. Fuller 2008, Peplow 2012, Swann and Allington 2009). Although much of this research has been published in stylistics journals and presented at stylistics conferences, it still remains to be seen how this research and more traditional stylistic analysis fit together. This is a question we will return to in the Future Directions section below. Before that, however, we summarise three studies within the NSR tradition: the *Discourse of Reading Groups* project led by Swann and Allington (Allington and Swann 2009, Swann and Allington 2009), Benwell's work in the *Devolving Diasporas* project (Benwell 2009), and Peplow's work on book groups as communities of practice (Peplow 2011).

The Discourse of Reading Groups investigated the significance of book groups in modern Britain, focusing variously on the content of the interpretations generated in book groups and on the ways in which argumentation is performed in this setting (Allington and Swann 2009, O'Halloran 2011, Swann and Allington 2009). The project considered the discourse used in sixteen face-to-face reading groups based in a variety of settings (e.g. prisons, private homes, workplaces), and two online groups. The aims of the project were two-fold: 'to understand reading groups as a contemporary cultural phenomenon' (Swann and Allington 2009, p. 247), and to offer an academic approach to readers and reading that moved away from the experimental methods discussed above and towards the naturalistic study of literary reading (2009, pp. 247–248).

The Discourse of Reading Groups study approached the recorded and observed data qualitatively (although O'Halloran [2011] combined a quantitative, corpus-based approach with a qualitative approach to the reading data). Swann and Allington (2009) used the qualitative software package *Atlas-ti*, running their transcribed spoken data through the programme. *Atlas-ti* facilitates thematic analysis and codifying, so the researchers divided the transcripts into episodes, each ending with a topic shift, and tagged these episodes according to codes decided upon by the researchers. The codes were established on the basis of the type of talk that frequently recurred in the meetings, and related to the content of the talk. Three of the most important codes were 'On book' (discussion on the specific book), 'Act of reading' (discussion of interaction with the text outside the meeting), and 'Interpretation' (evaluative judgements of the text). *Atlas-ti* allows for multiple tagging, so a passage of talk could be tagged with more than one code: for example 'I read it again yesterday because I enjoyed it so much' could be tagged with both 'Evaluation' and 'Act of reading' codes (Swann and Allington 2009, p. 252).

The main findings from *The Discourse of Reading Groups* study focused on the fundamentally social aspect of the talk conducted in reading groups. Swann and Allington concluded that readers' 'interpretational activity is contingent upon aspects of the contexts in which they read and is closely embedded within the sets of social and interpersonal relations' (2009, p. 250). In the book group context, interpretations of texts 'are collaboratively developed rather than being the property of individual speakers' (2009, p. 262). This propensity for co-construction in the reading groups reflects the importance of face-work for members (Goffman 1955), meaning that the act of discussing books in this group setting 'constitutes an interactional resource through which interpersonal relations are managed' (2009, p. 262). Talk in a reading group need not be merely talk about a book, therefore, but more generally an act of social engagement.

If these findings do not appear to be particularly closely-related to stylistic analysis, then this is because the groups in *The Discourse of Reading Groups* study were not particularly interested in discussing the language of literary texts. The Language code came to be 'foregrounded' when the groups were making evaluations of the texts (Swann and Allington 2009, p. 253), with readers often praising or criticising a text on the basis of the language choices made by the author (2009, pp. 255–260). However, readers were frequently tentative about making such comments on the language of the text. This talk tended to be developed over a number of turns, with various speakers contributing (2009, pp. 256–257).

Benwell (2009) was also published in the special reading group issue of *Language and Literature* and comprised a report of her work on the *Devolving Diasporas* project. Like Swann and Allington (2009), she approached reading groups from an ethnographic perspective, focusing on naturalistic data. Benwell similarly discussed the benefits and problems with approaching reading as it 'naturally' occurs (Benwell 2009, pp. 300–301), offering her own criticism of the experimental approach to reading. While she admits that her analysis of the reading groups discussion cannot 'afford a window onto the *originary* moment of reception', Benwell argues that she is able to capture 'shared discourses on particular texts, the place occupied by literary culture in everyday life, and cultural regimes of value informing the interpretations that are collaboratively arrived at' (2009, p. 301). Her dataset consisted of multiple reading groups' discussions of Andrea Levy's novel *Small Island*.

Benwell (2009) was interested in the various ways that the readers display their understanding of the world and how this view was negotiated with others in the group. As a novel focusing on a migrant population, *Small Island* provoked responses from readers relating to issues of race and national identity. Benwell considered the way that the readers' talk attended to 'commonsense anti-racism' when they offered interpretations of the novel. The readers often positioned themselves as anti-racist when analysing characters, pitting themselves against those characters who were regarded as overtly racist. Benwell concluded that for the readers '"commonsense anti-racism" is discursively achieved by a process of "othering" – the construction of an overtly racist group against which the speaker's values are implicitly contrasted' (Benwell 2009, p. 309). Like Swann and Allington, Benwell argued that the readers' discursive practices in the reading group extended beyond just the literary.

Benwell argued that we can 'theorise reading as an *activity*, embedded in cultural and political formations: collaborative, negotiated and partially determined by shared social practices and discourses' (Benwell 2009, p. 309 – emphasis in original).

Finally, Peplow (2011) was similarly interested in book group interaction as rhetorical, focusing on how particular discourse features and patterns of speech served to lend more credibility to the evaluations and the interpretations being put forward. Drawing on detailed transcript analyses, he found that three discourse features were particularly prominent in the talk of one book group: the turn-initial 'oh' particle (e.g. 'oh, I've known a lot of Irish people'), X then Y structures (e.g. 'at first I thought I hated it, then I loved it'), and invocations of category entitlement (e.g. a reader linking a character's experience with their own personal experience). Seeing the book group as an archetypal community of practice (for an overview, see Meyerhoff 2002), Peplow argued that these recurring discourse features and patterns of speech constituted the shared repertoire (or shared language) of a book group, which played an important role in creating and fostering group identity.

Although not a criticism of NSR studies per se, it should be clear that the three studies outlined above do not offer much in the way of traditional stylistic analysis. Generally speaking, the readers in these studies tend not to focus on the kind of fine-grained textual analysis in which stylistics is typically interested. Myers discusses this in his commentary piece of the 2009 reading group special issue of *Language and Literature*:

> These studies all, in different ways, give glimpses of the processes of reading. But they pose a problem, or maybe an opportunity, for stylistic analysis, because these readers do not necessarily address the concerns of literary stylistics, even when they are talking about *language*, *literature*, and *style*.
>
> *(Myers 2009, p. 338; emphasis in original)*

Of course, this is the price to be paid for conducting naturalistic studies: readers may not discuss the specific textual features in which the researcher is interested – indeed, readers in a book group may decide to only discuss the text for five minutes. Being committed to the ethnographic study of natural reading requires the researcher to be 'open' (Baszanger and Dodier 2004) to whatever data the readers provide and willing to suspend their hypotheses and expectations in light of this data. As Myers states, however, perhaps these natural studies of reading provide an opportunity for the field of stylistics. This opportunity may be found in combining the experimental and naturalistic methods. If many ESL studies are problematic because they fail to create natural reading environments for the readers and NSR studies are limited because they do not address the concerns of stylisticians, then a compromise may be found between the two. We discuss this in greater length in the Future Directions section below. Before that, however, we offer some practical recommendations for researchers interested in conducting studies of readers. We also offer suggestions for how researchers can make their findings applicable to the field of stylistics.

Recommendations for practice

By now it should be apparent that there are problems associated with all of the approaches to real reader data. Whether the researcher chooses to take an experimental approach or employ the naturalistic method depends on what they are interested in investigating. In this section we initially offer some recommendations for conducting experimental studies, and then move on to discussing recommendations for undertaking naturalistic studies of reading.

For the researcher who wishes to analyse the effect of a specific textual feature (foregrounding, metaphor, rhyme, metre etc.), the experimental approach is likely to be best. For advice on experiment design and the different data collection possibilities, see the Further Reading section at the end of this chapter. Researchers should be aware that having a reasonably good grasp of quantitative data handling may be beneficial for conducting experimental studies, particularly if they are planning to use a large number of participants. However, an extensive knowledge of quantitative data handling is by no means necessary and studies that rely heavily on such methods are likely to produce uninteresting and unintelligible results.

Given the criticism of 'textoids' both from within ESL (Graesser *et al.* 1997, pp. 165–166) and from without (Hall 2008, pp. 31–32), we recommend the use of whole, self-contained texts when conducting experimental research, where possible. For researchers who are interested in isolating and analysing the effect of a particular stylistic feature this may be difficult, and for obvious practical reasons using entire texts favours the study of poems (e.g. van Peer 1986) and short stories (e.g. Miall and Kuiken 1994) over novels, but we feel it is important to be able to make comments on real literary texts and readers' engagement with entire works of literature. For instance, Hakemulder's (2004) alterations to his experiment design, particularly his shift from using an extract from Rushdies's *The Satanic Verses* to using a Nabokov poem, shows not only the benefits of using a self-contained literary text but also that the results of experimental research can very much depend on the text that the participants are asked to read (2004, pp. 214–215).

Regardless of whether a researcher is conducting an ESL-inspired study or a NSR-inspired study, we believe it is important for them to draw on data from a variety of readers, who possess a wide-range of reading abilities and literary training. The ESL studies outlined in the previous section all used participants picked from a university context: students (undergraduate or graduate) and teachers. On the one hand this bias is quite predictable given that these studies are carried out by researchers based in universities and (in many cases) participants can be enlisted in exchange for course credit. Using such participants does, however, have a (potentially misguided) theoretical basis as well. There is the assumption in many experimental studies that the best way to investigate the thought processes underlying reading is to study those readers who are the most competent and the most highly trained – a view put forward by Harker (1994, p. 204). However, this is a limited approach to take to reading, and very likely the assumption about non-academic readers' competencies is incorrect, too. There is something to be said for researching beyond the academy as a good in its own right. Researchers need not necessarily be interested in probing issues of literary competence when using readers drawn from outside the university context, since engaging with the reading practices of the general public can potentially lead to a range of interesting findings – and, moreover, findings that have wide applicability.

When working with real readers, researchers need to ensure that they conform to their university or organisation's code of ethics. Specific policy on this differs between institutions and academic departments, so researchers should check the guidance on ethics for their particular department. Researchers will certainly need to produce consent forms for their participants to sign before taking part. These forms should give the participants a little information about the purpose of the study. On this note, we feel it is important for researchers working in this field to feed back their results to their participants after they have conducted a study. At the very least, researchers should debrief their participants immediately after they have taken part. Doing this will not only ensure that the researcher is complying with ethical guidelines; it also means that there is a greater likelihood that participants will feel happy with their treatment and will therefore be more likely to agree to take part in similar studies in the future.

Now we will turn to specific recommendations for taking the natural approach to readers. As mentioned earlier, this method is more suitable if the researcher is interested in studying reading 'as it comes'. Although conducting this kind of study may mean that the researcher is unable to address their initial research questions directly, there is no doubt that collecting such data will lead the researcher to make some fascinating findings. The NSR research contributions described above all focused on face-to-face book groups as the site of study, but research in this field need not be limited to this. The internet offers a number of opportunities for obtaining real reader data (e.g. online book groups, reading blogs, customer book reviews). Another possibility is to use university seminars (e.g. Allington 2012) or the school classroom (e.g. Eriksson Barajas and Aronsson 2009) as sites through which to study real reading.

For researchers planning to use book groups, it is worth heeding Allington's warning regarding the use of such data:

> It might be tempting to see them [book clubs] as prelapsarian interpretive communities uninfluenced by academic and other authority, but much social research would suggest this to be naive ... When we study reading group activity, then, we are not studying reading in the abstract, but a social practice with specific relationships to cultural legitimacy and to social stratification.
>
> *(Allington 2011, p. 319)*

Allington's point here is that book groups are not spaces from which researchers can necessarily gain unmediated access to real readers' literary interpretations and the cognitive processes that underlie these readings. Book groups may be long-running and well-established collectives in which particular relationships exist between the members, particular group identities may be salient, and certain types of interpretation are valued over others. This means that the responses that the readers offer are not easily decontextualised and may need to be seen in terms of surrounding conversational context and the relationships that exist between group members.

Future directions

In this chapter we have outlined two rather different approaches to real readers that are closely-related to stylistics research: the experimental ESL approach and the ethnographic NSR approach. We argued that both of these approaches have associated problems. As mentioned, questions have been raised regarding the methods of the ESL approach, specifically whether the experimental testing of readers creates 'artificial' reading situations (Allington and Swann 2009, Hall 2008), while the findings of NSR studies to date seem to have limited applicability for stylistics, not least because readers in natural contexts do not tend to focus on fine, linguistic detail when discussing and debating literary texts (Hall 2008, p. 32). Future work in the area of stylistics and real readers may seek to combine these two approaches, thus benefitting from the positive aspects of each approach and hopefully mitigating the problems of each method.

For instance, researchers could draw on a mixed-methodology when approaching a particular group of readers. A recording could be made of a group naturally discussing a particular text. Analysis of the responses gathered from this discussion could then be complemented with more experimental methods using the same text and the same readers. The researcher could conduct individual interviews with the readers at a point after the meeting, asking the participants to elaborate on particular passages of text that they referred to during the discussion – perhaps inviting them to pin-point words and phrases that led them to make their specific comments. To a certain extent, Fialho (2007) attempts this kind of mixed methodology in focusing on both quantitative and qualitative aspects of her reading data, but her study still errs very much on the experimental side.

Benwell (2009, p. 312) suggests that researchers should move 'dialectically between response and fictional text' when studying real reader responses. Future studies could therefore consider how textual features map onto the evaluations and interpretations that are revealed in the talk of readers. To date, Whiteley (2011) probably best accomplishes this balance between textual features and reader response. In her study, she enlisted three friends to read *The Remains of the Day* by Kazuo Ishiguro. Whiteley considered how the readers talked about the novel in a group setting, focusing specifically on how they identified with the characters. For some in the NSR field, the design of Whiteley's study may be a little too tightly controlled in that she selected the readers (rather than looking at a pre-existing book group), she picked the text, and she suggested the topics of conversation. However, these constraints allow her to look at specific elements of the text-occasioned readers' talk that interest her, thus making a direct contribution to stylistic analysis. Therefore, we believe that future studies could focus on similar themes in readers' talk, perhaps considering how readers in pre-existing book clubs go about reconstructing passages of foregrounded text and/or how readers go about adopting the perspective of characters in the their talk about texts.

Related topics

Emotion and neuroscience, linguistic levels of foregrounding in stylistics, quantitative methodological approaches, reader response criticism

Further reading

Language and Literature, 18 (3).

A special issue of this stylistics journal from 2009 containing nine pioneering NSR studies.

Miall, D., 2006. Empirical approaches to studying literary readers: The state of the discipline. *Book History*, 9, 291–311.

An excellent overview and critique of experimental research into literary reading.

Steen, G. J., 1991. The empirical study of literary reading: Methods of data collection. *Poetics*, 20, 559–575

A useful account of different research methods available to real reader researchers.

Swann, J., Peplow, D., Trimarco, P. & Whiteley, S., 2014. *Reading group discourse: Cognitive stylistics and sociocultural approaches*. London: Routledge.

Based within the NSR tradition, this book looks at reading groups across a range of different contexts: face-to-face, online, and in schools.

Zyngier, S, Bortolussi, M., Chesnokova, A., and Auracher, J., eds., 2008. *Directions in empirical literary studies*. Amsterdam: Benjamins.

A collection of papers based within the ESL tradition, some of which are experimental in nature.

References

Ali, M., 2004. *Brick lane*. London: Black Swan.

Allington, D., 2011. 'It actually painted a picture of the village and the sea and the bottom of the sea': Reading groups, cultural legitimacy, and description in narrative (with particular reference to John Steinbeck's *The Pearl*). *Language and Literature*, 20 (4), 317–332.

Allington, D., 2012. Private experience, textual analysis, and institutional authority: The discursive practice of critical interpretation and its enactment in literary training. *Language and Literature*, 21 (2), 211–225.

Allington, D. and Swann, J., 2009. Researching literary reading as social practice. *Language and Literature*, 18 (3), 219–230.

Barthes, R., 1977. *Image-music-text*. London: Fontana.

Baszanger, I. and Dodier, N., 2004. Ethnography: Relating the part to the whole. *In:* D. Silverman, ed. *Qualitative research: Theory, method, and practice*. London: Sage, 9–34.

Benwell, B., 2009. 'A pathetic and racist and awful character': Ethnomethodological approaches to the reception of diasporic fiction. *Language and Literature*, 18 (3), 300–315.

Bortolussi, M. and Dixon, P., 1996. The effects of formal training on literary reception. *Poetics*, 23 (6), 471–487.

Carter, R., 2004. *Language and creativity: The art of common talk*. London: Routledge.

Culler, J., [1975] 2002. *Structural poetics: Structuralism, linguistics and the study of literature*. 2nd edn. London: Routledge.

Cupchik, G. C., Oatley, K. and Voderer, P., 1998. Emotional effects of reading excerpts from short stories by James Joyce. *Poetics*, 25 (6), 363–377.

Dixon, P. and Bortolussi, M., 2008. Textual and extra-textual manipulations in the empirical study of literary response. *In:* S. Zyngier, M. Bortolussi, A. Chesnokova, and J. Auracher, eds. *Directions in empirical literary studies*. Amsterdam: Benjamins, 75–87.

Dixon, P., Bortolussi, M., Twilley, L. C. and Leung, A., 1993. Literary processing and interpretation: Towards empirical foundations. *Poetics*, 22 (1/2), 5–33.

Dorfman, M. H., 1996. Evaluating the interpretive community: Evidence from expert and novice readers. *Poetics*, 23 (6), 453–470.

Emmott, C., Sanford, A. J. and Morrow, L. I., 2006. Capturing the attention of readers? Stylistic and psychological perspectives on the use and effect of text fragmentation in narratives. *Journal of Literary Semantics*, 35, 1–30.

Eriksson Barajas, K. and Aronsson, K., 2009. Avid versus struggling readers: Co-construed pupils identities in school booktalk. *Language and Literature*, 18 (3), 281–299.

Fialho, O., 2007. Foregrounding and familiarization: Understanding readers' response to literary texts. *Language and Literature*, 16 (2), 105–123.

Fish, S., 1980. *Is there a text in this class? The authority of interpretive communities*. Cambridge, MA: Harvard University Press.

Fuller, D., 2008. Reading as social practice: The 'beyond the book' research project. *Popular Narrative Media*, 1 (2), 211–216.

Goffman, E., 1955. On face-work: An analysis of ritual elements in social interaction. *Psychiatry*, 18, 213–231.

Graesser, A., Millis, K., and Zwaan, R., 1997. Discourse comprehension. *Annual Review of Psychology*, 48, 163–189.

Green, J. and Bloome, D., 1995. Ethnography and ethnographers of and in education. *In:* F. Flood, S. Heath, D. Alvermann and D. Lapp, eds. *A handbook for literary educators*. New York: Macmillan, 181–202.

Hakemulder, J. F., 2004. Foregrounding and its effect on readers' perception. *Discourse Processes*, 38 (2), 193–218.

Hall, G., 2008. Empirical research into the processing of free indirect discourse and the imperative of ecological validity. *In:* S. Zyngier, M. Bortolussi, A. Chesnokova and J. Auracher, eds. *Directions in empirical literary studies*. Amsterdam: Benjamins, 21–34.

Hall, G., 2009. Texts, readers – and real readers. *Language and Literature*, 18 (3), 331–337.

Harker, W. J., 1994. Plain sense and poetic significance: Tenth-grade readers reading two poems. *Poetics*, 22 (3), 199–218.

Hartley, J., 2001. *Reading groups*. Oxford: Oxford University Press.

Iser, W., 1978. *The act of reading: A theory of aesthetic response*. Baltimore: John Hopkins University Press.

Leeds-Hurwitz, W., 2005. Ethnography. *In:* K. L. Fitch and R. E. Sanders, eds. *Handbook of language and social interaction*. London: Lawrence Erlbaum, 327–353.

Mailloux, S., 1982. Rhetorical hermeneutics. *Critical Inquiry*, 11 (4), 620–641.

Martindale, C. and Dailey, A., 1995. I. A. Richards revisited: Do people agree in their interpretations of literature? *Poetics*, 23 (4), 299–314.

Meyerhoff, M., 2002. Communities of practice. *In:* J. K. Chambers, P. Trudgill and N. Schilling-Estes, eds. *The handbook of language variation and change*. Oxford: Blackwell, 526–548.

Miall, D., 2006. Empirical approaches to studying literary readers: The state of the discipline. *Book History*, 9, 291–311.

Miall, D. S. and Kuiken, D., 1994. Foregrounding, defamiliarization, and affect: Response to literary stories. *Poetics*, 22, 389–407.

Mukařovsky, J., 1964. Standard language and poetic language. *In:* P. L. Garvin, ed. *A Prague School reader on esthetics, literary structure, and style*. Washington D. C.: Georgetown University, 17–30.

Myers, G., 2009. Stylistics and 'reading-in-talk'. *Language and Literature*, 18 (3), 338–344.

O'Halloran, K., 2011. Investigating argumentation in reading groups: Combining manual qualitative coding and automated corpus analysis tools. *Applied Linguistics*, 32 (2), 172–196.

Peplow, D., 2011. 'Oh, I've known a lot of Irish people': Reading groups and the negotiation of literary interpretation, *Language and Literature*, 20 (4), 295–315.

Peplow, D., 2012. Negotiating literary interpretation in the reading group. Unpublished PhD Thesis. University of Nottingham.

Pratt, M. L., 1982. Interpretive strategies/strategic interpretations: On Anglo-American reader-response criticism. *boundary 2*, 11 (1/2), 201–231.

Richards, I. A., 1929. *Practical criticism: A study of literary judgment*. New York: Harcourt Brace Jovanovich.

Short, M., 1996. *Exploring the language of poems, plays and prose*. Harlow: Longman.

Short, M. and van Peer, W., 1989. Accident! Stylisticians evaluate: Aims and methods of stylistic analysis. *In:* M. Short, ed. *Reading, analysing and teaching literature*. Harlow: Longman, 22–71.

Simpson, P., 2004. *Stylistics: A resource book for students*. London: Routledge.

Steen, G. J., 1991. The empirical study of literary reading: Methods of data collection. *Poetics*, 20, 559–75.

Stockwell, P., 2002. *Cognitive poetics: An introduction*. London: Routledge.

Swann, J. and Allington, D., 2009. Reading groups and the language of literary texts: A case study in social reading. *Language and Literature*, 18 (3), 247–264.

Swann, J., Peplow, D., Trimarco, P. & Whiteley, S. (2014) *Reading group discourse: Cognitive stylistics and sociocultural approaches*. London: Routledge.

Swann, J., Pope, R. and Carter, R., 2011. *Creativity in language and literature*. London: Palgrave.

van Peer, W., 1986. *Stylistics and psychology: Investigations of foregrounding*. London: Croom Helm.

van Peer, W., 2001. Justice in perspective. *In:* S. Chatman and W. van Peer, eds. *New perspectives on narrative perspective*. Albany: State University of New York, 325–336.

Wales, K., 2001. *A dictionary of stylistics*. 2nd edn. Harlow: Longman.

Whiteley, S., 2011. Text world theory, real readers and emotional responses to *The Remains of the Day*. *Language and Literature*, 20 (1), 23–42.

Wimsatt, W. K. and Beardsley, M. C., 1946. The intentional fallacy. *The Sewanee Review* 54, 468–488.

Zyngier, S., van Peer, W. and Hakemulder, J., 2007. Complexity and foregrounding: In the eye of the beholder? *Poetics Today*, 28 (4), 653–682.

28

Stylistics and film

Michael Toolan

Introduction

One difficulty with writing a handbook chapter under the title 'Stylistics and Film' is that stylistics as normally understood is centrally about language, and the specific consequences of particular ways of using language; but film is film, a recording of visual images onto a translucent surface that permits projection of those images onto a surface so that, typically, many can see the images. Language is not a necessary ingredient. Not that we should point to the silent movies of the early twentieth century as confirmation of this: these lacked sound (even if the projection was accompanied by live performance in the theatre, typically on piano or organ) but they did not lack language, since most contained written captions. The dominant venue or environment of film reception has shifted massively over the last one hundred years, too: first from the public theatre to the domestic television, and latterly to the computer screen, often displaying internet-based material. By convention we now understand that a film's images will (appear to) be moving and be accompanied by a sophisticated and synchronised sound track, and increasingly all of this will be recorded and reproduced digitally, with no real *film* (e.g. a translucent flexible strip coated with an emulsion of images) involved. However, even contemporary digital films, narrative or not, need not of necessity involve language. What would a stylistics of a language-less modern film be like? It is safe to say the question is rarely contemplated, and is remote from what most stylisticians concern themselves with. More plausible would be a *narratology* of language-less modern film, classifying and evaluating events and sequences, time manipulations, characterisation and point of view and world-shifts.

In a conjunction like 'stylistics and film', then, the term *film* is in practice typically a metonym for a particular kind of cultural artefact: the output of a recording, on film or in digital files, of a sequence of images and sounds (but not of smells, tastes, feels), which tell a fictional narrative; and, further (except in TV series), usually between one and two hours in duration. Thus, excluded from consideration, although they would need attention in a broader study of film, are such forms as film documentaries, TV and internet commercials, and most segments posted on YouTube and similar websites. This narrowing still leaves many marginal cases: filmed versions of operas and ballets, for example, are not yet explicitly excluded from attention, but few stylisticians who study film consider these genres, where film-independent kinds of expertise (music, singing, dance) seem to be more important than the specific affordances of film. A film of Shakespeare's play *Hamlet* falls within the core activity of the stylistic analysis of film, while a film of his contemporary Monteverdi's opera *The Coronation of Poppea* does not. There is a 'canon' of works to which film stylistics has been chiefly applied. It includes art films and feature films of the kind studied by the most celebrated scholars, critics and directors (Bordwell and Thompson, Eisenstein, Bazin, Truffaut, and Carroll), narrative film series broadcast on TV and also issued in DVD boxed sets or via internet download, and also some of the usually shorter and more digitally-dependent films only available on the web.

Yet another category of films might be mentioned here, which language-oriented stylisticians have never to my knowledge studied: the comparatively short films found in art galleries and museums, classified as 'installation art'. The stylisticians' disregard may be owing to these films' perceived remoteness from the written text, and a sense that they fall within the sister domain of art criticism and analysis; in addition, their status as narrative is often doubtful (there is no reason for film stylistics to focus exclusively on narrative films, but so far it has). Borderline between being film and digital poems or narratives are such internet-based works as Robert Kendall's *Faith* and Kate Pullinger and Chris Joseph's *Flight Paths*, where advancement from one (changing) screen to the next is dependent upon the viewer's mouse-click. That click is sufficiently similar to turning the page of a book and is sufficiently different from our typical film-viewing experience as to be decisive.

Within the multimodal world of a narrative film, the two main channels or media of communication are the visual and the auditory. If we follow multimodality scholars such as Kress and van Leeuwen we should not call the visual and auditory resources *modes*, because a mode for them is an organised set of semiotic resources for making meaning in a culture; so a written language would be a mode that exploited the visual *medium* in one way, while, perhaps, Western representational painting might be a distinct mode exploiting the visual medium in a different way. The auditory medium itself subdivides: audible speech (audible to the viewer), immediately symbolic, can be distinguished from all other kinds of sounds in the film. These non-speech sounds can be classified either as diegetic (naturally part of the depicted situation: the clink of cutlery during a dinner-party, the squealing of tires and roaring of engines during a car chase) or as extra- or non-diegetic (the frantic music accompanying a car chase, not emanating from within the scene but clearly an evaluative 'extra' added during the editing process: a resource infrequently used in live theatre where, perhaps, speech is even more important than in film).

There is a loose hierarchy of importance among these types of sound, with comprehensible speech the most important and non-diegetic sound the least so, but disruptions of this ranking are numerous. For example, diegetic non-speech sounds may be crucially important to the narrative, even when they occur in a way that is removed from ongoing verbal commentary, and perhaps 'represented' (rather than 'presented', that is, with identifiable source) in Martinec's terms (1998). Such a sound may be a 'kernel' in the telling of events – e.g. a gunshot, the first cries of new-born baby, the tolling of a bell or the playing of a wedding or funeral march. A particular kind of extra-diegetic sound familiar to all Western filmgoers will be non-diegetic orchestral music in the 'big budget' Hollywood narrative film. Regrettably, this has become one of the most hackneyed resources imaginable. At the time of writing, for example, Spielberg's *Lincoln* is being much commented upon in TV and radio arts programmes in the run-up to the Oscar awards for 2013, but the swelling 'grand-heroic' music reproduced from that movie sounds uncreatively similar to the grand-heroic swelling lines of hundreds of other commercial films of the past quarter-century (regardless, therefore, of differences of topic or era: at their core these films, recurringly tell of how 'a good man' – it is usually a man – has done 'good works'). Such over-familiarity and inter-substitutability (here of music, but potentially also of setting, shot-progression, dialogue, character-interaction and so on) are arguably reflexes of excessively generic film-making.

It is important to avoid treating the visual and the auditory media bifurcation as one in which language functions exclusively in the second. Language re-combines the two modes. In a typical film there are many forms of writing for the viewer to interpret, alongside the forms of speech the listener must process; in a typical feature film, a heavy input of writing comes soon after the first few minutes, in the opening credits. It is also widely assumed that the prominence of the visual in films means that this mode is more important to film comprehension and appreciation than the aural. However, there are some indicators that point to the aural on occasion being more important than the visual: where a film involves a good deal of character speech comprehensible to the audience, someone who attends a showing of that film with the visual mode removed (as a blind person does) may well get a fuller understanding of it than a viewer who has all the sound narration removed (as a deaf person does, although often with slight help by way of lip-reading). This may on occasion justify the claim that a blind person will tend more fully to understand a typical speech-rich film than a deaf person will. If these generalisations have any validity, they also point to the aural mode actually being more essential in film and TV narratives than the visual mode; and while the aural mode may comprise various kinds of sound, by far the most discursively rich and critical, usually, is the representation of understandable human speech. However, these claims concern comprehension only, and chiefly of content: absorbing a film's atmosphere and moods, and the sense of involvement it may foster in the viewer, clearly often relies heavily on a response to the richness of visual signs and non-speech sounds, in conjunction and in sequence. These claims also apply more where the dialogue we hear is, for want of a better term, significant: instrumental in plot-development, or highly indicative of character, or explanatory of background or motives. By contrast, we can imagine extended film dialogue that is phatic or inconsequential, such that blocked access to it has only a slight impact on film comprehension. Thus, there are many exceptions to the above generalisations, which also do not fit foreign language films, where the speech may be wonderfully clear to the listener, who nevertheless can make little sense of it and relies heavily on the visual mode for the subtitled translations as well as for the story-world representation.

In the remainder of this chapter I will focus at length on the difficulties and the challenges that we are faced with in trying to produce a stylistic representation of film, for it is here where much work still needs to be done by the stylisticians of the future.

Procedural challenges for a stylistics *of* film

> Style in cinema, then, is a set of such decisions by means of which I select or write the scenario; decide the objects and actors at which to point my camera; select the lens; design the lighting, costumes, make-up, decor (or accept those that are given); select film stock, f stop, shot metrage, angle, framing, and composition; design or accept the mise-en-scene; select, direct or accept actors; select the opticals, printing, and effects; select the sounds and decide their relationships to the images; and edit, etc, etc.
>
> *(Levaco 1974, p. 54)*

A stylistic analysis (of film) cannot mean simply a technical analysis (of which there will be innumerable kinds, emerging from film schools), but a technical analysis along the lines and with the assumptions enshrined in literary stylistic analysis. As Norgaard *et al.* note, stylistics of film is:

> The application of traditionally textual tools of analysis to the study of film and moving images … As is the case with textual stylistics, film stylistics aims for a more retrievable way of analysing cinematic forms based on frameworks which have already proven successful in the study of textual forms.
>
> *(Norgaard, Busse and Montoro 2011, p. 21)*

This in turn means that a stylistic analysis of a film must treat it as a communicative aesthetic event, just as such an analysis of a play would so treat it, adopting a suitably broad understanding of what 'aesthetic' and 'communicative event' may mean here. Like canonical communicative events, films are a complex integration of modes and factors, but typically they represent human actions and speech in specific and usually quite familiar or realist settings. Furthermore, reflecting their 'aesthetic' dimension, fictional narrative films are shaped by an acute selectivity of presentation, conducive to the 'telling' of a story and a sense of narrative arc.

In practice the engagement of stylistics with film has historically involved an assessment of the various semiotic resources used in feature-length narrative films, themselves often involving an adaptation from a novel or short story original, so as to identify what is distinctive in those resources and in their careful deployment in film. (See, as representative of such work, Forceville 2002, a study of the nonverbal means used to convey confusion in a film narrative, where that confusion was conveyed verbally – not simply reported – in the original novel.) Often the goal has been a 'grammar' of the main categories of choice that each channel or resource makes available (diegetic sounds, extra-diegetic sounds, lighting, editing, colour, granularity of image, point of view, and pace, for example). More specific topics have been less frequently addressed, at least from a specifically stylistic point of view: e.g. the construal of characters in the course of the narrative. This has been explored fairly systematically from various angles by stylisticians in relation to characters in written narratives, but much less so, and less systematically, in relation to those in films (or in plays in performance, for that matter). There are multiple explanations for this (it is not simple neglect), but chief of these is a recognition that narrative films (let alone films more generally) are not easily assimilated to an analysis that would remain recognisably and centrally stylistic. This in turn brings us back to the point that a stylistic analysis implies a systematic, demonstrable, potentially replicable and potentially falsifiable commentary on some part of the *verbal* texture of a text (usually literary, usually written), a commentary that particularly draws on one tradition or another within that broad field of enquiry known as linguistics.

Despite a century and more of film-making and film-viewing, it remains uncertain whether a thoroughgoing stylistics of film, on firm and enduring foundations, will emerge as distinct from a variety of efforts of transfer and application, i.e. of trying to use on films the verbal (especially written verbal) categories found useful in stylistic analysis of texts, and commenting on differences of affordance. This is essentially a comparativist enterprise, often reflecting an at least covert interest in literature-to-film adaptation, which I would summarise as 'stylistics and film', with the two terms conjoined and coordinated. It is telling that such comparative application rarely arises in relation to wordless music: I am not aware of attempts to import literary linguistic analytical categories and priorities into the analysis of symphonies and string quartets (e.g. a transitivity analysis of Beethoven's *Grosse Fugue,* a deictic or modality study of Sibelius's Fifth Symphony), although rhetorical analyses relating originally verbal style figures to music, and even narratological analyses of instrumental musical compositions, have considerable potential (pattern/repetition being at least as crucial to music as to verbal art). However, beyond the conjunction that we mostly witness at present – 'stylistics *and* film' – lies the question of whether an embedding relation – a 'stylistics *of* film' – is possible, and if not, what prevents this? These are the questions I explore further below, but before doing so I will make a couple of points about prose-to-film adaptations.

Much everyday commentary around film adaptations remains oriented to questions of 'fit', faithfulness, and commensurateness, despite the fact that standard opinion now insists that such evaluative comparisons are invidious or improper, each form – written narrative and film – needing to be judged on its own terms (see Stam 2005 for a representative recent account). To be set alongside that principle of autonomy, however, is the fact that in novel-film adaptation one version (the written one) is almost invariably prior and originary, taking precedence in a binary relation which, like most cultural binaries, develops a power/hierarchy asymmetry. Just such a negotiation between the theoretical autonomy of film adaptations, and their practical dependence and secondariness, can be seen in a discussion of good and bad adaptations by Salman Rushdie (2009), where he concludes that the best adaptations 'retain the essence' of the source text. So long, therefore, as we have adaptations (like translations) with an identified source text and a target text, and so long as sources precede and enable targets, no amount of argument will put adapters and translators on an *equal* footing with originators, but always on a different one (and occasionally a 'higher' one). Novel-film comparisons can hardly cease (so long as both forms are deemed to be rendering 'the same narrative'); but sharply evaluative comparison, where the forms and effects of one medium are dubiously judged against those of the other, may dwindle and come to be seen as part of a transitional twentieth-century reception of film. Arguably 'adaptation/translation' is itself one half of a suppressed binarism, the other partner being intertextuality. Adaptation is a more constraining and controlling process than intertextual appropriation. It is possible that the latter is marginalised as a cultural activity for that very reason, while 'faithful adaptation' is promoted as a result of its being more attractive to the wider social order than uncontrollable intertextuality (where faithfulness, ownership, and duty are inapplicable). Intertextuality is a freer, more creative and (ironically) more 'adaptive' principle which embraces cultural transmission, variation, change and recontextualisation, and does not insist on Shakespeare 'faithfully' adapting Holinshed, Joyce 'faithfully' adapting Homer and so on. It is a principle that recognises that every adaptation or translation is predicated in part on a dissatisfaction with the original – a dissatisfaction about the fact that, for all its merits, Joyce's 'The Dead' does not reach film audiences (whereas John Huston's work of the same name does), or that Lu Xun's stories are inaccessible to those who cannot read Chinese.

What would a stylistics of film aim to do?

By analogy with stylistics' goals in relation to literary texts, a stylistics of film could be expected to attempt to show how subjective impressions and intuitive responses of reasonably acculturated filmgoers are sourced in a range of foregrounded or patterned effects and techniques carefully achieved by the film-making team, and to underpin its account with arguments, evidence and texts. In this project, one area of great interest is that of shot composition and combination, the kinds of cut found in a film and the rhythm of their sequencing. Cutting and shot-combining and the meanings of the choices to a film-maker in this domain, I will argue, are a fascinating counterpart of the combinatorial logic behind the shaping of written narrative into punctuated sentences (or the signalling of a counterpart segmentation of the stream of speech by means of intonation choices).

A canonical stylistic analysis finds a 'striking' widely-agreed-upon effect in the work(s) of art of interest (restlessness giving way to calm, in a passage from a Raymond Chandler novel, or alienation and frustration in the opening of Hemingway's 'Cat in the Rain' story, for example). It then looks for a prominent linguistic pattern in the text, a foregrounded use of language or linguistic feature, which it proposes is the efficient cause of the readerly effect. Detailed textual analysis may be needed in the attempt to show 'but for' causation: but for the author's use of this or that precise pattern or foregrounded texture, the particular reader-confirmed effect would not have been achieved (or triggered, or induced). Time may also need to be spent on a full explanation of the instrumental pattern, its crucial characteristics (syntactically, phonologically, semantically, relative to co-text, and so on). Stylisticians have to be reasonably proficient or competent readers of literature, but their claim is to be especially competent and proficient scholars of language, particularly the written language of literary texts. I will say a little more here, relevant to the stylistic analysis of film I believe, about the stylistic prioritising – as I see it – of written language.

Some stylisticians may in principle be just as interested in the spoken language as in the written: the language of performed plays and poetry, for example. However, in practice the stylistics of spoken forms of literature (such as plays in performance) has mostly attended to those aspects that are discussible on the basis of a written transcript, which as the object of study and example replaces actual passages of speech – for example, studies of pragmatic effects and their linguistic sources, rather than the work's distinctively spoken dimensions. As for some of the prominent characteristics exclusive to speech, such as intonation patterns or variations in sonority, we find few stylistic studies of these. A quick search of the online catalogue for *Language and Literature*, now in its twentieth year, shows just two passing mentions of sonority (in articles about poetic rhyme and rhythm by Cureton 1994 and Hanson 2003 respectively). Intonation gets many more hits – forty-five in total – but on closer examination only three papers address it in any detail: Pople 1998, Cauldwell 1999, and Piazza 2010. By contrast, when a search with the written-language-exclusive term *paragraph* is executed 123 hits are returned; no doubt very few of these are papers that dwell on paragraphing to any great extent, but still it shows that the categories related to writing are prominent in the discourse of stylistics to a degree that those specific to speech often are not.

A stylistics of film seems compelled to grapple with the problem of having to work with a transcription, into the single, fixed and permanent modality of writing, of the multiplicity of kinds of meaningful communication that are coordinated and function progressively in film, with added uncertainty as to which of the kinds or strands are most important from one film to the next, or even from one shot sequence in a film to the next. Part of the problem relates to the fact that transcription is itself not a neutral act, as Ochs noted in a seminal article; it is 'a selective process reflecting theoretical goals and definitions' (Ochs 1979, p. 44). However, in addition to being necessarily selective, a transcription itself performs a foregrounding of some features and a backgrounding or silencing of others from the original communicative event. Driven by the researcher's interests, it performs an analysis while purporting to create the 'objective' material upon which an analysis can be conducted.

The discipline of film studies has clearly developed many of the things that Ochs called for in the study of child language, such as a set of conventions and a metalanguage for describing the verbal and nonverbal actions in a sequence. However, what is less clear is how that descriptive system (of types of shot, types of cut, types of transition, choices of lighting and depth of field, choices of extradiegetic sound, and so on – all the discriminations described in Bordwell and Thompson's *Film Art*, for example) can be used in a *stylistic* analysis of film, in the sense of an analysis treating a film narrative as a form of designed or crafted communication. This in turn is because in a film, as in a play or even a song, there is much more going on, much more involved, than that which is sponsored or given by the 'script' – whereas in relation to poetry and prose fiction, literary stylistics can proceed with reasonable confidence that the latter is the case. If I copy out Yeats's 'Sailing to Byzantium' I have not reduced it in any way; few would contend that my copied-out poem was not the poem itself. A useful test or standard to consider here is the 'reproducibility' of the original work from the transcript. An accurate and detailed transcribing of a poem or novel, even of a string quartet or a play, arguably assures us of being able to reproduce the original work itself; this is much less reliably true, it seems, with regard to reproducing a film from its detailed transcript. There is a necessary reduction and simplification in the devising of a suitable transcript of a narrative film, which some call logocentrism, others call 'entextualisation', but which in any case is inescapable if analysis, especially stylistically-minded analysis and argumentation, is to proceed. For an interesting critique of the methodologies and merits of two recent 'logocentric' studies of film dialogue (Kozloff 2000 and McIntyre 2008, from a film studies scholar and a stylistician respectively), see Richardson 2010; for broadly stylistic studies of the artifices of film dialogue, see Bednarek (2010) and Piazza, Bednarek, and Rossi (2011).

If I have dwelt at length on the difficulties of producing a written, readable, monomodal representation or 'capture' of the main things that have occurred, in combination and in sequence, during the film event, it is only because of the importance of the issues raised. The continuing difficulty with establishing a satisfactory framework for multimodal analysis should instruct us. Everywhere in discourse and communication studies the analyst confronts this difficulty, so profound theoretical considerations are at stake here. Ultimately the analyst has to acknowledge that no record 'captures everything important' in a film, song, or poem except a performance of the work under consideration – which gets you no further along in the task of analysis than you were before. So we are reminded that even a multi-strand transcription or score is a partial and reductive representation, good for some purposes but not all (and positively bad for some). Our hopes and illusions about written records giving us all the main information from a communicational event stem from writing's long use in the recording of speech, bolstered in the last century or more by the partial codifying of the phonetic units, pauses, pitch rises and falls and stress patterns used in particular speech events. However, written transcripts of speech events are also hugely reductive records, capturing certain 'main things', but only relative to prior decisions (a theory of speech meanings) about what the main things are. Among the innumerable factors that are not deemed 'main things' affecting the meaning and effects of speech events are the ambient lighting and the habitual pitch of speakers' voices: if you look for information about these, in standard discourse analytic or sociolinguistic speech transcripts, you will look in vain.

Main challenges on the way to a stylistics of film

When stylisticians look at film, they almost invariably do so by adapting the categories and some of the principles of linguistics, and – given their disciplinary background – it is hard to see them doing otherwise. If linguistics is a systematic study of our most complex semiotic resource, i.e. language, then it ought to be useful in the study of one large genre of semiosis, i.e. narrative film. At least, it ought to so long as language is seen as a branch of communication, with poems, mime, paintings and films as different exponents of the communicative impulse. Here it is helpful that there has been an opening out of much linguistics over the past forty years or more, and a parallel opening out of stylistics: both have broadened to acknowledge the social context of any linguistic act (so that consideration of the addresser and the addressee, at the very least, is recognised as crucial to the assessment of the act), and both have also come to pay more attention to humankind's cognitive dispositions, which might shape our communicative productions (literary or otherwise) in ways we either unthinkingly take for granted or are blithely unaware of. A stylistics which was once chiefly textual – using the core linguistic descriptive systems of phonology, morphology, syntax and semantics – now equally draws on sociolinguistics, pragmatics, and cognitive linguistic models.

Something of a similar broadening can be seen in many linguistic studies of films (at most, I suggest, a conjunction of stylistics and film). There is increasing study of aspects of film other than the verbal (spoken or written), and, where the verbal is attended to, there is a more frequent study of its sociopragmatic determinants (less frequently, its cognitive ones) rather than its core lexicogrammatical features. Quite a number of articles interested in one or another linguistic resource (often relating to discourse analytic or pragmatic phenomena) use segments of well-known film by way of naturalistic exemplification. Unless the film is minimally-edited documentary, the naturalism is often more apparent than real. In any case, these are not stylistic analyses of the film *qua* film, but rather a branch of sociolinguistics or pragmatics, where the film clip is chiefly attractive as high-quality and widely-available 'data'.

By the same token there tend not to be studies of final-rise intonation in the TV soap *Neighbours*, or of the spread of *aint* in the speech of Glaswegian-based films: the 'non-natural' character of film narratives will exclude this – even though studies of final-rise intonation in London teenage girls or of *aint* in Glaswegian ones may well cite such films as an important influence (see e.g. Freddi 2011 for a typical study, comparing formulaic filmic speech with formulaic naturally-occurring speech; see also Hodson 2014, an excellent study of dialect and identity in film and literature). Nor will we find, in studies of the same kinds of fictional film, studies of pseudo-clefts or subject-copying, inversions and deletions, or ergative verbs. These are all too 'core linguistic' to feel appropriate to film study. However, the same exclusion does not seem to apply to the more sociopragmatic topics, like accent-pride and -shame, illocution and perlocution, politeness strategies and face-threat or -maintenance, or patterns of pausing and interruption in conversation and their possible source in relations of power or affinity.

Among the chief challenges confronting a stylistics of narrative film are these three:

1. How to have a simultaneous, integrated tracking of at least these three co-occurring sequences: the visual stream (the sequence of shots, and their length in seconds), the speech stream, and the non-speech sound stream (the latter two synchronised with the schematic record of the visual sequence). In some ways this challenge is no different from the problem that confronts the linguist intent on a reasonably comprehensive discourse or conversation analysis of an interactional event between two or more participants. However, the selectivity and pragmatic exclusions in the latter situation are evident at the outset (especially in labels like *linguist* and *discourse*): a solution is reached where the speech, intonation and overlapping etc. is given in detail, gaze and gesture are more briefly reported, but the colour of interactants' clothing, the size of the room, the extent of ambient noise, the time of day, the air temperature and quality, and so on are deemed peripheral at best, and non-linguistic. However, films are made, not found, and it is not obvious that there is anything within them that is comparably peripheral or 'non-filmic'. Hence the long list of factors that film analysts feel justified in citing as contributory to the total effect, from granularity and definition to lighting and

contrast, depth of field, the clarity of speech, the rhythm of shots and cutting techniques, the quality of the acting, and so on and so forth.

2. How to have a grammar of at least these three streams, which can at once distinguish the contribution of signs from these different streams but also describes their integrated function. Various scholars continue to grapple with these issues, but no entirely satisfactory solution has emerged. Indeed, there is some sense that no satisfactory solution *can* emerge from such studies, since at the outset, in the name of analysis they segregate these different modes or streams, treating them as materially quite distinct so that their subsequent re-combination is bound to seem artificial.

3. How to have a grammar of these three streams when it is unclear that two of them (the visual and non-speech sounds) are amenable to grammatical analysis at all. Kress and van Leeuwen's *Reading Images* offered some basic grammar-like principles with which to interpret and classify images, but it is noticeable that even their principles and adaptations of systemic-linguistic ideas have been questioned, as forcing the fluidity of a two-dimensional image into a framework designed for the unidimensionality of language – and, perhaps more importantly, they offered a way of reading *fixed* images, not moving ones.

Ultimately the solution to the above 'simultaneity of semiotic streams' problem may lie in postulating the idea, somewhat supported by studies of selectivity of human attention, that the film-viewer directs their attention to now one, now another of the multiple channels or streams of semiosis, so that the latter are actually experienced as an interwoven unified sequence (cf van Leeuwen's (1993) discussion of the 'reading path' a reader may take through the fixed images and text on the printed page: reception of multi-modal film is clearly even more complex than the process van Leeuwen has in mind, and is neither reading nor a path). In a filmed sequence of heated dialogue between Elizabeth and Darcy in a film of *Pride and Prejudice*, for a few seconds we may focus chiefly on setting or on the characters' clothes (even though they have begun speaking comprehensibly, and there is ambient sound also), then switch our attention to the particular point that Darcy's words are making (and attending less to the persisting visual semiosis or non-speech sounds), and then switch to interpreting Elizabeth's face (now in medium closeup) as it reacts to Darcy's words, and so on; at the end of the exchange, even if the two protagonists are still in shot, we may attend chiefly to the non-diegetic sounds that have started up, and seem to evaluate much of what has just been shown happening. Some such account offers a kind of solution to the problem of the intractable multiplicity of semiotic resources, but of course it immediately raises the question of how these split-second decisions about primary-attention-shift are guided and constrained, whether supporting evidence of their real existence is available, whether communities of viewers tend to 'attention-shift' at the same places, and, if not, whether a stylistics of film is any nearer being put on a stable footing.

It may be objected that I am asking for too much, in asking for an integrated descriptive model of how moving images and speech, say, function together in film narration. It may be argued that in practice stylisticians studying film select one element among the interwoven many – the (varying) loudness of the soundtrack, or the politeness and face-threatening strategies used in a particular episode, or the effect of using steadicam sequences, etc. etc. – and in doing this they are directly mirroring what stylisticians of literature have long and routinely done, selecting just the transitivity or deictic-shift patterns, or the speech- and thought-presentation modes, or the pronouns or metaphor blends, as one small step along the way to a full analysis of a text's effects on readers. It is hard to dislodge this defence and its implicit criticism of literary stylistics, except to point out that there is considerably greater similarity of kind among the textual phenomena (transitivity, deixis, modality, reported discourse, etc. all being conceivable as interconnected parts of the language system) than among the film phenomena. As a result, when a stylistic analysis of a poem singles out deictic patterns (and not transitivity or modality or other systems) and argues for their foregrounded instrumentality in the literary effect, this is a singling-out of one among numerous comparable and interconnected linguistic systems. However, the systemic connection between Julia Roberts's range of facial expressions in a love scene and the musical sound-track that accompanies them is much harder to establish.

Some researchers have focused on what they call 'intersemiosis', the means by which the resources of multiple modes of signifying work together in integrated patterns so as to produce the meanings we find in films (Baldry and Thibault 2006, Martinec 1998, 2000, Bateman and Schmidt 2011, Tseng and Bateman 2012). Baldry and Thibault (2006), for example, propose a transcription method in which the analyst annotates adjacently on the page or screen for the occurrence in sequence of developments in sound, movement, colour, speech, and writing. A leading theorist in these respects is van Leeuwen; in *Speech, Music, Sound* (1999) he theorises the mode of sound as a social semiotic alongside that of images, and his 1999 study has been fruitfully taken up by other analysts. Van Leeuwen argues that sounds in everyday life and on film are susceptible to a ternary classification, as Figure (in hearer's focus), Ground (attended to as background), or Field (unattended background). In addition, the perceived loudness of a sound affects a listener's 'aural perspective' upon its source (louder generally being 'more important', although the independent factor of source-listener distance must also be taken into consideration). Van Leeuwen devises a fairly complex system network, but the ideas of focusing and distance seem central: those sounds we (realise we) are focusing on and which we treat as close to us rather than distant (whether that distance is physical or social or ideological) are the ones which are particularly semiotically significant.

As regards the basic challenge of devising a workable multi-mode transcription of the distinct but simultaneous and integrated strands of signification, one thing I am sure of is that such transcriptions must run across the page or screen horizontally (left to right or the reverse), and not vertically (where the different modes are displayed 'unnaturally' side by side). The roots of this reading preference are deeply cognitively embodied (our eyes being horizontally rather than vertically configured, for example), but they are amply confirmed by standard orchestral scores, where the contributions of the various instruments are stacked vertically and their simultaneous lines are mapped horizontally.

Working with postulated language-film equivalences

Because a stylistics of film logically must 'import' into its film analyses those categories and analytical resources it finds centrally useful in its analyses of literature, it is equally impelled to seek for counterparts where no direct transfer is possible. One such area of potentially illuminating loose equivalence, as I have indicated above and elsewhere, equates the film shot with the graphological sentence. Both can convey or represent 'one complete idea', both can be inflected by modality, both may record the kernel of 'one process' (an action, a mental reaction, an identification of one item), both may also evaluate or comment on the one main idea that has been communicated. Perhaps most critically of all, both typically come to an end in a matter of seconds, and must then be *joined* to a following sentence or shot, by means of a chaining that is also an overt demarcating or separating – even if the reader/viewer, absorbed in the narrative, does not particularly notice that periodicity or break. None of the above claimed equivalences intend to deny that on many occasions chunks that are much shorter than the graphological sentence – e.g. the phrase – may carry 'one complete idea and process'. Nor should we deny that in contemporary film, individual rapid film shots may be palpably incomplete, so that as a viewer you only feel you have grasped a 'complete idea or process' after you have watched a sequence of such shots. These exceptionalities must be acknowledged and addressed, while holding to the notion and explanatory usefulness of the shot-sentence equation if we are to operate with any kinds of commensurable unit between film and text.

The equivalence of film shot and grammatical sentence is just the first of many one might seek to identify and clarify (particularly if one wants to apply the categories of linguistic stylistics as fully as may be to the different construct that is film). It is hard to resist the inclination to seek counterparts or compensatory alternative resources in our categories of film-composition analysis with those familiar in the older tradition of text-grammatical analysis. Perhaps we should not resist. In which case, extending Kress and van Leeuwen's application of these categories chiefly to static images, we might seek to identify in film-narrative shots the equivalent of transitivity processes with their attendant roles: e.g. shots that approximate a relational process description that primarily represents a particular identification or attribute as carried by a focused-upon entity (a character, a building, a setting); or shots that chiefly represent a material process of doing or happening, affecting one entity but sometimes originating in a separate agentive entity (thus, two main participants), contextualised by a circumstantial background; or shots where an overt or inferable character's thoughts *about* or reactions *to* a projected identification or action or event, the viewer judges, is what is of primary importance. Thus here we would arguably have a film counterpart of mental process clauses, in a Hallidayan transitivity analysis. This last, of course – and everything to do with the representation of consciousness – is obviously difficult for film narration to achieve, but it is by no means impossible. It involves a suggestion on the part of the filmmakers and a deduction on the part of the viewer which arguably has a counterpart in written narratives in the veiled mental processing known as free indirect thought.

Recommendations for practice

Somewhere in America, there is a large estate, protected from prying eyes by a forbidding chain-link fence on which you will find affixed the blunt advisory, 'No Trespassing'. But they can't stop you looking. And if you look through the fence, and past the marvellous fretwork on the high gates at the entrance, you see primates of some sort – gibbons, perhaps – in a nearby enclosure, and high on a hill in the distance a gothic mansion fit for a fairytale or fable, redolent of faux-medieval Bohemia or Transylvania at its vampiric best. No sooner do these associations come to mind than our eyes notice a pair of empty gondolas, more fake than real, floating on something more like a miasmic swamp than a Venetian canal. Next we see a drawbridge (perhaps crossing the same swamp as before: everything is so dark it's hard to say) and then, equally random-seeming, a glimpse of a 'par 4' hole on a golf course.

Do you know the film that the above is derived from? Many readers – hopefully – will recognise the above as an attempted 'literary adaptation' of the opening ninety seconds or so of the film *Citizen Kane* (easily found, as are clips of many other classic films, on YouTube and similar websites). I make no claims for the fullness or accuracy of this 'novelisation':

inter alia, it attempts no direct reporting of the eerie music that is part of the opening sequence, and you can see how the camera's smooth panning, focusing, and cutting are clumsily matched by constructions like *no sooner than*, *if you look* and *next*. Nevertheless this is a useful exercise to sensitise one to the differences between literary and film narration.

1. Take any ninety-second opening segment of a well-known film (the opening, since this will be most manageable, experienced without prior narrated material), and translate it into written narration. Withholding any tell-tale title or character names for your composition, present your text to friends to see if they can identify the film original. Comparing your written narrative with the filmic original, you will find many topics worthy of further stylistic reflection, and many points where you have reported or not reported elements that another reader/viewer will question. To take one example arising from my Citizen Kane opening, above: I considered following the first phrase *Somewhere in America* with an equally vague temporal deictic, *some years ago*. Had I done so, I would have to have switched all subsequent finite verbs from present to past, and I wanted to avoid the sense of distance between scene, reporting viewer and reader, that past tense might have created. The point is, the language forces this tense-choice upon the writer, whereas film has no counterpart fixed system for marking temporal distance; it has, rather, a range of ways of signalling anteriority and posteriority. The camera cannot film now what happened yesterday.

2. Film trailers are everywhere on the internet, and form an interesting sub-genre in their own right. Take a small selection of trailers (three to five) from a single genre of films (e.g., adventure, rom-com, crime/gangster or biopics). Draw up a list of those factors identified elsewhere in this handbook as foundational to literary stylistics, which seem particularly important in the targeted type of trailer. A trailer is a kind of highly-controlled sampling, very different from the blurb that accompanies a novel. Your list of key factors in trailer-composition should enable you to describe trailer vs. blurb differences in stylistic detail.

3. The *Citizen Kane* opening and my novelising of it do not involve characters, but individuals are at the heart of film narration and therefore of a stylistics of film. To focus on just a small part of filmic characterisation, take a two-minute segment of film that focuses on a single character, and describe (with approximate timings) all the non-verbal sounds that accompany the shots involving that character, and in particular those where the character is in shot. What differences in characterisation might be suggested if the ambient sounds were radically different – or if there were little detectable accompanying sound at all? Muting an internet film-clip and substituting a very different sound-accompaniment (music or otherwise) is now quite feasible.

Final remarks and some future considerations

In light of the rough attempt I have offered above to apply the systemic-functional linguistic classification of transitivity (processes and participants) to the kinds of states and actions that a film narrates, we might see here a general project that stylistics could undertake. This would be to seek to express, as a grammar of typical choices, a reduction to classification of all the most instrumental types of choice that a film seems to involve (a grammar of perspective, a grammar of camera-angles, of degrees of close-up or distance from characters in shot, of shot-length variation, and so on). The kinds of 'design features' which one would need to map out in such a 'grammar' are exactly those features enumerated and discussed in an authoritative overview such as Bordwell and Thompson's *Film Art*. The difficulty then becomes not only the fact that so many distinct domains of choice in the course of film-making will be identified; there is also the difficulty that there is no clear hierarchy among them, or many constraints on how they interact. It may be argued that as much could be said about the analytical linguistic systems or categories we apply to literary texts: deixis, pronouns, aspect, modality, tense, transitivity, synonymy and so on. It is certainly true that a poem may select to good effect from a narrow part of the pronoun system, and these may seem quite independent in principle from the poem's modality or tense choices. But as I suggested earlier, coherent design can be claimed, where the pronoun choices and the modality and tense choices work together to achieve a particular effect. We might expect that a similar argument should be applicable in stylistic analysis of film, only with the difficulty that the claims will be made about the convergence or collective coherence of choices from systems that are inherently quite unrelated, and therefore are all the more difficult to bring together in a unified analysis: a particular recurrent lighting choice and its putative effect, a particular recurrent choice of speech act in the dialogue and its effect, a particular arrhythmia in the shot-lengths, a particular gesture enacted by one of the protagonists. In all this, the stylistic analyst is arguably re-stating, for purposes of explanation and understanding, the complex decisions and actions taken – perhaps not always with full deliberation – by the director, editor, actors and so on in creating the film in the first place.

However, whatever the level of 'translation' we find possible between the analytical systems of narrative-text grammar, say, and film narrative, it is important to recognise the importance of conventions of interpretation, genre, intertextual sense-making, mental scripts and idealised models, in our processing of everything we notice in the course of viewing a film. Film talk in the wider community – everyday discussions of film, film reviews in the press and on the internet, filmblogs and so on – routinely orient to these familiar scripts and schemes of interpretation, by means of which we classify film characters, situations, values, tones, and 'messages' by analogy and reference to deeply-entrenched types.

Independent of but underpinning the activity of analysing and evaluating text-to-film adaptations, a good deal of interest is directed towards examining the kinds of similarity and incommensurability that emerge when a written narrative (e.g. a story or novel) and a filmed narrative are compared. Both will represent events in explicit or inferable sequence (although the sequence of telling and therefore of reader/viewer processing may be distinct from the assumed sequence in which the events occurred: the famous double chronology of narrative), and successive events may be told in greater or lesser detail and at different temporal length, always with the possibility of telling several times over something that happened only once. However, we are as interested in characters as in events, and films have characters at least as much as novels do, notwithstanding the fact that the projection of characters in the two genres is profoundly difficult with stylistic consequences.

Against these, there are many respects in which film and novel have counterpart characteristics or analogies but not full similarity. As already suggested, since it is a powerful point of articulation, a point of local completion and resumption of the telling, the sentence boundary in written narrative, can be considered to have its counterpart in the shot boundary in film. Just as a subsequent sentence in a narrative must and will cohere with those that have gone before (and especially the immediately preceding one), a film shot will be expected to follow smoothly from previous shots and especially the most recent previous one (or it should depart from such 'smooth' continuity only with good reason – e.g. to mimic chaos, confusion, violence, surprise or outrage). However, in both cases there are possibilities of abrupt shift, of a kind that are not usually possible or attempted *within* a given shot or sequence. In other words, the film narrative shot, like the text narrative sentence, is a core – perhaps foundational – segment of narrative composition, with its own intrinsic coherence of content that cannot usually be radically disrupted. The foregoing points can only speak to norms in films and writing – narrative films comprising hundreds of internally-coherent shots which are judiciously sequenced in the editing process, and written narratives comprising hundreds of sentences similarly carefully adjoined. Exceptions to the above include films that purport to be made in one shot, novels without any internal sentence boundaries, or novels with extremely long and complex graphological sentences.

Another area where a counterpart relation might be suspected relates to characters' thoughts and feelings. Characters in film narratives are very often especially represented by their faces, and the focus on faces in film storytelling is inescapably prominent. This is arguably part and parcel of filmmaking's inescapable preoccupation with surfaces and exteriors, and the concomitant difficulty of moving 'all the way inward' into a character's mind, in the way that writing, especially twentieth century writing, has come so powerfully to simulate. We can begin thinking about this with remarks such as those of Virginia Woolf on the film versions of *Anna Karenina*, where Woolf adopts a contentious eye/brain-processing opposition: the details of Anna's (outward, of course) physical appearance are highly prominent, to the point of distracting us from the complexity of her inner conflicting impulses and judgements:

> The eye says: 'Here is Anna Karenina.' A voluptuous lady in black velvet wearing pearls comes before us. But the brain says: 'That is no more Anna Karenina than it is Queen Victoria.' For the brain knows Anna almost entirely by the inside of her mind – her charm, her passion, her despair. All the emphasis is laid by the cinema upon her teeth, her pearls, and her velvet.
>
> *(Woolf [1926] 1966, p. 270)*

Film cannot easily – that is, without noticeable artificiality – disclose to us a character's inner thoughts. Some films use voiceovers for this purpose, or else they have the character talk directly to camera, as if to a mirror; but neither convention has taken hold to the point of feeling 'natural' to viewers. Partly for that very reason, directors hire actors to play character roles who are gifted at using their faces (especially their eyes and mouth) to suggest kinds of complex thought, evaluative reaction and emotion. By contrast in written narratives, an array of modes including direct thought, free indirect thought and stream of consciousness can give the powerful impression of disclosing characters' thoughts in considerable detail, and for all their artificiality the narratives may be admired by readers as 'realistic' and life-like. Molly Bloom's long stream-of-consciousness passage at the close of Joyce's *Ulysses* is one of the most famous of these.

Finally, a major challenge for the stylistics of film is much like the challenge presented to the stylistics of postmodern and now globalised literary production: how to apprehend analytically its remorseless instabilities of form and grounding. As viewer and by extension as analyst, one has the illusion at least of terra firma with regard to story time and time-shifts, story place and place-shifts, in the bulk of films that mostly adopt continuity editing. However, in 'post-continuity films' there can be markedly fewer of the relative stabilities of temporal progression and orderliness, settings, character-perseveration, and consistency of narrational point of view that facilitate the analysis of pattern, foregrounding, and style. As one film theorist argues, the post-continuity films that succeeded what Bordwell (2002) identified as 'intensified-continuity' film compel the viewer to enter a 'space of flows', where there are speed-of-light transformations of time and space and character, all paralleling 'the endlessly modulating financial flows of globalised network capitalism … no longer tied to any concrete processes of production' (Shaviro 2010, p. 31). If the twentieth century was the century of film and television, in the twenty-first century new digital media are central to the shaping and reflecting of new forms of sensibility, new 'structures of feeling' (to use Raymond Williams's phrase). Such a shift in our artforms and in what we will learn to feel and regard as normal and natural is not itself new or surprising, but the reality of it will require new adjustments in a commensurate stylistic analysis of film.

Related topics

Drama and performance, functionalist stylistics, multimodality, speech and thought presentation, stylistics and translation

Further reading

Bordwell, D. and Thompson, K., 2012. *Film art: An introduction.* 10th edition, New York: McGraw Hill.

An admirably clear, systematic and accessible guide to the main components and systems which film-makers employ in the course of creating the aesthetic object that is a narrative film. Many of the terms and distinctions they use match closely with those central to literary stylistics and narratology (e.g. time manipulation, modality, foregrounding, and representations of agency and control).

Bateman, J. A. and Schmidt, K.-H., 2011. *Multimodal film analysis: How films mean.* London: Routledge.

An important study incorporating insights from multimodal analysis and systemic linguistics in the course of setting out a methodology for the empirical analysis of effects and meanings that can be argued to be intrinsic units in the composition of the films being subjected to analysis.

Piazza, R, Bednarek, M., and Rossi, F., eds. 2011. *Telecinematic discourse: Approaches to the language of films and television series.* Amsterdam/Philadelphia: John Benjamins Publishing Company.

The chapters gathered here all concentrate on the dialogue in films, but they do so from a range of perspectives and bring fresh insights to questions such as how characterisation is achieved multimodally in film, and how emotions are subtly projected.

Simpson, P., and Montgomery, M., 1995. Language, literature and film: The stylistics of Bernard MacLaverty's *Cal. In:* P. Verdonk, and J-J. Weber, eds. *Twentieth century fiction: From text to context.* London: Taylor and Francis, 138–164.

A clear and orderly discussion of some of the key stylistic changes to be found when the film version of a story is compared with the original version, MacLaverty's novel *Cal.* This accessible study shows how the film version copes with the challenge of conveying the specific (sometimes voyeuristic) point of view of a central character by means of shot-selection and framing rather than through words, as the written original does.

References

Baldry, A. and Thibault, P., 2006. *Multimodal transcription and text analysis: A multimedia toolkit and coursebook.* London: Equinox.
Bateman, J. A. and Schmidt, K.-H., 2011. *Multimodal film analysis: How films mean.* London: Routledge.
Bazin, A., [1958] 2009. *What is cinema?* trans., Timothy Barnard, Montreal: Caboose.
Bednarek, M., 2011. *The language of fictional television.* London: Continuum.
Bordwell, D., 1991. *Making meaning: Inference and rhetoric in the interpretation of cinema.* Cambridge MA: Harvard University Press.

Bordwell, D., 2002. Intensified continuity: Visual style in contemporary American film. *Film Quarterly*, 55 (3), 16–28.

Bordwell, D. and Thompson, K., 2012. *Film art: An introduction*. 10th edition. New York: McGraw Hill.

Cauldwell, R., 1999. Openings, rhythm and relationships: Philip Larkin reads 'Mr Bleaney'. *Language and Literature*, 8 (1), 35–48.

Culpeper J. and McIntyre, D., 2010. Activity types and characterisation in dramatic discourse. *In:* J. Eder, F. Jannidis, and R. Schneider, eds. *Characters in fictional worlds: Understanding imaginary beings in literature, film, and other media*. Berlin: De Gruyter, 176–207.

Cureton, R. C., 1994. Rhythm and verse study. *Language and Literature*, 3 (2), 105–124.

Eisenstein, S., 1949. *Film form: Essays in film theory*. Jay Leyda, trans. New York: Harcourt

Freddi, M., 2011. A phraseological approach to film dialogue: Film stylistics revisited. *Yearbook of Phraseology,* 137–162.

Forceville, C., 2002. The conspiracy in *The Comfort of Strangers*: Narration in the novel and the film. *Language and Literature*, 11 (2), 119–135.

Hakemulder, J., 2007. Tracing foregrounding in responses to film. *Language and Literature,* 16 (2), 125–139.

Hanson, K., 2003. Formal variation in the rhymes of Robert Pinsky's 'The Inferno of Dante'. *Language and Literature*, 12 (4), 309–337.

Hodson, J., 2014. *Dialect in Film and Literature*. London: Palgrave.

Kendall, R., 2003. *Faith*. Available at http://collection.eliterature.org/1/works/kendall__faith/index.htm (accessed 19 August 2013).

Kozloff, S., 2000. *Overhearing film dialogue*. Berkeley, CA: University of California Press.

Kress, G. and van Leeuwen, T., 2006. *Reading Images*. 2nd edn. London: Routledge.

Levaco, R., 1974. Eikhenbaum, inner speech and film stylistics. *Screen*, 15 (4), 47–58.

Martinec, R., 1998. Cohesion in action. *Semiotica,* 120/121 (2), 161–180.

Martinec, R., 2000. Construction of identity in Michael Jackson's 'Jam'. *Social Semiotics,* 10 (3), 313–329.

McIntyre, D., 2008. Integrating multimodal analysis and the stylistics of drama: A multimodal perspective on Ian McKellen's *Richard III. Language and Literature,* 17 (4), 309–334.

Nørgaard, N., Busse, B., and Montóro, R., 2011. *Key terms in stylistics*. London: Continuum.

Ochs, E., 1979. Transcription as theory. *In:* E. Ochs and B. Schieffelin, eds. *Developmental pragmatics*. New York: Academic Press, 43–72.

Piazza, R., 2010. Voice-over and self-narrative in film: A multimodal analysis of Antonioni's *When Love Fails* (*Tentato Suicidio*). *Language and Literature,* 19 (2), 173–195.

Piazza, R, Bednarek, M., and Rossi, F., eds., 2011. *Telecinematic discourse: Approaches to the language of films and television series*. Amsterdam/Philadelphia: John Benjamins Publishing Company.

Pople, I., 1998. Basil Bunting's 'Briggflatts': A case study in intonational prosody. *Language and Literature*, 7 (1), 21–38.

Pullinger, K. and Joseph, C., 2012. *Flight paths*. Available at http://flightpaths.net (accessed 19 August 2013).

Richardson, K., 2010. Multimodality and the study of popular drama. *Language and Literature*, 19 (4), 378–395.

Rushdie, S., 2009. Lost in translation. *The Weekend Australian*, 28–29 March, 4–6.

Shaviro, S., 2010. Post-cinematic affect: On *Grace Jones, Boarding Gate* and Southland Tales. *Film-Philosophy* 14 (1), 1–102.

Simpson, P., and Montgomery, M., 1995. Language, literature and film: The stylistics of Bernard MacLaverty's *Cal. In:* P. Verdonk, and J-J. Weber, eds. *Twentieth century fiction: From text to context*. London: Taylor and Francis, 138–164.

Stam, R., 2005. Introduction: The theory and practice of adaptation. *In:* R. Stam and A. Raengo, eds. *Literature and film: A guide to the theory and practice of film adaptation*. Oxford: Blackwell, 1–52.

Tseng, C. and Bateman, J., 2012. Multimodal narrative construction in Christopher Nolan's *Memento*: A description of analytic method. *Visual Communication*, 11, 91–119.

Truffaut, F., 1967. *Hitchcock/Truffaut*. New York: Simon and Schuster.

van Leeuwen, T., 1993. Genre and field in critical discourse analysis: A synopsis. *Discourse and Society*, 4 (2), 193–223.

van Leeuwen, T., 1999. *Speech, music, sound*. London: Macmillan.

Woolf, V., [1926] 1966. The cinema. *In: Collected essays. Vol. 2*. London: Hogarth Press, 268–272.

29

Multimodality and stylistics

Nina Nørgaard

Introduction

As demonstrated by the chapters in the present book, stylisticians study the way meaning is created through language in literature and other types of text – and they do so from a great variety of linguistic perspectives. Until recently the stylistic approach to text analysis has been predominantly logocentric in nature. However, as film analysis has caught the interest of a number of stylisticians (e.g. McIntyre 2008, Montoro 2010) and as technological developments in book production have caused a surge in literature that experiments with images, typography, colour, layout and so on, stylisticians have seen a need to expand the stylistic tool kit with tools geared towards handling the stylistic analysis of multimodal texts. So far, the new branch of *multimodal stylistics* would seem to have moved along two lines in particular: a cognitive approach, focusing on the cognitive impact of multimodal literature (cf. e.g. Gibbons 2012), and a social semiotic approach, which aims to develop 'grammars' for all the semiotic modes involved in meaning-making. The present chapter will be devoted to the latter. While both approaches obviously apply to the analysis of explicitly multimodal genres like film, drama performance, iconic poetry, comics, children's books, graphic novels and the art book, the analytical scope of this chapter will be the novel – explicitly multimodal novels as well as more traditional ones which most readers would probably tend not to think of as multimodal at all.

In short, the social semiotic take on multimodality builds on Halliday's functional linguistics and follows the multimodal credo that 'common semiotic principles operate in and across different modes' (Kress and Van Leeuwen 2001, p. 2). In *Reading Images* (1996) Kress and van Leeuwen thus explore the extent to which the fundamental ideas behind Halliday's approach to language are applicable to visual communication, and they develop a visual grammar which largely employs the same concepts and terminology as Halliday. Consequently, the addition of Kress and van Leeuwen's methodology to the stylistic tool kit will provide stylisticians with a consistent approach to – and terminology for – handling language *and* images. Following the pioneering work of *Reading Images*, modes such as typography (van Leeuwen 2005b, 2006), colour (Kress and van Leeuwen, 2002) and sound (van Leeuwen 1999) have been explored, too, and other modes await treatment in the future. In their later work, Kress and van Leeuwen (e.g. Kress 2010, van Leeuwen 2005a) turn from individual modes to looking at the meanings that come about as a result of multimodal semiosis. In *Multimodal Discourse* (Kress and van Leeuwen 2001) they approach multimodality from a new perspective by examining how meaning is created at four different levels, or *strata*: *discourse*, *design*, *production* and *distribution*. The present chapter draws particularly on the pioneering work by Kress and van Leeuwen, but the work of other proponents of social semiotic multimodal theory such as Baldry and Thibault (2006), O'Halloran (2005), Bateman (2008) and others should, of course, also be recognised.

In the following, I will sketch out a (preliminary) framework for a multimodal stylistic analysis of the novel, introducing respectively Halliday's approach to language and Kress and van Leeuwen's approach to other modes, accompanied by a brief exemplification. This will lead to a discussion of a number of critical issues entailed by this new branch of stylistics, followed by considerations about possible further directions of the field.

Multimodal stylistics and the novel

Hallidayan stylistics – A (meta)functional approach to language

Hallidayan linguistics focuses on the ways in which language may be seen to simultaneously express three types of meaning: experiential meaning (alternatively: ideational meaning), interpersonal meaning, and textual meaning. *Experiential meaning* (cf. Halliday 1994, pp. 106–175) concerns the way language represents – or rather constructs or construes – meaning as configurations of participants (typically nominals and pronominals), processes (typically verbals) and circumstances (typically adverbials). *Interpersonal meaning* (cf. Halliday 1994, pp. 68–105) refers to our social interaction through language. The way interlocutors use language in interaction is thus seen to construct and reflect their social roles in different contexts. This is mainly done through choices in mood and modality and by means of naming and vocatives. Mood choices (declarative, interrogative and imperative) reveal who 'gives' and 'takes' in conversation, whether it be information (statement or question) or goods-and-services (offer or demand). Modality reflects the speaker's commitment to what is said in terms of probability, usuality, obligation and inclination and may, for instance, reflect the degree of (un-)certainty or (im-)politeness of a given speaker in a particular interpersonal context. Finally, vocatives and naming carry interpersonal meaning since what we call other people in direct conversation and when we talk about them reflects our attitude to these people (and probably also to the people we are conversing with about them). The third type of meaning, *textual meaning* (cf. Halliday 1994, pp. 37–67), concerns the way we organise language into text. Here the Hallidayan focal points are theme-rheme structures and cohesion. Analysis of theme-rheme structures – i.e. of what comes first (theme) and what follows (rheme) in a sentence, as well as of 'thematic' patterns throughout a text – reveals how information has been organised in the text as well as the various foci of the speaker(s). Cohesion, on the other hand, is the textual resource that 'glues' the text together by means of the text-internal ties of conjunction, reference, ellipsis and lexical cohesion (i.e. repetition, synonymy and collocation).

When employed for the stylistic analysis of a literary text, Halliday's theory of language will reveal how the meaning of the text comes about as configurations of experiential, interpersonal and textual meaning. The analysis of experiential meaning may, for instance, reveal how different characters are constructed by means of the patterns of processes of which they are represented as the participant. While one character may be the participant of many material processes of doing/action and hence be projected as rather an active person (particularly if the processes are transitive, extending to other participants), another character may be construed as more passive as the participant of many relational processes of being and/or mental processes of perception. This is the case in James Joyce's short story 'Two Gallants' (1992) in which transitive material processes help construct one character, Corley, as a dynamic person of action, whereas the protagonist, Lenehan, is represented as more passive through configurations of him as the participant of many relational processes of being, mental processes of perception and intransitive material processes (for more comprehensive Hallidayan analyses of Joyce's story, see Kennedy 1982 and Nørgaard 2003).

In addition to experiential analysis, Hallidayan stylisticians are likely to examine how characters are construed interpersonally through the distribution of speech roles, mood choices, modality, vocatives and naming. As regards the distribution of speech roles and mood choices, analysis of these elements will reveal who is speaking and for how long, who is 'giving' and 'taking' in conversation and whether this is done straightforwardly, as it were, through congruent mood choices, or in grammatically incongruent ways – as a means of politeness, for example. An analysis of modality will throw light on the aspect of characterisation that concerns speakers' commitment to what is being said. While some characters – like people in reality – are likely to confidently state things as absolute (positive or negative) facts, others may tend to modalise as a result of uncertainty ('maybe she thinks you'll marry her', Joyce 1992, p. 45); for emphasis and/or to seem more certain than is actually the case ('that emphatically takes the biscuit', Joyce 1992, p. 45); or as markers of politeness ('if I may so call it', Joyce 1992, p. 44). The three examples just listed all occur in Lenehan's speech turns in 'Two Gallants' and are taken from a relatively large range of modality markers occurring in passages presenting his speech and thoughts. In contrast, Corley is constructed as a character who self-assuredly states things as absolute facts (positive and negative polarity) and only uses the kind of high probability modality that cannot easily be distinguished from non-modalised future expressions (e.g. 'She'll be there', 'I'll pull it off', Joyce 1992, p. 47). As regards the use of vocatives and naming in the story, it is worth noticing how Lenehan keeps using Corley's name – out of politeness, it seems, and to manifest and maintain their friendship – while Corley never uses Lenehan's name. Interestingly, the narrative passages conspicuously often refer to Corley as 'his [i.e. Lenehan's] friend' which clashes notably with the general impression the reader gets of their relationship.

As for textual meaning, the theme choices in 'Two Gallants' are relatively straightforward. Throughout the story, thematic prominence is given to setting in time and space and to the characters around whom the narrative evolves. At times, a constituent is promoted from its usual place in the syntax of the sentence to 'thematic' position (i.e. marked 'theme', cf. Halliday 1994, p. 44) with the effect of foregrounding and emphasis. Thus, for instance, when it is said about Lenehan that 'to appear natural he pushed his cap back on his head and planted his elbows on the table' (Joyce 1992, p. 51) a certain amount of emphasis is given to the fronted constituent and thereby to Lenehan's (and the story's) preoccupation with appearance (even if fronted adverbials are less marked in declaratives than fronted objects or subject complements). The choice of theme may hence be seen to play a role in characterisation. Joyce's use of the other textual resource, cohesion, is also mostly straightforward as is typical of literary realism, where the texture of a given text usually does not draw much attention to itself. However, in this highly cohesive text, one thing stands out in terms of cohesion: the way Lenehan and Corley refer to Corley's enterprise with the girl which lies at the crux of the story. Throughout the story, the two men refer to Corley's plan by means of the cohesively unresolved pronouns 'it' and 'that' (e.g. 'is she game for that', Joyce 1992, p. 46). In addition to giving the readers a sense that they are eavesdropping on a conversation, this somewhat conspicuous linguistic choice furthermore creates suspense and finally surprise when the last lines of the story reveal that the purpose of Corley's affair was neither romantic nor sexual, but to get money off the girl.

While the sections above make up only a sketchy introduction to Halliday's theory of language with cursory analytical exemplification, the motivation for their inclusion here is twofold: 1) to provide an outline of the linguistic theory upon which Kress and van Leeuwen base their visual grammar and their approach to other semiotic modes; and 2) to emphasise that even if modes other than wording are new and less explored in stylistics, language should not be forgotten altogether in our stylistic analysis.

The three metafunctions in visual communication

In *Reading Images*, Kress and van Leeuwen (1996) demonstrate how images, like language, may be seen to express – and hence be analysed in terms of – experiential, interpersonal and compositional meaning. As in language, *experiential meaning* in images is claimed to be structured as configurations of participants, processes and circumstances and the terminology used for analysis is largely the same as that used by Halliday in his functional grammar of language (cf. Kress and van Leeuwen 1996, pp. 43–118). This is particularly the case with narrative representations, i.e. processes of action (cf. Kress and van Leeuwen's overview 1996, pp. 74–75). It is worth noticing, however, that Kress and van Leeuwen's use of Halliday's terminology 'does not imply that images work in the same way as language; only that they can "say" (some of) the same things as language – in *very different ways*' (Kress and van Leeuwen 1996, p. 48; italics in original). Thus, for instance, action processes are realised by verbs in language and by vectors in images, but they can be transactional (i.e. extend from actor to goal) or non-transactional (i.e. no goal) in both modes.

In visual communication, *interpersonal meaning* (cf. Kress and van Leeuwen 1996, pp. 119–180) concerns the way the viewer is positioned in relation to the represented participants. The systems involved in analysing this are *gaze, angle of interaction, distance* and *modality*. Inspired by Halliday's work on verbal communication, Kress and van Leeuwen argue that images – like speech acts – can either 'offer' or 'demand'. When the participants in an image are represented as gazing directly at the viewer they 'demand' some kind of (fictional) engagement from the viewer, it is claimed, whereas the viewers are simply positioned as observers of information 'offered' to us when the participants are not represented as looking at us. Another means of positioning the viewer is *angle of interaction* – horizontally (frontality, profile, from behind and various oblique angles) as well as vertically (from above, eye-level, from below). Added to this, it has interpersonal implications in terms of intimacy or detachment whether we see the represented participants in a close shot, a medium shot or a long shot (i.e. the system of *distance*). Finally, Kress and van Leeuwen have introduced the concept of modality to the analysis of visual images which they see as yet another means of indicating to the viewer how the image should be taken. In visual communication, the modality scale goes from high modality – i.e. what it would have looked like if we had been there (cf. van Leeuwen's definition 2005a, pp. 160–177) – to representations which have been formally stylised (i.e. low modality) by decrease or exaggeration of one, some, or all of the following modality markers: articulation of detail, background, depth, light, shadow, tone and colour.

Compositional meaning (cf. Kress and van Leeuwen 1996, pp. 181–229) is Kress and van Leeuwen's visual counterpart to Halliday's textual meaning in language and refers to the spatial organisation of elements on the page. The key compositional principles are *information value*, *framing* and *salience*. *Information value* refers to the organisation of the page in terms of three different patterns which are seen as meaning-making in themselves: i.e. the placement of visual material on the page in terms of respectively a left/right, top/bottom or centre/margin principle of organisation. While Bateman (2008 p. 45) is right in querying the direct connection between compositional zone and ideological significance in Kress and van Leeuwen's equalling of left with 'given', right with 'new', top with 'ideal' and bottom with 'real', there may be a tendency for Westerners to interpret the zones in this way (especially in advertising, it seems; cf. Machin 2007, pp. 141–142). However, this would seem to be an area in need of more research for empirical substantiation. *Framing* refers to the ways in which elements in a spatial design may be connected and/or disconnected by means of frames and a couple of other features such as visual rhyme and contrast. The third compositional principle, *salience*, concerns elements that stand out in a visual composition and that which makes these elements stand out. Visual elements may be salient because of their relative size (whether big or small), colour, focus, tone and/or because they are foregrounded or overlapping other elements in the composition.

In multimodal stylistic analysis, Kress and van Leeuwen's visual grammar can be applied for detailed, consistent description and analysis of the visual images employed in novels like Foer's *Extremely Loud and Incredibly Close* (2005) and for inclusion of the book cover in our stylistic analysis. In the following, one of the many book covers of Kerouac's novel *On the Road* (1957), the Penguin edition from 1998, will serve as brief exemplification. The cover is displayed at www.beatbookcovers.com/kerouac-otr and can also be found through a Google search for 'On the Road Penguin 1998'. This is a top/bottom composition with a black top half which contains the name of the author, the title of the novel and a brief book review. The bottom features the experiential contents of a road, a couple of cars and a mountainous landscape which might well be American. The represented cars appear to be contemporary with the story and hence help to situate the narrative experientially in time. On closer scrutiny, the black top half of the cover turns out to be the underside of a car. This is the result of a rather unusual interpersonal vertical perspective from below and the interpersonal distance of a close shot which in combination allow the viewer to see only the underside of the car. As regards horizontal perspective, the viewer sees the cars from behind which creates an illusionary sense of moving in the same direction as the cars, going where they are going. Another interpersonal element of significance to the meaning created concerns the modality involved in the cover image. While the photographic nature of the image creates high modality, the articulation of colour and detail would seem to decrease the modality. The articulation of colour is characterised by high red colour saturation. To some extent, this results in what arguably looks like the faded colours characteristic of old photographs, hence supporting the experiential meaning of 'old'. At the same time, the dominant red tone of the image may also add the meaning of 'sunrise' or 'sunset'. As regards the modality involved by the articulation of detail, the significantly defocused nature of the representation of the road seen at the bottom is furthermore a typical signifier of movement at a certain speed.

Layout – The organisation of elements on the page

Another mode involved in the multimodal semiosis of the novel is that of layout, i.e. of the placement of elements on the page, how these elements relate to each other and the meanings created by these visual means. Although Kress and van Leeuwen's compositional meaning would seem to be the logical approach to analysing layout, the analysis of a novel reveals that the literary text (like other verbal texts of a certain length) differs somewhat from individual images and pages in isolation. Where Kress and van Leeuwen's compositional system of *information value* is clearly applicable to the analysis of individual images in a novel, it would seem to be less useful when it comes to analysing the layout of the pages of a novel which contain the verbal narrative. As a rule, it simply would not make sense to interpret the top part of the text of a random page in a verbal literary narrative as 'ideal' and the bottom as 'real', or even to think of such a page in terms of top and bottom. Nor does it make much sense to analyse such pages in terms of left and right/'given' and 'new'. This being said, a couple of exceptions arguably exist, as e.g. when it comes to the placement of chapter headings, which are usually placed at the top of a page and might be seen as 'ideal' in the sense of constituting the 'generalized essence of the information' (Kress and van Leeuwen 1996, p. 193). Similarly, footnotes are typically placed in the margin at the bottom of the page. Seeing that such notes conventionally consist of explanatory, factual information, it would not seem too farfetched to think of those as marginal and 'real' (cf. Kress and van Leeuwen 1996, p. 194). That this is in fact how we tend to perceive such notes becomes clear in the novel *Oracle Night*, when Paul Auster (2003) challenges the convention and the reader's expectations by letting footnotes to the main narrative of his novel develop into significant narrative sections in their own right, at times leaving the readers unsure whether to pursue the text or the footnotes in their reading.

The compositional concepts of *framing* and *salience* seem to bring more to the multimodal stylistic analysis of the layout of a novel. Even if the framing by whitespace around chapters, pages, sections, paragraphs and to some extent also sentences is probably so conventionalised that readers tend not to notice it much in their reading, such frames are nevertheless semiotic in their visual organisation of the novel into chunks of text of varying length. Arguably the sentence is visually less demarcated from its surroundings than paragraphs, sections and chapters. By including the sentence as a layout unit, I follow Bateman (2008) who sees the sentence as the smallest unit in his systematic analysis of layout. While the visual demarcation of the sentence, the paragraph, the section and the chapter is semiotic at the narrative level of the text where it signifies chunks of meaning of varying length, the framing of the page typically relates arbitrarily to the narrative contents of the text and is meaning-making at the level of production instead. It is thus usually of no consequence to the narrative where one page ends and another begins, but page margins are needed for the printing and binding of the novel, just as margins may vary in size for financial reasons. At its most extreme, perhaps, the latter was seen in England during WWII where the economic situation of the country actually led to legal requirements that text had to make up at least fifty-eight percent of a page in order to save paper (cf. Pedersen and Kidmose 1993, p. 86). Yet we also see this at the level of production and distribution in the case of cheap paperback novels where margins are often small to save paper and keep down expenses. At times, broader frames of white space around chunks of text furthermore indicate that these chunks somehow differ in nature from the main narrative into which they are 'inserted'. This is often the case with letters, recipes, newspaper clippings etc. (cf. e.g. Masters 2006 for examples and Nørgaard 2010b for analysis). The broader margins in such examples frequently combine with a different typography, font size, line spacing and thereby a different grey value – elements which in multimodal combination create a visual salience that interacts with wording to create the meaning of 'inserted, different text'.

Typography – What language looks like

Typography is the visual aspect of wording and is a semiotic mode in its own right. While often just employed to refer to the graphic side of printed type, 'typography' is here used in a somewhat broader sense, referring to all visual manifestations of writing, including printed type as well as calligraphy and handwriting. This liberal use of the term is motivated by the fact that a number of common semiotic resources appear to be at play in the semiosis that springs from the visual side of language, regardless of its materialisation. So far, the social semiotic approach to typography has addressed two areas in particular: how different typefaces may be described in terms of a number of *distinctive features* (van Leeuwen 2006), and how typographic meaning-making may be analysed in terms of a number of semiotic principles (van Leeuwen 2005b, Nørgaard 2009). In the multimodal stylistic approach to the novel, the semiotic typographic principles and van Leeuwen's distinctive features may be employed for analysis of the visual side of the narrative as well as of the typographic meanings created by the book cover.

Van Leeuwen's list of distinctive features (i.e. *weight*, *expansion*, *slope*, *curvature*, *connectivity*, *orientation* and *regularity*) is preliminary and may be adjusted. In my own work on typography, I miss features such as colour and edges and wonder why elements like serifs are decidedly not distinctive in van Leeuwen's view (2006, p. 151). These questions remain to be explored in future work. Nevertheless, the system provides us with a consistent descriptive system which allows us to capture the main characteristics of different typefaces.

While I am highly sympathetic to van Leeuwen's idea that typographic meaning-making may furthermore be described in terms of a number of semiotic principles, I am less convinced by his choice of principles: *metaphor* and *connotation* (for a discussion of van Leeuwen's approach, see Nørgaard 2009). Instead, I find the principles of *icon, index, symbol* (cf. Peirce e.g. in Martin and Ringham 2006) and *discursive import* (cf. van Leeuwen 2005a, 2005b) more useful. According to Peirce, the symbol is a sign which has no natural relation between its signifier and signified (or *representamen* and *object* in Peirce's terminology). In terms of typographic semiosis, one might argue that symbolic typographic meaning is at play when we read fictional narratives printed in conventional black type such as Palatino. It should be noted, however, that rather than being completely arbitrary, such conventional black typographic signs have come to mean 'typographically conventional'. The index is a sign whose meaning springs from some kind of physical or causal relation between the signifier and the signified as in the archetypical example of smoke and fire. Indexical typographic meaning occurs when a given typeface can be seen as a trace of its own coming into being. A recurring example of this in explicitly multimodal novels is the use of handwriting, as in Haddon (2003, p. 119) where the handwriting on an envelope is (fictionally) 'reproduced' and the narrator sees the circles (rather than dots) over the letter 'i' as a signifier of the person who wrote it. Another example is the use of Courier and other recognisable typewriter fonts to signify 'typewritten', for instance in the case of letters which are inserted into the narrative (e.g. Brenøe 1997). At the same time, these may also be seen as examples of the more general semiotic principle of *discursive import*, which is at play when a signifier, *in casu* a typographic signifier, and its connotations are 'imported' into a context where they did not previously belong. Finally, typographic iconicity is at play when typographic signifiers look like that which they signify – as, for instance, when the visual salience of majuscules is employed to signify the sonic salience of a 'raised voice' or 'shouting'. In other cases, a different typeface may be employed iconically to signal 'different text', as when a newspaper clipping or a recipe is inserted into the narrative. This visual signal obviously combines with wording and it is usually the latter mode that reveals to the reader exactly what kind of 'different text' we are dealing with. As a matter of fact, wording would often be enough to indicate that part of the narrative is a newspaper clipping. What happens when this is also signalled typographically by means of a recognisable newspaper font (and layout) seems intimately hooked up with the concept of modality, indicating that what we see is 'what we would have seen if we had been there' (cf. van Leeuwen 2005a, pp. 160–177). The high typographic modality functions as a kind of visual evidence which would seem to 'anchor' the narrative in reality, depending, of course, on its place on the modality continuum from some kind of reconstruction to actual reproduction in the shape of facsimile copy. At the same time, the ontological status of a (fictional) narrative may in some cases clash with the (seemingly) high modality of the typography. Where the insertion of handwriting, for example, would appear to authenticate the contents of a biographical novel, the use of handwriting in fiction is trickier as it will ultimately clash with the reader's knowledge that the character who assumedly wrote this by hand never existed. The question to be considered, of course, is also whether the high modality of handwriting or the like inserted into a typographically plain narrative would in fact be seen as high modality, or whether its clash with our genre expectations actually makes readers interpret it as low modality in the given context of a printed novel. Altogether, the use of images, special typography, layout and so on for the creation of authenticity by explicitly multimodal fiction automatically seems to entail a certain post-modern nudge by the author about the ability of such modes to authenticate the experiential contents of his or her narrative (cf. Nørgaard 2010a for further discussion of typographic modality; and Gibbons 2009 about the inherently metafictional nature of multimodal novels).

The materiality of the book – Exemplified by the semiotics of paper

Adding multimodal tools to the stylistic tool box enables us – and perhaps even invites us – to analyse not only the written verbal narrative and whatever use it makes of e.g. images and special typography, but also the book cover as indicated above as well as material elements such as the paper, printing and binding of the novel. The materiality of the novel has not yet been investigated to any great extent by multimodal scholars. In the following I will use paper as an example, indicating how this aspect of the novel may be semiotic in its own right.

While most readers probably know very little about paper quality and tend not to notice the paper much when they read a novel, work by experts in the field reveals that paper can be described and categorised in systematic ways not unlike other semiotic modes. Paper can thus be characterised in terms of its *type* (made of wood, rags, grasses, synthetic material), *thickness*, *relative weight*, *density* and *finish* (bleaching, coating, calendering and tinting) (cf. e.g. Mourier and Mourier 1999). Thus, paper arguably has its own 'grammar' just as language and visual images have theirs. However, the grammar of paper is mostly known and operable by experts in the field and largely unknown to lay people. According to van Leeuwen (2005b, p. 142), lay people's knowledge about and expertise on a given semiotic mode may change along with changes in the role played by the mode in our culture and our everyday lives. While this has been the case with typography – due, in particular, to the spread of the word processor – paper appears not (yet) to have gone through a similar development and consequently holds only a minor semiotic potential for most people. At this point, it would therefore not make much sense to develop a detailed 'grammar' of paper for the stylistic tool box. On the other hand, to completely ignore the possible meanings constructed by the paper on which a given novel is printed would run counter to the ideals of the multimodal – and hence also the multimodal stylistic – project. Instead, a fertile first step of relevance to a multimodal stylistic analysis of the novel would be to look out for and explore aspects of the choice of paper which are likely to be seen as semiotic even to people who are not experts in the field. One such aspect concerns the choice of matt or glossy paper. Where matt paper is fine for printed text, a glossy surface will be more suited for books with illustrations, for example. This has implications for explicitly multimodal novels which combine text and images. In Bantam Press's special illustrated edition of Dan Brown's *The Da Vinci Code* (2004), the choice of glossy paper clearly adds to the exquisiteness of the publication and seems an appropriate choice for the representation of the artworks, symbols, architecture and so on which are described in the novel. Coating and calendering thus enable a very high quality for the visual images, but unfortunately the reflection of light caused by the glossy surface interferes with the readability of the text. In Erlend Loe's novel *L* (1999) a similar problem has been solved by using matt paper for the verbal narrative and glossy paper for images. Interestingly the pages with illustrations have been placed together as sixteen glossy pages in the middle of the novel, resulting in a far more arbitrary linking of the images and the wording than is the case with Brown's novel, where the images occur in close proximity to the text with which they are associated. A fair guess would be that this aspect of Loe's novel is caused by a wish, or need, to keep costs down and would hence be seen as semiosis created at the level of production with a view to distribution and consumption.

Altogether, many readers probably have some sense of the general material quality of the edition of the novel they are looking at – a quality that comes about as a combination of the paper, printing and binding of the novel. While high quality editions may partly reflect the contents of the actual narrative by signalling that it is worth the exclusive 'wrapping', it first and foremost seems to be meaning-making at the level of *consumption*, where it signals something about the taste and financial capabilities of the owner of the book. Consumption may, in fact, be seen as a missing stratum in Kress and van Leeuwen's (2001) stratal model where only *discourse*, *design*, *production* and *distribution* are considered as meaning-making strata.

So far the multimodal stylistic tool box contains relatively few tools for analysing the meanings that come about as a result of material aspects of the novel. When developing new tools to cover this field we face the risk of developing descriptive systems that are so finely grained that they catch details which are in actual fact not perceived as semiotic – like, for instance, the question of whether the paper of a given novel has been made of wood, rags, grasses or synthetic material. On the other hand, stylisticians may (ideally) increase the general awareness of the meanings created by the various material elements of the novel through their work.

Critical issues and topics

The attempt to develop a multimodal stylistics entails a number of challenges. First of all, to do a multimodal stylistic analysis of a novel is potentially a very extensive project. In addition to the detailed analysis of the verbal text which is characteristic of the stylistic approach to literature, modes such as layout, typography, images and colour must be dealt with in an equally meticulous and stringent manner. Furthermore, elements like paper quality and the book cover also invite analysis. On top of this, the multimodal credo that 1+1>2 (cf. Baldry and Thibault 2006, p. 18) means that not only should all the modes be recognised, the analyst must also – and not least – examine the meanings that arise as a result of the interaction of all the different modes involved. Although this challenge needs to be acknowledged, it does not make a multimodal stylistic analysis all that different from more traditional stylistic (or other) approaches to text analysis. Just as in other types of analyses of long and/or complex texts, the analyst must choose a focus. Usually, the chosen focus is something that intrigues us in our reading – often a certain peculiarity of the text that seems to invite analysis. The important thing in this connection is to make our focus explicit and explain the analytical choices we make.

Another challenge involved in multimodal stylistics concerns the complex nature of the object of analysis and the extensive terminology and methodological apparatus required for analysis – even though a common terminology for the different modes is aimed at whenever possible. Consequently, many will find it a rather demanding task to acquire substantial knowledge about all the different modes involved in meaning-making. While one of the main strengths of the multimodal approach to communication is its acknowledgement of the semiotic potential of all the modes involved in a given text, this acknowledgement also poses a problem for the analyst as it is clearly impossible to be an expert on all modes at the same time. It is no coincidence that traditionally each mode has had its own experts: linguists being experts on language, typographers experts on typography, musicologist experts on music, and so on. The challenge of a theory – and a stylistic branch – which tries to encompass all modes is obviously to avoid ending up with academically weaker analyses than stylistic branches with a less complex focus. If we insist on the viability of a multimodal approach to text analysis, this is a problem that is difficult to solve. It is therefore essential that analysts acknowledge this weakness and make explicit the weak (and strong) spots of their analysis. Ideally, multimodal stylisticians should work as groups of people with different areas of expertise in order to qualify all aspects of the analysis as far as possible. If such practice is not feasible in real life, it should nevertheless remind us of seeking constructive feedback and advice from experts in modes where we lack proficiency ourselves.

At a recent stylistics symposium (*A Celebration in Style*, Nottingham University, April 8, 2011) it was suggested that stylisticians should stick to the core competence of their field, i.e. language. Although sympathetic to the scholarly concern behind this suggestion, I nevertheless find it problematic since the explicitly multimodal communicative reality we are facing today cannot be ignored. Instead, consistent detailed methods of analysis are needed to capture, describe, analyse and understand this 'new' reality – methods which may ultimately be implemented at all levels of education in order to further multimodal literacy (cf. e.g. Kress 2003). It would seem rather odd that stylisticians as experts on (various aspects) of communication should stay out of this enterprise. In addition, I find it hard to understand the notion that stylisticians would wish to preclude themselves from analysing novels that include modes such as images and special typography for their meaning-making – or analyse such texts without acknowledging the communicative work performed by these modes.

All this being said, multimodal stylisticians should take care not to forget the core competency of stylistics. So far there seems to be a tendency among practitioners of this new stylistic branch – myself included – to centre on modes other than language in our work. This is probably due to the fact that the inclusion of these modes is new to the field, but for a multimodal stylistic analysis of (say) a novel to be truly multimodal and truly stylistic, the mode of wording should not be neglected. Nor should we forget that even in explicitly multimodal novels, the majority of the meaning is still carried by the verbal text.

The last issue to be mentioned here concerns the extended notion of 'text' entailed by the multimodal take on text analysis. While an obvious strength of adding multimodal tools to the stylistic tool box is the consequent acknowledgement and inclusion of meanings made by modes other than language, this extension of the concept of the text makes our object of analysis less stable. Where the verbal narrative of a novel is relatively seldom changed from one edition to another, notably more changes appear if we consider the novel as a whole, since different editions typically involve differences in features such as layout, typography, paper quality and book cover. Some of these changes are likely to be seen as minor – or not seen at all – such as the change from one common black typography to another, but other changes like a different cover will probably be experienced as more radical. An example of this is Kerouac's *On the Road* which has been published in a considerable number of different editions, in English as well as in translation. On some of these covers the configuration of experiential visual elements relates to different aspects of the narrative contents of the novel. Other covers display images of the author, and yet others refer visually to the actual coming into being and the ontological status of the text itself – i.e. the scroll on which Kerouac typed the narrative. All these different covers clearly create different meanings which are suitable for different contexts. For the author to appear as the central element on the front cover, for instance, he would need to be famous enough to be recognised by potential buyers/readers of the book. This is not to say that images of unknown authors cannot occur on the cover of their books, but statistically this would be a rather unusual choice for a publisher to make. Other changes occur when a novel is republished in cheap paperback editions where elements such as the use of colour are changed at the level of production (e.g. Foer's *Extremely Loud and Incredibly Close*, 2005) – or the other way around: when a novel turns out to be so popular that more exclusive editions with illustrations etc. are subsequently published (e.g. Brown's *The Da Vinci Code*, 2004). If some might consider this instability an indication that stylisticians should stick to the analysis of wording, the multimodal (stylistic) approach would encourage us to acknowledge that the different editions of the book construct different meanings and that the actual edition of the book at hand will therefore have to serve as our object of analysis. Interestingly, the existence of different editions of a novel allows the analyst to make commutation tests that are based on real rather than imagined material. Instead of imagining what meanings would have been created if an element of the novel had been substituted by something else – had Foer's coloured typography been black, for example – the different editions of the novel allow us to investigate such differences through real data.

Recommendations for practice

1. Choose a visually conventional novel and use the tools provided above to describe how meaning is created by semiotic modes other than language. Also consider how these meanings interact multimodally with each other and with wording. Then repeat the exercise in relation to an explicitly multimodal novel (i.e. a novel that employs images, colour, special layout and typography for its meaning-making).
2. Find a couple of novels which employ special typography for their semiosis. Apply van Leeuwen's *distinctive features* and the semiotic principles of *symbol, icon, index* and *discursive import* to capture and describe these meanings.
3. Do a comparative multimodal analysis of the book covers of two (or more) editions of the same novel. For your analysis, use the tools presented above and preferably also draw on some of the references provided in the list below. Are there any similarities between the different covers? What are the main differences? How and to what extent do the meanings created by the book covers relate to the verbal narrative of the novel? Do any of the covers also signal 'author', 'publisher', 'genre', 'intended reader' or the like? How? Useful examples for analysis are the different editions of classic novels such as Kerouac's *On the Road*, of popular novels such as Fielding's *Bridget Jones's Diary*, or of the different editions of Rowling's novels about Harry Potter marketed to children and adults respectively.

Future directions

With the reservations expressed in the section on critical issues and topics above, I am still convinced that the combination of stylistics and multimodal theory and methodology is a promising route to follow if we wish to make detailed systematic analyses of multimodal literature and other types of text. Since Kress and van Leeuwen's approach to visual communication springs from and builds on Halliday's theory of language, the combination of the Hallidayan approach to the written verbal text and Kress and van Leeuwen's approach to the visual (and other modes) in multimodal stylistics ensures a consistency of research method and terminology across modes. It is, however, also possible to combine Kress and van Leeuwen's visual grammar and treatment of other semiotic modes with other stylistic approaches to the verbal text.

Where multimodal theory may contribute to the field of stylistics, the opposite would, in fact, also seem to be the case. An application of multimodal theory to a new domain such as literature may thus point to areas where the theory might be in need of adjustments. In my view this is the case with aspects of the multimodal approach to typography, for example (cf. Nørgaard 2009). In addition to this, the application of the multimodal approach to a new domain may point to areas where new descriptive systems are needed altogether, as indicated, for instance, by the section on the semiotics of paper above. Last but not least, the combination of multimodality and stylistics might furthermore (ideally) result in a strengthening of the linguistic part of more traditional multimodal analyses where multimodal scholars have so far tended to treat language less thoroughly than other modes.

In this chapter, I have focused on a multimodal stylistic approach to the novel. Further observations can obviously be made about the multimodal stylistics of poetry, drama, children's books and so on. Furthermore, different things will be brought to light by a cognitive (multimodal stylistic) perspective on text analysis (cf. e.g. Gibbons 2012). Altogether, the combination of stylistics and multimodal theory has opened up a large field of uncovered ground in terms of objects of analysis as well as theoretical work – and the fun has only just begun.

Related topics

Creative writing and stylistics, drama and performance, functionalist stylistics, stylistics and film, stylistics and comics, stylistics and hypertext fiction.

Further reading

Gibbons, A., 2012. *Multimodality, cognition, and experimental literature*. London and New York: Routledge.

This book presents a cognitive take on the analysis of explicitly multimodal novels and is thus particularly interested in the multimodal literary experience. It combines elements such as cluster analysis, vectors and reading paths from multimodality studies with components from cognitive poetics such as figure/ground, profiling, cognitive deixis, conceptual metaphor, conceptual integration and text world theory. The book first introduces central aspects of multimodality studies and cognitive poetics and Gibbons' fusion of the two into *multimodal cognitive poetics*. This is followed by illuminating analyses of four explicitly multimodal novels from the twenty-first century.

Kress, G. and Van Leeuwen, T., [1996] 2006. *Reading images: The grammar of visual design*. 2nd. edn. London and New York: Routledge.

This book is absolutely central to (social semiotic) multimodal stylistics. It provides a comprehensive and systematic grammar of visual communication, focusing on the ways in which visuals simultaneously represent the world (*experiential/ideational meaning*), position the viewer in relation to the represented participants (*interpersonal meaning*), and organise meaning through the placement of elements on the page (*compositional meaning*). The theoretical and methodological framework of the book is supported by an impressive number of examples, ranging from drawings, photographic images and paintings to three-dimensional objects such as sculpture, buildings and toys.

McIntyre, D., 2008. Integrating multimodal analysis and the stylistics of drama: A multimodal perspective on Ian McKellen's *Richard III, Language and Literature*, 17 (4), 309–334.

This article demonstrates how the traditional stylistic analysis of drama may be extended and enhanced by considering not only the meaning of the play text in isolation but also the meanings that come about multimodally in the actual performance of the play. In an analysis of the soliloquy scene from Ian McKellen's film version of Shakespeare's *Richard III*, McIntyre thus combines linguistic analysis with multimodal analysis of production elements, focusing in particular on visual transitivity patterns and the concepts of represented and interactive participants.

Nørgaard, N., 2011. Teaching multimodal stylistics. *In:* L. Jeffries and D. McIntyre, eds. *Teaching stylistics*. Palgrave Macmillan, 221–238.

The explicit aim of this book chapter is to provide suggestions for the teaching of multimodal stylistics. At the same time, it functions as an introduction to the field, touching on the semiosis involved by the modes of wording, layout, typopgraphy and images. While most of the analyses presented in this chapter concern the meaning-making of book covers, the methodological tools presented may equally well be employed for the analysis of narratives which – in addition to wording – make use of images as well as (special) typography and layout for their meaning-making.

References

Auster, P., 2003. *Oracle night*. New York: Henry Holt.

Baldry, A. and Thibault, P. J., 2006. *Multimodal transcription and text analysis: A multimedia toolkit and coursebook*. London and Oakville: Equinox.

Bateman, J., 2008. *Multimodality and genre. A foundation for the systematic analysis of multimodal documents*. Hampshire and New York: Palgrave MacMillan.

Brenøe, M., 1997. *David Feldts efterladte papirer*. Viborg, Denmark: Samleren.

Brown, D., 2004. *The da Vinci code. Special illustrated edition*. New York, London, Toronto, Sydney, Auckland: Doubleday.

Foer, J. S., 2005. *Extremely loud and incredibly close*. Great Britain: Hamish Hamilton.

Gibbons, A., 2009. I contain multitudes: Narrative multimodality and the book that bleeds. *In:* R. Page, ed. *New perspective on narrative and multimodality*. London: Routledge, 99–114.

Gibbons, A., 2012. *Multimodality, cognition, and experimental literature*. London and New York: Routledge.

Haddon, M., 2003. *The curious incident of the dog in the night-time*. London: Jonathan Cape.

Halliday, M. A. K., 1994. *An introduction to functional grammar*. 2nd edn. London, New York, Sydney, Auckland: Arnold.

Joyce, J., [1914] 1992. Two Gallants. *In: Dubliners*. London, New York, Victoria: Penguin.

Kennedy, C., 1982. Systemic grammar and its use in literary analysis. *In:* R. Carter, ed. *Language and literature. An introductory reader in stylistics*. London: George Allen and Unwin, 83–99.

Kerouac, J., [1957] 1998. *On the road*. London, New York, Victoria, Toronto: Penguin.

Kress, G., 2003. *Literacy in the new media age*. London and New York: Routledge.

Kress, G., 2010. *Multimodality. A social semiotic approach to contemporary communication*. London and New York: Routledge.

Kress, G. and van Leeuwen, T., 1996. *Reading images: The grammar of visual design*. 1st edn. London and New York: Routledge.

Kress, G. and van Leeuwen, T., 2001. *Multimodal discourse: The modes and media of contemporary communication*. London: Arnold.

Kress, G. and van Leeuwen, T., 2002. Colour as a semiotic mode: Notes for a grammar of colour. *Visual Communication*, 1 (3), 343–368.

Loe, E., 1999. *L*. Oslo: Cappelen forlag.

Machin, D., 2007. *Introduction to multimodal analysis*. London: Hodder Arnold.

McIntyre, D., 2008. Integrating multimodal analysis and the stylistics of drama: A multimodal perspective on Ian McKellen's *Richard III. Language and Literature*, 17 (4), 309–334.

Martin, B. and Ringham, F., 2006. *Key terms in semiotics*. London and New York: Continuum.

Masters, A., [2005] 2006. *Stuart. A life backwards*. London, New York, Toronto, Sydney: Harper Perennial.

Montoro, R., 2010. A multimodal approach to mind style: Semiotic metaphor vs. multimodal conceptual metaphor. *In:* R. Page, ed. *New perspectives in narrative and multimodality*. New York and London: Routledge, 31–49.

Mourier, M. and Mourier, E., 1999. *Bogdesign. Tilrettelægning af illustrerede bøger*. København: Den Gafiske Højskole/Forlaget Grafisk Litteratur.

Nørgaard, N., 2003. *Systemic functional linguistics and literary analysis. A Hallidayan approach to Joyce – A Joycean appraoch to Halliday*. Odense, Denmark: University Press of Southern Denmark.

Nørgaard, N., 2009. The semiotics of typography in literary texts: A multimodal approach. *Orbis Litterarum*, 64 (2), 141–160.

Nørgaard, N., 2010a. Modality: Commitment, truth value and reality claims across modes in multimodal novels. *Journal of Literary Theory*, 4 (1), 63–80.

Nørgaard, N., 2010b. Multimodality: Extending the stylistic tool kit. *In:* B. Busse and D. McIntyre, eds. *Language and Style*, Palgrave Macmillan, 433–448.

Nørgaard, N., 2011. Teaching multimodal stylistics. *In:* L. Jeffries and D. McIntyre, eds. *Teaching stylistics*. Palgrave Macmillan, 221–238.

O'Halloran, K., 2005. *Mathematical discourse. Language, symbolism and visual images*. London and New York: Continuum.

Pedersen, K. and Kidmose, A., 1993. *Sort på hvidt. En udviklingsrapport om typografi og læselighed*. Denmark: Den Grafiske Højskole.

Van Leeuwen, T., 1999. *Speech, music, sound*. London: MacMillan Press Ltd.

Van Leeuwen, T., 2005a. *Introducing social semiotics*. London and New York: Routledge.

Van Leeuwen, T., 2005b. Typographic meaning. *Visual Communication*, 4 (2), 137–143.

Van Leeuwen, T., 2006. Towards a semiotics of typography. *Information design journal + document design*, 14 (2), 139–155.

30

Stylistics and comics

Charles Forceville, Elisabeth El Refaie, and Gert Meesters

Introduction

Most scholars agree that comics should be considered a medium, not a genre (Chute 2008, Fingeroth 2007). McCloud, who used the comics format to show how comics create meaning, insists on a clear separation of form and content: 'The artform – the *medium* – known as comics is a *vessel* which can hold any *number* of *ideas* and *images*' (1993, p. 6, emphasis in original). Over the years, the comics medium has been used to tell a whole range of different stories, including horror, science fiction, and children's tales of 'funny animals', superheroes and adventurers. Since the early 1970s an ever-increasing number of comics creators has also been exploring the potential of the medium for more serious genres, such as history, reportage, memoir and biography.

Ryan suggests that what counts as a medium 'is a category that truly makes a difference about what stories can be evoked or told, how they are presented, why they are communicated, and how they are experienced' (2004, p. 18). In this chapter we explore the unique and less unique ways of presenting and evoking information and stories offered by the comics medium; in other words, its stylistics.

An August 2012 Google search for 'stylistics and comics' in various permutations yielded not a single hit, which supports our intuition that the burden for deciding what might qualify as a stylistics of comics is really on us. However, the fact that 'style in comics' yielded close to thirty thousand hits makes clear that we are by no means in uncharted territory. In relation to comics, 'style' is typically used to refer to the specific visual dimensions of the artwork, including choices such as drawing versus painting techniques, colour versus black and white, and realism versus abstraction. Comics style may also refer more broadly to such formal features as the layout of the page and the shape and arrangement of panels and speech or thought balloons. Examples of particular comics styles include Hergé's *ligne claire* ('clear line'), American underground 'comix', and Japanese manga. In these stylistic features the reader may find evidence of 'graphiation', the idiosyncratic gesture that produced a particular work (Marion 1993, discussed in Baetens 2001) and that offers 'a constant visual reminder of the hand of the illustration artist, much more so than the writer's traces' (Carney 2008, p. 195). Variations in style are also sometimes used within one album or even within the same panel to indicate 'degrees of certainty and nuances of attitude in relation to what is being recounted' (Miller 2007, p. 123), to add meaning by referring to other visual art, including other comics (Meesters 2010), or to distinguish between real life and fantasy (El Refaie 2010a).

Apart from such visual features, a consideration of stylistics in comics may also comprise the specific use of language in this medium. Comics can use words in the form of verbal narration in text boxes, as part of the landscape of the story world, to indicate sounds, and in speech and thought balloons. Here we will focus on those aspects of the verbal modality in comics that differ substantially from the use of language in other artistic media (e.g. prose fiction, film, theatre). For example, the use of speech balloons gives some of the written language of comics a distinctly 'oral' quality, as it is meant to be 'heard' rather than simply read (Barker 1989, p. 11, Khordoc 2001). What is also distinctive about the language of comics is that the boundaries between words and images are often blurred, with words assuming pictorial qualities and pictures often being characterised by a high level of abstraction (Beronä 2001). Onomatopoeic words, for instance, are visually integrated into the depicted world of the story. Titles are also sometimes used as an integral part of the pictorial landscape (Harvey 1996, pp. 80–85).

Our main goal is thus to provide a survey of the various categories of stylistic devices – whether verbal, visual, or multimodal – that are available to the medium of comics for communicating information and telling stories. This should help comics and multimodality scholars to detect stylistic patterns and idiosyncrasies.

We use 'comics' in a very broad sense. The typical comic consists of a sequence of at least two panels. A comic strip in a newspaper may comprise two to six panels, while an instalment in a magazine perhaps has a few dozen, and an album a few hundred. Multi-volume series may run into the thousands. All of these are, for our present purposes, regarded as 'comics'. We also consider the term to cover serious book-length comics for adults, which are nowadays often discussed and marketed under the label of 'graphic novels'. Although many regions of the world have thriving comics cultures, we focus here on European comics, with some attention being paid to North American comics and Japanese manga. Scholars are invited to test our insights and generalisations against other traditions, and where appropriate refine or adapt them. In our discussions we primarily have comics on paper in mind, but we are aware that there is a fast-growing body of webcomics. Finally, some of what we say here also applies to single-panel 'cartoons'.

Our general perspective is informed by the common-sense idea, rooted in Sperber and Wilson's 'relevance theory' (Sperber and Wilson 1995, Wilson and Sperber 2012) that comics makers are artistic communicators intent on conveying more or less specific narrative meaning to a mass audience. This means that most readers/viewers are expected to agree on the interpretation of most of the information provided, although there is always scope for individuals to 'read against the grain' or discover alternative meanings supported by inadvertently conveyed information – what Bordwell and Thompson (2008, p. 63) call 'symptomatic' meaning. (For more on relevance theory see Chapter 9 in this volume.)

Historical perspectives

Most scholars agree with Groensteen (2009, pp. 15–16) that the ninth art started with Rodolphe Töpffer's *Histoire de M. Jabot* (1833), although American scholars sometimes see the beginning of comic strips in newspapers, specifically Richard Outcault's Yellow Kid series (which ran from 1895 onwards in the *New York World* and then in the *New York Journal*), as a more important milestone. In Britain, modern comics developed out of the tradition of satirical monthlies such as *Punch* (from 1841). In any case, the second half of the nineteenth century saw the development of the art form, mostly in periodicals, more or less simultaneously in several parts of the world (Dierick and Lefèvre 1998). The twentieth century witnessed a growing popularity of the medium with the arrival of comic books in the US and albums in Western Europe. Comics in many countries started to target a young audience more specifically. From the late 1960s onwards, the medium has also rediscovered the adult audience it had served so effectively early in its history. The increasing availability of graphic novels in regular bookshops in recent years testifies to the much greater esteem in which such works are now held.

Comics stylistics as a scholarly discipline is still in its infancy, but some trail-blazers deserve to be mentioned. The first major publications in Europe were written by scholars interested in semiotics, such as Eco (1964) and Fresnault-Deruelle (1972). In English, comics artists gave an impetus to stylistic research by analysing their own medium. Eisner (1985) and McCloud (1993) were landmark publications in this respect. Recently scholars from diverse disciplines, including literary criticism, cognitive linguistics and communication science, have intensified the interest in comics' stylistic repertoire. There is a quickly expanding number of journals dedicated to comics, such as *Comics Journal, International Journal of Comic Art, Journal of Comics and Graphic Novels, European Comic Art* and *Scandinavian Journal of Comic Art*. Of interest is also *Comics Forum* (2009– at http://comicsforum.org/).

Key aspects of style in comics

In this section, we discuss the stylistic devices that artists have at their disposal to create narratively salient information. Inevitably, there is overlap in the list, and we make no claim to exhaustiveness.

Pages, panel arrangements and the gutter

In a mainstream comics' album the reader/viewer is expected to access the panels in a specific order, although in exceptional cases there may be some freedom. In the typical comic, panels are arranged in a regular grid pattern. They are normally read from left to right and from top to bottom, although, following Japanese reading conventions, manga pages and panels are read and viewed from right to left. The grid pattern format is frequently not followed by American superhero comics. Here a less strict reading direction applies, because panels may overlap, or be embedded in one another. Freedom with respect to the reading path is sometimes also exploited in graphic novels such as those by Chris Ware (see Sczepaniak 2010).

Comics panels typically have straight black borders, but this can vary to suggest alternative interpretations. For instance, a cloud-like wavy line might suggest a dream scene or a flashback (cf. Eisner 1985, pp. 44–50). The panels themselves usually vary between squares and rectangles. Sometimes a panel is bigger, taking up the space of two or more rows, or even an entire page, called a 'splash page'. Many artists occasionally or often deviate from the conventional panel form: panels can be round, oval or polygonal, forms that – much like balloon contours – may carry specific meaning. The choice of background colours in panels may be meaningful, too.

The fact that, as Eisner emphasised, comics deal 'with the arrangement of pictures or images' (1985, p. 5) makes the space between panels, the 'gutter', extremely important. In comics, unlike in film or prose fiction, a scene (roughly, an event unified by space, time, and the characters that are present) can only be conveyed by selected moments depicted in panels, often supported by verbal information. Movements and any other actions or events that are not represented in the panels 'happen' in the gutter. The relations between adjacent panels can be of different kinds (see McCloud 1993, pp. 70–72 and Cohn 2007 for two proposals). The gutter thus always requires the reader to *infer* some information. In mainstream comics this inferencing process is so unproblematic as to be, or at least to seem, completely automatic. On the basis of everything we know and believe as human beings, members of a culture, genre experts, and readers/viewers of the story at hand (together constituting our 'cognitive environment', Sperber and Wilson 1995, p. 38), we usually have little difficulty supplying the intended inferences. Of course, an artist may deliberately de-automatise this inferencing process, or else as idiosyncratic readers we may recruit presuppositions not envisaged by the artist or necessarily shared with fellow readers (for more on inferencing and applying the relevance theory model to comics, see Yus 2008).

In many comics, the page or the two-page spread is an important unit of meaning. Especially in European comics, the composition of panels on a page can resemble that of words in a paragraph or a sentence in prose. Since all panels on a page or two-page spread are visible at the same time, their interrelations allow for additional stylistic play. Peeters (1998, pp. 39–64) distinguishes between different types of page compositions; in one of them, the 'productive page', the composition appears to dictate the story instead of vice versa. Also, the final panel on a page can be used to end a scene or create a feeling of suspense. This happens most obviously with cliff-hangers in serial narratives, but can also be a way of pacing the story (Groensteen 2007, p. 29).

Several artists and scholars have noted the close association between time and space in the comics medium (Chute 2010, McCloud 1993, Miller 2003, Vice 2001), which chimes with the claim of conceptual metaphor theorists that there is a universal tendency to think about time passing in terms of movement through space, with the future in front of us, the present right by us, and the past behind (Lakoff and Johnson 1980, pp. 41–44, Lakoff 1993). Eisner (1985) has discussed the pace or 'rhythm' of comic book narratives by considering the number of panels dedicated to particular actions. The reader's perception of temporality may also be influenced by the arrangement, size, directionality and shape of panels on a page and by the space between panels, or by reiteration, overlap, and changes in perspective (Dittmar 2008, Groensteen 2007, Schneider 2010, Wolk 2007, pp. 181–202).

Comics also allow for every panel to enter into a relationship with any other panel in the book, forming complex strands of correspondences through 'braiding' (Groensteen 2001). These links can be established through visual or semantic similarities. Contrasting or merging different moments in time can be achieved by inserting visual representations of these moments within the same panel, or by juxtaposing them on the same or on facing pages (for a discussion of more sophisticated variations, see El Refaie 2010b).

Body types, postures, and facial expressions

Body shapes and postures tell us a lot about the depicted characters. There are typical ways in which a beautiful girl, a mean old man, an arrogant boss, and numerous other 'stock' types are depicted, even though a viewer may have to 'learn' the idiosyncratic manner in which a specific artist draws them. Moreover, artists need to ensure that their heroes and heroines and other recurring characters are immediately recognisable. Often this involves specific clothes and other props: Obelix sports blue-and-white striped pants, Tintin is accompanied by Milou, Lucky Luke wears a white cowboy hat and has a cigarette (nowadays a blade of grass) dangling from his mouth. In the case of autobiographical works, the medium offers artists the opportunity to represent their physical identities in ways that reflect their innermost sense of self by using a range of symbolic elements and rhetorical tropes to add layers of meaning to their self-portraits (El Refaie 2012a, 2012b, Mitchell 2010).

Physical activities (walking, throwing, fighting, giving, kissing etc.) are often depicted in highly stereotypical ways, although there is considerable freedom for individual artists to digress from these stereotypes. Since plot development depends on action, it is crucial that viewers correctly judge the nature of any physical activity. As movement can only be *suggested* in comics, the key moment of a movement needs to be chosen to convey the entire action – even more so in minimal 'stick-figure' comics. Finally, body postures often help signal emotions and mental states. Arm and hand positions are particularly revealing (Baetens 2004), because we can gesture and simulate much more accurately with our hands and arms than with other body parts. The manga album *Azumanga Daioh* exploits this in an unusual way: characters affected by emotion are sometimes depicted without hands, suggesting that their mental state makes them incapable of controlling their behaviour (Abbott and Forceville 2011).

For the correct assessment of mental states, facial expressions are possibly even more crucial. The depiction of eyes and mouths is especially informative. Based on the work of the psychologist Paul Ekman (2003) and the practitioner Gary Faigan (1990), McCloud (2006) demonstrates how the basic emotions of anger, disgust, fear, joy, sadness, and surprise can be visualised in comics as well as how they can be adapted to show various degrees of intensity, and combined to create other emotions and moods (see also Groensteen 2003, Eisner 1985). Tan (2001) suggests that conventional comics tend to use simple and highly exaggerated facial expressions to convey the universally recognisable basic emotions, which makes them transparent to readers of all ages and levels of literacy. The faces of characters in more complex graphic novels, he argues, typically reflect more ambiguous feelings, which require a higher level of interpretative work by the reader. Many manga *or* Japanese comics are characterised by the so-called 'super-deformed' style, which means not only that certain body parts (heads, eyes) may be depicted out of proportion or not at all (such as noses), but also that characters affected by emotion can suddenly have square eyes and mouths, looking like monsters (see Cohn 2010).

Most of this information is presented in a way that we are familiar with from real life. However, in many comics we see it in exaggerated, hyperbolic form. A face is not just red, it is lobster red; eyes do not just bulge, they almost pop out; bodies do not just shake, they seem to float above the ground or are depicted in overlapping images. Shinohara and Matsunaka (2009) note that angry characters in manga often have a 'popped-up vein'. The notion that this should be taken as a hyperbole which has acquired symbolic status transpires from the fact that such veins do not only occur in temples or foreheads, but also in unrealistic places (cheeks, hair, text balloons, or in mid-air).

Framing and angles in panels

Comics artists have various visual means at their disposal to suggest to their readers who is the most important character in the narrative and with whom they should identify or empathise. A simple but effective strategy for encouraging the reader to align with one character's perspective rather than another's is what the film scholar Murray Smith has termed 'spatial attachment': 'the way a narration may follow the spatio-temporal path of a particular character throughout the narrative, or divide its attention among many characters each tracing distinct spatio-temporal paths' (1995, p. 142). Social semioticians believe that there are several ways of establishing contact between the viewer of an image and the depicted persons (Kress and van Leeuwen 2006, pp. 114–153). These authors claim that in pictures, as in real life, distance reflects the quality of the relationship. A close-up thus suggests an intimate relation, while a medium shot implies a certain distancing. A long shot may suggest either an impersonal or a completely distant relationship. Where there is 'eye-contact' between a depicted character and the viewer, the former seems to be 'demanding' something of the latter, whereas lack of eye contact invites detached scrutiny of a person being on 'offer'. Looking at people from above gives the viewer symbolic power over them, an eye-level view suggests an equal relationship, and a low angle makes the depicted person appear more powerful. Finally, a full frontal view is thought to indicate a maximum degree of involvement and a profile view to suggest a sense of detachment.

Making a similar point with regard to self-portraits, Cumming argues that a fully frontal view of someone looking out at the viewer is the visual equivalent of direct address in written language, inviting 'the purest form of reciprocity' (2009, p. 26). The profile, by contrast, puts the self-portrait 'straight into the third person' (2009, p. 38). Historically, comics have generally evolved from showing characters' entire bodies in profile to more varied and dynamic ways of depicting them.

The equivalent of a first-person point of view can be achieved by showing a character from behind or over the shoulder, which seems to offer readers the opportunity to see the world through their eyes (Saraceni 2003). Comics artists can also make use of what in film is called an 'eyeline match', where 'shot A presents someone looking at something offscreen; shot B shows us what is being looked at. In neither shot are both looker and object present' (Bordwell and Thompson 2008, pp. 240–241). In comics, the shots are replaced by consecutive panels. In some comics, long sequences of events, dreams, fantasies, or memories are shown from a point of view that coincides completely with that of a single character, thus creating a particularly strong affiliation with him/her. Sometimes the character through whose eyes we see the events of a story remains completely absent visually and the reader only sees what he or she does, as in Daniel Clowes' short story 'The Stroll' (1990).

Speech and thought balloons

What comics characters say or think is usually represented in text balloons, although this text may also appear in blocks at the top or bottom of a panel, or underneath a row of panels. More often, however, this space is reserved for narratorial text that emanates from a non-character narrator or from a character-bound narrator (for more on this terminology see Bal 2009; see also Chapter 11 in this volume) looking back on events that are depicted in the panels in which s/he may him/herself appear.

Balloons can vary on a number of visual dimensions that potentially carry narrative significance. In Forceville *et al*. (2010), a corpus of some 4,000 balloons in six different comics albums was investigated, yielding the following variables: form; colour; tail-use; occurrence of deviant fonts; and inclusion of non-verbal material. The list below is largely based on the findings in that chapter.

Form. Normally, an album or artist has a standard balloon form. An oval with a tail linked to the speaking character is probably the most typical form, but the *Tintin* albums, for instance, have rectangles with bites taken out of their corners. What happens to be the standard balloon in an album is of no great import; what matters is that any deviations from a given standard may be meaningful within an album or artistic oeuvre. A *conventional* deviation is the thought balloon, which instead of a tail has 'thought bubbles' linking the balloon – perhaps featuring a cloud-like form – to the speaker. Another common deviation that is narratively salient is a balloon with spiky edges and often a sharp zigzag tail, which is associated with anger. Furthermore, electronically conveyed or amplified text (via a television, loudspeaker, mobile phone and so on) is often indicated in a balloon with a serrated contour.

Colour. The standard colour of a balloon is white, and the letters within it are black, in the same font. However, the balloon or elements in it (pictograms, letters) may be coloured. In European comics red is often a signal for anger. However, the colour of a balloon, like any of its other variables, sometimes has a 'local' significance only, for instance being associated with a specific character, or with a mental state. For example, in the Asterix album *The Roman Agent* (1972) anger is partly conveyed by green text balloons.

Deviant fonts and non-aligned letters. If one or more words in a balloon are rendered in a non-standard font, this is always meaningful. A word in bigger font, capitals, or bold face may indicate that it is emphatically pronounced, or shouted. By contrast, a smaller font perhaps suggests whispering, or fear. A 'dancing letter' text could be an indication that its source is drunk, or confused, or that the lines are sung.

Standalone non-letter marks. Particularly mainstream comics often feature text balloons with a standalone question mark or exclamation mark, conveying surprise or confusion (Meesters 2011). Other punctuation marks, mathematical symbols, or yet other signs one can find on a computer keyboard sometimes appear in a balloon. This is an interesting stylistic phenomenon, since these marks, while not really verbal, are nonetheless symbols with a coded meaning. An artist may decide not to use language in balloons, but still employ such symbols (e.g. in Lewis Trondheim's *Mister I*, 2005).

Tails. Typically, tails point to the speaker of the text in the balloons, who is him/herself visible in the panel. However, a tail may also point to a speaker who is not (yet) visible. This is often exploited as a source of surprise; not until the next panel, for instance, is the source of the spoken text revealed – a trick that works longer if that panel is on the next page, or in next week's magazine instalment. A tail may also *straddle* two panels.

Onomatopoeia and written words in the story world

Onomatopoeia, a style figure/trope from classical rhetoric, is 'the lexical process of creating words which actually sound like their referent' (Wales 2001, p. 277). It is thus one of those relatively rare linguistic phenomena where the form of a word is not arbitrary but motivated. Onomatopoeia is comics' device par excellence to suggest sound. The cross-cultural similarity in onomatopoeia is unsurprising, simply because (for instance) English and French animals – or Japanese ones, for that matter – presumably make the same noise, as do heavy doors being slammed, or objects being hit. That said, even then the match is only partial: the English cock crows 'cock-a-doodle-doo', the French one 'cocorico', and the Dutch one 'kukeleku'. Other sounds, such as sirens, train whistles, doorbells, or telephones, have stronger culture-specific dimensions. However, onomatopoeia need not be realistic: a large number of sound effects are creative in the sense that they are rarely present outside of comics and their form thus allows for a great deal of variation. Pollman (2001) describes the process of creating such onomatopoeias as 'inventing phonetics'. Frequently used onomatopoeias are conventionalised and thus become words in a language. This process fixes their form and prevents the variation caused by imperfect imitation of real word sounds with phonemes from a specific human language. Sometimes translated comics introduce new onomatopoeias in other languages. Since sound effects are often inscribed in the image, they are technically more difficult to change in a translated version than balloon text. Belgian publishers, often dealing with original comics in French that are subsequently translated into Dutch, sometimes gave their artists lists of onomatopoeias that would translate well into the target language. Despite such regulating translation policies by big publishers, some onomatopoeias from foreign comics have become absorbed in other languages. For example, *paw*, sometimes used for gunshots in English, has become frequent in French and Dutch comics, thereby partially replacing local onomatopoeias such as *pan* or *pang* respectively.

Onomatopoetic words in comics are often rendered in a font that at the very least deviates from standard fonts, but may also draw on visual qualities such as colour, non-aligned letters, and different sizes. Lettering in languages like Japanese can be integrated more easily into the image because of the pictorial quality of Japanese orthography. Possibly this feature of the Japanese writing system has contributed to the extension of onomatopoetic effects to cue even inaudible phenomena, such as 'silence' or 'blushing' (Pollman 2001). Written words such as road signs, posters, and all kind of names and labels may tell a lot about the story world. Some comics artists also use textual artefacts such as extracts from letters, maps and diaries in their work. In the case of non-fiction comics such documents are sometimes rendered in their original form, but more commonly they are reinterpreted through the artist's hand.

As Frahm (2003, no page number) points out, words and images in comics exist 'side by side on the same surface of the paper of the page', and are thus typically closely intertwined. For this reason word-image relations in comics are perhaps best understood in terms of a tension between sign systems that, for reasons of convention and expectation, are likely to be interpreted in distinct ways (Hatfield 2005, p. 37).

Pictograms and pictorial runes

We define 'pictograms' as stylised depictions of phenomena that are familiar from real-life phenomena or from other visual genres, but that have often acquired a more or less conventional meaning within the realm of comics. An isolated pictogram would thus have some basic meaning of its own when encountered outside of comics – a characteristic that distinguishes it from the pictorial runes to be discussed later. Examples of pictograms are $ ♥ (for many more examples see Gasca and Gubern 2001, pp. 312–411). Individual artists are likely to have developed their own style for depicting any specific pictogram. Moreover, artists may vary the standard depiction of a given pictogram creatively. Thus, the 'light bulb' pictogram for a sudden, bright idea can sometimes be a torch, or a spotlight, or a campfire instead. However, normally pictograms are used to depict protagonists' mental states: they can occur on their own as well as in multiples (either of the same or in combinations of different sorts), and they can appear both within and outside text balloons.

'Pictorial runes' is the name Kennedy (1982) suggested for 'non-mimetic graphic elements that contribute narratively salient information' (Forceville 2011, p. 875; see also Forceville 2005). Walker calls them 'indicia' (2000, p. 27). Pictorial runes are another device that helps comic artists visualise states and events that, in real life, would be inferred from other sources of information. We believe that runes comprise a limited number of items, with a fairly specific appearance and a more or less fixed meaning. Forceville (2011) made an inventory and counted the appearances of all the runes in a single *Tintin* album, paying attention to three dimensions: appearance (see Table 30.1), location, and orientation. This inventory can serve as a starting point for further systematic analysis of runes in the work of other artists, cultures, or periods.

Table 30.1 Stylised examples of pictorial runes used in *Tintin and the Picaros* (adapted from Forceville 2011, p. 877); the popped-up vein was identified in manga by Shinohara and Matsunaka (2009).

Speed lines	Three types of movement lines	Droplets	Spikes	Spiral	Twirl	Popped-up vein

Most importantly, pictorial runes are used to convey movement in a medium that can only portray the static. Movements can by and large be subdivided into movements of an animate agent or object through space ('speed lines') and movements of body parts (of animate agents) or elements (of objects) relative to those agents and objects ('movement lines'). The second major role of pictorial runes is to help convey characters' emotions and mental states. In this capacity, the runes appear around human (or anthropomorphised) characters' heads. The 'twirl,' 'spiral', 'droplet', and 'spike' all fulfil this goal, which thus comprises emotional affect, dizziness, drunkenness, and confusion. Interestingly the twirl is used both for motion and emotion, and this may well suggest a pictorial equivalent for the verbal similarity between the accompanying words, which both have the Latin root *movere* – to move (for more discussion of this idea see Forceville (2005, 2011). Other types of event whose interpretation by a comics reader is aided by pictorial runes are 'pain', 'sound', and 'smell'. The 'spikes' rune is also used as a generic 'attention-drawing' device: a halo-like circle of spikes around a person or object emphasises a person or object that might otherwise escape the attention of the comics reader.

We dare claim no exhaustiveness for either the types of runes identified or their functions, but we feel confident that the list presented above provides a good starting point for further analysis. Various problems beset attempts at systematic runic analysis, including the distinguishability of runes, the range of runes used, their combinability both with each other and with other stylistic devices, as well as the degree of precision with which a certain rune is used – problems that pertain to a specific artist's oeuvre no less than to comics styles and traditions generally.

Of course, many of these variables co-occur, and usually their precise meaning depends on this co-occurrence. Furthermore, it is to be realised that what has been sketched here are the norms and some common deviations from these norms. If and when a norm is clear, an artist may modify or depart from it. In American superhero comics, for instance, there is much more creative play with balloon form and colours than in European ones. For instance, the character in Dave Gibbon and Alan Moore's *Watchmen* (1987) that is transformed into Dr. Manhattan after an accident has a blue rim along the inner borders of his balloons: this type of balloon is uniquely associated with him. Albums that feature creative use of balloon variables and fonts are David Mazzucchelli's *Asterios Polyp* (2009) and Brecht Evens' *The Wrong Place* (2010). For more on creative exploitations of norms see Forceville (2013) and Meesters (2013); for a Deleuzian 'rhizome' reading of reading paths in Art Spiegelman's *In the Shadow of No Towers* (2004) and Chris Ware's *Building Stories* (2012), see Verwoerd (2013).

Recommendations for practice

1. Focus on an emotion (sadness, fear, disgust…) or a mental state (hopefulness, thoughtfulness, timidity…). Compare three or more different comics (or a single, long-running comic chronologically) and chart how this particular emotion/mental state is conveyed (via balloonic features, runes, onomatopoeia, colours, facial expressions, body postures…). Which features are the most crucial ones in order for readers to recognise the emotion/mental state? Are there recurring combinations? Which artist uses the largest spectrum? Has a given author's (or movement's, or tradition's) repertoire or preference changed over time? Are there cultural differences?

2. Irrespective of medium, it is essential to monitor who narrates a story, and whose literal and/or mental point of view is conveyed at any specific moment. Choose a mainstream comic album or graphic novel and consider the following questions: Is the narrator omniscient, objective or character-bound? Do we see what the narrator wants us to see, or are we aligned with a specific character? How are flashbacks signalled? Dreams? Are they signalled by visual, verbal, or verbal-plus-visual means?

3. Choose one comic that tells a fictional story (e.g. an adventure story for children, science fiction, horror) and one that tells a story from real life (e.g. a biography, autobiography, historical tale, or reportage). Are there any significant stylistic differences between them, and, if so, how might these relate to the two comics' different relationship with the 'real' or 'authentic'?

4. Find two comics of the same genre (e.g. Western, science fiction, autobiography), one serious and one funny. How is the difference in tone expressed and reinforced by stylistic means? What are the differences in the style of the illustrations? Are thought balloons, pictograms, runes and onomatopoeias equally ubiquitous in both comics? Why (not)?

5. Some comics' tendency to represent characters and their emotions through drawings that simplify and exaggerate salient features has, in the past, attracted much criticism, especially with respect to women and ethnic minorities. Choose a long-running comic (e.g. an American superhero comic) and trace the continuities and/or changes in how a particular category of people has been represented over the years. Alternatively, compare the depiction of a particular category of people across different kinds of comics (e.g. a superhero comic, a children's comic, a manga, and a graphic novel).

Future directions

While we hope to have grouped phenomena in intuitively plausible categories, we are aware that sometimes different choices could have been made. The borderline between pictograms and pictorial runes, for instance, may be a fuzzy one. However, as long as we accept that categorisation is done according to prototypes, this should not worry us overmuch.

Furthermore, it is clear that if a reader/viewer arrives at an interpretation that is somehow narratively relevant – whether pertaining to a character's emotions, motivations, or a state of affairs in the story-world – this happens most often as a result of *combining* signals from categories: an angry character's emotional state may well be cued as such by, say, her facial expression *and* bodily posture *and* runes *and* pictograms *and* balloon variables *and* panel forms *and* font sizes *and* onomatopoeia *and* the balloon text 'I am mad as hell!'

Studies of onomatopoeia could pave the way for other cross-cultural studies of the use of language. After all, mainstream European comics have been translated into many languages, offering great opportunities for comparison (e.g. Khordoc 2001, Kaindl 2004), while manga nowadays has a large international following. Other interesting avenues for research are the ways in which sentences are divided over different balloons emanating from the same speaker, or even different parts of a non-symmetrical balloon. Probably most such divisions respect clausal units, but enjambment-like divisions can be exploited for surprise effect.

We have shown that comics have a wide range of medium-specific stylistic devices to convey meaning. This meaning is predominantly recruited to tell a story, and thus our proposals are primarily informed by narratological concerns. However, meaning-creation may also serve argumentative or didactic purposes. Comics are increasingly seen as a medium that can relay 'factual' or 'documentary' information (e.g. *Logicomix*, Doxiadis and Papadimitriou 2009, *MetroBasel Comic*, Herzog *et al.* 2009, see also In 't Veld 2012). Comics elements such as balloons and runes are also used in educational books, brochures, and advertising.

We trust that the catalogue of comics stylistic elements presented here will function as a help for studies in different areas of research and teaching. First of all, of course, our proposals feed into the study of the history and theory of comics. All of the categories proffered invite questions as to when, where, and how the phenomena identified appear in specific strips or albums, movements, periods, genres, and cultures. Clearly there is always the possibility that some stylistic choices are symptoms of ideological biases. Studying specific corpora as well as conducting experimental research to test any theoretical findings are logical next steps (see Cohn 2013, Ojha *et al.* 2013). Moreover, because several of the categories (notably balloons, pictograms, and runes) have a standard repertoire of a fairly limited number of items and, perhaps, a rudimentary 'grammar' governing how these can be related to form patterned structures, we believe that the stylistics of comics are of interest to students of visual culture and multimodal discourse more generally.

'Narration' and 'focalization' and the multiple relations in which they can be hierarchically embedded are among the most complex and fascinating issues in narratology, and the ways in which the stylistic devices identified in this chapter can be deployed in their service deserves sustained study (see Chapter 11 in this volume for more on narratology). Finally, as with all systematic research of culturally meaningful discourses and structures, the analysis of comics will also be of interest to cognition studies (see Kukkonen 2013).

In this chapter we have mainly concentrated on elements of visual style that are typical of the medium of comics. However, clearly there are other angles that can be brought to bear on the topic. We will very briefly mention two of these. The first is a body of work associated with *Gestalt* theory (see Arnheim 1969, Smith 1996). The basic idea of *Gestalt* theory is that human beings are biologically inclined to favour certain spatial constellations above others. Other things being equal, we prefer symmetry, continuity, and centrality over asymmetry, discontinuity, and marginality. Bordwell and Thompson (2008, pp. 112–161) draw on such insights in arguing how a filmmaker can direct the viewer's attention by skilfully setting up the profilmic reality (*mise-en-scène*) and making it interact with camera positions, angles, and movements (see Chapter 28 in this volume for more on 'stylistics and film'). Comics artists can also draw on these hard-wired perceptive mechanisms – or subvert them.

Another pertinent field is the budding one of visual and multimodal rhetoric. Increasingly, the idea gains ground that many classical tropes and schemes, such as metaphor, metonymy, irony, hyperbole, antithesis, rhyme and so on, have pictorial and multimodal equivalents. However, while there is now a growing body of studies on metaphor, some of them specifically focusing on comics and cartoons (Eerden 2009, El Refaie 2009, Schilperoord and Maes 2009, Bounegru and Forceville 2011), work on other tropes is only just beginning (e.g. Teng 2009; see Forceville 2006 for some discussion and references, and see Wells 1998 for a list of tropes in animation film). The work on non-verbal rhetoric and on the stylistics of comics will undoubtedly be mutually beneficial. (See Chapter 1 in this volume for more on 'rhetoric' and Chapter 30 for more on 'multimodality'.)

Related topics

Cognitive poetics, corpus stylistics, emotion and neuroscience, literary pragmatics, metaphor and metonymy, multimodality, narrative fiction, relevance theory, rhetoric and poetics, stylistics and film, stylistics and translation

Further reading

Cohn, N., 2013. *The visual language of comics: Introduction to the structure and cognition of sequential images*. New York, NY: Bloomsbury.

This linguist and psychologist pushes the analogy between comics and language as far as he can. He demonstrates how the human drive to make and find meaning in all communication also governs the interpretation of comics. Cohn's terminology can be a bit intimidating, but the systematicity with which he builds up his tool kit is impressive.

Groensteen, T., 2007. *The system of comics*. Jackson, MS: University Press of Mississippi.

One of the best analyses of the mechanics of comics storytelling so far. This book deals extensively with panel and page composition and discusses the concept of braiding.

McCloud, S., 1993. *Understanding comics: The invisible art*. New York: Harper Perennial.

Thought-provoking theoretical book by a US comics artist on comics art in comics form, which gave a huge boost to comics scholarship worldwide.

Magnussen, A. and Christiansen, H. C., eds. 2000. *Comics & culture: Analytical and theoretical approaches to comics*. Copenhagen: Museum Tusculanum Press.

This collection draws together comics research by scholars from Europe and the USA. The main foci of the contributions are on the aesthetics of comics and their relation to other media, the analysis of specific works and genres, and discussions of the cultural status of comics in society.

Smith, M. J. and Duncan, R., eds., 2012. *Critical approaches to comics: Theories and methods*. New York: London.

The twenty-one chapters in this book, by a range of comics experts, are clustered under the headings 'form', 'content', 'production', 'context' and 'reception', and they sample the multifarious ways in which comics can be studied academically.

References

Abbott, M. and Forceville, C., 2011. Visual representation of emotion in manga: LOSS OF CONTROL IS LOSS OF HANDS. *In: Azumanga Daioh* Volume 4, *Language and Literature,* 20, 91–112.
Arnheim, R., [1954] 1969. *Art and visual perception: A psychology of the creative eye*. London: Faber and Faber.
Baetens, J., 2001. Revealing traces: A new theory of graphic enunciation. *In:* R. Varnum and C. T. Gibbons, eds. *The language of comics: Word and image*. Jackson, MS: University Press of Mississippi, 145–155.
Baetens, J., 2004. La main parlante. *Image [&] Narrative* 5 (1), http://www.imageandnarrative.be/inarchive/performance/baetens_main.htm (accessed 4 September 2012).
Bal, M., 2009. *Narratology*. 3rd ed. Toronto: University of Toronto Press.
Barker, M., 1989. *Comics: Ideology, power and the critics*. Manchester: University of Manchester Press.

Beronä, D. A., 2001. Pictures speak in comics without words: Pictorial principles in the work of Milt Gross, Hendrik Dorgathen, Eric Drooker, and Peter Kuper. *In:* R. Varnum and C. T. Gibbons, eds. *The language of comics: Word and image.* Jackson, MS: University Press of Mississippi, 19–39.

Bordwell, D. and Thompson, K., 2008. *Film art: An introduction.* 8th ed.. Boston: McGraw-Hill.

Bounegru, L. and Forceville, C., 2011. Metaphors in editorial cartoons representing the global financial crisis. *Visual Communication*, 10, 209–229.

Carney, S., 2008. The ear of the eye, or, do drawings make sounds? *English Language Notes*, 46, 193–209.

Chute, H., 2008. Comics as literature? Reading graphic narrative. *PMLA*, 123, 452–465.

Chute, H., 2010. *Graphic women: Life narrative and contemporary comics.* New York, NY: Columbia University Press.

Clowes, D., [1990] 2002. The stroll. *In: Twentieth century eightball.* Seattle: Fantagraphics Books, 17–21.

Cohn, N., 2007. A visual lexicon. *Public Journal of Semiotics*, 1, 53–83.

Cohn, N., 2010. Japanese visual language: The structure of manga. *In:* T. Johnson-Woods, ed. *Manga: An anthology of global and cultural perspectives.* London: Continuum, 187–202.

Cohn, N., 2013. *The visual language of comics: Introduction to the structure and cognition of sequential images.* New York, NY: Bloomsbury.

Cumming, L., 2009. *A face to the world: On self-portraits.* London: Harper Press.

Dierick, C. and Lefèvre, P., eds. 1998. *Forging a new medium: The comic strip in the nineteenth century.* Brussels: VUB Press.

Dittmar, J. F., 2008. *Comic-Analyse.* Konstanz: UVK.

Doxiadis, A. and Papadimitriou, C. H., 2009. *Logicomix.* London: Bloomsbury.

Eco, U., 1964. *Apocalittici e integrati.* Milano: Bompiani.

Eerden, B., 2009. Anger in *Asterix*: The metaphorical representation of anger in comics and animated films. *In:* C. Forceville and E. Urios-Aparisi, eds. *Multimodal metaphor.* Berlin: Mouton de Gruyter, 243–264.

Eisner, W., 1985. *Comics and sequential art.* Tamarac, FL: Poorhouse Press.

Ekman, P., 2003. *Emotions revealed.* New York, NY: Henry Holt.

El Refaie, E., 2009. Metaphor in political cartoons: Exploring audience responses. *In:* C. Forceville and E. Urios-Aparisi, eds. *Multimodal metaphor.* Berlin: Mouton de Gruyter, 173–196.

El Refaie, E., 2010a. Visual modality versus authenticity: The example of autobiographical comics. *Visual Studies*, 25, 162–174.

El Refaie, E., 2010b. Subjective time in David B's graphic memoir *Epileptic. Studies in Comics*, 1, 281–299.

El Refaie, E., 2012a. Of men, mice, and monsters: Embodiment and body image in David Small's graphic memoir *Stitches. The Journal of Graphic Novels and Comics*, 3, 55–67.

El Refaie, E., 2012b. *Autobiographical comics: Life writing in pictures.* Jackson, MS: Mississippi.

Evens, B., 2010. *The wrong place* [original title: *Ergens waar je niet wil zijn*, 2009]. M. Hutchison, L. Watkinson and R. Heppleston, trans. Montreal: Drawn and Quarterly.

Faigan, G., 1990. *The artist's complete guide to facial expression.* New York, NY: Watson-Guptill.

Fingeroth, D., 2007. *Disguised as Clark Kent: Jews, comics, and the creation of the superhero.* New York, NY: Continuum.

Forceville, C., 2005. Visual representations of the idealized cognitive model of ANGER in the Asterix album *La Zizanie. Journal of Pragmatics*, 37, 69–88.

Forceville, C., 2006. Non-verbal and multimodal metaphor in a cognitivist framework: Agendas for research. *In:* G. Kristiansen, M. Achard, R. Dirven, and F. Ruiz de Mendoza Ibáñez, eds. *Cognitive linguistics: Current applications and future perspectives.* Berlin: Mouton de Gruyter, 379–402.

Forceville, C., 2011. Pictorial runes in *Tintin and the Picaros. Journal of Pragmatics*, 43, 875–890.

Forceville, C., 2013. Creative visual duality in comics balloons. *In:* T. Veale, K. Feyaerts, and C. Forceville, eds. *Creativity and the agile mind: A multi-disciplinary exploration of a multi-faceted phenomenon.* Berlin: Mouton de Gruyter, 251–273.

Forceville, C., Veale, T. and Feyaerts, K., 2010. Balloonics: The visuals of balloons in comics. *In:* J. Goggin and D. Hassler-Forest, eds. *The rise and reason of comics and graphic literature: Critical essays on the form.* Jefferson, NC: McFarland, 56–73.

Frahm, O., 2003. Too much is too much: The never innocent laughter of the comics, *Image [&] Narrative* 4 (1), available at http://www.imageandnarrative.be/inarchive/graphicnovel/olefrahm.htm (accessed 4 September 2012).

Fresnault-Deruelle, P., 1972. *Dessins et bulles: La bande dessinée comme moyen d'expression*. Paris: Bordas.

Gasca, L. and Gubern, R., [1994] 2001. *El Discurso del Comic*. Madrid: Catedra.

Gibbon, D. and Moore, A., 1987. *Watchmen*. New York: DC Comics.

Goscinny, R. and Uderzo, A. [1972] 2004. *The Roman agent* [original title: *La zizanie*, 1970]. A. Bell and D. Hockridge, trans. London: Orion Books.

Groensteen, T., 2001. Le réseau et le lieu: Pour une analyse des procédures de tressage iconique. *In:* M. Ribière and J. Baetens, eds. *Time, narrative and the fixed image*. Amsterdam: Rodopi, 117–129.

Groensteen, T., 2003. *Lignes de vie: Le visage dessiné*. Saint-Egrève: Mosquito.

Groensteen, T., 2007. *The system of comics*. B. Beaty and N. Nguyen, trans. Jackson, MS: University Press of Mississippi.

Groensteen, T., 2009. *La bande dessinée. Son histoire et ses maîtres*. Paris: Skira Flammarion and La cité internationale de la bande dessinée et de l'image.

Harvey, R. C., 1996. *The art of the comic book: An aesthetic history*. Jackson, MS: University Press of Mississippi.

Hatfield, C., 2005. *Alternative comics: An emerging literature*. Jackson, MS: University Press of Mississippi.

Herzog, J., de Meuron, P. and Herz. M., 2009. *MetroBasel comic*. Basel: ETH Studio Basel. In 't Veld, L., 2012. Genocide in comics. *Comics Forum*, 17 February. Available at http://comicsforum.org/2012/02/17/genocide-in-comics-by-laurike-in-t-veld/ (accessed 4 September 2012).

Kaindl, K., 2004. Multimodality in the translation of humour in comics. *In:* E. Ventola, C. Charles, and M. Kaltenbacher, eds. *Perspectives on multimodality*. Amsterdam: Benjamins 173–192.

Kennedy, J., 1982. Metaphor in pictures. *Perception*, 11, 589–605.

Khordoc, C., 2001. The comic book's soundtrack: Visual sound effects in *Asterix*. *In:* R. Varnum and C. T. Gibbons, eds. *The language of comics: Word and image*. Jackson, MS: University Press of Mississippi, 157–173.

Kress, G. and Van Leeuwen, T., [1996] 2006. *Reading images: The grammar of visual design*. 2nd ed., London: Routledge.

Kukkonen, K. (2013). *Contemporary comics storytelling*. Lincoln, NE: University of Nebraska Press.

Lakoff, G., 1993. The contemporary theory of metaphor. *In:* A. Ortony, ed. *Metaphor and thought*. 2nd ed. Cambridge, MA: Cambridge University Press, 202–225.

Lakoff, G. and Johnson, M., 1980. *Metaphors we live by*. Chicago, IL: University of Chicago Press.

McCloud, S., 1993. *Understanding comics: The invisible art*. New York, NY: Harper Perennial.

McCloud, S., 2006. *Making comics: Storytelling secrets of comics, manga and graphic novels*. New York, NY: HarperCollins.

Magnussen, A. and Christiansen, H. C., eds. 2000. *Comics and culture: Analytical and theoretical approaches to comics*. Copenhagen: Museum Tusculanum Press.

Marion, P., 1993. *Traces en cases: Essai sur la bande dessinée*. Louvain-la-Neuve: Académia.

Mazzucchelli, D., 2009. *Asterios Polyp*. New York: Pantheon Books.

Meesters, G., 2010. Les significations du style graphique: *Mon fiston* d'Olivier Schrauwen et *Faire semblant, c'est mentir* de Dominique Goblet. *Textyles. Revue de Lettres Belges de Langue Française*. 36/37, 215–233.

Meesters, G., 2011. La narration visuelle de l'Association. De *Tintin* à *Lapin*. *In:* E. Dejasse, T. Habrand, G. Meesters and Group Acme, eds. *L'Association: Une utopie éditoriale et esthétique*. Brussels : Les Impressions Nouvelles, 123–131.

Meesters, G., 2013. Creativity in comics. Exploring the frontiers of the medium by respecting explicit self-imposed constraints. *In:* T. Veale, K. Feyaerts, and C. Forceville, eds. *Creativity and the agile mind: A multi-disciplinary exploration of a multi-faceted phenomenon*. Berlin: Mouton de Gruyter, 272–292.

Miller, A., 2007. *Reading bande dessinée: Critical approaches to French-language comic Strip*. Bristol: Intellect.

Miller, N. K., 2003. Cartoons of the self: Portrait of the artist as a young murderer – Art Spiegelman's 'Maus'. *In:* D. R. Geis, ed. *Considering Maus: Approaches to Art Spiegelman's 'survivor's tale' of the holocaust*. Tuscaloosa, AL: University of Alabama Press, 44–59.

Mitchell, A. A. 2010. Distributed identity: Networking image fragments in graphic memoirs. *Studies in Comics*, 1, 257–279.

Ojha, A., Forceville, C. and Indurkhya, B., 2013. Pictorial runes and their role in depicting emotions. Paper presented at 'Researching and Applying Metaphor' (RaAM) seminar on Metaphor, metonymy and emotions, Adam Mickiewicz University, Poznan, Poland, May.

Peeters, B., 1998. *Case planche récit: Lire la bande dessinée*. Tournai: Casterman.

Pollman, J., 2001. Shaping sounds in comics. *The International Journal of Comic Art*, 3, 9–21.

Ryan, M.-L., 2004. Introduction. *In:* M.-L. Ryan, ed. *Narrative across media: The languages of storytelling*. Lincoln, NE: University of Nebraska Press, 1–40.

Saraceni, M., 2003. *The language of comics*. London: Routledge.

Schilperoord, J. and Maes, A., 2009. Visual metaphoric conceptualization in editorial cartoons. *In:* C. Forceville and E. Urios-Aparisi, eds. *Multimodal metaphor*. Berlin: Mouton de Gruyter, 213–240.

Schneider, G., 2010. Comics and the everyday life: From *ennui* to contemplation. *European Comic Art*, 3, 37–63.

Sczepaniak, A., 2010. Brick by brick: Chris Ware's architecture of the page. *In:* J. Goggin and D. Hassler-Forest, eds. *The rise and reason of comics and graphic literature: Critical essays on the form*. Jefferson, NC: McFarland, 87–101.

Shinohara, K. and Matsunaka, Y., 2009. Pictorial metaphors of emotion in Japanese comics. *In:* C. Forceville and E. Urios-Aparisi, eds. *Multimodal metaphor*. Berlin: Mouton de Gruyter, 265–293.

Smith, K., 1996. Laughing at the way we see: The role of visual organizing principles in cartoon humor. *Humor*, 9, 19–38.

Smith, M., 1995. *Engaging characters: Fiction, emotion, and the cinema*. Oxford: Oxford University Press.

Smith, M. J. and Duncan, R., eds. 2012. *Critical approaches to comics: Theories and methods*. New York: London.

Sperber, D., and Wilson, D., [1986] 1995. *Relevance: Communication and cognition*. 2nd edn. Oxford: Blackwell.

Spiegelman, A., 2004. *In the shadow of no towers*. New York: Pantheon Books.

Tan, E. S., 2001. The telling face in comics strip and graphic novel. *In:* J. Baetens, ed. *The graphic novel*. Leuven: Leuven University Press, 31–46.

Teng, N. Y., 2009. Image alignment in multimodal metaphor. *In:* C. Forceville and E. Urios-Aparisi, eds. *Multimodal metaphor*. Berlin: Mouton de Gruyter, 197–211.

Töpffer, R., 1833. *Histoire de M. Jabot*. Paris: Dufrenóy.

Trondheim, L., 2005. *Mister I*. Paris: Delcourt.

Verwoerd, A., 2013. The future of *comics* is in the past. Unpublished MA Thesis. University of Amsterdam.

Vice, S., 2001. It's about time: The chronotope of the holocaust in Art Spiegelman's *Maus*. *In:* J. Baetens, ed. *The graphic novel*. Leuven: Leuven University Press, 47–60.

Wales, K., [1990] 2001. *A dictionary of stylistics*. 2nd edn. Harlow: Pearson.

Walker, M., [1980] 2000. *The lexicon of comicana*. Lincoln, NE: Authors Guild Backinprint.com Edition.

Ware, C., 2012. *Building stories*. New York: Pantheon Books.

Wells, P., 1998. *Understanding animation*. London: Routledge.

Wilson, D. and Sperber, D., 2012. *Meaning and relevance*. Cambridge, MA: Cambridge University Press.

Wolk, D., 2007. *Reading comics: How graphic novels work and what they mean*. Cambridge, MA: Da Capo Press.

Yus, F., 2008. Inferring from comics: A multi-stage account. *In:* P. Sancho Cremades, C. Gregori Signes and S. Renard, eds. *El discurs del comic*. Valencia: University of Valencia, 223–249.

31

Stylistics and hypertext fiction

Paola Trimarco

Introduction

While the history of hypertext fiction is a relatively short one, this genre has attracted considerable attention from stylisticians in recent years. Being created and read through computers, this type of digital text pieces together smaller, often multimodal texts, called nodes or lexia, through a series of hyperlinks. The reader clicks on the hyperlink in order to move from one lexia to another. Often the reader has more than one choice of hyperlink within a given lexia, and with each choice a different lexia appears. Each lexia contributes to a narrative, and there could be several in one hypertext, entering the storyline at any point. In such an interactive setting, each reader will undoubtedly have his or her own unique experience of the same hypertext.

The term 'hypertext' was coined by Theodore H. Nelson in the 1960s to describe 'non-sequential writing-text that branches and allows choices to the reader, best read at an interactive screen.' (Nelson 1981, cited in Landow 2006, p.3) Hypertexts, like other linking media, possess 'the potential qualities of multilinearity, consequent potential multivocality, conceptual richness ... and some degree of reader-centredness or control' (Landow 2006, p. 214). Such views lead naturally to comparisons between hypertext fictions and traditionally printed fiction: 'where printed genres are linear and hierarchical, hypertext is multiple and associative' (Bolter 2001, p. 42). While this is generally the case, it needs to be said that non-linear story telling is not unique to digital fiction, as shown in works such as Laurence Sterne's *Tristram Shandy*, *The Dictionary of the Khazars* by Milorad Pavic and James Joyce's *Ulysses*, to name but a few. Moreover, noting that we live in the late age of print, 'we depend in a variety of ways on our knowledge of print in order to read and write hypertexts (Bolter 2001, p.45). While many hypertexts include multimodal lexia, hypertext fictions involve reading words within sentences and paragraphs, and as will be illustrated below, these texts adhere to many of the conventions of their paper-based counterparts.

Following an overview of theoretical approaches and issues involving the reception of hypertext, this chapter describes the application of two approaches to hypertext fiction using two texts, Michael Joyce's *afternoon, a story* (1990), a seminal hypertext novel, and Caitlin Fisher's *These Waves of Girls* (2001), which won the Electronic Literature Award in 2001. These two texts have been chosen because they represent different types, or subgenres, of hypertext. Joyce's *afternoon* was created using Storyspace software and has characteristics unique to this platform; when reading *afternoon*, the reader sees a white screen with black typeface (see Figure 31.1) and can hit the enter key to go to another lexia. However, if they move their cursor over the words, they will discover some hidden hyperlinks. In either case, the reader does not know what theme or storyline the next lexia contributes to. Sometimes the new lexia provides a likely continuation of a narrative chain, but other times it does not. Also typical of Storyspace hypertexts are forward and back buttons and the history option in the menu. While these may appear to help avoid reader disorientation, the lack of semantic and linear connection between lexia can break the coherence of the various narrative lines. Other well-known Storyspace hypertexts include *Victory Garden* (Moulthorpe 1991), and *Patchwork Girl* (Jackson 1995).

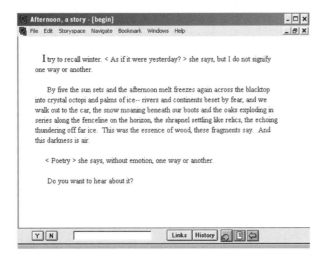

Figure 31.1 A screen image of a lexia from *afternoon, a story* by M. Joyce

These Waves of Girls, a web-based hypertext fiction, has more explicit links which give the reader a sense of the content of the next lexia, enabling an informed choice of one hyperlink over another. The opening pages of this hypertext include a navigational map of themes (see Figure 31.2). Also characteristic of web-based digital texts, *These Waves of Girls* uses more multimodal texts, mixing sounds and images with words. Other famous works published online include *Grammatron* (America 1998) and *Twelve Blue* (Joyce 1996), as well as hypertext short stories, such as 'Lies' (Pryll 1994) and 'Samantha in Winter' (Stephens 2004).

The two approaches applied to *afternoon* and *These Waves of Girls* in this chapter, cognitive stylistics and social semiotics respectively, have emerged in recent years as key approaches to analysing and appreciating hypertext fictions (Kress and van Leeuwen 2003, Schneider 2005, Landow 2006, Bell 2010, Trimarco, 2012). Cognitive stylistics focuses on the reader's mental representations. From this approach, so-called 'text world theory' will be applied. Social semiotics is a sociocultural method focusing on the social dimension of meanings attributed to the use of signs across modes. Here in this chapter it is employed to discuss the multimodal aspects of these hypertexts.

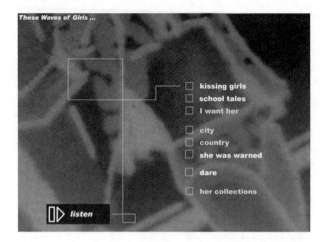

Figure 31.2 The first interactive screen of *These Waves of Girls*

Theorising hypertext fiction

Early approaches to hypertext tended to focus on the enigma of hypertext narratives and the interactivity imposed by these computer-based texts, giving the reader control of the narrative experience. The idea of the reader being actively involved in the creation of texts and meanings was seen to reflect Barthes' ideas of writerly texts and the 'death of the author'; indeed, the term 'lexia' was taken from Barthes (1974). Drawing from Barthes's distinction between readerly and writerly texts, some theorists claimed that printed texts were readerly, being more passive experiences for the reader, and hypertexts were writerly, where the reader's involvement makes the reader a writer as well (Landow 2006, Bolter 2001).

Other approaches in the early days of hypertext claimed that these texts followed postmodernist thinking. These theorists looked mainly to the writing of Derrida (1998), whose deconstructionism accounted for the open-ended and individualised interpretations of hypertext fictions, as well as other characteristics of hypertext such as repetition and references to other texts. Deconstruction also 'defies the notion of the author being the major source of literary input, who forces the reader into a purely perceptive framework' (Ensslin 2004, p.13). With reference to *afternoon,* Aarseth (1997) notes that this hypertext shares with postmodernism 'the metonymic mixing of fragments and genres, self-commentary and intrusions by the 'author', typographical variation, metaleptic breaks...' (p. 86).

As interests in hypertext came more into the domain of linguistics, these texts were still being viewed primarily from the perspective of readers' experiences of the new medium, set in contrast to the experiences of reading traditionally printed texts. Against this backdrop, Landow considered examining hypertext narrative along a number of axes: '1) reader choice, intervention, and empowerment; 2) inclusions of extralinguistic texts (images, motion, sound); 3) complexity of network structure; and 4) degrees of multiplicity and variation in literary elements, such as plot, characterization, setting and so forth' (Landow 2006, p. 217). Similarly, Schneider (2005) focused on three phenomena of hypertext fiction which distinguish it from print narratives: interactivity, non-linearity and coherence. Given the dominance of such issues in hypertext theory today, it is worth considering them for their influence on current stylistic approaches.

Reader empowerment

In terms of interactivity and reader empowerment, one feature of hypertext fiction that distinguishes it from print narratives is the use of a second person narration and the fact that 'the digital "you" features widely across digital texts' (Bell and Ensslin 2011, p. 312). The occurrence of the textual *you* in hypertext fiction operates at different levels. At one level it is no different from its appearance in printed texts, as a way of engaging the reader with the world of the text, an extended commentary of characters and plot, drawing the reader in for an evaluative stance. At another level, hypertext fiction can use the textual *you* to manoeuvre the reader across the text, addressing readers in order to make navigational choices, interrupting the building of the narrative or story world. For example, in *afternoon*, both levels of textual *you* occur. In one lexia we have 'I know how you feel. Nothing is more empty than heat…;' this is of the first level of reader involvement with the world of the text. In another example from *afternoon*, the first lexia introduces a fragment of the story and asks the reader 'Do you want to hear about it?' The reader can then respond 'yes' or 'no', each time going to a different lexia. Here, the textual *you* addresses the reader as navigator through the story.

Related to this is the idea that reading hypertext is more interactive than reading print text, since hypertext demands that readers help to construct the narrative, thereby empowering the reader. While readers often have choices to make as to which link they click, as noted in current hypertext theory, these links and lexia have been written by the author. The extent to which empowerment exists may reside in the rereading of these texts, a recognised feature of engaging with digital literature.

Complexity, non-linearity and multi-linearity

It is not unusual for a reader to begin a hypertext fiction with a lexia that appears to be in the middle of a story, with references to unknown characters and events which the reader might not learn more about until much later. It is also not unusual for hypertext fictions to appear to have many subplots or storylines, some of which appear unrelated. These points highlight perhaps the most written-about feature of hypertexts, their non-linearity and multi-linearity, both of which make for complex narratives.

Given the non-linearity of hypertext, theorists have asked if they can be said to have beginnings. Landow explains that while the typical hypertext narrative has a sense of beginning in the middle of the plot structure, most hypertext fictions 'take an essentially cautious approach to the problems of beginnings by offering the reader a lexia labelled something like 'start here' that combines the functions of the title page, introduction and opening paragraph' (Landow 2006, p. 227). Many web-based hypertext fictions, as noted above, start with a map or diagram for navigation. This vague sense of a beginning is akin to a table of contents, but the reader, unlike one viewing a table of contents in a printed book, would not know where the narrative begins.

A great deal has been written in hypertext theory about the lack of endings in these fictions. 'Unlike texts in manuscript or print, those in hypertext apparently can continue indefinitely, so one wonders if they can provide satisfying closure' (Landow 2006, p. 228). While this may be broadly speaking true, it is perhaps an oversimplification given the multilinear aspect of most of these hypertexts, which allow for closure of some narrative strands but not others, depending on the reader's experience and interaction with the text. Landow concedes this point by offering the idea that 'hypertext fictions always end because readings always end, but they can end in fatigue or a sense of satisfying closure' (Landow 2006, p. 229). Where a reading of a hypertext ends in fatigue, Aarseth notes when discussing *afternoon*:

> there is always a danger that its mechanical devices all but erase the poetical and narratological elements that are not directly effected through the technology. Instead of asking, What have I read? the critic might become preoccupied with the question, Have I read it all? and come to identify the task of interpretation as a task of territorial exploration and technical mastery.
>
> *(p. 87)*

Other, more recent approaches to hypertext have been considering issues of complexity and readability in light of the actual content, for example the narrative perspective, of the stories and not only the technological aspects behind reading them. Ensslin notes that '... the overall 'confusion' in the reader caused by hypertextuality, nonlinearity and non-closure contributes to the narrator's unreliability' (Ensslin 2012, p. 140) and a tendency for hypertext narratives to be presented through the vehicles of dreams, memories and the inner thoughts of a possibly unreliable narrator.

Multimodality

Reading hypertext, especially web-based hypertext, involves viewing and interpreting more graphic representations, such as a tree or network diagram or an image map, as well as more pictorial images than typically found in printed texts. According to Miall and Dobson (2001) who were responding to early hypertext theories, 'hypertext advocates are drawn to promote the visual over the verbal or abstract order of the book.' Drawing from studies on reading, Miall and Dobson argued that imagination plays an important role in reading traditional print text as well: 'Hypertext cannot offer to model the reader's mind. The author's associations are not those of the reader.' Moreover, Miall and Dobson (2001) suggest that hypertexts diminish the reading experience because images in the reader's mind are replaced by the images given, much in the same way that readers often find film adaptations of novels disappointing. The growing use of multimodal analysis, and as we will see later in this chapter, social semiotics, has recognised that the interpretation of images and sounds is integral to understanding and appreciating digitally-produced texts.

Coherence

The last of Schneider's phenomena for addressing hypertext fiction is the concept of coherence. As coherence has to do with the way a text makes sense and the extent to which it is well-formed, linguistic research that has examined coherence in hypertext fiction considers, among other things, the role of hyperlinks in these texts. As noted above, the different ways links are presented in relation to the lexia they connect is pivotal in distinguishing the two sub-genres of hypertext discussed in this chapter. Further to this, Tosca (2000) commenting first on Storyspace linking notes:

> Although it could be argued that even if the reader doesn't know what words are links, like in *afternoon,* she clicks the words that she suspects will yield more satisfying implicatures, so that she goes through the process even if her choices have no actual relationship to the results ... most hypertexts have explicit links, especially Web

hypertexts, as there is no way to get rid of the arrow changing shape to a pointed hand every time we fly over an active zone of the screen.

Early works on hypertext 'explored the possibility of defining relations between nodes, with an accompanying rhetoric emphasising the 'economy' of reading that such definitions may provide' (Miles 2002). This might be true for the everyday, non-fiction hyperlink found on most information websites, such as Wikipedia or BBC News sites; however, the hyperlinks that connect lexia in hypertext fiction operate in a greater variety of ways. For example, hyperlinks can go to the next episode of a story to help the reader navigate around a text, other hyperlinks suggest semantic associations between lexia, while others still appear totally unrelated. Furthermore, the fact that lexia can contribute to the structure of a hypertext in different ways also bears upon the potential function or meaning associated with a given hyperlink. Landow describes basic patterns of links made between lexia: (i) lexia to lexia unidirectional, (ii) lexia to lexia bidirectional, and (iii) string (words or phrases within a lexia) to lexia. These basic forms can be extended to include multiple lexia being linked to different hyperlinks within a given lexia (2006, pp. 13–18). Such variety of linking patterns could be suggesting that the connections between lexia hold a degree of the strength or weakness of association.

Given the complexity and possibilities for linking in hypertext, it is no surprise that many theorists have tackled this topic. Some theorists suggest that the links between lexias tend to be looser than the links between paragraphs, something confirmed by hypertext narrative readers, and this differs from the hyperlinking found in other digital texts, such as online news. 'Hypermedia as a medium conveys the strong impression that its links signify coherent, purposeful and above all *useful* relationships ... since hypermedia systems predispose users to expect significant relationships among lexia, those that disappoint these expectations tend to appear particularly incoherent and without significance' (Landow 2006, p. 153). Hypertext fiction that does not meet readers' expectations of hyperlinking can cause some confusion.

Hypertext linking has also been viewed in terms of semantic associations and the expectations of present day users of the internet. Bell (2010) notes that 'in a hypertext novel, words used as hyperlinks are often not indicative of the destination nodes to which they lead, so that any semantic associations are usually made, not in anticipation of the destination lexia, but in retrospect' (Bell, 2010, p. 12). This is especially the case when reading Storyspace hypertexts or those where the hyperlinked word or image does not indicate the linked lexia. As noted by Bell (2010), *afternoon* 'has no visible links so that readers must experimentally click within each lexia. In this case, the text inhibits rather than empowers them in their role as link chooser' (p. 12).

Aarseth suggests that hypertext is fiction, but not narrative; it is an alternative to narrative and can contain within it narration (1997, p. 85), which is true of other literary genres, such as poetry. Similar comments are made by Miles (2002): 'In a poem you can place any word in any other location (as you can with shots in narrative cinema), and there is clearly no need for formal syntactic and semantic rules of organisation for a poem (or a film) to be meaningful – that there may be such rules for some genres of poetry does not change this fact'. This would certainly seem to be the case in hypertext and suggests that hypertext linking ought to be considered as more analogous to poetry than to prose.

Summary of hypertext theories

To summarise this overview of hypertext theories, we can draw from Bell (2010) who distinguishes early hypertext theory from the current wave of hypertext by noting 'while the first-wave theory sees the medium as creating a powerful role for the reader, the second-wave has shown that the structure of the text, and the reader's role within it, represents a means of prohibiting her or him from fully engaging in the narratives that hypertext novels contain' (p. 15). While second-wave studies are more accurate in describing the role of the reader, the emphasis, as in the first-wave studies, has been more on the mechanisms of the hypertext medium than analysing the narratives per se. There have been 'few sustained applications to individual works' (p. 16). However, this is changing with more literary stylistic approaches to digital fictions.

A cognitive stylistic approach to *afternoon, a story*

Cognitive approaches are highly suitable for examining hypertexts as such approaches seek to understand the reader's experience of texts. According to Schneider (2005), 'using concepts provided by cognitive psychology, in which reading is viewed as information processing, these differences (between reading print and hypertext) can be described more satisfactorily than by relying on descriptions of the textual properties of hypertext' (p. 197). Cognitive stylistics, also known as 'cognitive poetics' (see Chapter 19 in this volume for more on this topic), is one of the newer areas of stylistics that has shifted the focus from frameworks based on text and composition to those based on the mind of the reader.

While there are various models of analysis within cognitive stylistics, what they have in common is the idea that while reading, the mind forms mental representations based on pre-existing knowledge and that these representations are modified by interacting with the new information provided in the text. Terms used to describe these mental representations include schemas, scripts and frames (for more on this, see Chapter 16 in this volume). Under the broad category of cognitive stylistics also resides text world theory, which is the main theory used in this analysis of *afternoon* (for an extended overview of text world theory, see Chapter 17 in this volume).

Cognitive approaches are also useful in analysing hypertexts given the experimental nature of many of these texts. As noted by Gavins and Steen (2003), one of the strengths of cognitive theories is that they can 'indicate those moments where default expectations are thwarted, in order to identify significant moments' for meaning making in the literary texts' (p. 10). This has been demonstrated in an analysis of surrealistic texts in printed media by Stockwell (2003) and can be applied where elements of a text do not fit into conventional paradigms of understanding. The surrealistic nature of many hypertexts often brings about meanings that are inferred or hypothesised. It is for this reason that we also turn to cognitive approaches which not only account for events explicit within texts, but those which are unrealised or speculative, as will be demonstrated below.

The actual content and themes of many hypertexts also tend to lend themselves to cognitive theories as these texts often reflect the working of the mind. Ensslin (2012) comments on the way writers have approached the 'hypertextual medium in terms of its affordances for the representation of conscious and subconscious cognitive processes such as memory, learning, imagination, dream, fantasy and nightmare but also the full spectrum of problematic psychological conditions ranging from personality crises through neurosis and trauma to psychotic conditions such as schizophrenia and multiple personality disorder' (p. 140). This description of many hypertexts is certainly apt for *afternoon*.

This much written-about example of hypertext fiction was first published in 1990 by Eastgate using Storyspace software, which comes in the form of an interactive CD-ROM. Essentially multilinear with non-linear strands, while it remediates printed texts by being composed of some 538 lexia, it appears like print as black text on a white background without any images as texts. *Afternoon* gives the reader a choice, in its opening lexia, of clicking <yes> to follow a default path through its nodes. This offers a more traditional, narrative route, from which the reader can surmise the story outline. This is one reader's account of *afternoon*:

> The first time I read *afternoon* I clicked my mouse haphazardly on any old word, and quickly grew disoriented. Realising I was lost, I began to carefully choose which words to click, but I usually couldn't understand the connection between the word I had chosen and the node to which it led me … After an hour or so of frustration I gave the whole thing up. It took several months before I got up the courage to have another go. This time I read the instructions … and was surprised to discover that a 'default' path existed through the nodes … the nodes make up a fairly traditional narrative … So for me to enjoy reading *afternoon*, I needed to give up my reader's choice and instead follow the author's arranged default reading, which was structured in the most conventional way a story can be told: chronologically. But after grasping a minimal version of the story, which the default reading gave me, I could fit new nodes into my constantly changing picture of the story.
>
> *(Walker 1999)*

Walker's description of her own reading process, though it does not address the specific lexia she encountered with her first reading, does exemplify how this reader's mind managed narrative schemas; after her expectations of chronological narrative and coherence were thwarted, being given a more linear narrative for the start of the main storyline enabled her to create mental representations that helped to form a story.

Other readers of *afternoon* have described a more complicated reading experience. As mentioned above, this particular hypertext fiction sometimes presents several links to other lexia within one lexia, but at other times there is only one path to follow. Sometimes the links draw lexia together which seem to share the same topic, while others do not. As a result, reading this hypertext fiction and piecing together its plots and sub-plots are similar to solving a puzzle.

Text world theory and afternoon

Having given consideration to the overall experience of reading *afternoon* in terms of schemas, we can now examine specific mental representations from *afternoon* using text world theory as a framework. This approach, developed by Werth (see Werth 1999), proposes three interconnected levels to describe the reception of narrative texts; these are discourse world, text world and sub-worlds.

A discourse world contains the participants of the language event, in these cases, the author(s) and the reader(s). Prototypically, a discourse world includes all of the information and background knowledge that participants have in their memories. However, as Stockwell (2002) points out, 'in order to prevent this mass of information being unmanageable in the framework, text world theory asserts that only the information that forms a necessary context, rather than all possible contexts, is used' (p. 136). This necessary information shared between author and reader grows with the reading of the text, in this case by reading new lexia. Every reader of *afternoon* will soon recognise the contemporary context of the story, which is part of the discourse world shared to a greater or lesser degree with the author.

A text world refers to the discourse at hand which participants construct in the communicative event. Gavins describes the text world as being formed by 'linguistic indicators contained within the discourse and by further inferences drawn from the participant's background knowledge and experience' (2003, p. 130). Text worlds can be further described as being made of 'world-building elements' and 'function-advancing propositions'. World-building elements account for the sense of time and place and the objects and characters of the text. Function-advancing propositions account for the states, actions and processes that move a story forward. Even though a text world for a hypertext will vary from reader to reader, some general points can be made. Whatever sequence of lexia a given reader experiences, it is likely they will meet the main characters which form the part of the text world. These are: Peter, who is a poet making his living as a technical writer; Wert, Peter's employer and friend; Lolly, who is Wert's wife; and Nausicaa, another employee, with whom Peter is having an affair. Two other characters referred to, who are integral to what might be described as the main story, are Peter's wife and son. Putting together information from several lexia, readers of *afternoon* soon learn that a confused, perhaps traumatised narrator, Peter, has discovered that his ex-wife and son were in a car accident. This event is generally treated as the main event of the story and is therefore a key feature of the text world.

Function-advancing propositions could be described more specifically as plot-advancing, scene-advancing, argument-advancing, and so on, with predicators about characters being seen as character-advancing. Given the formation of the schema of a car accident having taken place, an example of scene-advancing lexia would be the following:

Lexia title: 5

Cigarette butts and matted footprints mark the place where groups of on-lookers stood.... (ellipsis in original)

The use of the word 'on-lookers' fits into a schema or description of a place where an accident has occurred.

Other lexia appear which could be described as world-building elements, though their function in the text world is less straightforward. Consider the two lexia below:

1. Lexia title: Dora

   Zabriskie Point?

2. Lexia title: Bodhisattva Jizo

   A truck like this is the noiseless sutra of the Machine Essence. That sucker can crawl up mountains... (ellipsis in original)

Mental representations for these two lexia will vary from reader to reader and will depend on background knowledge of the United States, where Zabriskie Point is the name of a mountain range, and Buddhism, where 'Bodhisattva' means enlightened. Both of these lexia could form part of scenes and therefore could be treated as either scene-advancing or character-advancing. Alternatively, these could be regarded as snippets of direct speech or a couple of the confused memories of the main narrator, Peter, in which case they would be seen as 'world-switching', referring to a narrative moving between worlds within the text. These might appear to readers as flashbacks or flashforwards. Sub-worlds, developed from Werth (1999), refer to 'other worlds which depart from the parameters of the initial text world' (Gavins 2003, p. 131). Gavins (2007), however, refers to these as modal worlds, namely: 1) boulomaic modal worlds, which represent desires; 2) deontic modal worlds, which relate to obligations; and 3) epistemic modal worlds, which depict the hypothetical worlds, or possible worlds, set out by the narrator or characters.

While the characters of Peter, Lolly and Nausicaa narrate most of the lexia, other lexia still seem to have another omniscient narrator, which some readers claim is the writer himself. This is suggested by the self-reflexive lexia, which reads as follows:

> In my mind the story, as formed, takes on margins. Each margin will yield to the impatient, or wary, reader. You can answer yes at the beginning and page through on a wave of Returns, or page through directly – again using Returns – without that first interaction. These are not versions, but the story itself in long lines. Otherwise, however, the centre is all – Thoreau or Brer Rabbit, each preferred the bramble. I've discovered more there too, and the real interaction, if that is possible, is in pursuit of texture...

This commentary clearly takes the reader outside of the text world, with instructions for how to manage the hypertext reading experience which could arguably be treated as an 'actual world' interaction. However, the lexia also contains literary language, such as the elliptical 'each preferred the bramble,' as well as intertextual references to the writer Henry David Thoreau and the Brer Rabbit character from American folklore; such features keep this lexia rooted in the fictional story of *afternoon*, so perhaps it is best categorised as a world-switch, with elements of modal worlds contained within.

The creation and manipulation of modal-worlds is key to reading *afternoon*, where dreams and desires are abundant. Ensslin (2012) notes these points in her reading of *afternoon*:

> Whereas the 'Yes' trajectory is largely coherent and meaningful up to the point of Peter's looping thoughts surrounding the car accident, the 'No' scenario may be read in terms of a complete mental breakdown. It takes the reader on a journey through entirely disconnected sequences of quasi-feverish ranting, which grotesquely expose Peter's problematic sexual self-image, inferiority complex and, most importantly, irremediable feelings of guilt and loss.
>
> *(p. 141)*

In terms of character development, the 'Yes' trajectory could lead the reader to experience a somewhat flat character in Peter, while the 'no' trajectory is arguably round and, in the words of Schneider, 'psychologically opaque.'

It has been noted that with hypertext fiction, elements of a story which might at first appear to be sub-worlds, or world-switching to other worlds within the text world, could be reinterpreted with knowledge of other lexia into becoming part of the text world (Trimarco 2012). This feature of hypertext has also been observed by Miles (2002), noting that '…it is common for a narrative event or element to shift from an apparently minor to a major role (or the reverse) subject to our interpretation of later events and how we then apply these to our original schema.' Shifts between sub-world and text world can also occur with different readings of *afternoon*. Douglas (2001) recounts four readings of *afternoon*, where later readings were aided by insights gained from previous readings, previous paths followed and either stopped by the built-in link endings or by feeling too many narratives had presented themselves without resolve.

A similar description of the reading experience of *afternoon* comes from Bolter (2001), who observes that 'each of the many paths in *afternoon* seems to be a mixture of accident and the inexorable ... *afternoon* becomes the reader's story in a remarkable way, for the reader's desire to make the story happen and to make sense of what happens is inevitably inscribed in the story itself' (p. 128). These commentaries all suggest the necessity of a theoretical framework based on readers' cognitive experiences, where the reading experience itself contributes to the making of the story.

Social semiotics analysis of *These Waves of Girls*

Unlike *afternoon*, this web-based hypertext links its lexia in more explicit ways, relating lexia that either provide background information, continue a line of narrative, or are associative and describe the emotions of a character from the previous lexia. While these features would appear to make *These Waves of Girls* a less frustrating reading experience than *afternoon*, the work does have its critics. Landow (2006) refers to *These Waves of Girls* as a 'link intensive hyperfiction' (p. 200), which at the same time has a 'limited hypertextuality' because it has 'an organisational superstructure, a top-level branching structure that leads to multiple relatively isolated linear narratives' (p. 265). Similarly, Pope (2009) describes the reading experience for this hypertext as suffering from having too many explicit links to choose from 'and the perception in my reader-participants that there was no story at all.' While the 'intensive' hyperlinking might not suit some readers, this award-winning hypertext is highly regarded for its innovative use of images and sound alongside written text.

Given that *These Waves of Girls* is a multimodal text, it naturally lends itself to the framework provided by social semiotic analysis. Simpson and Mayr (2009) explain that social semiotics 'is concerned with the multi-semiotic or multimodal character of many texts in contemporary society and explores ways of analysing visual images ... and the relationship between language and visual images' (p. 87). In this approach, signs, whether linguistic or non-linguistic, are critically studied with the understanding that context is embedded in sign use and that signs are deployed strategically and function socially. When the reader starts *These Waves of Girls*, the social and cultural context of the internet environment is already present. The title and opening filmic sequence with the sound of girls laughing establishes some of the context used in interpreting the signs as the reader embarks on the hypertext. A few lexia into the story and the reader has already surmised that this fiction takes place somewhere in North America in the twentieth century. Given the presence of the main narrator, a young girl, readers are likely to draw meanings from social contexts related to childhood experiences, such as fears, being around other children and encounters with adults.

This approach has been developed using Halliday's systemic functional grammar (Halliday and Matthiessen 2004) as its base. Halliday's three metafunctions of language, the ideational, interpersonal and textual metafunctions, are employed as a way of analysing the signs from multimodal texts within their social contexts. Although Halliday originally formulated these metafunctions for linguistic structures, Kress and van Leeuwen (2006) have applied the approach to the detailed analysis of images. (See Chapter 3 in this volume for more on 'functionalist approaches to stylistics', and Chapter 29 for more on 'multimodal stylistic analysis'.)

The ideational metafunction deals with the way information and meaningful content is provided through the text. For the written text within a hypertext fiction this covers the characters and main story. In *These Waves of Girls*, part of the ideational metafunction encompasses the main story, which is about girls growing up and discovering their sexuality. The principle narrator, Tracey, tells the reader stories about her best friend Vanessa, other close friends, older school children and her enemies. The stories are often repeated in different lexia, sometimes by different narrators, assumed to be other children, and in ways that suggest they are rumours and gossip.

With images the information can be examined by considering what Kress and van Leeuwen (2006) refer to as presentational and conceptual patterns. Presentational patterns refer to participants in a narrative, which are visually created by vectors, the imaginary line the eyes tend to follow when viewing an image. Vectors can be formed by the direction of gaze of characters or the direction pointed out by objects, such as hands or guns. Leading the viewer's eyes to follow elements in an image in a particular way suggests that the participants are doing something, and are therefore forming part of a narrative. This has been described in more detail using Halliday's transitivity analysis, assigning 'processes' to the actions conveyed in these images and participant roles, such as agent and goal, to the participants (Kress and van Leeuwen 2006, Jones and Ventola 2010). In *These Waves of Girls*, images that suggest movement or action by the participants include those of girls playing and running and children boarding a school bus. Conceptual patterns refer to the participants' generalised characteristics such as class and age, which signify other ideational meanings. In this hypertext, the images of young girls convey generalised understandings.

The interpersonal metafunction accounts for the levels of friendliness and status difference which are communicated through the use of particular signs. With written texts there can be three areas to analyse for this: the dialogue between characters; the communication between the narrator and the reader; and any communication between the author and the reader. An example from a lexia of text from *These Waves of Girls* can be used to illustrate this (the ellipses appear in the original text):

> Next up, Mr. Anderson the science teacher. He welcomes us and begins his talk about science... but he lisps and science is an unfortunate word for him... Vivian is laughing, everyone's laughing. For a second I think about laughing but there he is on stage, like a sad dot from my balcony seat and he's trying to talk through the laughter like he doesn't hear it and every time an s comes the giggles swell and some kids behind us start hissing sss out to the front. I'm going to cry and I'm going to kill them.

The dialogue between the teacher lecturing to the students and the obvious status and age differences explains why the girls are laughing to each other about the teacher's speech impediment. The interpersonal metafunction is also realised between narrator and reader by the use of an informal tone and phrases such as 'next up'. Unlike *afternoon*, in this hypertext there is an absence of direct communication between author and reader.

When considering images, the interpersonal metafunction involves elements representing social relations between the producer, the viewer and the object (Kress and van Leeuwen 1996, p. 41). Images have the participants within the image and the interactive participants who create the image and the implied viewer. For example, if the image is of a person gazing directly at the implied viewer, this could be interpreted as a demand of some sort. Similarly, social distance between a human image and an implied viewer is suggested by the size of image and frame; for instance, a close-up conveys an intimate or personal social relationship, whereas a long shot suggests an impersonal relationship and so on.

In *These Waves of Girls* there is an image of a young girl (Figure 31.3), which appears in several of the lexia and conveys a degree of intimacy between image and viewer because it is so close-up and quite intense because only the eyes are shown. As these stare directly at the viewer there is a sense of demanding attention.

Figure 31.3 An image from *These Waves of Girls*

The textual metafunction relates to 'a world in which all elements of the text cohere internally, and which itself coheres with its relevant environment' (Kress and van Leeuwen 2006, p. 15). For the written text this would include how the reader moves between the lexia and how coherence and cohesion are achieved. Within *These Waves of Girls* many lexia have multiple links for the reader to choose from, and as mentioned earlier these are often explicit links which help to make the text coherent. This suggests that to some extent the reader actually creates some of the textual function themselves, since how they read the story depends on the choices they make. Moreover, the lexia also tend to have strong lexically cohesive elements, such as synonyms and hyponyms, making it obvious that the narrative continues through different lexia (although not usually chronologically).

In *These Waves of Girls* texts and images are arranged in a variety of ways that enable the creation of meanings. When describing such multimodal narratives, Hoffmann (2010) explains that 'The use of multiple semiotics codes in telling stories involves trans-semiotic relations between words, pictures and sound which may enrich the productive and perceptive opportunities of storytelling' (p. 1). Following on from a text describing a sexual encounter, a line of words goes across the screen in a continuous loop, reminiscent of street advertising, with the words 'and it was the most erotic year of my life'. Such a presentation of text shows the reader the importance of the encounter to the narrator. Elsewhere in the text images often overlap, creating a blurring between images to suggest unclear memories. When clicking on the 'Country' hyperlink from the front navigation page, the linking lexia is a full-screen image of a forest with a small text box in the middle. After clicking on the arrow within this text box more images of trees open up, overlapping one another. There are eight links which only open images of trees before the next lexia containing written text. From this arrangement of lexia the reader is given the impression of going further and further into the forest.

Similarly, textual arrangement creating the structure of this particular hypertext no matter the order in which the lexia are read, akin to reading *afternoon*, simulates the associative workings of the human memory. Moreover, as pointed out by Koshimaa (2004), 'following the hypertextually linked story fragments is very much like hearing a piece of gossip here and there. Some of the things are very hard to get by, whereas some stories you'll hear over and over again.'

Here I have outlined how social semiotics as a framework for analysing a web-based hypertext such as *These Waves of Girls* accounts for the role of social contexts in influencing meanings. Moreover, such an approach treats the different modes, written text, auditory speech and visual images, as in communication with each other.

Recommendations for practice

In this chapter we have approached two hypertext fictions, drawing from social semiotic and cognitive frameworks. You now have an opportunity to experience other hypertext fictions and develop your analytical skills by applying the same approaches. Choose one of these two stories, which are freely available online, and complete one or more of the exercises below.

- *The Virtual Disappearance of Miriam* (http://www.dreamingmethods.com/miriam/) by M. Bedford and A. Campbell (2000)
- *Twelve Blue* (http://www.eastgate.com/TwelveBlue/Twelve_Blue.html) by M. Joyce (1996)

1. Analyse your chosen text employing a social semiotic approach; this involves using Halliday's three metafunctions of language, the ideational, interpersonal and textual metafunctions. Consider how the textual metafunction in particular is different from fiction in printed texts.
2. Analyse your chosen text employing text world theory; you could begin by describing the discourse world, text world and sub-worlds that emerge from your reading of the story. Consider the role of world-switching when reading this hypertext; is it important in experiencing and interpreting the text?
3. If you have had the opportunity to read two or more hypertext fictions, write a short essay on one of these topics:
   a. Reader empowerment in hypertext
   b. Coherence in hypertext

If you are reading in a classroom setting, you may wish to compare your analyses, as every reader experiences hypertext fictions differently.

Future directions

In addition to being of interest to literary stylisticians, the stylistic analysis of hypertext fiction is taking root in literary studies, computer games design and creative writing. Furthermore, the presence of this form of fiction is continuing to grow with Web 2.0 technologies making production easier for writers. However, despite the growth in this genre of writing, it has been slow to enter academic and public discourse in the United Kingdom, unlike in Germany, Switzerland and the Americas (Ensslin 2007, p. 3).

Other cognitive approaches currently being employed to study hypertext include possible world theory, which has applications beyond literary studies. Cognitive-based literary theories hold the potential to investigate and explain how digital environments allow writers and readers to participate in imaginary and hypothetical worlds (Schneider 2005, p. 204).

Related topics

Cognitive poetics, functionalist stylistics, multimodality, text world theory

Further reading

Bell, A., 2010. *The possible worlds of hypertext fiction*. London: Palgrave Macmillan.

This book offers analyses of the major Storyspace hypertext fictions employing possible worlds theory.

Ensslin, A., 2007. *Canonizing hypertext: Explorations and constructions*. London: Continuum.

This book looks at the pedagogical possibilities for hypertext fiction.

Miall, D. S. and Dobson, T., 2001. Reading hypertext and the experience of literature. *Journal of Digital Information*, 2. Available at: http://journals.tdl.org/jodi/article/view/35

This online article looks at studies of actual readers' experiences with hypertext fiction.

Trimarco, P., 2012. Stylistic approaches to teaching hypertext fiction. *In:* M. Burke, S. Csábi, L. Week and J. Zerkowitz, eds. *Pedagogical stylistics: Current trends in language, literature and ELT*. London: Continuum, 158–176.

This book chapter describes a study involving undergraduate students reading 'Lies' by R. Pryll; the approaches employed are Labov's elements of narrative and text world theory.

References

Aarseth, E. J., 1997. *Cybertext: Perspectives on ergodic literature*. Baltimore: The Johns Hopkins University Press.

America, M., 1998. GRAMMATRON. Available at: http://www.grammatron.com/index2.html (accessed 9 August 2012).

Barthes, R., 1974. *S/Z*. Oxford: Basil Blackwell.

Bell, A., 2010. *The possible worlds of hypertext fiction*. London: Palgrave Macmillan.

Bell, A. and Ensslin, A., 2011. 'I know what it was. You know what it was': Second-person narration in hypertext fiction. *Narrative*, 19, 311–329.

Bolter, J. D., 2001. *Writing space: Computers, hypertext, and the remediation of print*. New York: Routledge.

Derrida, J., 1998. *Of grammatology*. Baltimore: Johns Hopkins University Press.

Douglas, J. Y., 2001. *The end of books – Or books without end?: Reading interactive narratives*. Ann Arbor: University of Michigan Press.

Ensslin, A., 2004. Reconstructing the deconstructed – hypertext and literary education. *Language and Literature*, 13, 307–333.

Ensslin, A., 2007. *Canonizing hypertext: Explorations and constructions*. London: Continuum.

Ensslin, A., 2012. 'I want to say I may have seen my son die this morning': Unintentional unreliable narration in digital fiction. *Language and Literature*, 21, 136–149.

Fisher, C., 2001. These waves of girls. Available at: http://www.yorku.ca/caitlin/waves/navigate.html (accessed 30 June 2012).

Gavins, J., 2003. Too much blague? An exploration of the text words of Donald Barthelme's Snow White. *In:* J. Gavins and G. Steen, eds. *Cognitive poetics in practice*. London: Routledge, 129–144.

Gavins, J., 2007. *Text world theory: An introduction*. Edinburgh: Edinburgh University Press.

Gavins, J. and Steen, G., eds. 2003. *Cognitive poetics in practice*. London: Routledge

Halliday, M. and Matthiessen, C., 2004. *An introduction to functional grammar*. 3rd edn. London: Hodder Education.

Hoffmann, C. R., 2010. *Narrative revisited: Telling a story in the age of new media*. London: John Benjamins Publishing Company.

Jackson, S., 1995. *Patchwork Girl*. Watertown, MA: Eastgate Systems.

Jones, C. and Ventola, E., 2010. *From language to multimodality: New developments in the study of ideational meaning*. London: Equinox Publishing Ltd.

Joyce, J., [1922] 2008. *Ulysses*. Oxford: Oxford University Press.

Joyce, M., 1990. *afternoon*. Watertown, MA: Eastgate Systems.

Joyce, M., 1996. Twelve blue. Available at: http://www.eastgate.com/TwelveBlue/ (accessed 9 August 2012).

Koshimaa, R., 2004. These waves of memories: A hyperfiction by Caitlin Fisher. Available at: http://elmcip.net/critical-writing/these-waves-memories-hyperfiction-caitlin-fisher (accessed 9 August 2012).

Kress, G. R. and van Leeuwen, T., 2006. *Reading Images: The grammar of visual design*. London: Routledge.

Landow, G. P., 2006. *Hypertext 3.0: Critical theory and new media in an era of globalization*. Baltimore: Johns Hopkins University Press.

Miall, D. S. and Dobson, T., 2001. Reading hypertext and the experience of literature. *Journal of Digital Information*, 2. Available at: http://journals.tdl.org/jodi/article/view/35 (accessed 28 June 2012).

Miles, A., 2002. Hypertext structure as the event of connection. *Journal of Digital Information*, 2. Available at: http://journals.tdl.org/jodi/article/view/48 (accessed 28 June 2012).

Moulthorpe, S., 1991. *Victory garden*. Watertown, MA: Eastgate Systems.

Pavic, M., 1984. *Dictionary of the Khazars*. New York: Vintage.

Pope, J., 2009. The significance of navigation and interactivity design for readers' responses to interactive narrative. Available at: http://dichtung-digital.mewi.unibas.ch/2009/Pope.htm (accessed 30 June 2012).

Pryll, R., 1994. Lies. Available at: http://users.rcn.com/rick.interport/lies/lies.html (accessed 9 August 2012).

Schneider, R., 2005. Hypertext narrative and the reader: A view from cognitive theory. *European Journal of English Studies*, 9, 197–208.

Simpson, P. and Mayr, A., 2009. *Language and power: A resource book for students*. London: Taylor and Francis.

Stephens, P., 2004. Samantha in winter. Available at: http://www.paulspages.co.uk/htext/saminwinter.htm (Accessed 9 August 2012).

Sterne, L., [1759] 1996. *Tristram Shandy*. Herefordshire: Wordsworth Editions.

Stockwell, P., 2002. *Cognitive poetics: An introduction*. London: Routledge.

Stockwell, P., 2003. Surreal figures. *In:* J. Gavins and G. Steen, eds. *Cognitive poetics in practice*. London: Routledge, 13–26.

Tosca, S. P., 2000. A pragmatics of links. *Journal of Digital Information*, 1. Available at: http://journals.tdl.org/jodi/article/view/23 (accessed 28 June 2012).

Trimarco, P., 2012. Stylistic approaches to teaching hypertext fiction. *In:* M. Burke, S. Csábi, L. Week and J. Zerkowitz, eds. *Pedagogical stylistics: Current trends in language, literature and ELT*. London: Continuum, 158–176.

Walker, J., 1999. Piecing together and tearing apart: Finding the story in afternoon. Available at: http://jilltxt.net/txt/afternoon.html (accessed 14 August 2012).

Werth, P., 1999. *Text worlds: Representing conceptual space in discourse*. London: Longman.

32

Stylistics, emotion and neuroscience

Patrick Colm Hogan

Introduction, definitions and usage

It may seem initially that the meanings of *stylistics*, *emotion*, and *neuroscience* are self-evident. However, there are complications and uncertainties in each case. It is important, therefore, to begin by explaining how each of these terms will be used in the current chapter. Following this, we will consider some of the limited work that has been done on emotion, style, and the brain. A third section outlines the varieties of emotion that enter into verbal art and related forms (such as film) at different levels. The subsequent section sets out some possibilities for a research programme in the study of emotion and style, focusing specifically on aesthetic response or the feeling of beauty. The chapter concludes with an example analysis based on the preceding theoretical discussion, followed by some brief reflections on possibilities for future study.

Emotion

Emotion is an ordinary language term. Therefore its meaning is intuitive, but also imprecise. In the following pages, 'emotion' refers to any motivational system, which is to say, a system that provides an impetus to self-conscious action. These motivational systems are neurologically defined, largely by subcortical structures, and they are open to prefrontal modulation (unlike reflexes). Emotion systems are closely related to what might be characterised as the 'pre-emotional' system of attentional orientation.

More precisely, emotion systems involve neural circuits that are activated by *eliciting conditions*. For example, in a story, the appearance of the hero's gun-wielding nemesis may be an eliciting condition for fear. Eliciting conditions may be external or internal and they may result from perceptions, memories, or imaginations, sometimes called 'simulations'. We tend to speak of eliciting conditions as if they were limited to environmental or somatic changes. However, environmental and somatic changes interact with predispositions on the part of the person experiencing the emotion. These predispositions range from enduring features of personality (such as high susceptibility to fright), to more limited moods, to relevant emotional memories. (Emotional memories are memories that revive the emotion of the initial experience.) Eliciting conditions are particularly important for the study of emotion and style. Indeed, they are perhaps the most important part of an emotion event for stylistic study. All the elements of eliciting conditions enter – including the personality of the reader, mood and so on, as Burke stresses (2011, p. 152) in slightly different terms.

Eliciting conditions lead to a variety of *outcomes*. These fall into three broad categories: *physiological*, *actional*, and *expressive*. Physiological outcomes are the changes in bodily conditions that accompany the activation of an emotion. These include, for example, alterations in heart rate, respiration, perspiration, and so on. These physiological outcomes are widely seen as providing the somatic conditions for what we experience as the *feeling* or *phenomenological tone* of an emotion. When we speak of having a certain emotion, we most often have in mind this phenomenological tone (e.g. what it feels like to be afraid). That feeling may be pleasurable or aversive. When we speak of the emotion produced by a work, including its style, we are almost necessarily referring to the phenomenological tone of a reader's experience. For our purposes, the importance of physiological outcomes *per se* is that they are relatively spontaneous and may be quite prominent in responses to works of art (in contrast with actional and expressive outcomes). Thus they are appropriate objects of empirical investigation (e.g. in skin conductance tests).

Actional outcomes are behaviours that have the purpose of altering or sustaining eliciting conditions. These are typically motor responses, but they may also be cognitive modulations. For example, the standard actional outcome when faced with fear-eliciting danger is flight. This aims to change the eliciting conditions by removing the danger. In the case of more distant threats, one may engage in 'mood repair' (see Forgas 2000, p. 258), such as distracting oneself from the danger by redirecting one's attention. Since the phrase 'actional outcomes' seems to imply motor involvement, we might adopt the less misleading phrase, 'condition modulating outcomes' or more briefly 'condition modulation'. Motor outcomes are largely absent from aesthetic emotion. Indeed, Norman Holland has drawn extensive conclusions from the relative immobility of readers, which we might view in terms of the inhibition of actional outcomes. On the other hand, aesthetic response undoubtedly does involve attentional reorientation and other forms of mood repair, and even some limited forms of actional outcomes (e.g. looking away from the screen during a movie). In principle, such condition modulation could be affected by stylistic elements and thus may be a legitimate feature of emotional stylistics, though it seems not to have been examined.

Expressive outcomes are external manifestations of the activation of an emotion system, such as weeping in the case of sorrow. However, they do not serve to alter the eliciting conditions directly. Rather, they serve to communicate emotion, perhaps altering the eliciting conditions indirectly. Expressive outcomes include facial expressions, posture, gait, pupil dilation, vocalisation, and so on. Emotion expressions are themselves eliciting conditions for emotions in observers. Expressive outcomes are clearly relevant to emotion in art – through, for example, the representation of emotionally expressive faces (see Plantinga 1999). They may have implications for emotion and style specifically – for example, if there is a connection between, say, emotional expression in vocalisation and features of pitch contour in a particular work.

Finally, it is important to note that much emotional response to literature is empathic. When the villain enters with a gun, the reader is not afraid for himself or herself, but for the hero. However, in the case of style, this is not the case. Our emotional response to style appears to be largely direct rather than empathic.

Neuroscience

Neuroscience is a fairly straightforward technical term. It refers to the integration of various sciences that contribute to our understanding of the brain. As such, the notion hardly requires elaboration. However, it is valuable to distinguish different ways in which neuroscience may enter into the study of emotion and style. These are basically the same ways in which it may enter into other areas of literary or artistic study.

The most obvious place where neuroscience and literary study may be integrated is in direct empirical research on literary response. For example, one might use brain imaging to examine the effects on variations in verse patterns. There has been valuable empirical research on literature and emotion, not always involving neuroscience. Moreover, only a limited amount of this research has focused on style. Such research should certainly be pursued more fully.

Most literary researchers do not have access to the equipment required for neuroscientific research. However, other ways of relating neuroscience and emotional stylistics are possible as well. Two seem particularly important. The first and most obvious is the extension to literary style of findings from other areas. Insofar as neuroscientific and related research establishes a general pattern in human emotion or cognition, we can assume that the general pattern applies to emotion or cognition regarding style, unless we have reason to believe otherwise. For example, Burke cites extensive evidence that human cognition generally involves structural anticipation based on past experience. Thus we have every reason to expect that 'skeletal echoes of previous styles, structures and rhythms that have affected a reader in the past' will be 'subconsciously channelled and brought to bear on concrete ... textual aspects of style during engaged acts of literary reading' (2011, p. 120).

The second use of neuroscience is, roughly, analogical extension. Certain sorts of operations appear to recur significantly, if often with functional differences, in various areas of brain operation. For example, neurons may have inhibitory or excitatory connections. In some cases, inhibitory connections may operate to enhance some features of a target. This is the case with lateral inhibition in the visual system, which serves to make the edges of objects more salient. One can certainly imagine something along these lines occurring in connection with, say, the perception of meter in verse. It is undoubtedly the case that our linguistic perception is generally 'cleaner' than the rather messy auditory signal that we receive (see Byrd 2011, p. 601). Thus a conjecture of something like 'pattern enhancement' seems quite plausible in the case of the experience of style. Analogical extension is obviously less rigorous than literal extension, and necessarily requires greater caution. However, it is potentially fruitful as well, particularly when combined with more direct, convergent research.

Style

Style is a term in ordinary language and a term of art in literary study. Unfortunately, the result seems to be that it ends up with the worst of both worlds. Specifically, many writers use the term as if it had a well-defined technical meaning, but they seem to vary widely in what they take that technical meaning to be. Burke, citing Verdonk (2002), characterises style as 'distinctive linguistic expression' and stylistics as 'the analysis' of such expression 'and the description of its purpose and effect' (2011, p. 123). Other writers adopt broader definitions, either explicitly or implicitly. For example, Jeffries and McIntyre include large areas of discourse analysis and pragmatics, as well as 'text comprehension' (2010, p. 1). In some uses, it becomes difficult to see how one might draw a principled distinction between stylistics and literary analysis generally, or even language study. Indeed, the field is in some ways even more encompassing than language study when, as in the present handbook, non-verbal or only partially verbal media are included, such as films and graphic fiction.

The preceding comments probably seem to constitute criticisms of the writers who have given expansive definitions of style and stylistics. However, theorists writing on stylistics must follow current practices. Insofar as practitioners of stylistics address discourse analysis, it is important to treat discourse analysis in the account of stylistics. Moreover, there is intrinsic reason to include at least some features of discourse analysis as a matter of style. It is also valuable to examine possibly cross-modal stylistic features. For example, Watling (1998) cites research that suggests 'that the neuronal firing patterns activated by listening to certain music styles bear similarities to those underlying certain thinking styles'. The connections appear to suggest cross-modal continuities in certain stylistic variations, such as inversion. Thus inclusiveness is not necessarily a bad thing. On the other hand, the value of inclusiveness only means that it is important to present a clear account of style in order to address its scope more adequately.

There are undoubtedly different ways in which style may be defined. Moreover, there are other places in this handbook where the issue is addressed thoughtfully and rigorously. I will present a definition that tries to capture the diversity just outlined. This attempt is not meant to give some single true account of style. Rather, it articulates how I will be using the term 'style', adding a further definition to those presented elsewhere in this volume.

First, we need to distinguish between levels of representation in a work. Cognition is a constructive activity. We do not merely know the world, including works of art. Rather, we process information at multiple levels. We have two separate levels of representation when we use one network of integrated information as one source in the construction of a distinct semantic, perceptual, or other cognitively integrated target. Thus we may be said to construct the story world of a narrative from the discourse of the narrative. (The story world is the events and situations as they 'really are'. The discourse is how those events and situations are presented. See, for example, Chatman 1980.) Similarly, we may be said to construct the discourse (and the story world) from the language of the work.

Given this, we may define style in the following way. Style is a distinctive pattern in features in one constructed level that are not determined by features at a lower level. For example, plot is part of discourse. Specifically, plot or emplotment is the selection and ordering of events and situations from the story world. Insofar as the ordering of events is not determined by the story world, we make speak of recurring patterns in that ordering as 'style of emplotment'. Similarly, insofar as diction is not determined by either discourse or story world, we may say that there is 'style of diction'. (One consequence of this definition is that all distinctive patterns in nonrepresentational works may count as style.)

This definition allows us to encompass a range of topics in stylistics, while also recognising that there are differences among them – for instance, style of plot is not the same as style of diction. Nonetheless, it is not quite adequate. It requires two addenda. First, the distinctiveness of the patterns may vary in the range over which it is distinctive. Thus the style (e.g. the diction) may be distinctive for a single work. Alternatively, the features in question may be distinctive for some group of works – an authorial canon, a movement, an historical period, and so on. Authorial distinctiveness is particularly important in that it is stressed by a number of writers, such as Holland, for whom the 'theme-and-variations style' is a matter of an author's (or reader's) 'identity' (p. 224). It was suggested perhaps most famously by Buffon (1753) in his much-quoted statement that 'the style is the man himself'. (On Buffon's views, as well as Proust's influential discussion of style in *Le temps retrouvé*, the reader may wish to consult Rueff 2010.) In each of these cases, the word 'distinctive' is intended to eliminate universal patterns resulting from the nature of the human mind. We would generally not wish to consider something stylistic if it is a pattern shared by all works or all authors.

The second addendum is the following. Not all levels are equally prototypical for the study of style. Specifically, prototypicality tends to decrease with the increased embedding of representations. Thus recurring features of story (relative to, say, genre) are generally seen as less 'stylistic' than emplotment and narration, while emplotment and narration are less exemplary of style than diction and sentence structure. The point is related to the fact that it is easier to isolate stylistic features for a work at the level of diction and sentence structure, whereas patterns in emplotment are more likely to be discernible only across works (e.g. in an authorial canon).

Research on style, emotion and the brain

Recent decades have witnessed a great deal of research on emotion and literature, much of it including attention to the brain. One consequence of the preceding definition, however, is that very little of this research can reasonably be considered stylistic. Perhaps the most prominent writer on literature and emotion is Martha Nussbaum. For example, her *Upheavals of Thought* (2001), considers a number of literary works in depth, examining their treatment of emotions, the relation between this treatment and empirical research (including neuropsychological research), and the ethical implications of both. However, as this suggests, Nussbaum focuses her attention almost entirely on highly 'embedded' representations, primarily theme and story. (Theme could be considered embedded in story, thus as even less a matter of style.) The same point holds for most of Keith Oatley's writings on literature and emotion, as well as Hogan's *What Literature Teaches Us About Emotion* (2011b). The latter draws on the neuropsychology of emotion, integrating it with representations of emotion in literature. The key point here is that his focus is on the story world – or even the real world as represented in the story world. Hogan's *The Mind and its Stories* (2003) and *Affective Narratology* (2011a) also treat emotion and literature. However, in these works, Hogan is concerned to isolate universal literary genres that guide an author's imagination of a story, thus arguably the most deeply embedded features of a narrative.

Some of Oatley's recent work on emotional intelligence could be thought of as bearing on style (though Oatley does not frame the research in that way). For example, one study presented two versions of a Chekhov short story to two test groups. One group received the story itself. The other group received a rewritten version of the story, now in the form of a court transcript. The former group had 'greater change in self-reported experience of personality traits' (Djikic *et al*. 2009, p. 24). However, it is difficult to say just what such self-reports tell us and what they might have to do with style, if anything.

There is work that explicitly considers style and the brain. However, in many cases the word 'style' is used differently. For example, Lengger and colleagues treated the behavioural and neurological results of giving test subjects 'stylistic information' when viewing paintings. The results are interesting. Giving 'stylistic information' appears to facilitate understanding of the works, but not their enjoyment. However, the one example they provide of such 'stylistic information' is a case of compositional 'procedures' (Lengger *et al*. 2007, p. 99) and intentions (e.g. challenging 'artistic authorship' [p. 99]). This seems to have only an indirect relevance to style as defined above or as ordinarily considered in stylistics.

Returning to literature, we find a similar case in Reuven Tsur's cognitive poetic work. Tsur discusses some universal tendencies of metrics, arguing that they derive from 'adaptation devices' of the human mind. For example, in the placement of a caesura, there is a cross-cultural tendency 'to prefer the 4 + 6 segmentation to the 6 + 4 segmentation in decasyllabic lines, irrespective of language and versification system' (2002, p. 72). The preference is a function of 'limitations of short-term memory' (p. 71). Tsur then states that 'style' occurs when ordinary 'cognitive processes' undergo 'freezing' into 'rigid formulas'. Tsur is therefore treating something very different – often a lexical or idiomatic requirement (his example is 'trick or treat', rather than the more logical 'treat or trick'). This is presumably excluded from style in the above definition.

Other work touches on style, but in a rather general way. For example, Young and Saver's valuable 'Neurology of Narrative' (2001) treats the effects of brain damage on narration. They explain that bilateral amygdalo-hippocampal system damage produces either 'arrested narration' or 'unbounded narration' (p. 76). These may appear to be two styles of narration in a robust sense. (I should note that Young and Saver are not claiming this.) However, the damage discussed by Young and Saver produces anterograde amnesia (the inability to store new memories). 'Arrested narration' simply means that one's autobiographical narration stops at the moment when one's memory stops, thus at the time of the injury. Unbounded narration involves confabulation for the period subsequent to the injury. The latter could be considered minimally stylistic, since telling something is not required by the absence of memories. Moreover, this does have some bearing on our understanding of style more generally, since it appears related to 'additional injury to frontal lobe structures responsible for monitoring of responses and inhibiting inaccurate replies' (p. 76). However, this seems to tell us only that some distinctive features of style may be a function of strictness or laxity in prefrontal monitoring. This is, of course, what we would have assumed anyway from the general operation of the brain.

Similarly, the other two effects of brain damage are 'undernarration' and 'denarration'. Undernarration is not actually a matter of recounting (as in the previous cases), but of simulating. Damage to orbitofrontal cortices impoverishes one's ability to generate multiple scenarios in simulation (e.g. imagining that if one asks for a raise, the boss might agree *or* might become angry and offended – as opposed to simply imagining that the boss agrees). This may bear on authorial creativity, and thus on creativity regarding style. However, it does not appear to have any special relevance to style. Denarration is a loss of affect after dorsolateral/mesial frontal damage. It clearly bears on the emotion aspect of our topic, but it also does not address style particularly.

There are certainly exceptions to these tendencies, in terms of work that does treat emotion, neuroscience, and style. We have already mentioned Burke (2011) on anticipation. The analyses of some writers on emotion and film point toward a brain-based understanding of stylistic features. To take a simple example, Plantinga's (1999) work on facial mirroring suggests that close-ups of faces may be more likely to provoke mirroring in spectators, thus generating intensified emotional response. Other aspects of film theory are consequential here as well. We will consider some elements of this below.

Art theory has some relevant cases also. Semir Zeki stresses ambiguity in his discussion of painting and sculpture. This at least might count as a feature of style. Zeki focuses on the ways in which paintings necessarily select very limited information from what we would call the story world. For example, a particular painting might represent a man and a woman talking. In the story world that we imagine for the painting there is a topic of conversation, a relation between the man and woman and so on, but these are not represented, thus leaving the work ambiguous. The difficulty is that this is true for such a large number of paintings from such diverse times and places that it is perhaps not very distinctive. Zeki's (2009) exploration of unfinished works of art is more promising in this regard. Zeki seeks to explain unfinished works by reference to the impossibility of realising a brain-generated ideal in some artefact, which is not precisely a stylistic issue. However, his concrete analyses are most suggestive when he treats 'unfinished' works as, in effect, finished, with the unshaped marble (for instance) manifesting the sculptor's stylistic choices.

Some work on neuropathology addresses style, but studies of this sort are often rather limited. For example, Bogousslavsky finds that Willem de Kooning's 'progressive dementia' resulted in a 'marked simplification of the previous painting structure' (2005, p. 110). Bogousslavsky finds de Kooning's creativity remained despite the dementia. In contrast with de Kooning, 'the reported stylistic changes in patients with frontotemporal dementia ... display ... an increased tendency to reproduce images semi-photographically' (p. 110). There are some interesting implications of this research, but it is difficult to interpret them. Clearly, more such research is needed.

Critical issues: Emotions and literature

Despite the relative limitations of current research in the area, there are great possibilities for a brain-based approach to emotional stylistics. However, to pursue this more fruitfully, we need to begin with a clearer sense of just what emotions are involved in literature generally. I say 'literature generally' because, by the preceding definition, the different levels of a literary work have at least some relevance to stylistic analysis. Moreover, the emotions of different levels interact. In other words, our emotional response to a stylistic device at one level is usually inseparable from the emotions represented at an embedded level. For instance, our emotional response to a feature of voice or diction is likely to be influenced by emplotment and by story events (e.g. whether the hero is in danger, suffering, rejoicing, or whatever). As it happens, there has been considerable work on emotion at the different levels of representation.

Any emotion may appear in the story world. However, research on universal genres (see Hogan 2003 and 2011a) suggests that the most fundamental organisation of the story world into a story already involves the privileging of some emotions over others. There are two main types of privileged emotions. First, there are the emotions that consistently drive the actions of the main characters in the universal genres. Characters do not simply act in response to immediate conditions, but are in most cases consistently motivated throughout the course of a work. The motivating forces are 'sustaining emotions'. There are also 'outcome emotions', which is to say, emotions that are relatively enduring at the end of the story. There are two outcome emotions – happiness and sorrow. (On sustaining and outcome emotions, see Hogan 2003, pp. 91–94.)

Perhaps the most prominent sustaining emotion in literature is attachment, the bonding of parents and children that recurs in friendship and in romantic love. It is the central emotion in two cross-cultural genres, those concerning romantic and familial separation and reunion. It is also an important motivating factor in revenge plots and even criminal investigation stories. Other recurring emotions include sexual desire, anger and hatred, and (roughly) pride – both individual and group-based. Sexual desire combines with attachment in the romantic plot. It also motivates the seduction plot. Individual and group pride underlie the two main components of the heroic plot. Anger and hatred underlie the revenge narrative.

With respect to readers or viewers, the sustaining and outcome emotions are entirely empathic. I am not in love with Juliet (or Romeo) when watching Shakespeare's play. Rather, I have an empathic response to their love for one another. Similarly, any happiness I have over a hero's triumph is, first of all, empathic happiness, just as my grief over his or her suffering is empathic sorrow.

The next level is that of discourse. Again, discourse comprises emplotment (what parts of the story are selected for communication and how they are arranged) and narration (who is speaking to whom). There are numerous emotions specific to discourse. The most important emotions for plot have been identified by Sternberg (1978) as suspense, curiosity, and surprise. The terms are not entirely parallel. We might rather distinguish two axes. First, there is an axis of story knowledge. Roughly speaking, complete story knowledge involves knowing the eliciting conditions of the sustaining emotions (and thus what prompts the main characters' actions to begin with), how these are resolved in outcome emotions, and the causal sequence leading from the former to the latter. Incomplete knowledge tends to provoke hope or fear (thus suspense) if we do not know the outcome. (For an insightful discussion of some complexities of suspense, see Tan 1996.) Incomplete story knowledge provokes curiosity if we know the outcome but not what precedes the outcome. Despite this difference, it seems clear that this curiosity may be suspenseful, involving fear or hope as well. In addition, we might isolate an axis of predictability where we would distinguish anticipated, unanticipated but retrospectively comprehensible, and unanticipated but anomalous developments. The second and third are forms of surprise. Note that incomplete knowledge tends to rely on empathic emotions whereas anticipation and surprise do not.

Narration is more straightforward. Insofar as the narrator is a character, we may have the usual range of emotional responses. However, the crucial emotional response to a narrator as narrator is one of trust or distrust. Note that this trust or distrust is not an empathic emotion.

Finally, above the level of narration emotion, there is artefact emotion, our emotional response to the work as a made object. The idea was explored by Tan (1996) and has been developed valuably by Plantinga (2009). Artefact emotion includes a range of non-empathic responses. For example, wonder over special effects in a film is a form of artefact emotion. For our purposes, the most important form of artefact emotion is aesthetic, prominently the feeling of beauty, although also the feeling of sublimity. We may refer to wonder over special effects and the like as emotional response to *skill*, while characterising aesthetic artefact emotion as a response to *style*. In connection with this, 'features of a work that provoke aesthetic artefact emotion' may serve as an alternative definition of *style*. It is, in effect, a correlate of the preceding definition, since features that are not determined by an embedded level are the features that mark a work as the product of choice, thus as an artefact.

Extending current research: The case of beauty

The first thing to recall in discussing emotional response to style, specifically aesthetic feeling, is that artefact emotions are partially dependent on story and discourse emotions. Again, a stylistic technique will not produce precisely the same emotional response when associated with the death of the hero as when it is associated with the union of lovers. For example, if (as Plantinga's 1999 work suggests) a close-up enhances facial mirroring, the viewer's emotion will differ depending on the emotion expressed by the character. Of course, artefact emotions are not wholly dependent on the emotional quality of the story or discourse. We may have aesthetic feeling (a feeling of beauty) when viewing a close-up whether the face is happy or sorrowful. Yet even this oversimplifies the situation, since it is clear that the emotional quality of the story may contribute to or detract from aesthetic response. To give a crude example, it is difficult to represent faeces in a beautiful way. Moreover, aesthetic feeling arises at each level. The most prototypical cases of aesthetic feeling may concern language or cinematography, but we speak frequently and accurately of a 'beautiful story' (meaning either a story or a plot, in the technical senses), as well as 'an ordinary story, beautifully told' (referring in at least some cases to narrational features).

In line with these points, we would expect the features particular to beauty to be closely related to distinctive features of style. At the same time, in analysing aesthetic feeling we would expect to find some eliciting conditions that are particular to beauty as well as some contributory emotions that result not from style proper, but from embedded representational features, prominently features of the story world. Finally, given the centrality of aesthetic emotion in verbal art, we might expect ancillary emotions to be drawn primarily from the set of dominant emotions at the story and discourse levels (rather than from emotions that appear only incidentally).

As it happens, there is a fairly rich body of research on aesthetic preference, though much of it is in visual art and music. In part, it fits well with the preceding analyses, while simultaneously extending those analyses. Specifically, there appear to be two key properties inspiring aesthetic feeling. One is pattern recognition, prominently pattern recognition in time. Treating music, Vuust and Kringelbach argue forcefully that 'anticipation/prediction' (2010, p. 256) is central to the experience of aesthetic pleasure. Specifically, they claim that such experience is a function of engagement of the brain's endogenous reward system (pp. 256, 266).

The research reported by Vuust and Kringelbach is somewhat unclear on the precise conditions for aesthetic feeling. They connect that feeling with both 'correct predictions' (p. 266) and 'violation of expectancies' (p. 263). I suspect that the apparent contradiction is best explained by the idea of non-anomalous surprise. Our most intense aesthetic responses to patterns are probably the result of not fully anticipating a result, but understanding the result retrospectively. This is what we would predict from the fact that pattern enjoyment is inhibited by habituation (see LeDoux 1996, p. 138 on habituation and reduced emotional response). The general point has been recognised by stylisticians, if somewhat more narrowly. For example, Burke explains that 'a significant part of stylistics concerns ... repetition and parallelism' or 'deviation' (2011, p. 124; recall that Burke emphasised anticipation as well). Empirical research on style and reader response is also consistent with these points. For example, Miall and Kuiken's (1994) work on defamiliarisation suggests the importance of overcoming habituation.

On the other hand, this may oversimplify the situation. It is probably the case that there are conditions in which aesthetic feeling is heightened by correct anticipation. These might particularly be cases where the prediction is not an object of focal attention but a sort of background constancy. For example, while concentrating on melodic variations, it may be best for our sense of the rhythm to be fairly constant, so as not to produce disorientation. Indeed, this may often be the case with rhythm or, more generally, with anticipatory properties that are strongly somatic rather than imaginative or simulative. Burke speaks suggestively of 'embodied rhythm' (2011, p. 128) and Watling (1998) reflects plausibly on kinaesthetic elements of music. Perhaps the constancy of confirmed anticipation is more bound up with motor routines, while the dulling effects of habituation are more bound up with processes that require attention. (In keeping with this, Frijda notes that habituation is linked with diminished attention [1986, p. 318].)

In short, there is reason to view unexpected pattern isolation as a feature of beauty, bound up with reward system activation, even if the precise operation of the unexpectedness is not fully clear. In literature, the point would seem to extend not only to, say, metre or imagistic parallelism, but also to features of narration and emplotment. Indeed, we initially isolated retrospectively comprehensible (thus non-anomalous) surprise as a feature of emplotment.

On the other hand, it seems clear that beauty is not only a function of pattern isolation. When we consider music or the music-like characteristics of literature, then temporal patterning is particularly salient. However, when we consider visual arts, then it becomes clear that we find beauty not only in sets of entities (e.g. sequences of notes). We also find beauty in single objects. Perhaps the most obvious case of this is the human face. Each of us considers some faces beautiful and others not. The general principle governing these responses is a matter of averaging (see Langlois and Roggman 1990). Thus the most beautiful face is the most average face or an approximation to a prototype. A prototype is an average across instances in one's experience (e.g. the prototypical bird is an average across birds; for a brief introduction to prototype theory, see Rosch 2011). The point about beauty is not confined to faces. For example, discussing studies of colour, Martindale and Moore report that 'more prototypical stimuli' are 'strongly preferred' (1988, p. 670). Similarly, Whitfield and Slatter (1979) treat research showing aesthetic preference for prototypical instances in furniture. On the other hand, prototypes are not always strict averages. They are often weighted by salient, differentiating characteristics. (For a striking case of such contrast, see Kahneman and Miller 1986, p. 143 on prototypical diet food.) It seems very likely that such weighting enters into our response to beauty, at least in some cases (e.g. male versus female). Indeed, this is precisely what Ramachandran's (2011) neural account of beauty suggests through the concept of peak shift. A peak shift is a shift in the direction of enhanced differentiating characteristics.

Given these points, we might refashion the preceding definition of style to read as follows: style is a distinctive pattern in features or a distinctive prototype approximation in one constructed level that is not determined by features at a lower level. Alternatively, we may simply consider prototype approximation to be a sort of pattern in which the patterned features are categorised as a single object.

Prototypicality may appear to violate the general dispreference for habituation. However, actual prototypical cases are not 'typical'. For example, no real face is perfectly average or prototypical. Rather, there are many clearly different faces that more or less approximate a prototype. The same point holds for prototypical characters ('beautiful characters'), prototypical (beautiful) scenes, and so on.

The mention of beautiful characters and beautiful scenes returns us to the issue of ancillary emotions. Given the list of emotions that are central to story structure, we might conjecture that our sense of beauty is enhanced by attachment relations (rather than, say, anger) at the level of the story. In fact, there is some neurological evidence for this. Nadal and colleagues discuss research on aesthetic feeling that 'found lower preference ratings associated with decreased activity of the caudate nucleus' (2008, p. 388; see Vartanian and Goel 2004). Research indicates that the caudate is 'associated with feelings of love' (Arsalidou and colleagues 2010, p. 47), including 'maternal' love (p. 50, see also Villablanca 2010, p. 95).

Thus the aesthetic response to beauty appears to be, first of all, a matter of reward response to unexpected patterning, including prototype approximation. This response bears primarily on style in the sense of features at one level that are not determined by features at some embedded representational level – thus prominently language or visual properties, to a lesser extent narration, and so on. This initial response is supplemented by empathic attachment feelings. One might conjecture that the sense of sublimity may rely more on feelings of pride than on feelings of attachment, though there does not seem to be any neurological evidence bearing on the topic.

It is worth remarking that this analysis posits universal processes for response to style and for aesthetic feeling. However, it in no way entails universality of actual responses. Our sensitivity to patterns will vary (e.g. with training); our propensities to habituation will differ also, as will the prototypes we form on the basis of our individual experiences. Our response to attachment relations is in part a function of our own emotional memories, which are necessarily not the same, and may diverge radically. As Raymond cautioned, 'The belief that all humans respond to and evaluate images in the same way has to be pitted against the obvious fact that people differ in what they value as art' (2003, p. 541). The preceding suggestions, though clearly only the most basic sketch of a possible research programme, at least have the advantage of avoiding that problem.

From theory to practice: A case of aesthetic response

In keeping with the preceding point about individual response, I will conclude with a brief discussion of a work that recently gave me the most intense aesthetic experience I have had in some time. This is a song and dance sequence, focused on a poem, that appears in the 1956 Hindi film *New Delhi*. (Readers wishing to see the sequence may find it easily on YouTube by searching for the first line, 'Muralī bairan bhayi, khanaiyā tori.') I do not necessarily expect readers to share my aesthetic response. The important point here is that stylistic features responsible for my intense feeling are amenable to analysis in terms of the principles just outlined.

The story of the film is a standard romantic tragi-comedy in which two people fall in love, are kept apart by their parents, but are eventually united. The woman is a dancer and the sequence in question takes place during a song and dance performance early in the relationship. The sequence begins and ends with classical south Indian dance. The style of this type of dance involves repeated halts or pauses. It is beautiful certainly, but – to exaggerate the point – it may appear to be a sequence of fixed poses and transitions among the fixed poses. To use an analogy, if this were poetry, it would be heavily end-stopped. This opening section is interrupted by the dancer glimpsing her beloved, who is seated in the audience. This precipitates a change to very fluid and much more free, but still classically influenced dance. It more or less represents the imagination and feelings of the dancer. In the story world, only the fully classical performance actually takes place. The contrast in styles is stressed by a number of features beyond fluidity. For example, both dances have a basic rhythmic cycle that is a multiple of three beats. However, the rhythm of the imaginary dance is presented in such a way as to make it ambiguous between an Indian rhythmic cycle and a waltz. In contrast, there is no hint of a waltz in the opening section. Initially, this change has a strongly dishabituating effect. On the other hand, the connection of the rhythm with a dance familiar to many audience members tends to make it more 'embodied', thus more of a background rhythm.

In keeping with the conventions of Indian classical dance, there are strong representational elements. These are partly naturalistic, but partly formalised. For example, the representation of Kṛṣṇa's flute involves extending the thumb and little finger of both hands (with the other three fingers folded down) and placing the little finger of the left hand on the thumb of the right hand to form a flute-like configuration, then positioning the hands to the right side of one's mouth, like a flute. While some of the gestures are more conventional than others, there is a degree to which they all abstract prototypical features of the represented objects or persons. In this way, the images of the dance, depending on the precise nature of the performance, may achieve significant prototype approximation.

The story context of the film is, as indicated, one of attachment. Moreover, the story within the song is perhaps the most prototypical love story of Hindu tradition, that of Kṛṣṇa and Rādhā. The song focuses on Kṛṣṇa's flute and recounts the terrible pain of the lovers in separation. In the story of the song, Kṛṣṇa's flute is what beckons Rādhā (thus the poem's speaker) to Kṛṣṇa, but also what reminds her of the impossibility of their enduring union.

The first line of the song and the refrain are 'Muralī bairan bhayi, khanaiyā tori', roughly, 'Flute has become the enemy, dark beloved, your'. The word order is strange, with the addressee and the possessive pronoun coming at the end of the line. Thus the phrasing is unexpected or surprising. Nonetheless, it forms part of discernible patterns. The obvious pattern is simply the syntactic sense. However, the enjambment with the following line is a sort of verbal echo of the fluidity found in the song and dance more generally. The repetition of the lines also contributes to the sense of a circling through the rhythmic cycle. The song partially avoids habituation through the partial disalignment of the syntax with the rhythm. I at least expect the first syllable of the syntactic phrase (the 'kan' of 'kanhaiyā') to fall on the first beat of the cycle, but it does not. There are also musical key changes during the verses, though the resolving pitch remains the same throughout. In addition, the main scale is ambiguous between the Indian rāga, Pīlū, and the Western harmonic minor. This too contributes to a sense of non-habituated but discernible patterning, as do such features as the near-rhyme on alternate words in the opening line, the assonance, alliteration and near alliteration, and so on. (There may also be a dishabituation in the caesura violating the universal tendency isolated by Tsur 2002.)

For me, there are two particularly exquisite moments in the sequence. Both involve the prototype approximations of dance. In the first, the poem refers to Rādhā in the paths of Brindavan grove. As this is sung, the dancer performs the swaying gesture of Rādhā walking through the grove while balancing a mimed water pot on her head. The momentary representation combines the great fluidity of the rest of the dance with a remarkable abstraction of the prototypical features of such a walk. The second striking moment occurs when the song explains that the 'natakhat', Krṣṇa, took her to the bank of the Jamuna river. (A natakhat is a rascal, but it also suggests someone who is a dancer, thus partially identifying the two lovers.) The image that follows is one of Krṣṇa's music passing through her heart. The sexuality of the scene is clear, but it is an implicit and frustrated sexuality. The dance gesture involves a representation of flowing water, in which the dancer bends back with undulating arm movements. For me, this beautifully conveys the prototypical elements of flowing water, suggests the arching of Rādhā's back in sexual union, and further contributes to the pattern of fluidity.

This sequence as a whole presents us with unexpected patterns in the foreground (music, verse, and dance), pattern confirmation 'embodied' in the background, and strong empathic attachment. All these are associated with stylistic features (as defined above). Again, not everyone will have the same response to the sequence as I do. However, those who do find the many levels of style beautiful are likely to be responding to the same types of features.

Future directions

The preceding analyses suggest that, with style as with other targets of psychological or neural processing, we are likely to find universal principles combined with idiosyncrasy of experience producing partially diverse responses. Both the universal processes and any non-universal patterns in individual response are possible topics for continuing study. As to universal processes, an area that particularly calls out for exploration is the relation between prototype approximation and unanticipated pattern isolation. There is an intuitive way in which prototype approximation may be understood as a matter of non-anomalous surprise (as indicated above). However, the relation can only be clarified by further examination of the precise nature of both. Put differently, it is theoretically inelegant to explain one type of response, aesthetic enjoyment, by two distinct types of operation. The emotional components of aesthetic response are also under-researched at the present time. There are suggestive, but very limited and ambiguous results.

Individual variation is typically less valuable as a topic of research, despite some individualistic reader response study. It is usually not terribly valuable to know that Jones has these particular preferences, while Smith has these other particular preferences. However, research on individual variation may be fruitful if it suggests patterns in aesthetic response that are not universal as such, but are not wholly idiosyncratic. For example, there may be connections between aesthetic response and degree of attachment security, or there may be distinctive ways in which authors or professional critics respond to literary works or films, either cognitively or emotionally.

Research in style, emotion and neuroscience is clearly very promising. It could prove to be one of the most fruitful areas of investigation in literary study generally. Now, it is only in its infancy.

Related topics

Cognitive poetics, drama and performance, rhetoric and poetics, narratology, stylistics and film

Further reading

Burke, M. and Troscianko, E. T., eds., 2013. *The Journal of Literary Semantics:* A special issue on 'Explorations in cognitive literary science', vol. 42 (2).

Four thought-provoking articles on style, rhetoric, literature, parallel processing and perception that not only explore what cognitive psychology and linguistics can offer literary studies (i.e. cognitive poetics), but crucially what literary studies can offer cognitive neuroscience (i.e. 'cognitive literary science' – for more on this term see the introductory article by Burke and Troscianko).

Burke, M., 2011. *Literary reading, cognition and emotion: An exploration of the oceanic mind.* New York: Routledge.

An interdisciplinary, arts and sciences study that sets out to chart what might be happening in the embodied minds of engaged readers when they sit down to read literature.

Hogan, P. C., 2013. *Ulysses and the poetics of cognition.* New York: Routledge.

A theoretical and interpretive work that draws on recent discoveries in cognitive science to explain the levels of thought and emotion, as well as narrative and stylistic features, in James Joyce's masterpiece *Ulysses.*

Plantinga, C., 2009. *Moving viewers: American film and the spectator's experience.* Berkeley, CA: University of California Press.

A thorough, cognitively-based examination of emotion in the aesthetic and thematic operation of film.

References

Arsalidou, M, Barbeau, E., Bayless, S. and Taylor, M., 2010. Brain responses differ to faces of mothers and fathers. *Brain and Cognition*, 74, 47–51.
Bogousslavsky, J., 2005. Artistic creativity, style and brain disorders. *European Neurology*, 54, 103–111.
Buffon (Georges-Louis Leclerc, Comte de Buffon), 1753. *Discours sur le style.* Available at http://pedagogie.ac-toulouse.fr/philosophie/textes/buffondiscourssurlestyle.htm
Burke, M., 2011. *Literary reading, cognition and emotion: An exploration of the oceanic mind.* New York: Routledge.
Burke, M. and Troscianko, E. T., eds., 2013. *The Journal of Literary Semantics:* A special issue on *Explorations in cognitive literary science.* Vol. 42 (2).

Byrd, D., 2011. Phonetics. *In:* P. C. Hogan, ed. *The Cambridge encyclopedia of the language sciences.* Cambridge: Cambridge University Press, 600–605.

Chatman, S., 1980. *Story and discourse: Narrative structure in fiction and film.* Ithaca, NY: Cornell University Press.

Djikic, M., Oatley, K. Zoeterman, S. and Peterson, J., 2009. On being moved by art: How reading fiction transforms the self. *Creativity Research Journal,* 21 (1), 24–29.

Forgas, J., 2000. Affect and information processing strategies: An interactive relationship. *In:* J. Forgas, ed. *Feeling and thinking: The role of affect in social cognition.* Cambridge: Cambridge University Press, 253–280.

Frijda, N., 1986. *The emotions.* Cambridge: Cambridge University Press.

Hogan, P. C., 2003. *The mind and its stories: Narrative universals and human emotions.* Cambridge: Cambridge University Press.

Hogan, P. C., 2011a. *Affective narratology: The emotional structure of stories.* Lincoln, NE: University of Nebraska Press.

Hogan, P. C., 2011b. *What literature teaches us about emotion.* Cambridge: Cambridge University Press.

Hogan, P. C., 2013. *Ulysses and the poetics of cognition.* New York: Routledge.

Holland, N., 2009. *Literature and the brain.* Gainesville, FL: PsyArt Foundation.

Jeffries, L. and McIntyre, D., 2010. *Stylistics.* Cambridge: Cambridge University Press.

Kahneman, D. and Miller, D. T., 1986. Norm theory: Comparing reality to its alternatives. *Psychological Review,* 93, 136–153.

Langlois, J. H. and Roggman, L. A., 1990. Attractive faces are only average. *Psychological Science,* 1, 115–121.

LeDoux, J., 1996. *The emotional brain: The mysterious underpinnings of emotional life.* New York: Touchstone.

Lengger, P., Fischmeister, F., Leder, H. and Bauer, H., 2007. Functional neuroanatomy of the perception of modern art: A DC-EED study on the influence of stylistic information on aesthetic experience. *Brain Research,* 1158, 93–102.

Martindale, C. and Moore, K., 1988. Priming, prototypicality, and preference. *Journal of Experimental Psychology: Human Perception and Performance,* 14 (4), 661–670.

Miall, D. S. and Kuiken, D., 1994. Foregrounding, defamiliarization, and affect: Response to literary stories. *Poetics,* 22, 389–407.

Nadal, M., Munar, E., Capó, M. A., Rosselló, J. and Cela-Conde, C. J. 2008. Towards a framework for the study of the neural correlates of aesthetic preference. *Spatial Vision,* 21, 379–396.

Nussbaum, M., 2001. *Upheavals of thought: The intelligence of emotions.* Cambridge: Cambridge University Press.

Plantinga, C., 1999. The scene of empathy and the human face on film. *In:* C. Plantinga and G. M. Smith, eds. *Passionate views: Film, cognition, and emotion.* Baltimore, MD: Johns Hopkins University Press, 239–255.

Plantinga, C., 2009. *Moving viewers: American film and the spectator's experience.* Berkeley, CA: University of California Press.

Ramachandran, V. S., 2011. *The tell-tale brain: A neuroscientist's quest for what makes us human.* New York: W. W. Norton.

Raymond, J. E., 2003. Review of R. L. Solso: The psychology of art and the evolution of the conscious brain. *Visual Cognition,* 12, 541–547.

Rosch, E., 2011. Prototypes. *In:* P. C. Hogan, ed. *The Cambridge encyclopedia of the language sciences.* Cambridge: Cambridge University Press, 680–682.

Rueff, M., 2010. 'Qu'est-ce que le style?' Lecture on 9 June at the Bibliotèque nationale de France. Available at: http://www.bnf.fr/fr/evenements_et_culture/anx_conferences_2010/a.c_100609_rueff.html

Sternberg, M., 1978. *Expositional modes and temporal ordering in fiction.* Baltimore, MD: Johns Hopkins University Press.

Tan, E., 1996. *Emotion and the structure of narrative film: Film as an emotion machine.* B. Fasting, trans. Mahwah, NJ: Lawrence Erlbaum.

Tsur, R., 2002. Some cognitive foundations of 'cultural programs'. *Poetics Today,* 23, 63–89.

Vartanian, O. and V. Goel., 2004. Neuroanatomical correlates of aesthetic preference for paintings. *Neuroreport,* 15, 893–897.

Verdonk, P., 2002. *Stylistics.* Oxford: Oxford University Press.

Villablanca, J., 2010. Why do we have a caudate nucleus? *Acta Neurobiologiae Experimentalis*, 70, 95–105.

Vuust, P. and Kringelbach, M., 2010. The pleasure of music. *In:* M. Kringelbach and K. Berridge, eds. *Pleasures of the brain*. Oxford: Oxford University Press, 255–269.

Watling, C., 1998. The arts, emotion, and current research in neuroscience. *Mosaic*, 31, 107–124.

Whitfield, T. and Slatter, P., 1979. The effect of categorization and prototypicality on aesthetic choice in a furniture selection task. *British Journal of Psychology*, 70, 67–75.

Young, K. and Saver, J., 2001. The neurology of narrative. *Substance*, 94/95, 72–84.

Zeki, S., 2009. *Splendors and miseries of the brain: Love, creativity, and the quest for human happiness*. Malden, MA: Wiley-Blackwell.

Index

Figures are shown by a page reference in *italics*, and tables are in **bold**.

Aarseth, E.J. 502, 504
Abbott, M. and Forceville, C. 333, 337
Abram, D. 314, 317, 320, 324, 325
Adams, Douglas (*Dirk Gently's Holistic Detective Agency*) 275–6
Adamson, S. 103
adjacency pairs 139, 143
aesthetics: and beauty 524–5; a case of aesthetic response 525–6; and cognition 314; and emotions 523–6; film as communicative aesthetic event 458; theory of 320–1
affective fallacies 68–9
Albakry, M. and Hancock, P.H. 337
Allington, D. 451
Allington, D. and Swann, J. 447–8
Apache *'agodzaahi* stories 324
Aristotle: catharsis 13–14, 15; character 253; constituents of drama 261; creative writing 425; metaphor 208; mimesis 13; plot structure 14–15, 253; poetics 13–14, 15, 208, 253, 425, 431; rhetoric 1–2, 18–19, 21, 24; tragedy 13–14, 254
artificial intelligence 268–9
arts: and cognitive approaches 313–14, 317; and stylistic analysis 521
attention 229–30
Atwood, Margaret (*The Handmaid's Tale*) 279
Austen, Jane: and free indirect thought 224, 379; *Pride and Prejudice* 139, 145–6, 200, 384
Auster, Paul (*The Brooklyn Follies*) 111
Austin, J.L. 120–1, 123, 259, 365–7, 411
authorship: authorial intention 169–70; forensic 330, 379–80; role of, hypertext fiction 502

Bakhtin, Mikhail 371, 426
Barthes, Roland 502
Bartlett, F.C. 268, 272
Bell, A. 505–6
Benwell, B. 448–9
Bergs, A. 315–16
Birch, D. and O'Toole, M. 63
Black, Max 210–11

blending theory: compression 300, 309; concept of 297–8; counterfactual constructions 304–5; decompression 300–1; emergent structures 298; future directions 310; generic space 298, 303–4, *304*; inputs 297–8, 304–6; and metaphor 435; optimality constraints 299; practical application (textual analysis) 301–9, *304*, *306*, *308*; as a process of meaning emergence 297–9; recommendations for practice 310; and translation 404; vital relations 300; XYZ constructions 298–9
Boase-Beier, J. 398
Boland, E. 402
Bolter, J.D. 500, 510
The Book of Eli (film) 123–5, 126–8, 129–30
Boulter, A. 426
Bousfield, D. 372
Boyd, B. 316
Brande, D. 437
Brontë, Emily (*Wuthering Heights*) 161–2
'Brooklyn vs. Manhattan,' New York City 106–7, 109–11
Brooks, A. 352
Brooks, Cleanth 68
Brown, Dan (*Angels and Demons*) 292–3
Brown, P. and Levinson, S.C. 118–19, 128–9, 372
Bruhn, M. 318
Bühler's model of communication *33*
Burke, M. 319, 335, 518, 524
Burrows, J. 379–80
Burton, D. 353–4
Busa, Roberto 379
Büscher, M. and Urry, J. 104–5, 106
Busse, B. 256, 385

Carter, R. 2, 95, 101, 245–6, 335, 379
Carter, R. and Nash, W. 429–30, 437
catharsis 13–14, 15
Celan, Paul: 'Heimkehr' 401–2; 'Stumme Herbstgerüche' 399
Cervel, Peña 217

characterisation: audience reading of 118–19, 130–1, *131*, 257–8; and film 468; Horace on 16; and language 130–1, *131*, 141–2, 201, 260; and multimodality 472–3; and narratology 201, 253–4; and plot 253–4; and psychological point of view 178; and schema theory 260, 274–5; and text world theory 290; top-down/bottom-up processing 130–2, *131*, 141
chick lit fiction 358
children's fiction 357
Chomsky, Noam 42, 284–5
Christie, Agatha 276
Cicero, Marcus Tullius 19
Citizen Kane (film) 36, 465–6
Clark, A.M. 330
Clark, B. 161
Clark, B. and Owtram, N. 170–1
Clark. U. and Zyngier, S. 247
cognitive (term) 313
cognitive approaches: discourse architecture of drama 258; and emotions 518; and metaphor 213–18, 219; overview 74–5
cognitive discourse grammar 285
cognitive fluidity thesis 317
cognitive linguistics: and blending 297; and cognitive poetics 192, 319; and metaphor theory 213–14, 216–17, 219; and text world theory 287
cognitive poetics: affective studies 319–20; and cognitive linguistics 319; and corpus stylistics 389; and creative writing 436; definitions 313–14; empirical/experimental approaches 318–19; future directions 325; historical perspectives 314–15; and the literary mind 316–17; and pedagogical stylistics 248; practical application (textual analysis) 321–4; sciences and arts/humanities relations 318; theoretical development 315–16; and translation 395–6, 403–4
cognitive pragmatics 375
cognitive stylistics: analysis, *afternoon, a story* (Joyce) 506–10; overview 501
cohesion (language) 47–50, **49**
collective consciousness 228–9, 231
colonialism 49–50, 60, 61
comics: body shapes and postures 488–9; future directions 494–6; historical perspectives 486–7; manga 333, 337, 488–9; as a medium 485; and narratology 490–1, 495; onomatopoeia 491–2; page composition 487–90; pictograms 492; pictorial runes 492–3, **493**; point of view 490; recommendations for practice 494; and relevance theory 486; style 485–6; text balloons 490–1, 493; use of language 486
communication: and metaphor 211–12; in reading groups 449; spoken language in film 460; in text world theory 287–8 *see also* conversation

analysis (CA); cooperative principle (CP); relevance theory; speech act theory
communities of practice 105–6
computational linguistic analyses 334
Conan Doyle, Sir Arthur 146–7
conceptual integration *see* blending theory
conceptual metaphor theory 214–16, 299, 315
Conrad, Joseph (*Heart of Darkness*) 195–6
context: and cognition 313–14; importance to text world theory 285; social, in linguistics 461–2
conversation analysis (CA) 136–8, 150–1, 258, 262
Cook, G 88, 245
Cooper, M.M. 143
cooperative principle (CP): conversational maxims 125–6, 142–4, 145–7, 212, 258–9, 368–9; long turns 372; overview 125–6, 136, 142 *see also* implicature, conversational
Corax 17, 23
corpus linguistics: concordances 380–2, *381*, *382*; and critical stylistics 418; quantitative research 334
corpus stylistics: clusters 385; and cognitive poetics 389; computational stylistics 379–80; concordances 382–3, *382*, 386–7; contextualising functions 386; counting and comparing 379–80; electronic texts 386–7; future directions 388–9; highlighting functions 386; key semantic domains 384; key words procedures 383–5; lexical bundles 385; local textual functions 386; overview 378–9; quantitative research 335, 380; and quantitative studies 330–1; recommendations for practice 388; semantic prosody 383; speech, thought and writing presentation 385; suspensions 387; term 378
Coward, Noël (*Private Lives*) 261–4
creative writing: Aristotle on 425; dialogism 426; figurative language 430–1; future directions 436–8; language/creativity relationship 437–8; mimesis and diegesis 425, 428–9, 431; and mind style 271; and narratology 426–8; Plato on 424–5; and point of view 432; recommendations for practice 431–2, 432–3, 434–5, 436; and relevance theory 170–1; and speech and thought representation 433–4, *434*; and stylistics 423–4, 430–1; use of metaphor 435–6
critical discourse analysis: and ideology 408–9, 410
critical stylistics: background 408; current research 417–18; equating and contrasting 414; exemplifying and enumerating 414; future directions 419; historical perspectives 410–11; ideational metafunction 409; implying and assuming 415; naming and describing 413; negating 416; prioritisation 415; representing actions/events/states 413–14; research methods

418–19; speech and thought representation 416–17; term 409–10; textual ideation 411; textual meaning 409, 410–11; textual-conceptual functions 409, 412–13, 419

Croce, B. 316, 320

Csábi, S. 217

Culler, Jonathan 42, 70–1, 73, 74

Culpeper, J.: on implicature in drama 147–8; key semantic domains 384; language and characterisation 130–1, *131*, 141–2, 201, 260; on relevance theory 371; and schema theory 272

Culpeper, J. *et al* (2003) 129, 130

Cumming, L. 490

Davies, B. 144

Davies, D. 246

deconstructuralism 36–7

defamiliarisation 35–6, 88, 279, 280

Dehaene, S. 317

deictic language 260, 289, 417

Demosthenes 18, 25

Derrida, Jacques 37, 212, 367, 502

deviation 89, 90–4, 108

diachronic stylistics 101–2, 102–3

dialogism 426

Dickens, Charles: *Bleak House* 183; *Great Expectations* 186; *Nicholas Nickleby* 382–3, *382*, 386

Dickinson, Emily: 'To Make Routine a Stimulus' 321–4; use of metaphor 217, 218–19; 'In Vain' 165

diegesis: and mimesis 425, 428–9, 431; sound in film 456–7; and the text world 432

discourse: and emotions 522–3; importance to text world theory 285; and literary language 365, 429–30; quantitative research 334; and stylistics 193–4, 519; and text types 91

discourse worlds 287–8

Djik, Teun van 364–5

Downes, D. and Rock, P. 89

drama: audience/reader roles 258; conversation analysis (CA) 258; current stylistic approaches 258–61; discourse architecture of drama 257–8; future directions 265; historical approaches 253–4; implicature 147–8; multimodal analysis 256–7, 258, 260–1; play text and the performance relationship 254–7, 436; recommendations for practice 265; and text world theory 293

dramatic irony 148–9, 258

dramatis personae, functions 37, *38–9*, 40–1, *41*

Dürrenmatt, Friedrich (*The Visit*) 368–9

echoic utterances 163–4

Eco, U. 207

EFL (English as a Foreign Language) 244–6

Eggers, Dave (*A Hologram for the King*) 234–5

Eisner, W. 487–8

Emmott, C. 192, 290

Emmott, C. *et al* (2006) 444–5

emotions: actional outcomes 517; and aesthetics 523–6; artefact emotion 523; attachment 522; beauty, concept of 524–5; a case of aesthetic response 525–6; defined 516; eliciting conditions 516–17; empathy 522; expressive outcomes 517; and film 521; future directions 527–8; and literature 520–1, 522–3; and narratology 523; physiological outcomes 517; privileged emotions 522; quantitative research 335; readers' affective responses 68–9, 318–20; and schema theory 273; and text world theory 291

empirical approaches 77–8

empirical study of literature (ESL) *see* ESL (empirical study of literature)

English as a Foreign Language (EFL) 244–6

enregisterment 107, 109–11

Ensslin, A. 506, 509

enthymemic reasoning 22

Erasmus of Rotterdam 20

ESL (empirical study of literature): criticism of 446–7; historical overview 441–2; methodology 441, 451; studies 443–6

ethnic studies approaches 75–6

ethnomethodology 137

ethos 22

Evenson, B. 428

event structures 354–5

explicatures 164–5

fabula 36–7, 426–7, 429, 431, 437

facework: face-threatening acts 129–30; and literary pragmatics 371–2; maintaining face 118–19; positive/negative face 128–9, 259; in reading groups 448

fairy tales: narrative studies (Propp) 37–41; and schema theory 270, 277–8

Fauconnier, G. and Turner, M. 298, 299

Faulkner, William (*As I Lay Dying*) 184–5

feminism: humour and sexist language 351; post-feminism 352–3, 358; and reader response theory 71; Second Wave feminism 350, 351, 352–3; Third Wave feminism 350–1, 353

feminist stylistics: deficit theory 349; difference theory 349; dominance theory 349; and event structures 354–5; feminist narratology 356–7; future directions 359; historical perspectives 347–8; language and gender studies 348–50; linguistic feminism 350–3; non-essentialist gender concepts 349–50, 356; non-verbal multimodal markers 356, 357–8; overview 346–7, 348; recommendations for practice 358–9; socially-constructed meanings 354, 355; and transitivity 353–4, 356

Fetterly, J. 71, 73, 74, 75

figurative language: and creative writing 430–2; metonymy 206–7, 211; personification 215; and relevance theory 163–4, 167; similes 208; synecdoche 207, 211 *see also* metaphor

film theory: and characterisation 468; diegesic sound 456–7; difficulties of stylistic analysis 457–9, 461–4, 466–7; and drama performances 265; and emotions 521; film shot and narrative 465–6, 467–8; film shots equivalence with sentences 464–5; installation art 456; and intersemiosis 464; as multimodal 456–7; prose-to-film adaptations 459; recommendations for practice 465–6; simultaneous semiotic streams 462–5; spoken language in 460; stylistics of film 459–61; taglines 90–5; temporal progression 468–9; term 455–6; and transitivity 465; use of transcriptions 460–1

Firth, J.R. 331

Fish, S. 72, 73, 74

Fisher, Caitlin (*These Waves of Girls*) 500–1, *502*, 510–12, *512*

Fitzgerald, F. Scott (*The Great Gatsby*) 184

Fleming, Ian (*Casino Royale*) 384–5

Fludernik, M. 104, 223, 232, 270

focalization: and creative writing 432; and narratology 191–2, 195–7, 428; and point of view theory 178–9, 195–200, 230–1; and readerly attention 230–1; and text world theory 290

Forceville, C. 492

foregrounding: defined 41; deviation 89, 90–4; ESL studies on 443–6; figure (term) 88; future directions 99; ground (term) 88; in historical texts 107–8; identification of and literary training 444; and metaphor 211; overview 87–9, 442–3; parallelism 94–5; style figures 25; text analysis 95–9; text fragmentation 444–5

formalism *see* Russian formalism

Four Weddings and a Funeral (film) 144

Fowler, Roger: mind styles 271; narratology 179–80, 181, 191, 193; point of view theory 177, 198–9

frame theory 98

free indirect discourse (FID) 433

free indirect thought 224–6, 229–32, 398

Freed, A. 349–50

Freeman, M. 214

Freemand, D. 217

Freud, Sigmund 70

Freytag, G. 254

Fuchs, C. 227

function-advancing propositions 289

functional stylistics: cohesion 47–50, **49**; future directions 64; historical background 46–7, 331; interpersonal metafunction 61–2, **62**; overview 45–6, 63; recommendations for practice 64; textual metafunction 47–50, 472, 473–4 *see also* ideational metafunction

functionalism 2, 41, 395

Furlong, A. 168

Gardam, Jane (*Bilgewater*) 197–8

Gardner, J. 430–1

Garfinkel, Harold 137

Gavins, J. 289, 290

gender, concepts of 347, 349–50, 356

gender studies approaches: and language 346, 348–50; and reader response theory 75–6

generative approaches 42, 178, 284–5

Genesis 22 302–9

Genette, G.: focalization 195, 196–7; homo/heterodiegetic narrators 178–9, 182; narrative features 192, 202, 203, 427–8; point of view theory 230, 428, 432

Gestalt theory 88, 495

Gibbons, A. 291

Gibbs, R.W. Jr 217–18

Goffman, E. 118, 128, 371

Golding, William (*The Inheritors*) 161

Gramling, D. and Warner, C. 375–6

grammar: grammatical deviation 92; modal grammar of narrative viewpoint 182–7; tense 202–3; *verba sentiendi* 179, 180, 181

graphological deviation 91–2

Greimas, A.J. 253

Grice, H.P.: conversational implicature 367–9; cooperative principle (CP) 125–6, 142–4; maxims applied to dramatic discourse 258–9; maxims of quality 125–6, 142–4, 145–7, 212, 258–9, 368–9; on metaphor 212; neo-Gricean approaches 151–2, 156, 162; and relevance theory 155–6 *see also* implicature, conversational

Gutt, E.-A. 398

Haddon, Mark (*The Curious Incident of the Dog in the Night-Time*) 146, 435

Haggard, H. Rider 47–50, **49**, 63, 65–7

Hall, G. 101, 446–7

Halliday, M.A.K.: language metafunctions 46–7, 409, 472–3, 510–11; socio-cultural dimension 331; textual meaning 473–4; theory of language 471–4; transitivity 50–5, 353–4, 356, 410–11, 413–14 *see also* ideational metafunction; interpersonal metafunction; textual metafunction

Halliday, M.A.K. and Hasan, R. 47, 48

Hamburger, Michael 399, 401–2

Hardy, Thomas: *Far From the Madding Crowd* 138–9, 185; *Tess of the d'Urbervilles* 200

Heaney, Seamus (*Digging*) 166, 167–8

Herman, D. 201

Herman, D. *et al* (2005) 176
heterodiegetic narrators 178–9, 182, 184–5, 428, 432, 433
heteroglossia 426
Hickey, L. 363
historical stylistics, new: future directions 113; and literary analysis 107–9; and literary discourse 103–4; and the mobility paradigm 104–6; modern-day relevance 101–2; and place-making 106–7, 109–10; and reader response theory 76; recommendations for practice 111–12
Hoffmann, C.R. 512
Hogan, P.C. 520
Holland, N. 70, 73, 74, 317–18
Holmes, J. 395
Homer (*The Iliad*) 425
homodiegetic narrators 178–9, 182, 184–5, 428, 432, 433
Hoover, D. 379
Horace 15–16
Horn, L. 151–2
humour studies: and feminist stylistics 351; quantitative research 334; and schema theory 271, 277–8
hypermedia 505
hypertext fiction: analysis, *afternoon, a story* (Joyce) 506–10; analysis, *These Waves for Girls* (Fisher) 510–12; author/reader roles 502, 503; future directions 513; historical perspectives 502; hyperlinks, role of 504–5; lexia 500, 505; multimodality 504; non-linearity/multi-linearity 503–4; recommendations for practice 513; theories of 502–6

iconicity 320–1, 402
ideational metafunction: behavioural processes 54; existential processes 54–5; in hypertext fiction 510–11; material processes 51–2, **51**; material processes, analysis (*King Solomon's Mines*) 55–61, **55–6**, 58–9; mental processes 52, **53**; overview 50–1, 409; process types, summary *55*; relational processes 53–4, **53**; verbal processes 54
implicature, conversational: and critical stylistics 415–16; defined 143–4; and dramatic discourse 259; and flouting maxims 148–50; and literary pragmatics 367–9; and relevance theory 159–60, **160**, 162–3, 165–6; and textual meaning 411–12; 'weak.' in translation 394
im/politeness theory 118–19, 128–30, 162, 259, 371–2
indexicality 107
Ingarden, R. 314
intentional fallacy 68–9
intermental thought 228–9, 231

International Poetics and Linguistics Association (PALA) 7, 249
interpersonal approaches 178, 179–81
interpersonal metafunction: in hypertext fiction 511; modal categories (*King Solomon's Mines*) **62**; modality 61–2, 472, 473
invariance hypothesis 215
irony: dramatic irony 148–9, 258, 262; ironical utterances 163–4
Iser, W. 71–2, 73, 74
Isocrates 18

Jakobson, Roman: associative functions of language *34*; career 32–3; and classical rhetoric 11; metaphor and aphasic patients 211; model of communication 33–4, *33*, 257; poetic function 34–5; on poetic function of language 331, 425–6; as structuralist 2; on translation 393, 395
James, Henry (*The Portrait of a Lady*) 224–5, 231
James, William 229–30
Jeffries, L. and McIntyre, D. 331
Ji, M. 337–8
Johnstone, B. 107, 109–10
Jones, F. 403
Joyce, James: *The Dead* 202; 'Two Gallants' 473–4
Joyce, Michael (*afternoon, a story*): background 500–1; cognitive stylistic approach to 506–10; coherence in 504–5; role of the reader 503; screen image from *501*; text world theory 507–10

kairos (*occasio*) 23–4
Kelman, James (*How Late It Was, How Late*) 433
Kennedy, J. 492
Kennedy, John Fitzgerald 299–300
Kerouac, Jack (*On the Road*) 475, 481
Keyes, Daniel (*Flowers for Algenon*) 95–9
King Solomon's Mines: Appendix, Ch. XIII in full 65–7; cohesive reference chain 47–50, **49**; material processes 55–61, **55–6**, **58–9**, 63; modal categories **62**
Kingsnorth, P. 297
Koestenbaum, W. 76
Koller, V. 357–8
Koshimaa, R. 512
Kövecses, Z. 215
Kress, G. and van Leeuwen, T.: multimodal semiosis 471–2; on page layout 87, 475–6; visual grammar 171, 474, 482, 511

Lahey, E. 291
Lakoff, G. 315
Lakoff, G. and Johnson, M. 214, 304
Lakoff, G. and Turner, M. 215, 216
Lakoff, R. 349

Lanchester, John (*Capital*) 227, 232–3
Landow, G.P. 500, 502, 503, 505, 510
language, literary: as characterisation device
    118–19, 130–2, 138–42, 145–7; and cognition
    318; deictic 260, 289, 417; and discourse 365,
    429–30; and gender studies 346, 348–50;
    literary language as distinct 241, 245, 429–30;
    and meaning-making 241, 245; poetic 32, 36,
    166, 320; political significance 350, 353;
    pragmatics 119, 362–3, 368 *see also*
    pedagogical stylistics; second language
    teaching
Language and Literature (journal) 204, 239, 301,
    332–5, **332**, 449
langue 409, 411
Larkin, Phillip 34–5
Leech, G.N. 94, 129, 363, 372
Leech, G.N. and Short, M.: metaphor 211;
    narratology 191, 192; point of view 195, 197,
    198, 200–1; sequencing 202; speech and
    thought presentation 222–4, **223**, **224**, 225
Leeuwen, T. van 463, 464, 477–8
Lefevère, A. 400
Leitch, V.B. *et al* (2001) 425
Levaco, R. 457
Lévi-Strauss, Claude 41
lexical pragmatics: and feminist stylistics 349;
    lexical bundles 385; lexical deviation 92–3;
    lexical priming 383; quantitative research
    333–4; and relevance theory 166–8
literacy 317–18
literariness: and poetic function 32, 34; and
    relevance theory 168–9; and schema theory
    273; and speech act theory 367
literary analysis: and cognitive approaches 315;
    dialogue, conversational structure 138–41,
    145–7; of drama 254–5; and emotions,
    research 520–1; free indirect thought (novels)
    224; and historical stylistics 107–9; history of
    243–4; and pedagogical stylistics 240, 244–5;
    and relevance theory 170; use of scientific
    methodology 329
literary discourse, genre conventions 103–4
literary pragmatics: basic schema 364–5;
    evolution of 363–4; and facework 371–2; and
    implicature 367–9; and im/politeness 371–2;
    overview 362–3; recommendations for
    practice 373–4; and relevance theory 370–1;
    and speech act theory 365–7 *see also*
    pragmatic stylistics
literary texts: concept of, multimodal analysis
    480–1; and human conceptual system 214; as
    long turns 372; metaphor as foregrounded
    deviation 211; as primary literary unit 365;
    and schema theory 273; and translation 394
Livia, A. 356
Locke, John 208

locution and illocution 123–5, 129, 366, 367,
    411–12
logos 22
Longinius 15, 16–17, 25, 36
Louw, W.E. 383

MacMahon, B. 162
Mahlberg, M. and McIntyre, D. 384–5
Mahlberg, M. and Smith, C. 384, 387
Mailloux, S. 69
A Man for all Season (play) 139–40
McCloud, S. 485
McEwan, Ian (*Atonement*) 79–81
McIntyre, D. 179, 180, 256, 257, 258, 260–1
meaning: and style 393–4; textual production of
    409
memory organisation packs (MOP) 269
Merleau-Ponty, M. 320
meronymic references 49
metafunctions: overview 46–7; in visual
    communication 474–5 *see also* ideational
    metafunction; interpersonal metafunction;
    textual metafunction
metaphor: as abuse of words 208; based on
    similarity 211; and cognitive approaches 213;
    comparison-metaphor 210; conceptual
    metaphor theory 214–16; conceptual tools
    216–18; as contextual change of meaning
    209–11, 212; the conventional view of 207; in
    conversation 211–12; and creative writing
    435; as fable 209; as foregrounded deviation
    211; historical perspective 207–8; image
    metaphors 216; interaction theory of metaphor
    210–11; metaphor identification procedure
    (MIP) 218; metaphor research 206–7, 213–14;
    metaphorical utterances 163, 167, 210,
    211–12; ontological metaphors 215;
    orientational metaphors 215; and philosophy
    212; and poetics 208, 211, 213, 214, 216, 217;
    and realism 211; recommendations for practice
    218–19; and relevance theory 212, 370; and
    rhetoric 207–8; and speech act theory 211–12;
    structural metaphors 215; substitution-
    metaphor 210; tenor 209–10; as transference
    208; and translation 398, 404; and *usure* 212;
    vehicle 209–10
metarepresentation 161–2
metonymy 206–7, 211
Miall, D.S. 318
Miall, D.S. and Dobson, T. 504
Miall, D.S. and Kuiken, D. 443–4
Miles, A. 505
Mills, S. 35, 192, 347–8, 352–3
Mills, S. and Mullany, L. 348, 350, 352
mimesis 12–13, 424–5, 428–9, 431
mind styles 271
Minsky, M. 269

Mithen, S. 317
mobility paradigm 101–2, 104–5, 109
modality: category A narratives 183–4; category
  B narratives 185–7; interpersonal
  metafunction 61–2; modal categories (*King
  Solomon's Mines*) 62, **62**; modal systems
  181–2; shading 183, 184; and text world
  theory 289, 290; as textual-conceptual
  function 416; and typography 478
Montoro, R. 358
moral accounting metaphor 304–5
Morris, C. 362
Mukařovský, Jan 41, 442–3
multimodal stylistics: analysis, *Private Lives*
  (Coward) 261–4; analysis, *These Waves for
  Girls* (Fisher) 510–12; as based on Hallidayan
  functional linguistics 471–4; compositional
  meaning 474–5; critical issues 479–81;
  experiential meaning 472–3, 474; and feminist
  stylistics 256, 257–8, 357–8; framing 475,
  476; future directions 481–2; in hypertext
  fiction 504; information value 475;
  interpersonal metafunction 472, 473, 474;
  metafunctions of visual communication
  474–5; multimodality of film 456–7, 462–4;
  page layout 475–6; and pedagogy 240; play
  texts analysis 256–7, 258, 260–1; quantitative
  research 340; recommendations for practice
  481; salience 476; semiotics of paper 478–9;
  as social semiotic approach 471; and text
  world theory 291–2, 293; textual metafunction
  473–4; typography 476–8
music, aesthetic appreciation 524
Myers, G. 449

Nahajec, L. 411, 418
narratology: and blending 301; and
  characterisation 201, 253–4; and comics 490–1,
  495; complication actions 128; and creative
  writing 426–8; diachronic stylistics 104; and
  discourse 193–4; and emotions 523; *fabula* and
  sjužet (narrative) 36–7, 426–7; fairy tales
  (Propp) 37–41; feminist narratology 356–7; and
  film theory 465–6, 467–8; and focalization
  191–2, 195–7; future directions 203–4; hetero/
  homodiegetic narrators 178–9, 182, 184–5,
  428, 432, 433; in hypertext fiction 505; modal
  grammar of narrative viewpoint 182–7;
  narration and brain damage 521; narrative voice
  428; narrator/narratee relationship 76–7; Plato
  on 12–13; and point of view theory 197–8; and
  reader response theory 76–7; recommendations
  for practice 203–4; and Russian formalism 32;
  and schema theory 270, 276–7; and stylistics
  191–3, 427; and tense 202–3; and translation
  404 *see also* focalization; point of view theory;
  speech and thought presentation

naturalistic study of reading (NSR) *see* NSR
  (naturalistic study of reading)
Nelson, T., H. 500
neo-Gricean approaches 151–2, 156, 162
neuroscience: acceptance of other literary worlds
  272; and literary analysis 317–18, 518; and
  schema theory 272–3; term 517–18 *see also*
  emotions
New Delhi (film) 525–6
new media discourse 101
Niffenegger, Audrey (*The Time Traveller's Wife*)
  274–5
non-verbal multimodal markers 256, 257–8
Nørgaard, N. *et al* (2010) 136
Nørgaard, N. *et al* (2011) 458
NSR (naturalistic study of reading): historical
  overview 442; methodology 441, 451; studies
  447–9
Nussbaum, M. 520

Oatley, K. 319, 437, 520
Ochs, E. 460
Ohmann, R. 367
oral storytelling 256
oration: styles of 1–2 *see also* rhetoric
Orientalism 49–50, 60, 61
Owen, Wilfrid ('Parable of the Old Man and the
  Young') 301–9
Owtram, N. 170–1

Page, R. 357
Paine, Thomas (*Common Sense*) 217
PALA (International Poetics and Linguistics
  Association) 7, 249
Palmer, A. 225, 228–9
parallelism 89, 94–5
Parker, Dorothy 362, 370–1
Parks, T. 400
parole 409, 411
pathos 22
pedagogical stylistics: and English language
  teaching (EFL) 244–6; future directions 248–9;
  historical perspectives 243–4; and non-English
  language teaching 247–9; and pragmatic
  stylistics 375–6; quantitative research 335; and
  technology 247; value of 240–3
pedagogical text world theory 293–4
Peer, W. van 329, 443
Peplow, D. 449
performances, play texts 254–6, 259–60
Petrey, S. 367, 372
Phelan, J. 77
phenomenology 318–19, 320–1
phonology 93–4, 333
Pietsch, M. 226–7
Pilkington, A. 166, 168
place-making 106–7, 109–10

Plath, Sylvia (*The Bell Jar*) 353
Plato 12–13, 18, 424–5, 429
play texts: multimodal analysis 256–7, 258, 260–1; and the performance 254–6
plot structure: Aristotle on 14–15, 253; historical approaches 253–4
plurimethodological studies 340
poesis 320
poetic function 34–5
poetic iconicity 320–1
poetics: Aristotle on (*Poetics*) 13–14, 15, 208, 253, 425; catharsis 13–14, 15; character 16; decorum 16; and metaphor 208, 211, 213, 214, 216, 217; mimesis 12–13; Plato on 12–13; recommendations for practice 27; Roman 15–17; and Russian formalism 32; the sublime 16–17; term 313
point of view theory: and comics 490; and creative writing 432; in drama 260; focalization 178–9, 195–200, 230–1; future directions 188; modal grammar of narrative viewpoint 182–7; and modality 181–2; and narratology 197–8; in *The Pale King* (Wallace) 230–1; psychological plane 177–81, 199; recommendations for practice 188; types of narration 175–8, 179–81, 199–200
politeness 118–19, 128–30, 162, 259, 371–2
possible worlds theories 285–7
Pragglejaz Group 218
pragmatic stylistics: defined 136, 362; enthymemic reasoning 22; and language use 119, 362–3, 365, 368; overview 362–3; and poetic effect 373 *see also* literary pragmatics
Prague School 32, 41–2, 331, 395
Prince, Gerald 76, 202
Private Lives (Coward) 261–4
Propp, Vladimir: functions of dramatis personae 37, *38–9*, 40–1, *41*, 253; narrative studies (fairy tales) 2, 37–41
prosody 314, 321, 323, 333, 383
prototypicality 525
psychoanalysis 70
psychology: attention, paying 229–30; evolutionary 316; and schema theory 268–9

quantitative methodology: descriptive research 336; explanatory research 338–40; explorative research 336; future directions 340; historical perspectives 330–1; recommendations for practice 340; research designs 335–6, 418–19; research examples, papers from *Language & Literature* 332–5, **332**; stylostatistics 330; univariate descriptive statistics 336–8
queer studies approaches 75–6
Quintilian (Marcus Fabius Quintilianus) 19

Rabinowitz, P. 77
Raskin, V. 271

reader response theory: and cognitive approaches 74–5; defining the readers 73; and empirical approaches 77–8; and feminism 71; future directions 81–2; and gender/ethnic/queer studies approaches 75–6; key theorists 69–72; and narrative/rhetorical approaches 76–7; overview 68–9, 73, 440–1; and pedagogy 78; quantitative research 335; on the reading process 73–4; and reception studies/new historical approaches 76; recommendations for practice 79–81; research, future directions 451–2; and text world theory 291, 293
readers: affective responses 68–9, 318–20; as meaning-makers 440–1; mixed-methodology research 451; non-professional readers, in research 291; research, recommendations for practice 449–51; role of, hypertext fiction 502, 503; and translation 395
reading groups: ESL studies on 443–6; NSL studies on 447–9; quantitative research 333
realism 211
reception studies 76
relevance theory: authorial intention 169–70; and autism spectrum disorders 146; and comics 486; communicative principle of relevance 157; and creative writing 170–1; decoupled representations 162; explicatures 164–5; figurative language 163–4, 167; future directions 171–2; implications 162–3; and implicature 159–60, **160**, 162–3, 165–6; lexical pragmatics 166–8; literariness 168–9; and literary analysis 170; and literary pragmatics 370–1; local and global inferences 168; and metaphor 212, 370; metarepresentation 161–2; overview 155–6; practical application (textual analysis) 159–60, **160**; processing effort 158; recommendations for practice 171; relevance-guided comprehension heuristic 156–8; salient inferences 160–1; strong/weak implicatures 370; and text analysis 158–68; and translation 398; writing and pedagogy 170–1
research methods: qualitative studies **332**, 333, 334, 418–19 *see also* quantitative methodology
rhetoric: ancient classical 1–2, 17–19; and democracy 17–18; five cannons of 20–5, **21**; future directions 28–9; learning, three stages of 25; and metaphor 207–8; modern 20, 23; and pedagogical stylistics 248; recommendations for practice 27; and Russian formalism 32; three genres of oratory 26
Rhetorica ad Herennium 23, **23**
rhetorical theory 77
Richards, I.A. 209–10, 441
Ricoeur, P. 212–13
Riffaterre, M. 395, 400
Rimmon-Kenan, S. 199, 201
'Rip Van Winkle' (story) 71

Romaine, S. 106
romance fiction 354–5
Rumelhart, D.E. and Norman, D.A. 269
Rushdie, Salman *(The Satanic Verses)* 367, 372
Russian formalism: and creative writing 425–6;
    development of 2, 31–2; formalist criticism
    68–9; future directions 43; and narratology 32;
    and poetics 32; and quantitative studies 330–1;
    recommendations for practice 42–3; and
    structuralism 2, 42; and translation 395
Ryan, M-L. 286, 485
Ryder, M.E. 354–5

Sacks, H. *et al* (1974) 137
Said, Edward 50
Sanford, A.J. and Emmott, C. 269–70
Saussure, Ferdinand de 46, 330, 409
Schaalje, G. B. *et al* (2012) 330
Schank, R.C. and Abselon, R.P. 269
schema theory: alien mind styles 275–6;
    assumption-making processes 274–5; attitude
    schemata 273; background 268–70; and
    characterisation 260, 274–5; culturally-specific
    knowledge 277–9; on drama and performance
    259–60; and fairy tales 270, 277–8; future
    directions 279–80; and humour 271, 277–8;
    intertextual schemata 270, 277–8; mind styles
    271, 275–6; motor schemata 273; and
    narratology 194, 270, 276–7; and other worlds
    271–2; scenarios 269–70, 276–7; schema
    refreshment 88, 273, 278–9; scripts 269;
    sensory schemata 273; socio-cultural schemata
    272; and standard inferences 274; story
    schemata 270; and text world theory 273; use
    of stereotypes 272
Schneider, R. 502, 506
Searle, J.R. 121–2, 126–7, 211, 259, 365, 366
second language teaching: and literary
    pragmatics 375–6; and pedagogical stylistics
    244–6, 247–8; and schema theory 272
Sell, R. 372
semantic deviation 92–3
Semino, E.A. 146, 271, 313
Semino, E.A. and Short, M. 385
Shakespeare, William: *Hamlet* 105, 148–9;
    Henry V 372; *Macbeth* 45, 63, 217; *Othello*
    149–50; Sonnet 73 206, 219; tragedies 254;
    Twelfth Night 162–3; use of schemata 272
Shklovsky, Viktor: criticism of 36–7;
    defamiliarisation 2, 35–6, 88; *fabula* and *sjužet*
    (narrative) 36–7, 426–7
Short, Mick: on deviation 41–2; direct/indirect
    quotation 416; discourse architecture of drama
    257–8, 265; dramatic dialogue 139–40, 140–1;
    narratology 192; parallelism 95; the
    performance of a play text 255–6; on stylistic
    analysis 2; teaching practice 246

Simpson, P.: on discourse 334; foregrounding
    88–9; modal grammar of narrative viewpoint
    182–7; modes of narration 179–81, 192, 193;
    point of view 177, 178, 417; on stylistics 2,
    31; on temporal arrangements 202–3;
    transitivity 414
Simpson, P. and Mayr, A. 510
Sinclair, J. 103
sjužet 36–7, 426–7
Sklar, H. 329
Slingerland, E. and Collard, M. 318
Smith, M. 489
Snow, C.P. 329
social semiotics: analysis, *These Waves for Girls*
    (Fisher) 510–12; overview 501
socio-pragmatic stylistics: analysis, *Private Lives*
    (Coward) 261–4
Socrates 18
Sophists 17–18
Sophocles (*Oedipus Rex*) 14–15
sounds, classification of 464
speech act theory: constatives 120–1;
    conversational implicature 143–4, 148–50; and
    dramatic discourse 259; felicity conditions
    120, 127–8, 366; form and force 123; future
    directions 133; intentionality 366–7; and
    literary pragmatics 365–7, 369; locution and
    illocution 123–5, 129, 366, 367, 411–12;
    maxims of quality 125–6, 142–4, 145–7, 212,
    258–9, 368–9; and metaphor 211–12;
    performatives 120–1, 365–6; recommendations
    for practice 132–3; types 121–2
speech and thought presentation: analysis (*The
    Pale King,* Wallace) 226–32; corpus stylistics
    385; creative writing 433–5, *434*; and critical
    stylistics 416–17; free indirect thought 224–6;
    future directions 234; historical perspectives
    222–4, **223**, **224**, 225; recommendations for
    practice 232–4
Sperber, D. and Wilson, D. 166, 370, 371, 486
Spolsky, E. 313–14
St André, J. 404
Starcke, B. 385
Stockwell, P. 88, 194, 331, 507
Stockwell, P. and Whitely, S. 291
Stoppard, Tom (*Rosencrantz and Guildenstern
    are Dead*) 144–5
structuralism 2, 42, 178
style: and creative writing 430–1; and genre
    conventions 103; and meaning 393–4; and the
    poetic sublime 16–17; in rhetoric 24–5; and
    translation 394
stylistic analysis: canonical analysis 460;
    overview 1–3, 363–4, 518–20; research
    methods 331–2
stylometry 379
stylostatistics 330, 331, 340

Sunderland, J. 357
Swann, J. 256
Swann, J. and Allington, D. 333
The Sweeney 120, 122–3, 132
Sweetser, E. 315
symbolism 32
synecdoche 207, 211
syntax 334
systemic functional linguistics (SFL) 410

Tan, E.S. 489
text analysis: meaning, *langue/parole* 409, 411; quantitative research 333; and relevance theory 158–68
text world theory (TWT): basic theory of 287–90; and creative writing 432, 436; diagramming 292; and diegesis 432; discourse worlds 287–8, 507; and emotions 291; enactors 290; function-advancing propositions 289, 508–9; future directions 293–4; historical background 284–5; modal worlds 289, 509; and multimodal stylistics 291–2, 293; and pedagogy 293–4; and possible worlds theories 285–7; practical application (textual analysis) 292–3, 507–10; and reader response theory 291, 293; and schema theory 273; self-implication 291; situational variables 289; sub-worlds 289–90, 509; and the text world 288–9, 507; and truth-conditional semantics 285–6; world switches 289; world-repairs 290; written communication 288
textual metafunction: and cultural significance (example) 48–50; defined 47, 472, 473–4; in hypertext fiction 512
textual-conceptual functions: defined 409, 412–13, 419; equating and contrasting 414; exemplifying and enumerating 414; hypothesising 416; implying and assuming 415; naming and describing 413; negating 412, 416; presenting others' speech and thoughts 416; prioritising 415; representing actions/events/states 413–14
Theatre of the Absurd 144–5
Thomas, B. 140
Thorne, B. and Henley, N. 349
Tiffin, C. and Lawson, A. 49
time, concepts of 23–4
Toolan, M. 139, 191, 193–4, 384, 423–4
Tosca, S.P. 504–5
Toury, G. 398
tragedy 13–14, 254
transitivity: analysis, *These Waves for Girls* (Fisher) 511; behavioural processes 54; existential processes 54–5; and feminist stylistics 353–4, 356; and film 465; material processes 51–2, **51**; mental processes 52, **53**; overview 50–1, *55*; participants 353–4; range element 52, 54; relational processes 53–4, *53*;

verbal processes 54, 410, 413–14 *see also* ideational metafunction; interpersonal metafunction; textual metafunction
translation: and blending 404; and cognitive poetics 395–6, 403–4; correspondence with film adaptation 459; defined 393; future directions 403–5; historical perspectives 394–7; internationalisation of 405; literary/non-literary texts 394; metaphors 398, 404; and narratology 404; onomatopoeia, comics 491–2; practical application (textual analysis) 400–2; recommendations for practice 402–3; and relevance theory 398; research study fields 397–9; as source of stylistic analysis 399–400; and style 394; stylistically-aware readings 401–2
truth-conditional semantics 285–6
Tsur, R. 213, 313, 314, 315, 319–20, 520–1
Turner, M. 316, 317
TWT *see* text world theory (TWT)
typography 476–8

underdeterminancy thesis 156
Uspensky, Boris 177, 179, 180, 198–9
usure 212

verba sentiendi 179, 180, 181
Viana, V. *et al* (2007) 385–6
Vico, Giambattista 209
Vinay, J.-P. and Darbelnet, J. 395
Vives, Juan Luis 20
Vuust, P. and Kringelbach, M. 524

Wales, K. 335, 355–6
Walker, J. 507
Wallace, C. 246
Wallace, David Foster (*The Pale King*) 226–32
Waugh, Evelyn 140
Weber, J.J. 375
Werth, Paul 217, 285 *see also* text world theory (TWT)
Whitely, S. 452
Widdowson, Henry 244–5
Wilson, D. 169–70
Wilson, D. and Sperber, D. 163–4
Wimsatt, W. Jr and Beardsley, M. 68
Wójcik-Leese, E. 319
Woolf, Virginia: on *Anna Karenina* (film) 468; free indirect thought (*Mrs Dalloway*) 225, 445; *To the Lighthouse* 196–7, 433, 434
worlds theories of modal logic 285
writing systems 317, 492

Young, K. and Saver, J. 521

Zimmer, B. 334
Zyngier, S. *et al* (2007) 445–6